AF600477

INCARDINATION AND EXCARDINATION OF SECULARS

THE CATHOLIC UNIVERSITY OF AMERICA
CANON LAW STUDIES
No. 145

INCARDINATION AND EXCARDINATION OF SECULARS

AN HISTORICAL SYNOPSIS AND COMMENTARY

A DISSERTATION

Submitted to the Faculty of Canon Law of the Catholic University of America in Partial Fulfillment of the Requirements for the Degree of

DOCTOR OF CANON LAW

BY

REV. JAMES THOMAS McBRIDE, A.B., J.C.L.
Priest of the Archdiocese of Philadelphia

WASHINGTON, D.C.
1941

Nihil obstat

CLEMENS V. BASTNAGEL, J.U.D.,
Censor Deputatus

WASHINGTONII, D.C., DIE 26 MAII 1941.

Imprimatur

✠ DIONYSIUS CARDINALIS DOUGHERTY, D.D.,
Archiepiscopus Philadelphiensis

PHILADELPHIAE, DIE 29 MAII 1941.

PRINTED IN THE UNITED STATES OF AMERICA
BY THE DOLPHIN PRESS, PHILADELPHIA, PA.

TO

MY ESTEEMED UNCLE

REV. JAMES T. HIGGINS

Whose Honor it Was
To be Enrolled as a Graduate Student Priest at
The Catholic University of America
The Year of its Foundation
and
Who Departed This Life
During his and its Golden Jubilee Year

FOREWORD

Early in the life of the Church it became apparent that a confinement of effort within territorial bounds would best promote the realization of world evangelization by the successors of the Apostles and their co-workers in the sacred ministry. A diocesan clergy was the result, subject in each territory to the jurisdiction of the ruling Bishop. Once thus organized, honorable reasons were not lacking from time to time for exchanges between dioceses of their clerical personnel. Canonical transfers of clerics and priests from one territory or diocese to another were allowed under regulation even from the early Christian centuries, as is witnessed by the canons of the provincial and general councils of the period.

Since attachment to a diocese in perpetuity was secured in the first instance through the medium of ordination, the disengagement of a cleric and his reattachment elsewhere was likewise considered achieved by the authorization of another Bishop to ordain the same cleric to a higher order in the new locality. Thus, sacred ordination had a close connection with canonical transfers, or with excardination and incardination as this process has since become known, and the close relationship of the two has never been severed. Legislation adopted by the Church for the latter process always involved the former. In fact, through most of the Church's history, the subject of incardination and excardination as such is not found at all in Church legislation, but must be sought out and gathered from various official pronouncements *De Ordine.*

It is true that much was written in centuries past on holy orders, and in particular about the proper Bishop for ordination and the ordination title, but very little was ever done in the way of abstracting from these two subjects the implicit legislation of the Church concerning excardination and incardination. Scant consideration was given to the matter by the canonists, and whatever few pertinent articles appeared in ecclesiastical periodicals were only phase treatments.

Meanwhile the basic law itself became more complicated with the passage of centuries. Five distinct periods may be discerned, in each of which a different discipline with reference to holy orders was enforced, and the greater part of these enactments were cumulative. Furthermore, every change in legislation potentially had four different effects according to the class of subjects to whom it was applicable, namely, to lay candidates for the clerical state, minor clerics, major clerics, and priests. Special laws, too, were enacted governing the canonical transfers of certain groups, such as clerics from foreign lands. A lack of uniform terminology throughout caused much confusion and added to the difficulty of a correct understanding of the common law. Various interpretations of the law when applied to particular cases gave rise to frequent contests in ecclesiastical courts to determine the diocese to which a cleric owed his allegiance, and these the Holy See was called upon again and again, even in the same particular instance, to adjudicate.

The Code of Canon Law clarified the situation very definitely by giving to the Church for the first time a clear-cut division of legislation on the two subjects, incardination and ordination, dealing with each under its own proper title, even though they still remained related subjects. This, however, did not settle all difficulties. The Code itself required interpretation in the light of a preceding legislation already ill understood, thus accentuating the long felt need for a general detailed study, both historical and canonical, of the whole field of legislation with regard to the excardination and incardination of clerics.

It is that need which the present work aims, however humbly and inadequately, to satisfy. To the writer's best knowledge it is a pioneer publication on the subject. The original purpose was to include in its scope the law concerning canonical transfers to and from Religious Institutes, but that was found infeasible. Accordingly, as its title indicates, it is restricted to the study of the incardination and excardination of seculars only, although it may be remarked that a separate study of the same question with respect to Religious is in process of preparation by another writer who himself is a member of a Religious Congregation.

Because of the fact that this is the first general treatise on the subject, it was thought advisable to incorporate in the footnotes much of the source material to invite a better criticism and evaluation of the conclusions herein reached in the more specialized and scientific studies that may follow.

The extensive treatment given to the subjects of the proper Bishop for ordination and the ordination title was made necessary because of the close nexus between ordination and incardination, and also because at the time this work was begun, in 1927, no treatise existed in the English language on those two fundamental related subjects. Since then, in the year 1935, a doctoral dissertation in English on the subject of the " Proper Bishop for Ordination " was published at the Catholic University of America, Washington, D. C., by the Reverend John M. Moeder, J.C.D., to whom, therefore, the humble apologies of the author are tendered for seemingly having transgressed on his canonical field.

More space, too, than may seem warranted has been given to the commentary on canon 114. The reason is that virtual incardination and excardination of clerics through the reception of a residential benefice, of which this canon treats, has been the source of more litigation in ecclesiastical courts than any other phase of the excardinatory process. It is the canon which is styled by one author " dangerous for unwary Bishops," because of the automatic way in which it secures its effect independently of their expressed will. It was felt, therefore, that a detailed examination of all the possible consequences of the application of canon 114 would serve to eliminate much of the previous misunderstanding about the virtual process of incardination upon which the aforesaid conflicts were based.

The research and assembly of source material for this work was accomplished during the years 1927-1929. In the long interval that elapsed between that and its final publication, during which time the writer was functioning as an assistant pastor in a busy city parish, it was inevitable that newer editions of many of the works consulted should emanate from the press. While some of these were procured and incorporated, it was found impossible to do so for all, but a comparison of a few of them and a scrutiny of the most recent Juridical Periodical Articles leads to the conclusion that the use of the older editions has not substantially affected the argument.

It is well recognized that incardination and excardination is a very practical subject, and in this study an effort has been made to provide the reader with a practical guide in the execution of these processes as well as with a basis of theoretical knowledge for such action. The formulae of letters and documents contained herein have been drawn up according to the latest prescriptions of ecclesiastical law; they are not obligatory, but merely indicative of safe practice. The various charts provided are intended to summarize and simplify the text so as to enable the reader to ascertain at a glance the law governing the more complicated phases of the entire problem. It is sincerely hoped that as a result of this work the history of incardination and excardination will be clarified and its present procedure simplified.

The writer is especially indebted to Rev. Clement V. Bastnagel, J.U.D., of the Faculty of the School of Canon Law, for his painstaking care and invaluable suggestions in correcting the lengthy manuscript of this work, and to all the Faculty members of the same School for their extreme kindness and sympathetic direction. He wishes to express his appreciation likewise to the personal staffs of the John K. Mullen of Denver Memorial Library at the Catholic University of America and of the St. Charles Borromeo Seminary Library at Overbrook, Pa., for the many willing and generous courtesies extended to him, and to the Reverends William D. Bruckmann, S.T.L., and Peter J. Klekotka, J.C.D., for the special assistance they rendered. Finally, he acknowledges his sincere gratitude to the Sisters of the Immaculate Heart of Mary and the priests attached to the parish of St. John the Baptist, Manayunk, Pa., including his former and present pastors, Rt. Rev. Msgr. Eugene Murphy, dec'd., and Rev. John J. McKenna, and his fellow Assistants, Revs. Connell Clinton, J.C.D., Ignatius C. Reynolds, James F. Connor, and Robert J. McVeigh, for the many sacrifices they made in his behalf, and also to all those who in any way helped to bring this work to a successful conclusion.

TABLE OF CONTENTS

SECTION I

HISTORICAL SYNOPSIS

CHAPTER I

The Terms *Incardination* and *Excardination*

ARTICLE I

ETYMOLOGY OF THE TERMS

The verb *to incardinate,* whenever used in an ecclesiastical sense from the sixth century to the time of the Code, invariably meant to perpetually attach a person, particularly a cleric, to a new diocese after he had been transferred from another, with a view to the engagement of his services as an ecclesiastic.

The verb *to excardinate,* appearing for the first time in the nineteenth century, meant, correlatively, to perpetually transfer a person from a diocese to which he already belonged.

Each of the two words is a compound of a preposition with the adjective *cardinatus.* This adjective was first used in the time of Caesar Augustus by an authority on architecture, Marcus Pollio Vitruvius,[1] and it has its root in the classical Latin word *cardo,* a hinge.[2] To understand the metaphorical use of the word *cardo,* it must be explained that a hinge originally consisted of a point-like extremity on one beam, requiring a cavity at the end of another, so that the former, inserted into the latter, could revolve. A door, for example, was made by erecting a strong vertical beam, with round, pointed projections at both ends, between two other beams placed horizontally, above and below the doorway, with cavities prepared in the ends of them in such a position that the projections of the vertical beam would fit into the cavities of the transverse beams, allowing the vertical beam a free, revolutionary movement. Sufficient paneling was then added to the vertical beam to cover the area of the doorway. Thus the door had two hinges or *cardines.* The

[1] *De Architectura Libri Decem ad Caesarem Augustum,* Lugduni (1552).

[2] Freund-Leverett, *Lexicon,* " cardo."

vertical beams were called *scapi cardinales,* that is, the beams bearing the *cardines* or points.[3]

The use of the word *cardo,* however, was not confined to a rotary object. It was a generic term applicable to the tenon and mortise principle of attaching one beam to another.[4] Consequently a beam was said to be *cardinated* if it had tenons or projections on its extremities making it possible for it to be attached in a fixed manner to another beam,[5] and the same was termed *intercardinated* when it was actually attached.[6]

ARTICLE II

SIGNIFICANCE OF THE WORD *Cardinal*

Authors are inclined to establish a real connection between the terms *incardinate* and *cardinal* so that in a general way *to incardinate* would always mean *to make a cardinal.* They are moved to do so by the coexistence of the two terms so frequently in the letters of Pope Gregory I as well as by their ap-

[3] "Fores ita compingantur, uti scapi cardinales sint ex altitudine luminis totius duodecima parte."—Vitruvius, *De Architectura,* Lib. IV, cap. 6, *De ostiorum et antepagmentorum sacrarum aedium rationibus,* p. 153. The uprights had to be one-twelfth longer than the aperture because of the jutting points.—*Ibid.,* Annotat., p. 156. Hence, too, the distinction between the male and female in a hinge: "In eo autem minus tympanum includatur *cardinibus* ex torno, *masculo* et *foemina* inter se coartatis, ita uti minus tympanum, quemadmodum epistomium, in maiore circumagendo arcte leniterque versetur."—*Op. cit.,* Lib. IX, cap. 9, *De horologiorum ratione,* p. 397; *ibid.,* Annotat., p. 399.

[4] ". . . regulae capitibus ad normam coagmentatos, et inter regulam et ancones a cardinibus compacta transversaria, . . . "—*Op. cit.,* Lib. VIII, cap. 6, *De perductionibus et librationibus aquarum, et instrumentis ad hunc usum,* p. 343. "Supra trabes collocentur capreoli cardinibus alius in alium conclusi, in altitudine excitati pedes IX. . . "—*Op. cit.,* Lib. X, cap. 20, *De testudine, etc.,* p. 440. On this passage the Annotator remarks: "*Cardinibus alius in alium conclusi*—Cardines hoc loco intelliguntur extremae capreolorum partes, quae in cavum induntur, quomodo cardinatum tignum dicitur capite proximo. Idem in postibus, trabibus, transversariis, scapis, parastatis intelligendum. Ipsum autem cavum nostri materiarii mortesiam, cardinem vero tenonem dicunt."—*Ibid.,* Annotat., p. 440.

[5] "Erigebantur et arrectaria duo compacta . . . coniuncta capitibus transversario cardinato tigno, et altero mediano inter duos scapos cardinato, et laminis ferreis religato: . . . "—*Op. cit.,* Lib. X, cap. 21, *De aliis testudinibus,* p. 441; Freund-Leverett, *Lexicon,* "cardinatus."

[6] "Eae [postes compactiles] concluduntur superne intercardinatis trabibus . . . "—Vitruvius, *op. cit.,* cap. 20, *De testudine ad congestionem fossarum paranda,* p. 440.

parent common stem. Before tracing the historical development of the verb *to incardinate,* therefore, it is the purpose of this Article to attempt to give a definite decision on the ancient meaning of the word *cardinal* and its bearing on the subject of this study.

There are four general opinions, each of which will be considered in turn.

1st. A cardinal meant any priest, deacon, (or even cleric) permanently attached to a church or diocese.

2nd. A cardinal meant a Bishop, priest, or deacon who, being forced because of persecution or some other reason to abandon the church or diocese to which he belonged by ordination, was temporarily attached to another church or diocese.

3rd. A cardinal was a Bishop, priest, or deacon attached to the principal church of the diocese, and in later years it included also those attached to any principal church within the diocese.

4th. A cardinal was the principal or ruling officer, whether Bishop, priest, or deacon of a diocese, church, oratory, or *diaconia,* who was at the same time permanently attached thereto.

1. *First opinion. A cardinal was any permanently attached priest or deacon.*—This opinion is advanced by a consultor of the Sacred Congregation of the Council,[7] by Hatch,[8] Sägmüller,[9] Devoti,[10] Creusen,[11] and Chelodi.[12] According to them, *to incardinate* meant to ascribe a priest or deacon permanently to a particular church.

This opinion is erroneous. In Chapter III of this study it will be shown that as early as the fourth century all clerics were

[7] On discussion of *Dubia* proposed on Aug. 21, 1897—*AkKR,* LXXIX (1899), 95-96.

[8] *Organization of Early Christian Churches,* (8th impression, London, 1918), p. 206, note 25.

[9] Art. "Cardinal,"—*Catholic Encyclopedia* (*Cath. Ency.*), III, 333 b.

[10] *Institutionum Canonicarum Libri IV* (*Instit. Can.*), (2 vols., Leodii, 1883), lib. I, tit. III, sec. II, § 23, note 4.

[11] Vermeersch-Creusen, *Epitome Iuris Canonici* (*Epit.*), (2. ed., 3 vols., Mechliniae-Romae: H. Dessain, 1924-1925), I, n. 307.

[12] *Ius de Personis* (*De Pers.*), (2. ed., Tridenti: Libr. Edit. Tridentum, 1927), n. 156.

permanently attached by law to the church of their first ordination and yet all were not designated as cardinals, for oftentimes mere priests were mentioned without such a title.[13]

2. *Second opinion. A cardinal was an exiled Bishop, priest or deacon temporarily placed in another church.*—The most recent and staunchest proponent of this theory was Tamagna,[14] who read that meaning out of the epistles of Pope Gregory the Great and who concluded, therefore, that *to incardinate* in the early ages meant the act of thus transferring a cleric temporarily.

His opinion is incorrect because: a) on one occasion a cardinal priest was constituted by ordination in his own church,[15] and b) in other cases such an interpretation would be repugnant to the rest of the context, e. g., where the clergy or people of a church asked the Pope to send them some particular individual as their cardinal priest, and were congratulated by the Pope on having asked for such a man.[16]

3. *Third opinion. A cardinal was a Bishop, priest or deacon (later on even a cleric) attached to the principal church of the diocese or, still later, to any principal church within the diocese.*—In other words, the term *cardinal* was understood to have primarily referred to a place, and only secondarily to the persons thereto attached. Bellarmine,[17] Wernz,[18] and De Meester [19] follow this view.

It lacks probability because even oratories, which were by no means principal churches, had their cardinals.[20]

[13] Cf., e. g., Greg. Mag., lib. I, epist. 15—*MPL*, LXXVII, 460-461; *ibid.*, epist. 53—*MPL*, LXXVII, 515; *ibid.*, epist. 78—*MPL*, LXXVII, 532; *ibid.*, epist. 81—*MPL*, LXXVII, 534; lib. IV, epist. 11—*MPL*, LXXVII, 679; lib. VI, epist. 12—*MPL*, LXXVII, 803.

[14] *Origini e Prerogative De' Cardinali*, cap. III, especially n. 49. He claimed that he followed Gonzales, Reiffenstuel, Lancellottus, Fleury, and Florente.—*Ibid.*, p. 98.

[15] Greg. Mag., lib. I, epist. 15—*MPL*, LXXVII, 460-461.

[16] *Ibid.*, lib. II, epist. 9—*MPL*, LXXVII, 545; *ibid.*, lib. III, epist. 13—*MPL*, LXXVII, 614-615; cc. 5-6, C. XXI, q. 1; *ibid.*, lib. III, epist. 14—*MPL*, LXXVII, 615.

[17] *De clericis*, lib. I, c. 16.

[18] *Ius Decretalium*, (3. ed., 6 vols., Prati, 1915), I, n. 359, ss.

[19] *Iuris Canonici et Iuris Canonico-Civilis Compendium* (*Compendium*), (ed. nova, Brugis: Sumptibus et Typis Societatis Sancti Augustini, 1923), II, n. 553.

[20] Greg. Mag., lib. IX, epist. 70—*MPL*, LXXVII, 1007; lib. XII, epist. 11—*MPL*, LXXVII, 1225-1226.

4. *Fourth opinion. A cardinal was a proper residential clerical Superior.*—He was the Titular and Primary Beneficiary of a place.[21]

This opinion is truly correct and best agrees with the usage of the term *cardinalis.* The scapi *cardinales* of Vitruvius,[22] be it remembered, where the word occurred for the first time, meant the beams bearing the *cardines* or points. Since Varro and Cicero used *cardines* to denote the points or poles of the earth; Pliny, in the first century, to denote the main points of the year separating the seasons; and Quintillian, in the same century, to describe the four quarters or points of the heavens,[23] it was but logical for the adjective *cardinalis* to become synonymous with *chief* or *principal,* as it did, at least by the fifth century, in the writings of the grammarian, Servius Honoratus.[24]

Applied ecclesiastically, *cardinalis* assumed the meaning of an important or principal cleric of a church. Its first known use as such was in the Council of Rome under Pope Sylvester in 314.[25] Efforts to trace it earlier in the Church are based on fragmentary accounts of the *Liber Pontificalis.* Thus Clement divided the City of Rome into seven Regions; Evaristus distributed the titles in the City of Rome to the priests; Hyginus

21 In a general way this opinion was defended by: Panvinius, *Romani Pontifices et Cardinales S.R.E.*, Appen. *De Episcopatibus, Titulis, et Diaconiis Cardinalium Liber* (*De Episcop.*), p. 51; Polydorus and Ciaconius—Kleiner, *Dissertatio de origine et antiquitate cardinalatus* (*Dissert. de orig. et antiq. card.*), cap. III, nn. 13-14 (Schmidt, *Thesaurus Iuris Ecclesiastici potissimum Germanici sive Dissertationes Selectae in Ius Ecclesiasticum* [*Thesaurus*], II, Dissert. IX); Thomassinus, *Vetus et Nova Ecclesiae Disciplina circa Beneficia et Beneficiarios* (*Eccl. Discip.*), P. I, lib. II, cap. CXV, nn. 2-6; Van Espen, *Ius Ecclesiasticum Universum* (*Ius Eccles. Univ.*), I, P. I, tit. 22, cc. 1, 6, 8; and others cited in Tamagna, *Origini e Prerogative De' Cardinali*, cap. III, n. 44.

22 Cf. *supra*, p. 2.

23 Freund-Leverett, *Lexicon*, "cardo."

24 *Ibid.*, "cardinalis."

25 "Presbiter autem cardinalis nisi in LXIV testibus non deponatur; diaconus cardinalis urbis Romae nisi in XXVII testibus non condemnabitur . . . "—Actio I, c. 3 (Mansi, *Sacrorum Conciliorum Nova et Amplissima Collectio*, II, 623; c. 2, C. II, q. 4); "Ut diaconi non essent plus vel amplius per parochiarum examen nisi duo et diaconos cardinales urbis Romae septem; . . . "—*Ibid.*, c. 6 (Mansi, II, 625); "A subdiacono usque ad lectores omnes subditi sint diacono cardinali viro reverentissimo, in ecclesia representantes ei honorem . . . "—*Ibid.*, c. 7 (Mansi, II, 625; c. 5, D. XCIII); Ferraris, *Biblioth.*, "Cardinales," Art. I, § 3.

put the clergy in order and distributed the posts of honor; Fabian distributed the Regions of the city to the deacons; Dionysius gave the churches to the priests; and Marcellus constituted twenty-five titles in the City of Rome, quasi-dioceses, for the baptism and penance of the multitude of pagan converts and for the burial of the martyrs.[26] Panvinius [27] understands the *titles* here spoken of to be the churches of Rome, which were placed in charge of priests, the *chief* of whom in each *title* was called the *cardinal priest.* In like manner, the *Regions* of Rome he understands to be seven sections of the city which were placed in care of deacons, so that each in his own Region would have exclusive care of the poor, the widows, and the orphans, but that when it became necessary to assign more than one deacon to a Region, the first or principal one in each section was called a *cardinal deacon,* and that these were the cardinal priests and deacons mentioned in the Council of Rome in 314.

Confirmation of this opinion is found also in the fifth century, when the term *cardinal Bishop* designated a Bishop who was a residential Superior in contradistinction to one who was only visiting. Pope Gelasius (a. 492-496) wrote to a Bishop Celestine authorizing him to go to another diocese in the capacity of a visitor, not as cardinal Bishop, and to confer the priesthood on Julian, a deacon of the church of St. Eleutherius.[28]

Considerable weight is further added to this opinion by the following observations: a) whenever a see was made vacant another Bishop was sent as *cardinalis sacerdos* or chief shepherd; [29] b) whenever the clergy and people were without a

[26] *Liber Pontificalis,* ed. Duchesne, I, pp. 123, 126, 131, 148, 157, 164. The supposed letter of Pope Anacletus to all Bishops (c. 2, D. XXII), in which the Apostolic See is called *cardo* "because by it all churches are ruled as a door is ruled by its hinge," on which text many authors relied in explaining the origin and meaning of the various derivatives of *cardo,* is Pseudo-Isidorean. — Cf. Hinschius, *Decretales Pseudoisidorianae et capitula Angilrami* (Lipsiae, 1863), p. 83.

[27] *De Episcopatibus, Titulis, et Diaconiis Cardinalium,* pp. 51-52.

[28] ". . . suprascriptum presbiterii honore decorabis, sciturus [eum] visitatoris, nomine te, non cardinalis creasse pontificis."—C. 3, D. XXIV. *Eum* is inserted into the text at the place indicated in the Roman edition of 1582.

[29] Greg. Mag., lib. I, epist. 79—*MPL,* LXXVII, 533; *ibid.,* lib. II, epist. 37—*MPL,* LXXVII, 575; c. 42, C. VII, q. 1; *ibid.,* lib. III, epist. 13—*MPL,* LXXVII, 614-5; cc. 5-6, C. XXI, q. 1.

cardinal Bishop they petitioned the Holy Father to send them one;[30] c) any Bishop, sojourning in another diocese, was forbidden to exercise the authority of a cardinal Bishop over the same;[31] d) after an oratory was built and consecrated, it was a matter for decision whether or not a resident priest should be placed in charge of it as a cardinal priest *(cardinalis presbyter)*;[32] e) on one occasion when a church was left not only without a chief shepherd but even without a priest to care for the dying, the neighboring Bishop was commissioned to go there and *ordain* a cardinal priest, two deacons, and in the parishes of the diocese three priests.[33]

From the foregoing it can well be concluded that the expression *to make a cardinal* was not interchangeable in meaning with the expression *to incardinate.*

ARTICLE III

Incardinate AND ITS SYNONYMS

The verb *to incardinate,* as an ecclesiastical expression, seems to have been used for the first time in the sixth century by Pope Gregory I. Various excerpts from his epistles in which it was used, especially in conjunction with the idea of "making a cardinal," are here given.

> Si eum post haec cardinalem facere volueris, nisi Pontificis sui cessionem solemni more meruerit, abstinendum ab omni *incardinatione* memineris, ...[34]

[30] Cf. *supra,* p. 4, footnote 16.

[31] Greg. Mag., lib. XIV, epist. 7—*MPL,* LXXVII, 1310; c. 3, D. XXIV.

[32] *Ibid.,* lib. II, epist. 12—*MPL,* LXXVII, 548; *ibid.,* lib. IX, epist. 70—*MPL,* LXXVII, 1007; *ibid.,* lib. XII, epist. 11—*MPL,* LXXVII, 1225-6.

[33] "Gregorius Balbino episcopo Rosellano. Pervenit ad nos quod Populanensis Ecclesia ita sit sacerdotis officio destituta . . . jubemus dilectioni tuae, ut, hujus praeceptionis auctoritate commonitus, memoratae Ecclesiae visitator accedas, ut unum cardinalem illic presbyterum et duos debeas diaconos ordinare. In parochiis vero praefatae Ecclesiae tres similiter presbyteros, quos tamen dignos etc."—Greg. Mag., lib. I, epist. 15 (*MPL,* LXXVII, 460-1).

[34] Greg. Mag., lib. 1, epist. 83 (italics inserted)—*MPL,* LXXVII, 536.

Gregorius Agnello episcopo de Fundis, qui nunc in civitate *incardinatus* est Terracinensi.[35]

C. 5. Relatio cleri simul et populi Terracinae degentis nos ualde letificat, ob hoc, quod de tua fraternitate bona testatur. Et quia defuncto pontifice suo Petro sibi *cardinalem* postulant te constitui *sacerdotem*, eorum desideria necessario conplenda preuidimus ... Quicquid uero de predictae rebus ecclesiae uel eius patrimonio, seu cleri ordinatione promotioneue, et omnibus generaliter ad eam pertinentibus sollerter atque canonice ordinare facereque prouideris, liberam habebis, quippe ut sacerdos proprius, modis omnibus facultatem.

C. 6. Illud quoque fraternitatem tuam scire necesse est, quoniam sic te predictae Terracinensis ecclesiae *cardinalem* esse constituimus *sacerdotem*, ut et Fundensis ecclesiae pontifex esse *non* desinas, nec curam gubernationemque eius pretereas, quia ita fraternitati tuae sepe dictae Terracinensis ecclesiae curam iniungimus ut Fundensis ecclesiae tibi iura potestatemue nullo modo subtrahamus.[36]

Pastoralis offitii cura nos ammonet, destitutis ecclesiis proprios constituere sacerdotes, qui gregem dominicum pastorali sollicitudine gubernare debeant. Propterea te Iohannem ab hostibus captiuatum Lesimanae ciuitatis episcopum in Squillitana ecclesia *cardinalem* necesse duximus statuere *sacerdotem*, ut et susceptam semel animarum curam intuitu futurae retributionis inpleas. Et licet tua sis hoste inminente depulsus, aliam, que a pastore uacat, debes ecclesiam gubernare, ita tamen, ut si ciuitatem illam hostibus liberam effici et Domino protegente ad priorem statum contigerit reuocari, in eam, in qua *prius ordinatus es*, ecclesiam reuertaris; sin autem predicta ciuitas continua captiuitatis calamitate premitus, in hac, in qua es *incardinatus* a nobis, debeas ecclesia permanere.[37]

Praesentium lator Felix *diaconus*, cum nullatenus in haereticorum dogma lapsus sit, nec a catholica fide discesserit, pravis illectus adversus Constantinopolitanam synodum suspicionibus, in Istricorum se separatione removerat. Qui cum Romam venisset, recepta a nobis juvante Domino ratione, excessum suum, recepta

[35] Title to lib. III, epist. 13 (italics inserted)—*MPL*, LXXVII, 614.

[36] Greg. Mag., lib. III, epist. 13 *ad Agnellum Episcopum* (italics inserted)—Cc. 5-6, C. XXI, q. 1.

[37] Greg. Mag., lib. II, epist. 37 *Ioanni Episcopo Squillatino* (italics inserted)—*MPL*, LXXVII, 575; c. 42, C. VII, q. 1.

Dominici corporis communione, correxit. Quia ergo, . . . non in haeresim incidit, . . . imbecillitati ejus atque necessitatibus consulentes, maximeque sustentationi ejus pietatis intuitu providentes, in tua Ecclesia Syracusana eum praevidimus *cardinandum*; sive ut officium diaconatus expleat, seu certe ut sola ejusdem officii pro sustentanda paupertate sua commoda consequatur, in tuae fraternitatis volumus hoc pendere judicio.[38]

Fraternitatem tuam a nobis petisse recolimus, ut Gratianum ecclesiae Enafrenae *diaconem* tuae concederemus ecclesiae *cardinandum*. Et quoniam nec episcopum, cui obsecundare debeat, propria habet ecclesia, hoste scilicet prohibente, quo suum debeat ministerium exhibere, peticionem tuam non preuidimus differendam. Idcirco scriptis tibi presentibus eum necessario duximus concedendum, habiturus licentiam illum *diaconum* nostra interueniente auctoritate ecclesiae tuae, Deo propitio, constituere *cardinalem*.[39]

A brief study of these excerpts will show that in every epistle Pope Gregory used the word *cardinate* or *incardinate* to refer to the act of *transferring* a Bishop, priest, or deacon to a church or diocese different from his native church, but always in the capacity of a cardinal, i. e., as a residential Superior. However, the converse is not true, namely, that in his letters every constitution of a cardinal priest or deacon was termed an incardination, especially when the cleric was to be made a cardinal priest or cardinal deacon in the very church of his first ordination.[40]

The Roman Correctors of the Decree of Gratian add weight to this belief,[41] as does also John the Deacon in the seventh

[38] *Ibid.*, lib. IV, epist. 14 (italics inserted)—*MPL*, LXXVII, 684.

[39] *Ibid.*, lib. VI, epist. 11 *Fortunato Episcopo Neapolitano* (italics inserted)—*MPL*, LXXVII, 802; c. 5, D, LXXI. *Cardinandum* is a correction inserted in the Roman edition.

[40] Cf. *supra*, pp. 6-7, footnotes 28, 33; c. 6, D. LXXIV.

[41] "Cardinandum: Antea legebatur: ordinandum. Emendatum est ex ipsa epistola. Cardinare vero, seu cardinalem constituere (quod est in fine huius capitis), ita videtur B. Gregorius accepisse, ut canonicam translationem significet. Nam quum tempore S. Gregorii canon 6 concilii Chalcedonensis accurate observaretur, ut nullo modo daretur alicui locus in ecclesia (qui nunc titulus vocatur) nisi simul ad eum locum ordinaretur, quum aliquis iam ordinatus, necessitate aliqua in aliam ecclesiam transferebatur, ut in illa in eodem gradu, quo in prima ordinatus erat, deserviret, in secunda dicebatur incardinari; quod ex isto nunc indicato loco patere potest, et ex l. 3, epist. 14 et alibi."—*Notationes Correctorum*, c. 5, D. LXXI.

century when, writing the life of Gregory the Great, he says of him that he took care to incardinate in vacant sees those Bishops who had to abandon their own sees, and that those whom he could not readily incardinate he sent to other Bishops for sustenance, and that he was very prudent in incardinating clerics of other dioceses either into his own diocese or into the dioceses of others.[42]

From the seventh to the end of the eleventh century no variation in the meaning of the term is in evidence.[43]

From the twelfth to the eighteenth century it did not appear in official documents at all, e. g., in the Decretals of Gregory IX, the canons of the Councils, particularly of Trent, Papal Bulls or Letters, or even in the Latin lexicons of the period.[44] Only a few exceptions occur, such as in the provincial Synod of the Greek Maronites held on Mount Libanus in 1736,[45] and in a letter sent to all the Bishops of Etruria in connection with their convention at Florence in 1786-1787.[46]

Widespread use of the term *incardination* along with its correlative *excardination* began only in the latter part of the nineteenth century. It was the Roman Curia which adopted it in

[42] *Vita S. Gregorii*, lib. III, §§ 15, 16, 19—*MPL*, LXXV, 133.

[43] "Synodale, ut episcopus alterius civitatis in alia Ecclesia possit *incardinari*."—*Liber Diurnus Romanorum Pontificum*, cap. III, t. 11 (*MPL*, CV, 77); Adrian II, a. 868, ep. 7—Mansi, XV, 823-824; *ibid.*, ep. 11—Mansi, XV, 828; Hincmar, Abp. of Rheims, a. 874, *Capitula in Synodo Rhemis data*, cap. 1—*MPL*, CXXV, 795; John VIII, a. 876, ep. 13 *ad Bituricenses*—Mansi, XVIIa, 13; *ibid.*, ep. 14 *ad episcopos Provinc. Bitur.*—Mansi, XVIIa, 14; Adam, Canon of Bremen, XI cent., *Gesta Hammaburgensis Ecclesiae Pontificum*, cap. 215—*MPL*, CXLVI, 626; Ivo of Chartres, XI cent., ep. 131, *ad Wilgrinum*—*MPL*, CLXII, 140; Urban II, a. 1092, ep. 71—*MPL*, CLI, 356-7; Mansi, XX, 671.

[44] Gerardi Joannis Vosii *Etymologicon Linguae Latinae* (Amstelodami, 1662); Ambrosii Calepini *Dictionarium* (*ed. noviss.*, Lugduni, 1681); Basilii Fabrii Sorami *Thesaurus Eruditionis Scholasticae* (Hagae-Comitum, 1735); *Vocabularium Latinum et Italicum* (Romae, 1792); *Totius Latinitatis Lexicon* Aegidii Forcellini, (Schneelbergae, 1831).

[45] ". . . Nemo presbyterum vel clericum ab aliena dioecesi ad propriam transferat, . . . vel eum in propria *incardinet* ecclesia, nisi consensum dante ordinario . . . "—Italics inserted. *Constitutiones et Canones*, P. III, cap. IV, n. 24 (Mansi, XXXVIII, 193).

[46] "Tutti i sacerdoti, che abbiano benefizio residenziale, dovrebbero essere *incardinati* alla chiesa, dove sia fondato il loro benefizio, . . ."—Italics inserted. Sec. XXI (Mansi, XXXVIII, 1004-5).

its discussions and responses, but which broadened its meaning so as to include the permanent attachment of any cleric or, in later years, even of a lay person to a new diocese after his transfer from another.[47]

America, a vast new missionary field, requiring the acquisition of many priests from abroad, had much to do with the development of the terminology for canonical transfers. In 1829 the First Provincial Council of Baltimore used the classical Latin word *cooptare* (to receive or admit into a body) to designate the transfer and enlistment of a foreign cleric in the service of a church here.[48] This and another expression, namely, *incorporare,* were used here throughout the major part of the nineteenth century until it became the practice of the Church to use the term *incardination* exclusively.[49]

The Code of Canon Law in canon 111, §2, however, has given to the term a more comprehensive meaning than it ever had before. To be *incardinated* now means to be permanently attached or admitted to the clergy of a diocese, whether by transfer from elsewhere or by initial tonsure in one's own diocese.[50]

[47] S.C.C., *Solutionis seu Excardinationis,* 18 dec. 1869 et 19 feb. 1870—*ASS,* V (1869), 477-478, where the Commentator discusses the word; S.C.C., *Taurinen., Adscriptionis seu Incardinationis,* 25 aug. 1877—*ASS,* X (1877), 485-491; S.C.C., *Viglevanen seu Mediolanen., Excardinationis,* 8 maii 1886—*ASS,* XIX (1886), 122-125; S.C.C., decr. "*A primis,*" 20 iulii 1898—*ASS,* XXXI (1898-1899), 49 ss.; *AER,* XX (1899), 179 ff.; S.C. Ep. et Reg., *Viterbien., Excardinationis,* 14 iulii, 1905—*ASS,* XXXIX (1906), 207 ss.; S.C.C., decr. "*Vetuit,*" 22 dec. 1905—*ASS,* XXXVIII (1905-1906), 407 ss.; S.C.C., *Romana et Aliarum,* 15 sept. 1906—*ASS,* XXXIX (1906), 486 ss.; S.C.C., decr., 24 nov. 1906—*ASS,* XXXIX (1906), 600 ss.; *AER,* XXXVI (1907), 292; S.R.R., *Londonen.,* 9 ian. 1912—*AAS,* IV (1912), 249 ss.; S.C.C., *Bismarckien. et Aliarum,* 31 ian. 1913—*AAS,* V (1913), 34 ss.; S.R.R., Decis. XXII, 17 apr. 1913—*Decisiones seu Sententiae,* V, 249 ss.; S.C.C., *Dioecesis T.,* 27 ian., 1917—*AAS,* X (1918), 18 ss.

[48] *Decreta,* n. II—Mansi, XXXIX, 295.

[49] I Plenary Council of Baltimore, a. 1852, *Decreta,* n. 9—Mansi, XLIV, 675; II Provincial Council of New Orleans, a. 1860, *Decreta,* n. 9—Mansi, XLVIII, 23; II Plenary Council of Baltimore, a. 1866, *Decreta,* nn. 108-9, 121, 314—*Conc. Plen. Balt. II Acta et Decreta,* pp. 75, 78, 166; I Provincial Council of Quebec, a. 1851, *Decreta,* n. XIII—Mansi, XLIV, 585; III Plenary Council of Baltimore, a. 1884, *Decreta,* nn. 62-3—*Acta et Decreta Conc. Plen. Balt. III,* p. 32.

[50] Vermeersch-Creusen, *Epitome,* I, n. 202; Wernz-Vidal, *Ius Canonicum ad Codicis normam exactum* (*Ius Can.*), II *De Personis* (2. ed., Romae: Universitas Gregoriana, 1928), n. 58.

ARTICLE IV

Excardinate AND ITS SYNONYMS

The preposition *ex* prefixed to the ancient adjective *cardinatus,* already analyzed,[51] gives the notion of one thing being detached from another. *To excardinate* in ecclesiastical language vividly represents the release of a cleric from the diocese to which he antecedently belonged. Though the etymology is old, the term is new. It did not appear in any important Church laws or documents prior to the nineteenth century, and is not mentioned in the major Latin lexicons.[52] After 1865, the Roman Curia used it frequently in the sense just defined, just as it did its correlative *incardination.*[53]

The idea of detaching a cleric from one diocese in order to subject him to another is as old as the establishment of the territorial divisions of the Church. This will be fully discussed in Chapters III and IV. All that pertains to the present Article is to note the synonyms which were used to express what is now termed *excardination.* There were many. Very often the words *transire* (to pass over), *transferre* (to transfer), *migrare* (to change one's habitation), *discedere* (to depart), and *recedere* (to go away from) are found in the text of the canons of the various councils, and it is apparent from the context that they signify a canonical change of diocese.[54]

In the Ancient Period of the Church "dimissorial letters" *(litterae dimissoriae)* was recognized as a traditional, accepted

[51] *Supra,* p. 2.

[52] Gerardi Joannis Vosii *Etymologicon Linguae Latinae*; Ambrosii Calepini *Dictionarium*; Du Cange, *Glossarium*; Basilii Fabri Sorani, *Thesaurus Eruditionis Scholasticae*; *Totius Latinitatis Lexicon* Aegidii Forcellini; Harper's *Latin Dictionary*; Freund-Leverett, *Lexicon.*

[53] *ASS,* I (1865), 361-2, note 1; *supra,* p. 11, footnote 47. Summary of responses given by the Bishops of the world on matters of ecclesiastical discipline to be treated in the Vatican Council, Quaest. IX, n. 245—Mansi, XLIX, 354-5; S.C.C., *Resp.* 29 maii 1880—*ASS,* XIII (1880), 522-526.

[54] E. g., IV Counc. of Carthage, a. 398, cap. 27—Mansi, III, 953; Council of Chalcedon, a. 451, c. 10—Mansi, VII, 362; c. 3, C. XXI, q. 2; II Counc. of Nice, a. 787, c. 10—Mansi, XIII, 429, 751; Synod of Szabolcs, Hungary, a. 1092, cap. 18—Mansi, XX, 769; Provincial Council of Tours, a. 1583, tit. 14—Mansi, XXXIVa, 834.

term for excardination,[55] though the meaning of dimissorial letters after the twelfth century and also in the Code is vastly different.[56] Sometimes the letters by which a cleric was released from his diocese were called *formatae,*[57] *Apostoli,*[58] or *Commendatitiae,*[59] and in the nineteenth century they received still other new names, such as *litterae excorporationis,*[60] *litterae remissoriales,*[61] *litterae discessoriae,*[62] *litterae discessoriales,*[63] and *exeat.*[64]

One of the beneficial effects of the Code was to establish technical terminology in the entire sphere of Canon Law. Because of its specific use in canons 111 to 117, *excardination* is now the sole term employed to designate the perpetual release of a secular cleric from a diocese as a concomitant effect of his canonical attachment to another diocese or of his perpetual affiliation with a Religious Institute.

55 Thomassinus, *Eccl. Discip.*, P. II, lib. I, cap. V, n. 5; Bingham, *Antiq.*, Bk. II, ch. IV, n. 5; Bk. VI, ch. IV, n. 4; Gasparri, *De Sacra Ordinatione*, n. 863; Ojetti, *Synopsis Rerum Moralium et Iuris Pontificii*, II, n. 1805.

56 Moeder, *The Proper Bishop for Ordination and Dimissorial Letters*, pp. 41, 79 ff.

57 Thomassinus, *Eccl. Discip.*, P. II, lib. I, cap. V, n. 5; Bingham, *Antiq.*, Bk. II, ch. IV, n. 5.

58 Du Cange, *Glossarium*, "Apostoli."

59 VI Council of Paris, a. 829, lib. I, cap. 36—Mansi, XIV, 561-2; Glossa in c. 5, X, *de clericis non resident.*, III, 4.

60 I Provincial Council of Westminister, a. 1852, *Decreta*, cap. XXIX, n. 7—Mansi, XLIV, 750.

61 S.C.C., 22 iun. 1871—*ASS*, VI (1870), 495.

62 S.C.C., litt. ency. (*ad Epp. Ital. et Amer.*) 27 iul. 1890—*Collectanea* S. C. P. F., n. 1734, §4.

63 S. C. Consist., decr. "*Ethnographica studia,*" 25 mar. 1914—*AAS*, VI (1914), 182 ss.

64 III Plenary Council of Baltimore, a. 1884, *Decreta*, n. 67—*Acta et Decreta Conc. Plen. Balt.* III, p. 34.

CHAPTER II

Episcopal and Parochial Organization

Many brilliant works on this subject already exist. It is to the purpose of this study here and now only to give to the reader a brief framework of facts and conditions in a chronological order, to provide a background of easy reference for the correct understanding of what is to follow.

ARTICLE I

BEFORE 300

1. The East

The Apostles were not circumscribed by any territorial limits in the exercise of their spiritual authority. They acted as protectors and visitors to the Christian foundations in various cities. Divinely authorized to transmit their powers, they associated with themselves in the ministry men like Timothy and Titus, Barnabas and Luke, and constituted others in certain capacities variously designated as Bishops (ἐπίσκοποι),[1] priests (πρεσβύτεροι),[2] or presidents (προιστάμενοι).[3] Some of these, at least, were the first Bishops of the Catholic Church, who were set to rule and ordain others.[4]

The *Bishops* of the second century already were jurisdictionally limited to the flock over which they were placed, as, for instance, Ignatius of Antioch and Polycarp of Smyrna. No exact territory was assigned as yet, but they were established

[1] *Acts*, XX, 28; *Phil.*, I, 1; 1 *Tim.*, III, 2; *Titus*, I, 7.

[2] *Acts*, XI, 30; XIV, 22; XV, 2, 4, 6, 22, 23; XVI, 4; XX, 17; XXI, 18; 1 *Tim.*, V, 17, 19; *Titus*, I, 5.

[3] 1 *Thes.*, V, 12; *Rom.*, XII, 8.

[4] *Acts*, XX, 28: "Attendite vobis, et universo gregi, in quo vos Spiritus sanctus posuit episcopos regere Ecclesiam Dei, quam acquisivit sanguine suo." *Titus*, I, 5: "Huius rei gratia reliqui te Cretae, ut ea, quae desunt, corrigas, et constituas per civitates presbyteros, sicut et ego disposui tibi."

as residents in the important cities where the major Christian communities existed, and the sphere of their influence over nearby smaller cities and villages was the indeterminate extent of their jurisdiction.[5] By the year 250 it seems reasonably certain that every city of importance had become the residence of a Bishop.[6]

The place of worship in Apostolic times was the private house, as can be deduced from St. Paul's epistles.[7] By legacy or gift, some such places must have become the property of the Church, for St. Ignatius of Antioch repeatedly spoke of the Bishop's church in the city.[8] Likewise, he left no doubt that the Bishop alone was the episcopal pastor of the entire city; that to his church all the faithful had to come on days of divine worship to attend the only eucharistic sacrifice, celebrated by him alone, and to receive from his hands the sacraments.[9]

Other clergy than the Bishop embraced priests, deacons, and those who had received only minor orders,[10] which latter in-

[5] St. Ignatius of Antioch (a. 117) addressed his epistles only to the churches of the largest cities, and never made mention of any other than the Bishop's church, thus, for example: "... Sicut ergo Dominus sine Patre nihil facit ... sic etiam et vos sine episcopo, sive presbyter, seu diaconus, sive laicus. Non ergo aliquid rationabile vobis videtur extra ipsius sententiam; tale etenim iniquum est et Deo inimicum ... Omnes adunati ad templum Dei concurrite, sicut ad unum altare."—*Ad Magnes.*, cap. VII, 1-2 (*MPG*, V, 668); *idem, ad Smyr.*, cap. VIII, 1—*MPG*, V, 713.

[6] In Egypt alone there were one hundred bishoprics by the time of the Synod of Alexandria (a. 324)—Funk, *Manual of Church History*, I, 34; Van Hove, "Diocese," —*Cath. Ency.*, V, I; Natalis Alexander, *Historia Ecclesiastica Veteris Novique Testamenti* (*Hist. Eccl.*), t. VII, cap. V, art. VI.

[7] 1 *Cor.*, XI, 22; *Rom.*, XVI, 1, 4, 5; *Coloss.*, IV, 15; 1 *Cor.*, XVI, 19; *Phil.*, I, 2; Bingham, *Antiq.*, Bk. VIII, ch. I, n. 13 (t. II, pp. 369-70).

[8] See footnote 5 immediately above. Pliny the Younger, proconsul of Bithynia, related to Emperor Trajan, about the year 112, concerning the Christians: "They assemble before dawn at a fixed hour and all together sing a hymn to Christ as to God."—*Epist. X, 97* (Lesêtre, *La Paroisse*, p. 11).

[9] See above on this page, footnote 5.

[10] Priests and deacons were certainly in existence, as one can gather from the New Testament as well as from the rules concerning them in the early fourth century councils and synods, e. g., c. 13 of the Synod of Neocaesarea (a. 314-25)—Mansi, II, 541-2; Synod of Ancyra, a. 314, c. 13—Hardouin, II, 275-6. Some minor orders were in existence in the second century, for St. Ignatius Martyr, a. 117, wrote to the Antiochians: "Saluto Hypodiaconos, Lectores, Cantores, Janitores, Laborantes,

cluded chanters *(cantores)* and grave-diggers *(laborantes)*. These were to assist, or, in the case of priests, to substitute for, the Bishop in the many phases of church worship.[11]

Rural Bishops, later known as *chorepiscopi* (χωρεπίσκοποι), were the established delegates of the city Bishops for the evangelization of the villages wherever the number of Christians warranted it.[12] They enjoyed some episcopal powers, but were dependent on the city Bishop, and were the pastors of the first country churches, having about them priests, deacons and minor clergy, who aided them while they celebrated the sole sacrifice in the rural town.[13]

This Period saw the beginning of Religious in the Church, when in the third century men like St. Paul of Thebes and St. Anthony fled into the desert places of Egypt to find more intimate union with God by living a spiritual, mortified life in solitary huts, and by seldom communicating with the outside world. They received the name of anchorites *(anachoretae)* or hermits *(eremitae)*. Obviously they were not clerics.[14]

2. *The West*

Persecution made the problem of organization more difficult than in the East. The Christians were forbidden to meet in any regular place, so in Rome they chose private homes *(tituli)* and

Exorcistas."—Thomassinus, *Eccl. Discip.*, P. I, lib. II, cap. XXX, n. 2. All the present minor orders are listed in the third century in a letter of Pope Cornelius to Fabian, Bishop of Antioch, a. 252,—Eusebius, *Hist. Eccl.*, l. VI, c. 43 (*MPG*, XX, 622). The subdiaconate, be it remembered, is still a minor order in the Oriental Church and was in the Latin Church until the twelfth century—Many, *De Sacra Ordin.*, n. 8, 3°, 4°. *Tonsurati* did not exist prior to the fourth century.

[11] Pighi, *Institutiones Historiae Ecclesiasticae* (*Institutx.*), I, p. 13.

[12] Cf. Synodal letter of the Bishops of the Council of Antioch, a. 269—Eusebius, *Hist. Eccles.*, l. VII, c. 30 (*MPG*, XX, 709-20), in which mention of rural Bishops is made. Cf. also the listing of *chorepiscopi* as an established institution in the early councils of the fourth century, e. g., Synod of Ancyra, a. 314, c. 13—Hardouin, II, 275-6; *Council of Nicaea*, a. 325, c. 8—Hardouin, I, 326; Mansi, II, 671-2.

[13] Bastnagel, *The Appointment of Parochial Adjutants and Assistants* (Washington, D. C.: The Catholic University of America, 1930), pp. 7-9.

[14] Chelodi, *Ius de Personis*, n. 246; Vermeersch-Creusen, *Epit.*, I, n. 538; Fanfani, *De Iure Relig.*, n. 8; Schäfer, *De Relig.*, n. 10; Huddleston, "Monasticism,"—*Cath. Ency.*, X, 461d; Fortescue, "Eastern Monasticism,"—*Cath. Ency.*, X, 467-8.

cemeteries or catacombs *(cymiteria)* as their places for divine worship.[15] The Bishops, nevertheless, were installed in important cities at such a rapid pace that sixty of them from Italy alone attended a synod at Rome under Pope Cornelius (†253);[16] eighty-seven were brought together for the III Synod of Carthage in Africa in 256,[17] and at the Spanish Council of Elvira in 305 there were nineteen present.[18] As in the East, they were the pastors over the entire city, and everyone from city and country alike worshipped wherever the Bishop celebrated.[19]

The city clergy attached to the Bishop's church alone included among the minor orders at least lectors, exorcists and acolytes,[20] whose functions were a preparation for the clergy proper.[21] The country districts, too, had their priests and even their churches,[22] though there are no traces of *chorepiscopi.*

Monasticism did not exist as yet in the West.

15 De Rossi, *Roma Sotteranea Cristiana,* I, 199 ss.; II, 478 ss.; Fanning, "Church maintenance,"—*Cath. Ency.,* III, 762; Pighi, *Instituts.,* I, pp. 58-9; Duchesne, *Liber Pontif.,* I, pp. 126, 157.

16 Eusebius, *Hist. Eccl.,* l. VI, c. 43, n. 2—*MPG,* XX, 615.

17 Funk, *Manual of Church History,* I, p. 34.

18 *Loc. cit.*

19 Justin, *Apologia,* I, 67: "... et qui praeest, preces et gratiarum actiones totis viribus emittit, et populus acclamat, *Amen,* et eorum, in quibus gratiae actae sunt, distributio fit et communicatio unicuique praesentium, et absentibus per diaconos mittitur . . ."—*MPG,* VI, 430. Tertullian, *De Baptismo,* cap. 17: "Superest de observatione quoque dandi et accipiendi baptismi commonefacere. Dandi quidem habet ius summus sacerdos, qui est episcopus; dehinc presbyteri et diaconi, non tamen sine episcopi auctoritate, propter ecclesiae honorem, quo salvo, salva est pax..."—*MPL,* I, 1217; Cyprian, *Epistolae,* ep. 33: ". . . ut ecclesia super episcopos constituatur ..., et omnis actus ecclesiae per eosdem praepositos gubernetur."—*Corpus Scriptorum Ecclesiasticorum Latinorum* (*Corpus Vindobonense* = *CV*), III, 2, 566; Justin, *Apologia,* I, 67: "... Ac solis, ut dicitur, die omnium sive urbes sive agros incolentium in eumden locum fit conventus..."—*MPG,* VI, 430.

20 Thomassinus, *Eccl. Discip.,* P. I, lib. II, cap. XXX, nn. 5-6, where he cites Tertullian and Cyprian.

21 *Ibid.,* n. 8.

22 The Council of Elvira, a. 305, bore the names of priests attending with the names of their villages appended, and also spoke of the deacon in charge of the people in the country.—Mansi, II, 29; *ibid.,* cap. 77—Mansi, II, 18.

ARTICLE II

300 TO 500

1. *The East*

This was a period of great activity in the organizational progress of the Church. A term παροικία (a parish, i. e., a city and its neighborhood) was used for the first time to designate the territory of a Bishop.[23] It was later superseded, however, by the western term *dioecesis* (διοίκησις or *diocese*), which the Roman Empire was using for its divisions in civil government. Originally this term meant the "managing of a house," then "management" or "government" in general and, finally, in Roman Law, "the territory under the government of a city *(civitas)*" where a Roman ruler resided. Since a Bishop's territory was coextensive with the latter, the civil term *diocese* became an ecclesiastical one as well.[24] So closely, in fact, did the Church follow the districts of the highly organized Roman Empire to achieve well-defined episcopal territories that it even modified the boundaries of a diocese to agree with the modification of the civil district.[25] For a long time, however, the term *dioecesis* was not in universal use, and the term *parochia* is to be found along with it almost indiscriminately.[26]

The Bishop's position as chief pastor of an entire city did not change during this Period, and there were even laws enacted

[23] Council of Ancyra (a. 314), c. 18—Mansi, II, 265, 513; Council of Nicaea (a. 325), c. 16—Mansi, II, 675; c. 2, C. VII, q. 1; Council of Antioch (a. 341), c. 3—Mansi, VI App., 1160; c. 24, C. VII, q. 1; Council of Sardica (a. 343), c. 1 —c. 1, D. LXXI; Apostolic Canons 14-15—Mansi, I, 31; Bingham, *Antiq.*, Bk. IX, ch. II, n. 1.

[24] Van Hove, "Diocese," *Cath. Ency.*, V, 1. It was thus used in the Councils of Antioch (a. 332), c. 9—c. 2, C. IX, q. 3; Sardica (a. 343), c. 1—c. 1, D. LXXI (though the ancient Latin edition contains the word *parochia* instead—Mansi, VI App., 1150); and in the Council of Constantinople (a. 381), c. 2: "Qui sunt super dioecesim episcopi, nequaquam ad ecclesias, quae sunt extra praefixos sibi terminos, accedant, nec eas hac praesumptione confundant."—Mansi, III, 566-67; Hartzheim, *Concilia Germaniae*, I, 167.

[25] Council of Chalcedon (a. 451), c. 17—Mansi, VII, 365; Van Hove, "Diocese," —*Cath. Ency.*, V, 1; Duchesne, *Christian Worship*, pp. 12-13; Bingham, *Antiq.*, Bk. IX, ch. II, nn. 1-2.

[26] Lesêtre, *La Paroisse*, pp. 1-2; Van Hove, *loc. cit.*; Bingham, *ibid.*, ch. VIII, n. 1.

which expressly forbade the placing of Bishops in villages where a priest alone would suffice.[27] The strict unity of the eucharistic sacrifice, as well as the growth of the Church, is seen from a letter of Pope Leo I to Dioscorus, the Bishop of Alexandria, permitting him to have more than one Mass in a day to accommodate the crowds.[28]

City churches other than the cathedral were slow in being established; they made their appearance only after the formation of the country parishes. There is evidence in this Period that more than one church did exist at least in the episcopal cities of Alexandria[29] and Constantinople.[30] In the former city each church also had its own priest,[31] but apparently they were not permitted to celebrate Mass.[32] If other cities had any subsidiary churches it is likely that they were served by priests from the Bishop's cathedral.[33]

Country or rural churches in the more important towns answered a need which could not be satisfied by the Bishop himself. That is the reason for the earlier institution and multiplicity of country parishes. The rural Bishops were their residential pastors, but these Bishops were still subject to the city Bishop.[34] They were empowered to confer minor orders in their country churches,[35] but not major orders, since that was a faculty reserved to the urban Bishop.[36] They continued to

[27] Council of Sardica (a. 343), c. 6—Mansi, III, 10; Council of Laodicaea [a. 320], c. 57—Mansi, II, 573; Leo I (a. 446), ep. 12—*MPL*, LIV, 647.

[28] Epist. IX, cap. 2—Mansi, V, 1142; Thomassinus, *Eccl. Discip.*, P. I, lib. II, cap. XXII, n. 5.

[29] Epiphanius, *Haeres.* 69, n. 1—*MPG*, XLII, 202; *ibid.*, 68, n. 4—*MPG*, XLII, 190; Thomassinus, *Eccl. Discip.*, P. I, lib. II, cap. XXII, n. 1.

[30] Justinian (a. 527) observed that there were three churches there without proper clergy—Novell. III, c. 1.

[31] Epiphanius, *Haeres.*, *loc. cit.*; Thomassinus, *Eccl. Discip.*, *loc. cit.*

[32] St. Athanasius had to defend himself for having celebrated Mass in a certain church before it had been completely built—*Apol. ad Constant.*, n. 14 ff. (*MPG*, XXV, 611 ff.); Thomassinus, *ibid.*, n. 4.

[33] Bingham, *Antiq.*, Bk. IX, ch. VIII, n. 5.

[34] Council of Antioch (a. 341), c. 10—Mansi, II, 1312.

[35] *Ibid.*, cc. 24-25.

[36] *Ibid.*, c. 10.

have with them priests and minor clergy to assist in the sacrifice of the Mass and the administration of the sacraments.[37]

In addition to the country churches, other religious places, needing the services of priests or clerics, were increasing. These comprised filial churches or chapels of ease in the hamlets, chapels of martyrs which were erected at their tombs, poor houses or hospitals, hospices for travellers, and monastery chapels.[38]

A sharp distinction was being drawn between the clerical orders and the offices (stewards, defenders of the churches, etc.), the former alone being constituted as clergy by the imposition of the hands of the Bishop, the latter requiring merely promotion.[39]

Apparently the sustenance of the clergy had been cared for in the East, similarly as in the West, by a monthly division of the common fund, made up of the contributions of the faithful from all the churches and chapels subject to the urban Bishop, and administered by an *Oeconomus*. In the year 460 at Con-

[37] Council of Neocaesarea [a. 314], cc. 13-14—Mansi, II, 541-544; Council of Nicaea (a. 325), c. 8—Mansi, II, 671; Council of Antioch (a. 341), c. 10—Mansi, II, 1311; Council of Sardica (a. 343), c. 6—Mansi, VI, 1143; Council of Laodicaea [a. 320], c. 57—Mansi, II, 573. Athanasius (a. 326-373) declared that in the large villages near Alexandria there were a number of churches with proper priests—*Apologia contra Arianos* (*MPG*, XXV, 385-400).

[38] Council of Chalcedon (a. 451), c. 10—Mansi, VII, 362; c. 3, C. XXI, q. 2; *ibid.*, c. 19—Hardouin, II, 603, 607. St. John Chrysostom, Bishop of Constantinople (a. 397-407), had exhorted rich people in the country to build churches or chapels and have a priest and deacon or other clerics to offer the Holy Sacrifice there on Sundays and have the Divine Office—*In Acta Apos.*, Homily 18—*MPG*, LX, 141-150; Thomassinus, *Eccl. Discip.*, P. I, lib. II, cap. XCII, n. 9. It was in these small hamlets that the Councils cited above (p. 19, footnote 27) forbade the placement of a Bishop where a priest would be sufficient. St. Jerome (*Dialog. cont. Lucifer.*, c. 4) said that it was the custom for people who had been baptized by priests or deacons in villages or remote places to have the Bishop come and impose hands on them in order to receive the Holy Ghost. Some lived so far away that they died before the Bishop could come.—Bingham, *Antiq.*, Bk. IX, ch. VI, nn. 21-22.

[39] Council of Laodicaea [a. 320], c. 24—Mansi, II, 568; Council of Chalcedon (a. 451), c. 2—Mansi, VII, 373. Recipients of both orders and offices, however, were liable to any penalties levelled against clerics, according to St. Basil's epistle to Amphilochius of Iconium.—Epist. CCXVII, c. LI (*MPG*, XXXII, 795). Cf. Thomassinus, *Eccl. Discip.*, P. I, lib. II, cap. XXXIV, in which this subject is fully discussed.

stantinople there appeared the first evidence of a change in the system, when Marcianus, the *Oeconomus* for Gennadius, Archbishop of Constantinople, ordered each separate church and its clergy to retain their own offerings.[40]

A new development in the religious life occurred in this period. About the year 318, St. Pachomius in Egypt adopted with his followers a community, instead of a solitary, life, and they acquired the name of cenobites *(coenobitae)*. This new form of religious life, because of its superior advantages, met with the greater favor of the Church. In the succeeding centuries the houses where the cenobites lived, called *monasteria*, were intended primarily and solely for those who wished to sanctify themselves, and not for pursuants of some secondary purpose, such as that of teaching, of preaching, and the like. The monks indulged in various forms of manual work such as agriculture, writing, and weaving, but always in such a way as not to distract the mind from prayer. All of them were laymen; it would have been foreign to their aims to serve the churches as clerics. Their spiritual needs were supplied by the diocesan clergy. That is the meaning of the *monasteria* to which some clerics were assigned at ordination.[41]

2. *The West*

The term " diocese " (*dioecesis*, διοίκησις), which for ages has signified the territory subject to a Bishop's jurisdiction, originated in the West, denoting a Roman civil district. Its first ecclesiastical usage anywhere with its present significance occurred during the fourth century at the Council of Arles in France (a. 314),[42] and continued during that and the follow-

[40] Theodorus Lector thus wrote of Gennadius: " Designavit Gennadius Marcianum Oeconomum, qui mox atque Oeconomus esset factus, quae in unaquaque Ecclesia offerebantur, ab ejus loci Clericis accipi decrevit. Ad id enim usque tempus cuncta accipiebat Ecclesia Magna."—*Eccles. Hist.*, lib. I, n. 13 (*MPG*, LXXXVI, 171-174); Natalis Alexander, *Hist. Eccl.*, t. IX, cap. VI, art. V; Bingham, *Antiq.*, Bk. V, ch. VI, n. 1.

[41] Council of Chalcedon (a. 451), c. 6—Mansi, VII, 362; Bingham, *Antiq.*, Bk. VIII, ch. I, n. 1; Eusebius, *Hist. Eccl.*, l. II, c. 17.

[42] *Epistola Synodi*, " *Placuit* "—Mansi, II, 469; Bingham, *Antiq.*, Bk. IX, ch. II, nn. 1-2.

ing century in official documents with increasing regularity.[43] A diocese was as accurately defined in the Church as a civil district was in the Roman system, sometimes embracing more than one city together with the surrounding country. No Bishop was allowed to molest another by invading jurisdictionally his domain.[44]

Apparently city churches other than the cathedral existed both at Rome and at Hippo,[45] but in both cities they were dependent institutions, merely created to relieve the cathedral church of its increasing number of ministrations of baptism and penance. Priests were not permitted to celebrate Mass in them on Sundays, but received from the Bishop, through the medium of acolytes, the *fermentum,* or elements consecrated by the Bishop himself, thus demonstrating the unity of Catholic sacrificial worship.[46] The city churches did have, however, their own priests and clergy for the administration of baptism and penance, as can be inferred from the wording of a letter of

[43] II Council of Carthage (a. 390), c. 5—c. 50, C. XVI, q. 1; III Council of Carthage (a. 397), c. 42—c. 51, C. XVI, q. 1; V Council of Carthage (a. 401), c. 5—Mansi, III, 969; Council of Tours (a. 461), c. 9—Mansi, VII, 946.

[44] Council of Arles (a. 314), c. 17—Mansi, II, 473.

[45] In the *Liber Pontificalis* of Duchesne there is contained the following brief extract from the life of Pope Marcellus (a. 308-309): "Hic fecit cymiterium Novellae, via Salaria, et XXV titulos in urbe Roma constituit, quasi dioecesis, propter baptismum et paenitentiam multorum qui convertebantur ex paganis et propter sepulturas martyrum."—I, p. 164; Thomassinus, *Eccl. Discip.*, P. I, lib. II, cap. XXI, n. 11. St. Augustine mentions three churches in the city of Hippo —Epist. 110 (*MPL*, XXXIII, 419-421); Bingham, *Antiq.*, Bk. IX, ch. II, n. 5.

[46] The life of Pope Siricius (a. 384-99) states: "Hic constituit, ut nullus presbyter Missas celebraret per omnem hebdomadam, nisi consecratum Episcopi loci designati susciperet declaratum, quod nominatur fermentum."—*MPL*, CXXVIII, 110; Thomassinus, *Eccl. Discip.*, P. I, lib. II, cap. XXI, n. 12. A letter of Pope Innocent I (a. 416) to Decentius, Bishop of Gubbio in Umbria, Italy (Ep. 25, n. 8), relates: "De fermento vero quod die dominica per titulos mittimus superflue nos consulere voluisti, cum omnes ecclesiae nostrae intra civitatem sint constitutae. Quarum presbyteri quia die ipsa propter plebem sibi creditam nobiscum convenire non possunt, idcirco fermentum a nobis confectum per acolythos accipiunt, ut se a nostra communione maxime illa die non iudicent separatos. Quod per paroecias fieri debere non puto, quia nec longe portanda sunt sacramenta: nec nos per coemeteria diversa constitutis presbyteris destinamus et presbyteri eorum conficiendorum ius habeant atque licentiam."—Hardouin, II, 797-8; *MPL*, XX, 556. Cf. Funk, *Manual of Church History*, I, § 23.

Pope Innocent I to Decentius, Bishop of Gubbio,[47] and from the subscriptions to the first Synod of Rome (a. 499), e. g., "*Valens, presbyter, tituli Sanctae Sabinae subscripsi,*" and "*Paulinus, presbyter, tituli Julii subscripsi.*"[48]

The institution of country churches developed rapidly during this Period. Unlike the practice in the East, they were not ruled by rural Bishops, but by diocesan priests, who were sent out to reside in the towns and villages assigned to them with various powers of preaching, baptizing, and administering extreme unction.[49] In 416 there is the first record of permission granted by the Pope to rural parishes to have Mass celebrated by their own resident priests as an exception from the

[47] Cf. preceding footnote 46.

[48] Mansi, VIII, 235; Hefele, II, 625; Hardouin, II, 961-2.

[49] *In Spain*: the Synod of Elvira (a. 300-306), c. 77, contained the names of 24 priests and their rural assignments, e. g., "Maurus, presbyter de Illiturgi; Natalis, presbyter de Orsuna; Lamponius, presbyter de Carula"—Mansi, II, 29; Thomassinus, *Eccl. Discip.*, P. I, lib. II, cap. XXII, n. 8. By the same Synod (c. 19) the clergy were commanded to reside continuously within the places of their ministry, and (c. 32) the priests were granted the faculty of receiving the sick and dying back into communion with the Church—Mansi, II, 9-11; Thomassinus, *ibid.*, n. 2. The I Council of Toledo (a. 400), c. 20, instructed the rural priests to obtain the holy oils for their churches from the Bishop before Easter by sending deacons or subdeacons to fetch them.—Mansi, III, 1002; Hardouin, II, 1044. The Council of Tarragona (a. 516), c. 8, ordered the Bishops to visit their dioceses once a year, because it had been found that some diocesan churches go to ruin—Mansi, VIII, 542; Bingham, *Antiq.*, Bk. IX, ch. VI, nn. 21-22.

In Africa: The Letters of St. Augustine (a. 390-430) mention a number of churches and parishes in his own diocese of Hippo-Regius—Epistolae 203, 212, 236, 240 (*CV*, LVII, 315-17, 371-72, 523-25, 559-60; *MPL*, XXXIII, 938, 965, 1033-34, 1051). The IV Council of Carthage (a. 398), c. 36, ordered every priest of the diocese to come to the Bishop for chrism at Easter—Bingham, *Antiq.*, Bk. IX, ch. VI, nn. 21-22. The V Council of Carthage (a. 401), c. 5, forbade a Bishop to leave his principal church to betake himself to another church of his diocese—*Ibid.*; Mansi, III, 971.

In France: The I Council of Vaison (a. 442), c. 3, commanded the priests to obtain annually from their Bishop the consecrated oils they needed for baptism and extreme unction—Mansi, VI, 453. The I Council of Orange (ab. 441), c. 1, seems to have given the parish priests the faculty of even confirming repentant heretics at the point of death—Mansi, VI, 434.

In Italy: In the Roman Synod under Innocent I in 402 rural priests were acknowledged to have the right to baptize and to administer extreme unction—C. 7 (Mansi, III, 1134-39).

general law of receiving the elements already consecrated by the Bishop.[50]

An interesting sidelight on this Period, and one which increases respect for the priesthood and gives a better appreciation of the canonical legislation on their transfers, is the length of time required to become a priest. According to the Council of Caesarea (a. 314) a candidate for the priesthood was required to be thirty years of age.[51] Later in the same century the stipulated age was increased to thirty-five.[52] The long period of probation which this rule entailed was to be spent in the exercise of the various minor orders.[53] All the minor orders, therefore, were in existence and the rite by which they were to be conferred was definitely established, as well as the duties of each.[54] The office of chanters *(psalmistae* or *cantores)*, sometimes listed among the clergy, was of sacerdotal, not episcopal, appointment, and probably was simply conferred on those who were clerics already.[55]

The minor orders entailed actual work, so that individuals could not reasonably discharge the duties of all of them simultaneously or even of each separately,[56] but at least they received all of them, since the important factor was the proof of each individual's virtuous life and his obedience to authority,

[50] Innocent I, Epist. 25 *ad Decent. Eugub.*, n. 8.—Hardouin, II, 797-8; *MPL*, XX, 556. Cf. *supra*, p. 22, footnote 46.

[51] Funk, *Didascalia et Constitutiones Apostolorum*, II, 1.

[52] Cf. letter of Pope Siricius to Himerius, Bishop of Tarragona, Feb. 10, 385, n. 13—*MPL*, XIII, 1142-1143.

[53] Cf. Thomassinus, *Eccl. Discip.*, P. I, lib. II, cap. XXXV, n. 5.

[54] IV Council of Carthage (a. 398), cc. 5-9—Mansi, III, 951; Thomassinus, *Eccl. Discip.*, *ibid.*, cap. XXXIV, n. 13; Bingham, *Antiq.*, Bk. III, ch. II-V. Tonsure did not exist as a rite, though the monks began to practice it, and the IV Council of Carthage (a. 398), c. 44, foreshadowed it when it forbade clerics to let their hair grow long.—Thomassinus, *op. cit.*, P. I, lib. II, cap. XXXVII, nn. 9-12.

[55] IV Council of Carthage (a. 398), c. 10—Mansi, III, 952; Thomassinus, *ibid.*, n. 12.

[56] Pope Siricius (a. 384-399) demanded that clerical candidates exercise the functions of either lector or exorcist before they became acolytes and proceeded through the various interstices.—Epist. 1, cc. 9, 10 (Thomassinus, *Eccl. Discip.*, P. I, lib. II, cap. XXXIV, n. 9).

as ascertained by a period of probation in at least some of the preparatory orders.[57]

Where did the clergy dwell during this time? From the above it should be clear that the priests lived at or near the cathedral which they served, or at the city or country church to which they had been assigned. The sending of deacons or subdeacons for the holy oils suggests that each church had its inferior clerics in residence, where they performed their duties and received instruction. In the latter part of the fourth century the first evidence of a diocesan seminary appeared in the West when St. Eusebius, the Bishop of Vercelli in Italy, united monastic with clerical life and led with the clergy of his city a common life modelled upon that of the Eastern cenobites.[58] St. Augustine, a half century later, instituted in his own Episcopal house *(domus Episcopi)* a monastery for the clergy of his diocese of Hippo-Regius, where they all lived together, possessed things in common, and ate at the common table,[59] and St. Augustine refused to ordain anyone unless he entered that monastery.[60] In this institution the instruction of the younger members was entrusted to the older of them.[61]

The sustenance of all the clerics of the diocese was provided for by a division of all the offerings which were regularly being sent to the cathedral from all its subsidiary churches. In the poorer districts the clerics helped to support themselves by manual work or agriculture.[62]

[57] Innocent I (a. 402-417), in Epist. 4, c. 5, stated: "Nec cito quilibet Lector, cito Acolythus, cito Diaconus, cito Sacerdos fiat. Quia in minoribus Officiis si diu perdurent, et vita eorum pariter et obsequia comprobantur."—Thomassinus, *ibid.*, cap. XXXV, n. 7. St. Ambrose's life was known so well already that he received, according to Paulinus, all the orders up to and including the episcopacy within eight days.—Thomassinus, *ibid.*, n. 14.

[58] Ott, "Eusebius, Saint,"—*Cath. Ency.*, V, 614; Funk, *Manual of Church History*, I, § 60.

[59] Possidius, *Vita Augustini*, c. 11—*MPL*, XXXII, 42; *ibid.*, c. 25—*MPL*, XXXII, 54; St. Augustine, *Sermones De Diversis*, Sermo CCCLV, cap. 1—*MPL*, XXXIX, 1569; *ibid.*, Sermo CCCLVI, n. 2—*MPL*, XXXIX, 1575; Natalis Alexander, *Hist. Eccl.*, t. IX, cap. VI, art. III; Vieban, "Ecclesiastical Seminary,"—*Cath. Ency.*, XIII, 695 b.

[60] *Sermones De Diversis*, Sermo CCCLV, cap. 1—*Loc. cit.*

[61] Funk, *Manual of Church History*, I, § 60.

[62] Funk, *op. et loc. cit.*; Natalis Alexander, *Hist. Eccl.*, *ibid.*, art. V.

Monasticism, as just stated, was borrowed from the East and was imitated for the first time in the fourth century in the cathedral communities at Vercelli in Italy, and at Hippo. Both Eusebius and Augustine, their respective Bishops, are honored, therefore, as the founders of the Canons Regular of St. Augustine.

ARTICLE III

500 TO 1100 [63]

The notable features of these centuries were:

1) The development of rural churches into the status of parishes.
2) The establishment of a common life for clerics in rural parishes and in the Cathedral schools of the cities.
3) The creation of *precaria* and benefices.
4) The new significance of a title of ordination.
5) The adoption of tonsure as a ceremony of initiation into the clerical life.
6) The recognition of lay patronage.
7) The promotion of rural filial chapels into parishes.
8) The abolition of rural Bishops *(chorepiscopi)*.
9) The formation of city parishes.
10) The spread of cenobitic monasticism and the foundation of Clerical Religious Institutes.

Rural Mother Parishes.—The country churches in both the East and the West in the preceding Period, namely, 300 to 500, were not independent parishes, because in the East, at least prior to the year 460,[64] and in the West, at least prior to the year

[63] In interpreting the legislation of this Period it is to be noted that both terms *dioecesis* and *parochia* were employed to signify the jurisdictional territory of a Bishop. Thus *dioecesis* was used in the III Council of Orleans (a. 538), c. 15: "Episcopus in dioeceses alienas ad alienos clericos ordinandos vel consecranda altaria irruere non debet."—Mansi, IX, 16; IV Council of Toledo (a. 633), c. 35—Mansi, X, 628-9; c. 11, C. X, q. 1; Council of Ravenna (a. 997), c. 3—Mansi, XIX, 220-1. *Parochia* was used in the *Capitula* of Pope Hadrian (a. 785), c. 18—Hartzheim, I, 253; VI Council of Arles (a. 813), c. 24—Mansi, XIV, 62; Council of Ravenna (a. 997), c. 3—Mansi, XIX, 220-1; Epistle of Pope Urban (a. 1088-99) to Hugo, Archbishop of Lyons—c. 10, C. IX, q. 2.

[64] Cf. *supra*, pp. 20-21.

419,[65] their priests lacked the power of administration over their church property, were limited in their spiritual functions, and lacked definite boundaries for their ministrations. From the sixth century onward this condition changed and the churches in the principal country towns developed into real parishes. Bishops, accustomed to administer the funds of all churches by a quadruple division—for the clergy, the Bishop, the poor, and the maintenance of the buildings—were now being forbidden from having any share in the offerings made to the other diocesan churches.[66]

In the East, the Church, which had entered into a period of temporal prosperity following the peace of Constantine, was beholding everywhere the voluntary erection of oratories and chapels through the devotion and munificence of wealthy individuals, who endowed the same to insure their perpetuity.[67] The same was true in the West during the Merovingian reign when the grand-parishes came into existence.[68] The responsibility of providing divine worship and spiritual ministrations in these many chapels and oratories devolved upon the large country parishes within whose general territory they had been erected. This served three purposes: a) it caused a finer determination of the relative rights of the mother and filial churches; b) it made exact boundaries imperative; and c) it created an urgent need for clergy and particularly for priests in the country parishes, either to act as delegates of the rural pastor or to reside as chaplains at the minor *tituli*.[69]

65 Cf. next footnote.

66 II Council of Braga [*alias* III, a. 572], c. 2, "*Placuit*"—Mansi, IX, 839; Council of Hippo-Regius (ab. 419), c. 9: "Ut episcopus matricis non usurpet quicquid fuerit donatum ecclesiis, quae in dioecesi constitutae sunt."—Labbe-Cossart, *Sacrorum Conciliorum Nova et Amplissima Collectio*, IV, 442; Bingham, *Antiq.*, Bk. VIII, ch. I, n. 12. Various epistles of Pope Gregory the Great, however, show that many Bishops throughout the sixth century still administered all the funds—cf. Natalis Alexander, *Hist. Eccl.*, t. X, cap. VI, art. VI.

67 Justinian, Novell. LVII, 2; CXXIII, 18.

68 Hinschius, *System des kath. KR.*, II, 262 ff.

69 Coady, *The Appointment of Pastors*, pp. 16-18; Bastnagel, *The Appointment of Parochial Adjutants and Assistants*, pp. 19, 26-28. The Trullan Synod at Constantinople (a. 692), c. 31, is a sample of the restriction of parochial rights on

Community life for clerics.—To supply the priests and clerics necessary in the rural districts of the West there arose a custom, first in Italy, and then elsewhere, to have the candidates live with and be educated by the resident priest.[70] This had long since been the custom under the rural Bishops in the East, who were even able to ordain their candidates as far as major orders. When they were fit for orders, and especially for the priesthood, they were presented, by the rural Bishop or his archdeacon in the East, or by the resident priest or pastor in the West, to the city Bishop for ordination. The consequent plurality of priests at a country parish caused the title *archipresbyter* to be attached to the pastor.[71] Sometimes also he was called the "cardinal priest."[72]

Quasi-Seminaries or Cathedral Schools answered the same purpose in the cities, in imitation of the early establishments of Bishops Eusebius of Vercelli and Augustine of Hippo.[73] Some idea of the size of these undertakings is gained from Victor,

chapels of ease in the East—Mansi, XI, 955. In a certain "mixed synod" under Tissilo of Bavaria in 772 it was decided that the Bishop should designate clearly how many and which villages, towns or hamlets each parish priest should govern —*MPL*, XCVII, 523, 710.

[70] Thus the III Council of Vaison (a. 529), c. 1, adopted this practice for the diocese of Arles: "Hoc enim placuit, ut omnes presbyteri, qui sunt in parochiis constituti, secundum consuetudinem, quam per totam Italiam satis salubriter teneri cognovimus, juniores lectores quantoscumque sine uxore habuerint, secum in domo, ubi ipsi habitare videntur, recipiant: et eos quomodo boni patres spiritaliter nutrientes, psalmos parare, divinis lectionibus insistere, et in lege domini erudire contendant: ut et sibi dignos successores provideant, et a domino praemia aeterna recipiant."—Mansi, VIII, 726; IV Council of Toledo (a. 653), c. 24—Mansi, X, 626; Council of Merida (a. 666), c. 18—Mansi, XI, 85.

[71] E.g., the II Council of Tours (a. 567), c. 19, speaks of "*archipresbyteri*" and "*reliqui presbyteri et diaconi et subdiaconi vicani*"—Mansi, IX, 797; Council of Rheims (a. 630), c. 19: ". . . ut in parochiis nullus laicorum archipresbyter praeponatur: sed qui senior in ipsis esse debet, clericus ordinetur."—Mansi, X, 597; XI Council of Toledo (a. 675), c. 14: "Necessarium duximus instituere ut ubi temporis, vel loci, sive cleri copia suffragatur, habeat semper quisquis ille canens Deo vel sacrificans, post se vicini solaminis adjutorem: ut si aliquo casu ille qui officia impleturus accedit turbatus fuerit, vel ad terram elisus, a tergo semper habeat qui eius vicem exequatur intrepidus."—Mansi, XI, 145; Council of Nantes (IX cent.), c. 8—Mansi, XVIII, 168.

[72] *Supra*, p. 5.

[73] Thus St. Gregory the Great established such a congregation at the Apostolic Palace in the VI century—John the Deacon, *Vita Gregorii*, l. II, c. 11 (*MPL*,

Bishop of Vita, in the province of Byzacium in Africa, who relates that the number of clergy in the Cathedral church of Carthage in the sixth century amounted to almost 500.[74] In some places, at the time of Charlemagne, religious monasteries were utilized to impart this instruction.[75]

Precaria and Benefices.—To educate clerics for its church and many subordinate chapels was not the only problem of the rural parish of the sixth and subsequent centuries; it had to sustain them as well. The laws of the Period took care to require the payment of the tithes to the rural mother church; but gifts of lands were multiplying and rendering some readjustment necessary. The endowment of some chapels on noblemen's estates, which perpetually provided for both chapel and clergy who ministered in it, made it appear desirable for all churches to be endowed.[76] As the next best solution, a portion of the church's lands, known as a *precarium,* was assigned to each cleric, and while he lived he had the right to the income from it. At his death it simply reverted to the common fund.

There was no marked distinction in these allotments of land revenues to clerics until the eleventh century. Then it was that each allotment was made a distinct entity—a perpetual foundation for the support of one cleric. When the cleric who was in possession of it died or in some way lost it, the same became *vacant* and could be bestowed on another cleric. Allotments of this sort were known as benefices *(beneficia)* or prebends *(praebenda)*.[77]

Title of Ordination.—Even the minor clergy, therefore, needed a *precarium* or, later on, a benefice, in order to insure

LXXV, 92). It became a matter of law to have them in Spain and France, e. g., II Council of Toledo (a. 531), c. 1—Mansi, VIII, 785; IV Council of Toledo (a. 633), cc. 22-23—Mansi, X, 630; VI Council of Toledo (ab. 645)—Thomassinus, *Eccl. Discip.*, P. I, lib. III, cap. V, n. 3; III Council of Tours (a. 813), c. 12—Hardouin, IV, 1025; Thomassinus, *ibid.*, nn. 1-9; Vieban, "Ecclesiastical Seminary,"—*Cath. Ency.*, XIII, 695 c.

74 *Historia Persecutionis Africanae Provinciae,* III, 34—*CV,* VII, 89.

75 Thomassinus, *Eccl. Discip.*, P. I, lib. III, cap. VI, n. 1.

76 Such a wish is expressed in the Synodal Statutes of the diocese of Rheims (a. 627-630), cc. 12, 21—Mansi, X, 599-600.

77 Many, *De Sacra Ordin.*, n. 134; Creagh, "Benefice,"—*Cath. Ency.*, II, 474.

their sustenance before they could be promoted to orders by the Bishop. In former years the particular church itself or *titulus* was the cleric's guarantee of livelihood. Since the benefice now became that guarantee it, in turn, inherited the designation of *the title.* As a consequence, a *title* came to mean, for both diocesan and religious clerics, the source of sustenance rather than the place of employment.[78]

Minor clerics also were held high in esteem. In the Capitulary of Charlemagne [79] lay people were ordered to respect them as they do God Himself. The minor clergy received at this time only those orders which they could actually exercise,[80] and they began their education for the priesthood in boyhood, which qualified them for the order of subdiaconate at the age of twenty.[81]

Clerical Initiation by Tonsure.—Tonsure was not a distinct ceremony of initiation into the clerical state, but was connected with the reception of the first minor order, that of Lector or Porter.[82] As such it had existed in the East from the end of the fourth century, and in the West from the end of the fifth century. There was a distinct separation of the form of tonsure from the minor orders no later than the sixth century,[83] after which it served as the actual ceremony of initiation into the clerical state.

[78] Many, *op. cit.*, nn. 132-134.

[79] L. VII, c. 390—Mansi, XVII bis, 1109.

[80] Thomassinus, *Eccl. Discip.*, P. I, lib. II, cap. XXXII, nn. 6-7.

[81] Natalis Alexander, *Hist. Eccl.*, t. X, cap. VI, art. IV, n. 1; II Council of Toledo (a. 531), c. 1: "De his quos voluntas parentum a primis infantiae annis in Clericatus officio, vel Monachali posuit, pariter statuimus observandum, ut mox cum detonsi vel ministerio Lectorum contraditi fuerint, in domo Ecclesiae sub Episcopali praesentia a Praeposito sibi debeant erudiri. At ubi octavum decimum aetatis suae annum compleverint, si gratia eis castitatis Deo inspirante placuerit, hi tanquam appetitores arctissimae vitae levissimo Domini jugo subdantur; ac primo Subdiaconatus Ministerium probatione habita professionis suae a vigesimo anno suscipiant."—Mansi, VIII, 785; Thomassinus, *Eccl. Discip.*, P. I, lib. III, cap. V, n. 1.

[82] Thomassinus, *op. cit.*, P. I, lib. II, cap. XXXII, nn. 1-2; Many, *De Sacra Ordin.*, n. 10; Pope Siricius, Epist. 1, cc. 9-10—*MPL*, XIII, 1142-1143.

[83] Cf., *e. g.*, *Lexikon für Theologie und Kirche*, "Tonsur."

Lay Patronage.—The authority of the Bishop to know, approve of and ordain the candidates for the various parishes in his diocese received a serious challenge as a result of the endowment and the building of churches and oratories by the nobility. It required many laws to register the Church's protest against the founders for choosing their own clergy for the churches they built and for having them ordained by alien Bishops. The result of the struggle was the official recognition in the sixth and seventh centuries of the right of Lay Patronage, by which the Church agreed to let the founders have the privilege of nominating or presenting a cleric from among those eligible in the parish, provided that their choice was ratified by the Bishop of the place.[84]

Rural Filial Parishes.—Beginning with the ninth century, the little filial chapels in the country were recognized as independent parishes also. Their pastors became resident, their funds distinct. The right of patronage now meant more than the presentation of an assistant priest in a parish; it meant a voice in the choice of a pastor.

A plurality of priests at a mother parish in the country districts was no longer needed. The title of archpriest disappears, but non-sacerdotal clerics still remain in residence.[85]

Rural Bishops abolished.—A similar development of country parishes took place in the East after the rural Bishops as an institution were abolished at the Second Nicene Council in the year 787.[86]

City Parishes.—The churches in the cities were not raised to full parochial status until the eleventh century.[87]

Monasticism and Clerical Religious Institutes.—The great father of Western Monasticism was St. Benedict (a. 480-543), who adopted the cenobite idea and founded a great monastery at Monte Cassino, between Rome and Naples, in 529. The rule

[84] Coady, *The Appointment of Pastors*, pp. 26-27.

[85] Bastnagel, *The Appointment of Parochial Adjutants and Assistants*, pp. 28-29.

[86] C. 14—Funk, *Manual of Church History*, I, § 62.

[87] De Meester, *Compen.*, II, n. 805; Wernz-Vidal, *Ius Can.*, II, n. 721; Badii, *Institute.*, I, n. 269; Boudinhon, "Parish,"—*Cath. Ency.*, XI, 501.

of life which he mapped out for the monks became for centuries the standard for all the Religious of the West.[88] Here, too, the monks were laymen striving for spiritual perfection, and their monasteries were supplied with religious services by the diocesan clergy. It was the monks who first began the practice of wearing the tonsure, and it was the secular clergy working amongst them who brought the practice into general use by imitation.[89]

Necessity dictated that, when monasteries were far from the parochial church, a few monks with the requisite qualities could be ordained to the priesthood to provide for divine services in their own chapels, and, in fact, it seems, from a letter of Pope Gregory I to Bishop Candidus, that even to supply a shortage of priests in the diocese monks who were worthy could be elevated to the priestly dignity.[90]

In the West, moreover, the religious life was subject to a gradual evolution in form, and one of the products of this was the Clerical Religious Institute, in which all or most of the individual Religious were clerics or priests. The origin of such a type of Institute, known as the Canons Regular, is variously dated from the tenth to the twelfth century, when the canons of some Cathedral Chapters started a common life under the rule of St. Augustine and bound themselves by vows, thus making the religious life subservient to their status as priests.

ARTICLE IV

1100 TO THE CODE

The episcopal and parochial organization of the Church was now complete, just as it is today. Hence, the legislation occupied itself with ways and means of making it function more perfectly and smoothly; it concentrated on the management of the parishes. More solicitude was exhibited that clerics be decently and honorably sustained than that they spend long

[88] Chelodi, *Ius de Personis*, n. 246.

[89] Thomassinus, *Eccl. Discip.*, P. I, lib. II, cap. XXXVII, n. 12.

[90] Bastnagel, *The Appointment of Parochial Adjutants and Assistants*, p. 21; Bingham, *Antiq.*, Bk. VII, chs. I-II.

periods of probation at a definite church in the exercise of each order received.[91]

Just as the promotion of rural filial chapels to the status of parishes, beginning with the ninth century, had lessened the need for priests at the rural mother parishes, so now the expansion in the numbers of the faithful due to missionary endeavor reversed the trend, and created a demand for priest assistants to work along with, but under the authority of, the pastors of the parishes in the care of souls.[92] Furthermore, the prodigious increase in the number of city churches[93] enhanced very much the importance of the priest cleric, so that the imparting of a better education to minor clerics became of far greater importance than the practical service which these minor clerics might render at the church of their original assignment. This resulted in clerics being excused from their churches for five or more years to attend classes at the Universities, which had begun to flourish in the thirteenth century.[94]

Recognizing the fall in the morale of the clerics due to their daily association with laymen at the Universities, the Church in the Council of Trent (a. 1563)[95] decreed the institution of seminaries in all dioceses of the world, so that thenceforth candidates for the priesthood from the country as well as from the city parishes would be completely segregated from all other students, their entire time would be engaged in study, discipline, and spirituality, and their service to the cathedral or to the church to which they had been assigned originally would be

[91] Cf. cap. 5 of the III Lateran Council (a. 1179) under Pope Alexander III—Mansi, XXII, 220; c. 4, X, *de praebendis et dignitatibus*, III, 5. This decree inaugurated a whole series of similar provincial laws.

[92] Bastnagel, *The Appointment of Parochial Adjutants and Assistants*, pp. 37-38.

[93] *Ibidem*, footnote 3, Henry Adams is quoted as follows: "According to history, in a single century between 1170 and 1270 the French built 80 cathedrals and nearly 500 churches of the cathedral class, which would have cost, according to an estimate made in 1840, more than five thousand millions to replace. Five thousand million francs is a thousand million dollars, and this covered only the great churches of a single country." (Munro-Sontag, *The Middle Ages* [The Century Historical Series], p. 385).

[94] Cc. 4-5, X, *de clericis non residentibus in Ecclesia vel praebenda*, III, 4.

[95] Sess. XXIII, *de ref.*, c. 18.

reduced to a minimum (". . . *cathedrali et aliis loci ecclesiis diebus festis inserviant.*").

The sustenance of the cleric was to be provided by either a benefice or patrimony, and benefices could be conferred on boys as young as fourteen years of age.[96] The law did not absolutely require a benefice or guarantee of support, however, until the first major order was to be received.[97] Oftentimes a parish was conferred *in titulum* on a cleric who had not yet been ordained a priest, with the proviso that he be elevated to the subdiaconate within a year. Such a titular was called a *plebanus.* The Bishop would then have to provide for the care of souls through the medium of a suitable vicar until the titular became a priest.[98] To understand this strange procedure, it must be remembered that lay patronage had to be recognized in the conferment of a great many benefices[99] and, if the nominees were otherwise capable and worthy, the Bishop had to accept them and confer on them the vacant parishes. Lay patronage was never completely abolished, but the Church has modified it somewhat to her own advantage, and has been striving for centuries to induce the patrons voluntarily to renounce their traditional right.

In this Period, when the support of the clerics assumed greater importance than their residence or service, absolute ordinations, i. e., without fixity of residence, gave to the world a wealth of ecclesiastics, and made it the problem of each pastor to select and appoint his own assistant priests from their number. This seems unique now, but from the thirteenth century onward common law itself gave to the parish priest that right. All authors admit it, and even the Council of Trent reiterated it in these words: " Episcopi, etiam tamquam apostolicae Sedis delegati, in omnibus ecclesiis parochialibus, vel baptismalibus, in quibus populus ita numerosus sit, ut unus rector non possit suf-

[96] Conc. Trid., sess. XXIII, *de ref.*, c. 6.

[97] C. 4, X, *de praebendis et dignitatibus*, III, 5.

[98] C. 34, *de electione et electi potestate*, I, 6, in VI°; Thomassinus, *Eccl. Discip.*, P. I, lib. II, cap. XXXIII, n. 8.

[99] In the diocese of Paris, for example, in the twelfth century, the Bishop had the freedom of appointment to only two hundred and fifteen out of four hundred and sixty-nine parishes.—Lesêtre, *La Paroisse*, pp. 64-66.

ficere ecclesiasticis sacramentis ministrandis, et cultui divino peragendo, cogant rectores, vel alios, ad quos pertinet, sibi tot sacerdotes ad hoc munus adiungere, quot sufficiant ad sacramenta exhibenda, et cultum divinum celebrandum."[100] A regular contract had to be entered into between the pastor and his prospective assistants as to the time-period of their service, their duties, rights, emoluments and the like.[101] Though the first reversal of this came as early as 1677 at Freising, where the Curia claimed the appointment and transfer of assistants was its own proper right, nevertheless, the practice still remained in other dioceses and countries until the nineteenth century, and in a few, e. g., in Colombia, S. A., in Central America, and in the canton of Lucerne in Switzerland, it persists to the present day.[102]

Religious Institutes took another important step forward in this Period. The great Mendicant Orders came into existence in the early part of the thirteenth century, and new Religious Orders of various types rapidly multiplied. It then became a practice to unite some parishes of the diocese with certain religious monasteries or convents in such a way that thereafter the religious monasteries or convents possessed the title to the parishes, and acquired thereby both the right to receive their revenues and the perpetual obligation of the care of souls within them, which they would satisfy through the appointment of vicars from their own Religious Institute. This was called *plena incorporatio vel unio.*

Another form of union, called *minus plena,* gave to them the right to the revenues but required that they employ a diocesan priest as their vicar—one whom the Bishop would appoint upon their recommendation.

100 Sess. XXI, *de ref.*, c. 4.

101 For a full discussion of this cf. Bastnagel, *The Appointment of Parochial Adjutants and Assistants*, pp. 45 ff.

102 *Ibid.*, pp. 52-58.

CHAPTER III

The Initial Diocesan Attachment of Laymen

The involved history of the legislation of the Church on the incardination and excardination of its secular clergy is most logically treated by giving separate consideration to the two classes of persons subject to it, namely, laymen and diocesan clerics.

Though the term *incardination*, as was shown in Chapter I, has always signified the attachment of a cleric to a new diocese after a canonical transfer, yet, it is the original bond with a diocese, contracted at the time of the layman's induction into the clerical state, that must be severed in order to effect a canonical transfer. Rightly, therefore, does the contraction of that original bond receive prior consideration in this treatise. It is logically followed by the story of clerical incardination and excardination.

ARTICLE I

REASON AND NECESSITY OF A PERMANENT BOND BETWEEN DIOCESAN CLERICS AND THEIR BISHOP

A Bishop has in his diocese two distinct classes of subjects, the laity and the clergy. For the laity, their domicile or habitation within the boundaries of a diocese has always constituted a bond between them and their Bishop, obliging them to obey him as their spiritual ruler. Yet, this bond has mostly been of a very restricted nature and could be exchanged with comparative ease. For the clergy, the case is vastly different. They are not merely a congregation of persons being guided to eternal salvation, but a very special group of men with divinely constituted powers and a very definite purpose for being within a diocese. There are a number of reasons why they should be bound to their Bishop and to their diocese in a much more permanent and rigid way than the laity.

1. *The People's Reason—Service of Their Spiritual Needs*

A Pastor of souls, like the shepherd of a flock, should be stationary in his position. By years of intimate association he, like the Master, should know his sheep and they should know him. His best work for souls is accomplished when there exists between him and his people this close mutual relationship. If there were no secure bond between the clergy and their Bishop and it were the rule rather than the exception for priests to be changing from one diocese to another, the people's spiritual welfare would suffer. As far as their interests are concerned, therefore, a permanent bond between their clergy and Bishop is most desirable.

2. *The Bishop's Reasons*

A) *Peace among Bishops.* — From the standpoint of the Bishop, there are four reasons for a permanent bond between him and his clerics. The first of these is to keep peace among Bishops by having their rights over their clerics mutually recognized and respected in perpetuity. After a Bishop has borne all the labor and expense in procuring and educating clerics, justice would be lacking if there were no bond to prevent other Bishops from taking from him the fruits of his labor. This was the reason expressed in some of the early councils for the enactment of legislation concerning clerical attachment.[1]

B) *Obedience of Clergy.*—The second reason is to insure the docile obedience of the clergy. If there were nothing to bind them permanently to a diocese, the clergy could easily and successfully assert their own will over their Bishop, for they could always arbitrarily desert the diocese. With a permanent bond, however, the Bishop has an exclusive power over them, and so they are placed under the constraint of obedience.

C) *Prevention of Avaricious Ambition.*—In the third place, the Bishop needs a satisfied and contented clergy if they are to be effective. This is secured if they know that they are so bound

[1] Cf. e. g., Council of Sardica (a. 343), c. 18—Mansi, III, 29; I Council of Carthage (a. 348), c. 5—Mansi, III, 155.

to their assigned places that they cannot look for more lucrative positions elsewhere. This reason is likewise adduced for early legislation on the subject.[2]

D) *Restraint on Unworthy Clerics.* — A Bishop is bound in conscience to ordain only worthy ministers of the altar. He may be deceived in some candidates, but their bad morals and character, if any, become well known to him as long as they are under his watchful eye, living within and discharging their duties in his diocese. He is then in a position to restrain the unworthy ones permanently from receiving any further advancement in holy orders.[3]

3. *The Clergy's Reasons*

Finally, for the sake of the clerics themselves, there are two very good reasons for the existence of a special bond which will associate them in a permanent manner with a Bishop and his diocese.

A) *Permanent Employment.* — The first of these is that it provides them with permanent employment in the spiritual ministry. The powers of Orders are not conferred for any other purpose than that they be exercised, and that under proper ecclesiastical authority. Clerics are not ordained *honoris causa,* but rather to be active workers and co-operators in the propagation of the Christian faith. It ill becomes them to be idle, not exercising the sacred powers which are theirs, not assigned to any definite religious work, and wandering or traveling around without any definite abode or Superior. This arouses scandal and brings the clerical state into disrepute despite its high dignity. Such clerics have been known for centuries as *vagi* or *acephali* and have been universally abominated.

[2] Cf. e. g., IV Council of Carthage (a. 398), cap. 27—Mansi, III, 953; *Epistola S. Leonis Magni ad Aquilejensem Episc.* (a. 442), cap. 5: "...ut in integrum revoces, admonemus: ut unusquisque non ambitione illectus, non cupiditate seductus, non persuasione hominum depravatus, ubi ordinatus est, perseveret..."—Mansi, V, 1115.

[3] Hallier, *De Sacris Electionibus et Ordinationibus ex Antiquo et Novo Ecclesiae Usu* (*De Sacris Elect. et Ordin.*), P. II, sec. V, cap. III, art. I, n. 7—Migne, *Theologiae Cursus Completus* (Hereafter to be cited as *MTC*), XXIV, 980-981.

If there were no law regulating the ordination of laymen to the clerical state; if Bishops could ordain them at will, without regard to the need for their services and without having to assign them to definite places, the result would be the existence of a vast number of idle clerics wandering around without employment. This, in fact, was the result during the period when Church legislation ceased to require the perpetual assignment of clerics to particular churches.[4] The ordinary regulation, which requires at the time of ordination the assignment of every cleric to a definite place of service, not only binds the cleric to his diocese in a permanent way, but also keeps the number of clerics in a diocese equal to the number of places where their services can well be utilized, and thereby also assures the people of having constant spiritual care and assures the cleric of having permanent employment of his sacred powers.[5]

B) *Permanent Sustenance.* — Another reason why, for the cleric's sake, a stable bond of ecclesiastical assignment exists is to assure him of being perpetually sustained through his spiritual labors, so that he does not have to beg, or to pursue some menial occupation unworthy of his state, in order to gain a livelihood.[6] Holy Scripture itself gives testimony to the right of a cleric to be sustained by those to whom he ministers,[7] but it is necessary that he have a place in which to labor in order that he might receive this sustenance. By being assured permanent employment through clerical assignment, he is at the same time assured the sustenance which proceeds from it.

[4] Cf. *infra*, pp. 75-77.

[5] Cf. Thomassinus, *Eccl. Discip.*, P. II, lib. I, cap. IX, n. 2; Many, *De Sacra Ordin.*, n. 133.

[6] This was the purpose of the Council of Trent in requiring an assured service of the diocese from all major clerics, as it is explained in Sess. XXI, *de ref.*, c. 2: "Cum non deceat eos, qui divino ministerio adscripti sunt cum Ordinis dedecore mendicare, aut sordidum aliquem quaestum exercere: . . ." Cf. also *Innocentius III Zamorensi Episcopo*—C. 16, X, *de praebendis et dignitatibus*, III, 5.

[7] 1 Cor., IX, 11-14.

ARTICLE II

THE PROPER BISHOP FOR THE FIRST ORDINATION AND ATTACHMENT OF LAYMEN

Five periods of history are given in order to render easier the study of the chief pieces of legislation concerning the title by which a Bishop became the proper Bishop for a layman's ordination, i.e., by which he received the undisputed right to promote a layman to the clerical state. In the beginning, only one title was unquestionably recognized. Thereafter, the Church progressively accepted two, three, and finally four such titles. The only one which remained constant throughout was the title of origin, i.e., on the basis of the place of one's original habitation.

1. *Ancient Law (Before 1100)*

Proper Bishop of Origin

During the first millennium, it is difficult to decide with certainty what, if any, was the accepted law. A wealth of legislation on the proper Bishop for *clerics* only serves to accentuate the grand silence concerning the proper Bishop for *laymen*. For this reason authors of the past generally concluded that laymen had no particular Bishop whom they could consider proper for their initial reception of orders, but were free to travel and to settle down wherever a Bishop could be found who was willing to accept them.[8] To substantiate their claim they adduced the examples of Origen, Jerome, Paulinus, and Augustine, who had been received into the clerical state in foreign dioceses without any complaint *ad rem* being registered by their Bishops at home; they also pointed out the fact that the councils and synods were silent on penalties against Bishops for ordaining alien laymen.

Against this theory there is opposed the whole tenor of the early Christian organization and discipline. With Hinschius,[9]

[8] Thomassinus, *Eccl. Discip.*, P. II, lib. I, capp. I, II, V; Riganti, *Commentaria in Regulas, Constitutiones et Ordinationes Cancellariae Apostolicae*, Commen. in reg. XXIV, § III, n. 1; Hallier, *De Sacris Elect. et Ordin.*, P. II, sec. V, cap. III, art. VI, n. 2—*MTC*, XXIV, 1003; *ibid.*, art. I, nn. 13-20—*MTC*, XXIV, 969-975.

[9] *System des katholischen Kirchenrechts*, I, 86.

Wernz,[10] and others,[11] it is found more convincing to accept the view that laymen also had a proper Bishop for ordination, and that he was ordinarily the Bishop of their place of *origin* or *original domicile*, i.e., of the place where their parents had an established residence at the time of the son's birth. Witness the following excerpts from laws proper to the East and to the West, including Africa, Italy, Spain, and France, during the first eleven centuries:

a) Council of Elvira, Spain, (ab. 305), cap. 24: "Omnes qui peregre fuerint baptizati, eo quod eorum minime sit cognita vita, placuit, ad clerum non esse promovendos in alienis provinciis." [12]

b) Epistle of Pope Julus I (336-352) to the Oriental Bishops, n. 6: "Nullus episcopus alterius parochianum praesumat retinere, aut ordinare absque eius episcopi voluntate, vel iudicare, salva tamen in omnibus apostolica auctoritate; quia sicut irrita erit eius ordinatio ita et dijudicatio." [13]

c) I Council of Carthage (a. 348), c. 5: "Ut clerici et laici in alterius ecclesia non ordinentur. Privatus episcopus Begeselitanus dixit: Suggero sanctitati vestrae, ut statuatis, non debere clericum alienum ab aliquo suscipi sine litteris episcopi sui, neque apud se detinere: sed nec laicum usurpare sibi de plebe aliena, ut eum ordinet sine conscientia ejus episcopi, de cujus plebe est. Gratus episcopus dixit: Haec observantia pacem custodit: nam et memini sanctissimo concilio Sardicensi similiter statutum, ut nemo alterius plebis hominem sibi usurpet: sed si forte erit necessarius ordinationi, ut de vicino homo sit necessarius, petat a collega suo, et concessum habeat." [14]

d) V Council of Carthage (a. 401), cap. 13: "Item placuit, ut si quis de alterius monasterio receptum, vel ad clericatum promovere voluerit, vel in suo monasterii constituere; episcopus qui hoc fecerit, a ceterorum communione sejunctus, sue tantum plebis communione contentus sit: et ille neque clericus, neque praepositus perseveret." [15]

[10] *Ius Decretalium*, II, n. 26.

[11] E. g., Moeder, *The Proper Bishop for Ordination and Dimissorial Letters*, pp. 23-25.

[12] Mansi, II, 10; c. 4, D. XCVIII.

[13] Mansi, II, 1185; c. 36, *Apost. Cans.*—Mansi, I, 35.

[14] Mansi, III, 155; c. 6, D. LXXI.

[15] Mansi, III, 971. Some Bishops, e. g., St. Augustine of Hippo in 390, had instituted diocesan *monasteries* for their clergy. Cf. *supra*, p. 25.

e) Council of Rome (a. 402), c. 16: "Praeterea etiam laici dicuntur a communione cognita causa seclusi, et ab alio episcopo clerici facti. Hoc jam super omne malum est. Unde aut conventi corrigant, qui talia ausi sunt facere, ita ut removeantur hi quibus indigne ordo collatus est, aut ad nos nomina eorum deserantur, ut sciamus a quibus nos abstinere debeamus." [16]

In other words, lay persons who have been excluded from Orders by their own Bishop may not be received into the ranks of the clergy elsewhere.

f) I Council of Orange (a. 441), c. 9: "Si qui autem alienos cives, aut alibi consistentes ordinaverint; nec ordinati in ullo accusantur, aut ad se eos revocent, aut gratiam ipsis eorum impetrent, cum quibus habitant." [17]

g) In the Eastern Roman Empire since the time of Arcadius, and in the Western Roman Empire since the time of Justinian, it had been incorporated as a part of the civil law that the clerics of a church were to be recruited from its surrounding locality.[18]

h) The Synod of Merida, Spain (a. 666), c. 18: "... Proinde instituit haec sancta synodus, ut omnes parochitani presbyteri, juxta ut in rebus sibi a Deo creditis sentiunt habere virtutem, de ecclesiae suae familia clericos sibi faciant: quos per bonam voluntatem ita nutriant, ut et officium sanctum digne peragant, et ad servitium suum aptos eos habeant." [19]

Therefore, the rural parish priest was to select from the subjects of his parish his presentees to the Bishop for ordination.

i) Council of Mainz, Germany (a. 888), cap. 14: "Nullus episcopus alterius parochianum praesumat retinere aut ordinare absque ejus voluntate, vel judicare, quia sicut ejus irrita erit ordinatio, ita et judicatio; quoniam censemus alterius nullum judicis, nisi sui, sententia teneri. Nam qui eum ordinare non potuit, nec judicare ullatenus potest." [20]

j) Council of Ravenna, Italy (a. 997), c. 3: "Nemo nostrum alterius dioecesenses, v. parochianos recipere, aut promovere, seu retinere praesumat, sine canonicis epistolis ..." [21]

[16] Mansi, III, 1139.

[17] Mansi, VI, 437. Since it is the Bishop of the laymen's domicile who is outraged, it is he who should later be conciliated.

[18] Cf. Codex Theodosianus, XVI, 2, 33; Codex Justinianus, I, 3, 11. Cf. also Mansi, XVIII, 169.

[19] Mansi, XI, 85.

[20] Mansi, XVIII A, 68.

[21] Mansi, XIX, 220; Thomassinus, *Eccl. Discip.*, P. II, lib. I, cap. VII, n. 2.

k) Epistle of St. Anselm, Archbishop of Canterbury, to Atserus, first Archbishop of London (a. 1094): "... Rogo sanctitatem vestram quatinus regnum illud vestro sancto studio emundetis ab apostatis, ut nullus alienigena ibi recipiat aliquem Ecclesiasticum Ordinem: quia illi qui ab Episcopis suis repelluntur, illuc pergunt, et execrabiliter ad diversos ordines sacrantur." [22]

Throughout the above it is patent that there was a distinction between *plebs sua* and *plebs aliena,* and that it was forbidden for a Bishop to ordain a layman *de plebe aliena* without at least some permission from that layman's Bishop. To be numbered amongst a people even when far away from them presupposes that one either originated in their native locality or ordinarily dwells amongst them. Canon 9 of the I Council of Orange (*f* above) shows that it was the latter, namely, the place where they were living (*cum quibus habitant*), which counted; and none of the citations made above insinuates the existence of more than one proper Bishop. Canon 24 of the Council of Elvira (*a* above) discounts baptism as the deciding factor,[23] and the Theodosian and Justinian Codices (*g*) together with the Synod of Merida (*h*) simply substantiate what in Chapter II above was stated to be the universal practice of the Church, namely, that clerics were trained for their ministry from early youth in that particular church near which they lived, which indicates that it must have been the Bishop of the place where they had their original domicile who was qualified to accept them as laymen. The Council of Rome (*e*) reveals the reason which formed the basis for this discipline—to protect the Church from the unworthy.

It would be a glaring contradiction for the Church to be so strict about the place where people received the sacraments of Penance and Holy Eucharist that they could not communicate away from home without commendatory letters from their home Bishop, and to be so liberal about the sacrament of Holy Orders that they could receive it anywhere. The authority of

[22] Mansi, XVIII B, 1556. *Alienigena* = a stranger, foreigner, one born in or belonging to another country, an alien—Freund-Leverett, *Lexicon,* "alienigena."

[23] Augustine Bachofen to the contrary—*A Commentary on the New Code of Canon Law,* IV, p. 418.

a Bishop over his diocesans (i. e., residents) was so inviolable even in the fourth century that many laws were enacted forbidding a strange Bishop from entering another Bishop's territory and exercising the pontificals, and especially from ordaining the other Bishop's subjects.[24] Now, may one not also conclude that it was equally an affront to lure the other Bishop's diocesans away for ordination elsewhere?

Even if Bishop Julianus of Uzaritan was ordered to restore a proper citizen of his own city to Bishop Epigonius of Bulla, who had baptized, educated, and ordained the same, it must be noted that Julianus had commended the still unbaptized youth to Epigonius in the first place, whereupon the youth had changed his place of habitation.[25] Why should Bishop Julianus have to commend the youth, except that he was considered to have authority over him as an inhabitant (*proprium civem sui loci*), and why did he attempt to reclaim him later, except that he knew that a Bishop had a right over those who ordinarily dwelt in his territory?

The cases of Origen, Jerome, Paulinus, and Augustine are simply examples of absolute ordinations and do not disprove the above stated thesis. In fact, Origen's case (a man minus physical integrity raised to the clerical state) only serves to show into what blunders a Bishop other than the one of the layman's native and permanent domicile could fall when he presumed to ordain a layman from another diocese.

Hallier adduces canon 9 of the I Council of Orange (*f* above) to prove that provincial laws even placed their approval on Bishops ordaining lay aliens if they saw fit, and he confirms his

[24] Council of Antioch (a. 341), c. 13: "Nullus episcopus ex alia provincia audeat ad aliam transgredi ad promotionem ministerii aliquos in ecclesiis ordinare, licet consensum videantur praebere nonnulli nisi literis tam metropolitani quam ceterorum qui cum eo sunt episcoporum rogatus adveniat, et sic ad actionem ordinationis accedat."—Mansi, II, 1323; Hefele, I, 517; *ibid*., c. 22: "Episcopus alienam civitatem quae non est illi subjecta, non adeat; nec ad possessionem accedat quae ad eum pertinet super ordinationem cuiusquam; nec constituat presbyteros, aut diaconos alteri subjectos episcopi, nisi forte consilio et voluntate regionis episcopi."—Mansi, II, 1326; Hefele, I, 519-520.

[25] Cf. Thomassinus, *Eccl. Discip*., P. II, lib. I, cap. I, n. 2; Hallier, *De Sacris Elect. et Ordin*., P. II, sec. V, cap. III, art. I, nn. 14-16—*MTC*, XXIV, 970-1.

theory with many examples, e. g., Martin Sabaria, born in Pannonia, baptized in Amiens, but raised to the clerical state and attached to the see of Poitiers by Hilary; Epiphanius, native of Palestine, but ordained by the Bishop of Salamis in Cyprus; Alexander of Cyrene, ordained by St. John Chrysostom of Constantinople, and later made Bishop of Basilinopolis; Pinianus, a Roman, who on a visit to Augustine at Hippo-Regius was coaxed by the people there to swear that he would never become a cleric in any other church but theirs; St. Patrick of Brittany, ordained by Martin, Bishop of Tours; Walfrid of England, who was tonsured by Delphinus of Lyons; and Evagrius of Egypt, ordained by Gregory Nazianzen at Constantinople. Yet, after all these cases have been cited, the author admits that the laws which prohibit Bishops from ordaining lay aliens mean that the Bishops cannot do so as long as the laymen continue to reside in a place alien to the territory of the Bishop who would like to have them, but that by a long period of residence in a new diocese they would become proper subjects in it and could then be tonsured by the new Bishop.[26]

2. *Medieval Law (1100–1563 [C. of Trent])*
Proper Bishops of Origin and of Acquired Domicile

A common error of authors is to confuse the proper Bishop for the first ordination with him who is authorized to confer higher orders on an already initiated cleric. All those who write on this Medieval Period immediately call attention to a change of discipline when Pope Clement IV (a. 1265–1268) recognized two proper Bishops, the one of the cleric's place of origin and

[26] "Hinc tot poenis, tot censuris, tam ordinantes alienum clericum quam ordinatos ab alieno episcopo, alio scilicet ab eo a quo primum in clerum allecti sunt, perculsos supra legimus, cum nullam in ordinantes alterius civitatis *laicum* inflictam poenam legamus; solummodo ordinationem irritam, sicut et judicationem ab eo qui alterius parochianum ordinarit aut judicarit, declaratam advertimus in dubiis quisbusdam Calixti et Julii I Epistolis; quae tamen declaratio hanc interpretationem patitur, ut, quamdiu alterius est parochianus, ab episcopo ordinari non possit, ubi vero *habitatione diuturna* parochianus episcopi alicujus loci effectus fuerit, possit ab eo ordinari; sicut ob minus diuturnam habitationem, non dubium est quin ab episcopo diverso ab episcopo originis suae quivis judicari possit."—Hallier, *De Sacris Elect. et Ordin.*, P. II, sec. V, cap. II, art. I, nn. 19-20 (*MTC*, XXIV, 973-975). Italics inserted.

the other of the diocese where the cleric held a benefice,[27] and to still another change when Pope Boniface VIII (a. 1294–1303) added a third proper Bishop—the Bishop of the cleric's domicile.[28] Few pause to consider further whether these changes applied to *lay* candidates for tonsure as well as to ordained clerics. Room for doubt as to their double application is found in the very wording of the two decrees, both of which expressly set out to solve a problem of *clerics* being ordained to higher orders in alien dioceses.[29] Since these decrees make no mention of the ordination of *laymen*, it is safe to say that they were not to be applied equally to the same, as the succeeding pages will attempt to demonstrate.

Prior to the law of Clement IV, there are various citations which clearly indicate that a layman had a single proper Bishop, and that he was the Bishop of the place where the layman was considered a native.

Michael III, Patriarch of Constantinople (ab. 1167), in order to overcome the abuse of Bishops invading other dioceses to ordain candidates or, in their own territories, of imposing hands on laymen from other dioceses, proposed a discussion of the question in a council of Bishops, and gave as his own the view that certain sacraments could be administered by a Bishop not only on his own subjects but also on outsiders present in his diocese, whereas the sacrament of orders could be conferred only on his own subjects, thus:

> Deinde de ea re sententiam facere cupientes, invenimus eos quidem, qui mysteriis non sunt initiati, fidei rationem docere et catechizare; deinde sic etiam illuminatione dignari ac divina etiam et vivifica mysteria impertire fidelibus, qui sunt ex quacumque regione, hoc esse commune officium judicavimus, et in iis qui ex propria regione accedunt, et iis etiam qui ex aliena regione veniunt: manus autem imponere, et sacros ordines conferre, non iis qui

[27] C. 1, *de temp. ord.*, I, 9, in VI°.

[28] *Ibid.*, c. 3.

[29] "Saepe contingit, quod nonnulli clerici, vinculo excommunicationis adstricti . . ."—*Ibid.*, c. 1. "Quum nullus clericum parochiae alienae praeter superioris ipsius licentiam debeat ordinare: . . . "—*Ibid.*, c. 3.

> undequaque veniunt, sed iis solis qui sunt ejus dioecesis, unicuique antistiti canone cautum est, ne inter eos confusio, seditioque versetur, a quibus et ordo, et pacis bonum, aliis quoque certa debet regula tradi.[80]

He further showed who the proper Bishop of laymen was when he said that ordination was not open to everyone, but only to the selected few, and that the choice of candidates would have to be made by the Bishop who could know them better and could investigate them more easily. Furthermore, as soon as they were ordained they would have to serve the church of their ordination and, he argues, " where could they serve better than in the church which nourished them; where could they rule better than in the church where they themselves had learned to obey?" For these reasons he issued an edict that thenceforward any one who had come from the City of Constantinople and, in violation of the law, temporarily had gone elsewhere to some Bishop to be ordained, would not be permitted to perform sacred ministrations in any other diocese than the one where he had improperly procured his own ordination. This, he thought, would be sufficient punishment for such disobedient laymen, since they would naturally have the hope and expectation of exercising their orders in their home diocese, and it would forever be denied them.[81]

Balsamon, the Greek canonist (a. 1150–1195), in response to a query by Mark, Archbishop of Constantinople, whether penalties levelled against Bishops for ordaining alien clerics applied also for ordaining alien laymen, wrote:

> De laicis autem simul quaesitum est, in S. Constantinop. Sunodo, etc. Et facta est synodalis subnotatio ex aequo puniri eum, qui ex aliena provincia ordinat laicum, praeter episcopi ipsius sententiam.[82]

[80] Hallier, *De Sacris Elect. et Ordin.*, P. II, sec. V, cap. III, art. II, n. 9—*MTC*, XXIV, 987.

[81] *Ibid.*, nn. 9-10—*MTC*, XXIV, 986-7.

[82] *Jur. Orient.*, t. I, pp. 382-383—Thomassinus, *Eccl. Discip.*, P. II, lib. I, cap. V, n. 11.

In England and France the following canons sufficiently express the truth that a Bishop had the exclusive right to say whether or not his native laymen should be advanced to the clerical state:

> Council of London [or Westminster, a. 1125], cap. 10: "Nullus episcoporum, alterius praesumat parochianum ordinare aut judicare: unusquisque enim suo domino stat aut cadit: nec tenetur aliquis sententia non a suo judice prolata."[33]
>
> Council of Montpellier, France (a. 1258), cap. 2: "Nullus episcopus de caetero praetextu ratihabitionis, cujuslibet alterius dioecesanum aliquem absque licentia sui episcopi tonsurare audeat, nec ipsum multo fortius ad minores, v. majores ordines promovere."[34]

In the latter part of the thirteenth century there were issued the papal declarations, already alluded to, of Clement IV (a. 1265–1268) and of Boniface VIII (a. 1294–1303), which are now quoted:

> Saepe contingit, quod nonnulli clerici, vinculo excommunicationis adstricti, aut apostatae, seu irregulares, vel alias ordinum sacrorum susceptione indigni, suam patriam, in qua de his habetur notitia, fugientes, se in remotis partibus faciunt ad huiusmodi ordines promoveri. Nos igitur, volentes animarum ipsorum periculis obviare, statuimus, ut nullus episcoporum Italiae de cetero aliquem ultramontanum clericum ordinare praesumat, nisi a nobis specialem licentiam habeat, vel ab episcopo, de cuius dioecesi traxit originem ordinandus, vel in cuius dioecesi beneficiatus exsistit, per eius patentes literas, causam rationabilem continentes, quare ipsum nolit aut nequeat ordinare. Eos vero, quos contra praemissa contigerit ordinari, manere volumus absque spe dispensationis super hoc a sede apostolica obtinendae suspensos, ac ordinantes poenitentia condigna puniri, omnibus nostris poenitentiariis inhibentes districti, ne absque licentia nostra speciali cum taliter ordinatis dispensent, vel suas eis tradant literas, per quas cum ipsis debeat dispensari.[35]

[33] Mansi, XXI, 332.

[34] Mansi, XXIII, 990; Thomassinus, *Eccl. Discip.*, P. II, lib. I, cap. VII, n. 3.

[35] Clement IV—C. 1, *de temp. ord.*, I, 9, in VI°.

> Quum nullus clericum parochiae alienae praeter superioris ipsius licentiam debeat ordinare: superior intelligitur in hoc casu episcopus, de cuius dioecesi est is, qui ad ordines promoveri desiderat, oriundus, seu in cuius dioecesi beneficium obtinet ecclesiasticum, seu habet (licet alibi natus fuerit,) domicilium in eadem. Inferiores quoque praelati, religiosi vel alii, nisi eis, quod suos clericos aut subditos possint a quo voluerint episcopo facere ordinari, a sede apostolica specialiter sit indultum, vel officialis episcopi, quum ad hoc se ipsius officium non extendat, huiusmodi nequeunt licentiam impartiri. Episcopo autem in remotis agente, ipsius in spiritualibus vicarius generalis, vel, sede vacante, capitulum, seu is, ad quem tunc temporis administratio spiritualium noscitur pertinere, dare possunt licentiam ordinandi.[36]

In analyzing the first of these decrees, namely, that of Pope Clement IV (a. 1265–1268), it is found that he enumerates only two dioceses from which a *cleric* [37] might have come, that in which he originated or that in which he was beneficed. Even if it be supposed that he was beneficed in a diocese different from that of his origin, one is forced to conclude that he could not have received tonsure in any but the diocese of origin, because by law a benefice could not have been conferred on him while he was still a layman. That means that there was only one proper Bishop for laymen, namely, the Bishop of the place of the layman's origin, which may well be described as his "original domicile"; and the recommendation implied in this decree is that a layman should remain in his fatherland (*suam patriam*) and receive all his orders there where he is well known.

The second decree, a quarter of a century later, by Pope Boniface VIII (a. 1294–1303), did not differ substantially from the first, except that it added another possible diocese to those from which a *cleric* might have come, namely, the diocese in which he had acquired a domicile different from his original one. It is apparent that the cleric could have acquired such a domicile *before* becoming a cleric, because in this Period the Bishop of the place of origin did not have as much authority over laymen as he formerly enjoyed, and, hence, he could not

[36] Boniface VIII—C. 3, *de temp. ord.*, I, 9, in VI°.

[37] Cf. *supra*, pp. 45-46.

prevent laypeople from moving away from his diocese if they so wished. But the cleric could also have acquired a new domicile *after* being raised to the clerical state, because at this time no title of ordination was necessary for tonsure, no assignment to a special church was required; and, hence, no obligation of residence prevailed except diocesan, and it could be dispensed from by the written permission of the Bishop.[38] For instance, the following case was submitted to Navarrus (Martino de Azpilcueta), a jurist of the sixteenth century (a. 1491–1586): " An Hispanus ortus Compluti et ibi ordinatus ad minores, qui postea mansit Tiburi tribus annis, et servivit episcopo ejus possit ordinari ad ordines superiores per episcopum Tiburtinum?" His answer was that the aforesaid cleric could be licitly ordained by the Bishop of Tivoli or by any Bishop to whom he would issue dimissorial letters, even though the cleric had remained only three years, more or less, at Tivoli, as long as he had the intention of remaining there perpetually.[39]

Though this decree of Pope Boniface dealt only with *clerics*, a simple process of argument shows that implicitly it recognized as proper *lay* subjects of a diocese not only the men who had never left it from the time of their birth, but also those who had acquired a domicile in it by moving into it from elsewhere. In both cases they were to look to its Bishop as their proper Bishop for ordination. This, it is declared, was not a new enumeration, but was used by certain canonists and theologians before the time of Boniface VIII.[40] It is even believed that the omission of any reference to the Bishop of the place of acquired domicile in the decree of Pope Clement IV did not signify that in his time " acquired domicile " was not a basis upon which a proper Bishop for ordination could be secured, for his decree did not forbid the ordination by a Bishop in Italy of a cleric who had come from beyond the Alps and had acquired a domicile in Italy. Rather, this decree specified the Bishops from

[38] *Infra*, pp. 77-78.

[39] Consilio 2, in 2 edit. de Temporibus ordinat.—Hallier, *De Sacris Elect. et Ordin.*, P. II, sec. V, cap. III, art. IV, n. 9 (*MTC*, XXIV, 997).

[40] Hallier, *ibid.*, art. II, n. 3—*MTC*, XXIV, 982.

whom dimissorial letters should be obtained in just such a case. Even if the cleric in these circumstances had come from a diocese beyond the Alps wherein he had only an acquired domicile, it must be presumed that he abandoned that domicile in order to acquire a new one in Italy, and, therefore, it could hardly be expected that he would need dimissorial letters from a Bishop who no longer possessed authority over him.[41]

The introduction of several bases of competency by which a Bishop could become the proper Bishop to ordain a layman or cleric was a natural outgrowth of changed times. In the Ancient Period, not even a lay person could leave a diocese, even for a time, without Testimonial Letters. The Bishops communicated often with one another by means of letters, carried by minor clerics, through which they were able to warn each other of those whom they had excommunicated or who were infected with heresy and the like. In this Period, on the other hand, Bishops had ceased their frequent exchange of epistles; laymen were able to go where they pleased without letters; and clerics even asserted their right to travel when they were not given a church to occupy them at home. The life and morals of laymen, who had long since moved away from the place of their birth, became totally unknown to the Bishops of the place of origin; investigation of the same seemed well nigh impossible; and so it was left to the Bishop of the place to which they had gone, i.e., to the Bishop of the place where they had an acquired domicile, who now knew them better, either to tonsure them himself on his own responsibility or to grant permission for them to be tonsured after he had certified to their fitness.[42]

The important question now was, "How long does it take for a stranger to acquire a domicile?" In order to be able to confer a sacrament so tremendously important as Holy Orders, a Bishop would need to have a permanent jurisdiction over the subject, even as the Bishop of a candidate's original domicile always had. It was agreed that the stranger should necessarily have the intention to reside perpetually in the new place. The

41 *Ibid.*, art. IV, n. 4—*MTC*, XXIV, 994-5.

42 *Ibid.*, art. IV, nn. 1, 2—*MTC*, XXIV, 992 ss.

emperors Diocletian and Maximian had well defined domicile when they said: " In eodem loco singulos habere domicilium non ambigi, ubi quis larem rerumque ac fortunarum suarum summam constituit: unde rursus non sit discessurus, si nihil avocet; unde cum profectus est, peregrinari videtur; quo si redit peregrinari jam destitit." [48] This definition was accepted and applied by the civil laws and the jurists of succeeding ages.

As long as the intention of perpetually remaining was present, even one moment of residence was considered enough. The intention, however, was difficult to prove. Probable presumptions had to be relied upon. For example, if the candidate lived at his father's home, if he transferred to the place a large part of his goods, if he accepted a position requiring residence, or if he actually lived there for ten years, it was presumed that he intended to remain in the place.

In all cases, Bishops had to be careful in ordaining by virtue of this title, since strangers coming into a diocese to be ordained could easily be suspected of perpetrating fraud. It is not difficult to conclude that candidates were not able to change domiciles as readily as one might be led to believe.

Since laymen had two possible titles by virtue of which they could secure a proper Bishop, namely, those of origin and of acquired domicile, the question arises, " Were both Bishops simultaneously competent?" According to the letter of the law, yes. However, the precise purpose of establishing several proper Bishops was the desire to pass on to that Bishop, to whom the investigation into the life and morals of the candidate would be easiest, the responsibility of tonsuring the candidate or of authorizing him to be tonsured. As long as the candidate stayed in the diocese of his origin *A*, the Bishop of *A* was solely competent to tonsure him. But, when he left his original domicile *A* and spent ten years acquiring a domicile at *B*, the Bishop who could best investigate his character then was the Bishop of *B*, who ought to be his sole proper Bishop as long as the candidate remained at *B*. If, however, before applying for tonsure he should again move to *C* and after ten years ask to be made

[48] C. X. 40 (39) 7.

a cleric there, then the Bishop of *C* would be solely competent for the ordination, would inherit also the problem of ascertaining the candidate's character, and would have to proceed very cautiously before tonsuring him. It is hardly credible that the Bishop of *A*, who had not seen or known the candidate since boyhood, if suddenly approached by the candidate now living at *C*, would consent to tonsure the same on his own authority. Strictly considered, then, though there is nothing to indicate that both the Bishop of origin and the Bishop of the place of acquired domicile were not simultaneously competent, in practice only the one where the candidate actually lived exercised his right. This opinion seems to be substantiated by the Council of Aquileia (a. 1282),[44] and by a decree of Pope Boniface VIII (a. 1294–1303) concerning the ordination of lay aliens,[45] in both of which decrees the language used presupposes only one proper Superior over a layman, and that the one who has a fuller knowledge of his flock.

To those who would interpret Pope Clement's or Pope Boniface's decrees in the sense of giving to a layman a proper Bishop in whatever diocese he became beneficed, the reply must be made that, though youths as young as seven could receive bene-

44 "Considerantes quod aliqui, non ut divinis insistant obsequiis, sed ut privilegio clericali muniti declinent in perpetratis seu perpetrandis malitiis judicium seculare, clericari procurant; statuimus, ut nullus Episcoporum nostrae Provinciae alicui de aliena Civitate, vel Dioecesi absque litteris sui Dioecesani, qui agnitionem habere debet sui pecoris pleniorem, primam tonsuram conferre praesumat. Qui autem praesumpserit, per annum ab executione collationis hujusmodi sit suspensus."—Cap. *Ne quis episcopus* (Mansi, XXIV, 434).

45 "Nullus episcopus vel quivis alius infanti, nisi forte religionem intraret, seu illiterato, sed nec absque sui superioris licentia homini dioecesis alienae, clericalem praesumat conferre tonsuram, nec etiam coniugato, nisi volenti religionem intrare aut ad sacros ordines promoveri, prout est sacris canonibus diffinitum. Qui vero contra fecerit, ut in eo, in quo peccaverit, puniatur, per unum annum a collatione clericalis tonsurae duntaxat noverit se suspensum."—C. 4, *de temp. ord.*, I, 9, in VI°. According to the Provincial Council of Béziers (a. 1310), cap. 1 (Mansi, XXV, 359), the implied purpose of this canon of Pope Boniface VIII was to ward off from the clerical state those men who desired to be clerics for fraudulent reasons rather than out of devotion and those who were involved in some irregularity or who ought not to be tonsured because of some impediment of law. For this to be achieved, it was both desirable and necessary to the mind of Pope Boniface that laymen have as their sole proper Bishop for the conferring of tonsure the Superior of that diocese in which they lived.

fices during the Medieval Period, it was necessary for them to be in the clerical state first,[46] and that could be conferred only by the Bishop of their native or acquired diocese.

Passerini tried to find a loophole in this procedure with the argument that, if he conferred a benefice on a lay youth from another diocese in the same act as he tonsured him, a Bishop would be within the law; but Pignatelli vigorously opposed this opinion and warned that it would open the way to all kinds of abuses contrary to the purpose of the papal decrees.[47]

3. *Tridentine Law (1564–1694)*

Proper Bishops of Origin, of Acquired Domicile, and of Familiaritas

The Council of Trent did not enact any law clearly and decisively indicating who was to be considered the proper Bishop for the ordination of laymen and clerics. From a comparison of pertinent texts of its chapters, however, one can gather the following:

[46] Creagh, "Benefice,"—*Cath. Ency.*, II, 475-6; Thomassinus, *Eccl. Discip.*, P. II, lib. I, cap. VII, n. 4.

[47] Pignatelli, *Consultationes Canonicae*, t. III, consult. XIII, n. 14, *finis*. Reiffenstuel likewise insisted on the law being obeyed in order to avert serious consequences, thus: "Certum est, quod unusquisque non nisi a proprio Episcopo sit ordinandus, nullusque possit ordinare extraneum, nec etiam primam Tonsuram huic conferre absque proprii Superioris licentia.... Et merito: tum, ut dissensiones evitentur, quae suboriri possent inter Episcopos, si unus alterius subditos eodem ignorante, ac saepius invito, ordinare praesumeret, can. 1, D. 71. Tum, ut obvietur malitiis hominum, atque indigni, et ignorantes ad sacros Ordines non promoveantur, qui alioquin Clericales Ordines, quos a propriis Episcopis forsan sibi jam denegatos dolent, aut ex certis impedimentis canonicis sibi denegandos fore merito verentur; ab extraneis Episcopis, nullamque de ipsorum defectibus notitiam habentibus, in animarum suarum perniciem, et Ecclesiastici Ordinis dedecus, recipere praesumerent."—*Jus Canon. Univ.*, t. I, in c. 4, X, *de temp. ordin.*, I, 11, n. 77. That they were correct in their opinions can be seen from the later wording of the Constitution "*Speculatores*" of Innocent XII, Nov. 4, 1694, n. 3: "... decernimus, et declaramus, nulli Episcopo... licere exterum quempiam... ad Clericalem Tonsuram promovere, cuiusvis Beneficii Ecclesiastici ei statim ac tonsura huiusmodi insignitus fuerit conferendi, seu ad quos is a Patronis iam praesentatus, seu nominatus fuerit, praetextu, etiamsi Beneficium praedictum de novo ea expresse adiecta lege fundatum fuisse constiterit, ut quis immediate post Clericalem characterem susceptum ad illud instituatur;..."—*Codicis Iuris Canonici Fontes*, n. 258. Hereafter this collection will simply be cited as *Fontes*.

1. Everyone had to be ordained by his proper Bishop or with the dimissorials of the same.[48]

2. Titular Bishops especially, without dioceses of their own, were not to confer tonsure or any order without the express consent of the candidate's proper Prelate.[49]

3. Initiation into the clerical state was taking place at a very tender age, since the requisites were that the candidate have already received the sacrament of confirmation, know the rudiments of faith, be able to read and write, and be reasonably reliable in the sincerity of his purpose.[50]

4. No one was to receive a benefice unless he was already tonsured and at least fourteen years of age.[51]

5. A new title of proper Bishop was recognized, namely, that of intimate association with the Bishop's domestic retinue, which required three years' residence in the very household of the Bishop. This was termed *familiaritas*. As soon as the Bishop tonsured a member of his official household he became the young cleric's proper Bishop for higher orders by the title of benefice, for it was required that along with tonsure a benefice be immediately conferred on the candidate.[52]

6. Abbots and non-episcopal exempt Prelates could not tonsure or ordain any but their own regular subjects; neither could they issue dimissorials for secular clerics.[53]

7. No one was to be ordained at all unless in the judgment of his own Bishop he would be useful or necessary for some church or holy place, to which he had to be assigned.[54]

8. Every cathedral was to have near it or in some convenient place, to be selected by the Bishop, a college containing a certain number of boys of that same city or diocese (or province, if the

[48] Sess. XXIII, *de ref.*, c. 8.

[49] Sess. XIV, *de ref.*, c. 2.

[50] Sess. XXIII, *de ref.*, c. 4.

[51] *Ibid.*, c. 6.

[52] *Ibid.*, c. 9.

[53] *Ibid.*, c. 10.

[54] *Ibid.*, c. 16.

diocese was small) who would be at least twelve years of age and would show good evidences of a priestly vocation. They were to be supported and instructed in religion and church discipline according to classes, tonsured, and vested in the clerical garb, and were to form thereby a perpetual seminary of ministers of God.[55]

Though the words *Bishop of domicile* are not used, it can certainly be gleaned from the texts that the proper Bishop for a lay youth was the one in whose city or diocese this youth lived and to whose seminary he would go for instruction and tonsure, or else the Bishop under whose charge he was engaged as a member of the household.

It is of interest to note that, since boys could be tonsured as young as twelve years of age at this time, as was just pointed out in the matter of seminaries, the Bishop of the place of domicile of a lay aspirant to the clerical state would in almost every case be identical with the Bishop of origin. It could not happen otherwise unless the boy's parents moved their established home within that brief span of their son's life.

True it is that many texts of the Period speak only of the Bishop of the layman's *origin* or of the city from which he sprung, and ignore the factor of domicile. However, the *origin* of a layman, which so often occurs as a basic title for determining the proper Bishop for ordination, does not mean simply the place where a male youth was born, but rather the place where the youth's parents at the time of his birth had their established residence or domicile. *Origin*, in other words, merely signifies *original domicile*. The practice in France substantiates this interpretation. By an agreement of all the Archbishops and Bishops of France in 1635 the title of "origin" was adopted as the sole title of competence for a Bishop to ordain a layman—a practice which was an exception to the universal custom—and the French hierarchy abided by this agreement for more than two hundred years.[56] If a youth applied for admis-

[55] *Ibid.*, c. 18.

[56] Many, *De Sacra Ordin.*, nn. 47-49. Even prior to 1635 this practice existed in some dioceses—Cf., e. g., the Provincial Council of Narbonne (a. 1609), cap. 21 (Mansi, XXXIV B, 1499a).

sion to the clerical state in a diocese where he had only an acquired domicile, he was referred back to the Bishop of his origin, for the reason that origin was considered far easier and swifter to prove than domicile was. Yet, if the youth had been perchance born in a place outside his father's domicile, perhaps even outside France itself, it was to the Bishop of the place where the father had his domicile at the time of his son's birth that the young candidate was sent for his initiation into the clerical state.[57] Thus it is seen that even in France, *origin* really meant *original domicile.* To clarify this fact the latter term is frequently used in this study.

In other countries, the Bishop of the place of the layman's acquired domicile as well as the Bishop of his place of origin was recognized as competent to elevate him to the ranks of the clergy, and even in France the Bishops sometimes used this right.[58]

It was now, after the Council of Trent, that difficulties arose anew precisely on the question of domicile. As long as the layman still resided where he had been born, it was apparent which Bishop could tonsure him. When, however, he left his place of birth, how long did he have to live in a new diocese before acquiring its Bishop as the proper Bishop for his initiation into the clerical state?

In Mexico a custom had arisen whereby lay candidates, when they came into a new diocese seeking orders, simply took an oath that it was their intention to remain in the new location, and this was considered sufficient for establishing a domicile, whereupon the new Bishop on the strength of that title would tonsure them. The Council of Mexico (a. 1585) abolished this practice in the following words: " . . . interdicit haec synodus,

[57] " Ob hanc itaque difficultatem probandi domicilii, itemque ob ejus incertitudinem . . . consulto in Gallia ab ordinatione clericorum qui alibi nati sint, episcopi sibi temperare solent, non quod, ut opinor, id sibi interdictum putent, sed quod originis probatio facilior sit et expeditior, ad cujus proinde episcopum remittunt, nisi in extranea quis patria, vel extra paternum domicilium fortuito natus sit, quo casu domicilii, quod originis locum quodammodo obtinet, rationem habent, et ordines iis conferunt qui apud eos domicilium habuerint."—Hallier, *De Sacris Elect. et Ordin.*, P. II, sec. V, cap. III, art. IV, n. 10 (*MTC*, XXIV, 998).

[58] Many, *De Sacra Ordin.*, n. 49.

ne quisquam ad titulum hujusmodi ordinetur, aut ordinari permittatur, nisi per tantum tempus in ea dioecesi vitam duxerit, ex quo probabile sit velle se ibi permanere."[59]

A finer distinction, and one which is still used, was made by the I Council of Siena in Italy (a. 1599), which required of those seeking tonsure or major or minor orders ten years' residence to acquire a domicile, thus: "Primo igitur quisque probet, se ex legitimis nuptiis procreatum esse, vel saltem dispensationem de impedimento natalium accepisse; deinde, ius dioecesis sibi competere, ratione vel originis vel ecclesiastici beneficii quod in dioecesi obtineat, vel domicilii decennatis, vel alia demum quavis legitima causa; . . ."[60] It was left, however, for the next Period to settle definitely these difficulties.

4. *Innocentian Law (1694–1906)*
Proper Bishops of Origin, of Acquired Domicile, and of Familiaritas

The clearest expression thus far from any authoritative source of what is meant by the various proper Bishops for ordination is found in the Constitution "*Speculatores*" issued by Pope Innocent XII on November 4, 1694.[61] In this document it is clearly stated, among other things of importance, that the proper Bishop for the tonsuring of a layman is the Bishop of the candidate's place of origin, or of his present domicile, or of the place where the candidate resides in his domestic association with the Bishop's household; and that no Bishop can ever claim competency to tonsure a lay extern merely on the strength of a benefice that he is going to confer at once on that layman.[62]

The *origin* of the lay aspirant was the determining factor as long as he or, in the case of a minor, his father did not move from the diocese where he had actually been born. If he was born while his father was on a temporary sojourn, then his place of origin was legally considered the same as the diocese of his

[59] Lib. I, tit. IV, sec. *De modo conferendi ordines et literas dimissorias*, c. 2—Mansi, XXXIV B, 1036.

[60] Cap. XV *De sacramento ordinis*, n. 3—Mansi, XXXVI B, 536.

[61] *Fontes*, n. 258.

[62] *Ibid.*, nn. 3, 6—*Loc. cit.*

father's origin, i.e., where his father had been living prior to the journey.[63] If, however, the youth's father had moved away from the legal place of his son's birth and had stayed long enough in the second place, i.e., where the son was actually born, to contract a new domicile, then no longer was the origin of the father to be the deciding factor, but rather the newly contracted domicile, in determining the proper Bishop for the administration of tonsure to the youth.

> At si Pater in alieno loco, ubi eius filius natus est, tamdiu, ac eo animo permanserit, ut inibi vere Domicilium de iure contraxerit, tunc non origo Patris, sed Domicilium per Patrem legitime ut praefertur, contractum pro Ordinatione eiusdem filii attendi debeat.[64]

In the legislation of Pope Innocent XII it is stated that to obtain an ecclesiastical *domicile* the candidate must: a) reside in the diocese for at least ten years and fortify by an oath his intention of remaining there; or b) transfer to the place the greater part of his belongings and household furnishings and reside there for some considerable time, sufficient to demonstrate his intention of staying there permanently, which intention he must likewise fortify by an oath.[65] Even to these stringent precautions, it is prescribed in addition that the Bishop of the place of the layman's origin have Testimonial Letters from any diocese where the lay candidate stayed long enough to become liable for the contraction of a canonical impediment; and in the second case, it is prescribed that the Bishop of the place of the layman's domicile have Testimonial Letters from the Bishop of the place of the candidate's origin, if departure did not take place until the youth was fourteen years of age.[66]

Finally, if the candidate left his place of origin or his place of domicile to live in the household of a third Bishop, he would still not lose the former proper Bishop, but, after completing

[63] Innocentius XII, const. "*Speculatores*," 4 nov. 1694, n. 4—*Fontes*, n. 258.

[64] *Ibid.*, n. 5.

[65] *Loc. cit.*

[66] *Loc. cit.*

three years of service in the third Bishop's employ, the latter would also become his proper Bishop by the title of *familiaritas* and could tonsure him, provided that this same Bishop obtained Testimonial Letters from one or the other of the previous proper Bishops and had a benefice to confer on the youth within a month afterwards.[67]

This classic law became the norm by which all cases were judged and the model for provincial legislation for the next two centuries or more.[68] Some points of it received greater eluci-

[67] *Ibid.*, n. 6.

[68] Thus the Provincial Synod of the Ruthenians (a. 1720), cap. 7: "In propria vero dioecesi neminem promovere pariter audeat alienae dioecesis subditum, sine licentia, ac literis Dimissorialibus sui superioris, episcopi scilicet, tam originis, quam domicilii, juxta Constitutionem a S. M. Innocentio XII, quae incipit: Speculatores, hac de re editam, actis synodalibus inserendam, et sub poenis in eadem constitutione tam contra ordinantem, quam contra ordinatum praescriptis."—Mansi, XXXV B, 1500; the Provincial Synod of the Maronites held on Mount Libanus (a. 1736), *Constitutiones et Canones*, P. II, cap. XIV, n. 8: "In propria vero dioecesi neminem promovere episcopus potest, qui alienae dioecesis subditus sit, sine licentia ac literis dimissorialibus sui superioris, episcopi scilicet tam originis, quam domicilii, juxta constitutionem ab Innocentio XII, summo pontifice, editam sub poenis in eadem constitutione tam contra ordinantem, quam contra ordinatum, praescriptis . . ."—Mansi, XXXVIII, 130; *ibid.*, P. III, cap. IV, n. 24: "Nemo alienae dioeceseos clericum ordinet, neque etiam laicum ad ordines suscipiendos in propria dioecesi admittat, nisi domicilium, ut supra, contraxerit, vel nisi ordinarius consensum in scriptis dederit."—Mansi, XXXVIII, 193; the Council of Soissons, France (a. 1849), *Decreta*, tit. X, cap. I: "'Unusquisque a proprio episcopo ordinetur,' Episcopus igitur non conferat ordines nisi sibi subditis, aut ratione originis aut ratione domicilii, quod ordinandus acquisivit in alia quam suae originis dioecesi, aut ratione beneficii aut titulo familiaritatis; quemadmodum statutum est constitutione Innocentii XII, quae incipit: Speculatores."—Mansi, XLIII, 594a; the II Plenary Council of Baltimore (a. 1866), tit. V, cap. VIII, n. 317: "Juxta Ecclesiae mentem, quae ex saepe repetitis Canonici Juris sanctionibus manifeste eruitur, unusquisque a proprio Episcopo ordinandus est. Quo nomine appellatur Episcopus, cui subditur ratione sive originis, sive domicilii. Locus originis dicitur urbs, oppidum, aut pagus, ubi quis naturaliter ortus est, scilicet ubi pater verum domicilium habet. Si autem alibi per accidens nascatur, v. g. occasione itineris, legationis, mercaturae, vel cujusvis alterius temporalis morae, tum nullatenus hujusmodi fortuita nativitas, sed vera tantum et naturalis patris origo erit attendenda. Quo si pater in alieno loco ubi filius nascitur, tandiu eoque animo permanserit, ut inibi domicilium de jure contraxerit, tunc non origo patris, sed domicilium pro filii ordinatione attendi debet."—*Conc. Plen. Balt. II. Acta et Decreta*, pp. 167-168. See also S. C. C., decr. "*A primis*," 20 iulii 1898: ". . . Cum autem de huiusmodi titulis disceptaretur, Innocentius XII app. litt. incipientibus "*Speculatores*" datis die 4 nov. 1694, determinavit ac constituit quo sensu et extensione iidem essent accipiendi ad eum effectum, ut quis proprius fieret alicuius Episcopi subditus, quo legitime ordinari valeret. Quae constitutio ut suprema lex deinde habita est, eaque duce omnes quaestiones diremptae."—*ASS*, XXXI (1898-9), 49 ss.; *AER*, XX (1899), 179 ff.; *Fontes*, n. 4307.

dation and definition from the discussions which it excited. Thus, the place of origin of a lay youth was shown to mean the place where his parents had their domicile.[69] A recently baptized lay convert was to consider as his Bishop of origin the Bishop of the diocese wherein the baptism took place.[70] The " considerable time " required to acquire a domicile after transferring one's goods and furnishings to a new location was interpreted by custom to mean three years.[71] Whenever a layman had two domiciles, the Bishops of both places of domicile were to be considered the proper Bishop for his ordination, i. e., he could exercise the power of choice between them.[72]

Petitions were made at intervals to the Sacred Congregation of the Council to relax, at least temporarily, some of the provisions of the Constitution "*Speculatores.*" Some of these petitions, emanating from widely scattered sections of the globe and as late as the end of the nineteenth century, certainly prove that this classic law enjoyed a wide enforcement throughout the entire Innocentian Period.[73]

69 Tolomeus Cioffi's parents had retained their domicile at Melfi with the intention of returning there, but were journeying when Tolomeus was born. Melfi was not the legal place of origin of the father of the youth, but was the place where he had acquired a domicile. The S. C. C. decided that Tolomeus had a right to be tonsured by the Bishop of Melfi on the strength of the title of origin—S. C. C., *Melphiensis,* 23 feb. 1901 (*ASS,* XXXIII [1900-01], 541-6).

70 II Plenary Council of Baltimore (a. 1866), tit. V, cap. VIII, n. 317: ". . . In neo-baptizatis, ex haeresi aut infidelitate conversis, locus originis censetur ille, in quo Baptismum accipiunt. Ita enim a Paulo III constitutum fuit, et ita se habet praxis Curiae Romanae."—*Conc. Plen. Balt. II. Acta et Decreta* (Baltimorae: Murphy, 1894), p. 168.

71 Cf. S. C. C., *Bononien. seu Ferrarien. Ordinationis,* 14 nov. 1733, in which the case is decided on the strength of three years' residence with the transfer of belongings—*ASS,* VI (1870), 579 ss. Cf. also S. C. C., *Manizalen.,* Jan. 21, 1905, where the decision rendered refused to recognize a three years' stay as sufficient for seminarians, who had no house furnishings to transport and whose intention was conditional on their success in being promoted—*ASS,* XXXVII (1904-05), 775-780; Gasparri, *De Sacra Ordin.,* II, n. 832.

72 II Plenary Council of Baltimore (a. 1866), tit. V, cap. VIII, n. 318: "...Si quis duo habeat domicilia, poterit ab utriuslibet loci Episcopo Ordines petere, quia uterque *proprii* Episcopi loco habetur."—*Con. Plen. Balt. II. Acta et Decreta,* p. 168.

73 Thus the Bishop of Algiers won the right to retain a cleric, Aemilius Strub, whom as a lay candidate for tonsure he had received from Strasbourg, the diocese of the youth's origin, educated for six years and finally tonsured without even

When the number of the faithful in the vast territories of the United States of America increased beyond the point where their spiritual needs could be supplied by a native clergy, it seemed a distinct benefit of Divine Providence to have multitudes of ecclesiastical candidates from abroad seek this country as a spiritual field. In order that this boon might not become an instrument for evil instead of for good, the Ordinaries of the United States were warned that every alien layman seeking tonsure had to present dimissorial and Testimonial Letters from the Bishop of his place of origin. In addition, however, there was made on Feb. 25, 1896 this special requisite for lay candidates coming to the United States of America from Poland, even though latterly they had been inhabitants of Italy: that they should exhibit Testimonial Letters from the Sacred Congregation for the Propagation of the Faith, which would certify to their freedom of departure, immunity from censures, and good morals.[74]

Testimonial Letters from the Bishop of origin, because it had become a custom in Algiers to consider six years sufficient for a domicile.—S. C. C., *Argentinen. et Algerien.*, 7 iulii 1833 (*ASS*, XVI [1883], 249-262). Though it was impossible for seminarians to contract a domicile in a seminary of another than their native diocese until they had spent ten years in it (cf. *supra*, p. 59), yet a temporary permission for three years was granted to the Bishop of the newly erected diocese of Manizales, Colombia, S. A., to ordain his seminarians who had come from other dioceses without dimissorials from the proper Bishops of their place of origin or of domicile, even though their intention of remaining in Manizales had been conditioned on their success in receiving ordination—S. C. C., *Manizalen.*, 21 ian. 1905 (*ASS*, XXXVII [1904-05], 775 ss.). In 1883 a lay youth, changing his residence at age 12 from Vasto, his place of origin, to Ortona, where he stayed ten years, was allowed to be considered a subject for tonsure in Ortona, even though the Bishop of his place of origin, viz. Vasto, who was still recognized by the youth as his proper Bishop, was unwilling for the youth to be tonsured under the circumstances. It was impossible for a boy of twelve to establish a legal domicile; hence, it was his place of origin that still counted. But he was poor, and Ortona needed priests; so the permission was granted provided that he took an oath to stay at Ortona—S. C. C., *Vasten. et Ortonen.*, 1 dec. 1883 (*ASS*, XVI [1883], 398-401).

[74] Instr. (*ad Epp. Stat. Foed. Americ.*), 25 feb. 1896: ". . . Sacra Congregatio per praesentes literas omnibus et singulis R̃mis Ordinariis Statuum Foederatorum Americae Septen. notum facit sequentem regulam in posterum servandam esse, ut scilicet nullus sacerdos, vel ad statum ecclesiasticum candidatus, ex Polonia oriundus, etiamsi ex Italia vel alia dioecesi mediate migraverit, in clerum dioecesanum admittatur, nisi testimoniales literas exhibeat hujus S. C., quibus de legitima discedendi a dioecesi facultate, de immunitate a censuris, nec non de bonis moribus praesentandi plane constet."—*Collectanea S. C. P. F.*, n. 1918. This regulation was changed in 1908—Cf. *infra*, p. 64.

5. *Pre-Code Law (1906–1917)*
Proper Bishops of Origin, of Acquired Domicile, of Familiaritas, *and of Quasi-Incardination*

The most important development in this Period was the introduction of a new basis or title of proper Bishop for the ordination of laymen, namely, the Bishop of *quasi-incardination.* It came as a direct result of a change in legislation for the higher ordination of clerics, as contained in the Sacred Congregation of the Council's Decree "*A primis*" of July 20, 1898.[75]

The Constitution "*Speculatores*" had defined the Bishops of the places of origin, of domicile, of *familiaritas,* and of a conferred benefice as proper for the further ordination of tonsured clerics. Its requisites for the acquisition of a domicile were stringent, making the introduction of contrary customs a foregone conclusion. The "*A primis*" canonized and regulated some of these customs for clerics only. Logical sequence called for consideration and regulation of the contrary customs by which laymen established domiciles by abbreviated methods, and this was exactly what happened. The Sacred Congregation of the Council answered those Bishops who had submitted doubts in the matter with the promise of a pertinent decree.

The decree was issued on November 24, 1906.[76] As far as the subject matter of this Article is concerned, it amounted to a universal and perpetual derogation from that portion of the Constitution "*Speculatores*"[77] which had prescribed the conditions for the acquisition of a domicile by which a proper Bishop for the conferring of initial tonsure could be obtained. It legitimized the custom whereby laymen were considered proper subjects of a Bishop for the conferring of tonsure as soon as they arrived in a new diocese, and even before they had ever arrived, as long as their former Bishop had granted to the new Bishop letters conceding the perpetual dismissal of said laymen and testifying to their worthiness for the clerical state. The

[75] *ASS,* XXXI (1898-9), 49 ss.

[76] *ASS,* XXXIX (1906), 600 ss; *AER,* XXXVI (1907), 292 ff.; *NRT,* XXXIX (1907), 12.

[77] *Scil.* n. 5—*Fontes,* n. 258.

only portion of n. 5 of the "*Speculatores*" that was retained was the oath to be taken by the candidates that they would remain perpetually in the new diocese. A layman fulfilling the conditions of the decree obtained by the title of quasi-incardination a new proper Bishop, who could then on his own authority either tonsure the layman or issue dimissorials for the same.

This decree together with the "*A primis*"[78] and the "*Vetuit*"[79] supplanted, after 1908, the former Instruction of the Sacred Congregation for the Propagation of the Faith to the Ordinaries of the United States of America[80] with regard to the special requisites demanded of lay ecclesiastical candidates from Poland for acquiring a proper Bishop for the conferring of tonsure in the United States of America.[81]

Since the decree remained in force until the Code was published, there were, from 1906 to 1917, four potential titles by which a layman's proper Bishop for the conferring of tonsure was determined, namely, by reason of origin, of domicile, of *familiaritas*, and of quasi-incardination. It was within the power of the layman himself to seek tonsure from that Bishop whose basis of competency best suited his individual case.

A fuller discussion of the last important change in legislation whereby the title of quasi-incardination was introduced is reserved for the section on the Quasi-Excardination and Quasi-Incardination of Laymen.[82]

ARTICLE III

TITLE OF ORDINATION FOR LAYMEN

In the brief sketch of the organizational development of the Church in Chapter II, it was shown that, even in the second century, Bishops had already associated with themselves major

[78] S. C. C., July 20, 1898—*ASS*, XXXI (1898-9), 49 ss.; *Fontes*, n. 4307.

[79] S. C. C., Dec. 22, 1905—*ASS*, XXXVIII (1905-06), 407 ss.

[80] *Supra*, p. 62.

[81] *AAS*, II (1910), 102; Pius X, Const. "*Sapienti Consilio*," 29 iun. 1908—*AAS*, I (1909), 7-19; *Fontes*, n. 682.

[82] Cf. *infra*, pp. 89 ff.

and minor clerics to share the work of spreading the faith. This collaboration grew proportionately with the Church. The most fundamental concept of a cleric was that of a man to work for the dissemination of the faith under the direction of a Bishop. An idle cleric was an anomaly. Every city which had a Bishop installed in it, every new town or village that had a parish started within it, every chapel of ease or martyr's tomb that was erected, created a need for one or more priests or non-sacerdotal clerics as assistants, chaplains, or custodians. The Bishop met the need by ordaining some of his more worthy lay subjects to the clerical state; and the clerics, upon receiving the very first minor order, were assigned, each to the particular church which was to be his field of labor for life.

At Rome, private dwellings were the first form of city churches.[83] Over its doorway each bore the inscription or title *(titulus)* of its owner or builder. When such a house, by donation or legacy, became the property of the Church, and was used exclusively for religious worship, it retained, at first, the name of the owner as a suitable designation, e. g., *titulus Julii Pudentis*. Afterwards, it might receive a saint's name as its proper designation, e. g., *titulus Sanctae Sabinae;* and the cleric assigned to its service was said to have it as his *title,* or to be *intitulated.*[84] That practice of designation soon spread elsewhere, so that every layman, as soon as he was ordained to the clerical state, had to be given a title, by which was meant a church or religious place which needed his ministry. Such was the original concept of the title of ordination.[85]

Since all clerics participated in an equal monthly distribution of a specified portion of the entire diocesan funds collected from all the churches,[86] a cleric's title of ordination was likewise his perpetual guarantee of sustenance, but only secondarily so. One who was ordained absolutely, on the other hand, had no church assigned to him, and, hence, had no share in the distribu-

83 *Supra,* p. 16.

84 *Supra,* pp. 22-23.

85 Cf. Moeder, *The Proper Bishop for Ordination and Dimissorial Letters,* pp. 3-4.

86 *Supra,* pp. 20, 25.

tion of the offerings of the faithful; but absolute ordinations were outlawed from the very beginning.

It is the purpose of this Article to trace the fluctuations which the ordination title for laymen underwent in the progress of the ages.

1. *The First Five Centuries*

Little is known of the ways in which the Church allotted, utilized, and supported its clerics until the beginning of the fourth century, whereupon the perpetual assignment of every cleric, not merely to a diocese, but even to a particular church, is seen to have been prescribed everywhere with the utmost rigor.[87] This canonical attachment bound the cleric not only to service, but also to personal residence, in recompense for which he was listed on the *canon* or *catalogue* of beneficiaries of the diocesan fund. All clerics, minor as well as major, were included. The services of the minor clerics were not so important, e. g., their functions of acting as church janitors, of being messengers between Bishops, servers at the Mass, bearers of the *fermentum,* etc., but they were preparing for the sublime order of the priesthood in a practical way and in the very church where later they could expect to exercise their priestly functions.[88]

The first clear expression of this discipline in the West was in the I Council of Arles (a. 314),[89] and the first in the East was in the Ecumenical Council of Nicaea (a. 325), which required that clerics who seceded from their churches (i. e., dioceses) be forced to return to them.[90] In the Council of

[87] I. e., to the cathedral church, or to an established rural church, though in some dioceses, such as Constantinople and Alexandria in the East, or Rome and Hippo in the West, it might also have been an assignment to one of the auxiliary, but subordinate, city churches. Cf. *supra,* pp. 19, 22.

[88] Cf. *supra,* pp. 20, 24, 25.

[89] Tit. Ut ubi quisque ordinatur, ibi permaneat. C. 2: "De his qui in quibuscumque locis ordinati fuerint ministri, in ipsis locis perseverent."—Mansi, II, 471.

[90] C. 16: "Quicumque temere et inconsiderate, nec Dei timorem prae oculis habentes, nec ecclesiasticum canonem scientes presbyteri vel diaconi, vel quicumque omnino in canone recensentur, ab ecclesiis secesserint, ii in aliena ecclesia nullo modo recipi debent, sed omnino cogendi sunt in suas ipsorum parochias redire: ..."— Mansi, II, 675; c. 23, C. VII, q. 1.

Antioch (a. 341) it was ruled that any cleric who left his diocese to go elsewhere was forbidden to minister any longer,[91] and if he refused to return when ordered to do so by his Bishop he was to be degraded irrevocably from his ministry.[92] The Council of Mileve in Africa (a. 416) indicated that even the lowest grade of cleric, the lector, had an office to perform in the church of his ordination.[93] St. Leo the Great, in an epistle to the Bishop of Aquileia (a. 442), forbade the arbitrary transfer of any cleric from one church to another, and admonished clerics to persevere where they had been ordained.[94] This, like the other instances referred to below, in which a permanent residence in one church is prescribed, indicates that the clerics of any order were occupied in the church where they resided.

The classical law, however, prescribing a definite place of employment in the sacred ministry for every ordained cleric is found in the Council of Chalcedon (a. 451), especially in canon 6, which states:

> Nullum absolute ordinare nec Diaconum, nec Presbyterum, nec omnino aliquem eorum, qui sunt in ecclesiastica ordinatione, nisi specialiter in Ecclesia civitatis, vel in possessione, vel in Martyrio, vel Monasterio ordinandus praedicetur: et eos vero, qui

[91] C. 3: "Si quis presbyter, vel diaconus, vel quilibet clericus, deserta sua ecclesia, ad aliam transeundum esse crediderit, et ibi paullatim temptet, quo migravit, perpetuo permanere, ulterius ministrare non debet, praesertim si ab episcopo suo ad revertendum fuerit exhortatus."—C. 24, C. VII, q. 1; Mansi, VI Appen., 1160. The text of this canon as edited by Mansi contains the expression "*derelinquens suam parrociam*," which, however, referred to a "diocese." Cf. *supra*, p. 18.

[92] "Si forte evocatus a proprio Episcopo, ut revertatur ad propriam, et correptus non audiat, et permanserit inquietudine, omnino degradari eum a ministerio, et nullam eum spem habere ad revertendum."—Mansi, *loc. cit.* In the Decree of Gratian this penalty is rendered "*omnimodis ab officio suo deponi debere.*"—C. 24, C. VII, q. 1.

[93] C. 15: "Item placuit, ut quicumque in ecclesia primum vel semel legerit, ab alia ecclesia ad clericatum non teneatur."—Mansi, IV, 331; c. 3, D. LXXII.

[94] Cap. 5: "Illam quoque partem ecclesiasticae disciplinae, qua olim a sanctis Patribus et a nobis saepe decretum est, ut nec in Presbyteratus gradu, nec in Diaconatus ordine, nec in subsequenti officio Clericorum ab Ecclesia ad Ecclesiam cuiquam transire sit liberum, ut in integrum revoces, admonemus: ut unusquisque non ambitione illectus, non cupiditate seductus, non persuasione hominum depravatus, ubi ordinatus est, perseveret: "—Mansi, V, 1115.

absolute ordinantur, definit sancta Synodus irritam habere hujusmodi ordinationem, et in actu invalidam, ad injuriam ordinantis.[95]

In other words, this meant that no cleric was to be ordained *absolutely,* that is to say, no one was to be ordained, even to the lowest grade of cleric, unless he were especially assigned to the usual single city church, the cathedral, to a church in the rural towns of the diocese, to one of the chapels erected over the tombs of martyrs, or to a chaplaincy in a monastery of Religious. This law has come down through the centuries as the strictest model of a perpetual bond between cleric and diocese, for it not merely assigned clerics to the general service of the diocese, but limited and confined their ministry for life to one particular church or position. Canons 10 and 20 of the same Council substantiate this view, because they command that clerics be content to remain in the service of the church of their first ordination.[96]

Residence.—The laws of the period, too, were very clear in exacting personal residence. Thus, clerics were forbidden to depart from their diocese arbitrarily in order to take up their abode elsewhere, and, if they did so, either they were to be forced to return or various punishments were to be visited

[95] Mansi, VI, 1226; c. 1, D. LXX. There are other interpretations of this canon in which "*praedicetur*" is rendered "*designetur*" or "*pronuntietur,*" which, according to some, would make the canon refer to the public announcement of the ordination in the church (Mansi, VII, 362, 375), and, in fact, the version of it in the Decree of Gratian unmistakably presents that meaning. However, the phrase "*absolute ordinantur,*" which had a very definite meaning, namely, to be ordained without a title, i. e., without a place of employment and sustenance, is a key to the correct interpretation, and, indeed, the Fathers of the Council of Trent understood the canon in the sense of clerical assignment (sess. XXIII, *de ref.*, c. 16). The declaration of invalidity here made against ordinations without a title meant suspension from the exercise of the order received—Moeder, *The Proper Bishop for Ordination and Dimissorial Letters*, pp. 6-7.

[96] C. 10: "Non licere clerico in duarum civitatum ecclesiis eodem tempore in catalogum referri, et in ea in qua a principio ordinatus est, et in ea, in quam, tanquam ad majorem, confugit, propter inanis gloriae cupiditatem: eos autem qui hoc faciunt, propriae ecclesiae restitui, in qua ab initio ordinati sunt, ut illic solum ministrent."—Mansi, VII, 362; c. 3, C. XXI, q. 2; c. 20: "Clericos in ecclesiis ministerio fungentes, quemadmodum jam statuimus, non licere in alius civitatis ecclesia ordinari: sed illa esse contentos, in qua ab initio ut ministrarent, digni habiti sunt."—Mansi, VII, 366; c. 4, D. LXXI.

upon them.[97] Only with the permission of their Bishops was such a departure for clerics possible,[98] and this permission was needed even for temporary journeys away from the church or diocese.[99] In addition to these clear citations of the law of the period there are others which at least insinuate rather plainly the necessity of personal residence.[100] The only circumstance for which the rigor of the law was relaxed was that in which the cleric necessarily had to leave his country as well as his church and diocese because of exile or loss of citizenship.[101]

[97] Apostolic Canons, c. 15: "Si quis presbyter aut diaconus aut quilibet e catalogo clericorum relinquens suam parochiam ad aliam abieret et omnino demigrans in alia parochia commoretur praeter sui episcopi voluntatem, hunc iubemus non amplius sacris ministrare, praesertim si episcopo ad reditum adhortanti non obtemperaverit, in ordinis desertione perseverans verumtamen ut laicus ibi communicet." — Funk, *Didascalia et Constitutiones Apostolorum*, I, 569, who also places these canons about the year 400 (*op. cit.*, Proleg., XV); *Epistola S. Leonis Magni ad Septimum Episc. Altinensem* (a. 442), cap. II: "Circa quos etiam illam canonum constitutionem praecipimus custodiri, ne ab his Ecclesiis, ad quas proprie pertinent, sinantur abscedere, et pro suo arbitrio ad loca sibi non deputata transire."—Mansi, V, 1116; Council of Chalcedon, c. 5: "De episcopis, vel clericis, qui a civitate in civitatem transeunt, placuit eos qui editi sunt a sanctis patribus canones, vires obtinere."—Mansi, VII, 362; c. 26, C. VII, q. 1; II Council of Arles (a. 452), c. 13: "Nullus cujuscumque ordinis clericus, non diaconus, non presbyter, non episcopus, quacumque occasione faciente, propriam relinquat ecclesiam; sed omnimodis aut excommunicetur, aut redire cogatur."—Mansi, VII, 880.

[98] II Council of Carthage (a. 398), cap. 27: "Ut episcopus de loco ignobili ad nobilem per ambitionem non transeat, nec quisquam inferioris ordinis clericus... Inferioris vero gradus sacerdotes, vel alii clerici, concessione suorum episcoporum possunt ad alias ecclesias transmigrare."—Mansi, III, 953; Council of Angers, France (453), c. 1: "Clericis non liceat... de loco ad alium sine episcopi permissione transire."—Mansi, VII, 900; I Council of Tours (a. 461), c. 11: "Si quis vero clericus, absque episcopi sui permissu, derelicta ecclesia sua, ad alium se transferre voluerit locum, alienus a communione habeatur."—Mansi, VII, 946.

[99] I Council of Tours (a. 461), c. 12: "Clerici non absque sacerdotum suorum commendatione, ad alias provincias seu civitates ambulare disponant."—Mansi, VII, 946; Council of Laodicaea (between 343 and 381), c. 42: "Non oportet sacerdotem vel clericum sine jussione sui pontificis iter ingredi."—Mansi, II, 581.

[100] E. g., I Council of Arles (a. 314), c. 2—Mansi, II, 471; Epistle 167 of Pope Leo the Great to Rusticus (a. 441), c. 1: "Aliter vana habenda est ordinatio, quae nec loco fundata est, nec auctoritate munita."—Mansi, VI, 400; Synod of St. Patrick in Ireland (a. 450), c. 3: "Clericus vagus non sit in plebe."—Mansi, VI, 515.

[101] Council of Chalcedon (a. 451), c. 20: "Clericos in ecclesiis ministerio fungentes, quemadmodum jam statuimus, non licere in alius civitatis ecclesia ordinari: sed illa esse contentos, in qua ab initio ut ministrarent, digni habiti sunt: praeter illos qui amissa sua patria, in aliam ecclesiam necessario transierunt."—Mansi, VII, 366; c. 4, D. LXXI.

Sustenance.—Since clerics from the time of their first ordination were assigned to the permanent service of one certain church, it followed that from natural equity they should be sustained in life from the fruits of their labors as long as they persevered in the church where they were assigned, for the laborer is worthy of his hire, and even in apostolic times the principle was recognized that " they who serve the altar partake with the altar." [102] A layman could hardly be expected voluntarily to assume the perpetual yoke of a cleric without a dependable guarantee of sustenance, and yet nowhere is it read that the candidate for orders had to have the means of supporting himself from his own funds. Neither would it have been just for so many and such great penalties to be leveled against recalcitrant clerics for not returning to their diocese at the call of their Bishop whom they deserted, if that Bishop had not provided them a livelihood. The laws then in existence confirm this rational deduction. They forbade clerics arbitrarily to desert one church or diocese for another through ambition, cupidity, or self-seeking.[103] Now there would have been no place for these evils in the transfer of clerics unless clerics had been receiving emoluments from the churches or places which they were serving and, despite these emoluments, had cherished the evil desire of reaping greater fruits in the service of some other diocese.[104] The Council of Chalcedon (a. 451) forbade

[102] 1 Cor., IX, 13.

[103] IV Council of Carthage (a. 398), cap. 27: "Ut episcopus de loco ignobili ad nobilem per ambitionem non transeat, nec quisquam inferioris ordinis clericus."—Mansi, III, 953; Epistle of St. Leo the Great to the Bishop of Aquileia (a. 442), cap. 5: "Ut unusquisque non ambitione illectus, non cupiditate seductus, non persuasione hominum depravatus, ubi ordinatus est, perseveret: ita ut si quis sua quaerens, non quae JESU CHRISTI, ad plebem et Ecclesiam suam redire neglexerit, et ab honoris privilegio, et a communionis vinculo habeatur extraneus."—Mansi, V, 1115; Epistle of St. Leo the Great to Anastasius, Bishop of Thessalonica (a. 446), Cap. IX: "Si autem longius recessit, tui praecepti auctoritate revocabitur: ut nec cupiditati, nec ambitioni occasio relinquatur."—Mansi V, 1183. Of only doubtful value is the fictitious 2nd epistle of Pope Clement to James, the brother of the Lord, in which he states that many useless clerics are a grave burden to the ordainer.—C. 4, D. XXIII.

[104] Thomassinus held that the reason why so many clerics deserted their churches for others was the hope of getting the same *remuneration* without the same *labor* as in their proper churches.—*Eccl. Discip.*, P. II, lib. I, cap. XIX, n. 9.

clerics who had been transferred from one church or diocese to another to partake any more in the things of the former church,[105] which certainly shows that they did partake of the goods of the church which they served. Furthermore, it is historically certain that during these centuries a regular distribution of the revenues of each church was made amongst the clerics by the Bishop.[106]

2. *From 500 to 1100*

This was a period of gradual eclipse in the importance that once attached to the services of minor clerics. Sacerdotal ministrations became more and more the public pastoral demand. More attention was being paid to the proper preparation of candidates for the priesthood than to their practical services as clerics in the minor orders. With community life and instruction for clerics gaining headway in both rural and city districts, it was inevitable that, for laymen ascending to the clerical state, the title of ordination would be of lessening importance. Yet, some type of ministry at the church of the first ordination and assignment was still required,[107] and the same contempt for

[105] C. 10: "Sed si jam quispiam ex alia in aliam ecclesiam translatus est, nihil prioris, ecclesiae vel eorum quae sub ea sunt martyriorum, vel ptochotrophiorum, vel xenodochiorum rebus communicare."—Mansi, VII, 362; c. 3, C. XXI, q. 2.

[106] Cf. Claeys-Bouuaert, *De Canonica Cleri Saecularis Obedientia*, p. 204, note 4. *Supra*, pp. 20, 25.

[107] Council of Valencia (a. 524), cap. 5: "Hoc etiam placuit, ut vagus, atque instabilis clericus, . . . si episcopi, a quo ordinatus est, praeceptis non obedierit, ut in delegata sibi ecclesia officium dependat assiduum; quousque in vitio permanserit, a communione, et honore privetur."—Mansi, VIII, 622; II Council of Seville (a. 619), c. 3: "Tertia definitione ad nos oblata precatio est a reverendissimo fratre nostro Cambrane, Italicensi episcopo, pro quodam clerico Israssando, qui deserens ecclesiae cultum suae, in qua dicatus ab exordiis infantiae fuerat, ad ecclesiam Cordubensem se contulit . . . Non aliter et de clericis, qui in agro ecclesiae operantur, canonum decreto praecipitur; nisi ut ibi permaneant, ubi coeperunt. Ideoque placuit, ut si quis clericus ministeriis ecclesiae propriae destitutis, ad aliam transitum fecerit, compellente ad quem fuerit sacerdote, ad ecclesiam quam prius incoluerat remittatur."—Mansi, X, 557-8; c. 2, C. XXI, q. 2; Council of Verona (a. 755), c. 12: "Clericos in ecclesia militantes, sicut jam constitutum est, non licere in alterius civitatis ecclesia, vel in potestate laicorum militare, sed ibidem permanere, in qua principio ministrare meruerunt."—Mansi, XII, 582-3; II Council of Nicaea (a. 787), c. 15.—Mansi, XIII, 433; Capitulary of Charlemagne and Louis the Pious, l. VII, cap. 393: "Clerici cujuslibet gradus in quibuscunque locis ordinati fuerint Min-

clerical "*vagi*" or "*acephali*" was shown,[108] including that new brand of "*acephali*" who, instead of being attached to the service of some church, were ingloriously subject to laymen and even to women in the courts of princes.[109]

Residence.—Whatever may be said of the service which clerics were to render to the church of their ordination, one thing is absolutely clear—that during this second period they were bound by the inexorable law of remaining and residing in the diocesan church in which they had been first ordained and where they were in training for the priesthood. They could not perpetually leave this church without the permission of their Bishop, nor could they even travel unless he sanctioned it. Right up to the twelfth century the provincial and particular councils, mindful of the famous sixth canon of Chalcedon, merely stated that no cleric was permitted to leave his own church to go to another, that he was to remain in the church where he had begun, and that if he did leave unlawfully he was to be regarded as a *vagus* or fugitive and was to be returned to his proper church.[110]

istri, ad eadem loca pertineant, atque in ipsis locis perseverent."—Mansi, XVII^B^, 1110; Council of Frankfurt (a. 794), cap. 26—Mansi, XVII^B^, 267; Council of Meaux (a. 845), c. 52: "Qui vero ex nostris parochiis aut ad titulum, aut absolute, ordinari petuntur, nullatenus ordinentur, nisi aut in clero certo et religioso, vel etiam in civitate, saltem uno anno immorentur, ut de vita et conversatione atque doctrina illorum certitudo possit agnosci."—Mansi, XIV, 831; Council of Piacenza (a. 1095), cap. 15—Mansi, XX, 806; c. 2, D. LXX; Council of Clermont (a. 1095), cc. 12-13—Mansi, XX, 817.

[108] Council of Mainz (a. 813), c. 22—Mansi, XIV, 71.

[109] Council of Melfi (a. 1089), c. 9—Mansi, XX, 723.

[110] II Council of Toledo (a. 531), c. 2—Mansi, VIII, 785; V Council of Orleans (a. 549), c. 5—Mansi, IX, 129-30; II Council of Seville (a. 619), c. 3—Mansi, X, 557-8; c. 2, C. XXI, q. 2; Council of Hereford (a. 673), cap. 5—Mansi, V, 129; XIII Council of Toledo (a. 683), cap. 11—Mansi, XI, 1073-4; The Trullan Synod of Constantinople (a. 692), c. 17—Mansi, XI, 951; c. 1, C. XXI, q. 2; Council of Verona (a. 755), c. 12—Mansi, XII, 582-3; II Council of Nicaea (a. 787), c. 15—Mansi, XIII, 433; Council of Frankfurt (a. 794), cap. 25—Mansi, XVII^B^, 267; Canonical epitome given to Charlemagne at Rome in 773 by Pope Adrian I: *Eccles. Reg.*, c. 15—Mansi, XII, 859; *Regulae apud Antiochiam*, c. 3—Mansi, XII, 864; *Ecclesiastical Constitutions*, cap. 18—Mansi, XIII, 1083; *Capitulary of Charlemagne and Louis the Pious*, l. VII, cap. 393—Mansi, XV^B^, 1110; Council of Mainz (a. 813), c. 31—Mansi, XIV, 72; VI Council of Arles (a. 813), c. 24—Mansi, XIV, 62; VI Council of Paris (a. 829), l. I, cap. 36—Mansi, XIV, 561-2; Council of Meaux

Sustenance.—The transfer of the administration of the revenues of each church from the Bishop to the church itself, which began to be adopted after the fifth century,[111] consolidated in one spot the two elements of the ordination title, but at the same time brought the secondary element of sustenance into such prominence as to overshadow the primary—a trend which was destined to make history. Some parishes even within a diocese would now be considered more remunerative than others, creating a restlessness on the part of the less fortunate clergy and exciting their cupidity.[112]

Some clerics tried to equalize the scales by having themselves included on the catalogue of beneficiaries of two or more churches simultaneously—a practice which had to be condemned.[113] As a remedy, wherever filial chapels were unable by their own resources to sustain their clerics, the obligation was placed upon the mother church to provide for them.[114]

(a. 845), c. 50—Mansi, XIV, 830; Council of Vernon (a. 845), cap. 4—Mansi, XVIII^B, 16; Council of Tribur (a. 895), c. 28—Mansi, XVIII^A, 146; Council of Authie, France (a. 916), cap. 27—Mansi, XVIII^A, 329; Council of Gerona (a. 1069), c. 9—Mansi, XIX, 1071; Council of Piacenza (a. 1095), cap. 15—Mansi, XX, 806; c. 2, D. LXX.

111 *Supra*, p. 27.

112 II Council of Nicaea (a. 787), c. 15: "Clericus ab instanti tempore non connumeretur in duabus ecclesiis. Negotiationis enim est hoc et turpis commodi proprium, et ab ecclesiastica consuetudine penitus alienum... Unusquisque ergo secundum apostolicam vocem, in quo vocatus est, in hoc debet manere, et in una locari ecclesia. Quae enim per turpe lucrum in ecclesiasticis rebus efficiuntur, aliena consistunt a Deo."—Mansi, XIII, 433; XIII Council of Toledo (a. 683), cap. 11—Mansi, XI, 1073-4.

113 Cf. II Council of Nicaea (a. 787), c. 15, in preceding footnote; Council of Clermont (a. 1095), c. 12: "Ut nulli clericorum liceat deinceps in duabus civitatibus duas praebendas obtinere, cum duos titulos non possit habere."—Mansi, XX, 817; Council of Piacenza (a. 1095), cap. 15: "...Omnino autem in duabus aliq... titulari non liceat, sed unusquisque in qua titulatus est, in ea tantum canonicus habeatur. Licet enim episcopi dispositione unus diversis praeesse debeat ecclesiis, canonicus aut praebendarius, nisi unius tantum ecclesiae, quae conscriptus est, esse non debeat . . ."—Mansi, XX, 806; c. 2, D. LXX.

114 Council of Piacenza (a. 1095), cap. 15: "...Si quae tamen capellae sunt, quae suis redditibus clericos sustinere non possint, earum cura aut dispositio praeposito maioris ecclesiae cui capellae subditae esse videntur, immineat, et tam de possessionibus, quam et de ecclesiasticis capellarum officiis ipse provideat."—Mansi, XX, 806.

To simplify the problem of sustenance, and to give, as far as possible, security to all clerics, equal to that enjoyed by those of endowed chapels, each church began at this time, as was seen, to divide its land possessions into portions *(precaria)*, the revenues from which would guarantee livelihood to as many clerics as there were *precaria.*[115] As long as the Bishop of a church did not accept for ordination to the clerical state any more laymen than his church could provide for with *precaria,* the situation was well in hand; but some Bishops were going beyond their limit. For them restraining laws had to be passed.[116] When these laws were violated a new pass was reached—clerics ordained, indeed, with a title, but without a source of livelihood. The Church now had to insist that a Bishop have a definite source of sustenance to confer on a man before he could ordain him.[117] The *precaria* were made distinct entities, known as benefices *(beneficia)* or prebends (*praebenda*), which had the character of retaining their identity perpetually, regardless of the physical personality of their possessors. One of these benefices or prebends belonging to a definite church had to be *vacant* (i. e., without a possessor) before the Bishop could proceed to ordain a new cleric for that church, and the vacant benefice or prebend then had to be conferred upon the new cleric. In this way, about the end of the eleventh century, the *benefice* or *prebend* itself became known as the *title of ordination.*[118]

[115] *Supra*, p. 29.

[116] "Non liceat ulli episcopo ordinare clericos, et eis nullas alimonias praestare, sed duorum alterum eligat: vel non faciat clericos, vel si fecerit, det illis unde vivere possint."—C. 2, X, *De praebendis et dignitatibus*, III, 5; *Capitulary of Charlemagne and Louis the Pious*, l. VI, cap. 127: "Ne passim Episcopus multitudinem Clericorum faciat, sed secundum meritum vel reditum Ecclesiarum numerus moderetur."—Mansi, XVII^{B}, 944; Council of Rome (a. 853), c. 9: "Itaque in congregandis clericis modus discretionis teneatur, videlicet, ne plus admittantur, quam facultas rerum eis canonice adtributa sufficere possit."—Mansi, XIV, 1004.

[117] *Supra*, pp. 29-30.

[118] Cf. e. g., Council of Clermont (a. 1095), c. 12: "Ut nulli clericorum liceat deinceps in duabus civitatibus duas praebendas obtinere, cum duos titulos non possit habere."—Mansi, XX, 817.

3. *1100 to the Council of Trent*

If the Church thought that the new system of benefices would provide for the sustenance of every cleric, she was soon disabused of the idea. A benefice had to be a large enough portion of a church's goods that the annual income alone would be sufficient to support a man for a year. The number of them was, therefore, very limited, insufficient by far to provide every existing cleric with one. Provincial councils had to be content, then, with requiring only candidates for major orders to have them.[119] Even that was too strict for some Bishops who, in their anxiety to have a large number of clerics because of the honors accorded to the clerical state, ordained many even to major orders without having any vacant benefices to confer on them, that is to say, ordained them without any title of ordination. The result was that the Church became overrun with clerical *vagi* and *acephali.*

It was to remedy this condition that Pope Alexander III in the III General Council of the Lateran (a. 1179) issued a famous decree to the effect that any Bishop who ordained a man to the diaconate or priesthood without a certain title would have to support the same out of his personal resources until the cleric obtained a title, unless the subject had enough material wealth to provide for himself from his own resources or from his patrimony.[120] Though issued with the best of intentions of outlawing clerical vagrants by restraining Bishops from ordaining men to sacred orders without any title at all, this decree was misconstrued as an official declaration of a new policy with regard to the title of ordination, namely, that it was no longer to be identified with a benefice alone, but was

[119] Council of London (Westminster, a. 1125), cap. 8: "Nullus in presbyterum nullus in diaconum, nisi ad certum titulum ordinetur. Qui vero absolute fuerit ordinatus, sumpta careat dignitate."—Mansi, XXI, 331; Council of Abernethy, Scotland (a. 1172), decr. 6: "Item sacerdotes non ordinentur sine certo titulo."—Mansi, XXII, 140.

[120] "Episcopus, si aliquem sine certo titulo, de quo necessaria vitae percipiat, in diaconum vel presbyterum ordinaverit, tamdiu ei necessaria subministret, donec in aliqua ecclesia ei convenientia stipendia militiae clericalis assignet, nisi talis forte ordinatus de sua vel paterna hereditate subsidium vitae possit habere."—C. 4, X, *de praebendis et dignitatibus*, III, 5; Mansi, XXII, 220.

also to include any guarantee of sufficient income to support a cleric, even if it were the cleric's own patrimony.

From that time on to the Council of Trent the ecclesiastical laws insisted on a title of ordination (either a benefice or patrimony) solely for sacred orders.[121] The subdiaconate was included in this regulation by Pope Innocent III in 1198.[122] Hence, no title whatever was required of laymen ascending to the clerical state, although some canonists tried to extend the need for one also to minor orders, but without success.[123]

[121] Council of London (a. 1200), cap. 6—Mansi, XXII, 716; Innocent III, *Epistle to the Archbishop of Besançon*: "Tuis quaestionibus respondemus, quod clericos in minoribus ordinibus constitutos, de patrimonialibus bonis habentes unde possint congrue sustentari, etsi nondum fuerint beneficium ecclesiasticum assecuti, dummodo aliud canonicum non obsistat, ad superiores poteris ordines promovere." — C. 23, X, *de praebendis*, III, 5; Council of an uncertain location in Spain (a. 1215), c. 3: "Praecipimus ne quis promoveatur in subdiaconum, diaconum, vel presbyterum, nisi habeat competens secundum qualitatem terrae beneficium ecclesiasticum, vel saltem sufficiens patrimonium, ad cujus quasi titulum ordinatur. Et qui aliter ordinaverit, competenter provideat eidem in necessariis, vel a repraesentatiore ipsius ordinato faciat provideri, donec ei competens beneficium fuerit assignatum."—Mansi, XXII, 1090; IV General Council of the Lateran (a. 1215), c. 3: "... portio presbyteris ipsis sufficiens assignetur."—Mansi, XXII, 1019; Council of Narbonne (a. 1228), c. 9—Mansi, XXIII, 23; Council of Béziers (a. 1246), c. 26: "Ut presbyteris idonea et sufficiens portio assignetur in ecclesiis."—Mansi, XXIII, 697; Synod of Exeter (a. 1287), cap. 8: "Religiosis ac saecularibus clericis districte praecipimus, ne aliquos de confratribus suis ad sacros ordines nobis audeant praesentare: nisi eis ante ordinum susceptionem in sufficienti et perpetuo titulo velint et valeant providere." —Mansi, XXIV, 796; Council of Prague (a. 1346), cap. *De aetate et qualitate ad sacros ordines*: "... praelati ex sui officii debito diligenter inquirant, ... utrum habeat perpetuum beneficium ecclesiasticum, vel sufficiens patrimonium volens ad sacros ordines promoveri." — Mansi, XXVI, 78; Council of Lyons (a. 1449), cap. 13: "Praelati neminem promoveant ad sacros ordines, nisi quem constabit obtinere beneficium ecclesiasticum, vel actualiter habere patrimonium ... "—Mansi, XXXII, 96; Council of Avignon (a. 1455), c. 17—Mansi, XXXII, 188; Constitutions of Nicholas Francus, Bishop of Treviso and Apostolic Legate (a. 1491), Tit. *Poena episcopis imposita etc.*—Mansi, XXXV, 1556; Council of Mainz (a. 1549), cap. 81 *De promovendis ad sacros ordines*: "... Nec quisquam ordinandus recipiatur, nisi ad certum titulum ecclesiastici beneficii, quod sit perpetuum, a quo non possit ad inordinatum alicujus placitum amoveri, aut cui de proprio patrimonio sufficienter sit provisum." —Mansi, XXXII, 1430; Council of Narbonne (a. 1551), c. 8: "Itaque nemo sacros ordines consequatur cui speciatim destinata ad victum bona non sint; sive a sacerdotio, seu beneficio aliquo sive a patrimonio petantur."—Mansi, XXXIII, 1254.

[122] C. 16, X, *de praebendis et dignitatibus*, III, 5; cc. 23, 37, X, *de simonia*, V, 3. Cf. also the evidence in the above footnote.

[123] Thus the 6th canon of the Council of Chalcedon is found in c. 1, D. LXX, and the Glossa states: "In ordine autem Romano fit mentio talis pronounciationis,

Stephen, Bishop of Tournay (a. 1135-1203), when requested by the reigning Pontiff to express his views on this question, said that to exact a title for minor orders would be a new and unusual custom; that it was impossible for the Bishops to remember all those on whom they had conferred minor orders or deaconship by giving them benefices. "Better by far," said he, "to renounce ordaining than to impose upon one's self such weighty responsibilities." [124]

Some minor clerics, it is true, especially those nominated by lay patrons, were receiving even curatial benefices, but they had to be so far advanced in the clerical state as to be ready to receive the subdiaconate within a year; meanwhile vicars appointed by the Bishop supplied the curacy.[125] It is also possible that prebends or non-curatial benefices were possessed by some clerics in minor orders, as can be deduced from the Council of Trent's reforms in discipline, one of which required the *beneficiati* to be at least fourteen years of age.[126] But the great majority of tonsured clerics were without any title at all and, hence, were not actively serving any particular church. In any event, the eleventh century rise of city parishes had served to decentralize the sacred functions performed at the cathedrals and had reduced the services of the clerics in their colleges to a minimum.

Residence.—Since it was curatial benefices which required personal residence at the church in which they were founded, tonsured clerics, being mostly non-beneficed, were not bound to any residence save diocesan. They still could not leave their

episcopi nomine per archidiaconum factae: De titulo S. Stephani eligimus Petrum ad lectorem ad eundem titulum." Likewise the following ancient law was incorporated in the Decretals: "Non liceat ulli episcopo ordinare clericos, et eis nullas alimonias praestare, sed duorum alterum eligat: vel non faciat clericos, vel si fecerit, det illis unde vivere possint."—C. 2, X, *de praebendis et dignitatibus*, III, 5. No conciliar law, however, is found requiring a title for inferior clerics, e. g., in the Councils of Montpellier (a. 1258), cap. 2—Mansi, XXIII, 990; Béziers (a. 1310), cap. 1—Mansi, XXV, 359; Lyons (a. 1449), cap. 2—Mansi, XXXII, 94.

124 Epistle 194 to the Pope—*MPL*, CCXI, 477.

125 Cf. c. 34, *de electione et electi potestate*, I, 6, in VI°, where Boniface VIII in 1298 expressly allowed this.

126 Sess. XXIII, *de ref.*, c. 6.

diocese to go elsewhere without their Bishop's written permission.[127] Many of them received such permission for periods of five to seven successive years to attend the Universities, because the Bishops were anxious to have a cultured clergy.[128] Those who kept their residence within the diocese at cathedral colleges were simply spending their time in study and in preparation for the priesthood.

The decree of Pope Clement IV (a. 1265-1268), mentioned above in connection with the proper Bishop of ordination,[129] had a considerable loosening effect on even this diocesan bond of residence, for, in recognizing as a proper Bishop for ordination the Bishop of the diocese in which a cleric possessed a benefice, even though it was not the diocese where the cleric's parents originally had their domicile, it left open the conclusion that, if a cleric, even a mere *tonsuratus*, were not beneficed by the Bishop at tonsure, he was free to obtain another proper Bishop by securing a prebend in another diocese, and his first Bishop could not prevent him from going to the new diocese as long as the first Bishop's church would not suffer damage thereby.[130]

Sustenance.—Most of the *tonsurati*, having no ordination title, had to live on their own resources or on the charity of their proper Bishop. In consequence of this, it is understandable that they could go to another diocese if they secured a title there.

[127] National Synod of Esztergom, Hungary (a. 1114), cap. 19—Mansi, XXI, 103-4; letter of Alexander III (a. 1159-1181) to the Archbishop of York—c. 5, X, *de clericis non residentibus in ecclesia vel praebenda*, III, 4; Council of Constantinople (a. 1171), cap. II—Mansi, XXII, 123-128; Provincial Council of Fritzlar (a. 1246), cap. 10—Mansi, XXIII, 728; Synodal Constitutions of the Diocese of Valencia (a. 1255), Cap. *De Clericis ordinandis*—Mansi, XXIII, 892; decree of Gregory X in the General Council at Lyons—c. 2, *de temporibus ordinationum et qualitate ordinandorum*, I, 9, in VI°. Cf. also the stern indictment of clerical "*vagi*," popularly known as "Eberhardini," in the Provincial Council of Mainz (a. 1261), c. 17—Mansi, XXIII, 1085-6.

[128] Cc. 4-5, X, *de clericis non residentibus in Ecclesia vel praebenda*, III, 4; c. 34, *de electione et electi potestate*, I, 6, in VI°.

[129] Pp. 45, 48.

[130] Hofmann, *Die Excardination einst und jetzt*—*ZkT*, XXIV (1900), 399 ff.; Claeys-Bouuaert, *De Canonica Cleri Saecularis Obedientia*, p. 206.

4. *Council of Trent to the Code*

The Council of Trent wanted to prevent clerics of all orders from being idlers or wanderers. It retained the law that every candidate for major orders must have a title of ordination, but added that, regardless of what title it might be, even if it were patrimony or pension, his services must be judged necessary or useful for the churches of the diocese and he must be definitely assigned to one of them.[181] This discipline was simply reiterated by all the Church councils right up to the Code.[182] No title

[181] Sess. XXI, *de ref.*, c. 2: "... statuit sancta Synodus, ne quis deinceps clericus saecularis, quamvis alias sit idoneus moribus, scientia, et aetate, ad sacros Ordines promoveatur, nisi prius legitime constet, eum beneficium ecclesiasticum, quod sibi ad victum honeste sufficiat, pacifice possidere... Patrimonium vero, vel pensionem obtinentes ordinari posthac non possint, nisi illi, quos episcopus judicaverit assumendos pro necessitate, vel commoditate ecclesiarum suarum . . ."; sess. XXIII, *de ref.*, c. 16: "Cum nullus debeat ordinari, qui judicio sui episcopi non sit utilis, aut necessarius suis ecclesiis; sancta Synodus, vestigiis sexti canonis Concilii Chalcedonensis inhaerendo, statuit, ut nullus in posterum ordinetur, qui illi ecclesiae, aut pio loco, pro cujus necessitate aut utilitate assumitur, non adscribatur, ubi suis fungatur muneribus, nec incertis vagetur sedibus. Quod si locum inconsulto Episcopo deseruerit, ei sacrorum exercitium interdicatur."

[182] Provincial Council of Rheims (a. 1564), *statutum* 12—Mansi, XXXIII, 1296; Provincial Synod of Ravenna (a. 1568), tit. *De ordine,* cap. 5: "Animadvertant etiam episcopi, ne sacris ordinibus aliquem initient, qui vere ecclesiasticum beneficium, pensionem, vel patrimonium ejus victui sufficiens, juxta ejusdem concilii decretum, non obtineat."—Mansi, XXXV^A, 622; Synodal Statutes of the Diocese of Besançon (a. 1571), stat. *De examine ordinandorum*, n. 8: "Ad subdiaconatum. Promovendi ad ordinem subdiaconatus primo exhibeant titulum beneficii aut pensionis, vel patrimonii sufficientis, cuius copiam relinquent penes sigilliferum curiae. Sub patrimonii vero titulo vel pensionis, non alios ordinabit episcopus, quam quos maxime necessarios vel utiles iudicaverit ecclesiae."—Mansi, XXXVI^B, 63; *ibid.*, n. 14: "... nullus in presbyterum ordinabitur, qui ecclesiae aut pio loco non inscribatur; ut illic suo fungatur munere, nec incertis vagetur sedibus."—Mansi, XXXVI^B, 64; Synodal Constitutions of the Polish Province of Gniezno (a. 1577), l. I, tit. *De temporibus ordinationum*—Mansi, XXXVI^B, Appen. I, 675; Provincial Council of Toledo (a. 1582), *Actio Tertia, decretum* 32—Mansi, XXXVI^B, 176-7; *ibid.*, *decretum* 31: "Ne quis sacris ordinibus initietur, nisi beneficium ecclesiasticum aut patrimonium vere obtineat."—Mansi, *op. et loc. cit.*; Provincial Council of Bordeaux (a. 1583), tit. 14, *De sacramento ordinis*—Mansi, XXXIV^A, 760; Provincial Council of Sorrento (a. 1584), cap. XXVI, n. 15: "Subdiaconatus ordinem suscepturus haec ultra praedicta demonstrabit, videlicet: ... quod aetatem ... habeat, ac titulum de iure requisitum ut supra."—Mansi, XXXVI^B, 296; Council of Mexico (a. 1585), l. I, tit. IV, c. 1—Mansi, XXXIV^B, 1035; Provincial Synod of Cambrai (a. 1586), tit. X, cap. 4: "Forma vero juramenti, quod prestare tenebuntur ii, qui patrimoniali titulo ad ordines promovebuntur, sit haec: Ego N. juro, quod in acquisitione bonorum meorum patrimonialium, ad quorum titulum sum promovendus ad sacros ordines,

was required for the lay candidate for tonsure or for the cleric who was about to receive any minor order. They were all, however, to be kept busy in some definite religious place. In

nulla fraus aut dolus intercessit: . . . "—Mansi, XXXIV^{B}, 1238; I Provincial Council of Fermo (a. 1590), cap. XVIII, n. 2—Mansi, XXXVI^{B}, Appen. I, 904; Prov. Counc. of Avignon (a. 1594), tit. 19—Mansi, XXXIV^{B}, 1341; Prov. Counc. of Aquileia (a. 1596), rubrica XI *De vita et honestate clericorum*—Mansi, XXXIV^{B}, 1401; Prov. Counc. of Naples (a. 1699), *Constitutiones*, tit. III, cap. VII, n. 4: "Qua in re sancta synodus, sacrosancti Tridentini concilii praeceptis inhaerens, mandat, ut nemo ad sacros ordines promoveatur, nisi ecclesiasticum beneficium ad sustentationem sufficiens iuxta taxam synodalem suae dioecesis pacifice possederit. Ad titulum vero patrimonii ii solum ordinentur, ad quos admittendos aut necessitas aut utilitas ecclesiae compulerit . . . "—Mansi, XXXVI Ter, 749; Provincial Synod of the Ruthenians at Zamose, Poland (a. 1720), tit. III, cap. 7: "Nullus praeterea saecularis ordinetur, qui non habeat titulum perpetuum sufficientis ecclesiae, alioquin ille ab exercitio ordinum suspensus sit; . . . "—Mansi, XXXV^{B}, 1502; National Synod of the Greek Melchites held in the Monastery of the Holy Saviour (a. 1790), *Acta et Decreta*, sess. 23, sec. c: "Cum sacrorum ordinum receptioni praemitti oporteat diligens examen accurataque probatio de scientia et moribus quibus instrui debeant ordinandi, haec nostra sancta synodus decrevit: . . . c) Quem ultima hac experientia probaverit episcopus non promovebit praeterquam ad ecclesiam aliquam determinatam, ut canones praescribunt, ei suppeditando quae ad sumptus fuerint necessaria; . . ."—Mansi, XLVI, 646; III Prov. Counc. of Baltimore (a. 1837), *Decreta*, I: "Cum, ex apostolico indulto, consueverint plerumque clerici saeculares ordinari, in his Foederatis Provinciis, titulo missionis, monemus episcopos ut eos tantum eo titulo ad sacros ordines evehant, qui idonei sacris missionibus videantur, vel alias religionis profectui, episcopi iudicio, inservituri, . . . " —Mansi, XXXIX, 349; Prov. Counc. of Avignon (a. 1849), *Decreta*, tit. IV, cap. VII, n. 3: "Praeterea, iuxta eiusdem concilii Tridentini mentem, vehementer optat synodus, ut nullus clericus secularis ad sacrum subdiaconatum promoveatur, quoad fieri poterit, sine titulo ecclesiastico, nisi prius legitime constet ab illo titulum patrimonialem possideri. Si vero deficiat titulus praedictus, accedat, ex apostolicae sedis indulgentia, episcopi dispensatio."—Mansi, XLIII, 748; Patriarchal Counc. of Jerusalem (a. 1849), *Decreta, Prima Parte*, cap. VI, c. 1: "Richiedendo la disciplina antica e permanente della nostra santa chiesa greca orientale dai pastori delle diocesi di non conferire ad alcuno dei loro sudditi gli ordini sagri, se non per servire gli altari delle chiese note ed esistenti nelle loro diocesi che hanno dei particolari popoli, le di cui anime sono servite da questi ordinati sopra quelle chiese come veri curati di giurisdizione ecclesiastica originale o ordinaria, non delegata, e che servono li suddetti altari durante la loro vita e vivono dai diritti delle loro stole e dalle volontarie elemosine, che a loro si danno dai parrocchiani e dagli altri, conforme alle consuetudini orientali, . . . "—Mansi, XLVI, 1046-7; I Prov. Counc. of Westminster (a. 1852), *Decreta*, cap. XXI, n. 5: "Ut aliquis modus statuatur quo clericus, titulo patrimonii ad subdiaconatum promotus, decentem sustentationem habeat, patres censent neminem ordinari debere nisi habeat legaliter certum redditum quadraginta ad minus librarum sterlinarum . . . "—Mansi, XXXIII, 741. Cf. also decr. S. C. P. F. *de ordinat.*, 21 apr. 1852—I Prov. Counc. of Westminster, Appendix I, n. 16 (Mansi, XLIV, 770); S. C. P. F., 14 martii 1853—*Ibid.*, Appendix I, n. 17 (Mansi, *loc. cit.*).

case they were fortunate enough to have a benefice or prebend, that would give them their locale of service, where at the same time they would prepare for higher orders. If they were non-beneficed, they had to attend some school, seminary, or University to study for the priesthood; and, if they could not do that, they were to be assigned by the Bishop to the service of some definite church, but had to support themselves; otherwise they were denied the *privilegium fori.*[183] To provide for the training and sustenance of the many non-beneficed inferior clerics the Council of Trent made obligatory the erection of a seminary in every diocese, and required that the students receive tonsure, wear the clerical garb, spend their time and energies in study, give a nominal service to the cathedral and to other churches of the diocese on feast days, and be supported, if rich, by their own resources, but, if poor, by the seminary's administrative fund. This fund was to be made up, partly of the moneys set aside in some churches of the diocese for the education of clerical aspirants, and partly of a tax on all the benefices, prebends, praestimonia, ecclesiastical foundations, and revenues of whatsoever type in the entire diocese.[184] This classic law made the training and sustenance of minor clerics a diocesan project, and, consequently, paved the way for the future title of " service of the diocese " rather than of service of one particular church as had been the case in former years. Naturally, it would take years before every diocese would be able to have its own seminary, but the mind of the Council of Trent was that every layman advancing to the clercial state but not residing in a seminary was to be assigned to that particular church or holy place for the necessity or utility of which he was being accepted by the Bishop.[185]

Considerable confusion resulted from this last Tridentine provision, contained in the 16th chapter of the XXIII reform session. The penalty against the cleric who deserted his place of assignment—" *ei sacrorum exercitium interdicatur* "—cer-

[183] Conc. Trid., sess. XXIII, *de ref.*, c. 6.

[184] *Ibid.*, c. 18.

[185] *Ibid.*, c. 16. See text above, p. 79, footnote 131.

tainly would seem to indicate that the law applied only to those in sacred orders, but chapter 11 of the same Session showed that it was to include all inferior clerics as long as they were not away somewhere engaged in study. Hence, it may be presumed that even in the diocesan seminary clerics were to be assigned to some church, to which they were to go on Sundays and feast days to help the pastor, according to the functions of their respective orders.[136] The dioceses in Italy understood the decree in this sense.[137] The diocese of Naples even

[136] "... cathedrali, et aliis loci ecclesiis diebus festis inserviant..."—*Ibid.*, c. 18.

[137] II Prov. Counc. of Milan (a. 1569), decr. 24—Mansi, XXXIV^A^, 112-3; *ibid.*, tit. II, decr. 28—Mansi, XXXIV^A^, 120; Prov. Counc. of Genoa (ante 1574), *Decreta*, cap. XII, n. 3: "Et quoniam ad ordines nullos promoveri quemquam oportet, qui non certae alicui ecclesiae addicatur, propterea, scribae meminerint ab ordinariis quaerere ordinationum tempore, qui quisque sit ecclesiae adscribendus; nec ante litteras collati ordinis testimonium continentes tradant, quam eisdem ecclesiis adscribantur..." —Mansi, XXXVI^B^, Appen. I, 577; Prov. Synod of Naples (a. 1576), *Constitutiones et Decreta*, cap. XIX: "... Quilibet clericus in ea, cui semel adscriptus est, ecclesia resideat, atque inibi sua obeat munera, nec sine dimissoriis proprii ordinarii literis alio vagetur, suique ordinis actum exerceat..."—Mansi, XXXV^B^, 825; II Counc. of Ravenna (a. 1582), tit. *De sacramento ordinis*, n. 10: "Clerici omnes, cum ad aliquem ordinem promoventur, per episcopum certae ascribantur ecclesiae, in qua suorum ordinum functiones obeant, illasque in ea tali pietate praestent, ut digni habeantur, qui ad altiorem gradum ascendant, nec ulterius promoveantur, nisi legitime episcopo fidem fecerint, se in ecclesia, cui adscripti sunt, pie ac diligenter praestitisse impositas sibi functiones, aut per eos non stetisse quin eas praestiterint."—Mansi, XXXVI^B^, Appen. I, 842; Prov. Counc. of Sorrento (a. 1584), cap. V, n. 31: "Sacerdotes omnes et clerici, alicuius certae ecclesiae ministerio non addicti, in maiorem vel parochialem ecclesiam, cuius fines habitant, dominicis festisque diebus ad divina celebranda conveniant, nisi legitime excusentur."—Mansi, XXXVI^B^, 278; *ibid.*, cap. XXVI, n. 8—Mansi, XXXVI^B^, 296; Prov. Counc. of Benevento (a. 1599), tit. XXIX, cap. 2: "Clerici, qui certae ecclesiae non sunt adscripti, curent episcopi, ut dominicis et festis diebus, parochialibus presbyteris, intra quorum ecclesiarum fines habitaverint, vel ecclesiasticum beneficium obtinuerint, aut alteri ecclesiae, prout ipsis videbitur, inservire debeant. Illi vero, qui certis ecclesiis adscripti sunt, ad illas conveniant, et eas functiones expleant, quas ipsis episcopi praescripserint, ne vagi populo scandalo sint..."—Mansi, XXXVI^B^, 443; Prov. Counc. of Benevento (a. 1693), *Constitutiones*, tit. VI, n. 3 *Modus in clericorum numero adhibendus*: "... Quocirca sancta synodus episcopos omnes enixe hortatur, ne numerosum gregem effraenata clericorum multitudine sibi parent, sed eos dumtaxat promoveant, quos utiles et necessarios suis ecclesiis agnoscunt, et illud Hieronymi effatum prae oculis habeant: 'Diaconos paucitas honorabiles; presbyteros turba contemptibiles facit.'"—Mansi, XXXVI Ter, 552-3; Counc. of Rome in the Lateran Basilica (a. 1725), tit. VII, cap. 2: "Clericali insuper Tonsura nullus initietur, nisi eodem tempore Ecclesiae illi adscribatur, pro cujus servitio debet ordinari. Si qui vero sint, etiam minoribus, aut sacris Ordinibus insigniti; qui

went beyond it by requiring a benefice also for the reception of first tonsure;[138] and Innocent XIII so enforced it in Spain that in 1723 he required all the Bishops of Spain immediately to supply all the assignments which their predecessors had neglected.[139] But scarcely any other part of the world at all considered the decree as applying to any but major clerics,[140] and, even when applied solely to major clerics, the widely divergent replies, received at Rome in 1869 from the Bishops of the world to the question how this chapter of the Council of Trent concerning universal clerical assignment was being observed in their dioceses, showed that most of the Bishops interpreted the chapter in the sense of assignment to the service of a diocese

nulli certae Ecclesiae fuerint adscripti, Episcopi adscriptionem hujusmodi, etiam a suis Praedecessoribus omissam, suppleant, et pro arbitrio servitium, toties quoties opus fuerit, praestandum designent: quam adscriptionem, quando eos, qui jam promoti, extra Dioecesim, vel studiorum causa, vel alia ab Episcopis probata, commorantur, ad tempus, ipsimet Episcopis benevisum, differri posse indulgemus..." —Mansi, XXXIV^B, 1862.

138 Prov. Counc. of Naples (a. 1699), *Constitutiones*, tit. III, cap. VII, n. 5: "Ne quis clericatu initiatus et sufficienti deinde sustentationis titulo destitutus; aut ab ecclesiastico statu turpiter recedere, aut cum eiusdem dedecore mendicare, aut sordidum aliquem quaestum exercere cogatur: mandat sancta synodus, ut inviolabilis observantia dioecesis Neapolitanae de non admittendo ad primam tonsuram quemquam, nisi de beneficio conferendo aut patrimonio constiterit, ad totam provinciam extendatur, iuxta tamen taxam synodalem cuiuscumque dioecesis."—Mansi, XXXVI Ter, 749. The same was required in Spain by Innocent XIII—Const. "*Apostolici ministerii*," 23 maii 1723, n. 2 (*Fontes*, n. 280).

139 Const. "*Apostolici ministerii*," 23 maii 1723, nn. 2, 3, 4—*Fontes*, n. 280.

140 A few Councils outside Italy required assignments for all clerics, e. g., Prov. Counc. of Rouen (a. 1581), cap. *De episcoporum officiis*, n. 6—Mansi, XXXIV^A, 633; Prov. Synod of Cambrai (a. 1586), tit. X, n. 6: "Omnes qui ordinantur, alicui ecclesiae adscribantur; et in proximi ordinis susceptione examinentur singuli, num in iis ecclesiis, quibus adscripti fuerint, suas functiones obierint. Singuli autem ordinati in suis ordinibus ministrare teneantur: sacerdotes quidem, frequenter celebrando: reliqui per vices, diebus maxime solemnioribus, sacerdotibus ministrando." —Mansi, XXXIV^B, 1239; Prov. Synod on Mount Libanus (a. 1736), *Constitutiones et Canones*, p. II, cap. 14, n. 12: "Quum ordinatio ita clericum potestati et jurisdictioni episcopi, a quo consecratur, vindicet, ut, illo aut invito aut inscio, nihil ex iis, quae ad divina spectant, pertentare possit; et clericus quisque particulari cuidam ecclesiae sic alligetur, ut residere in ea teneatur, ac officia omnia ibi exhibere, quae recepto ordini conveniant, ac vicissim ex praestitis officiis jus habeat ad portionem, quae sustentationi congruat: hinc duo secundum canones sequuntur, primum, ut nullus clericus sine titulo ecclesiae ordinetur; alterum, ne quis ex una ad aliam ecclesiam transeat."—Mansi, XXXVIII, 132.

rather than of a particular church.[141] A more detailed explanation of how and when this interpretation of the Tridentine decree originated and how it finally gave birth in the nineteenth century to the extraordinary title of ordination by reason of "service of the diocese" is reserved for the section on the title of ordination for diocesan clerics.[142]

ARTICLE IV

THE CEREMONY OF INITIAL ENLISTMENT

The special bond between a diocesan cleric and his Bishop, the reasonableness of which was explained above,[143] quite obviously is contracted as soon as a layman becomes a cleric. It has been seen that already in the second century not only priests and deacons, but also some of the minor orders, were in existence, the completion of their number being reached in the following century, and a man who received any one of them was numbered among the clergy.[144] By the fourth century, the clergy in the East were clearly distinct from kindred ecclesiastical officers, such as "defenders of the churches," because clerics were constituted by the imposition of the hands of the Bishop instead of by mere promotion as were the lesser officers.[145] In the West, at the same time, the rite by which each minor order was to be conferred was definitely established, but not so any relative priority of reception of them. The order to be received first depended upon the custom of the province, the ability of the candidate, and the specific needs of the particular church for the service of which he was to be accepted.[146] Usually it was the order of lector which was received first, but,

141 Vatican Council, p. I *Monumenta Praesynodalia*, A, XXI, *quaestione* IX—Mansi, XLIX, 349-357.

142 Cf. *infra*, pp. 148-151.

143 Pp. 36-40.

144 *Supra*, pp. 15-16, 17.

145 *Supra*, p. 20.

146 *Supra*, p. 24.

no matter which it was, the bond with the Bishop commenced the moment the first imposition of hands took place.[147]

More of the effects of that bond will be reviewed in Chapter IV, where the proper Bishop for clerics will be discussed,[148] but suffice it to say here that as soon as a Bishop became, in his own right, the proper Bishop for the higher ordination of a man by legitimately conferring on him his first minor order, that Bishop inherited for himself and his successors in the episcopal see a strict right over the services of the *ordinatus* to such an extent that no other Bishop could usurp the cleric without the first Bishop's permission. The type of functions the cleric was to exercise was determined by the order conferred. The church or place for the exercise of these functions was known beforehand, because the Bishop did not act unless a certain church could use a cleric, and then the candidate was ordained either actually in that church or at least for its service. Even the rural Bishops, it will be recalled, had the power to confer minor orders in the churches of the country towns where they were located, and by that act the *ordinati* became attached to their particular rural Bishop's country church.[149]

The usual procedure was for the layman to seek enlistment in the service of the church near which he lived, and where he was well known, in much the same fashion as do the altar boys of

[147] Council of Nicaea (a. 325), c. 16—Mansi, II, 675; c. 23, C. VII, q. 1; Council of Hippo (a. 393), c. 19: "Ut clericum alienum, nisi concedente ejus Episcopo, nemo audeat vel retinere, vel promovere in ecclesia sibi credita. Clericorum autem nomen etiam Lectores retineant."—Mansi, III, 922; III Council of Carthage (a. 397), c. 21: "Ut clericum alienum, nisi concedente ejus episcopo, nemo audeat vel retinere, vel promovere in ecclesia sibi credita. Clericorum autem nomen etiam lectores, et psalmistae, et ostiarii retinent."—Mansi, III, 883; c. 2, D. LXXII; Canons of the Apostles (ab. 400), cc. 15, 16—Funk, *Didascalia et Constitutiones Apostolorum*, I, 569. St. Augustine had ordained Timothy a lector, and he afterwards went to another Bishop, Severus, and was ordained to the subdiaconate by him after promising with an oath never to leave him. Augustine, seeking the return of his cleric, wrote to Severus, persuading him to send back Timothy, so that both Timothy's oath and the law, by which a cleric belonged to the Bishop who first ordained him, would be kept inviolate.—Thomassinus, *Eccl. Discip.*, P. II, lib. I, cap. II, n. 7.

[148] Pp. 98-116.

[149] *Supra*, p. 19.

current times. It took many years for him to reach the priesthood,[150] but, when he did reach the requisite age, it was in, or at least for, the church which he knew so well and had served so long that he was ordained. His years of service were as a practical seminary career, spent in the city cathedral under the supervision of the Bishop and of the archdeacon, or in a rural church under the guidance and tutelage of the resident priest, whose deacon he would one day become and whose place eventually he would inherit.

No mention is made of clerical tonsure until late in the fourth century, and then only in the East.[151] Clerics were merely obliged, according to the doctrine of St. Paul, not to wear their hair long: "Doth not even nature itself teach you that a man indeed, if he nourish his hair, it is a shame unto him?"[152] In the West, in the fourth century, Optatus even condemned the Donatists for having shorn the hair of priest prisoners;[153] and the IV Council of Carthage (a. 398) forbade clerics the culture of their hair, but said nothing of a ceremony of tonsure, although it diligently prescribed ceremonies for all the holy orders.[154]

The real genesis of tonsure was among the monks of the fifth century; clerics followed their lead. At first the monks observed moderation in all things and let their hair grow. Later, some of the more austere, wishing to be despised by carnal men, either cut their hair in a very unconventional way or else sheared it off completely.[155] There is clear proof that the wearing of the clerical tonsure was a familiar custom, at least in Gaul, during the latter fifth and in the sixth century. For Sidonius Apollinaris (a. 431-489) wrote that the Bishop Germanicus had his hair cut "in the shape of a wheel" (*"in rotae speciem"*);

[150] *Supra*, p. 24.

[151] *Lexicon für Theologie und Kirche*, "Tonsur."

[152] 1 Cor., XI, 14.

[153] Thomassinus, *Eccl. Discip.*, P. I, lib. II, cap. XXXVII, n. 5.

[154] C. 44: "Clericus nec comam nutriat, et barbam radat."—Mansi, III, 955; Thomassinus, *ibid.*, n. 9.

[155] Thomassinus, *ibid.*, nn. 11-12.

and, according to St. Gregory of Tours, St. Nicetius († 570), a French Benedictine monk, was miraculously designated from birth for the clerical state, being born with a fringe of hair like a "*corona clerici.*"[156] This was taken for an omen and the clerical *corona* was adopted in the monastery. Many of the Bishops had been educated in religious monasteries and wished to introduce the customs of the monks into the diocesan clergy.[157] When finally it became of obligation, the wearing of the tonsure by secular clerics commenced from the day of their first minor ordination. It was not later than the sixth century that it became a distinct but supplemental rite performed by the ordaining Bishop as a part of the minor order ceremony, even as it still is in the Greek Church.[158] Finally it became an entirely distinct ceremony of initiation into the clerical state.

The first clear legislation on the wearing of the tonsure is to be found in the IV Council of Toledo (a. 633) which states in canon 41: "Omnes clerici, vel lectores, sicut levitae, et sacerdotes detonso superius toto capite, inferius solam circuli coronam relinquant: non sicut hucusque in Galliciae partibus facere lectores videntur, qui prolixis, ut laici, comis, in solo capitis apice modicum circulum tondent. Ritus enim iste in Hispania hucusque haereticorum fuit. Unde oportet, ut pro amputando ecclesiae scandalo, hoc signum dedecoris auferatur, et una sit tonsura, vel habitus, sicut totius Hispaniae est usus. Qui autem hoc non custodierit, fidei catholicae reus erit."[159]

In the Gregorian Sacramentary there is included under the heading *Orationes seu Oratio ad Clericum faciendum* a rite consisting in the cutting of hair.[160] Similarly in the *Liber Pontificalis* one reads of an *oratio clericatus,* which seems to be the same rite, and is distinct from ordination itself.[161] A dis-

[156] Addis and Arnold, *Catholic Dictionary* (12. ed., [1928]), "Tonsure."

[157] Thomassinus, *ibid.*, nn. 2-14.

[158] *Lexicon für Theologie und Kirche,* "Tonsur."

[159] Mansi, X, 630.

[160] *MPL,* LXXVIII, 212.

[161] Vita Stephani III (a. 768-772): "Compulerunt eum (nempe Georgium episcopum) orationem clericatus eidem Constantino tribui";—ed. Duchesne, I, 468; Vita Zachariae (a. 741-752)—*ibid.*, 434.

tinct rite of tonsure is apparent also in the Council of Meaux (a. 845),[162] and in the treatise *De Sacramentis* by Hugh of St. Victor (a. 1142).[163]

Complete certainty, however, that first tonsure was a special rite, distinct from any order, that it was to be performed by the proper Bishop of ordination, and that by it the clerical order was conferred, was given for the first time by Pope Innocent III in the year 1210.[164] A strict regulation that no Bishop without due authorization should attempt to confer tonsure on any layman who was not his proper subject was made in the same century by the Council of Montpellier (a. 1258),[165] and by Pope Boniface VIII.[166]

No sooner had tonsure alone become the ceremony of initiation into the clerical state than the assignment of new clerics to particular churches was abandoned by reason of the change already effected in the ordination title of laymen.[167]

The Council of Trent recognized tonsure as the gateway to the clerical state, and endeavored to bring about a restoration of the old discipline by which each cleric from the very time of his ascent to the clerical state became attached to the service of a definite church.[168] However, its efforts were practically

[162] C. 58: "Canonicorum autem, qui in parochiis tonsurantur, et erudiuntur, interdum etiam et ordinantur, sine auctoritate (episcopi) dignitas regalis in suum periculum non dignetur recipere . . ."—Mansi, XIV, 832.

[163] L. II, p. III, cc. I, II, III, V—*MPL,* CLXXVI, 421 ss.

[164] "Cum contingat interdum, quod laici, ad monasteria convolantes, a suis abbatibus tonsurentur, requisisti an clericatus ordo in tonsura hujusmodi conferatur. Super quo tibi respondemus, quod, cum in septima synodo sit statutum, ut lectores per manus impositionem licentia sit unicuique abbati . . . faciendi, . . . per primam tonsuram, juxta formam Ecclesiae datam, a talibus clericalis ordo confertur."—C. 11, X, *de aetate et qualitate et ordine praeficiendorum,* I, 14.

[165] Cap. 2: "Nullus episcopus de caetero praetextu ratihabitionis, cujuslibet alterius dioecesanum aliquem absque licentia sui episcopi tonsurare audeat, nec ipsum multo fortius ad minores, vel majores ordines promovere."—Mansi, XXIII, 990.

[166] "Nullus episcopus vel quivis alius . . . absque sui superioris licentia homini dioecesis alienae, clericalem praesumat conferre tonsuram . . ."—C. 4, *De temporibus ordinationum et qualitate ordinandorum,* I, 9, in VI°.

[167] *Supra,* pp. 75 ff.

[168] Sess. XXIII, *de ref.,* c. 16.

nullified by its concomitant decree on the erection of seminaries for *tonsurati*.[169]

It was the bestowal of a benefice on a *tonsuratus* which now had the effect of assigning him a specific church or place for his ministry. Tonsure did nothing more than this: it enlisted the subject in the clergy of the *diocese* of the proper Prelate in such a rigid way that thereafter the cleric could not change his domicile to another diocese without that Prelate's permission. Wherever, after the Council of Trent, the non-beneficed *tonsurati* were attached to a particular church, it was done by a distinct act of the Bishop, such as that required of the Bishops of Spain by Pope Innocent XIII,[170] and the service required of the clerics in the parishes to which they were thus specifically assigned was only elementary assistance of the priests on Sundays and feastdays. There were very few dioceses in the world, however, where the Bishops made these special assignments of mere tonsured clerics to definite churches, and that was still the state of affairs up to the promulgation of the Code.

ARTICLE V

THE QUASI-EXCARDINATION AND QUASI-INCARDINATION OF LAYMEN

The number of his own lay subjects that a Bishop could accept for the clerical state was not unlimited. At the time when the title of ordination meant a particular church or religious place in which to perform one's ecclesiastical functions, he could legitimately impose hands on as many only as he could practically use in the churches of the diocese. This is evident from the early laws against absolute ordinations, i. e., ordinations conferred without any assignment.[171] Later, when the title of ordination became synonymous with a guaranteed source of sustenance, he was forbidden to confer *major* orders on more clerics than the resources of the diocese could provide for, and,

169 *Ibid.*, c. 18.

170 Const. "*Apostolici ministerii*," 23 maii 1723, nn. 2, 3, 4—*Fontes*, n. 280.

171 Cf. *supra*, pp. 66-68.

consequently, in his prudence he had to restrict also the number of admissions to the clerical state.[172] Many Bishops, through imprudence, filled their clerical ranks with hosts of useless men, which brought ignominy upon the clerical state itself, and forced the Council of Trent to insist again upon the old rule of universal assignment, although of a much less rigorous type than formerly.

The vocations in a diocese never were limited to the needs of the diocese. Divine Providence is therein displayed, since a surplus of vocations redounds to the aid of the missionary cause. Youths who despair of being accepted into the clerical ranks of their own diocese look elsewhere for a field of labor. For obvious reasons they cannot always expect their parents to move their domicile to achieve this, and so there is often present an honorable reason for the transfer by mere letters of laymen from less needy to more needy dioceses. Such a transfer is called *quasi*-excardination, because, strictly considered, the term excardination can be used only of clerics, since they alone are said to be incardinated in a diocese. Correlatively, the act of accepting an alien layman is termed *quasi*-incardination.

Quasi-excardination might be defined as the juridical transfer to another Bishop of the right which a proper Bishop for ordination has over a lay subject. In other words, it is still another title by virtue of which a Bishop may become the proper Bishop for a layman's ordination.

In the first eleven centuries, when there was only one proper Bishop for the ordination of laymen, namely, the Bishop of the layman's origin, if a man did not want to serve his life as a cleric under the Bishop of his place of origin, his only recourse was to obtain from his proper Bishop permission (probably written) for another Bishop to raise him to the clerical state, and probably also to all future orders whenever that Bishop saw fit to do so, and to assign him to some church or place in that second diocese. Evidence of this is seen in such expressions as "*absque eius episcopi voluntate,*" "*sine conscientia ejus episcopi,*" "*absque ejus* [i. e., *alterius episcopi*] *voluntate,*" "*sine*

[172] Cf. *supra*, pp. 75 ff.

canonicis epistolis," which are contained in the canonical prohibitions against the ordination of lay aliens.[173]

From the twelfth century to the Council of Trent, when the Bishops of the place of origin and of acquired domicile were both recognized as proper Bishops for laymen, and in addition the Bishop of a conferred benefice was regarded as proper for clerics, the discontented or superfluous lay aspirant to the clerical state had two possible means of escape from his diocese of origin: one was to have his family (if he was a minor) move away from their original domicile and acquire a new domicile elsewhere, by which after a long period of residence, amounting to about ten years, the layman would become subject *quoad ordinationem* to the new Bishop; the other was to have his original Bishop tonsure him or issue dimissorial letters for the same without any title of ordination, which rendered him a potential candidate for a benefice in another diocese, upon receiving which the Bishop under whom he accepted the benefice would become his proper Bishop.

After the Council of Trent, still another avenue was opened —he could become a member of the episcopal household under another Bishop and, after three years, become that Bishop's proper subject for tonsure. Also, the papal Constitution "*Speculatores*" had considerably eased the requirement for the legal acquisition of a new domicile, but it still necessitated at least three years' residence.

All of these processes were long and difficult. They were not suited to meet the problems of the nineteenth century, in which dioceses in need of clerics were sometimes thousands of miles away from those which had more than enough clerics. The result was that customs sprung up of acquiring domiciles by abbreviated methods, in contradiction to the rigid rules of the "*Speculatores.*" These afforded an occasion for the Holy See to liberalize the law, first for clerics, and afterwards for laymen. By the Decree "*A primis*" of the Sacred Congregation of the Council, dated July 20, 1898,[174] *clerics* received a

[173] *Supra,* pp. 41-43.

[174] ASS, XXXI (1898-9), 49 ss.; *Fontes,* n. 4307.

new proper Bishop by virtue of the title of incardination, i. e., by mere letters of transfer from one diocese to another, which was in reality a much abbreviated method of acquiring a new domicile. But, dealing with *laymen* only in passing, the decree stated:

> 6°. Denique quoad laicos, aut etiam quoad clericos, qui excardinationis beneficio uti nequeunt vel nolunt, standum esse dispositionibus const. "Speculatores" quae, nihil obstante praesenti decreto, ratae ac firmae semper manere debent.

The ambiguous wording of this paragraph left an uncertainty about the lawfulness of transferring *laymen.* Did the relative clause "*qui excardinationis beneficio uti nequeunt vel nolunt*" modify "*clericos*" only or also "*laicos*"? If the former, then lay transfers had to conform to the strict prescriptions of the "*Speculatores*"; if the latter, the lawfulness of transferring laymen by letter was also recognized, at least implicitly. Opinion was divided,[175] and paved the way for a threshing out of the difficulty and a final settlement of the question.

It was the problem of supplying candidates for the priesthood in the foreign mission fields which had given rise to this new difficulty. The Bishops charged with the problem had very few native vocations. Yet, the dioceses with a plentiful supply of volunteers were hundreds and even thousands of miles distant. There was need of some method to bring the willing lay candidates of the well populated distant dioceses under the direct control of the Bishops in the mission countries, so that these could ordain, or cause to be ordained, as many candidates as they could place, whenever they saw fit to do so. According to the existing law, the lay candidates could not become proper subjects of the mission Bishops until they had acquired a domicile by three years' residence in the mission fields. After that they would have to travel back to some established seminary for training under the control of their new Bishop, and, after ordination, would have to make the journey again to their destination. With such great distances inter-

[175] Many, *De Sacra Ordin.*, n. 71.

vening, this was an impossible demand on young laymen. The result was that the Bishops were forced to solve the problem in their own way, even though it was not strictly a legal one.

Early in 1899 various Bishops of these mission countries, sensing the possible conflict between the custom in their territories and the provisions of the Decree "*A primis,*" submitted their difficulty for solution to the Sacred Congregation for the Propagation of the Faith, and asked that their custom in this matter be legitimized.[176] This custom may be briefly summarized as follows: They were frequently accepting for service in their missions lay candidates from foreign countries. In order to save expense, however, the ordination and incardination of such candidates was effected in an arbitrary manner. The release of the candidate from his proper diocese, and his incardination into the territory of the new Bishop, was accomplished by an exchange of letters between the Bishops. Then, the candidate was sent for his education to a college near his former diocese, where in due time he was tonsured and ordained to the priesthood, whereupon he proceeded to the mission territory of the receiving Bishop. Despite the fact that he had lost his former proper Bishop and, according to the requirements of the Constitution "*Speculatores*" for the acquisition of a domicile, could not yet consider the receiving Bishop as his proper Bishop for tonsure by reason of domicile, nevertheless, the missionary Bishop receiving him considered him from the beginning as a proper subject in virtue of the above process, and authorized both his tonsure and his higher ordination. Hence, the missionary Bishops were seeking the legitimation of the custom of quasi-excardinating and quasi-incardinating laymen, i. e., through the medium of mere letters.

Likewise, in February, 1899, the Bishop of Ratisbon sent to Rome for solution a similar difficulty. According to him, there had long been in vogue in Germany the custom of granting letters of excardination *(litterae dimissoriales)* to laymen, so that they could be permanently received into another diocese and become proper subjects for tonsure immediately upon setting foot

[176] S. C. C., *Romana et aliarum,* 15 sept. 1906—*ASS,* XXXIX (1906), 486 ss.

in it, without having to observe the conditions of the Constitution "*Speculatores*" for the establishment of a domicile or for the title of *familiaritas*.[177] It was asked, therefore, whether such letters conceded before the promulgation of the Decree "*A primis*" were valid or not, and, if valid, whether or not such letters could be validly given in the future.

Both of these difficulties, that of the missionary Bishops and that of the Bishop of Ratisbon, were discussed together by the Sacred Congregation of the Council, and the reply was given that everything would be provided for in a new general decree.[178] The promised decree was issued on November 24, 1906. Because of its importance it is here reproduced:

> Decretum de excardinatione et sacra ordinatione.
>
> Decreto diei 20 mensis Iulii 1898, quod incipit "A primis" Emi. S.C. Concilii Patres, probante v.m. S.P. Leone XIII, circa "excardinationem et incardinationem" clericorum eorumque subsequentem ordinationem, haec quae sequuntur statuerunt:
>
> (Then follows a complete quotation of the Decree "*A primis*").[179]
>
> Sed pluribus in locis mos iam pridem invaluerat ut quaedam litterae quasi excardinatoriae, seu excorporationis aut exeat nuncupatae, laicis quoque traderentur, eodem ferme modo ac pro clericis fieri consueverat: quibus litteris Episcopus originis laicum suae dioecesis subditum dimittebat, et ius nativum, quo pollebat eum in clericalem statum adscribendi, in alium Ordinarium transferre eique cedere videbatur: et vicissim hic illum suscipiens eum proprium subditum sibi facere, et qua talem ad primam tonsuram et ss. Ordines promovere libere posse arbitrabatur, quin aut ratione domicilii aut ratione familiaritatis subditus sibi esset iuxta Constitutionis "Speculatores" praescripta.
>
> Porro evulgato decreto "A primis", de huius praxis legitimitate disputari coepit, et plura dubia hac de re ad S. Sedem delata sunt.
>
> Quapropter de mandato SSmi quaestione semel et iterum in hac S. Congregatione examinata, tandem die 15 Septembris 1906

[177] *Ibid.*, 487 ss.

[178] *Ibid.*, 498-9.

[179] See text below, pp. 217-218.

Eñi Patres censuerunt, permitti posse, si Sanctitas sua id probaverit, ut praefatae litterae, quibus laici a propria dioecesi dimittuntur, ab Ordinariis concedantur, earum vi extradioecesanus fieri proprius valeat Episcopi benevoli receptoris, et hoc titulo ad clericalem tonsuram et ad ss. Ordines ab eo promoveri; dummodo tamen,

1°. dimissio ab Episcopo proprio ex iusta causa, in scriptis et pro determinata dioecesi concedatur.

2°. Acceptatio ne fiat nisi servatis regulis quae pro clericis incardinandis statutae sunt, et superius sub num. II, III, IV, et V recensentur; et servato quoque decreto "Vetuit" diei 22 Decembris 1905 quoad alumnos a seminariis dimissos.

3°. Sed iuramentum ad tramitem Constitutionis "Speculatores" requisitum, praestandum esse ante clericalem tonsuram. Verum cum obligatio permanendi in dioecesi non propria, eique in perpetuum serviendi, ante maiorem aetatem non sine difficultatibus et periculis suscipi possit, cavendum esse ab Episcopis ne ad clericalem tonsuram admittant qui aetate maior non sit.

Facta autem de his omnibus relatione SSño D.N. Pio Papae X ab infrascripto Secretario in audientia diei 16 Septembris 1906, Sanctitas Sua deliberationem Eñ. Patrum probavit et confirmavit, mandavitque ut evulgaretur per litteras S. C. Concilii, ut omnibus ad quos spectat lex et regula esset, contrariis quibuslibet minime obstantibus.[180]

By this decree the quasi-excardination of lay persons from one diocese and their quasi-incardination into another through the medium of letters was made lawful, provided that certain conditions were observed. These conditions were: 1st. That the quasi-excardination be for a just cause, that it be made in writing, and that it be given for a determined diocese only; 2nd. That the quasi-incardination of laymen observe the same rules as those which applied to the incardination of clerics in the Decree "*A primis,*" and that it observe the Decree "*Vetuit*" concerning the reception of lay persons who had been dismissed from other seminaries; [181] and 3rd. That the oath, prescribed by the Constitution "*Speculatores*" for the acquisition of a domi-

[180] *ASS*, XXXIX (1906), 600 ss.; *AER*, XXXVI (1907), 292 ff.

[181] S. C. C., 22 dec. 1905—*ASS*, XXXVIII (1905-06), 407 ss.

cile, be taken by the candidate before he receive tonsure, and that no one so incardinated be admitted to tonsure until he reach his majority.

1. *Special Requisites for the Reception of Dismissed Seminarians*

In order to prevent anyone from receiving sacred orders who was not well proved in character and morals, Pope Pius X issued, through the Sacred Congregation of the Council, on December 22, 1905, the Decree "*Vetuit,*"[182] just referred to above, which laid down special conditions for Ordinaries to follow, even if they only received into their seminaries clerics or laymen from other dioceses. The conditions were:

1st. That in the future no local Ordinary is to receive into his seminary a subject of another diocese, whether lay or cleric, unless he shall have inquired and ascertained by secret letter from the proper Bishop of the candidate whether the same was ever dismissed from his proper Bishop's seminary. If he finds it so, without entering into the reasons or the justice of the proper Bishop's action, the local Ordinary is to exclude him.

2nd. If he has already in good faith admitted some who concealed their previous dismissal from another seminary, as soon as he learns of their status he is to advise them to leave. If, however, they wish to stay and he permits it, they are to be incardinated and ordained according to the canonical regulations, but, once they are ordained to the priesthood, they are forbidden to return and establish a stable domicile in the diocese from the seminary of which they have been dismissed.

3rd. He is not to allow back in his diocese anyone who, after having been dismissed from his seminary while in major orders, afterwards entered a Religious Institute.

4th. He is not to admit into his diocesan seminary any students who have been dismissed from any Religious Institute, unless first he shall have obtained from their former moderators secret information in writing as to their morals, nature, and ability, and shall have ascertained that there is nothing about them which would make them unsuited for the clerical state.

[182] *ASS*, XXXVIII (1905-06), 407 ss.

2. *Special Requisites for the Reception of Foreign-born Laymen in the Dioceses of the United States of America*

Between the years 1896 and 1908 the reception in the dioceses of the United States of America of lay candidates for the priesthood who had originated in Poland, including those who had lived for a time in Italy after having left their fatherland, was governed by a special instruction of the Sacred Congregation for the Propagation of the Faith of February 25, 1896.[183] It required that these candidates be provided with Testimonial Letters from the Sacred Congregation for the Propagation of the Faith certifying to their freedom of departure, immunity from censures, and their good morals. By the Constitution "*Sapienti Consilio*" of Pius X on June 29, 1908,[184] this instruction was withdrawn as a norm in favor of the Decrees "*A primis,*"[185] "*Vetuit,*"[186] and that of November 24, 1906.[187]

183 *Collectanea S. C. P. F.*, n. 1918. Cf. *supra*, p. 62.

184 *AAS*, I (1909), 7-19; *Fontes*, n. 682. Cf. also *AAS*, II (1910), 102.

185 S. C. C., 20 iul., 1898—*ASS*, XXXI (1898-9), 49 ss.

186 S. C. C., 22 dec., 1905—*ASS*, XXXVIII (1905-06), 407 ss. Cf. *supra*, p. 64.

187 *ASS*, XXXIX (1906), 600 ss.

CHAPTER IV

Incardination and Excardination of Diocesan Clerics

ARTICLE I

THE PROPER BISHOP FOR ORDINATION OF DIOCESAN CLERICS

The identity of the proper Bishop for the initial ordination of a layman has been fully discussed in the last chapter. But to whom was a cleric to look for his reception of higher orders up to and including the priesthood? That is the subject to be studied here; and properly so, because it has an important bearing on the transfer of clerics from one diocese to another.

1. *Ancient Law (Prior to 1100)*

Proper Bishop of Origin

As soon as a layman had been accepted and raised to the clerical state by the Bishop of the place of his origin, that same Bishop, who performed this initial ceremony by the imposition of hands, became the cleric's sole and permanent proper Bishop for all future higher ordinations. No other Bishop was permitted to entice the new cleric away from that diocese, to receive him as a fugitive, to retain him, or to ordain him to any higher order. To do so was equivalent to stealing most precious property, and was prohibited under severe penalties against both the usurping Bishop and the disobedient or recalcitrant cleric. The first record of this law is found in canon 16 of the Council of Nicaea (a. 325), in which also any higher ordination of the cleric usurped is declared to be void.[1] The same law is pro-

[1] "Sin autem etiam ausus fuerit quispiam eum, qui ad alium pertinet surripere, et in ecclesia, non consentiente proprio episcopo, a quo recessit qui in canone censetur, irrita sit ordinatio."—Mansi, II, 675; c. 3, D. LXXI. "*Irrita*" here, as elsewhere in the early period, meant "void" as to the execution of the orders, not as to their reception. On this point cf. Wernz, *Ius Decretalium,* II, n. 91, note 31; Thomassinus, *Eccl. Discip.*, P. II, lib. I, cap. IX, n. 1.

pounded in clearer language in the Council of Sardica (a. 343);[2] and from then on it is repeated and renewed at frequent intervals in both the general and the particular councils of different countries, thus showing its universal acceptance.[3] Canon 3 of the

[2] C. 18: "Januarius Episcopus dixit. Illud praeterea statuat sanctitas vestra, ut nulli Episcopo liceat alterius civitatis clericum sollicitare, et in suis parrochiis ordinare. Universi dixerunt: Quia ex his contentionibus solent nasci discordiae, prohibet omnium sententia, ne quis hoc facere audeat"; *ibid.*, c. 19: "Osius Episcopus dixit. Et hoc universi constituimus, ut quicumque ex alia parochia alienum ministrum sine conscientia vel voluntate sui Episcopi voluerit in ordine promovere, non sit rata ejus ordinatio. Quicumque autem hoc usurpare temptaverit, a fratribus et coepiscopis nostris et admoneri debet et corrigi."—Mansi, VI, Append., 1150; c. 1, D. LXXI.

[3] Thus, in *Africa*: I Counc. of Carthage (a. 348), c. 5: "Privatus episcopus Begeselitanus dixit: Suggero sanctitati vestrae, ut statuatis, non debere clericum alienum ab aliquo suscipi sine litteris episcopi sui, neque apud se detinere": — Mansi, III, 155; c. 6, D. LXXI; Counc. of Hippo (a. 393), c. 19: "Ut clericum alienum, nisi concedente ejus Episcopo, nemo audeat vel retinere, vel promovere in ecclesia sibi credita."—Mansi, III, 922; III Counc. of Carthage (a. 397), c. 21, which merely repeats c. 19 of the Counc. of Hippo—Mansi, III, 883; c. 2, D. LXXII; IV Counc. of Carthage (a. 398), cap. 27: "Inferioris vero gradus sacerdotes, vel alii clerici, concessione suorum episcoporum possunt ad alias ecclesias transmigrare."—Mansi, III, 953; Counc. of Telepte (a. 418), c. 6: "Clericum alienum nullus audeat ordinare."—Mansi, IV, 380; *ibid.*, c. 7: "Abjectum Clericum alter non suscipiat."—Mansi, *loc. cit.*

In *Italy*: Counc. of Turin (a. 397), c. 7: "Nec illud praetermittendum fuit, quod synodi sententia definitum est, ut clericum alterius secundum statuta canonum nemo suscipiat, neque suae ecclesiae licet in alio gradu audeat ordinare, neque abjectum recipiat in communionem."—Mansi, III, 862; Roman Synod under Eugene II (a. 826), c. 18—C. 1, D. LXXII; Counc. of Benevento (a. 1091), c. 3—Mansi, XX, 739.

In *Spain*: I Counc. of Toledo (a. 400), c. 12: "Item ut liberum ulli clerico non sit, discedere de episcopo suo, et alteri episcopo communicare."—Mansi, III, 1000; Counc. of Valencia (a. 524), cap. 6—Mansi, VIII, 622; Counc. of Merida (a. 666), cap. 12—Mansi, V, 82.

In *Portugal*: II Counc. of Braga (a. 563), cap. 8—Mansi, IX, 778.

In *France*: Counc. of Angers (a. 453), c. 9: "Aliis quoque episcopis aliorum clericis gradum augere non liceat."—Mansi, VII, 901; II Counc. of Arles (a. 452), c. 13: "Quod si aliquo commorationis tempore, invito episcopo suo, in aliena ecclesia habitans ab episcopo loci clericus fuerit ordinatus hujusmodi ordinatio irrita habeatur."—Mansi, VII, 880; I Counc. of Tours (a. 461), c. 9: "...ut si quis episcopus...aut clericos ab aliis ordinatos promovere praesumat, ab universorum fratrum et consacerdotum suorum communione se alienum efficiendum non dubitet..."—Mansi, VII, 946; *ibid.*, c. 11: "Si quis vero clericus, absque episcopi

Council of Antioch (a. 341), furthermore, shows that the proper Bishop so controlled his clerics that he could call them back to his diocese, even though they had already left it without permission, and they were specially punished if they did not obey.[4] There can be no doubt that even the new cleric in the lowest grade of orders was included in all this legislation, because the context consistently directs the cleric to persevere in the place of his *first* ordination and not to look to be received by any other Bishop; in some instances also it is expressly stated that lectors are included in the law.[5]

That which is concluded from a study of the councils is further confirmed by the epistles of the Popes of this period.

sui permissu, derelicta ecclesia sua, ad alium se transferre voluerit locum, alienus a communione habeatur."—Mansi, *loc. cit.*; IV Counc. of Arles (a. 524), c. 4—Mansi, VIII, 627; Counc. of Clermont (a. 535), c. 11—Mansi, VIII, 861; Counc. of Châlon sur Saone (a. 650), c. 13—Mansi, X, 1192; Counc. of Rouen (a. 1048), c. 9—Mansi, XIX, 753.

In *Germany*: Counc. of Mainz (a. 813), c. 22—Mansi, XIV, 71.

In the *East*: Counc. of Chalcedon (a. 451), c. 20: "Si qui autem episcopi post hoc decretum, clericum qui ad alium episcopum pertinet susceperint, placuit esse excommunicatos, eumque qui susceptus est, et eum, qui suscepit, donec clericus qui migravit, in suam ecclesiam redeat."—Mansi, VII, 366; c. 4, D. LXXI.

4 "Si forte evocatus a proprio Episcopo, ut revertatur ad propriam, et correptus non audiat, et permanserit inquietudine, omnino degradari eum a ministerio, et nullam eum spem habere ad revertendum. Si autem degradatum pro hac culpa suscipiat eum alius Episcopus, et ille culpatur a communione Synodo, eo quod destruat dispositiones ecclesiasticas."—Mansi, VI, Append., 1160; c. 24, C. VII, q. 1. Cf. also *Canones Apostolorum*, cc. 15, 16, where the words of this Antiochene canon are repeated almost *verbatim*—Funk, *Didascalia et Constitutiones Apostolorum*, I, 569. The same is shown from the epistle, quoted below (footnote 7), of St. Leo the Great to Anastasius, Bishop of Thessalonica, cap. IX—Mansi, V, 1183.

5 E. g., in the Counc. of Hippo (a. 393), c. 19: "Ut Clericum alienum, nisi concedente ejus Episcopo, nemo audeat vel retinere, vel promovere in ecclesia sibi credita. Clericorum autem nomen etiam Lectores retineant."—Mansi, III, 922; and in the III Counc. of Carthage (a. 397), c. 21—Mansi, III, 883; c. 2, D. LXXII, in which the same words are repeated with the following amplification: "Clericorum autem nomen etiam lectores, et psalmistae, et ostiarii retinent." On this, Thomassinus (*Eccl. Discip.*, P. II, lib. I, cap. I, n. 1) comments as follows: "Quae postrema verba non oscitanter pratereunda. Docent enim luculentissime, minimo quolibet ordine accepto quemlibet clericum ordinatori episcopo ita adstrictum fuisse, ut citra ejus assensum non posset jam alteri sese episcopo adglutinare."

Thus, Innocent I (a. 404), in a letter to Victricius, Bishop of Rouen, states that no one can take a cleric from another diocese unless the cleric's Bishop is willing to grant the permission.[6] The same is repeated by St. Leo the Great (a. 446), with the additional comment that he who seeks or keeps another Bishop's cleric is guilty of a grave injury, because he takes from his brother that which is very useful and precious.[7] Adrian I (a. 785) forbids clerics to depart from their Bishop and to transfer to another;[8] and Urban II (a. 1088-1099) declares that clerics who were ordained, contrary to the canons of the Church, by Bishops of other dioceses than their own may be received back in their new grade by their proper Bishop, provided that their life is otherwise worthy and that they do penance for the offense committed against their church.[9]

The civil laws, too, add their testimony to the general conclusion.[10]

[6] Tit. VII: "Ut de aliena ecclesia clericum ordinare nullus usurpet, nisi ejus episcopus precibus exoratus concedere voluerit. Hoc etiam synodus statuit Nicaena, ut abjectum ab altero clericum altera ecclesia non recipiat."—Mansi, III, 1034; c. 2, D. LXXI.

[7] "Alienum Clericum, invito Episcopo ipsius, nemo suscipiat, nemo sollicitet: nisi forte ex placito caritatis id inter dantem accipientemque convenerit. Nam gravis injuriae reus est, qui de fratris Ecclesia id quod est utilius aut pretiosius audet vel allicere, vel tenere. Itaque si intra provinciam res agitur, transfugam Clericum ad suam Ecclesiam Metropolitanus redire compellet. Si autem longius recessit, tui praecepti auctoritate revocabitur: ut nec cupiditati, nec ambitioni occasio relinquatur."—*Epist. ad Anastasium Thessalonicensem Episcopum*, cap. IX (Mansi, V, 1183). Cf. also *Epist. ad Episcopos Metropolitanos per Illyrici provincias constitutos* (a. 446), cap. IV: "Illud quoque pari observantia ad sacerdotalis concordiae vinculum ab omnibus volumus custodiri, ut nullus Episcopus alterius Episcopi Clericum sibi audeat vindicare, sine illius ad quem pertinet cessione..." —Mansi, V, 1175; and what is supposed to be an epistle to Rusticus, Bishop of Narbonne (a. 446): "Alienum clericum invito episcopo ipsius nemo suscipiat."—C. 1, C. XIX, q. 2.

[8] "Ut nullus clericus ab episcopo suo recedat, et ad alium se transferat."—*Capitula Ingilrammo Mediomatricae urbis episcopo tradita*, cap. 66 (Mansi, XII, 913).

[9] *Letter to Hugh, Archbishop of Lyons*—C. 10, C. IX, q. 2.

[10] E. g., *Caroli Magni Leges, cum Pontifice Romano et Synodali Concilio* (a. 774-814), cap. 6—Mansi, XII, 895; *Capitula Excerpta ex Lege Longobardorum* (a. 801), capp. XL-XLI—Mansi, XVII Bis, 355.

The only exception to the bond between a cleric and the Bishop who raised him to the clerical state that is found during this first period is in the case of a cleric who was converted from heresy to the Catholic faith by a Bishop other than his ordaining Bishop, and who subsequently becomes desirous of attaching himself to the diocese of that Bishop who converted him.[11]

A few examples on record of the permanent bond which existed betwen a cleric and his proper Bishop make interesting illustrations of the application of the law. A certain Bishop, Julian, of Uzaritan, Africa, had sent to another Bishop, Epigonius, of Bulla, a very poor boy, who was an unbaptized resident of his district. Epigonius was so moved by charity for the boy that he not only baptized him, but also bore all the expenses of his education and literary training, and finally ordained him lector. Then Julian, without consulting Epigonius, took him back to himself and ordained him deacon. Epigonius protested, and took his case before the council, which thereupon ordered Julian to restore the cleric to the Bishop who first ordained him.[12] Again, St. Augustine had ordained Timothy a lector; but the latter afterwards went to another Bishop, Severus, and caused himself to be ordained a subdeacon, finally promising Severus on his oath that he would never leave him. In reclaiming the cleric, Augustine wrote a letter persuading Severus to order Timothy to come back, so that he would not have to violate his oath by leaving the new diocese voluntarily and at the same time would not be guilty of violating the primary law which bound all clerics to the Bishop who first ordained them.[13]

[11] I Counc. of Toledo (a. 400), c. 12: "Item ut liberum ulli clerico non sit, discedere de episcopo suo, et alteri episcopo communicare: nisi forte ei, quem episcopus alius libenter habeat de haereticorum schismate discedentem, et ad fidem catholicam revertentem."—Mansi, III, 1000.

[12] I Counc. of Carthage (a. 348), c. 44—Mansi, III, 156. Cf. Thomassinus, *Eccl. Discip.*, P. II, lib. I, cap. I, n. 2; Hallier, *De Sacris Elect. et Ordin.*, P. II, sec. V, cap. III, art. I, nn. 14-16—*MTC*, XXIV, 970-1.

[13] "Christum consulas tuae menti praesidentem, utrum homo, qui in ecclesia meae dispensationi credita jam legere coeperat, et non semel, sed iterum et tertio, non fuisse lector possit, et debeat judicari, . . . Non vereor, ne parum intelligas,

2. *Medieval Law (1100 to the Council of Trent)*

Proper Bishops of Origin, of Acquired Domicile, and of Benefice

This was the period of absolute ordinations, that is to say, the period wherein no titles of ordination, no places of assignment, were required for the initial ordination of laymen by the Bishop of their place of origin. The new clerics, being for the most part non-beneficed, were not bound to any particular place of residence, but were only required to stay within the diocese,[14] which was only a natural consequence of their bond with the ordaining Bishop. They were subject to his dominion, whether or not they were fortunate enough to possess a benefice in his diocese, so that they could not be received into any other diocese without his permission; [15] but, if they had a good reason, they were able to leave his diocese and establish a domicile elsewhere. Even if they possessed a benefice in the diocese, it was in the Bishop's power to permit them to absent themselves from the diocese for some years to attend a University without forfeiting the income from their benefice.[16] Furthermore, he alone could either legitimately ordain them to higher orders or give permission for them to be so ordained.[17]

quantus aditus aperitur ad dissolvendum ordinem ecclesiasticae disciplinae, si alterius ecclesiae clericus, cuicumque juraverit, quod ab ipso non sit recessurus."—*Epist. LXIII Ad Severum* (*MPL*, XXXIII, 232). Cf. Thomassinus, *Eccl. Discip.*, P. II, lib. I, cap. II, n. 7.

[14] *Supra*, pp. 76-78.

[15] National Synod of Esztergom in Hungary (ab. 1114), cap. 19—Mansi, XXI, 103-4; *Letter of Pope Alexander III to the Archbishop of York*—C. 5, X, *de clericis non residentibus in ecclesia vel praebenda*, III, 4. Cf. also the provision of the Provincial Council of Mainz (a. 1261), c. 17 (Mansi, XXIII, 1085-6), that all such written permissions be subject to diligent scrutiny and approval by the receiving Bishop—a measure made necessary because of the number of forgeries that were being perpetrated in them.

[16] *Alexander III Eboracensi Archiepiscopo*—C. 5, X, *de clericis non residentibus in ecclesia vel praebenda*, III, 4; *Innocentius III Altissiodorensi Episcopo*—*Ibid.*, c. 12.

[17] Council of London (a. 1138), c. 7—Mansi, XXI, 512; Counc. of London (a. 1175), c. 5—Mansi, XXII, 148; Provincial Counc. of Fritzlar (a. 1246), cap. 10—Mansi, XXIII, 728; Synodal Constitutions of the Diocese of Valencia (a. 1255), cap. *De Clericis ordinandis*—Mansi, XXIII, 892 c; *Constitutiones Walteri De Kirkham*

Since benefices were scarce, one good reason for a cleric's leaving his diocese of origin was to receive a benefice in another diocese. He thereby became a subject of the second diocese, but not *quoad ordinationem* (prior to the time of Clement IV); for that he still depended on the Bishop of his place of origin, whose subject he would again become if he ever lost or resigned the acquired benefice.

Sometimes the Bishop of origin had to refuse either to ordain or to grant permission by *litterae dimissoriae* for the higher ordination, especially to sacred orders, of his native cleric, because the cleric had become irregular, fallen under censure, apostatized, or otherwise had shown himself unworthy. To escape this obstacle the cleric would sometimes leave his native locality where his evil reputation was public knowledge, and travel to distant dioceses, where his character was unknown, with the hope of securing some Bishop to confer sacred orders on him without the permission of his proper Bishop of the place of his origin. Presumption in a matter so important is incredible, and yet apparently some Bishops were presuming the authorization of the Bishop of origin to ordain such unworthy ones, bringing untold damage upon the Church as well as upon the souls of the sacrilegious recipients.

It was to avert such terrible dangers with their possible eternal consequences that Pope Clement IV (a. 1265-1268) issued the decree requiring Bishops in the dioceses of Italy to have the special permission of the Pope or of the Bishop of the diocese where the cleric originated or of the diocese where he was already in possession of a benefice, together with letters clearly stating why they would not or could not ordain him, before these Italian Bishops could promote, especially to sacred orders, a cleric who came to them from other parts of Europe.[18]

The unusual feature of the decree was that the Pope apparently recognized the Bishop of the diocese in which a cleric had

Episcopi Dunelmensis (a. 1255)—Mansi, XXIII, 899 e; Synodal Statutes of the Diocese of Gerona (a. 1261), cap. 12—Mansi, XXIII, 931; Provincial Counc. of Mainz (a. 1261), cap. 32—Mansi, XXIII, 1091.

[18] C. 1, *de temporibus ordinationum et qualitate ordinandorum*, I, 9, in VI°. For complete text, see above, p. 48.

a benefice as having the right to ordain or to give to another Bishop the permission to ordain that cleric. This in itself was not new, for in the ancient law the Bishop could not ordain a candidate unless he had a church to which he could assign the same. But, for the first time in history, there were now two simultaneous titles by which different Bishops became equally competent to ordain the same cleric. No longer, then, was a cleric bound so absolutely to the Bishop of his place of origin, for he was at liberty to find a new proper Bishop by the acquisition of a benefice in another diocese, as long as he was not already beneficed in the first, and no permission was necessary for the process,[19] except that of the Bishop in whose diocese the newly acquired benefice existed.[20]

It is to be noted that no qualifications whatever were specified by Pope Clement IV as to the type of benefice which would give rise to this new title of proper Bishop. Canonists concluded that any acquired benefice, whether residential or simple, would suffice to create the title, even if it were classified only among the *praestimonia;* that it did not matter whether it was possessed *in titulum* or *in commendam,* as long as the cleric actually possessed it and did not have just a title to it; that it mattered not how large or small its revenue was; and, finally, that even a plurality of compatible benefices, obtained in different dioceses by the same individual, though contrary to original church discipline, would now result in the simultaneous multiplication of the title of proper Bishop *ratione beneficii* among the Bishops who conferred these benefices, giving to each of these Bishops an equal right to promote to higher orders the common clerical recipient of their beneficence.[21]

The only restrictive provision agreed upon by episcopal practice was that the benefice must not be one received *in fraudem,* that is, that an insignificant or non-residential benefice, obtained by the candidate in order to escape an examination by his proper

[19] Claeys-Bouuaert, *De Canonica Cleri Saecularis Obedientia,* pp. 206-7.

[20] *Constitutions of the Church of Ferrara* (a. 1332), const. 14—Mansi, XXV, 908.

[21] Hallier, *De Sacris Elect. et Ordin.,* P. II, sec. V, cap. III, art. V—*MTC,* XXIV, 1000-1001.

Bishop of origin or of domicile, must not be countenanced. Fraud could easily be suspected, for instance, when the beneficial revenue did not exceed four ducats, or when the benefice obtained was non-residential and its possessor never actually resided either in it or in the diocese which controlled it. Though the fact could not be denied that Bishops could claim as proper subjects for higher ordination the clerics who held simple benefices in their dioceses, the danger to the Church from such action was well apprehended. The probability was that such subjects never intended to exercise sacred orders in that diocese wherein they held merely a simple benefice; otherwise they would be interested enough to remain there. If, despite this inherent danger, the Bishop of the simple benefice conferred sacred orders on them, the result was that the Bishop of their place of origin or of their domicile, where they were actually residing, suffered the infliction of sacred ministers whose higher ordination he had not authorized, yet whom he could not legally command to depart from his diocese. The need of having clerics rooted to the very diocese where they received holy orders was thus appreciated more and more, and was the cause for the renewal in the Council of Trent of the Council of Chalcedon's ancient law which insisted on clerical assignment within the diocese where the ordination took place.[22]

The institution of the new title which provided a proper Bishop *ratione beneficii* did not destroy the bond of the cleric with the first ordaining Bishop, for as long as the cleric did not receive a residential benefice in another diocese he still belonged to the first ordaining Bishop and could not establish his domicile elsewhere without that Bishop's permission.[23] The relaxing

[22] Cf. Hallier, *De Sacris Elect. et Ordin.*, P. II, sec. V, cap. III, art. V—*MTC*, XXIV, 999-1002, where this subject is extensively treated for this particular period.

[23] Synod of Bayeux (a. 1300), cap. 111—Mansi, XXV, 80; Council of Nogaro (a. 1303), c. 1—Mansi, XXV, 111; Council of Marciana (a. 1326), cap. 2—Mansi, XXV, 776; Provincial Counc. of England (a. 1509), Tit. *De clericis peregrinis*—Mansi, XXXI A, 374-5; Counc. of Sens (also called Parisian) (a. 1528), *Decreta Morum*, n. 5—Mansi, XXXII, 1185-6; Provincial Counc. of Canterbury (a. 1529 ff.), *Statuta et Ordinationes, De qualitate ordinandorum*—Mansi, XXXV A, 332 c; Provincial Counc. of Narbonne (a. 1551), c. 13—Mansi, XXXIII, 1256.

effects of this change of legislation might easily be misunderstood and overestimated, and in fact are by several canonists. As was stated above,[24] benefices, being scarce, were not usually conferred on any except major clerics, for whom alone ordination titles were required, and so the proper Bishops of origin and of acquired domicile were hardly in danger of losing a great number of their minor clerics until it was time for these to receive the subdiaconate, and then the Bishops were able to retain their clerics by supplying the same with benefices in their own dioceses. It is true that there were great numbers of clerical *vagi* roaming about the European continent in the Medieval Period, but they were mostly priests and clerics already in major orders, and their prevalence was due to the introduction into the Church of patrimony as a legitimate title of ordination rather than to this cause, as will be shown in a later article.[25]

The title of proper Bishop by acquired domicile, which was canonized for the first time by Pope Boniface VIII [26] has already been explained,[27] and it has also been shown why and how it applied to already tonsured clerics.

What was said there about the length of time necessary to acquire a domicile applied as well to any *cleric* who for some good reason, e. g., health, wanted to move to another diocese than that in which he had been tonsured. The question which spontaneously occurs is, Who was that cleric's proper Bishop during the long period of time necessary for acquiring the new domicile? The answer is: his Bishop of origin *A*, whom he could not possibly lose as his proper Bishop no matter where he travelled. If, some years later, after having acquired a new domicile and with it a new proper Bishop *B*, he should again move to still another diocese, he would thereby lose his proper Bishop *B* but would still be subject for ordination to the Bishop of origin *A*, until, after ten years, he acquired the new proper

[24] Pp. 75-76.

[25] *Infra*, pp. 131-133.

[26] C. 3, *De temporibus ordinationum et qualitate ordinandorum*, I, 9, in VI°. For complete text, cf. above, p. 49.

[27] *Supra*, pp. 49 ff.

Bishop *C*, and even then he would simultaneously retain Bishop *A* as a proper Bishop.

A further complication of status arose if the cleric acquired two domiciles simultaneously, e. g., one for winter and one for summer, for then the episcopal Ordinaries of both places became his proper Bishop for ordination.

The conclusion, then, is that from the year 1100 to the Council of Trent, a cleric could be subject to Bishops for ordination purposes on three distinct bases, namely, by reason of origin, of acquired domicile, and of possessed benefice; and, correlatively, these same three factors served as titles for the proper Bishop in his ordination of clerics to holy orders. Numerically there might have been more than three proper Bishops for one cleric, since a cleric might have had, in addition to the above, a Bishop of the place of his summer domicile and several Bishops governing various simple benefices which he simultaneously possessed. All of these were, strictly taken, equally and simultaneously competent to ordain, though in practice it is quite reasonable to suppose that no one of them would exercise the right to issue dimissorial letters for the conferring of any order on the subject cleric except the one in whose diocese the cleric was actually living or from whose diocese he had obtained permission to absent himself for study at a University.

3. *Tridentine Law (1564-1694)*

Proper Bishops of Origin, of Acquired Domicile, of Benefice, and of Familiaritas

The only new title added to the list by which a Bishop became the proper Bishop for the ordination of a cleric during this period was that of *familiaritas*. It was officially introduced by the Council of Trent in 1563.[28] The idea, however, was far from new. The I Council of Orange (a. 441) had given Bishops the right to pass second judgment on rejected clerics of other Bishops, by having those rejected come to live with them, and,

[28] Sess. XXIII, *de ref.*, c. 9: "Episcopus familiarem suum non subditum ordinare non possit, nisi per triennium secum fuerit commoratus; et beneficium, quacumque fraude cessante, statim re ipsa illi conferat: consuetudine quacumque, etiam immemorabili, in contrarium non obstante."

after a period of trial and a consultation with their former Bishop, to raise these same to higher orders if they saw fit to do so.[29] The same rule was repeated by the II Council of Arles (a. 452).[30] It is probable that from these canons Bishops conceived the idea that they could ordain another's cleric without the permission of the proper Bishop, provided that the cleric became attached to their domestic household where he could be closely observed. After a time, even the consultation of the cleric's proper Bishop on the subject of promoting the cleric to higher orders was omitted. This practice gave rise to a general custom, which the Council of Trent canonized within duly indicated restrictions *(consuetudine quacumque, etiam immemorabili, in contrarium non obstante)*.[31] The custom of a Bishop to confer a benefice on a cleric whom he had employed in his episcopal household and whom he desired to ordain to a higher order arose a considerable time prior to the Council of Trent. The *Glossa*, which comments on the word *figmento* in c. 2, *de temporibus ordinationum et qualitate ordinandorum*, I, 9, in VI° (a decree of Gregory X, at the II General Council of Lyons in 1275, in which penalties were laid on Bishops who presumed to ordain lay aliens on any pretext), reveals the existence of the custom, and even reprehends it as a fraudulent method of gaining control over an alien cleric.[32] Nevertheless this custom also became canonized by the Council of Trent.

After the Council of Trent, the title of *familiaritas* came to mean the following: A Bishop could bring into his episcopal residence as a servant either a cleric or a layman who was not a subject of his diocese. After three complete years of service the Bishop became competent to tonsure, or, in the case of a cleric, to confer the next order, on this member of his household, but

[29] C. 8: "Si quis alibi consistentem clericum ordinandum putaverit, prius definiat, ut cum ipso habitet. Sic quoque non sine consultatione ejus episcopi, cum quo ante habitavit eum, qui fortasse non sine causa diu ab alio ordinatus non est, ordinare praesumat."—Mansi, VI, 437.

[30] C. 35—Mansi, VII, 882.

[31] Sess. XXIII, *de ref.*, c. 9.

[32] Cf. Hallier, *De Sacris Elect. et Ordin.*, P. II, sec. V, cap. III, art. V, n. 8.—*MTC*, XXIV, 1101.

in either case, apart from all deceit, he immediately had to confer on the promoted cleric a genuine benefice, by which conferment he became the proper Bishop over the cleric by the title of benefice. Hence the title of *familiaritas* lasted only for that one act of ordination. This privilege was naturally denied to titular Bishops.[33]

The title of proper Bishop by reason of a conferred benefice was very considerably and appropriately restricted by the Council of Trent, which decreed that thenceforward no one should be ordained to any order unless, in the judgment of his Bishop, he would be useful or necessary to the churches of the diocese, and would be assigned to whatever church or place the Bishop had in mind for him, where he was to perform his duties in canonical residence.[34] This decree of the Council was apparently aimed at the proper Bishops *ratione beneficii.* It did not take away their title, but equivalently said: " If you ordain a man, keep him in your diocese." No matter whether the benefice, by the conferring of which the Bishop became the proper Bishop, was a residential or a non-residential one, the cleric ordained by a proper Bishop *ratione beneficii* had to be assigned to residence and service within the diocese, and his future promotion in orders was made dependent on how he discharged these duties.[35] No cleric could have more than one benefice, unless the second was a simple one to make up for the insufficient revenue of the first, but in no case could they both be residential.[36] Hence in this period the cleric could not have two proper Bishops by reason of benefice; he had to choose the one in whose diocese he was going to serve. Fourteen was the minimum age for the recipient of any type of benefice,[37] and twenty-five was the minimum for the recipient of any dignities which had the care of souls attached.[38] For all inferior curatial benefices

[33] Sess. XIV, *de ref.*, c. 2.

[34] Sess. XXIII, *de ref.*, c. 16.

[35] *Ibid.*, cc. 11, 13.

[36] Sess. XXIV, *de ref.*, c. 17.

[37] Sess. XXIII, *de ref.*, c. 6.

[38] Sess. XXIV, *de ref.*, c. 12.

there was required an age that proved suitable for the beneficiary to exercise the care of souls personally.[39]

It is no secret that the law of the Council of Trent which insisted on every cleric being assigned to some church was more honored in the breach than in the observance. But the law at least effected that Bishops were keeping within the diocese the clerics ordained by themselves, especially after the erection of diocesan seminaries became more and more widespread.

4. *Innocentian Law (1694-1898)*

Proper Bishops of Origin, of Acquired Domicile, of Adequate Benefice, and of Familiaritas

The accurate definitions of the titles of proper Bishop by reason of origin and of acquired domicile, which were at length promulgated officially by Pope Innocent XII in his Constitution "*Speculatores*"[40] have received sufficient mention above,[41] and were as valid for clerics as for laymen, except that clerics needed their proper Bishop's permission for a change of domicile.[42] What most interests one here is the more precise requisites concerning the title of proper Bishop by reason of benefice, which were also included in this famous document, pertinent parts of which are now reproduced:

> N. 3. . . . Licet vero Clericus ratione cuiusvis Beneficii in aliena Dioecesi obtenti subiici dicatur Iurisdictioni illius Episcopi, in cuius Dioecesi Beneficium huiusmodi situm est, eam tamen de caetero hac in re inconcusse servari volumus Regulam, ut nemo eiusmodi subiectionem ad effectum suscipiendi Ordines acquirere censeatur, nisi Beneficium praedictum eius sit redditus, ut ad congruam vitae sustentationem, sive iuxta Taxam Synodalem, sive, ea deficiente, iuxta morem Regionis pro promovendis ad Sacros Ordines, detractis oneribus, per se sufficiat, illudque ab Ordinando pacifice possideatur, sublata quacumque facultate supplendi, quod

[39] Sess. VII, *de ref.*, c. 3.

[40] November 4, 1694—*Fontes*, n. 258.

[41] Pp. 58-59.

[42] Cf. S.C.C., Resp. (*Excardinationis*), 29 maii 1880—*ASS*, XIII (1880), 522 ss. Note, however, that the conclusions of the analyst in this case are incorrect.

> deficeret fructibus eiusdem Beneficii cum adiectione Patrimonii etiam pinguis, quod ipse Ordinandus in eadem, seu alia quavis Dioecesi obtineret: ac Episcopus sic Ordinans tam de praedictis Testimonialibus Literis, quam de reddittu Beneficii huiusmodi expressam in consueta collatorum Ordinum attestatione mentionem facere debebit.

In order that a cleric's possession of a benefice might entitle the Bishop of the diocese in which it existed to become the proper Bishop for the ordination of its possessor, therefore, two things were necessary:

1. Its revenue had to be adequate, after necessary expenses had been deducted, to provide decent sustenance in conformity with the standards of clerics in sacred orders, as judged by the synodal tax or by the custom of the region, without requiring any patrimony whatsoever to be added to it. Perpetuity, however, was not required.[43]

2. It had to be held in peaceful possession, i. e., untrammeled by contesting claims or litigation.

When these conditions were fulfilled the Bishop who controlled the benefice, before proceeding to ordain, had to procure Testimonial Letters from the Bishop of the cleric's original domicile, as well as from the Bishop of any new domicile that the cleric had acquired, concerning his birth, age, morals, and life; and these the Bishop who became proper by reason of the benefice had to keep in the archives of the Chancery. Afterwards, the same Bishop had to make mention both of the Testimonials received concerning the cleric's character and of the revenue of the benefice in the certificate which was given to the cleric in testimony of the orders conferred on him.

In the constitution of Innocent XII it was also established beyond doubt that even clerics could be employed by outside Bishops in their household, who could thus become the proper Bishops for such clerics' next ordination. The requirements were:

[43] S.C.C., *Pientina seu Ilcinen.*, 18 iul. 1733—quoted in *ASS*, VI (1870), Appen. X, 498-510.

1st. That the Bishop retain the cleric in actual service in his own episcopal house and support him for a period of three complete years.

2nd. That the Bishop obtain Testimonial Letters as to the cleric's birth, age, morals, and life from the Bishop of the cleric's original domicile and from the Bishop of any new domicile that the cleric might up to that time have acquired.

3rd. That at least within a period of one month from the day of ordination the Bishop confer upon the cleric a benefice which would fulfil the two requirements stated above, namely:

a) that the revenue of the benefice be sufficient, after necessary expenses were deducted, to provide decent sustenance in conformity with the standards of clerics in sacred orders, as judged by the synodal tax or by the custom of the region, without requiring any patrimony whatsoever to be added to it; and

b) that it be held in peaceful possession, without any pending litigation.

4th That in the certificate of ordination mention be made of the title of *familiaritas* and of the Testimonials received as to the character of the cleric.[44]

5. *Pre-Code Law (1898-1917)*

Proper Bishops of Origin, of Acquired Domicile, of Adequate Benefice, of **Familiaritas**, *and of Incardination*

The nineteenth century developed still another title of proper Bishop for the ordination of clerics, namely, that of incardination, reference to which was made in the article on quasi-incardination of laymen,[45] since the genesis of both was alike. Up to that time, if a cleric had a good reason for wanting to transfer from his diocese of origin, in which also he had been tonsured, to become a priest elsewhere, there were three courses open to him after securing permission of his Bishop of origin to leave the diocese: 1) to acquire a domicile in the place of his choice, which would take at least three years; 2) to get possession of an adequate benefice in the same, which might take many years of

[44] Const. "*Speculatores*," n. 6—*Fontes*, n. 258.

[45] *Supra*, pp. 91-92.

waiting; 3) to become affiliated with the household of the Bishop of the place to which he wished to go; and even such affiliation would have to last for three years before the Bishop would become his proper Bishop, even assuming that the latter was willing and had an adequate benefice to give him. Obviously each of these courses was difficult. Bishops, who were in urgent need of major clerics whom they could ordain to the priesthood in a short time to fill vacancies in their dioceses, could not withstand the delays involved in a strict observance of the law. They solved their problem of obtaining clerics by what they termed *excardination* and *incardination,* which was nothing more than an abbreviated method whereby such clerics could acquire a new domicile in their diocese merely by a declared intention of perpetually remaining in it, fortified by an oath.

The clerics who wanted to leave their own diocese and exercise their life's ministry in another sought and obtained from their present Bishop a full and perpetual release, called excardination, and, fortified with that, they petitioned the Bishop of the diocese of their choice for an immediate affiliation with his diocesan clergy, called incardination, which he would concede as soon as they took the oath, required by the Constitution "*Speculatores,*" for the election of a domicile. By that act they would immediately become his proper subjects whom he could raise to higher orders at once on his own authority by the title of incardination. This soon gave rise to many controversies, causing the whole question to be submitted to Rome for adjudication. On August 21, 1897, the following *dubia* were proposed to the Sacred Congregation of the Council:

I. An clerici incardinati ex ipso facto incardinationis et electionis domicilii iuramento confirmatae statim ad S. Ordines promoveri possint in casu.

II. An et quomodo providendum in casu.

The response, given on December 11, 1897, was: "Provideatur per Decretum."[46]

The promised Decree was the "*A primis,*" issued by the Sacred Congregation of the Council on July 20, 1898,[47] in which in-

[46] *AkKR,* LXXIX (1899), 101.

[47] *ASS,* XXXI (1898-9), 49 ss.; *Fontes,* n. 4307. For full text see below, pp. 217-218.

cardination was made a new title for the gaining of a proper Bishop for the ordination of clerics, provided that certain rules were followed. These rules were:

1. Excardination cannot licitly be given except for just causes, and it does not completely take effect until incardination in another diocese has been put into execution.

2. Incardination must be performed by a Bishop, not orally, but in writing, and even that must be absolute and perpetual, without any expressed or implied conditions attached, so that the cleric becomes entirely subject to the new diocese after having taken an oath to remain in it permanently, similar to the oath prescribed by the Constitution "*Speculatores*" for the acquisition of a new domicile.

3. Incardination cannot be effected unless it is first clear from a legitimate document that the alien cleric seeking it has been perpetually dismissed from his native diocese, and opportune testimony has been obtained, secretly if necessary, from the Bishop who is releasing him as to his birth, life, morals, and studies.

4. Those incardinated into a diocese in this way can, indeed, be promoted to orders. Since, however, no one should be ordained hastily, the Bishops should recognize it as their duty to decide in each case whether, after all things have been considered, the newly incardinated cleric is such that he can be safely ordained at once without any further trial or whether he should be subjected to a longer period of probation. They should furthermore remember that, just as according to the Council of Trent no one was to be ordained who in the judgment of his Bishop would not be useful or necessary to his churches, so too now no new cleric should be incardinated except in view of the necessity or benefit of the diocese.

5. In incardinating clerics of a foreign tongue and nationality Bishops must proceed with greater caution and strictness, and never should they receive such clerics unless they have first sought and obtained from the respective Ordinaries of the candidates secret and favorable information concerning these foreign clerics' life and morals. This duty binds the conscience of the incardinating Bishop under pain of grave sin.

6. Finally, as to laymen, or also as to clerics who are either unable or unwilling to use the benefit of excardination, the provisions of the Constitution "*Speculatores*" must be obeyed, which, notwithstanding this present decree, must always remain binding.

ARTICLE II

VARIATION AMONG PROPER BISHOPS

1. *Ancient Period*

In ancient church law, prior to the twelfth century, there was no possibility of receiving different orders from various proper Bishops, since there was only one proper Bishop for the ordination of any man, namely, the Bishop of the place of his origin, or the one in whose territory the man's parents had their established residence at the time he was born. It was to this Bishop that the candidate had to apply, not only for his first minor ordination, but also for all subsequent grades including the priesthood.[48]

2. *Medieval Period*

The first official recognition of a second proper Bishop for a *layman* was given by Pope Boniface VIII (a. 1294-1303), when by decree he admitted the right of the Bishop of a candidate's acquired domicile, as well as that of the Bishop of the candidate's place of origin, to grant permission for the ordination of the same subject.[49] In successive periods of the Church's history two other titles for the gaining of a proper Bishop by laymen came to be recognized, namely, *familiaritas* and quasi-incardination.

Despite this potential multiplicity, in many instances a candidate would still have only one proper Bishop, that is to say, when he still lived in the legal place of his birth and was never transferred to another Bishop by official letters or by introduction as a member into such Bishop's official household. In other cases, where changes like these had actually taken place, the candidate

[48] *Supra*, pp. 40-45, 98-102.

[49] C. 3, *De temporibus ordin.*, I, 9, in VI°. Cf. *supra*, p. 49.

would have several proper Bishops, and technically could select any one of them to confer his first order; but practically, as has been seen, there would be no choice, since he would be expected to approach for tonsure that Bishop whose title as proper Bishop best applied in his individual case, i. e., the one in whose diocese he was then actually residing as a subject, who in consequence of this residence knew him best.[50]

A far more difficult problem is the question of the practical use of a multiplicity of proper Bishops for *clerics* and the factor of lawfulness in varying from one to the other in each new ascent in holy orders. Though some phases of this have already been treated in preceding Chapters, it will be helpful to consider the question more thoroughly in an article by itself.

Prior to 1100 the only proper Bishop for a *cleric* was the one who had legitimately conferred on him the first order, i. e., the Bishop of his place of origin. The possibility of two proper Bishops for *clerics* was officially introduced for the first time in history by Pope Clement IV (a. 1265-1268),[51] who attributed equal power over a cleric's ordination to the Bishop in whose diocese the cleric obtained a benefice. Twenty-five years later Boniface VIII added also the title of acquired domicile. Since it was possible for an individual to have two domiciles and several manual benefices in different dioceses simultaneously, the same cleric might have six or seven distinct proper Bishops.

To understand this seeming incongruity, one has to be mindful of the scarcity of titles of ordination for minor clerics during this period of history, and of the wide use of patrimony as a title of ordination even for major clerics. Without a title to keep him busy and fixed to a definite spot, without any financial support or aid from the diocese, the cleric was free to find other Bishops who could better use his services and render aid in his sustenance, thereby becoming his proper Bishops, and anyone of them could be appealed to for his reception of higher orders.

The only restriction on the cleric's liberty was that he must not select or obtain a proper Bishop *in fraudem,* i. e., through

[50] *Supra,* pp. 52-53.

[51] C. 1, *De temporibus ordin.,* I, 9, in VI°. Cf. *supra,* p. 48.

some flimsy reason on the strength of which he would evade a real examination for fitness by the proper Bishop who knew him best, or by virtue of which, after being rejected at home, he would be ordained abroad.[52]

To exemplify, let it be supposed that a lay youth, Paul, was born in diocese *A* and in due time was received into the clerical state by its Bishop, but no benefice was assigned to him and he was to receive his education for the priesthood in some school or University at his parents' expense. A few years later his parents move to diocese *B*, which is considered to offer a more healthful climate, and they take Paul, their clerical son, with them to continue his studies in a school within diocese *B*. Paul merely needed a routine permission from the Bishop of *A* to change his domicile, but it is that same Bishop of *A* who must issue the dimissorials for Paul's reception of the minor orders, at least during the ten succeeding years until Paul has acquired a domicile in diocese *B*, whereupon the Bishop of *B* also becomes his proper Bishop and can confer the subdiaconate on him by his own proper authority, using patrimony for the ordination title. Then Paul becomes acquainted with the Bishop of diocese *C*, who gives him a manual benefice, not requiring residence. No permission is needed from the Bishop of *B* for him to accept such a benefice, and now the Bishop of *C* can promote him to the diaconate. Let it be supposed that still another Bishop, who has more churches to supply than he has clerics, offers Paul a residential benefice in *D*. Paul can accept that, too, without any permissions being needed, and it will serve two purposes, to become, first of all, his title of ordination in place of patrimony, and to make him a subject of the Bishop of *D*, who can now properly ordain him to the priesthood. Paul thereby becomes attached to diocese *D* for life, or at least he cannot leave it to accept a residential benefice elsewhere unless the Bishop of *D* is willing to let him go.

This is only one of many ways in which Paul could have received different orders from different Bishops. It might even have come to pass that he disliked his domicile in diocese *B* and

[52] Cf. *supra*, pp. 105-106.

independently of his parents moved back to the diocese of his origin *A*, in which also he might have received a residential benefice, giving the Bishop of *A* the right to ordain him on two counts, namely, by reason of origin and by reason of benefice.

On the other hand, if Paul's parents had moved to *B*, not really for reasons of health, but because Paul had been rejected as unworthy of receiving higher orders from the Bishop of *A*, then Paul's use of the Bishop of acquired domicile *B* would have been *in fraudem* and therefore unlawful, though valid.

3. *Tridentine Period*

In the Council of Trent one more proper Bishop was added to the list—the proper Bishop *ratione familiaritatis,*—but other decrees of this Council limited very much the former freedom of clerics in receiving holy orders from various Bishops. That practice could not help but prove harmful to the Church, since a cleric rejected by one Bishop could be accepted by some other, who would soon be sought after by many other incompetent candidates as having the reputation of being more carefree in his demands and consequently less exacting in his examination. The general discipline of the Church was set in jeopardy.[53]

Most of all there was need of restricting the right of a Bishop to ordain by reason of a benefice being obtained in his diocese, since that offered the greatest opportunity for fraud and occasioned the use of a wide latitude in the successive variation of the proper Bishops for ordination. Origin and domicile were standard titles. Tonsure was received on the score of one or the other in accordance with the candidate's continuance in or departure from the place of his birth. The title of *familiaritas* gave the layman a chance to cast his future clerical lot with a Bishop of his acquaintance, though this Bishop ruled over a diocese far removed from the home diocese of the candidate. But once tonsure had been received, there was not much room for any successive variation in the proper Bishops for ordination except through the repeated employment of the title of benefice. It took ten years to acquire a domicile, three years to become a

[53] Hallier, *De Sacris Elect. et Ordin.*, P. II, sec. V, cap. III, art. V, n. 10—*MTC*, XXIV, 1002.

familiaris of a Bishop, but no extension of time at all to receive a benefice in another diocese and thus become subject to its Bishop by reason of it. Sometimes the conferred benefice would be of mean and paltry character; sometimes it did not require residence even within the diocese where it existed. A multitude of such benefices obtained by one person in different dioceses gave a multitude of Bishops an equal right to ordain the same individual.[54] Clerics could be ordained to the priesthood on the authority of Bishops in whose dioceses they had never set foot either in actuality or in intention. It is easy to see how a cleric could practice fraud in having himself ordained despite the wishes of his native Bishop of origin or of domicile.

In remedying this evil the Council of Trent did not expressly change the requisites inherent in the benefice itself. Any type of benefice would still make its possessor in the matter of ordination a subject of the Bishop who controlled the benefice, though it is to be recalled that before a benefice could become a title of ordination for the reception of major orders it had to be adequate in providing the proper sustenance for its possessor. But any Bishop who conferred any order, no matter by what title he claimed to be the proper Bishop of the cleric, had to have a position where he could use that cleric and had to assign him to that place. No further order was to be conferred unless the candidate had properly exercised the functions assigned to him in his earlier reception of orders.[55] Apparently this affected most of all those who had obtained manual or simple non-residential benefices in alien dioceses for ordination purposes. Practically, it limited the title of the proper Bishop *ratione beneficii* to cases in which residential benefices were held, since the possessor of a manual benefice had to come to the diocese where it existed and had to be enlisted in clerical service while residing there if he wished the Bishop of that diocese to confer any order on him. Through an imitation of canon 6 of the Council of Chalcedon (a. 451)[56] this demand of the Council of Trent had the lofty

[54] Garcia, *De Benef. Eccles.*, p. II, cap. IV, n. 2.

[55] Sess. XXIII, *de ref.*, cc. 16, 11, 13.

[56] Mansi, VI, 1226; c. 1, D. LXX.

purpose of requiring every clerical candidate to select at the outset the diocese where he wanted to exercise his life's ministry so that he might receive all his orders there where he was best known. This, it was felt, would do the least injury to the Church. A cleric was not prevented from receiving several benefices, but only one of them could be used for ordination purposes.

The clerical assignment law of the Council of Trent did not block the possibility of a successive variation of proper Bishops, but held it under better control. Though even the simple cleric, tonsured in his diocese of origin, was to be assigned to some church or place within that diocese, he was not prevented from changing his domicile along with his parents, but he had to have his original Bishop's permission. Similarly, permission from his Bishop of origin or of acquired domicile was now needed for him to accept a benefice which would entail his leaving his home diocese, unless his Bishop at home had neither beneficed him nor assigned him to some definite service.[57] If, with the necessary permit, he did accept a benefice in another diocese, there was nothing to prevent him from receiving higher orders from the Bishop of that diocese as long as there was no fraud present. This was decided by the Sacred Congregation of the Council for the diocese of Fondi on Jan. 23, 1666. The *dubia* proposed were: " 1°. An in suscipiendis ordinibus sit permissa variatio, ita ut qui ab episcopo originis seu domicilii tonsura aut altero ex minoribus ordinibus initiatus fuit, possit ad alium ordinem minorem ab episcopo beneficii promoveri? 2°. An sit permissa variatio in ascensu ab acolythatu ad subdiaconatum? 3°. An sit permissum subdiacono in promotione ad diaconatum, vel diacono in promotione ad sacerdotium variare? " The response of the Sacred Congregation of the Council was: " Variationem in unoquoque ex praenarratis casibus, dummodo in fraudem non fiat, licitam esse." [58]

[57] Pignatelli, *Consultationes Canonicae*, t. III, consult. LVI, nn. 2-3; Bouix, *Tractatus De Episcopo*, V. II, p. V, cap. XXIV.

[58] Found in *Causa Pisanae,—Thesaurus Resolutionum*, V, 204; Gasparri, *De Sacra Ordin.*, II, n. 854. Cf. Riganti, *Comment. in Reg. Cancell. Ap.*, *Reg.* XXIV, § III, n. 84.

Once a cleric was assigned to a church or place in his new diocese by reason of the title of benefice, he lost his former Bishop of domicile, and could not vary again, either to the Bishop *ratione originis* in order to regain him as his proper Bishop, or to the Bishops *ratione alius beneficii aut familiaritatis* in order to acquire them in a similar capacity, unless the existing proper Bishop *ratione concessi beneficii* gave him express permission to do so. The same was true if a cleric received one order from his proper Bishop *ratione familiaritatis,* because that Bishop was required in consequence of such ordination to benefice his subject and to assign him to a definite clerical service in the diocese.

A layman, however, who was rejected for tonsure by his proper Bishop *ratione originis aut domicilii* could not acquire a proper Bishop *ratione beneficii* who would confer tonsure upon him in view of his being presented for a benefice in another diocese, since laymen were incapable of possessing benefices and the mere presentation would not give an alien Bishop any right over another's diocesan.[59] A layman's recourse was to become associated with the official household of some other Bishop and prove himself worthy through three years of service.

4. *Innocentian Period*

After the Constitution " *Speculatores* " of Innocent XII [60] had become the universal law on the matter of proper Bishops for ordination, the question of possible variation became very much clarified. There were still four titles by which Bishops could claim clerics as proper subjects for ordination, but one of these, the *titulum beneficii,* was circumscribed in such manner as only to comprise benefices which, without any supplementary patrimonial revenue, proved adequate for the cleric's proper sustenance.[61] Apparently the Tridentine law which demanded the

[59] The following doubt was proposed to the Sacred Congregation of the Council: " An laico cui a proprio episcopo fuit denegata prima tonsura, possit ipsa prima tonsura conferri, vel concedi litterae dimissoriales ab Ordinario alterius dioecesis coram quo ipse laicus praesentatus fuit ad beneficium ecclesiasticum " ? The response was: " Non posse."—*Mutinensi,* 26 ian. 1658 (Gasparri, *De Sacra Ordin.,* II, n. 855).

[60] Nov. 4, 1694—*Fontes,* n. 258.

[61] *Ibid.,* n. 3; *supra,* pp. 111-112.

assignment of every cleric to a church or place in the diocese of the ordaining Prelate was renewed, since the constitution expressly stated so with regard to all previous conciliar legislation not opposed to its new prescriptions.[62] Especially was this true of clerics elevated to major orders with patrimony as a title.[63]

The lawfulness of receiving different orders from various proper Bishops was expressly acknowledged in the constitution in several places. Thus, in order that a cleric who had been tonsured or who had received minor orders in the diocese of his origin or of acquired domicile might be raised to higher orders by his proper Bishop *ratione beneficii,* he had to obtain from the Bishops of his origin and of his domicile Testimonial Letters as to his birth, age, morals, and life, and these, after being scrutinized, had to be preserved by the proper Bishop *ratione beneficii* in the Chancery archives, and, moreover, mention of them had to be made in the certificate that furnished testimony of the orders conferred. The same had to be done before the proper Bishop *ratione familiaritatis* could further ordain in his own right another Bishop's cleric.

Likewise the Constitution " *Speculatores* " not only permitted, but ordered, the proper Bishops *ratione originis et domicilii,* when receiving back their clerics who had been raised to higher orders by other Bishops, no matter by what title, to subject the same to an academic examination and diligently to scrutinize the Testimonial Letters of the orders they had received elsewhere, in order to be sure that they conformed to the prescriptions of this constitution; and if the Bishops were not satisfied, they were to suspend the clerics from the exercise of the orders thus received for as long a time as would seem expedient.[64]

62 " Hinc est quod Nos ex commissae Nobis Divinitus Apostolicae servitutis munere, abusus, fraudes, ac scandala huiusmodi penitus, et omnino e medio tollere, ac irreligiosam contrafacientium audaciam, quantum Nobis ex alto conceditur, compescere, et reprimere volentes, necnon fel. rec. Urbani VIII contra male ordinantes, et male ordinatos, quae incipit: *Secretis,* aliorumque Romanorum Pontificum Praedecessorum nostrorum, ac etiam Conciliaribus hac in re editis Constitutionibus, et Ordinationibus inhaerentes, illasque quoad ea, quae praesentibus non adversantur, quatenus opus sit, innovantes: . . ."—*Ibid.,* n. 3.

63 *Ibid.,* n. 1.

64 *Ibid.,* n. 7.

Riganti states[65] that these Testimonial Letters were required of the proper Bishops *ratione originis et domicilii,* not merely to testify to the good morals of the candidate, but also for two other reasons: 1st. that the native proper Bishop who tonsured the cleric might thereby give his consent for the cleric to leave the church of his former assignment; and 2nd. that the native proper Bishop might be made certain of the ordination of his subject, especially since he had to issue these Letters also for major orders, even though he had formerly given them for minor orders, and the ordinand in the meantime had not gone back to him.[66]

Certainly it is to be noted that beyond these Testimonial Letters the "*Speculatores*" makes no mention of any formal permission being required from the proper Bishops *ratione originis aut domicilii* for a cleric to accept a benefice or become associated with a Bishop's household in an alien diocese. However, it does not take into consideration at all: a) the transfer of a *cleric* from his diocese of origin to that of an acquired domicile; or b) the transfer of a cleric from a diocese in which he possessed a residential benefice to another diocese in which he wished to accept a similar one.

a) With respect to the first of these omissions, a cleric could make such a transfer with the permission of his Bishop, just as he had been able to do since the twelfth century; but, while there was a right, there was no obligation on the part of the Bishop *ratione domicilii* to receive him into his clergy or to raise him to higher orders. If the cleric sought orders, the Bishop *ratione domicilii* might insist on dimissorials (*litterae dimissoriae*), and not merely on Testimonials, from the Bishop *ratione originis,* so that the cleric in his new status would still belong to the clergy of his original diocese. Thus at Rome in the middle of the nineteenth century it was the custom that any cleric originating elsewhere and settling in the Eternal City could not be incorpor-

[65] *Comment. in Reg. Cancell. Ap., Reg. XXIV,* § III, n. 94.

[66] This he states was the mind of the Sacred Congregation of the Council, *Firmana seu Luretana* ordinationis, 14 dec. 1705—*Op. et loc. cit.*

ated with the Roman clergy without a formal decree from the Cardinal Vicar of Rome, which was difficult to obtain.[67]

b) With respect to the second unmentioned transfer, it may be that the diocese of residential benefice was considered also the diocese of acquired domicile, and therefore subject to the same rules; but it is also true, as will be seen below, that a cleric possessing such a benefice could not leave the diocese against the will of its Bishop.

Thus, the sole obstacle to the use of a possible variation in this period, as in the preceding one, was fraud, as is apparent from official decisions of the Roman Curia [68] as well as from the common opinion of contemporary authors.[69] Such fraud might be perpetrated: 1) against the canon law itself, as when a cleric in minor orders, in order to avoid an examination by his proper Bishop or to escape giving proof of patrimony, would have a benefice with a revenue inadequate for his decent sustenance conferred on him elsewhere with the intention of being promoted to sacred orders; [70] or when a cleric, after being barred from the reception of higher orders by one proper Bishop because of a canonical impediment, would succeed in becoming ordained by another proper Bishop through concealment of the defect; or 2) against the rights of the Bishop, as when the cleric seeking to receive orders from another proper Bishop: a) had already been educated in a seminary or University at the expense of the present Bishop's diocese, because through that circumstance there existed a quasi-contract to remain there; or b) had received a major order for the title of the mission (*titulus missionis*) or its equivalent, whereby he assumed under oath the obligation of remaining; or c) was already in possession of a

[67] Gasparri, *De Sacra Ordin.*, II, n. 857.

[68] E.g., S.C.C., *Aquipendien. seu Clusina*, Diaconatus, 13 nov. 1717; *Pisina seu Clusina*, Ordinationis, 26 ian. 1732—*Thesaurus Resolutionum*, V, 204; Gasparri, *De Sacra Ordin.*, II, n. 854.

[69] E.g., Gasparri, *op. cit.*, nn. 853-859; Many, *De Sacra Ordin.*, n. 42; Riganti, *Comment. in Reg. Cancell. Ap.*, *Reg. XXIV*, § III, nn. 81-84; Pignatelli, *Consultationes Canonicae*, t. I, consult. XXXVIII; Petra, *Commentaria ad Constitutiones Apostolicas*, In const. unicam Urbani II, sect. 1, n. 64 (t. I, p. 186).

[70] Riganti, *op. cit.*, n. 72.

residential benefice in his present diocese, which therefore he could not desert against his present Bishop's will.[71]

5. *Pre-Code Period*

In the Pre-Code period (i. e., after 1898), a fifth title for the gaining of a proper Bishop was added—that of incardination. No changes or limitations were placed upon the other four categories, so that variation among them was still licit as long as it was not fraudulently used.[72] The title of incardination, however, when once obtained, rendered all future variation unlawful. The cleric who became subject to a Bishop by this method was absolutely and perpetually affiliated to his diocese, and the union was sealed by an official document and fortified by an oath.[73]

ARTICLE III

TITLE OF ORDINATION FOR DIOCESAN CLERICS

The evolution of the concept of the title of ordination from a place of one's spiritual ministry to a guarantee of one's perpetual sustenance was sufficiently explained above.[74] In like

[71] Bouix, *Tractatus de Episcopo*, V. II, p. V, cap. XXIV, § III. Fraud was not considered present if he was merely assigned to some church and sought permission to be raised to higher orders by another proper Bishop, as is seen from this case: John Rossetti had received tonsure, minor orders, and subdiaconate from his proper Bishop *ratione originis* at Fabriano, Italy, for the necessity and utility of a parochial church. Then he obtained a perpetual chaplaincy, over which his father and others had *ius patronatus*, in the diocese of Nocera. When he sought ordination to the diaconate and priesthood from the Bishop of Nocera, his former Bishop refused to grant Testimonial Letters. Whereupon the *dubium* was presented to the Sacred Congregation of the Council: "An liceat episcopo beneficii conferre subdiacono Joanni Rossetti ordines diaconatus et presbyteratus absque litteris testimonialibus sui Ordinarii"? The response given was: "Affirmative, facto verbo cum SSmo."—Gasparri, *De Sacra Ordin.*, II, nn. 716, 857; Many, *De Sacra Ordin.*, n. 42.

[72] Wernz, *Ius Decretalium*, II, n. 28, Scholion II.

[73] "Incardinationem faciendam esse ab Episcopo non oretenus, sed in scriptis, absolute et in perpetuum, id est nullis sive expressis sive tacitis limitationibus obnoxiam; ita ut clericus novae dioecesi prorsus mancipetur, praestito ad hoc iuramento ad instar illius quod Constitutio "Speculatores" pro domicilio acquirendo praescribit."—S.C.C., decr. "*A primis*," 20 iul. 1898, 2º—*ASS*, XXXI (1898-9), 49 ss.; *Fontes*, n. 4307.

[74] Pp. 64-74.

manner enough was said of the ancient necessity of a title of ordination for every cleric, and of the restriction of that necessity, after the twelfth century, to candidates for sacred orders alone.[75] It remains to discuss in detail which guarantees received the general approval of the Church as titles of ordination after the eleventh century change in the term, and which thereby merited the designation of "canonical titles."

1. *Titles Recognized by Common Law*

Benefice, patrimony, and pension

A. Benefice

This was the first title to be officially so recognized. There are some who even trace its origin back to the Council of Chalcedon (a. 451) wherein they find in the law of clerical assignment in canon 6 the essential features of a benefice, i. e., a place to exercise a spiritual ministry coupled with a perpetual right to share in the material fruits thereof. The word is not found in use, however, until the eleventh century, when the portions of the fruits of ecclesiastical properties were made and kept separate entities. From that time on it always received first and principal mention, giving everyone to understand that it was the primary and most important title. An important instance of this is found in the Council of Trent, thus:

> . . . statuit sancta Synodus, ne quis deinceps clericus saecularis, quamvis alias sit idoneus moribus, scientia, et aetate, ad sacros Ordines promoveatur, nisi prius legitime constet, eum beneficium ecclesiasticum, quod sibi ad victum honeste sufficiat, pacifice possidere.[76]

Not any type of benefice, therefore, fulfilled this function. It had to meet certain specifications.

1°. Requisites for a benefice to be a legitimate title of ordination

From the above quoted chapter of the Council of Trent the following deductions may be made:

[75] Pp. 64-80.

[76] Sess. XXI, *de ref.*, c. 2.

a) The benefice, to be a legitimate title of ordination, had to be actually possessed before the cleric received sacred orders (*nisi prius legitime constet eum beneficium ecclesiasticum . . . pacifice possidere*). Hence, mere promise, nomination, presentation, election, collation, or anything short of actual possession were not sufficient. This was not a new feature; it had been generally the same from the time benefices were instituted.[77]

b) It had to be peacefully possessed (*pacifice possidere*), i. e., without any controversy over its ownership or possession. An exception to this would be a benefice, the fruits of which were being contested only in part, provided that the balance of it would be sufficient for the possessor.[78]

c) It had to be adequate for the honorable livelihood of the cleric (*quod sibi ad victum honeste sufficiat*). It is to be noted that: (1) This had to be determined by each Bishop for his own diocese. Usually in the diocesan synod an amount would be stipulated as adequate for the decent sustenance of each cleric in that diocese. It was called the "synodal tax," even though in some places it might have been fixed outside of a synod.[79] In the absence of any declaration of the amount of the synodal tax, the standard for judging the adequacy of a benefice would be the custom of the diocese. Thus at Paris the synodal tax

[77] Note the expressions of some of the ante-Tridentine Councils, thus: "Praecipimus ne quis promoveatur in subdiaconum, diaconum, vel presbyterum, nisi habeat competens secundum qualitatem terrae beneficium ecclesiasticum, . . ."—Council of an uncertain place in Spain (a. 1215), c. 3 (Mansi, XXII, 1090); ". . . praelati . . . diligenter inquirant, . . . utrum habeat perpetuum beneficium ecclesiasticum, vel sufficiens patrimonium volens ad sacros ordines promoveri . . ." — Council of Prague (a. 1346), Cap. *De aetate & qualitate ad sacros ordines* (Mansi, XXVI, 78); "Praelati neminem promoveant ad sacros ordines, nisi quem constabit obtinere beneficium ecclesiasticum, vel actualiter habere patrimonium, et eodem beneficio vel patrimonio realiter et pacifice gaudere, . . ."—Council of Lyons (a. 1449), cap. 13 (Mansi, XXXII, 96); ". . . praecipimus, ut nullus episcopus clericum aliquem in subdiaconum, aut diaconum, vel presbyterum ordinet, . . . nisi prius eidem episcopo legitime constiterit, quod dictus clericus ordinandus beneficium ecclesiasticum sufficiens habuerit, . . ." — Constitutions published by Nicholas Francus, Bishop of Treviso and Apostolic Legate (a. 1491), Tit. *Poena episcopis imposita clericos sine sufficienti titulo in aliena dioecesi ordinantibus* (Mansi, XXXV, 1555-6).

[78] Schmalzgrueber, *Jus Ecclesiasticum Universum* (12 vols., Romae, 1843-1845), lib. I, tit. XI, n. 54.

[79] Benedict XIV, *De Synodo Dioecesana*, lib. XII, c. 9, n. 1.

was 400 francs; at Bologna 40 Roman gold coins; at Rome 60.[80] From time to time it was necessary to change the amount of the tax according to fluctuations in the cost of living. Likewise the tax in the country could be different from that in the city. A benefice exceeding or equalling the tax was acceptable, as also the one which did not quite measure up to it, as long as the discrepancy was slight; but a Bishop could never dispense from this requirement of adequacy when the benefice yielded a notably lower revenue than the indicated tax, because that would be the same as ordaining without a title. (2) It was the synodal tax of the cleric's diocese of domicile that had to be equalled by the revenue of the benefice, even though the holdings of the benefice from which the revenue accrued were located in another diocese. (3) An inadequate benefice could lawfully be supplemented by another benefice or by patrimony, but in the latter event the other conditions necessary for the use of patrimony as a title had to be verified.[81] (4) The benefice had to be adequate in its revenue after all certainly foreseen and definitely fixed expenses were taken out; extraordinary expenses, however, did not thus have to be taken into account.[82] Sometimes a pension had to be paid out of the revenues of a benefice. Manifestly it was only what was left that could be used for the sustenance of the cleric, and that residue had to be adequate for that purpose.[83]

[80] Gasparri, *De Sacra Ordin.*, I, n. 597; Many, *De Sacra Ordin.*, n. 137.

[81] The following doubt was proposed by the diocese of Guadalajara to the Sacred Congregation of the Council in 1589: " An clericus, alioquin idoneus, habens beneficium de per se insufficiens, sed, juncto patrimonio, habeat quod sufficiat ad honestam vitae sustentationem, possit promoveri "; the response, given on Oct. 24, 1589, was: " posse juxta formam Concilii, sess. XXI, cap. II." — Gasparri, *De Sacra Ordin.*, I, n. 598.

[82] Riganti, *Comment. in Reg. Cancell. Ap.*, *Reg. XXIV*, § III, n. 126.

[83] For a long time it was argued *pro* and *con* whether the stipends for obligatory Masses attached to the benefice could be considered as fixed expenses and therefore be deducted. Those defending the affirmative said that in the case of a long illness the beneficiary would have to pay out all such stipends to another priest, leaving insufficient revenue for himself. The negative defenders said that ordinarily a beneficiary profited by all his stipends; only extraordinarily would he be sick for a long time and the law did not take such emergencies into account. The Sacred Congregation of the Council settled the difficulty, after several replies to the diocese of Rimini,

d) The benefice had to be perpetual in character. This is not expressly stated in the Tridentine chapter under consideration,[84] but it is easily deducible from the purpose of the law, which was to insure every major cleric a permanent livelihood, and also from the regulation, to be cited below, that no cleric could ever resign a benefice unless he had another title to take its place. Some particular councils added perpetuity to the expressed conditions of this title,[85] and the Sacred Congregation of the Council in its interpretative responses frequently confirmed the same,[86] which was likewise the common opinion of authors.[87] By way of exception, if a cleric possessed a manual benefice, and the patron who held the right to remove the beneficiary agreed never to remove the cleric, the benefice could be considered as actually perpetual in character in the individual case if the Bishop prudently so judged.[88]

2°. Conditions for the resignation of a benefice held as a title of ordination

The Council of Trent stated the case in these words: " Id vero beneficium resignare non possit, nisi facta mentione quod ad illius beneficii titulum sit promotus; neque ea resignatio ad-

Italy, dated August 8 and 29, 1722, and May 15 and July 17, 1723, with the final response: "esse relinquendum arbitrio et conscientiae Ordinariorum."—*Thesaurus Resolutionum*, II, 213, 221, 309, 338. The Ordinaries thenceforward could settle such questions in each individual case or by diocesan decree.

[84] Sess. XXI, *de ref.*, c. 2.

[85] E.g., Council of Prague (a. 1346), cap. *De aetate & qualitate ad sacros ordines & curata beneficia promovendorum:* ". . . praelati . . . diligenter inquirant, . . . & utrum habeat perpetuum beneficium ecclesiasticum, vel sufficiens patrimonium volens ad sacros ordines promoveri . . ."—Mansi, XXVI, 78; Council of Mainz (a. 1549), cap. 81: ". . . Nec quisquam ordinandus recipiatur, nisi ad certum titulum ecclesiastici beneficii, quod sit perpetuum . . ."—Mansi, XXXII, 1430; Council of the Province of Gniezno, Poland (a. 1577), *Constitutionum Synodalium*, l. I, tit. *De temporibus ordinationum:* ". . . praelati . . . diligenter inquirant . . . utrum habeat perpetuum beneficium ecclesiasticum . . . volens ad sacros ordines promoveri";—Mansi, XXXVI Bis, Appen. I, 675; Provincial Synod of the Ruthenians (a. 1720), tit. III, cap. 7: ". . . Nullus praeterea saecularis ordinetur, qui non habeat titulum perpetuum sufficientis ecclesiae, . . ."—Mansi, XXXV Bis, 1502.

[86] Riganti, *Comment. in Reg. Cancell. Ap., Reg.* XXIV, § V, nn. 32-33.

[87] Many, *De Sacra Ordin.*, n. 137; Gasparri, *De Sacra Ordin.*, I, n. 600.

[88] Riganti, *op. et loc. cit.*, nn. 34-35.

mittatur, nisi constito quod aliunde vivere commode possit; et aliter facta resignatio nulla sit."[89] Hence for the validity of the resignation two things were necessary: a) in the act of resignation mention had to be absolutely and expressly made of the fact that the cleric was ordained to hold title to this benefice; and b) it had to be proved by authentic documents that the cleric had sufficient means from some other source on which he could live, e. g., from some other adequate benefice or from patrimony. This meant that the Bishop had to declare in an official written document that such and such patrimony or such and such a benefice was adequate for this cleric's future sustenance and that as Bishop he was now constituting the same as a new title of sacred ordination and was substituting it in place of the former title, now resigned. The necessity of these formalities was confirmed by many decisions of the Sacred Congregation of the Council and of other Sacred Congregations, which indicated the constant practice of the Roman Curia.[90]

B. Patrimony

1°. Origin and nature of it

When Pope Alexander III in the III General Council of the Lateran (a. 1179) issued the famous decree that any Bishop who ordained a cleric to the diaconate or priesthood without a certain title would have to support the same out of his own funds until the cleric obtained a title, unless, perchance, the

[89] Sess. XXI, *de ref.*, c. 2.

[90] Thus, to the proposed doubts: "1° An ordinatus ad titulum beneficii teneatur in illius resignatione individualiter exprimere se fuisse ad illius titulum ordinatum; 2° An haec individua expressio suppleatur per assertivam: *Forsan ordinatus;* 3° An constare debeat per probationes concludentes resignantem habere quo commode vivere possit; 4° An haec probatio censeatur adimpleta per solam confessionem juratam resignantis; 5° An resignans teneatur aliud beneficium habitum, vel alia bona subrogare beneficio resignato; 6° An haec subrogatio facienda sit per episcopi declarationem"; the Sacred Congregation of the Council, in *Lancianen.*, 9 Febr. 1726, replied: "Ad 1um affirmative; ad 2um negative, et ad mentem: mens fuit ut haec resolutio habeat locum in futuris resignationibus; ad 3um, 5um, et 6um affirmative; ad 4um negative."—*Thesaurus Resolutionum*, III, 271-3; Gasparri, *De Sacra Ordin.*, I, n. 608. For other decisions of S. C. C. cf. Monacelli, *Formularium*, ed. Romae (1713), t. I, p. 70, n. 2; t. II, p. 72, n. 18; t. IV, p. 80, n. 440. Cf. also S. C. de Prop. Fide, 1 sept. 1856 (reviewed in *Instructio de titulo S. Ordinationis*, 27 apr. 1871, n. 11)—*Collectanea S. C. P. F.*, n. 1369.

cleric had enough resources of his own or from his father's inheritance on which to live,[91] his Holiness did not intend to imply that thenceforward a secular cleric could be ordained *in sacris* without a benefice, provided only that he had enough patrimony for his own livelihood. Rather the intention was to penalize any Bishop for performing an absolute ordination, but to release the Bishop from the penalty if the one thus ordained had sufficient personal money to support himself. Ambiguous wording, however, gave rise to the aforesaid interpretation. Scarcely twenty years later, Stephen, Bishop of Tournay († 1203), writing to Pope Celestine III (or Innocent III), said: "Quidam etiam, quibus sunt propriae facultates, ut inde vivere possint, ordinari tamen expetunt, ut pro titulo, secundum dispensationem sacrorum canonum, rebus propriis utantur." [92] This showed that at that early date patrimony was already considered on the authority of the Church to take the place of a title.

A few years later, in 1208, Pope Innocent III permitted the Archbishop of Besançon to ordain rich clerics to sacred orders without a title, thus: "Tuis quaestionibus respondemus, quod clericos in minoribus ordinibus constitutos, de patrimonialibus bonis habentes, unde possint congrue sustentari, etsi nondum fuerint beneficium ecclesiasticum assecuti, dummodo aliud canonicum non obsistat, ad superiores poteris ordines promovere." [93] Soon patrimony was not only considered as taking the place of, but was actually being called, a title (*titulus patrimonii*), as though it were on exactly the same footing as the only true and proper title of benefice. Thus, in the Council of Beziers (a. 1233), canon 6 states: "Sine titulo patrimoniali centum solidorum Turonensium ad minus, vel ecclesiastico beneficio competenti, sicut in jure canonico cautum est, ordinandus de cetero nullatenus admittatur." [94]

[91] Cap. 5—Mansi, XXII, 220; c. 4, X, *de praebendis et dignitatibus*, III, 5.

[92] *Epist. 194 Ad papam—MPL*, CCXI, 477.

[93] C. 23, X, *de praebendis et dignitatibus*, III, 5.

[94] Mansi, XXIII, 271. The Glossa shows evidence of the same, for in interpreting the words "*sive possessionis*" of the sixth canon of the Council of Chalcedon, in c. 1, D. LXX, it incorrectly took them to mean "someone ordained for the title of patrimony," whereas "*possessio*" really meant "village."

In succeeding years the use of this title occasioned much harm for the Church, for the possession of wealth was confused with a divine vocation, since all candidates enjoying such wealth could easily be ordained *in sacris* with it as their title of ordination, and, not being bound to serve any definite church or place, as were those who had a residential benefice as their title, they became *vagi*, spending their lives in idleness, and involving themselves in many scandals.

The Council of Trent had to correct these abuses. Some Bishops wanted to abolish the title altogether and return to the discipline of the Council of Chalcedon. Others objected, for the reason that their people would be deprived of priests, because of the lack of church funds in the form of benefices; and so the fathers of the Council adopted the compromise of retaining patrimony as a title, but of restricting at the same time the liberty of Bishops to employ it as a title for ordination.[95] The pertinent texts are: "Patrimonium vero, vel pensionem obtinentes ordinari posthac non possint, nisi illi, quos episcopus judicaverit assumendos pro necessitate, vel commoditate ecclesiarum suarum . . ."; [96] and " . . . sancta Synodus, vestigiis sexti canonis Concilii Chalcedonensis inhaerendo, statuit, ut nullus in posterum ordinetur, qui illi ecclesiae, aut pio loco, pro cujus necessitate aut utilitate assumitur, non adscribatur, ubi suis fungatur muneribus, nec incertis vagetur sedibus. . . ." [97] These regulations were later renewed by Pope Innocent XI through an encyclical letter of the Sacred Congregation of the Council on May 13, 1679,[98] and by Pope Innocent XII in the Constitution "*Speculatores*" on Nov. 4, 1694.[99] Lest there be

[95] Theiner, *Acta Genuina SS. Oecumenici Conc. Trid.*, II, 565-6; Many, *De Sacra Ordin.*, n. 134.

[96] Sess. XXI, *de ref.*, c. 2.

[97] Sess. XXIII, *de ref.*, c. 16.

[98] "Deinde per has circulares litteras episcopis omnibus sanctissimum Tridentinum decretum in memoriam reduci mandavit, quatenus omnes illud sancte custodiant, sciantque non aliter ordinandum ad titulum patrimonii vel pensionis, nisi cum Ecclesiae necessitas vel commoditas id exigat: qua in re prudens episcopi timoratumque judicium servari debebit."—Riganti, *Comment. in Reg. Cancell. Ap.*, *Reg.* XXIV, § V, n. 109; Gasparri, *De Sacra Ordin.*, I, n. 596.

[99] N. 1—*Fontes*, n. 258.

any shadow of doubt about their continuance in effect, the Sacred Congregation of the Council was asked whether by virtue of certain Apostolic Briefs a cleric could be ordained for the title of patrimony as a solace to his parents, even though he would not be necessary or useful to the churches of his diocese, and the answer was "*Negative.*" [100]

From the language of the Tridentine ruling on this matter [101] it is apparent that patrimony was only a subsidiary title, which was to be used by way of dispensation, for: 1) it could be used only when the cleric had not an adequate benefice, and the expectation was that such a benefice would be substituted for it as soon as obtained (". . . atque illa deinceps sine licentia episcopi alienari, aut extingui, vel remitti nullatenus possint, donec beneficium ecclesiasticum sufficiens sint adepti; vel aliunde habeant unde vivere possint: antiquorum canonum poenas super his innovando."); [102] and 2) it could be used only when the Bishop judged that its possessor really answered to the necessity or utility of the churches in the diocese.

2°. Requisites for patrimony to be a legitimate title of ordination

a) It had to be truly and actually posesssed, as the Council of Trent expressly prescribed (". . . *eo quoque prius perspecto, patrimonium illud, vel pensionem vere ab eis obtineri . . .*").[103] Whenever the ordinand's patrimonial title was created out of his own goods there was no difficulty on this score. He merely designated which particular portion of his goods he wanted to donate to that sacred purpose, so that it could be kept separate and inalienable. When, however, it was the cleric's parents or even strangers who wished to constitute the sacred patrimony by a donation of their goods, it was a more difficult problem to

[100] Giraldi, *Expositio Iuris Pontificii*, II, sect. 55; Gasparri, *op. et loc. cit.*

[101] Sess. XXI, *de ref.*, c. 2.

[102] *Ibid.* This is likewise confirmed by frequent responses of S. C. C., e. g., *Sorana*, 26 ian. 1669, and *Camerinen.*, 4 aug., 1685—Monacelli, *Formularium*, tit. XIII, form. 3, n. 6 (t. II, p. 71).

[103] Sess. XXI, *de ref.*, c. 2.

determine whether or not the cleric could be said to be truly and actually in possession of the title. Explaining this, the Sacred Congregation of the Council, in 1573, said the donation had to be "*vere, absque ulla fraude, et in forma juris valida.*" This excluded any patrimony which was false, fictitious, borrowed, null, unjust, or liable to restitution or to dissolution. Further explanation of what was meant by these is given by D'Annibale [104] as follows: Patrimony is *false* if it does not exist, i. e., if the goods or the documents assigning the same or the names of the donors are only imaginary; *fictitious*, if the goods really exist, but were not set aside with the intention of constituting a patrimony; *borrowed*, if the patrimony is constituted on the condition that later on all revenues ever received from it will be returned, or that the ordained cleric will not accept its revenues; *null*, if it is infected with invalidity for some reason, e. g., when it is given by an insane person; *unjust*, if its constitution did not observe the legal forms, e. g., if the donation was made by a private agreement only; *liable to restitution*, if the one constituting it was not free to do so, e. g., if he had not yet reached his majority or was under constraint of treachery or force; *liable to dissolution*, if changed circumstances would not allow it to continue, e. g., if the donor who was without heirs at the time of the patrimonial bestowal later acquired special obligations towards heirs.

From the way in which the Council of Trent [105] speaks of patrimony, namely, that it is not subject to alienation or extinction until an adequate benefice or other means of livelihood has been acquired by the cleric, it is apparent that alienation under proper conditions was legally possible. Hence it was entirely legitimate for patrimony to be constituted with the condition that the title was to be returned as soon as the possessor secured an adequate benefice.[106]

By the words "*eo quoque prius perspecto*" the Council placed on the Bishop the obligation of judging whether or not the

[104] *In Const. Apostolicae Sedis*, n. 144, not. 32.

[105] Sess. XXI, *de ref.*, c. 2.

[106] S. C. C., *Ravennaten.*, 19 iulii 1783—*Thesaurus Resolutionum*, LII (1783), 147-152. Cf. Many, *De Sacra Ordin.*, n. 139.

patrimony fulfilled the two specified conditions. In order to overcome all danger of fraud it was in his power to establish various other precautionary measures of his own determination, such as Pope Benedict XIV did when he was Archbishop of Bologna, e. g., to post in the parochial church a list of whatever goods were designated as patrimonial, or to have the ordinand and even additional witnesses swear to the existence and sufficiency of these goods.[107]

b) It needed to be adequate in its purpose of sustaining the cleric, which also was prescribed in the Tridentine ruling (". . . *taliaque esse, quae eis ad vitam sustentandam satis sint* . . ."). This meant that its annual revenues had to be equal in amount to the sum specified by the synodal tax or by the customary usage of the diocese wherein the cleric had his domicile, similarly as for the case in which a benefice constituted the title for ordination, and also that the adequacy of the patrimonial income had to be properly certified by appropriate documents.[108]

c) It was necessary that it be made up of definitely assured and naturally permanent goods, which would effectively continue to be available for the life-time of the cleric whose livelihood was being guaranteed by them. Hence, a patrimonial title for ordination could not be derived from such uncertain and insecure considerations as manual Mass stipends, from personal enterprise and industry on the part of a cleric, e. g., in the art

[107] Benedictus XIV, *Inst. Eccl.*, XXVI, nn. 20 ss.; Many, *op. cit.*, n. 140. An example of such an oath is given in the Provincial Synod of Cambrai, France (a. 1586), thus: "Ego N. juro, quod in acquisitione bonorum meorum patrimonialum, ad quorum titulum sum promovendus ad sacros ordines, nulla fraus aut dolus intercessit: quodque illa vere possideo, neque in posterum directe aut indirecte alienabo, nisi fuerit mihi de beneficio ecclesiastico aeque sufficienti provisum: quo casu id ipsum non faciam sine consensu mei episcopi, in litteris ipsius alienationis specialiter exprimendo: beneficium autem, quod in dicti tituli mei locum successerit, sine simili consensu non resignabo. Ita me Deus adjuvet, & haec sancta Dei evangelia."—Tit. X, cap. 4 (Mansi, XXXIV Bis, 1238).

[108] Honorante, *Praxis Secretariae Tribunalis*, cap. VIII, not. X. An example of the sum specified by the synodal tax is found in the I Provincial Council of Westminster in England (a. 1852), *Decreta*, cap. XXI, n. 5, where it is stated that in order to be adequate the title of patrimony had to furnish an annual income of 40 £ sterling—Mansi, XLIV, 741.

of painting or music, or from mortgaged possessions, unless the latter would still supply a sufficient surplus after the mortgage was retired in full.[109]

d) It was necessarily made up of immovable goods or their equivalent.[110] The former, bearing annual revenues, were preferable, because of their particularly stable character which guaranteed an assured income. The latter, however, sufficed. These latter consisted, for example, in governmental rentals, in private rentals which were founded on real immovable property, in a personal pledge of support from a donor which at the same time was made real by means of a mortgage raised on his goods in order to oblige his heirs as well,[111] or also in lay chaplaincies which were constituted permanently or at least for the life-time of their occupants.[112]

3°. Alienation of patrimony

The Council of Trent thus treats of the alienation of patrimony: ". . . atque illa [patrimonium et pensio] deinceps sine licentia episcopi alienari, aut extingui, vel remitti nullatenus possint, donec beneficium ecclesiasticum sufficiens sint adepti; vel aliunde habeant unde vivere possint: . . ." [113] From this there can be gathered two conditions as necessary for a valid alienation: (a) a new title, in the form of an adequate ecclesiastical benefice or of a new patrimony or pension, had to be acquired previous to the alienation; and (b) the permission of the cleric's Bishop had to be obtained. This was the tenor of many decisions of the Sacred Congregation of the Council in 1638, 1652, etc.,[114] even though the alienation had observed all the solemnities of

109 S. C. C., *Seguntina*, Oct. 1589—Garcia, *De Benef. Eccles.*, p. II, cap. V, n. 125; Honorante, *op. cit.*, cap. III, not. III.

110 S. C. C., *in Sypontina*, 29 nov. 1670—Pallottini, *Collectio Resolutionum S. C. Concilii*, XV, 6, n. 19.

111 S. C. C., 8 iun. 1704—Riganti, *Comment. in Reg. Cancell. Ap.*, Reg. XXIV, § V, n. 122; Benedictus XIV, *Inst. Eccl.*, XXVI, n. 11.

112 Benedictus XIV, *loc. cit.*

113 Sess. XXI, *de ref.*, c. 2.

114 Cf. Benedictus XIV, *Inst. Eccl.*, XXVI, nn. 28-29.

the civil law. All substitutions of titles had to be made by the authority of the Bishop, even when the cleric wished to exchange his patrimonial title for the title of benefice.[115] Likewise, without the consent of his Bishop, the cleric could not lease his patrimony, use it as security or bail, or otherwise change it.[116] Of the two stipulated conditions, however, the former was more important, for as long as the cleric had fulfilled the first, but not the second, his alienation of patrimony was valid, but unlawful.

C. Pension

1°. Origin and nature

This title made its official appearance for the first time in the Council of Trent.[117] It lay midway between a benefice and patrimony in its structural character. A pension was a sum of money which had to be paid annually out of the revenues of some foundation, whether ecclesiastical or lay. In the former case, when it was paid out of the revenues of a benefice, it was called an ecclesiastical pension; in the latter case, when it was paid out of the rents derived from a lay person's estate, it was called a lay pension. An ecclesiastical pension, when constituted in perpetuity by an episcopal decree as deriving from the revenues of a church and as due to be conferred on a cleric by canonical institution, did not differ from a benefice and was governed accordingly. The same, when it was constituted as deriving only temporarily from the revenues of a church, and when for a reasonable cause it was assigned to someone by the authority of the Superior, was a canonical pension, such as is spoken of here, and could be a title of ordination if it became a fixed arrangement for the lifetime of its possessor. A lay pension did not differ from patrimony and followed the same rules.[118]

[115] S. C. C., 14 feb. 1662; 12 iul. 1687; *in Oretana*, aug. 1604; *in Terracinen.*, 20 iul. 1619—Monacelli, *Formularium*, tit. III, form. 8, n. 1; tit. XIII, form. 3, n. 18. Cf. Gasparri, *De Sacra Ordin.*, I, n. 608.

[116] Gasparri, *op. et loc. cit.*

[117] Sess. XXI, *de ref.*, c. 2.

[118] Gasparri, *De Sacra Ordin.*, I, n. 593.

Practically the same as pension was the title of administration in Mexico. There, the faithful were bound to make certain determined offerings to the pastor on the occasion of various ecclesiastical functions, and these formed the dowry of the parochial benefice. A certain portion of this dowry, definitely determined by each diocese, had to be given to the priests who acted as assistants or coadjutors to the pastor in the parish. The assignment of a priest to this or that office, which gave him a quasi-part in the administration of the church, together with that priest's right to the aforesaid share, or pension, was called the title of administration. There was an immemorial custom in Mexico of ordaining to sacred orders for that title, and the Sacred Congregation of the Council sustained it.[119]

There is good reason to hold, too, that clerics anywhere who were assigned to a church and received a share of its revenues could likewise consider such an adjustment as a title of ordination under the name of a pension, as long as the various conditions were fulfilled.[120]

2°. Requisites for canonical pension to be a legitimate title of ordination

The Council of Trent placed the title of pension on the same level with that of patrimony ("*Patrimonium vero vel pensionem obtinentes* . . ."). Hence it was only a subsidiary title, which could not be used unless there was no benefice available, and even then only when the Bishop judged the cleric would be necessary or useful for his churches. Hence, too, it followed all the regulations just laid down for the legitimacy of patrimony as a title, and for the alienation of the same.

2. *Titles Contrary to Common Law*

After the Council of Trent no other new titles of ordination for diocesan clerics were incorporated in the common law. Any others which might arise would simply need Apostolic Indults to be used, since they would be exceptions to the law. As a

[119] In *Chiapensi,* 21 iun. 1879—*ASS,* XII (1879), 569; Gasparri, *op. cit.,* I, n. 607.

[120] Gasparri, *loc. cit.*

matter of fact, two classes of these, for secular clerics, actually did develop: the title of the mission (*titulus missionis*), in places subject to the jurisdiction of the Sacred Congregation for the Propagation of the Faith, and the title of the service of the church (*titulus servitii ecclesiae*) or of the service of the diocese (*titulus servitii dioecesis*) and other kindred ones, in non-missionary places which were not under the jurisdiction of the aforesaid Sacred Congregation. The supreme law for both these classes was the pontifical Indult by which they were conceded. From that alone could be learned the circumstances in which they could be used, the rights and obligations attached to them, and the length of time, or the number of cases, for which they were conceded.

In all other instances, where there were no canonical titles available, and where no pontifical Indult was conceded, a dispensation had to be sought from the Sacred Congregation of the Council, which usually contained the clause, " Ut episcopus curet meliori quo potest modo eorum sustentationi consulere, ne cum ordinis dedecore mendicare cogantur."

Two of these uncanonical titles must be examined more in detail because of their wide use, especially in the United States of America, namely, the title of the mission, and that of the service of the diocese.

A. Title of the Mission

1°. Its origin

Near the close of the sixteenth century Roman Institutes were founded for the propagation of the faith in mission countries. A total lack of benefices in these lands, as well as a lack of patrimony on the part of clerics willing to volunteer their priestly labor for the missions, necessitated some unusual step to be taken to guarantee the perpetual sustenance of such clerics before they assumed sacred orders. On April 22, 1579, the English College at Rome was erected, and, in the Bull of erection, Pope Gregory XIII granted it a series of privileges, including the following: " Eisdem alumnis, ut, de licentia protectoris ac dicti collegii rectoris consensu, et examine praecedente . . .

etiam absque suorum Ordinariorum literis dimissorialibus, ac sine aliquo beneficii vel patrimonii titulo . . . ad omnes, etiam sacros et presbyteratus ordines promoveri . . . libere et licite valeant, indulgemus . . ." [121]

Authors consider this the beginning of the "title of the mission." [122] The expression "*titulus missionis*," however, appeared for the first time in the Constitution "*Sacrosanctae*" of Pope Urban VIII, April 12, 1631, in which the use of that title was conceded for the students of the Irish College at Rome.[123] Later, the same Pope, Urban VIII, by the Constitution "*Ad uberes*" of May 18, 1638, extended the use of that same title to all the colleges subject to the Sacred Congregation for the Propagation of the Faith,[124] on the grounds that the alumni of these colleges could receive their sustenance from the voluntary offerings of the faithful in those missions to which they would devote their priestly labor. In the course of time even regions where the episcopal hierarchy was established received the Indult, e. g., the Bishops of the United States of America received it for various five-year periods,[125] as did also the Bishops of Canada, England, Scotland, and Ireland, at various times.[126] In fact, prior to 1908, it was the usual title for which the clergy in the United States of America were ordained.

The title of the mission might, therefore, be defined as the very right which clerics, ordained for that title, enjoy of receiv-

[121] *Bullarium Magnum*, II, 459.

[122] Wernz, *Ius Decretalium*, II, n. 91; Honorante, *Praxis Secretariae Tribunalis*, cap. XVII, p. 171.

[123] De Martinis, *Ius Pontificium de Prop. Fide*, P. I, t. I, p. 128; Many, *De Sacra Ordin.*, n. 145.

[124] *Bullarium Pontificium Sacrae Congregationis de Propaganda Fide*, Romae, 1839, I, 91; De Martinis, *op. et loc. cit.*, p. 173.

[125] Conc. Provin. Balt. III (a. 1837), *Decreta*, n. 1—Mansi, XXXIX, 349; Indultum S. C. de Prop. Fide, 3 oct. 1852—Mansi, XLIV, 680; *Conc. Plen. Balt. II. (a. 1866), Acta et Decreta*, tit. III, cap. II, n. 89. An appeal of the hierarchy in the United States to have the faculty for a twenty-year period was denied in favor of a shorter period in the General Instruction of S. C. de Prop. Fide, *De Decretis Concilii Corrigendis*, 24 ian. 1868, and in that Sacred Congregation's decree of the same date—*Conc. Plen. Balt. II. (a. 1866), Acta et Decreta*, p. cxxxix, n. 14, and p. cxlvii.

[126] Many, *op. cit.*, n. 145.

ing the necessaries of life from the ministry to which they have been, or will be, assigned in some particular mission.

2°. The required oath

a) *Its formula.* To make certain that the missions, from which clerics, ordained for this title, received their sustenance, would also be adequately served, the Holy See constantly required the *ordinandus titulo missionis* to take an oath, before he received the subdiaconate, that he would perpetually serve the mission for which he was, or would be, destined. This had been the practice for all the students of the Pontifical Colleges, and was clearly declared to be the law for all in the Instruction of the Sacred Congregation for the Propagation of the Faith *de titulo S. Ordinationis*, April 27, 1871, n. 8.[127] In order to keep uniformity, the following formula for this oath was prescribed:

> Ego N. Filius N. Dioecesis vel Vicariatus N. spondeo, et iuro, quod postquam ad Sacros Ordines promotus fuero, nullam Religionem, Societatem, aut Congregationem regularem sine speciali Sedis Apostolicae licentia, aut S. Congregationis de Propaganda Fide ingrediar, neque in earum aliqua professionem emittam.
>
> Voveo pariter et iuro, quod in hac Dioecesi, aut Vicariatu (vel in Missione cui S. Sedi vel S. Congregationi de Propaganda Fide me destinare placuerit),[128] perpetuo in divinis administrandis laborem meum ac operam, sub omnimoda directione et iurisdictione R. P. D. pro tempore Ordinarii, pro salute animarum impendam, quod etiam praestabo, si cum praedictae Sedis Apostolicae licentia Religionem, Societatem, aut Congregationem regularem ingressus fuero, et in earum aliqua professionem emisero.
>
> Item voveo, et iuro, me praedictum iuramentum, et eius obligationem intelligere, et observaturum. Sic me Deus adiuvet et haec Sancta Dei Evangelia.[129]

[127] *Collectanea S. C. P. F.*, n 1369; *Acta et Decreta Conc. Plen. Balt. III.*, Appendix, p. 207.

[128] The form in parenthesis was to be used by those who had not yet been attached to any mission.

[129] *Acta et Decreta Conc. Plen. Balt. III.*, Appendix, p. 209.

Not only was this oath to be taken before an official, such as the rector of the college or seminary, but a copy of it in the handwriting of the candidate was to be transmitted to the Bishop. The above Instruction was really given as a final answer to various appeals from the Bishops of the United States of America for liberal exceptions to the law. Among other things, the fathers of the I Provincial Council of St. Louis (a. 1855),[130] and those of the II Plenary Council of Baltimore (a. 1866),[131] had asked the Holy See to allow the title of the mission to be used here without the oath, since they felt this oath was acting as a deterrent on missionary vocations, and was no longer needed to accomplish its original purpose. A refusal of this petition was contained in the decree of the Sacred Congregation for the Propagation of the Faith, Jan. 24, 1868,[132] and was incorporated as well in the Instruction of 1871 just cited.

b) *Its Obligations.* From the wording of the formula of the oath and from interpretations and responses of the Sacred Congregation for the Propagation of the Faith it can be gathered that the ordinand thereby obliged himself: 1) Not to enter any regular Order without special permission of the Holy See or of the Sacred Congregation for the Propagation of the Faith. The reason for this was to let the Holy See judge, after hearing the views of the Ordinary of the locality, whether or not the necessity of the mission to which the cleric was attached was so great that he could not be spared, for the public good would always have to take precedence over the private.[133] It is quite probable that this provision was included in the oath to provide for the special needs of the United States of America, where the early Provincial Councils had complained of secular priests abandoning the missions to enter Religious Orders. 2) To devote his priestly labor perpetually to the salvation of souls in the diocese or vicariate to which he was assigned and under the complete

130 *Decreta*, n. 3—Mansi, XLVII, 313.

131 *Conc. Plen. Balt. II. (a. 1866), Acta et Decreta*, tit. V, cap. VIII, n. 323.

132 Cf. *Conc. Plen. Balt. II. (a. 1866), Acta et Decreta*, p. cxlvii.

133 Instructio S. C. de Prop. Fide, 27 apr. 1871, n. 10—*Collectanea S. C. P. F.*, n. 1369.

direction and jurisdiction of its Ordinary. Hence also without the special permission of the Holy See or of the Sacred Congregation for the Propagation of the Faith he could not transfer to another diocese or enter any Religious Congregation with only simple vows, since that would no longer be under his Ordinary's jurisdiction. Proof of this statement is afforded by the Instruction of the Sacred Congregation for the Propagation of the Faith of April 27, 1871, n. 13,[134] and by that same Sacred Congregation's responses to the Bishop of Natchez, Mississippi, on Feb. 4, 1873.[135] 3) To work perpetually for the salvation of souls in that same diocese or vicariate, even if by special permission he should later enter a Religious Order or Congregation. This is evident from the clause "*quod etiam praestabo etc.*" included in the oath. Hence, without an extra special permission of the Holy See he could not enter any Religious Institute which did not do missionary work in that same territory, and if he did enter such a Religious Institute he was to be dismissed.[136] 4) To go wherever he was sent by his Ordinary, even temporarily to another diocese, province, or religious community. This would be in accordance with his promise to be under the complete direction of his Ordinary, and it would not violate other parts of the oath, for he would not become incardinated in the other diocese, but only lent to it, and he would not take any vows in the religious community. Hence the Bishop could recall such a cleric at any time and, conversely, the cleric could petition a recall.

c) *Its Partial Relaxation.* As indicated in the formula of the oath, the territory to which an ordinand obliged himself for life was a single diocese or vicariate.[137] In England all dioceses

[134] *Loc. cit.*

[135] Ad 4um et 5um—*Collectanea* S. C. P. F., n. 1400; *Acta et Decreta Conc. Plen. Balt. III.*, Appendix, pp. 209-211.

[136] Declaratio S. C. de Prop. Fide, 8 apr. 1661, n. 4: ". . . Quod si alumni religionem aliquam ingredi voluerint, quae huic muneri [missionum] minime vacet, vel, quantumvis vacaverit, aut munia in fundatione collegii praescripta in ea exercere, aut nationibus quibus se devoverunt prodesse non concedatur, aequum prorsus erit ut ab ea excludantur."—*Collectanea* S. C. P. F. (1893), n. 361.

[137] *Acta et Decreta Conc. Plen. Balt. III.*, nn. 60-61.

formed a single ecclesiastical province. Its Bishops, therefore, sought and obtained from the Holy See a relaxation from the oath to the extent that it would oblige the ordinand to stay perpetually in the province rather than in just one diocese.[138] A few months later, the Archbishop of Baltimore, acting in the name of all the Bishops of the United States of America, sought and obtained a similar relaxation.[139] This made it possible for clerics, ordained after 1885 for the title of the mission in England or in the United States, to be excardinated and incardinated into another diocese of the same province without either taking a new oath or having recourse to the Holy See for permission, but solely by having a new title of the mission conferred upon them with the consent of both their former and their new Bishops. Those already ordained for the title of the mission prior to 1885 were also enabled to change dioceses within the province without recourse to the Holy See, but they had to take the new oath of service to the province, as well as have a new title conferred on them.

3°. Nature of the " title of the mission "

a) *It was extraordinary.* This follows from the fact that it was contrary to the common law, and was allowed by special Apostolic Indult only in those places where the common law on titles could not be observed, because of the lack of canonical ones, and where there was urgent need, nevertheless, of clerics in sacred orders. To make use of the Indult in an individual case when a canonical title was at hand, was lawful, indeed, but not expedient. Grave warning was given by the Holy See that even where the Indult obtained, it was to be used only sparingly, not for every candidate who sought the missionary field, for, it said, if St. Paul's admonition " *manus nemini cito imponendae* " was true in general, it certainly applied with greater force with respect to those who were assuming the arduous task of an apostle. Hence, it was to be used only in favor of those who,

[138] Decr. S. C. de Prop. Fide, 18 aug. 1885—*Collectanea* S. C. P. F., n. 1640.

[139] Decr. S. C. de Prop. Fide, 30 nov. 1885—*Collectanea* S. C. P. F., n. 1641; *Acta et Decreta Conc. Plen. Balt. III.*, p. civ.

by good natural qualities, by docility, by uprightness of intention, by aptitude for learning, by progress in sacred studies, by integrity of moral character, and by contempt of worldly things, gave promise of becoming zealous preachers of the gospel; and the responsibility for observing this warning was left squarely on the conscience of the clerics' Superior.[140] Though the use of the title of the mission was granted for a term of years, Bishops were exhorted as far as possible to introduce other canonical titles in its place.[141]

b) *It could be lost.* While a cleric ordained for this title received thereby a right to be sustained from the voluntary offerings at his mission, he lost that right if he became unworthy of exercising the sacred ministry, just as the possessor of a benefice could be punished for a crime by being deprived of his benefice. That was the burden of a response of the Sacred Congregation for the Propagation of the Faith to the Bishop of Natchez, Mississippi, on Feb. 4, 1873, ad 1um, wherein to the question: " Utrum et quomodo declarandum sit, sacerdotes titulo missionis ordinatos, qui se indignos reddiderunt sacri ministerii exercendi, hoc titulo privari; neque Ordinarium teneri ad sustentationem illis praebendam "; the Sacred Congregation replied: " In casu, prout exponitur, praevia declaratione eiusmodi Sacerdoti ab Episcopo facienda, et quamdiu praedictus Sacerdos in sua prava vivendi consuetudine perseveret, nullum exhibens sincerae resipiscentiae signum, Episcopum non teneri ad sustentationem illi praebendam. Seiunctim autem a resolutione dubiorum per epistolam significetur Ordinario (eidem Episcopo), ut ad dictam declarationem non deveniat, nisi postquam paternis ac repetitis monitis eiusmodi Sacerdotem ad resipiscendum frustra invitaverit, atque de eius criminibus et publica diffamatione probationes certas etiam extraiudicialiter conquisitas sibi comparaverit, quas in casu recursus exhibere valeat Sacrae Congregationi." [142]

[140] Instructio S. C. de Prop. Fide, 27 apr. 1871, nn. 6-7—*Collectanea* S. C. P. F., n. 1369; *Acta et Decreta Conc. Plen. Balt. III.*, pp. 206-7.

[141] Instructio S. C. de Prop. Fide, *ibid.*, n. 14.

[142] *Collectanea* S. C. P. F., n. 1394; *Acta et Decreta Conc. Plen. Balt. III.*, pp. 209-211.

In other words, the privation of title was not immediate. First, a warning had to be given by the Bishop to the delinquent priest; and, if he remained contumacious and unrepentant, the Bishop was released from the obligation of providing him support. However, the Bishop was advised not to be satisfied with one warning, but to make frequent paternal appeals to the unfortunate man, and to fortify himself with unchallengeable proofs of the delinquent's misdeeds and public disrepute, even if these proofs were obtained extrajudicially, so that he would have something to show if the case would ever be taken to Rome.

c) *It could be supplanted.* Since the title of the mission was an extraordinary title, it not only could, but also had to be supplanted as soon as possible by a canonical title; but permission of the Holy See was required for that substitution, for it presupposed a release from the oath. The same was true if a cleric was deprived of the title by his Ordinary. The one so stripped of his title did not become suspended, but was to be compelled by the Ordinary to substitute another legitimate title in its place,[143] unless there were no other titles available, in which case this particular ruling of the Instruction did not apply.[144] Whenever missionaries relinquished their positions, they of course lost the title of that mission which they had served, and, if they took up the same work in another mission field, they had to get the title of the new mission conferred on them by the authority of the Holy See; [145] but, after 1885, priests in the United States of America could supplant their mission title with another in the same province without having to approach the Holy See.

[143] S. C. de Prop. Fide, instr., 27 apr. 1871, n. 11—*Collectanea S. C. P. F.*, n. 1369; *Fontes*, n. 4878.

[144] S. C. de Prop. Fide (Natchez), 4 feb. 1873, ad 2um—*Collectanea S. C. P. F.*, n. 1394; *Fontes*, n. 4881.

[145] S. C. de Prop. Fide, instr., 27 apr. 1871, n. 13—*Collectanea S. C. P. F.*, n. 1369; *Fontes*, n. 4878.

B. Title of Service of the Church or Diocese

1°. Origin and history

When the Constituent Assembly in France (a. 1789) overthrew the constitution, and, in the Declaration of the Rights of Man, proclaimed freedom of worship, "all superfluous treasures of the Church were confiscated for the good of the country, and as still greater financial resources were needed, the whole of the Church property was, on the motion of Talleyrand, Bishop of Autun, placed at the disposal of the nation." [146] From this alienation of the material goods of the Church was born a serious problem—how to sustain the clergy of the nation without endangering the decency due their clerical state. Ecclesiastical law required every aspirant to sacred orders to have a title, and expected every Bishop to ordain as many clerics as would be needed or at least would be useful in his churches. Yet, in France at the close of the eighteenth century, canonical titles were scarcely existent, and still the many parochial churches could not be allowed to languish without spiritual ministrations. In such an urgent necessity the Bishops, from the time of the Concordat in 1801, began on their own authority a custom of ordaining to sacred orders without any title as many clerics as they thought would be necessary or useful to their dioceses.[147] Later, the Holy See kindly granted them the permission to dispense from the Tridentine law concerning titles of ordination whenever they saw fit.[148] At the same time they were warned that, if available, the canonical titles of patrimony or pension should be used. Previously the civil law, entitled "*Articles Organiques,*" on April 8, 1802,[149] had made that course very difficult, by prohibiting the Bishops from conferring sacred orders on anyone unless he could prove that he had patri-

[146] Funk, *A Manual of Church History,* II, § 198.

[147] Many, *De Sacra Ordin.,* n. 146.

[148] Provinc. Counc. of Soissons (a. 1849), *Decreta,* tit. X, cap. II—Mansi, XLIII, 594; Prov. Counc. of Bordeaux (a. 1850), *Decreta,* tit. III, cap. VII, n. 1—Mansi, XLIV, 87.

[149] Art. 26.

mony with an annual revenue of 300 francs.[150] Various dioceses in their statutes expressed the Bishops' contempt for that civil law by determining on a synodal tax which was considerably less than the one the state had required, even less than what was actually necessary for sustenance, in order to have some semblance of a title of ordination. Likewise, because of the danger of destitution in old age for those who were ordained without titles, the provincial councils asked that there be started and maintained in every diocese a separate ecclesiastical fund or treasury for the express purpose of taking care of major clerics in sickness and in the extremities of old age.[151]

Clerics who were ordained without a title were usually kept in the seminary at diocesan expense until they reached the priesthood, whereupon the Bishop assigned them to some sacred office, such as that of parochial assistant or chaplain, whence they could easily derive a livelihood, and they were not removed from that office without being assigned to another in its place. Since the dioceses in France were large, there was a sufficient number of such offices in every diocese so that the Bishop could readily assign one to every priest. Hence, a priest in his youthful and active years was guaranteed a livelihood, at least from the diocese as a whole, instead of from one church or particular foundation. When he grew ill or feeble and was unable to fill an office, his support until death was provided for either by a government pension or by a regular allowance from an established ecclesiastical fund. Since, then, the Bishop of the diocese was standing responsible for his cleric throughout life, the cleric, though ordained without a canonical title, could really be said to possess an uncanonical one at least, which might be termed the *title of service of the church or diocese.*

Elsewhere, too, similar plans were used to guarantee the clerics' livelihood. Thus, there was the custom in Mexico, declared in 1879 to be immemorial, and approved by the Sacred Congregation of the Council, by which the clergy were assigned to sacred

[150] This was revoked by Napoleonic decree, Feb. 24, 1810, art. 2—Many, *De Sacra Ordin.*, n. 147.

[151] Many, *op. et loc. cit.*

offices by their Bishop and in turn received a right to share in a portion of moneys contributed on the occasion of various spiritual ministrations at the parochial churches where they served.[152] Though called the *title of administration*, this did not differ in any essential from the title of *service of the church or diocese*, and in its origin dates from about the same time that the latter made its appearance in France.

Prior to the Vatican Council (a. 1869-1870), a questionnaire was sent out to the Bishops of the world, seeking their views on what disciplinary matters needed to be discussed or changed. In reply to the questions how that Tridentine Law which required the assignment of every cleric to a definite church [153] was being observed, and whether or not it should be changed, half of the Bishops of the world replied that in modern times that type of assignment was impractical, gravely inconvenient, and often impossible, and that they were better supplying the needs of their churches by requiring every major cleric to serve within the diocese, and particularly to fulfill whatever office or position would be temporarily assigned to him.[154] As a result, in the scheme of constitutions to be proposed for the examination of the fathers of the Council there was contained [155] the recommendation that, wherever the canonical titles of benefice, patrimony, and pension were lacking, there should be allowed the use of patrimony which did not meet all the canonical requirements, as long as it was judged adequate; and if even that could not be obtained, Bishops should be authorized to ordain for the title of " service of their own diocese or church," and to provide for those so ordained an ecclesiastical office by means of which they could be decently supported. No action was taken on this at the Council, but the recommendation received practical recognition.[156] Thus, the Plenary Council of Latin

[152] S. C. C., *Chiapensi*, 21 iun. 1879—*ASS*, XII (1879), 569; cf. *supra*, p. 139.

[153] Sess. XXIII, *de ref.*, c. 16.

[154] *Summarium responsorum ab episcopis datorum de gravioribus disciplinae ecclesiasticae capitibus in concilio tractandis*, Quaestio IX—Mansi, XLIX, 349-357.

[155] Cap. III, n. 14, *De titulis ordinationum*—Mansi, LIII, 746-7.

[156] Peries, " Titulus Ordinationis,"—*AER*, XIII (1895), 353.

America (a. 1900) mentioned the title of service of the Church as being sufficient and legitimate for that region.[157] Moreover, when on June 29, 1908, Pope Pius X by his Constitution "*Sapienti Consilio*" withdrew from subjection to the Sacred Congregation for the Propagation of the Faith the countries of England, Scotland, Ireland, Holland, Canada, Newfoundland, and the United States of America,[158] and placed them under the common law, the question arose as to what title of ordination should then be used in these countries, and which Sacred Congregation would have competence over them. The Sacred Congregation of the Consistory, on November 12, 1908,[159] replied that it itself would be competent for them, and that in place of the title of the mission they were thenceforth to use the title of service of the Church. The decision of Pope Pius X to this effect was conveyed to the Apostolic Delegate in the United States of America by an Indult through the Papal Secretary of State on January 2, 1909.[160] Accordingly, even wherever clerics had already received sacred orders for the title of the mission in this country they were to have it changed into the new title of service of the Church.

2°. Nature

a) *Difference between it and the title of the mission.* It is difficult to find any fundamental difference between this title and that of the mission. In both the cleric had a right to receive sustenance from the voluntary oblations of the people in the

[157] *Acta et Decreta Concilii Plenarii Americae Latinae in Urbe Celebrati A. D. 1899*, Decreta, tit. V, De Sacramentis, cap. VII, n. 582: "Secluso speciali indulto, nemo ad sacros Ordines promoveri potest nisi titulo *ecclesiastico* vel *patrimoniali* de honesta sustentatione provisus sit. In nostris autem regionibus sufficit titulus administrationis seu ministerii sive *servitii Ecclesiae*, iuxta Decretum Sacrae Congregationis Concilii, diei 21 Junii, 1879, quod in Appendice inserendum jussimus." Cf. *ASS*, XII (1879), 569-576.

[158] § 1, 6°, n. 2—*Fontes*, n. 682; *AAS*, I (1909), 12.

[159] *AAS*, I (1909), 148-152.

[160] "In risposta alla sua lettera del 14 Decembre teste decorso, N. 420-d., mi reco a premura di significare alla S. V. Illm̃a, che il Santo Padre ha stabilito, che d'ora innanzi, in tutti codesti Stati Uniti d'America Settentrionale, i Chierici promovendi al Suddiaconato sieno ordinati "titulo servitii ecclesiae" anziche "titulo missionis" come fu fatto finora."—*AER*, XL (1909), 329.

office or mission where he labored; in both, too, there was the absence of any perpetual foundation with an annual yield to serve as the cleric's absolute guarantee of sustenance. The one important difference was that the title of service of the Church or diocese was introduced in a country only after a native clergy was well established, so that, though those who were ordained for it had to be content with a fluctuating income from a voluntary source, the field where they were laboring was ordinarily the diocese of their origin or domicile, whereas those ordained for the title of the mission were understood to be leaving their home to labor for life in foreign fields. The latter was naturally a more rigorous and self-sacrificing form of service, and called for an oath perpetually to remain on the mission, in order to bolster up the will-power of the candidate as well as to protect the mission from being abandoned; but there was not the same need for an oath in the case of the cleric who was destined to serve the diocese in which he had his domicile at the time of his ordination.

b) *It was an extraordinary title,* since it originated from an almost entire lack of canonical ones, and was not permitted for any country except by special Indult, such as that extended to the Bishops of the United States of America.[161] Hence, as soon as a diocese which employed this title could again avail itself of canonical titles it would have to discontinue the use of this extraordinary title.

c) *No special oath was required.* As just noted above in *a,* there was not the same reason for exacting an oath as there was in the case of the mission title. Among other questions, submitted to the Sacred Consistorial Congregation after the Constitution "*Sapienti Consilio,*" it was asked if the students of the Roman Colleges of those countries which had been removed from the jurisdiction of the Sacred Congregation for the Propagation of the Faith would still have to take the oath of the mission, and if the students of the same countries attending the Urban College for the Propagation of the Faith would have to take it, and the answer on November 12, 1908, was that they would still

[161] *Loc. cit.*

have to take an oath, but that a new formula would be prepared and published.[162] Yet, less than a year later, when it was asked if the clerics of the United States of America who were being promoted to sacred orders for the title of service of the Church would have to take an oath binding themselves to the service of their own church or diocese, the response was: " Negative, nisi ad id adigantur in casibus a iure communi praescriptis; facta tamen obligatione alumnis, qui gratuito in bonum dioecesis aluntur, promissionem scriptam emittendi, sese fideliter inservituros esse propriae dioecesi." [163]

d) *The rights it conferred.* Since a Bishop who ordained clerics for this title was really ordaining without any canonical title, the old penal law of Pope Alexander III [164] applied, namely, that he himself would have to sustain them until they obtained a benefice, unless they had sufficient patrimony by which to live. Consequently he was their guarantee of a livelihood, and if he was unwilling or unable to assign them to an ecclesiastical office, he had to give them enough on which to live, unless they already had sufficient of themselves.[165]

e) *It could be lost.* The right of the cleric to sustenance was part of an implicit quasi-contract in which the Bishop assumed the obligation of sustaining the cleric and the cleric assumed a similar obligation of exercising his sacred ministry in the diocese. Hence, if the cleric, by any grave fault of his own, rendered himself incapable or unworthy of the sacred ministry, he violated his part of the contract, and thereby automatically released the Bishop from the other. The same did not happen when clerics, through no fault of their own, but by sickness, accident, invalidity, or old age, became incapable of working, because these eventualities were in the very nature of things, and, hence, were foreseen and included in the contract, so that the Bishop was still bound to provide such clerics support.[166] If the contract

[162] *AAS*, I (1909), 148-152; *Fontes*, n. 2056.

[163] S. C. Consist., 6 aug. 1909—*AAS*, I (1909), 687; *Fontes*, n. 2061.

[164] C. 4, X, *de praebendis et dignitatibus*, III, 5.

[165] Many, *De Sacra Ordin.*, n. 148.

[166] Many, *op. et loc. cit.*

was broken by the cleric's fault, the Bishop could not act too arbitrarily, but had to follow the instructions as to procedure given by the Sacred Congregation for the Propagation of the Faith in similar losses of the mission title,[167] by giving repeated warnings, by using many paternal admonitions, and finally, by providing himself with documentary proof of the cleric's misdeed.

f) *It could be supplanted.* When a cleric who had been ordained for this title sought to be excardinated from his diocese into another, there was need for the substitution of a new title of service of the Church or of the diocese, because the effective achievement of such an intention implied a quasi-contract with a new Bishop. But, since the absence of an oath precluded all need of dispensation from it, such a substitution could be effected by the two Bishops concerned.

ARTICLE IV

METHODS AND REQUISITES FOR THE EXCARDINATION AND INCARDINATION OF DIOCESAN CLERICS

So involved is the interlinking of this specific phase of the general subject of this study with that of proper Bishops for ordination, of ordination titles, and of the obligation of residence on the part of clerics, that it seemed a distinct advantage to compile, for clarity's sake, accompanying schedules of the interrelations of all these, coördinated both as to periods of history and as to grades of orders. The subject matter of this article follows the chronological order of the schedules, a parallel study of which will assist the reader, it is hoped, in finding the way through this canonical labyrinth.[168]

1. *Ancient Period (Prior to 1100)*

A. Minor and Major Clerics

A young man initiated into the clerical state by his sole proper Bishop, namely the proper Bishop by reason of the can-

[167] *Supra*, pp. 146-147.

[168] These coördinated schedules are to be found at the end of the historical section of this work, viz., pp. 263 to 284.

didate's origin or original domicile, belonged to that Bishop for the rest of his life, and in obedience to the same spent all his days in the one church or pious place to which he was assigned at the very first ordination. Every religious place in the Bishop's territory needed the services of clerics, but in every place also there were native men willing to come forward and offer themselves as candidates for the clerical state in order to perform those services. Hence there seemed little need for intra-diocesan, much less extra-diocesan, transfers of the clergy.[169] However, it so happened that occasionally a city or territory was captured by infidels and its clergy was forced to leave. These clerics then had to be distributed among other dioceses, perhaps only for a while, but sometimes also for life. Not infrequently, too, as years went on, a Bishop was in need of one or more clerics in a certain grade of orders, and these he sought from a neighboring Bishop. The result was the canonical transfer of the clerics.

The only way in which a canonical transfer could take place was by means of letters from the first Bishop committing the cleric perpetually to the second Bishop and at the same time authorizing the second Bishop to confer all future orders on the candidate whenever he would judge it proper. The reason for the authorization to ordain was founded in the fact that there was, as already noted, only the one proper Bishop for the ordination of any cleric, i. e., the Bishop of the cleric's place of origin. Though the receiving Bishop eventually acquired the cleric as his own, he still depended on the first Bishop for his authority to raise this cleric to higher orders. For that reason these letters were called " dimissorial " (*litterae dimissoriae*), but, unlike the temporary authorization to confer one or several orders in the present day (also known as *litterae dimissoriae*), these letters were perpetual. From various characteristics they also received the names of: *commendatitiae,* because they recommended the morals and life of the cleric; *formatae,* because their wording followed a general formulary; *canonicae,* because they were authoritative and legal; or *reverendae,* because they usually com-

[169] The migrations of clerics from church to church which were forbidden in so many early councils applied in many instances to changes attempted within the diocese without the Bishop's authorization.

menced with the title "*Reverendo*" or "*Reverendissimo*" before the name of the addressee.

An example of these *litterae dimissoriae perpetuae*, illustrative of their proper contents and form, was published by the Bishops of the Council of Nicaea (a. 325) and was incorporated in the Decree of Gratian as a model for later centuries.[170] Accordingly, in the councils of the period one reads that it was forbidden for any cleric to transfer to another diocese without the "letters," the "concession," or the "permission" of his Bishop, all of which expressions meant *dimissoriae*.[171]

To overcome the possibility of fraud there was adopted at the same Council of Nicaea a system by which Bishops could be assured of the genuinity of the letters presented to them by alien clerics through a series of Greek alphabetic characters in-

[170] "Sanctissimo in Christo fratri summa dulcedine karitatis amplectendo A., illius civitatis episcopo, Υ., illius ecclesiae presul, perpetuae beatitudinis optat in Christo salutem. Ω. Υ. Α. Ω. De cetero noverit sancta fraternitas vestra, quod iste clericus, Hermannus nomine, nostra in parrochia instructus ac detonsus, parvitatem nostram rogavit, quatinus illi commendaticias litteras conscriberemus, quibus vestrae celsitudini commendatus sub tuitione vestri regiminis degere posset; cuius voluntati consentientes secundum canonicam auctoritatem litteras ei dimissorias dedimus, per quas et ipsi concedimus, ut sub vestro magisterio divinae servituti insistens suae deserviat utilitati, et vobis licentiam tribuimus, ut, si dignum eum iudicaveritis, ad sacros ordines promoveatis. Commendatum ergo eum curae vestrae suscipite, et nostris ex partibus absolutum in vestrarum ovium numero custodite. Quas litteras, ut vigore veritatis firmatae indubitanter a vobis suscipiantur, litteris grecis, ut canonica docet auctoritas, confirmare sategimus. Sancta Trinitas vestram beatitudinem ad regimen sanctae suae ecclesiae perpetualiter bene valere concedat, Ἀμήν. —C. 2, D. LXXIII.

[171] E. g., I Council of Carthage (a. 348), c. 5: "Ut statuatis non licere clericum alienum ab aliquo suscipi sine litteris episcopi sui, neque apud se retinere."—Mansi, III, 155; c. 6, D. LXXI; III Counc. of Carthage (a. 397), c. 21: "Clericum alienum, nisi concedente ejus episcopo, nemo audeat vel retinere vel promovere in ecclesia sibi credita."—Mansi, III, 883; c. 2, D. LXXII; Counc. of Tours (a. 460), c. 11: "Si quis vero clericus, absque episcopi sui permissu derelicta ecclesia sua, ad alium se transferre voluerit locum, alienus a communione habeatur."—Bruns, *Canones apostolorum et conciliorum saec. IV-VII* (Berolini, 1839), II, 141; V Counc. of Orange (a. 549), c. 5: "Ut nullus clericum seu lectorem alienum, sine sui cessione pontificis, vel promovere vel sibi quibuslibet conditionibus audeat vindicare."—Mansi, IX, 129-130; VI Counc. of Paris (a. 829), lib. I, cap. 36: "Priscis temporibus, quando jura canonum suum servabant vigorem, nullus clericorum parochiam suam, in qua divinae militiae devinctus erat, relinquere, et ad aliam sine episcopi sui commendatitiis litteris et epistolis, quas mos canonicus formatas appellat, audebat quoquomodo pergere."—Mansi, XIV, 561-2.

corporated in the document, each of which had a special significance. The protection lay either in the fact that the characters were kept secret among the Bishops alone, or in the fact that they had to be written in a Bishop's own hand.[172]

One of the Greek characters signified the name of the Bishop to whom the letters were addressed, and another the city in which he was located. In other words, there were no *dimissoriae* issued to a cleric without his definite destination being known, lest he become " a lost and wandering sheep." This meant that a request first had to be received from another Bishop for a named or unnamed cleric.[173] It also signified that whenever the request for *dimissoriae* came from the cleric himself he already had an understanding with the Bishop to whom

[172] For fuller discussion cf. Hallier, *De Sacris Elect. et Ordin.*, P. II, sec. V, cap. III, art. X,—*MTC*, XXIV, 1035 ss.

[173] An example of such a request was the one received by Bishop Aeneas of Paris from Hincmar, Bp. of Rheims, for a cleric named Berno: " Hincmarus nomine, non merito, Remorum episcopus, ac plebis Dei famulus, dilecto fratri et venerabili episcopo Aeneae salutem. Nostri fratres de monasterio S. Dionysii per licentiam domini abbatis H. Ludovici, ad educandum etque erudiendum commiserunt mihi quemdam adolescentem nomine Bernonem, quem vestra fraternitas acolythum ordinavit, propterea quoniam sine vestra licentia eum nolumus in nostra Ecclesia diuturno tempore immorari, petimus dilectionem vestram, ut de illo nobis litteras canonicas faciatis, quatenus eum in Ecclesia nostra possimus regulariter ordinare."—Hallier, *ibid.*, n. 8—*MTC*, XXIV, 1045. In the I Council of Carthage (a. 348), c. 5, it is stated that an alien cleric was not to be received or retained without the letters of his Bishop, " sed si forte erit necessarius ordinationi ut de vicino homo sit necessarius, petat a collega suo, et concessum habeat."—Mansi, III, 155; c. 6, D. LXXI; in the epistle of Pope Innocent I (a. 402) to Bishop Victricius: " Ut de aliena ecclesia clericum ordinare nullus usurpet, nisi ejus episcopus precibus exoratus concedere voluerit."—Mansi, III, 1034; c. 2, D. LXXI; by Pope Leo I, epist. 82 [84] to Anastasius of Thessalonica, cap. 9: " ut alienum clericum invito episcopo ipsius nemo suscipiat, nemo sollicitet, nisi forte ex placito charitatis id inter dantem accipientemque conveniat."—Hallier, *De Sacris Elect. et Ordin.*, P. II, sec. V, cap. III, art. X, n. 7 (*MTC*, XXIV, 1044-45). Likewise, it appears that Simplicianus, a holy Roman priest, was given by Pope Damasus at the request of St. Ambrose; also that a legation was sent by Bishop Aurelius of Carthage and the other Bishops of Africa to Pope Anastasius and to Venerius, Bishop of Milan, asking that they aid the Church of Africa, which at the time was laboring under a shortage of clerics; and that it was probably in answer to that appeal that Paulinus, the lector of Milan, who wrote the life of St. Ambrose, was sent to Carthage, where he was made a deacon by Fortunatus, and where he wrote also the life of St. Augustine—Hallier, *op. et loc. cit.*

he wished to go.[174] However, even if the request came from a Bishop, no cleric was given *dimissoriae* against his own will, since the transfer of a cleric was like the adoption of a child, wherein the will of the child had to be considered.[175]

Though the Bishop of the cleric's place of origin was the only competent authority to issue these *dimissoriae*, it sometimes happened that the incardinating Bishop who received the cleric later reconceded the same to a third Bishop, in which case he passed on also his committed authority to ordain the subject. An example of this is found in the *dimissoriae* issued in the year 768 by Luitadus, Bishop of Vinchy, to Wenilo, Archbishop of Rouen, in which he reconceded a deacon, Wlfadus, who had formerly been committed to him by Ebbo, Bishop of Rheims.[176]

[174] The example given above (cf. footnote 170) is an illustration of this, as is also the case of the following *dimissoriae* of Durandus, Bishop of Auvergne, to Rodulfus, Archbishop of Tours: "Comperiat dilectio vestra quod hic praesens subdiaconus, quem manu propria consecravimus misericorditer formatam a nobis expetit epistolam, et omnem auctoritatem canonicam, sicut inter dantem et accipientem fieri oportet; quatenus hac auctoritate securus, jure vestrae ditioni subjici valeret. Cujus petitionibus annuentes, mittimus nobilitati vestrae hanc epistolam canonica institutione formatam, ut quem sanctitatis vestrae amodo custodiae rogando committimus, cum libera nostra concessione ad quodcumque officium, seu ad quemcumque gradum visum fuerit, promoveatis, et omnem quam erga eum hactenus potestatem nobis licuit exercere, sit vobis licitum. Et ut nullus in vestro animo scrupulus haesitationis remaneat, ea signa quae sancti patres in Nicaeno concilio statuere in ejusmodi epistolis scribendis, in primis et ultimis annotavimus."—Hallier, *op. et loc. cit.* (*MTC*, XXIV, 1048). It is likewise a conclusion from the Synod of Rome (a. 826), c. 18: "Episcopus subiecto sibi sacerdoti, vel alii clerico, nisi ab ipso postulatus, dimissorias non faciat, ne quis quasi perdita aut errans inveniatur."—C. 1, D. LXXII. Note that the Glossa renders this passage "*ab alio postulatus*," and interprets it to be the request of the receiving Bishop.

[175] Thus Pope Gregory the Great refused to consecrate Florentine, a Roman subdeacon, as Bishop of Naples against his own will, and also recalled to his original diocese of Syracuse a subdeacon, named Cosmas, who was not satisfied with the place where he had been sent.—Hallier, *op. et loc. cit.* (*MTC*, XXIV, 1044).

[176] Π. Υ. Α. Reverendissimo et sanctissimo Patri Weniloni Rothomagensi archiepiscopo, Luitadus Vinciensis episcopus, aeternam in Domino salutem. Optarem, valde, si nobis spatia terrarum sinerent, fraternum et amicissimum vobiscum habere colloquium, atque de nostris communibus opportunitatibus tractare; sed quia id prolixitas itineris denegare videtur, vestram sanctitatem humiliter exoro ut mei memoriam coram sancto altari habere dignemini, vestraeque me commendare Ecclesiae, quoniam vestram charitatem jam in gremio Ecclesiae nostrae recepimus, et pro vobis quotidianis precibus Deum exoramus. Ceterum comperiat sanctitas vestra, quemdam fratrem nostrum, et filium Ecclesiae nostrae nomine Wlfadum subdiaconum, me petente, traditum mihi per litteras, quas ecclesiastica consuetudo formatas appellat, a vener-

B. Priests

The only point of difference in the transfer of a priest was the absence of any authorization to ordain. Here, then, were dimissorial letters (*litterae dimissoriae*) which were really and solely letters of excardination. The Bishops of the Council of Nicaea adopted a standard formulary for this also, and it is likewise to be found in the Decree of Gratian.[177]

abili Ebbone quondam Remensi archiepiscopo; et quia impendentibus quibusdam causis, postquam mihi traditus erat, in propria remansit Ecclesia, me suggerente, ordinavit eum idem Ebbo in gradu diaconatus. Nunc autem quia scitis eum propter causas necessarias in partibus vestris morari, sicut mihi commendatus erat, vobis eum committo, vestraeque custodiae et prudentiae delego, et ut ad majores gradus eum provehatis, suppliciter exoro; credimus enim quoniam et sapientia, et mores ad hoc dignum eum indicant. Commendamus igitur vestrae beatitudini, Ecclesiaeque vestrae, praefatum fratrem nostrum Wlfadum, et de profectu ejus petimus vos laetari in aeternum. At sicut mos ecclesiasticus est et inventum ac constitutum a trecentis decem et octo in Nicaena synodo episcopis, formatam epistolam facientes, ut in nomine sanctae et individuae Trinitatis nostrum opus largitionis et dimissionis hujus nostri dilecti fratris roboratum fructuosius et utilius fieret, in supputatione calculationis assumpsimus prima elementa Graeca Patris, et Filii et Spiritus sancti Π, Υ, Α, quae octogenarium et quadringentesimum et primum significant..."—Hallier, *op. et loc cit.*, n. 8 (*MTC*, XXIV, 1047).

177 "In nomine Patris Π., et Filii Υ., et Spiritus sancti A. Π. Walterio Spirensi episcopo ego Burchardus sanctae Vormaciensis ecclesiae devotus gregis Christi famulus, in Deo vero summae felicitatis beatitudinem. Cum sancta catholica ecclesia prompta sit sequi documenta evangelica, que dicunt: 'Qui recipit prophetam in nomine prophetae, accipiet mercedem prophetae, et qui recipit iustum in nomine iusti, mercedem iusti accipiet, etc.' et Apostolus iubeat hospitalitatem sectari, et necessitatibus sanctorum virorum communicare; tamen propter eos, qui cauteriatam habent suam conscientiam, dicentes se esse simplices, cum sint astutia diabolica repleti, et pro opere pietatis dicunt se de loco ad locum transire, cum sint sua malicia faciente fugitivi, et dicunt se esse ministerio sacro insertos, cum non sint: statutum est a sanctis Patribus, neminem clericum alienum et ignotum recipi ab aliquo episcopo, et inthronizari in sua ecclesia, nisi habeat a proprio episcopo epistolam, que in canonibus nominatur Formata. Ideo notum facimus fraternitati vestrae, quod presens frater noster, harum litterarum portitor, nomine Hermannus, non pro sua nequicia expulsus est a nobis, sed postulantibus fratribus, eo quod ex familia nostra fuit et noster baptizatus, fecimus ei libertatem receptam in cornu altaris canonice, et ordinavimus eum ad gradum presbiterii. Cui etiam has dimissorias sive commendaticias litteras facimus, et eum ad vestram dilectam fraternitatem dirigimus, ut in vestra parrochia sub vestro sacro regimine et defensione consistere valeat. Ego, inquam, Burchardus humilis episcopus, in nomine Patris, et Filii et Spiritus sancti, et in unitate sanctae ecclesiae, in qua Petro datum est ius ligandi atque solvendi, absolvo Hermannum presbiterum de civitate Vormaciensi indictione X, et licentiam do vobis inthronizandi eum in quacumque ecclesia vultis vestrae parrochiae..."—C. 1, D. LXXIII.

2. *Medieval Period (1100 to the Council of Trent)*

A. Minor and Major Clerics

The story of the introduction in the year 1179 of the title of patrimony for ordinands has already been recounted.[178] It had the effect of loosening the bond between Bishop and cleric, because it removed for the latter the necessity of a particular office and of residence in the diocese, and that with the full benediction of the law. Scarcely a century later, it has likewise been seen, two additional proper Bishops of ordination were introduced, namely those of the cleric's acquired domicile and of the cleric's attained benefice.[179] This further loosened the bond, because it supplied the cleric with not only a legal method, but even a motive and an impetus, to leave his diocese if it did not suit him. The age became one of absolute ordinations. Minor clerics needed no ordination title whatever, and major clerics could substitute their own funds for one.

Even those who had benefices were not all obliged to residence thereat. In the early part of the period every benefice and prebend was considered as requiring the presence of the beneficiary.[180] However, the multiplicity of clerics absent on leave to attend the Universities, the institution of special benefices, known as *praestimonia,* precisely to be conferred on clerics absent for a just cause, such as for studies, and the gradual evolution by universal custom of simple benefices from residential [181]

[178] *Supra,* pp. 75 ff.

[179] *Supra,* pp. 45 ff.

[180] Thus in the letter of Pope Innocent III to the Patriarch of Constantinople in 1206 only a just and necessary cause with the consent of the Bishop would excuse from residence—C. 10, X, *de clericis non residentibus in ecclesia vel praebenda,* III, 4. This entire title deals with the subject.

[181] Evidence of this is found in those texts which forbade a plurality of simple benefices, e. g., in c. 6, X, *de praebendis,* III, 5; *ibid.,* c. 13: "Et illud est omni rationi contrarium, ut unus clericus in una ecclesia vel in diversis ecclesiis plures dignitates vel personatus obtineat, quum singula officia in ecclesiis assiduitatem exigant personarum." Boniface VIII (a. 1294-1303), in c. 15, *de rescriptis,* I, 3, in VI°, stripped the simply beneficed of the right of the fruits if they were absent, even for studies.

to non-residential ones[182] brought an end to the strict bond of all beneficiaries with the Bishop, and gave a large degree of freedom to all those who had not yet succeeded in obtaining benefices that were residential. It causes little wonder, then, that the writers of the period taught the doctrine that any cleric who was not in possession of a residential benefice was free to go to another diocese to obtain one without needing any permission from his Bishop. This applied to any cleric in minor orders who had no ordination title whatever, as well as to any minor or major cleric who either had patrimony as his title, or whose benefice was a non-residential one.[183] Once a cleric obtained such a residential benefice, he became *ipso facto* canonically transferred to the diocese in which it existed, because then he came under the authority and jurisdiction of the new Bishop in all that pertained to the benefice, and could never resign it and leave that diocese without that new Bishop's permission. Similarly, he acquired the said Bishop as his proper Bishop for future ordination, and was able to use the new benefice for his ordination title.

By a far greater reason, a cleric like the above could acquire a new domicile in another diocese or obtain a simple benefice anywhere without his Bishop's permission, because he was considered free to leave his original diocese.[184] By doing so, however, he did not necessarily effect a canonical transfer. The Bishops of the place where the cleric had acquired a domicile or held a simple benefice were enabled to act as his proper Bishops, but were not required to do so. In other words, even after the

[182] Panormitanus, *Commentaria super quinque libros Decretalium* (5 vols., Lugduni, 1547), ad c. 17 (*clericos*), X, *de clericis non residentibus*, III, 4, n. 3; Pirhing, *Jus Canonicum in V Libros Decretalium distributum* (ed. noviss., 5 vols., Dilingae, 1722), lib. IV, tit. III, nn. 16-17.

[183] Cf. e. g., Abbas Antiquus, *Lectura aurea super quinque libris Decretalium* (Argentinae, 1510), ad. c. 23 (*Tuis quaestionibus*), X, *de praebendis*, III, 5, who held that anyone ordained for the title of patrimony could not be kept in the diocese against his will. Similarly, Nicolaus de Tudeschis, writing under the name of Abbas Panormitanus, ad c. 5 (*Fraternitati*), X, *de clericis non residentibus in ecclesia vel praebenda*, III, 4, says in n. 4: "Clericus saecularis vel laicus non sunt ita subjecti proprio episcopo quominus possint transferre domicilium et acceptare alibi beneficium, sine licentia praelati."

[184] Panormitanus, *loc. cit.*

cleric resided for ten years in a new diocese or obtained a simple benefice in a new diocese, the Bishop of the place did not have to consider that cleric as one of *his* clerics, and the candidate would still have to seek further promotion in orders from the Bishop of his place of origin. On the other hand, if either of these two proper Bishops, namely, of the place of the acquired domicile or of the place of the simple benefice, wanted to keep the cleric he could promote the latter to higher orders on his own authority and sooner or later confer on him a residential benefice as an ordination title, and thereby effect the canonical transfer.

In the event that a cleric was already in possession of a residential benefice in his original diocese, he could not become canonically transferred elsewhere without the explicit permission of the Bishop of his place of origin, by which permission the cleric became authorized to resign his benefice and to accept another one elsewhere, thereby completing the transfer. No permission was needed for him to accept a non-residential benefice elsewhere, though such permission was required for the purpose of changing his domicile. Yet, either of these two latter ways of legally departing from the diocese of his origin would not become canonical transfers until he received a residential benefice from one of the two new proper Bishops.

B. Priests

The same exact procedure was valid also for priests, with the exception that they could not acquire any new proper Bishops for ordination, because the right of conferring of any higher order was preëmpted exclusively by the papal authority.

3. *Tridentine Period* (*Council of Trent to 1694*)

A. Minor and Major Clerics

The Council of Trent set itself the task of restricting the number of clerics, particularly priests, within a diocese, so that no longer would there be the same liberty of departure that existed in the Medieval Period, which had resulted in abuses and scandals detrimental to the Church. The first scheme drawn up for submission to the Council was entitled "*Ad moderandum numerum sacerdotum.*" It was the idea of one of the participating Bishops to have the Church return to the ancient practice of ordaining only those clerics for whom there were available ecclesiastical sources of revenue, and, correspondingly, some church or religious place wherein the regular performance of their sacred functions would be obligatory in return for their sustenance. The Bishops of the kingdom of Naples, of Dalmatia, of Greece, and of other places where the benefices were few and meagre, objected to this on the grounds that, if they could not have more priests than could be supported by the revenues at hand, many of their people would be left without pastors. Their objection was heard; the caption indicative of the method of reform was altered, and a less drastic course was adopted. One decree [185] aimed to reduce the multitude of clerics by requiring that those who were without benefices but who sought ordination for the title of patrimony or pension could be ordained only if the Bishop judged that they would be necessary or useful to his churches. The second decree [186] struck at the abuse of vagrant clerics by ordering that no cleric be ordained who would not be assigned to, and be obliged to serve and reside at, that church or religious place for the necessity or utility of which the Bishop was accepting him, and that if he left that place without the consent of the Bishop he was to be suspended from the exercise of his sacred orders.[187]

The first of these decrees, therefore, opened the way for a Bishop to thwart the ordination of needless clerics. No matter how much patrimony or what large pensions they enjoyed, he could refuse them ordination unless and until there was a need for their clerical services. The second decree gave him the power of binding to personal residence all those clerics, including even the merely tonsured, who were not already so bound by their possession of residential benefices.

185 Sess. XXI, *de ref.*, c. 2.

186 Sess. XXIII, *de ref.*, c. 16.

187 Pallavicini, *Vera conc. tridentini historia* (Antwerpiae, 1673), p. III, lib. XVII, c. 9.

How poorly this second decree was enforced has already been seen. In Italy itself the councils insisted on it,[188] as did also a few councils in France and elsewhere,[189] but in the world at large it never received general acceptance, except insofar as it was understood to apply in the matter of assigning to the service of the entire diocese such clerics who were already in major orders.[190]

In retrospect it seems logical that this decree should have met with the fate it suffered, because the Council of Trent had at the same time prescribed the institution of seminaries throughout the world, and these, when started, rendered practically useless any assignment to particular churches of those not yet ordained priests. In fact, the Council itself seemed to indicate that assignment was not of importance for those who were away studying in a seminary or University.[191]

The question of primary interest here is the following: How far did the law of the Council of Trent restrain clerics who held

[188] Cf. *supra*, pp. 82-83.

[189] Cf. *supra*, p. 83, footnote 140.

[190] Cf. *supra*, p. 84, footnote 141. Testimony to the lack of the decree's enforcement in Spain is rendered thus by Garcia (a. 1618): "Quae adscriptio non videtur observari nec esse in usu."—*De Benef. Eccles.*, p. II, cap. V, n. 103. The same can be gathered readily from the Constitution "*Apostolici ministerii*" of Innocent XIII, May 23, 1723 (*Fontes*, n. 280), in which the Bishops of Spain were ordered to make up for the failure of their predecessors by effecting the omitted assignments at once. A trace of its enforcement is found in the Counc. of Toledo (a. 1582): "...ideo, haec sancta synodus, oecumenicae synodi Tridentinae praecepto inhaerens, statuit, ut quicumque posthac ad sacros ordines titulo patrimonii aut pensionis promovebuntur, eius ecclesiae servitio addicantur, cui tanquam necessarii aut utiles sunt ordinati. Ea vero deputatio in literis ordinum testimonialibus adscribatur, ut visitatores a singulis eius ministerii rationem exigant."—*Actio* 3ª, *decretum* 32 (Mansi, XXXVI Bis, 176-177). Benedict XIV alluded to the non-observance of the decree (*De Syn. dioec.*, lib. XI, c. 2, n. 13), and even the Sacred Congregation of the Council revealed the same, e. g., in *Valentina*, 29 iun. 1628: "...episcopum teneri adscribere ad servitium ecclesiae clericum in minoribus constitutum vel prima tonsura initiatum petentem adscribi."—Barbosa, *Summa apostolicarum decisionum*, coll. 295, n. 13, and in other declarations wherein that Sacred Congregation stated that the assignment had to be made in the very act of promotion, because anyone who was ordained for the title of patrimony and was not assigned to any church at the time of the ordination could not be assigned afterwards (Garcia, *ibid.*, n. 101).

[191] Sess. XXIII, *de ref.*, cc. 6, 11, 18.

no residential benefices from leaving their dioceses to become attached elsewhere? From an examination of the available testimony, the answer is that, wherever Bishops followed the decree and formally assigned each cleric, the liberty of leaving the diocese to become attached elsewhere ceased, and such a cleric was bound to his diocese just as firmly as the one who possessed a residential benefice; whereas in those dioceses where the assignment was neglected the clerics enjoyed almost the same freedom of departure as they had in the Medieval Period, the only restriction being that now they were at least to seek the permission to depart.

The Sacred Congregation of the Council itself led the way for this opinion. Adhering to the letter rather than to the spirit of the law, it decided: "Clericum, qui certo loco non est adscriptus, ab episcopo suo non posse invitum retineri, ne a sua dioecesi recedat et alibi parochiam accipiat." [192] In still another case it declared: "Talem (clericum) vero teneri, antequam vadat ad residentiam, petere ab episcopo proprio licentiam, quam ille non potest denegare." [193]

The authors of the period followed the Sacred Congregation in its interpretation of that clause of sess. XXIII, *de ref.*, c. 16 ". . . Quod si (adscriptus) locum inconsulto episcopo deseruerit, ei sacrorum exercitium interdicatur." Thus, Fagnanus (a. 1661) wrote:

> Cap. 16, sess. 23 loquitur de eo qui in sua ordinatione permisit se adscribi ac tamquam servum adscriptitium mancipari servitio ecclesiae, pro cujus utilitate est ordinatus. Unde non mirum, si eo casu locum deserere non potest, inconsulto episcopo.[194]

He interpreted *inconsulto episcopo* to mean *sine consensu episcopi* and warned that this was a change from the medieval law, in accordance with which the only ones who could not freely leave the diocese were those who held residential benefices, whereas

[192] In *Ariminen.*, 5 dec. 1574—Richter, *Canones et decreta conc. tridentini, declarationes ac resolutiones*, p. 207, n. 3.

[193] In *Ferrarien.*, 12 iun. 1604—Richter, *loc. cit.*

[194] *Commentaria in Libros Decretalium* (5 vols., Romae, 1661), ad c. 4 (*admonet*), X, *de renunciatione*, I, 9, n. 27.

according to the Tridentine law also those who were assigned to any church were under a similar restriction.[195] Garcia (a. 1618) said the same:

> Si clericus nullum beneficium habet in titulum requirens residentiam aut nulli loco sit adscriptus, ab omnibus episcopis recipi potest et ejus ordinarius dimissoria concedere debet.[196]

Similarly, Pignatelli (a. 1700) wrote:

> Itaque, si sint adscripti servitio alicujus ecclesiae, non poterunt discedere absque licentia sui Episcopi, juxta Concilium Tridentinum (sess. 23, c. 16); ubi decernitur quod tales non debent locum deserere, inconsulto Episcopo, id est, sine consensu Episcopi . . . Quod si deseruerint, sacrorum exercitium est eis interdicendum, ad praescriptum sexti canonis Concilii Chalcedonensis, qui . . . a Tridentina Synodo innovatur, dicto capite 16. . . . Hinc, hujusmodi limitationibus salvis, licet clerici habeant beneficium simplex, possunt tamen Ordinarii eos hortari, non cogere, ad frequentandam ecclesiam et chorum; . . . Multoque minus prohibere potest eis (Episcopus) sub poena suspensionis ipso facto incurrenda, ne exeant e loco sine licentia.[197]

Other authors, in view of the wide neglect of the assignment of clerics, did not even mention formal assignment at ordination as a way of keeping clerics rooted to their dioceses, and adhered instead to the medieval discipline that all non-residentially beneficed clerics were free to depart.[198]

[195] "Nec tales debent locum deserere inconsulto Episcopo, id est, sine consensu Episcopi, prout haec verba exponuntur hic (i. e. in c. 4) et in capite *cum plantare, de Privilegiis.* Quod si deseruerint, sacrorum exercitium est eis interdicendum, ad praescriptum sexti canonis Concilii Chalcedonensis, qui a Tridentina Synodo innovatur dicto cap. 16 (Sess. 23). Unde cavendum est a modernis collectoribus . . . , dum, aliis relatis, dixerunt, presbyteris et clericis non habentibus beneficium in titulum, personalem residentiam requirens, licitum esse ire quo velint, et Ordinarios teneri litteras commendatitias concedere. Hoc enim est contra praecitatum Concilii decretum."—*Ibid.*, n. 15.

[196] *De Benef. Eccles.*, p. II, cap. V, n. 102.

[197] *Consultationes canonicae*, t. III, consult. LVI, n. 3.

[198] E. g., Barbosa, *de Officio et potestate Episcopi* (2 vols., Lugduni, 1656), p. II, allegatione 21, n. 5: "Nec sunt denegandae (*commendatitiae litterae*) ab Episcopo sacerdotibus et clericis qui non habent beneficia in titulum residentiam requirentia, prout etiam decisum refert Armendarus . . . Et iterum in S. Congregatione Cardinalium

From the common agreement of these opinions one can infer that, though a cleric was assigned, he could, nevertheless, be transferred to another diocese by obtaining a residential benefice in the same, provided that he first received permission from his Bishop to depart.[199] This permission was in the form of commendatory letters (*litterae commendatitiae*). The Bishop could refuse to give them on the ground that the cleric was necessary or useful to the churches of the diocese, and then the cleric could have recourse to a higher authority, where it would be decided whether or not his cause for departing was just and reasonable, as it would be, for example, if he was suffering from ill health caused by the climate, if he was not getting enough from his extraordinary title of patrimony or pension for his proper sustenance, or if his work in a new diocese would be much more useful or valuable than it was in the old. If his cause was just,

negotiis Episcoporum et Regularium praeposita, decretum fuit illos non posse revocare subditos ecclesiasticos alibi degentes, nec eos cogere; sed teneri litteras eis dare extra volentibus morari, si ratione beneficii non adstringerentur in sua dioecesi residere. Dicit ita in causa propria obtinuisse Campanilla... Sic etiam in facti contingentia respondisse asserit Aloysius Riccius (*in Praxi fori eccles.*, decis. 598 et resol. 524). Ubi ampliat ad clericum obtinentem simplex beneficium, qui etiam non poterit cogi residere in dioecesi ubi illud habet, sed poterit ire quo vellet, et ita dicit in Rota decisum."; Pirhing, *Jus Canon.*, lib. I, tit. XXII, n. 3: "Episcopus vero non potest denegare litteras commendatitias aut testimoniales presbyteris aliisque clericis, si intra vel extra dioecesim peregrinari, vel omnino discedere velint, nisi habeant in titulum beneficia requirentia residentiam, ut declaravit Sacra Congregatio Concilii... ; quamvis olim, cum essent pauciores clerici, et omnes intitulati, non poterant discedere ab ecclesia sua, praesertim in longinquum, sine jussu Episcopi, vel facultate ab eodem obtenta; ut constat ex capite *si qui vero* (23, C. 7, q. 1) desumpto ex Concilio Nicaeno, can. 16; et ex Concilio Laodicensi, can. 41."; Schmalzgrueber, *Jus Eccles. Univ.*, lib. I, tit. XXII, n. 2: "Cum communi (sententia) dicendum, quod episcopi teneantur per se loquendo hujusmodi clericis dare litteras commendatitias, si has ex peregrinationis, aut etiam domicilii vel dioecesis mutandae causa petant."

199 Prov. Counc. of Rheims (a. 1564), stat. 12—Mansi, XXXIII, 1296; Prov. Counc. of Rouen (a. 1581), cap. *De episcoporum officiis*, n. 6: "... nec ullus ordinetur, qui illi ecclesiae; aut pio loco, pro cujus necessitate aut utilitate judicio sui episcopi assumitur, non ascribatur, ubi suis fungatur muneribus. Ut postea in omnibus literis ordinum susceptorum apponatur, ordinatos ad talem ecclesiam, a qua sine episcopi licentia in scriptis tradenda, non liceat ad alienam etiam ejusdem dioecesis transire."—Mansi, XXXIV A, 633; Prov. Counc. of Tours (a. 1583), tit. 14: "... omnibus clericis, saltem uno sacrorum ordinum charactere insignitis, etiam musicis prohibemus, ne sua domicilia, aut paroecias deserant vel relinquant, inconsultis suis episcopis, capitulis aliisve ecclesiasticis, quibus sunt adscripti et absque causae (cur id fiat) expressione et cognatione, scriptoque probata licentia debiteque attestata."—Mansi, XXXIV A, 834.

the higher authority would order the Bishop to issue the *litterae commendatitiae;* if not, it would sustain the Bishop's refusal, but inject the condition that he should provide for the assigned cleric a suitable source of revenue. Many such decisions are to be found in the *Thesaurus Resolutionum.*[200]

The unassigned cleric could transfer to another diocese by obtaining a residential benefice in the same after having sought from his Bishop commendatory letters, containing, as they did, a recommendation of his life and morals together with an authorization to any Bishop to receive him and use him in his diocese. These letters could not be denied him under the circumstances.[201]

The residentially beneficed cleric was no more free to change dioceses than he was in the preceding period. All authorities agreed on that. He needed not only the permission of his Bishop to resign his benefice (under penalty of censure),[202] but also

[200] Bouix, *Tractatus De Episcopo,* V. II, p. V, cap. XXIV, § II.

[201] Cf. *supra,* p. 165, footnotes 192, 193. Counc. of Salisbury, England (a. 1569), const. XXIX, cap. 1: ". . . districte prohibemus, ne aliquem alienae provinciae presbyterum, neque etiam eum, qui licet provincialis fuerit, de una tamen in alteram dioecesim etiam eiusdem provinciae peregrinatur, in vicarium, provisorem, cooperatorem aut capellanum, in ecclesia vel beneficio suo, nec non in castra, villas seu domos pro exercendo officio sacerdotali assumant, non ad divina, nisi devotionis causa, et visis formatis in forma fide digna, admittant, nisi sufficienter et in scriptis doceat, et coram officialibus, archidiacono aut decano nostro aliquo rurali, sub cuius ditione morabitur, de susceptione omnium ordinum, tam minorum quam maiorum, fidem faciat, offeratque litteras testimoniales, ab episcopo suo, aut illo, ex cuius dioecesi proxime recessit, continentes quidem, quod in fide catholica et unitate sanctae Romanae ecclesiae permanserit, et in ea adhuc duret; item, a quo victus sive sustentationis honestae provisionem seu titulum habeat, nec non et ultimam causam, quare in hanc provinciam nostram se receperit."—Mansi, XXXVI A, 222-223.

[202] C. 4, X, *de renunciatione,* I, 9: "Universis personis tui episcopatus ecclesiasticis sub districtione prohibeas, ne ecclesias tuae dioecesis ad ordinationem tuam pertinentes absque assensu tuo intrare audeant aut detinere, aut te dimittere inconsulto. Quodsi quis contra prohibitionem tuam venire praesumpserit, in eum auctoritate nostra et tua fretus canonicam exerceas ultionem." Concerning this decretal Fagnanus says: "Ejus auctoritatem requiri in dimissione beneficii, quae requiritur in illius assecutione, ut hic . . . Unde is demum potest auctoritatem praestare renuntiationi, qui potest invitum destituere . . . Nota ibi, te dimittere inconsulto, consilium aliquando poni pro consensu vel auctoritate, ut hic . . . Non enim ad beneficium dimittendum sufficit Praelatum consulere, sed oportet illius consensum obtinere."—Ad c. 4 (*admonet*), X, *de renuntiatione,* I, 9, nn. 2-3. Conc. Trident., sess. XXI, *de ref.,* c. 2.

Testimonial Letters certifying to his legal resignation of the same, and *litterae commendatitiae*, which contained not only a recommendation of the cleric but also permission for him to receive a residential benefice from the Bishop of another diocese. As soon as the residential benefice was conferred by the Bishop of the new diocese on a cleric who was in possession of such *litterae testimoniales* and *litterae commendatitiae* from his proper Bishop the canonical transfer was complete. As in the case of the assigned cleric, the Bishop could refuse the *commendatitiae* to a cleric whom he needed, but only if the cleric's reason for departure was unjust and unreasonable and if the Bishop himself was willing to support the cleric out of assured church funds.[203]

The simply beneficed cleric did not need his Bishop's permission to resign his benefice, because a simple benefice was conferred solely in the interest of its incumbent, who could receive it or resign it at will, since it exacted no personal service or residence. By acquiring a residential benefice elsewhere, a cleric automatically resigned his simple benefice,[204] and could transfer to the other diocese, provided that he received his native Bishop's *litterae commendatitiae*, if he had been formally assigned to

[203] Cf. *supra*, p. 166, footnote 198. Pius V in his Constitution "*Quanta Ecclesiae*," Apr. 1, 1568, § 3, recognized as a legitimate cause for resignation of a benefice the possessor's promotion to another, thus: "Episcopi, et alii facultatem habentes, eorum dumtaxat resignationes recipere, et admittere possint, qui aut senio confecti, aut valetudinarii, aut corpore impediti, vel vitiati, aut crimini obnoxii, censurisque Ecclesiasticis irretiti, aut nequeunt, aut non debent Ecclesiae, vel beneficio inservire; seu qui unum illud, vel plura beneficia obtinuerint, vel quos ad aliud contigerit promoveri";—*Fontes*, n. 125.

[204] Fagnanus, ad c. 4, X, *de renuntiatione*, I, 9, nn. 25 ss.: "Aut agitur de beneficio cui nullum est annexum certum personale servitium: et tunc, quia in hoc casu horum beneficiorum collatio fit principaliter ad utilitatem illorum quibus conferuntur, provisi de illis (modo non impediantur ob contenta in Concilio Tridentino, sess. 21, cap. 2, et in cap. *cum secundum, de Praebendis*) videntur posse eadem invito superiore resignare; per regulam quod quisque potest ei renuntiare, quod pro se principaliter est introductum... Cum hodie beneficia simplicia personalem residentiam non requirant, ex generali consuetudine..., ex eorum resignatione superior nullum potest praetendere interesse: nam nec ea obtinentes potest ut resideant in episcopatu cogere; ut alias censuit S. Congregatio Episcoporum ac Regularium negotiis praeposita. Unde non est ratio quare sic provisus cogi possit ut beneficium invitus retineat."

some church or pious place, or at least sought these testimonials, if he had not been so assigned.[205]

Finally, any cleric who had not yet attained the priesthood might obtain a canonical transfer mediately by first acquiring a new proper Bishop for ordination, who in time might incardinate him by giving him a residential benefice. As has already been seen, the association of a cleric with a Bishop in his household for a term of three years became, during this period, one of the ways of obtaining a proper Bishop of ordination. There were, then, three categories of proper Bishops for ordination over and above that of the Bishop of the cleric's place of origin, namely, the Bishops who gained such a status by reason of the cleric's acquired domicile, by reason of the benefice attained by the cleric, and by reason of the latter's association with some Bishop's household for a period of at least three years. A minor cleric, or also a major cleric who had not yet received the order of priesthood, could, therefore, with the permission of his native Bishop, change his domicile or become associated with some outside Bishop's household, and could, even without the permission of his native Bishop, acquire a simple benefice in some other diocese. The proper Bishops thus acquired by the cleric could raise him to higher orders, but the question of his incardination in the new diocese remained contingent upon the kind of benefice conferred on him: the conferring of a residential benefice implied incardination; the conferring of a non-residential benefice did not. But the residential benefice could not be conferred on the cleric at any later time as an act altogether distinct from the ordination unless the cleric had previously obtained, or at least sought, the *litterae commendatitiae* in accordance with whether he had been, or had not been, holding an assignment in his home diocese.

Since the " title of the mission " had also been introduced during this period, it must be noted that clerics who received

[205] Note that a cleric whose place of origin was in diocese *A* could hold a simple benefice in diocese *B* without ever having set foot there, and thereupon could acquire a residential benefice in diocese *C*. In the latter event he automatically resigned the benefice in diocese *B*, but in addition needed a testimonial for his departure from his native diocese *A* if he had received some assignment there.

the subdiaconate or diaconate for the title of the mission could not be transferred to another mission without the special permission of the Sacred Congregation for the Propagation of the Faith [206] as well as the permission of the Ordinary of the diocese or mission territory which they were leaving.[207]

B. Priests

In the various passages just cited from councils and authors the word *presbyter* occurs along with *clericus,* showing that the same interpretation of the law applied equally to both clerics and priests.[208]

The law which forbade Bishops to ordain anyone for the title of patrimony or pension unless such a person was judged necessary or useful in the administration of the diocesan churches [209] applied especially to priests. It was noted above that the very title of the contemplated reform measure as prepared for the Council of Trent was "*Ad moderandum numerum sacerdotum.*" [210] In case, then, that any priests in a diocese could not be employed in some necessary or useful spiritual service, there was a greater reason for them than for clerics to be allowed to transfer to another diocese to secure priestly employment, especially when they were unassigned at home, or when, though they were assigned, they had to rely on their patrimony or on a

[206] Cf. *supra,* p. 144.

[207] The wording of their oath indicates this: "Voveo et juro, quod in hac dioecesi . . . perpetuo in divinis administrandis, laborem meum ac operam, sub omnimoda directione et jursidictione R. P. D. pro tempore ordinarii . . . impendam"; —*Supra,* p. 142; and this was definitely decided by the S. C. de Prop. Fide on July 7, 1828—Zitelli, *Apparatus juris ecclesiastici,* p. 197.

[208] E. g., Bouix, *Tractatus De Episcopo,* V. II, p. V, cap. XXIV, § II, n. 2: "Hinc, verbi gratia, si quis presbyter, ordinatus ad titulum patrimonii, et simul adscriptus servitio ecclesiae cathedralis, nominetur ad canonicatum, parochiamve, aut ad aliquod officium ecclesiasticum, in aliena dioecesi, poterit acceptare. At nequibit discedere absque Episcopi licentia. Quod si Episcopus licentiam hanc deneget, poterit dictus presbyter ad superiorem auctoritatem recurrere, verbi gratia, ad Archiepiscopum. Et tunc expenditur an causa discedendi quam allegat presbyter vere justa sit ac rationabilis: sit talis sit, cogitur Episcopus ad dandam postulatam licentiam."

[209] Conc. Trident., sess. XXI, *de ref.,* c. 2.

[210] Cf. *supra,* p. 163.

simple benefice as their means of support, because their course of studies was over, and the valuable time and powers of their priesthood would otherwise be rendered nugatory to a considerable extent.[211] Hence, the only conditions which could justify a Bishop in withholding the *litterae commendatitiae* from one of his priests who desired to accept a residential benefice and become incardinated elsewhere were: a) if the priest's services proved useful or necessary for the churches of the diocese; [212] b) if a suitable sustenance from an ecclesiastical source, such as an office was assured him; and c) if the priest's reason for departure was neither just nor reasonable. But, even when justified in refusing, the Bishop could still grant the permission to depart as a favor.

Priests ordained *titulo missionis* and destined for, or laboring in, mission territories were unable to obtain a canonical transfer without special permission of the Holy See or of the Sacred Congregation for the Propagation of the Faith, as well as permission of the Ordinary of the diocese or vicariate from which they were to depart, after having secured another Bishop willing to receive them.[213]

4. *Innocentian Period* (*1694-1898*)

A. Factors Which Bound the Cleric to His Diocese More Securely

1°. Decrease in number of benefices

In the course of this period the Church at large suffered a great diminution in the number of its benefices, both residential and simple. An example of this, already cited,[214] was the con-

[211] Bouix, *ibid.*, n. 3.

[212] S. C. C. in *Tinen.*, 15 mart. 1625, censuit posse episcopos, ob ecclesiae necessitatem presbyteris ordinatis titulo patrimonii interdicere, ne ipsam ecclesiam deserant atque alterius ecclesiae servitio se addicant, absque ejus licentia.—Richter, *Declarationes ac Resolutiones*, p. 207, n. 4.

[213] Cf. *supra*, p. 144.

[214] P. 148. Cf. also Bouix, *Tractatus De Episcopo*, V. II, p. V, cap. XXIV, § IV.

fiscation and later alienation in 1789-1791 of all Church property in France. A similar suppression of benefices occurred in Belgium,[215] while in England and North America no real curatial benefices were to be found at all.

The direct result was the almost complete extinction of that numerous class of clerics who, by reason of the simple benefices they held, were not burdened with the care of souls, but only with such duties as celebrating or serving Mass or reciting the Divine Office—a group who were conceded to have comparative liberty to change dioceses, since such benefices imposed no obligation of residence and established no special bond or connection between the beneficiary and the diocese controlling the benefice.

Another result was the provision which it forced Bishops to make for the many major clerics who were *needed* for the adequate spiritual care of the people of a diocese, but who had neither benefice nor patrimony.[216] Such provision was made by the introduction of new titles of ordination. In other words, the decree of the Council of Trent that no one be ordained unless he was needed in or could prove useful to the diocese was now being fulfilled to the letter. Though there were but few residential benefices to which to assign major clerics and priests, there were plenty of ecclesiastical offices, and the new titles of ordination guaranteed the sustenance of the appointees. Formerly, *officia* without endowments for their incumbents were practically non-existent, and received scant consideration from the canonists, who were accustomed to treat the entire subject of clerical sustenance under the one title "*De praebendis et beneficiis.*" Now it was discovered that laws which had been

[215] In an appeal to Pope Gregory XVI for a new title of ordination in Belgium, the Bishop of Bruges, in 1845, wrote in part: "Concilii tridentini sanctio . . . in Belgio usque ad gallicas perturbationes integre custodita, difficilior servatu evasit, postquam, suppressis injuria temporum ecclesiasticis collegiatis ac beneficiis simplicibus penitus exstinctis, clerici ad sacros ordines assumendi plerumque bonis patrimonialibus destituti reperiantur."—Refertur in folio *Brugen.* tituli sacrae ordinationis, 24 aug. 1850 (*Thesaurus Resolutionum*, CIX, 295).

[216] The Bishop of Bruges related that, at most, only a third of his *ordinandi* were provided with sufficient patrimony—*Loc. cit.*

made to govern the residence, resignation, and transfer of the vast body of beneficiaries would affect in the strict sense only that smaller portion of the clergy who were still fortunate enough to come under that technical category. Hence, there is noticeable in this period of history a very decided change on the part of canonists in their interpretation of the laws, which was so extended by them as to cover also that category of the clergy who filled ecclesiastical offices without conjointly possessing an ecclesiastical benefice.[217] This change was adopted by the Roman Congregations as well, so that every cleric, whether he enjoyed a benefice or merely held an ecclesiastical office, was now considered bound so closely to his diocese and to its Bishop that he could not leave the diocese without his Bishop's permission.

2°. New titles of ordination

The story of the introduction of new titles of ordination during this period was given above.[218] This adaptation came as a result of the vast reduction in the number of benefices, especially in France and Belgium, at the close of the eighteenth century.[219] Bishops, mindful of the old penal law which prescribed that he

[217] Cf. Claeys-Bouuaert, *De Canonica Cleri Saecularis Obedientia*, pp. 217-219. Bouix, in arguing for a broader interpretation of the law of residence, so that it would apply not only to beneficed priests but also to those who merely held ecclesiastical offices, writes: " Si admittenda sit sententia posse clericos non adscriptos, nec ullum obtinentes beneficium residentiam exigens, invito episcopo dioecesim suam deserere, sequitur, verbi gratia, quoad hodiernum Galliae clerum, posse presbyteros omnes praeter canonicos et beneficium parochiale obtinentes, e suis respective dioecesibus migrare, quin obstare possint proprii ipsorum episcopi. Non enim servatur in Galliis tridentina praescriptio singulos qui ad ordines promoventur, alicujus ecclesiae servitio adscribendi. Unde dicti presbyteri de iis sunt qui nec dicto servitio sunt adscripti, nec ullum obtinent beneficium residentiam requirens. Sequitur insuper cogi non posse dictos presbyteros ad obeunda ecclesiastica munia quae ipsis respectivi eorum episcopi committere vellent: quia si jus habeant a dioecesi discedendi, hoc ipso jus habent munia haec in dioecesi non obeundi. Sequitur tandem eosdem presbyteros, si praefata munia jam acceptaverint, posse invito episcopo ea dimittere. Nam, cum non adfuerit obligatio acceptandi, censendi sunt acceptasse libere, et salva facultate ea dimittendi."—*Tractatus De Episcopo*, V. II, p. V, cap. XXIV, § IV.

[218] Pp. 148-151.

[219] The appeal of the Bishop of Bruges to Pope Gregory XVI in 1845 is a good illustration of the condition.—See p. 173, footnote 215. Cf. also Bouix, *op. et loc. cit.*

who ordained a man without a canonical title would have to support him himself,[220] were forced, nevertheless, in many instances to violate the prescriptions of the common law, especially that of the Council of Trent, by ordaining without any title those whom they absolutely needed to minister to their people. Since the Bishop himself, then, became the guarantor of their sustenance, he made provision for them as he saw fit. Some of the Bishops sought to have their own method of sustaining their untitled clergy recognized and approved by the Holy See, which would be nothing short of canonizing it as a title. This Rome refused to do. The unusual methods employed were still considered as derogatory to the common law, and were permitted only by pontifical dispensation, and that ordinarily for only a limited period of time or a restricted number of cases.[221] Other Bishops simply proceeded on their own initiative using their own scheme and calling it a title, so that a legitimate custom contrary to the common law was gradually and, in view of the impossibility of conforming to the common law, no doubt deliberately effected in the diocese.[222] In Mexico there was an immemorial

[220] C. 24, X, *de praebendis et dignitatibus*, III, 5.

[221] The Bishop of Bruges (a. 1845) wanted Rome to approve his method of quasi-patrimony as a title, whereby each ordinand would contribute at least two hundred francs towards a common treasury to take care of priests when they became old and inactive. The question proposed to the S. C. C. was: "An sit concedendum episcopo oratori indultum promovendi clericos ad sacros ordines absque legitimo et sufficienti titulo; ita ut sit approbanda institutio novae tituli ordinationis formae?" The response was: "Negative, et providebitur in casibus particularibus."—*Thesaurus Resolutionum*, CIX, 320. How Rome did provide in particular cases is seen from a faculty granted to the same Bishop by S. C. Ep. et Reg. on May 14, 1860: "... ut cum aliis centum clericis a titulo s. ordinationis dispensare valeat, ita tamen ut eos curet de aliquo beneficio vel ecclesiastico officio providere, vel saltem meliori, quo potuerit, modo ... eorum sustentationi consulere ..."—Gasparri, *De Sacra Ordin.*, I, n. 601.

[222] In France after 1801 there arose a custom of ordaining *titulo obedientiae*, which might be explained thus: "... ea nimirum lege, ut semper et quacumque data occasione, ad dioecesis ministerium praesto sint praesuli vocanti, qui illis de necessariis providebit."—[Icard]., *Praelectiones Iuris Canonici* (Paris, 1859), II, p. 32, n. 293. In Belgium, the dioceses of Ghent, Tournai, and Liége, as well as Bruges were using the title *quasi-patrimonii*; in Namur it was the title *servitii*; in some dioceses of Italy, according to the synod of Ancona (a. 1883, n. 140): "... coguntur episcopi implorare indultum nonnullos clericos ad sacros ordines promovendi etiam sine ulla ecclesiastica provisione, sed tantum servitii ecclesiae titulo."—*AkKR*, LV, 70.

custom of ordaining for the title *administrationis,* as explained above,[223] and the Sacred Congregation of the Council in 1879 approved it as a title for that country,[224] although it is possible that the approbation was granted because *administration* was so close to the canonical title of *pension* as to be almost identical with it.

Where there were no legitimate customs in this matter, the Holy See supplied the Bishops with the general permission to dispense from the law of canonical titles whenever they saw fit, as it did progressively for the Bishops of Reims, Avignon, Soissons, Bordeaux, Sens and Auch.[225] Clerics ordained to major orders without a canonical title were supported and educated in seminaries up to the time of their priestly ordination, whereupon the Bishops, finding that it best solved their own problems to use these new priests as a mobile force within the diocese, assigned each one to a separate ecclesiastical office, wherever the need was greatest, and changed them to other offices when and as it was found expedient. Though they were ordained without a canonical title, the diocese itself was their source of support, and the Bishops, therefore, spoke of them as having the title *servitii dioecesis.* This was in contradistinction to the ancient title *servitii ecclesiae,* in which a particular church was the cleric's source of sustenance,—a title which was now no better than an extraordinary one, despite the attempt to restore it through the pertinent law of the Council of Trent.[226]

223 P. 139.

224 In *Chiapensi,* 21 iun. 1879—*ASS,* XII (1879), 569; Gasparri, *De Sacra Ordin.,* I, n. 607.

225 Cf. Conc. Remense (a. 1849), tit. X, c. 2; Avenionense (a. 1849), tit. IV, c. V, n. 3; Senonense (a. 1850), tit. III, c. 7; Auscitanum (a. 1851), n. 96—*Coll. Lac.,* IV, col. 125, 341, 893, 1189; Conc. Suessionense (a. 1849), tit. X, cap. II—Mansi, XLIII, 594; Conc. Burdigalense (a. 1850), tit. III, cap. VII, n. 1—Mansi, XLIV, 87.

226 "Titulus servitii Ecclesiae qui olim ordinarius erat, prout supra adnotatum fuit, et postea evasit extraordinarius, iis quandoque conceditur, qui cum Beneficio ecclesiastico vel pensione careant, aut patrimonialia aliaque bona non possideant, ea lege ordinantur, ut alicui Ecclesiae sint mancipati, ex cuius servitio et eleemosynis a piis Christifidelibus elargiendis substentari possint, et ab eadem Ecclesia nullo

A great many of the Bishops who answered the questionnaire prior to the Vatican Council (a. 1869-1870) had promoted the idea of a title *servitii dioecesis* as best suited to modern needs,[227] and so in the schema "*De titulis ordinationum*" prepared for submission to the Council there was included the recommendation that, in whatever dioceses the Bishops were unable to observe the common law, they could ordain "*titulo servitii suae dioecesis seu ecclesiae et de ecclesiastico officio providere, quo decenter sustentari* (*clerici*) *valeant.*"[228] Though no formal action was taken, this became the common practice of the Church.

In all these various types of ordination titles, which could be summed up under the generic name *servitii dioecesis,* there is one feature in common—that they were derogations of the common law, not in favor of the cleric, as patrimony was, but in favor of the faithful of the diocese, in order that these would not be bereft of sacred ministers to supply them with the consolations of their religion. Hence any cleric who was elevated to major orders for any such title was certainly ordained for the necessity or utility of the churches of the diocese, and thereby entered into a quasi-contract with his proper Bishop to reside in and serve those churches after his promotion to sacred orders—a promotion to which otherwise he would have no right.[229]

unquam tempore amoveri vel ipsi recedere nequeant, nisi aliter eis provisum fuerit; quo titulo ut suis clericis sacros ordines conferret, s. m. Sixtum V. Patriarchae Venetiarum indulsisse constat."—S. C. de Prop. Fide, instr. *de titulo ordinationis,* 27 apr. 1871, n. 5 (*Collectanea S. C. P. F.*, n. 1369).

[227] Cf. *supra,* p. 150, footnote 154.

[228] Cap. III, n. 14—Mansi, LIII, 746-7. Here, as elsewhere in later documents, the titles *servitii dioecesis* and *servitii ecclesiae* seem to be considered synonymous, e. g., in the Code of Canon Law, can. 981, §§ 1, 2.

[229] Claeys-Bouuaert, *De Canonica Cleri Saecularis Obedientia,* p. 229. The previously cited schema "*De titulis ordinationum,*" prepared for the Vatican Council, after rehearsing the law that no one should be ordained except for the necessity or utility of the Church, adds: "Multo magis servari eadem regula debet in iis, qui nullo alio quam dioecesis titulo ordinantur, cum is ipse profecto operam in ea praestandam indicet, quae absque necessitate vel saltem utilitate non concipitur." —*Coll. Lac.*, VII, col. 670. Again, in the Council of Colocza, Hungary (a. 1863), one reads: "Qui ex indulto apostolico, in servitium dioecesis absque titulo ordinantur presbyteri, servire dioecesi obligantur, usque dum de causa canonica inhabiles fiant aut declarentur."—*Coll. Lac.*, V, col. 686.

3°. Gratuitous seminary education

The diocesan or provincial seminary, instituted by the Council of Trent to assume the work of training clerics for all the churches of the diocese instead of having each church to train its own, was always, according to the tenor of the decree, to be a place of free education except for those rich enough to pay for themselves.[230] In order to make it so, the Council imposed a strict tax on all benefices and ecclesiastical revenues of any kind to aid in forming in each diocese the seminary's administrative fund. Since it was a diocesan enterprise, naturally it was expected that the diocese would profit by it later in the service rendered to the diocese by its ordained alumni. Yet the only requirement of candidates for admission was a well founded hope that they would devote themselves perpetually to the ecclesiastical ministry. Nothing specific was set down about the location of that ministry.

The problem which now occurred was: Has the diocese a strict claim on the cleric gratuitously educated in its seminary, so that he must either serve the diocese perpetually, or reimburse it if he seeks to return to the world, to enter religion, or to become excardinated?

In the absence of anything specific in the Tridentine decree itself which might serve as a solution for the problem, an affirmative argument might be offered in the following way: Diocesan seminary training of clerics is a corporate effort on the part of all the churches of a diocese to do what was formerly accomplished by each church separately. In the latter instance, each church was the ordination title for its own clerics, and everyone admitted that no cleric was free to abandon his title at will. In the former instance, then, all the churches that make up the diocese should be considered an ordination title, and hence also no cleric who was gratuitously educated at their expense should be allowed to desert them at will. Some authors took the extreme view that a cleric could not desert his diocese,

[230] Sess. XXIII, *de ref.*, c. 18: "... Pauperum autem filios praecipue eligi vult; nec tamen ditiorum excludit; modo suo sumptu alantur, et studium prae se ferant Deo, et ecclesiae inserviendi."

even to enter religion, until he had served it for a determined and notable period of time.[231] The Bishop of Algiers, in a case before the Sacred Congregation of the Council on July 7, 1883,[232] contended that the custom in his diocese was for gratuitous clerical education to be considered a regular ordination title, binding those who received it to serve the diocese. On the strength of this argument the Sacred Congregation of the Council even reversed its original decision and recognized the Bishop's right to retain a certain cleric, Aemilius Strub, as his own by reason of gratuitous seminary education, even though the said cleric was not his by reason of origin. Similarly, the Sacred Congregation of the Council in *Solutionis seu Excardinationis*, Feb. 19, 1870,[233] recognized the right of the Bishop of a priest's place of origin to still retain the priest, Livius, because of the fact that he had been educated gratis at the seminary in the diocese of his place of origin, even though he had already given that diocese seven years of his labor and now had a professorial chair offered to him in a University in another diocese.

In order to answer the problem adequately, however, three hypotheses should be considered: 1st. when nothing definite has been said or intimated to the clerical candidate about the assumption of an obligation to the diocese in return for his free education; 2nd. when the synodal statutes or legitimate custom require of the gratuitously educated clerics either service of the diocese or reimbursement of the same; and 3rd. when the founder of the seminary or the donor of a burse stipulates the condition that those benefited by these gratuities who later desert the service of the church or diocese be bound to restitution to the diocese.

1st Hypothesis (nothing definite said).—As long as a poor boy had the right intention upon entering the seminary, he

[231] Cf. e. g., Daris, *Praelectiones Canonicae*, IV, 60: "Clericus qui sumptibus seminarii alitur, tacitum iniit contractum cum episcopo, scilicet, laborandi in ministerio sacro sub directione episcopi saltem per notabile tempus. Is igitur clericus contractui stare tenetur, nec ante determinatum tempus sacrum ministerium derelinquere potest sine consensu episcopi, etiam ad amplectendum statum religiosum."

[232] *Argentinen. et Algerien.*—*ASS*, XVI (1883), 249-262.

[233] *ASS*, V (1869), 472-479.

could not be prevented, on this score of free education at least, from leaving the service of the diocese for an honorable reason, either during or after his seminary career, and could not be forced to recompense the seminary, since he did not violate any law. If, however, he was rich and received his education gratuitously, he could be compelled to restore its cost, for the Council of Trent [234] did not command the dioceses to educate such; [235] so, also, if he was poor, but did not have the intention of persevering, or left the seminary for a dishonorable reason, e. g., because of expulsion, he could be bound in justice to reimburse the diocese.[236]

2nd Hypothesis (diocesan statutes or custom obliges).—If a cleric left the diocese which educated him in order to enter the religious life, he would not be abandoning the clerical state, but rather binding himself more strictly. It is every man's right to strive for perfection, and while he may renounce his right, it must be done in no uncertain way. Positive law again and again has recognized a secular cleric's right to enter religion, even against the will of his Bishop, and the Holy See has repeatedly insisted on that freedom.[237] Wherefore, it was re-

[234] Sess. XXIII, *de ref.*, c. 18.

[235] Monacelli, *Formularium*, tit. XIII, form. 7, n. 19.

[236] St. Charles Borromeo (a. 1538-1584) had ruled for his seminary: "Si quis, decursu temporis, de statu mutando consilium caperet, etiamsi de religione ingredienda cogitaret, de eo archiepiscopum... statim certiorem faciat. Peccaret enim, si in seminario hoc animo viveret, in alium finem consumens, quod ad operarios pro hujus ecclesiae auxilio sustentandos est constitutum."—Nilles, *De libertate clericorum religionem ingrediendi*, p. 112.

[237] The synodal statutes of the diocese of Cesena, Italy, had prescribed: "...ut si vel religionem aliquam, aut congregationem ingredi voluerint, vel ad statum laicalem redire, sumptus seminarii refundere deberent," but the S. C. C. (d. 26 febr. 1695) ordered the clause about entering religion to be deleted—Monacelli, *Formularium*, supplement to t. II, n. 108. In 1882 a certain Bishop of Bavaria had made a ruling that he would not ordain to the priesthood any cleric of his diocesan seminary who would not previously oblige himself in writing: 1st. to serve the diocese at least for six years; and 2nd. to restore to the diocese the expenses of his education (2000 marks) in case he wished to leave it for any reason whatever after the six years were completed. Four deacons refused to sign the promises, and Pope Leo XIII, through the S. C. pro Negot. Eccl. Extraord., settled their case by having them appeal to the Bishop for ordination according to the mind of the Supreme Pontiff, which was thus revealed to them: "Voluntas est S̃mi Patris,

garded as contrary to the cleric's right and to the mind of the Church for any diocesan statutes or custom to exact from a candidate for a secular seminary any promise to repay the seminary in case he later wished to embrace the religious life.

If the abandonment of a diocese by a cleric meant his return to the lay state, he could certainly be bound by statute or custom to restore the money spent on him. There was nothing against law or justice in the adoption of statutes to that end,[238] and the approval of the Holy See was not lacking, as may be seen from the above-mentioned case of the diocese of Cesena, Italy,[239] and from that of the abbacy of Nonantola, Italy, which asked: " An servandae sunt constitutiones synodales, quibus cavetur dandam esse ab alumnis fidejussionem de restituendis alimentis et expensis pro eis factis, casu quo ipsi, propria culpa, ad sacrum presbyteratus ordinem non promoveantur? " to which the Sacred

ut quatuor diaconi scribant proprio ordinario exprimentes sensus filiales obsequii, implorantes gratiam ordinationis, . . . promittentes fideles futuros se esse quoad obedientiam quam ipsi promittent recipientes ordinem presbyteratus, devovendo se servitio dioecesis cum zelo et perseverantia, si non placeat Deo seipsos vocare aliquando ad statum majoris perfectionis."—Nilles, *op. cit.*, p. 121.

[238] The Prov. Synod of Malines, Belgium (a. 1609), tit. XX, cap. 4, decreed: " Singuli in sua ad seminarium assumptione declarabunt se habere animum ad statum ecclesiasticum; et insuper promittent, se, cum idonei invenientur, id muneris in ecclesia Dei subituros quod nos ipsis injungemus, aut refusuros expensas, quibus seminarium affecerint."—Claeys-Bouuaert, *De Canonica Cleri Saecularis Obedientia,* p. 249, not. 4. The Prov. Synod of Bordeaux (a. 1583) required every seminarian to have a bondsman who would be willing to pay the expenses of his seminary training if he did not persevere in the ecclesiastical state—Hardouin, *Conciliorum collectio regia maxima,* X, 1383. The Prov. Synod of Naples (a. 1699), tit. X, n. 10, required a pledge from the students and their parents that they would make good the expenses of their board, both in case they abandoned the clerical state and in case they refused an office or duty assigned to them by the Bishop—*Coll. Lac.*, I, col. 229. The III Prov. Counc. of Cincinnati, U. S. A. (a. 1861), ruled as follows: " Decreverunt patres exigendam esse ab omnibus alumnis seminariorum infra sex menses post inceptam philosophiam, seriam promissionem iuxta normam collegiorum pontificiorum eos nempe constitutiones seminarii observaturos, ordines sacros suscepturos, quando superioribus visum fuerit, confectisque studiis, in propria dioecesi ad nutum ordinarii in divinis exercendis perpetuo mansuros. Insuper statuerunt ab iisdem exigendam esse eodem tempore promissionem scriptis exaratam, se proprio ordinario totam pecuniae summam, eorum educatione expensam, restituturos, si qua a suscipiendis ordinibus resilierint."—*Decreta,* n. 5 (Mansi, XLVIII, 366).

[239] P. 180, footnote 237.

Congregation of the Council, on Dec. 1, 1685, replied: "Affirmative, ita ut pro pauperibus sufficiat obligatio conjunctorum." [240]

When the cleric's action in leaving the service of the diocese which had educated him gratis was prompted by a desire to be excardinated to another diocese, natural equity was not served unless the second diocese recompensed the first, especially if this diocese was in need of clerics.[241] Though this particular problem is not mentioned in most diocesan synodal statutes, the mind of Rome can be discerned as requiring service or restitution, from its manner of solving the cases cited above of the Sacred Congregation of the Council, namely, *Argentinen. et Algerien.*, July 7, 1883, and *Solutionis seu Excardinationis*, Feb. 19, 1870,[242] in the first of which the Sacred Congregation of the Council's original decision was to grant excardination from the diocese of free clerical training "*facta compensatione expensarum*," but its later reversal of opinion was that, under the circumstances, nothing short of diocesan service itself would satisfy justice for the free training and support which the cleric, Aemilius Strub, had received in Algiers.

3rd Hypothesis (founder or donor stipulates restitution).—Nothing militated against a donor stipulating how his money was to be used. If his wish was to help train priests for this or that particular diocese, he could make it effective by a prior condition that anyone accepting his largess be bound to stay in

[240] Monacelli, *Formularium*, supplement to t. II, n. 108.

[241] The II Plen. Counc. of Baltimore (a. 1866) commanded this to be done in the case of students transferring from one seminary to another, thus: "Experientia docet saepius evenire, ut alumni unius seminarii in aliud migrent, sive quia ad ministerium haud idonei judicantur, sive disciplinae severioris fuga, sive tandem ex animi inconstantia et levitate. Praecipimus igitur, ut nemo hujusmodi in posterum in seminarium quodvis admittatur, nisi secum afferat literas testimoniales ab Episcopo et superioribus seminarii ex quo recens egressus est. Quod si eum hactenus Episcopus ille aut superiores seminarii suis sumptibus aluerint, ex justitia recuperare debent ab Episcopo aut superioribus seminarii, ad quod transiit, tantum quantum in ipso educando impensum fuit."—*Conc. Plen. Balt. II., Acta et Decreta*, n. 180; this was renewed in III Plen. Counc. of Baltimore (a. 1884)—*Acta et Decreta Conc. Plen. Balt. III.*, n. 176.

[242] P. 179, footnotes 232-233.

the diocese or repay the amount spent on his training.[243] Anyone accepting a gratuity under such terms equivalently entered a contract binding on him in justice. If the founder or donor wished to forestall in his stipulated condition any desertion of the diocese even for entry into religion, he would have to state so explicitly, whereupon the cleric accepting the condition and binding himself by contract would equivalently renounce his right to enter the religious state.[244] There could be circumstances, however, wherein even a contract of this nature would cease binding, e. g., when the cleric's salvation would otherwise be endangered.[245]

4°. Oaths of diocesan service

Though the Holy See decreed that an oath perpetually to serve their mission should be taken by all those who were ordained *titulo missionis,* it did not favor the exaction of a similar oath outside mission territories by any subordinate power.[246] Each Bishop had ordinary means in common law to retain his clerics as long as they were necessary or useful, and these rendered an oath superfluous. Besides, sometimes excardinations were to be recommended, and then oaths would be obstacles.

Some dioceses obliged their clerics by particular law or custom to make a promise to labor in them for a certain determined

[243] In two cases where founders had placed such conditions for those returning to the lay state, viz., *Tiburtina,* 11 mart. 1752, and *Ferrarien.,* 20 ianuar. 1821, the S. C. C. did not interfere—Lucidi, *De visitatione sacrorum liminum,* II, pp. 341-2.

[244] "Nam religiosum statum amplecti est tantum de consilio; quod autem contractum ab ipso initum expleat, est de praecepto."—Bouix, *Tractatus de Jure Regularium* (2 ed., Bruxellis, 1867), I, p. 550.

[245] Cf. Claeys-Bouuaert, *De Canonica Cleri Saecularis Obedientia,* pp. 246-253, in which a more complete discussion of this whole question may be found.

[246] S. C. C., 15 apr. 1628, answered that a Bishop could not exact from his clerics before their priestly ordination a promise to serve a certain church, when they possessed only a simple benefice not requiring residence—Barbosa, *Summa apostolicarum decisionum,* coll. 295, n. 12. In 1861, however, when the U. S. A. was still under the S. C. P. F., the III Prov. Counc. of Cincinnati required a serious promise to this effect.—Cf. *supra,* p. 181, footnote 238.

period of time.[247] The unhappy result was that after that period expired they were considered as having discharged their entire obligation and as being freed of further service in the diocese.[248]

Even when such promises were exacted, they had to be understood as not excluding one's freedom to enter religion. In 1859 a Bishop in France had asked Pope Pius IX for permission to prohibit his secular clerics from entering any Religious Institute for a period of three years from their priestly ordination, and the Sacred Congregation for the affairs of Bishops and of Religious Orders refused the petition as unprecedented.[249] Likewise, in the incident of the Bishop of Bavaria in 1882 [250] the four deacons were sustained in their objection to making a promise of six years of unconditional service, because their right to enter religion, if God so called them, had to be safeguarded; and an extra promise to serve the diocese was unnecessary, since everyone receiving the priesthood had to promise obedience to his Bishop.

B. Minor and Major Clerics

1°. Their diocesan stability

Several characteristics of clerical life demanded a less stringent discipline for them than for priests. Attendance at seminaries removed them from parishes; their assignment to a church had become a formality meaning little more than serving Mass in a definite church on Sundays and feast days; their necessity or utility to the diocese referred rather to the future. They still had four possible proper Bishops for ordination, so that if they were refused by one for an insufficient reason they still had to

247 E. g., the Synod of Paderborn in 1867 obliged the students of the seminary to at least a three-year period of service after ordination—Cap. XLIV, n. 5 (*AkKR*, XX, 398).

248 So it was in many dioceses of Italy—Nilles, *De libertate clericorum religionem ingrediendi*, p. 113.

249 *Collectanea in Usum Secretariae Sacrae Congregationis Episcoporum et Regularium* (A. Bizzarri, Romae, 1885), (*Collectanea S. C. Ep. et Reg.*), pp. 669-670.

250 Cf. *supra*, p. 180, footnote 237.

be allowed the liberty of seeking another. A title of ordination was unnecessary until they reached major orders, and then it might be a simple benefice, patrimony, or pension, none of which, as such, required residence.

All authorities agreed that a cleric could not leave his diocese without permission, but they still contended that that permission, in the form of *litterae commendatitiae,* could not be refused to one who was non-beneficed and unassigned.[251] If he was assigned or beneficed, the Bishop for a just cause could refuse to let him leave.[252] This was the constant principle on which the Sacred Congregation of the Council settled disputes occasioned by the interpretation of sess. XXIII, *de ref.*, c. 16, as far as clerics alone were concerned.[253]

[251] E. g., Schmalzgrueber: "Cum communi (sententia) dicendum, quod Episcopi teneantur per se loquendo hujusmodi clericis dare litteras commendatitias, si has ex peregrinationis, aut etiam domicilii vel dioecesis mutandae causa petant."—as cited by Bouix, *Tractatus De Episcopo,* V. II, p. V, cap. XXIX, § IV; Monacelli: "De honestate requiritur licentia (pro discedendo e dioecesi) non autem de necessitate. Nam litterae hujusmodi commendatitiae pro discessu a dioecesi, iis qui non habent officium, beneficium aut aliam obligationem personalem, servitium et residentiam exigentia, nunquam sunt denegandae... Nisi tamen ageretur de ordinatis ob necessitatem ecclesiae: nam isti locum inconsulto Episcopo deserere non possunt."—*Formularium,* tit. IV, form. 6, n. 1. Of like tenor was the response of S. C. Ep. et Reg., *Castri Maris,* 8 maii 1716, in which question VIII was: "An Sacerdotibus, et Clericis dictae Civitatis non obligatis ad Curam, neque ad residentiam, volentibus alio se transferre absque licentia Episcopi teneatur idem Episcopus concedere litteras commendatitias in casu...?" to which the response was: "Ad octavum, non esse denegandas, nisi cum rationabili causa." — *Fontes,* n. 1832; *Collectanea S. C. Ep. et Reg.,* pp. 303, 304.

[252] Pignatelli stated: "Itaque, si sint adscripti servitio alicujus ecclesiae, non poterunt discedere absque licentia sui Episcopi, juxta Concilium Tridentinum (sess. 23, c. 16); ubi decernitur quod tales non debent locum deserere, inconsulto Episcopo, id est, sine consensu Episcopi... Quod si deseruerint, sacrorum exercitium est eis interdicendum, ad praescriptum sexti canonis Concilii Chalcedonensis, qui... a Tridentina Synodo innovatur, dicto capite 16."—*Consultationes canonicae,* t. III, consult. LVI, n. 3. S. C. C., in *Fulginatensi,* 19 ianuarii 1805: "Quanquam ex Decreto Clementis XI probari nequeant resignationes beneficiorum, nisi accedente *attestatione* Ordinarii, attamen si compertum sit, eumdem nulla subeunte justa causa repugnasse, quominus resignatio concedatur, tum solet Summus Pontifex sua uti auctoritate, ut sine testimonialibus resignationes hujusmodi concedat; uti tradit Rigantius, in commentario ad regulam 45 Cancellariae, n. 34 et seq., tomo 3."—Pallottini, *Collectio Resolutionum S. C. Concilii,* III, 235, n. 171; Bouix, *Tractatus De Episcopo,* V. II, p. V, cap. XXIX, § III.

[253] Note the following decisions of S. C. C.: *Larinen.*, 20 aug. 1732, that a Bishop can prohibit under certain punishment any ecclesiastic, even in minor orders, from

The extraneous factors spoken of above[254] later tightened the bond to the diocese even of the unassigned cleric, so that no longer could it be stated categorically that he was free to leave. For example, if he had enjoyed the gratuitous education of his diocese for a number of years, or had received major orders *titulo servitii dioecesis,* he remained bound to the diocese even though he was not assigned to any particular church or office.[255]

2°. Methods of excardination and incardination

There were three chief ways in which a simple cleric could be canonically transferred to another diocese: a) by the acquisition of a residential benefice elsewhere with the proper letters (*commendatitiae*) of his present Bishop; b) by letters of ex-

leaving the diocese without permission of the Ordinary—Richter, *Conc. Trident.*, sess. XXIII, *de ref.*, c. 16, *Declar. et Resol.*, n. 1; *Segnen.*, 13 sept. 1749: "An decretum episcopi factum in visitatione, quo prohibetur, ne clerici (ascripti) discedant a dioecesi sine licentia eiusdem episcopi in scriptis habenda sub poena suspensionis, sustineatur, et quatenus affirmative: An liceat dicto episcopo sine iusta causa discessum denegare in casu . . . ," to which the S. C. C. replied: "Affirmative ad primam partem in casu de quo agitur; negative ad secundam et amplius."—*Thesaurus Resolutionum*, XIX, 83; Richter, *Conc. Trident., Declar. et Resol.*, n. 2; *Amerina*, 8 maii 1756, that clerics ordained for the necessity of the church and assigned to it cannot leave without express permission, and any opinion to the contrary is reprobated—*Thesaurus Resolutionum*, XXV (1756), 37-38; opinion confirmed, July 17, 1756 (*ibid.*, p. 53). The same decision was rendered 12 aug. 1871—*Thesaurus Resolutionum*, CXXX (1871), 543-550. This nullified the theory of Antonius De Martinis, who had held: ". . . si clericus qui habet simplicem adscriptionem ecclesiae alicui, consulto Episcopo abiret, discessus licentiam ab eo quaerendo, Concilio (Tridentino) satisfaceret: nec dicatur, quod in hoc casu Episcopus licentiam denegaret, cum id de jure peragere non possit, ut censuit S. Congregatio."—as cited by Bouix, *ibid.*, § IV, p. 281. In the acts of the preparatory commission on disciplinary matters for the Vatican Council (a. 1869) it appears that the consultors were satisfied that no new law was needed, but only a more faithful observance of the old law: "Ora intorno a siffatta questione i reverendissimi consultori opinarono che le ordinazioni dei canoni già esistenti sono per sè sufficienti, qualora siano esattamente osservate, a raggiungere lo scopo voluto dal Tridentino, ad impedire al chierico l'illegittimo abbandono della chiesa a cui trovasi ascritto o della diocesi, a frenare la facilità delle escardinazioni ed incardinazioni dei chierici, sicchè non sia mestieri di emanare nuovi decreti, e solo tornare espediente di inculcare gravemente ea fedele osservanza degli antichi."—*Congressus* XL (Mansi, XLIX, 893).

[254] Pp. 172-184.

[255] Note that for a similar reason the cleric, Aemilius Strub, was ordered to remain in Algiers.—Cf. *supra*, p. 179, footnote 232.

corporation (also known as *dimissoriales* or *excardinatoriae*); and c) indirectly, by acquiring a new proper Bishop.

a) *Residential benefice.*—From what was said above about the scarcity of these benefices in the nineteenth century, and about the multiplication of seminaries, it must be concluded that for clerics still in training this was not any longer a usual method. In order to take possession of such a benefice legally and conclude the transfer, the cleric had to have the *litterae commendatitiae* of his Bishop, which, besides a permission to leave, certified to his birth, age, life and morals, the absence of impediments, etc., so that any other Bishop, to whose diocese the cleric travelled, was authorized not only to receive him, but also to confer on him an office or benefice, if he so chose.[256] Clerics occupying residential benefices in other dioceses without having obtained these letters could be recalled under pain of censure.

The difficulty of obtaining the necessary *litterae commendatitiae* depended on how necessary the cleric was to his present diocese. If he himself or his friends were supplying the patrimony or pension for his support, and if as yet he had not been assigned to any church, it was presumed that he was not necessary to his diocese, and the Bishop could not refuse to give him the letters. If, on the other hand, the cleric had been assigned to a church where his future labor would be necessary, or if he was already occupying a residential benefice, the Bishop could refuse to grant him *litterae commendatitiae,* because then he was considered indispensable.

In the latter event, if the cleric still wanted to depart, recourse had to be made by him to the Holy See, which either sustained the Bishop's refusal or requested the Bishop to grant the letters.

[256] S. C. de Prop. Fide, resp. 20 apr. 1873: "Graviter itaque tulit S. C. P. F. quod non semel ad eius aures pervenit, quandoque in Ecclesiis Missionum contingere ut facile in dioeceses recipiantur presbyteri et clerici quin litteras commendatitias praedictas afferant, immo et sine iisdem ab una ecclesia discedant et in aliam transmeare audeant... Quapropter ne similibus damnis via in posterum pateat, omnino mandat S. Congregatio omnibus Episcopis in locis missionum degentibus nec non Vicariis ac Praefectis Apostolicis ut omni tergiversatione seposita, litteras commendatitias suorum Episcoporum a clericis et sacerdotibus peregrinis exigant";—*Collectanea* S. C. P. F., n. 1400; *Acta et Decreta Conc. Plen. Balt. III*, Appen., pp. 211-212.

The Holy See did not decide "*pro gratia*" unless it was clear: 1st. that the diocese could dispense with the cleric without suffering damage to souls; 2nd. that the cleric was not receiving a suitable sustenance; and 3rd. that the cleric's reason for departure was just and reasonable, for example, because his health was endangered by the climate of his present locality, or because his parents had moved to another diocese and needed his help. In such instances, if he had been educated in the first diocese gratuitously, the condition was added that he reimburse it before leaving.

When the cleric desiring the transfer was already in possession of a residential benefice in his own diocese, he had to resign it according to law,[257] and also had to bring to the new Bishop a testimonial of the resignation. Obviously, the new Bishop also became the proper Bishop for his future ordination.

b) *Letters of excorporation.*—The genesis of the practice of excardinating clerics by letter was explained in Chapters III and IV.[258] Though it can hardly be doubted that the custom was of long duration before it was made a part of the common law by papal decree, nevertheless, little is read about it prior to that time. The following case is found as far back as 1848 and illustrates the procedure: When the Archbishop of Naples had continually refused to elevate to major orders a certain acolyte in his diocese because he judged the candidate unworthy, the cleric brought his case to Rome, petitioning the Sacred Congregation of the Council for the favor either of being ordained or of being excardinated to another diocese where he could be ordained. After the Sacred Congregation had found, upon investigation, very favorable testimony as to the life and character of the cleric, appropriate recommendations were made to the Archbishop, who replied that he could not give his consent to the excardination on account of a glaring abuse in Naples by which, as he stated, ". . . omnes mali clerici ab archiepiscopo rejecti, obtenta excardinatione, in alias dioeceses pergebant, ubi brevi tempore sacerdotes facti, Neapolim revertebantur et in

[257] Cc. 1-15, X, *de renunciatione*, I, 9.

[258] Pp. 91-92, 113-114.

familiis suis viventes ludibrium et angustias archiepiscopo parabant." Since, however, the Ordinary of the Abbacy Nullius of the Most Holy Trinity of Cava, near Naples, was willing to receive the acolyte into his clergy, the Sacred Congregation of the Council gave the following as its final response: "Emisso prius juramento de animo fideliter permanendi in abbatia Nullius SS. Trinitatis, pro gratia excardinationis . . ., ita ut valeat ab eodem ordinario (scil. abbate) ad omnes ss. ordines servatis servandis . . . promoveri, dummodo, postquam fuerit promotus, ordines non exerceat in dioecesi Neapolitana absque consensu archiepiscopi, etiamsi cappellaniam vel beneficium in eadem possideat; facto verbo cum Sanctissimo." [259]

By proper analysis of this case it will be found that the favor granted did not differ from the letters of excardination which became the normal legal procedure in 1898 by the Decree "*A primis.*" The acolyte had not yet moved to the new Abbacy; yet, its Ordinary was empowered to raise the cleric to sacred orders on his own right, without any period of residence being exacted of the cleric, but with only an oath to remain permanently. This was the fundamental notion of letters of excardination for clerics—an abbreviated method of acquiring a new domicile and proper Bishop.

Evidence of what seems to be excardination of clerics by letters is also found in the IV Provincial Council of Baltimore (a. 1840) when it decreed: "Commendamus episcopis libros habere in quibus accurate recenseantur ordinationes, clericorum ex aliis dioecesibus in suas cooptationes, designationes pastorum, tituli ecclesiarum, aliaque omnia quae ad statum ecclesiasticum respiciunt." [260]

c) *Indirect method: acquisition of a new proper Bishop.*—There still was, as always, this avenue of escape for any discontented cleric. Granted that he became a cleric in the diocese of

[259] In *Neapolitana,* 15 iulii 1848—Lingen et Reuss, *Causae selectae in S. C. C. propositae per summaria precum ab a. 1823 usque ad a. 1869* (Ratisbonae, 1871), pp. 4-7.

[260] *Decreta,* n. IX—Mansi, XXXIX, 368. The same was copied by the II Plen. Counc. of Baltimore (a. 1866)—*Conc. Plen. Balt. II.* (a. 1866), *Acta et Decreta,* t. III, cap. II, n. 92.

his origin, he could still acquire a new domicile, an adequate simple benefice, or a Bishop to receive him in his household, with the knowledge and consent of his present proper Bishop; and in each case it was possible for him to become incardinated in the diocese of his new proper Bishop, if and when the same conferred on him a residential benefice.[261]

It may seem odd that a *cleric* could change his domicile, with of course the permission of his former Bishop, but this was the most common form of excardination for clerics not yet ordained to the priesthood.[262] In fact some Bishops were so alarmed at alien clerics residing in their dioceses that they attempted to exclude them for the sole reason that they did not belong there, until the Sacred Congregation for the affairs of Bishops and of Religious Orders, on Dec. 17, 1839, admonished them that such clerics could not be expelled, since reasonable causes warranted their remaining.[263]

[261] Gasparri, *De Sacra Ordin.*, II, nn. 853-859.

[262] The following cases of the Roman Congregations will exemplify this truth: 1) S. C. C., *Januen.*, 30 ianuarii 1830, in which two seminarians of Genoa, complaining of their poverty and ill health, sought permission to depart from their diocese to set up a domicile in Bobbio, where a certain benefactor pledged sacred patrimony for both of them. The S. C. C. replied: "Quoties ordinarius januensis nec locum, in quo oratores absque valetudinis detrimento studia perficere possint, assignare, nec titulum pro s. ordinatione eis suppeditare valeat, et postquam constiterit de legitima constitutione tituli s. ordinationis, pro gratia . . . , facto verbo cum Sanctissimo."—Lingen et Reuss, *Causae selectae*, p. 7. 2) S. C. Ep. et Reg., *Neapolitan.*, 16 iulii 1841, in which the Bishop of Sora raised an objection to the ordination to the priesthood of a certain deacon of the diocese, because for four years he had been staying at Naples, where he held a position as prefect in a college. To the Bishop's demand that he return to his diocesan seminary the deacon replied that he was too poor to reimburse the Neapolitan seminary, and that he was in ill health. The S. C. Ep. et Reg. replied: "Scribatur episcopo sorano ad mentem; mens est: 'che s'insinui a Mons. vescovo o di accordare l'escardinazione o le dimissorie.' "—*Collectanea S. C. Ep. et Reg.*, pp. 475-476. 3) S. C. C., Resp. (*Excardinationis*) 29 maii 1880, in which a cleric R, of diocese S, obtained permission in 1875 to go to Naples for his theological studies. While there, circumstances made it reasonable for him to endeavor to remain there perpetually, because his father transferred his home and goods to that city, where also someone promised him patrimony, of which he was destitute, on condition of his celebrating Mass there. Accordingly, he asked his Bishop of S for excardination to Naples, who refused and ordered him to come back to his own diocesan seminary. The cleric appealed to S. C. C. for excardination, which replied: "Pro gratia, facto verbo cum Sanctissimo."—*ASS*, XIII (1880), 522 *ss.*

[263] *Collectanea S. C. Ep. et Reg.*, p. 89.

The practice, however, of clerics going to and remaining at Rome itself, and of establishing a domicile there, was becoming an abuse which was draining many dioceses of their priests. Pope Leo XIII, at the repeated instance of many Bishops, struck at and remedied the abuse through a decree of the Sacred Congregation of the Council, "*Anteactis temporibus*," Dec. 22, 1894.[264] In this he made it impossible for clerics of an alien diocese to establish a domicile at Rome without the express permission of the Supreme Pontiff, to be granted through the Sacred Congregation of the Council. Those who were then in Rome were to return home after a month, unless they were bound to residence by a title of benefice or office already possessed, or had already acquired a domicile at Rome, through a long period of residence there, with the tacit or express permission of their Bishops. No cleric of another diocese was to be given any office or duty, requiring residence at Rome, without the permission of the Holy Father as well as the testimonial and commendatory letters of his Bishop; and those living in Rome for studies, or permitted by their Ordinaries to go there for other reasons, were to return home as soon as their business was finished, and were not to attempt staying under some specious plea, such as that of insufficient sustenance at home.

An adequate simple benefice acquired by a cleric in an alien diocese did no more than subject the possessor to the new Bishop in all things pertaining to it, and empower said Bishop to confer orders on him, after receiving the testimonials of his original Bishop. No permissions were needed to acquire a simple benefice, since it did not take the cleric out of his proper diocese at all, not even for residence, much less for incardination. Whensoever the new Bishop of the place where the simple benefice had been acquired wanted to attach the cleric to that same diocese, he had to resort to one of the other methods just explained.

In order that a cleric might become excardinated through his association with the household of some Bishop it was required: 1st. that he obtain permission from his present proper Bishop—the Bishop of the cleric's place of origin or of his acquired

264 *ASS*, XXVII (1894-1895), 373 ff.

domicile—to leave the diocese for the sake of entering the service of some Bishop in that Bishop's own household; 2nd. that he spend three years of service in the household of that Bishop; and 3rd. that his service be satisfactory enough to make that Bishop willing, not only to confer the next order on him and to bestow on him an ordinary benefice (as was required in every ordination by virtue of the title of *familiaritas*), but to install him in a residential benefice, the authorization to accept which was understood to be contained in the original permission whereby he lawfully engaged himself in that particular Bishop's household service.

3°. Special requisites for certain groups

a) *Subdeacons and deacons ordained* titulo missionis.—By reason of their oath these were still under the control of the Sacred Congregation for the Propagation of the Faith, as in the preceding period,[265] but in 1885 there was a relaxation granted for both England and the United States of America to the extent that there could be excardinations of such clerics in these countries to other dioceses within their same province without needing permission from the Sacred Congregation for the Propagation of the Faith.[266]

b) *Foreign-born clerics emigrating to the United States of America, especially from Poland.*—The Holy See recognized that it was very important, in the transfer of candidates for the priesthood to dioceses thousands of miles away, to follow the regulations of ecclesiastical law so wisely laid down by the Church. Accordingly, the Sacred Congregation for the Propagation of the Faith issued an instruction to the Bishops of the United States of America on February 25, 1896, to remind them of the requisites for receiving such clerics, and to amplify these same requirements.[267] The instruction dealt particularly with priests and candidates for the priesthood, whether clerical or lay, who had originated in Poland, even though latterly they lived

[265] Cf. *supra*, pp. 170-171.

[266] Cf. *supra*, pp. 144-145.

[267] *Collectanea* S. C. P. F., n. 1918. Cf. *supra*, p. 97.

for a while in Italy or elsewhere. For clerics of any nation who had not yet been ordained priests and who were desirous of becoming linked with the clergy of some diocese here, it reminded the Bishops that they should require from them the *litterae dimissoriales et testimoniales* of the Ordinary of their place of origin. But, for those who had originated in Poland, it decreed that the Bishops should not admit them unless they were provided with Testimonial Letters from the Sacred Congregation for the Propagation of the Faith which plainly attested to the liberty of their departure, certified their freedom from censures, and gave assurance of their possession of good morals.[268]

The Bishops of Italy were equally warned by Pope Leo XIII, a few years later, not to confer sacred orders on any foreign youths, especially those from Poland, without the authentic Testimonial Letters of their proper Ordinary, namely, when these youths, who originated in Poland, were acquiring new proper Bishops in Italy through a change of domicile, and especially not to give these clerics *litterae commendatitiae* to the Bishops of America without the previous permission of the Sacred Congregation for the Propagation of the Faith.[269] The instruction of 1896 was withdrawn in 1908 [270] in favor of three decrees of the Sacred Congregation of the Council, the "*A primis*," [271] the "*Vetuit*," [272] and that of November 24, 1906.[273]

C. Priests

1°. Diocesan stability strengthened

The Tridentine discipline continued for priests until the beginning of the nineteenth century. A priest who had been assigned to a church at ordination could not leave it without

[268] Cf. *supra*, p. 62, footnote 74.

[269] S. C. de Prop. Fide, *Litterae circulares ad Italiae Ordinarios*, 2 maii 1898—*ASS*, XXXI (1898-99), 320.

[270] Pius X, Const. "*Sapienti Consilio*," June 29, 1908—*AAS*, I (1909), 7-19; *Fontes*, n. 682.

[271] July 20, 1898—*ASS*, XXXI (1898-99), 49 ss.; *Fontes*, n. 4307.

[272] Dec. 22, 1905—*ASS*, XXXVIII (1905-06), 407 ss.; *Fontes*, n. 4327.

[273] *ASS*, XXXIX (1906), 600 ss.; *Fontes*, n. 4330.

his Bishop's permission.[274] If he was neither beneficed nor by any other duty held to residence, he was free to leave the diocese without permission, and the Bishop was bound to issue *litterae dimissoriales* for him.[275] Those who possessed benefices could

[274] Benedict XIV, ep. "*Ex quo,*" 14 ian. 1747, § 11, concluded this even from that solemn promise of obedience and reverence which, for a thousand years back, every priest was required to make in the hands of his ordaining Bishop: "Neque porro Nos pro nuda inanique formula habendam esse putamus solemnem illam obedientiae, et reverentiae sponsionem, quam Presbyter facit in manibus Episcopi ordinantis, iuxta vetustissimum Ecclesiae morem, ante mille annos indubitanter servatum; ut ex antiquis Ritualibus colligitur, quae expendit Catalanus *ad Pontificale Romanum*, Tom. I, pag. 149 in notis ad § 29. Quin immo libenter agnoscimus, Presbyterum, huiusmodi promissionis vigore, ea lege, inter alias, adstrictum teneri, ut a servitio Ecclesiae, cui in ordinatione addictus fuerit, discedere nequeat sine licentia Episcopi";—*Fontes*, n. 374. S. C. C., *Segnensis*, 13 sept. 1749—the Bishop had forbidden any cleric to depart from the diocese without his permission. Some priests objected on the grounds that they had no benefice or duty requiring residence, and that the obligation of serving a church without recompense ceased at priestly ordination. The Bishop stated that the names of all of them were inscribed on the clerical roll of the cathedral church, from which, in fact, they received a token of recompense on the occasion of funerals and anniversaries. The doubt proposed to the Sacred Congregation was: "An decretum Episcopi, quo prohibetur ne clerici discedant a dioecesi sine licentia ejusdem Episcopi, in scriptis habenda, sub poena suspensionis, sustineatur?—Et quatenus affirmative, an liceat dicto Episcopo sine justa causa discessum denegare?" and the response was: "Affirmative ad primam partem in casu de quo agitur: negative ad secundam et amplius."—*Thesaurus Resolutionum*, XIX (1750), 83. S. C. C., *Amerina*, 8 maii 1756—Ignatius Torretti had been ordained and assigned to the service of a certain parochial church, where he was unwilling to remain. To the question whether he could leave against his Bishop's will, the answer was: "Negative, assignata congrua per Episcopum."—*Thesaurus Resolutionum*, XXV (1756), 37.

[275] S. C. Ep. et Reg., *Castri Maris*, 8 maii 1716, to dub. VIII: "An Sacerdotibus, et Clericis dictae Civitatis non obligatis ad Curam, neque ad residentiam, volentibus alio se transferre absque licentia Episcopi teneatur idem Episcopus concedere litteras commendatitias in casu etc.?" responded: "Ad octavum, non esse denegandas, nisi cum rationabili causa."—*Collectanea S. C. Ep. et Reg.*, pp. 303-304; *Fontes*, n. 1832. S. C. Ep. et Reg., 26 martii 1784, commanded a certain Bishop to issue *litterae commendatitiae* for a cleric's transfer under the circumstances here considered—*Anal. Jur. Pont.*, serie 8 (1866), col. 1959. The same Sacred Congregation on May 18, 1795, ordered a priest who had received a residential benefice elsewhere without his Bishop's permission to go back temporarily and ask for the permission, whereupon he could reassume his new benefice—*Loc. cit.* Though it is not expressly stated, probably he was assigned in his home diocese without possessing an adequate benefice or some other title of assured income, and thus the obtaining of a residential benefice elsewhere was regarded as a just cause, in the presence of which the Bishop could not deny him the intermediate permission for his transfer.

not leave, of course, without first being permitted to resign, but such a resignation could not be rejected without a just cause.[276]

If that same discipline had been followed after the collapse of the beneficial edifice, doubtless the world would have been filled with vagrant priests. As Bouix stated, when discussing whether or not in the nineteenth century the unassigned and unbeneficed priests were free to depart, acceptance of the affirmative view could have drained France of almost all its priests.[277] Very noticeable was the change in the *stylus Romanae Curiae* by virtue of a stricter interpretation of the already existing common law. The nineteenth century rules adhered to in solving difficulties were:

1st. Every priest, even the non-beneficed and unassigned, was bound to residence and service in his diocese as long as he was given an office or sacred duty and a suitable source of support from the particular church; and

2nd. Permission to depart from a diocese could be given to any priest, but only for a just and reasonable cause.

Examples of the application of the first rule by the Roman Curia in solving cases are:

a) S.C.C., *Nucerina* residentiae et suspensionis, 19 sept. 1818. The Bishop had placed on a priest, ordained for the title of patrimony and unassigned in the diocese, the obligation of remaining in the diocese under pain of *ipso facto* suspension. The priest, thinking such a mandate was invalid, since he had not even an ecclesiastical office, departed from the diocese and appealed to Rome. The Sacred Congregation of the Council answered that the precept of the Bishop would have to be observed, provided that the Bishop assigned to the priest a suitable source of support (*congrua sustentatio*); furthermore, it said that the priest had incurred an irregularity for having exercised

[276] S. C. C., in *Fulginatensi*, 19 ianuarii 1805: "Quanquam ex Decreto Clementis XI probari nequeant resignationes beneficiorum nisi accedente *attestatione* Ordinarii, attamen si compertum sit eumdem, nulla subeunte justa causa, repugnare quominus resignatio concedatur, tum solet Summus Pontifex sua uti auctoritate, ut sine testimonialibus resignationes hujusmodi concedat";—Bouix, *Tractatus De Episcopo*, V. II, p. V, cap. XXIV, § III.

[277] Cf. *supra*, p. 174, footnote 217.

his sacred orders at a time when he had already been under the *ipso facto* censure of suspension.[278]

b) S.C.C., *Nucerina,* 19 sept. 1818. The Bishop of Nocera, in 1803, had issued an edict that all ordinands had to be assigned to their own parochial church or to some other one at the discretion of the Bishop, and that if they left this place they would incur suspension *ipso facto.* A certain priest, ordained for the title of patrimony, afterwards absented himself from the diocese and refused to return at the command of the Bishop. The Sacred Congregation of the Council decided that the Bishop's mandate was valid, that the priest had to return, and, furthermore, that he had incurred suspension by his action.[279]

c) S.C.Ep. et Reg., *Amerina,* 12 feb. 1819. A priest of the diocese of Amelia had obtained a parish in the diocese of Todi. It was asked of the Sacred Congregation for the affairs of Bishops and of Religious Orders: " 1. An sacerdos de quo parere teneatur amerino episcopo eumdem ad suam dioecesim revocanti? Et quatenus affirmative, 2. An idem sacerdos cogi possit ad acceptandum archipresbyteratum collegiatae cujusdam ecclesiae eidem ab episcopo amerino oblatum? " to which it replied: " Ad 1um, affirmative; ad 2um, sacerdos de quo commendetur episcopo et ad mentem; mens est, quod episcopus provideat sacerdotem de congrua sustentatione." [280]

d) S.C.C., *Amerina,* 14 dec. 1822. A priest, Hippolytus Fossati, holding a choral benefice in the cathedral chapter of Amelia, while on vacation at Rome resigned his benefice, and his resignation was accepted by the Office of the Apostolic Datary. When his vacation period was over he asked the Sacred Congregation of the Council for an extension of his absence from the diocese on account of illness. The Bishop of Amelia objected to this, told the Sacred Congregation of the Council of the great shortage of priests in his city and asked that the priest be required to return to his diocese where he could

278 *Anal. Jur. Pont.,* serie 8 (1866), coll. 1940-1943; *Thesaurus Resolutionum,* LXXVIII (1818), 250 ss.

279 *Anal. Jur. Pont., ibid.,* coll. 1944-1945; *Thesaurus Resolutionum, ibid.,* 262 ss.

280 *Collectanea S. C. Ep. et Reg.,* p. 413.

be of help at least in offering Mass on feast days. To the question: "An et quod tempus sit oratori concedendum Indultum absentiae?" the Sacred Congregation of the Council replied: "Affirmative donec convalescat."[281] Hence, even though the priest was without a benefice, he was still bound to serve in the diocese as long as there was an office which could be assigned to him which guaranteed a source of income.

e) S.C.C., *Nucerina,* 15 martii 1828. A priest, ordained for the title of patrimony and in possession of a parochial benefice in Nocera, later acquired a parish in another diocese without his Bishop's consent. The Sacred Congregation of the Council ordered him to return to his own diocese, and declared that he had incurred suspension and irregularity.[282]

f) S.C.C., *Reatina,* 26 ian. 1833. Gaspar Brizi received tonsure in his original diocese of Rieti. Some time later, at Rome, he joined the Society of the Priests of the Mission (Lazarists or Vincentians), where also he received minor and major orders for the title of patrimony supplied by his parents in Rieti. Afterwards, he left the Congregation, which he was free to do, and returned to his diocese of birth, where he was given the position of teaching youths, for which there was a foundation with an obligation of two Masses a week, but for which the appointee was removable *ad nutum* of the town councilors. The priest, Brizi, held this post for five years; but, when the archpresbyteral parish "Montis Boni" in the diocese of Sabina had become vacant, he entered the *concursus* and won it; whereupon, he took possession of the parish through an Apostolic Letter, and soon was made Vicar Forane. The Bishop of Rieti refused permission for him to leave the diocese on the grounds that there was an archpresbyteral parish in his own diocese that he could have.

The case was brought to the Sacred Congregation of the Council, and on the priest's behalf it was argued: 1. that he had not been assigned in Rieti at the time of tonsure, nor at the time of the minor and major orders, because then he was in a Re-

[281] *Thesaurus Resolutionum,* LXXXII (1822), 278.

[282] *Anal. Jur. Pont.,* serie 8 (1866), coll. 1947-1950.

ligious Institute; 2. he was not held in Rieti by any residential benefice, because his teaching position was revocable *ad nutum;* and 3. past decisions of the Sacred Congregation of the Council, in 1574 and 1604, in similar cases, decreed that a cleric in Brizi's circumstances was free to depart from his diocese at will.

Despite all this, to the question: " An et quomodo sacerdos Gaspar Brizi cogi possit ut in dioecesim Reatinam revertatur," the response was: " Affirmative, dummodo de congrua eidem ab Episcopo provideatur." [283]

g) S.C.C., *Causa solutionis et excardinationis,* 18 feb. 1869 et 19 feb. 1870. A certain priest, Livius, whose seminary education for ten years was at the expense of the diocese of his origin, after serving the diocese as teacher for one year and seminary professor for six years, obtained a three-month leave of absence. During it he acquired a position of professor in a certain University, and at the end of his specified leave refused to return. The Bishop suspended him, and appealed to the Sacred Congregation of the Council that the priest be forced to return, or at least be made to restore the expenses of his education. The response was: " Posse cogi ad revertendum in propriam dioecesim, modo absolutionem a censuris obtineat eique de congrua provideatur." [284]

h) S.C.C., *Calaritana seu Uxellen.* excardinationis et nominationis, 29 ian. 1887. A priest who was a Canon Theologian of the Cathedral of Alais, France, and who taught dogmatic theology and sacred Scripture in the seminary, was elected, after a *concursus,* to the dignity of Canon Penitentiary of the Cathedral of Cagliari, Italy. The Bishop of Alais refused to grant consent for the election to be ratified on the ground that the Canon was necessary to his own diocese. The Canon alleged ill health and his long period of service as his excuse for desiring the change, and the Bishop of Cagliari offered to give a priest from that diocese to take the Canon's place. But to the question: " An excardinatio et electio sit admittenda in casu? " the Sacred

[283] *Thesaurus Resolutionum,* XCIII (1833), 28-35; Richter, *Conc. Trident.,* p. 208, n. 9; Bouix, *Tractatus De Episcopo,* V. II, p. V, cap. XXIV, pp. 284-5.

[284] *ASS,* V (1869), 477-479.

Congregation of the Council replied: "Negative, et fiat novus concursus." [285]

Examples of the application of the second rule by the Roman Curia in the solution of cases are:

a) S.C.C., *Bojanen. et Thermularum,* 12 dec. 1885. A priest, William, of the diocese of Boiano, accepted a temporary position as a preacher in the diocese of Termoli with the consent of his own Bishop, given orally for an indefinite period. His success was such that the people of the parish of St. Mary in Termoli wanted him as pastor, and the Bishop of Termoli consented. When excardination was asked for, the Bishop of Boiano objected on the grounds that William was necessary to his diocese of origin because of a shortage of clergy there, and that, besides, he was in possession of a benefice, or a share in the revenues of the diocese of his origin, by which he was bound to personal residence. Furthermore, the Bishop of Boiano declared that he had never given William permission to leave at all.

In favor of excardination, William produced two witnesses to his Bishop's oral permission to leave, and the new Bishop claimed that he would have trouble with the parish in question if William were not permitted to remain.

The Sacred Congregation of the Council responded: "Scribatur episcopo bojanensi ad mentem: nempe videri s. congregationi adesse causas sufficientes concedendi excardinationem; informet tamen s. congregationem super redditibus quos actu possidet sacerdos de quo, et si habet rationes in contrarium producat." [286]

b) S.C.C., *Viglevanen. seu Mediolanen.* excardinationis, 8 maii 1886. Martianus, a priest of the diocese of Vigevano, Italy, was educated gratis for two years at his own seminary, after which, while still a student, he received permission to go to Milan, because of his health, and because a pastor there awaited his help. Later, he was ordained by his original Bishop for the title of a chaplaincy at Milan, but under the condition of supplying it by a vicar. Frequently he received oral permission from the Bishop of his place of origin to be absent from that

[285] *ASS*, XX (1887), 34.

[286] *ASS*, XVIII (1885), 504-506.

diocese, so that most of his time was spent at Milan. Several times, also, he did not return when told to do so by his Bishop.

The first request for excardination met with the response on Feb. 16, 1884: "Lectum, et orator absque mora pareat mandatis episcopi."[287]

However, Martianus, reintroducing the case, claimed that the diocese of Vigevano did not lack priests, that he had no residential benefice in it, that he had received an inheritance in Milan, where also his title of ordination was located, that on the testimony of four doctors he had been and still was suffering from ill health, and that it was because of ill health that he had not always been able to return to Vigevano at the command of the Bishop.

Since these *preces* seemed to contain just and reasonable causes, the Sacred Congregation of the Council, on May 8, 1886, reversed its former decision and said: "Excardinationem esse ab ordinario concedendam."[288]

c) S.C.C., *Nucerina* excardinationis, 23 iul. 1887. A priest, originating in the diocese of Nocera, and educated in the seminary there for three years, afterwards completed his studies in the seminary of Frascati and there received sacred orders. Then he fixed his domicile at Rome, and stayed there many years, until in 1887 the Bishop of Nocera recalled him. He sought from the Sacred Congregation of the Council the favor of excardination, asserting that by reason of his changed domicile he no longer belonged to the diocese of his place of origin, and furthermore, that the position which he had obtained at Rome was necessary for him, so that he could sustain his parents.

Evidently because he was not needed in Nocera, had not been receiving any sustenance from there, and his reasons were just and reasonable, the Sacred Congregation of the Council responded: "Pro gratia."[289]

d) S.C.C., S. *Jacobi de Chile et Serenen.*, 25 ian. 1896. A priest, Germanus Donoso, having acquired a domicile before

[287] *ASS*, XVI (1883), 534.

[288] *ASS*, XIX (1886), 118-121.

[289] *ASS*, XX (1887), 309-312.

ordination in the diocese of La Serena in Chile, and having been ordained for the title *servitii Ecclesiae,* sought an indult of excardination to the archdiocese of Santiago, the place of his origin. He had given his service to La Serena for many years, and, with the permission of his Ordinary, had dwelt for eighteen years in Santiago, where he was growing old and sickly. The Bishop of La Serena refused excardination because of the title of service of the Church and the shortage of priests, which, indeed, were legitimate reasons, but, on account of the priest's peculiar circumstances, judged to be just and reasonable excuses, the Sacred Congregation of the Council, after first refusing, finally responded: "Supplicandum Sanctissimo pro gratia excardinationis."[290]

Particular laws incorporated these rules and helped to make them universal. Thus, priests who had been ordained for the title of patrimony were now no longer considered free in the matter of residence.[291] Pope Leo XIII's Decree "*Anteactis temporibus,*" issued through the Sacred Congregation of the Council on December 22, 1894,[292] which complained of the multitude of priests and clerics establishing domiciles at Rome, reminded the Bishops that, through the prescriptions of the Council of Trent, especially sess. XXI, *de ref.,* c. 2, and sess. XXIII, *de ref.,* c. 16, they still had remedies of common law to restrict this license. Because of the necessity of their churches, it was pointed out, the Bishops still had the right to forbid their priests, even those ordained *titulo patrimonii,* from deserting their proper diocese. If some priests had already departed without their respective Bishop's permission, the Bishop could still recall them, even if these priests had obtained a residential benefice elsewhere, in fact even if they had obtained one at Rome itself through an Apostolic Letter, as long as a suitable source of livelihood could be offered them in their own diocese.

290 *Thesaurus Resolutionum,* CLV (1896), 85; *ASS,* XXIX (1896-1897), 31-35.

291 Cf. e. g., Prov. Counc. of Westminster (a. 1852), decr. 21—*Coll. Lac.,* III, 936; the Council of Colocza, Hungary (a. 1863)—*Ibid.,* V, 686; and the Plenary Council of Scotland (a. 1886), n. 22—*AkKR,* LXI, 248.

292 *ASS,* XXVII (1894-1895), 373 ss.

To help the Bishops enforce this, the Sovereign Pontiff laid down various new prescriptions: thenceforward no priest or cleric of an alien diocese could establish a stable domicile at Rome without the express permission of the Holy Father, granted through the Sacred Congregation of the Council, etc.[293]

It is easy to see, then, how rigidly a Bishop could hold his priests in the diocese. If a Bishop elevated one of his native clerics to the holy priesthood, the presumption at once was that, in accordance with the Council of Trent, the new priest would be necessary or useful to that diocese, and all the Bishop had to do to retain the priest was to assign the individual to an ecclesiastical office or position with a suitable source of sustenance.

If one of the other proper Bishops raised the cleric to the priesthood, the Bishop of the cleric's place of origin still had first option on him and could claim him for his own diocese in the same way, that is, by assigning and sustaining him. Failing in that, he could not refuse to let that proper Bishop who had actually ordained the priest assign and sustain the same and thereby acquire control of him.

This, of course, was the rule whenever a case was considered apart from the complication of titles of service, gratuitous seminary education, and oaths or promises to serve, all of which had to be taken into consideration in any particular case.

2°. Methods of excardination and incardination

For priests, these methods were simple and clear. They could not acquire any other proper Bishop outside of excardination and incardination. Though it appears that they could acquire a domicile outside their diocese, this did not mean excardination, for, in virtue of the Decree "*Anteactis temporibus*,"[294] their Bishops could recall them, and the residential benefice obtained by them in the meantime connoted no change of proper Bishops, unless the permission of the Bishop of the native diocese had intervened.

[293] Cf. *supra*, p. 191.

[294] Cf. *supra*, p. 201.

There were, therefore, only two ways by which *priests* could be canonically transferred:

a) By the acquisition of a residential benefice in another diocese with the *litterae commendatitiae* of their proper Bishop;

b) By letters of excorporation or excardination (also called *dimissoriales* or *remissoriales*) of their present Bishop, accepted in perpetuity by the Bishop of the new diocese.

In the United States of America there was also a variation of this latter method known as " presumptive incardination."

a) *Acquisition of a residential benefice.*—If a priest was superfluous in his own diocese, it was not only possible, but desirable, for him to obtain priestly employment elsewhere in a way which would also guarantee him his livelihood, as had been the wish of the Church from the beginning.

Sometimes residential benefices were conferred by Bishops; at other times by the Holy See itself through the Office of the Apostolic Datary. If the benefice was to be conferred on the one who proved the most successful in a *concursus,* then no restrictions as to diocese were placed on the contestants. It was taken for granted that a right to the benefice would be acquired first and permission to take possession of it would be obtained afterwards. Since all residential beneficiaries were under the complete jurisdiction of the Bishop of the diocese where their benefices were founded, the very acquisition of such benefices by alien clerics, with the permission of the Bishops of their present dioceses, amounted to a transfer of allegiance and of obedience. In other words, such a procedure effected a cleric's excardination from his native diocese and his incardination in the diocese where the residential benefice was established.

In the earlier part of this Innocentian Period, any priest who was not already bound to residence in his own diocese by reason of some benefice or sacred office was free to accept a residential benefice elsewhere, and his Bishop was bound to consent.[295] Later discipline required every priest, no matter whether or not he was employed in his own diocese, to obtain his Bishop's written permission (*litterae commendatitiae*) before he could validly

[295] Cf. *supra,* p. 194.

accept such a benefice in another diocese. This permission could be refused: 1. if the priest's services were necessary or useful for his own diocese, as demonstrable by his assignment to some ecclesiastical office; 2. if he was receiving a suitable revenue from the church where he labored; or 3. if his cause for leaving was unjust or unreasonable, e. g., if it was inspired only by ambition or cupidity, or on a false plea of ill health, etc.

b) *Letters of excorporation or excardination.*—A strange phenomenon in this whole subject is that the practice of ceding priests to other Bishops *in perpetuum* through the instrumentality of letters, known as *formatae* or *dimissoriae*, existed in the Ancient Period of the Church,[296] but that afterwards, with the exception of the formula of such letters in the *Corpus Iuris*,[297] nothing is read about them until the nineteenth century.

Letters of excardination for *inferior clerics* in that century differed in principle from those of the Ancient Period, but not so those for *priests*. In the latter case it was merely required that the first Bishop transfer by document all his rights over the priest to another Bishop who was willing to accept him. It has been seen [298] that in the Ancient Period the Bishops had to adopt unique measures to prevent deception. Much more so were various precautionary measures necessary in these latter days, when the number of transfers was so large and the destinations oftentimes so far distant.

§ 1. *Acceptance* **in perpetuum** *of letters of release.*—It was the North American continent, and particularly the United States of America, which popularized in this late period the practice of transfer by letters. There was not much else that could be done. Residential benefices here were non-existent; hence neither could transfers be effected through their acquisition.

The first Provincial Council of Baltimore (a. 1829) outlined the procedure as follows:

[296] Cf. *supra*, p. 159.

[297] C. 1, D. LXXIII.

[298] *Supra*, pp. 156-157.

II . . . cooptari autem declaramus quemlibet ex aliena dioecesi advenientem, statim ac testimoniales et dimissoriales litterae, praesulis, cui proxime subditus erat, munitae auctoritate, ab ipso sacerdote ordinario cui se subiicere velit, exhibentur, et ab eodem in perpetuum acceptantur. . . .

III. Enixe hortamur praesules omnes huius provinciae ne concedant facultates sacra munera exercendi sacerdoti aliunde venienti, nisi afferat testimoniales seu dimissoriales litteras, praesulis, cui proxime subditus fuerat, auctoritate firmatas; nec etiam concedant eas facultates sacerdoti huiusmodi, si, absque causa sufficienti, distulerit ultra sex menses praesulem eligere, cuius auctoritati et iurisdictioni in perpetuum subiaceat. Hoc autem decreto nolumus derogare privilegiis a s. sede quibusdam religiosis societatibus et missionariis apostolicis concessis.[299]

In these two decrees the following regulations may be discerned: 1. the priest transferring had to have the *litterae dimissoriales* of his present proper Bishop; 2. he had to have the *litterae testimoniales* of the same; 3. these letters had to be signed by the Bishop "*a quo*"; 4. the priest was free to choose his diocese of destination after receiving the *dimissoriales;* 5. six months' time was granted to him for the choice; and 6. the letters had to be seen and accepted perpetually by the Bishop "*ad quem.*"

Other particular councils in the course of the century adopted the same plan, though sometimes they used a different terminology; and throughout one finds an effort to correct the weaknesses of the law. A written permission from the Bishop "*a quo*" to leave the diocese permanently had to be obtained, whether it be termed *litterae dimissoriales,*[300] a mere *licentia exeundi,*[301] *litterae excorporationis seu excardinationis,*[302] or

[299] Mansi, XXXIX, 295.

[300] E. g., I Counc. of Port of Spain, Central America (a. 1854), *Decreta,* sec. II, n. 1: "Sacerdotes, qui ministerii exercendi desiderio, nostras dioeceses petunt, non admittantur, nisi litteras dimissoriales rite confectas habeant."—Mansi, XLVII, 66; Council of Latin rite Bishops at Smyrna, Asia Minor (a. 1869), *Decreta,* sec. III, cap. I: "Sacerdotes exteri ne admittantur in dioecesim, nisi prius litteras dimissoriales rite confectas proprii episcopi ordinario loci exhibuerint."—Mansi, XLII, 320-321; S. C. Ep. et Reg., resp. *Rottenburgen.,* 26 martii 1886—*ASS,* XIX (1886), 87 ss.

[301] E. g., I Prov. Counc. of Quebec (a. 1851), *Decreta,* n. XIII: "Nullus extraneus sacerdos ut membrum cleri dioecesani admittatur, quin prius, praeter

litterae discessoriales seu discessoriae.[303] Likewise, it was continually held necessary for the Bishop "*ad quem*" to be informed and satisfied about the birth, age, life, and character of the priest he was to receive by some sort of written testimony (*commendatitiae, testimoniales, testimonium,* etc.).[304] To secure this knowledge in time, provision was made that the two Bishops concerned get in touch with each other by letter before the transfer took place, independently of the priest seeking it, and have an honest exchange of ideas regarding him.[305] No

licentiam exeundi, exhibuerit litteras commendatitias recens scriptas, et a proprio episcopo subsignatas."—Mansi, XLIV, 585.

[302] E. g., I Prov. Counc. of Westminster (a. 1852), *Decreta,* cap. XXIX, n. 7: "Sacerdos, a dioecesi cui est addictus discedere volens, debet muniri litteris excorporationis sui ordinarii, neque episcopus alienum sacerdotem sine talibus litteris suae dioecesi aggregare possit."—Mansi, XLIV, 750; I Counc. of Halifax (a. 1857), *Decreta,* tit. XIX, n. 7: ". . . nec etiam alienum sacerdotem suae dioecesi aggregare potest episcopus, sine consensu et litteris excorporationis ordinarii sui . . ."—Mansi, XLVII, 523.

[303] E. g., S. C. C., Encyclical Letter to the Bishops of Italy and America, 27 iulii 1890, nn. 2, 4—*Collectanea S. C. P. F.,* n. 1734. The same Sacred Congregation in its *disceptatio synoptica* on June 22, 1871, named and defined the letters for a canonical transfer as follows: "Litteras excardinatorias, quas alii remissoriales appellant, quaeque in eo consistunt, ut aliquis a proprio Episcopo libere e sua dioecesi abire sinatur, ut ab alieno Episcopo in suum Clerum cooptetur, . . ." — *ASS,* VI (1870-1871), Appendix X, 489-490.

[304] Cf. *supra,* footnotes 300-301. See also II Plen. Counc. of Baltimore (a. 1866), n. 122: "Cavendum itaque Episcopis, ut si quando necessitate cogente, ad admissionem hujusmodi Sacerdotum (scil. ex aliis dioecesibus praesertim Europae advenientium) devenire opus fuerit, nonnisi habitis de eorum probitate ac doctrina indubiis testimoniis recipiantur."—*Conc. Plen. Balt. II., Acta et Decreta,* p. 78.

[305] I Plen. Counc. of Baltimore (a. 1852), n. 9: "Ne sacerdotes vagi et ignoti nimis facile admittantur ad sacra munera obeunda cum animarum periculo, nolumus sacerdotes ex Europa advenientes in clerum nostrum cooptari, nisi litteris suorum episcoporum prius missis, consensum episcopi in cuius dioecesim transire desiderant, obtinuerint."—Mansi, XLIV, 675; this was approved by the II Plen. Counc. of Balt. also.—*Conc. Plen. Balt. II., Acta et Decreta,* tit. III, cap. IV, n. 121. Cf. I Counc. of Port of Spain, Central America (a. 1854), *Decreta,* sec. 2[a], n. 1: ". . . Priusquam vero aliquod ipsis (scil. sacerdotibus advenis) committatur officium, ad ordinarium tum dioeceseos, ex qua discesserunt, tum illius in qua sacros ordines receperunt, litterae mittantur oportet, ut de eorum moribus et anteacta vita notitia secura habeatur; nec aliquid, nisi post responsionem acceptam, circa eos definiatur."—Mansi, XLVII, 66; Counc. of Latin rite Bishops at Smyrna, Asia Minor (a. 1869), *Decreta,* sec. III, cap. I, n. 3: "Ubi sacerdotes in aliam dioecesim se conferant animo ibi manendi et sacrum ministerium exercendi, priusquam ipsis aliquod committatur officium, ad ordinarium dioecesis ex qua discesserunt litterae mittantur oportet, ut de eorum moribus et anteacta vita notitia secura habeatur, nec aliquid, nisi post responsionem acceptam, circa eos definiatur."—Mansi, XLII, 320-321.

office was to be conferred on the immigrant priest until this had been done.[306]

Though in 1829 *litterae dimissoriales* apparently were not addressed to any particular Bishop, in as far as it was left to the excardinated priest to travel around and find a diocese to his liking with a willing Bishop, this was soon found to be fraught with difficulties. The Church had repeatedly shown its abhorrence of vagrant clerics, whose wandering about revealed their lack of any fixed residence; yet, the employment of general *dimissoriales* tended to invite a recurrence of this old evil.[307] The " remedy " used was a return to the ancient practice of the Church,[308] which required that the identity and the consent of the Bishop "*ad quem*" be known before *dimissoriales* were issued.[309]

[306] The province of St. Louis also decreed that when one of these immigrants had been dismissed by any Bishop of the province for bad morals, he could not be incardinated into any of the other dioceses of the province until he had shown signs of true repentance and constant amendment.—II Prov. Counc. of St. Louis (a. 1858), *Decreta*, n. 5: " Ut malis quae ex vagis sacerdotibus oriri solent obviam fiat, consulendum est episcopis ut decretum IX concilii Baltimori habiti anno salutis 1852 stricte servent, etiam quoad sacerdotes qui alicui dioecesi in his Foederatis Statibus iam adscripti, in aliam transire velint; adeo ut neminem ad sacra munia exercenda admittant, multo minus in clerum cooptent dioecesanum, qui ab aliquo episcopo huius provinciae ob pravos mores dimissus fuerit, nisi dederit verae poenitentiae et constantis emendationis signa." (Mansi, XLVII, 628-629.)

[307] I Counc. of Halifax (a. 1857), *Decreta*, t. XIX, n. 7: "... Et quoniam in America plurima scandala et incommoda obveniunt ob numerum sacerdotum vagantium, qui, quamvis litteris excorporationis seu testimonialibus muniti, huc et illuc discursant sine ulla fixa sede, ita ut reipsa contra ecclesiae disciplinam per longum tempus sine aliquo superiore existant, huic malo succurrere volens, haec synodus enixe hortatur episcopos, ut, omni quo possint modo, remedium opportunum adhibeant, et tali deordinationi finem imponant."—Mansi, XLVII, 523.

[308] Cf. *supra*, p. 157.

[309] VII Prov. Counc. of Baltimore (a. 1849), *Decreta*, n. V: "Statuunt patres nullum harum provinciarum sacerdotem, ad aliam dioecesim transire volentem, a proprio episcopo dimittendum, nisi certo constet eum ab alio episcopo esse recipiendum. Si qui autem in posterum aliter dimissi fuerint, non recipiantur."—Mansi, XLIII, 411; I Plen. Counc. of Baltimore (a. 1852), *Decreta*, n. 9: "Ne sacerdotes vagi et ignoti nimis facile admittantur ad sacra munera obeunda cum animarum periculo, nolumus sacerdotes ex Europa advenientes in clerum nostrum cooptari, nisi litteris suorum episcoporum prius missis, consensum episcopi in cuius dioecesim transire desiderant, obtinuerint."—Mansi, XLIV, 675. These decrees were approved in the II Plen. Counc. of Balt. (a. 1866)—*Conc. Plen. Balt. II., Acta*

§ 2. *Formal incardination in the United States of America.*—Feeling the need of a definite and uniform mode of procedure in these canonical transfers of priests from one diocese to another, the III Plenary Council of Baltimore (a. 1884), acting for the ecclesiastical provinces of the United States of America, officially constituted and approved two methods of transfer called, respectively, *formal* and *presumptive* incardination. Each of these methods will be examined in turn.

Formal incardination, the first of the two, was established in the following decree:

> N. 63. Formalem [incardinationem] declaramus eam esse, quae per actum Episcopi documento signatum efficitur, qui sacerdotem alienae dioecesis, dummodo utique literas commendatitias et excardinationis a suo Episcopo afferat atque exhibeat, in clerum suum adscribit. Haec tamen adscriptio non statim facienda est, cum quis admitti in aliquam dioecesim postulat, quocumque titulo ordinatus fuerit, sed Episcopus eum inter trienii spatium in ministeriis sacris exercendo ad tempus probabit, exquirendo interim peculiares informationes ab Ordinario, a quo fuerat dimissus. Exigere tamen poterit experimentum ultra triennium, sed non ultra quinquennium, quo in casu Episcopus hoc suum propositum ulterioris probationis sacerdoti in scriptis significare debet, antequam triennium expiret. Priusquam vero triennale vel quinquennale experimentum absolvatur, si illum idoneum reperiat, expresso decreto dioecesi adscribat; idque Episcopo, cui ille proxime subditus fuit, significet. Ex communi vero consilio et consensu utriusque Episcopi atque ipsius sacerdotis, poterit is ex propria dioecesi excorporari et in alteram incorporari absolute et immediate, praetermisso probationis tempore.[310]

et Decreta, nn. 120-121. See also III Plen. Counc. of Baltimore (a. 1884), n. 67: "... Simul decernimus quod, sicut nullus sacerdos exterus in dioecesim adscribendus est, priusquam literas dimissoriales proprii Episcopi rite confectas Ordinario loci exhibuerit, ita neque has literas ulli sacerdoti a suo Episcopo dandas esse, nisi certo constet, eum ab alio Episcopo in dioecesim fore admittendum."—*Acta et Decreta Conc. Plen. Balt. III.*, pp. 34-35; S. C. Ep. et Reg., resp. *Rottenburgen.*, 26 martii 1886—*ASS*, XIX (1886), 87 ss.; S. C. C., Litt. ency. (*Ad Epp. Ital. et Amer.*), 27 iulii 1890—*Collectanea S. C. P. F.*, n. 1734, in which, not only the consent to receive, but also the promise to assign the priest to some ecclesiastical duty was required.

[310] *Acta et Decreta Conc. Plen. Balt. III.*, pp. 32-33.

Formal incardination, therefore, was more than acceptance *in perpetuum* of the priest's letters of release. It was concluded solely by a document signed by the receiving Bishop, in which he incorporated a priest of another diocese with his own clergy. It was not to be done hastily. The priest first had to present the *litterae commendatitiae et excardinationis* of his own proper Bishop. Then, the receiving Bishop was to give him a probationary appointment in the sacred ministry for any period up to three years, no matter what his title of ordination had been. If a longer period of trial was considered desirable, the receiving Bishop had to inform the priest of that in writing before the initial three-year term expired; but under no circumstances was the trial period to be extended beyond five years. Meanwhile, the Bishop "*ad quem*" was to inquire more particularly about the candidate's character and morals from the Bishop "*a quo*." If the priest's work or reputation was unsatisfactory, he was to be sent back to his proper diocese; if, however, the receiving Bishop was satisfied with the priest, he was to signify the same, before the probationary period was completed, by a formal, signed document, incorporating that priest in his own diocese. Still the priest remained a subject of his former Bishop until written word of his formal incardination in the new diocese had been transmitted to and received by the excardinating Bishop. As is apparent, incardination by this method was not absolute from the outset, but rather conditional.

In cases wherein both Bishops and the priest to be excardinated agreed, however, formal incardination could be applied and made effective immediately, without any period of probation.

Elsewhere in the world, a conditional incardination likewise existed, but followed no set terms. Letters of excardination would be issued to a priest by his proper Bishop, who previously made sure that another Bishop was ready to receive him, whereupon the priest, armed with his letters of excardination, would go to the new diocese and receive a provisory appointment there for an indefinite period, with the promise that he would be incardinated if he fulfilled a certain condition, namely, that his conduct proved him to be worthy. If he felt that he had fulfilled his part of the contract and yet the Bishop "*ad quem*" had failed to act, recourse to the Holy See was open to him.[311]

§ 3. *Presumptive incardination in the United States of America.*—This was a secondary provision of the III Plenary Council of Baltimore (a. 1884), designed to protect the priests, who were serving their probationary appointments in anticipation of formal incardination in one of the dioceses of the United States of America, from the injustice of being completely forgotten or neglected by the Bishop who had admitted them to his diocese in a provisory way. According to it, if, when the

[311] For example, John Nepomucene W. originated in the diocese of Rottenburg, Germany, but acquired a new domicile in Detroit, U. S. A., and was educated and ordained there. Three years later he asked for letters of excardination, which his Ordinary gave only after hearing from the Bishop of W's place of origin that he was inclined to incardinate W. In Rottenburg, W. was appointed a pastor, but only in a provisory way, the condition of incardination being that his conduct after a long time prove him worthy. In this he failed, and repeatedly he was warned by the Bishop of Rottenburg that he was not incardinated. His case was taken to Rome, and the S. C. Ep. et Reg., resp. *Rottenburgen.*, 26 martii 1886, replied that his incardination in Rottenburg was not certain, but that he should be commended to the charity of both Bishops—*ASS*, XIX (1886), 87 ss. In another case, Rudolph R., who originated in the archdiocese of Cologne, joined a Religious Congregation, in which he was thereafter educated, and from whose Superior General he received *dimissoriae* for sacred orders while he was still a novice. Three months later, with the permission of the Superior, he left the Congregation to find a benevolent Bishop. At Limburg he was promised incardination on condition that he produce his diocesan dismissal from the Archbishop of Cologne as well as his religious dismissal from the Superior General of the Religious Institute. He did receive a provisory appointment in Limburg, but fulfilled the latter part only of the incardinatory condition. A year later, he was suspended perpetually and ordered to leave Limburg, and the question arose as to which Bishop would have to support him. To the question: "An et cui incumbat onus finem imponendi vitae vagae Sacerdotis R., eique alimenta suppeditandi in casu?" the S. C. Ep. et Reg., *Colonien. seu Limburgen.*, 24 feb. 1893, responded: "Affirmative ad Episcopum Limburgensem." —*ASS*, XXV (1892-1893), 627-634. This seemed to grant incardination despite an unfulfilled condition attached to the contract, and likewise to contradict the law that a youth entering religion belongs to the Bishop of his place of original or acquired domicile until he has made his *perpetual* profession. Yet, the same Sacred Congregation for the Affairs of Bishops and Religious Orders in a decree of June 7, 1899 (*ASS*, XXXVII [1904-1905], 240-241) presumed that Superiors General of Congregations with simple vows, who have received by Indult of the Holy See the temporary permission of granting *litterae dimissoriae*, may do so for those who have made only their *first* profession and have not yet been assigned to any particular house. Relying on this, the Congregation must have decided in the above case that the dismissal from the Archbishop of Cologne was not necessary, and that Rudolph R. had legally fulfilled his condition of incardination in Limburg.

three or five-year period of trial was ended, the receiving Bishop had not made known his intentions with regard to the priest whom he had been trying out, either by plainly and openly refusing to incardinate, or by signing a formal document of incardination, he was presumed by law to have accepted and incardinated the candidate, and this was known as " presumptive incardination." The important decree of the Council by which this method was instituted was as follows:

> N. 66. Praesumptam incardinationem haberi declaramus, si Episcopus elapso triennio vel respectivo quinquennio probationis, actum adscriptionis formalem omiserit. Qui enim eo elapso tempore, clericum qui dioecesi adscribi petierat, nec formaliter admittit nec admittere plane diserteque recusat, jure praesumitur adscripsisse. Quod quidem valet etiam pro ordinatis titulo missionis, quo in casu juramentum praestitum in aliena dioecesi, censetur pro nova esse servandum ... [312]

It is to be noted that this was strictly a subsidiary method of incardinating by letters, and was valid only for the United States of America. It had nothing to do with the method of incardination by the reception of a residential benefice, which, as already pointed out, could hardly obtain in the United States

[312] *Acta et Decreta Conc. Plen. Balt. III.*, p. 34. De Becker, in an article entitled " The Admission of Secular Priests into a Diocese in the United States," (*AER*, XVIII [1898], 135-159), argues, and rightly it seems, that this type of incardination, being only a *presumptio juris*, as the Council (*loc. cit.*) expressly states, must be based on fact, and that that basis would be destroyed if the receiving Bishop's mind was shown, within a sufficiently short time after the trial period was over, to be opposed to the incardination of the candidate; in which case no presumptive incardination could take place. But, the receiving Bishop's will would rightly be presumed as favorable if a considerable period elapsed without his saying anything. To make presumptive incardination to be decided by the minute hand of the clock on the closing day of the trial period would be involving it in formalities as rigid as those for formal incardination. It would bring up questions of unstamped envelopes, wrongly delivered or forgotten mail, and a host of others. It would be making the same mistake as was made by the interpreters of the decrees of the Council of Trent, who insisted that clerical assignment did not take place unless the Bishop in a formal sentence declared that he was hereby assigning cleric *A* to church *B*, even though *A* actually labored in *B* for years at his command. Note also that " *statim* " in the Council of Trent (sess. XXIII, *de ref.*, c. 9) was interpreted in the Const. " *Speculatores* " of Innocent XII thus: ". . . statim, hoc est, saltem intra terminum unius mensis."—*Fontes*, n. 258, § 6.

where there were so few, if any, benefices. Hence it was immaterial whether or not the trial appointment at the very outset was specifically stated to be made only for the time being (commonly called a *pro tem.* appointment); immaterial also whether the appointment was to a pastorate, to an assistancy or to a mere administrative function; it resulted in incardination if, within a reasonable time after the period specified by the law had been completed, the receiving Bishop had said nothing to the probationed priest or to his former Bishop by way of either acceptance or rejection. In a matter so important it was not good to have to depend on a presumed will, so difficult to prove in law. Yet, the apparently intended purpose of the method was laudable—to prevent the waste of priests' lives in multiple trial periods prolonged far beyond the legal limit. It kept the Bishops mindful of those priests who were laboring in their dioceses with the hope of becoming incardinated some day, and made the Bishops more careful to give those priests a timely warning if they did not intend to incardinate them.

In both the formal and presumptive methods of incardination there was usually a lapse of time, which could be as long as five years, between the issuance of the letters of excardination and the formal or implied incorporation in the new diocese. No matter how complete and unconditional in their wording these letters of diocesan dismissal were, and no matter whether they were issued abroad or in this country, they were in no sense to be considered as effective until the correlative incardination process was completed, that is, in the case of the formal process, until the Bishop "*a quo*" had received from the Bishop "*ad quem*" an authentic notice that he had signed a document incardinating the priest, or, in the presumptive process, until the time limit of the trial period had elapsed without any word being received by the probationed priest or his Bishop from the Bishop "*ad quem.*" Throughout the trial period the "excardinated" priest still remained subject to the Bishop of the diocese from which he came, and continued so until somewhere the process of incardination was completed for him.[313]

[313] *Acta et Decreta Conc. Plen. Balt. III.* (a. 1884), n. 67.

With so much depending on that formal document of acceptance it was desirable that uniformity be observed in the formulae of excardination and incardination throughout the United States of America, and for this the III Plenary Council of Baltimore expressed an urgent desire, though it did not reduce it to law.[314]

3°. Special requisites for certain groups

a) *Priests ordained* titulo missionis.—As in the preceding period, these priests could not be excardinated without special permission from the Sacred Congregation for the Propagation of the Faith, in addition to the regular permission of their proper Ordinary.[315] If they attempted to effect a transfer otherwise, they violated their oath and became guilty of grave sin, from which they could not be absolved until they had made reparation. If they remained obstinate, they might possibly incur suspension *ipso facto,* and any attempted incardination elsewhere might possibly be null and void, namely, when the law of their proper diocese or province included such sanctions.[316]

To effect a canonical transfer for priests of this group through letters of excardination, the correct process, as outlined by the III Plenary Council of Baltimore (a. 1884),[317] was the same as for priests ordained for other titles, except that the Bishop "*ad quem*" had the obligation of applying to the Sacred Congregation for the Propagation of the Faith six months prior to his intended incorporation of the candidate in his diocese (i. e., during the period of trial) to ask that it dispense the candidate from his present oath of service. When that was granted, the Bishop "*ad quem*" received from the candidate a new oath in favor of the diocese of destination and kept a signed copy of the

[314] *Ibid.*, n. 68.

[315] Cf. *supra*, p. 172.

[316] E. g., II Prov. Counc. of New Orleans (a. 1860), *Decreta*, n. 9—Mansi, XLVIII, 23.

[317] Nn. 63, 64.—*Acta et Decreta Conc. Plen. Balt. III.*, pp. 32-33. *Mutatis mutandis*, the same process could be applied whenever the excardination was to be effected by the conferring of a residential benefice in a new diocese with the permission of the Bishop of the old.

same in the Chancery archives. Then, after the formal incardination, he sent the Bishop "*a quo*" the usual notification that he had signed the document of reception.

In the event that the incardinating Bishop failed to apply for the dispensation from the oath, and even failed to act at all, prior to the expiration of the probationary time limit, it was not only presumed that the priest was incardinated, but it was also presumed that the former oath then applied to the new in place of the old diocese.[318]

After 1885, the oath as taken in all the dioceses in England and the United States of America was considerably broadened in its scope,[319] so that for excardinations within the same ecclesiastical province dispensations from Rome were no longer necessary, since the new oath had been taken with a view to serve the entire province.

b) *Priests emigrating to the United States of America from Italy.*—In an Encyclical Letter to the Bishops of Italy and America, sent through the Sacred Congregation of the Council on July 27, 1890,[320] Pope Leo XIII imposed certain special regulations for this group in order to put an end to some abuses that had arisen in the past. They were:

1st. If any Italian priests who had already emigrated to the United States of America were delinquent, the local Bishops, acting, if need be, as delegates for the Apostolic See, were to institute summary processes against them according to the method described in the sacred canons.

2nd. From 1890 on the Bishops and Ordinaries of Italy were absolutely forbidden to give their secular priests letters of excardination to emigrate to America.

3rd. Only by way of exception could emigration to the United States be permitted in an individual case for some priest, mature in age, endowed with the necessary sacred knowledge, and having a just cause for wanting to go; and even then, the

318 *Ibid.*, n. 66.

319 Cf. *supra*, pp. 144-5, 192.

320 *Collectanea* S. C. P. F., n. 1734.

responsibility for that priest would be on the conscience of the Bishop sending him.

Such a one would have to have Testimonials of the moral integrity of his priestly life and of a true ecclesiastical spirit in his zeal for the salvation of souls, so that there would be a well-founded hope of his edifying by word and example the new flock to which he was to minister, and a moral certainty that he would never disgrace the priestly dignity by engaging in any menial or indecorous avocations.

4th. After all these qualifications had been certified, the Italian Bishop or Ordinary was to negotiate directly with the Bishop "*ad quem*" in America, and obtain from him in advance a formal acceptance of the said priest together with a promise of assigning him to some function of the ecclesiastical ministry.

The entire case was then to be submitted to the Sacred Congregation of the Council for its approval. If it gave consent, then the Bishop could issue the letters of excardination, secretly communicating at the same time to the American Bishop personal notes or characteristics of the emigrating priest to prevent any deception in the identity of the individual.

If the priest in question ever wanted to be transferred later from this to another diocese in America, he would have to have another permit from the Sacred Congregation of the Council.

5th. Under no conditions were any exceptions to be made in favor of priests of the Oriental rite in Italy for emigration to America.

6th. In the case of an Italian priest who wished merely to visit America temporarily for some personal and honorable reason, it was sufficient, as long as there was no obstacle in the way, for his proper Ordinary to grant him a written temporary permission (not to exceed one year), in which would be included the cause of the journey together with the condition that, after the expiration of the leave of absence, if he had neither returned nor obtained an extension of his leave of absence, he was *ipso facto* suspended *a divinis*.

7th. Priests who enjoyed some special apostolic privilege in this matter were not included in these regulations.

c) *Foreign-born priests emigrating to the United States of America, especially from Poland.*—The instruction of the Sacred Congregation for the Propagation of the Faith, which was issued to the Bishops of the United States of America on February 25, 1896,[321] affected the emigration of foreign-born priests as well as clerics. It reminded the Bishops here of the obligation of any incoming foreign-born priest to be fortified with his Ordinary's written permission to depart, and a Testimonial Letter of his freedom from censures and of his good morals. For priests who had originated in Poland, even though they had been later incardinated for some time in a diocese in Italy or elsewhere, the Sacred Congregation for the Propagation of the Faith added this special prerequisite for their emigration to the United States of America and their incardination in any diocese here: that they bring Testimonial Letters of the Sacred Congregation for the Propagation of the Faith, plainly certifying to their liberty in departing, their freedom from censures, and their enjoyment of good morals. Care, too, was exercised by the Sacred Congregation for the Propagation of the Faith that the Bishops of Italy would not be deceived in receiving and ordaining these men without genuine Testimonials from the Bishop of their place of origin.[322]

Other decrees were substituted to cover this subject after 1908.[323]

5. *Pre-Code Period (1898-1917)*

A. The Decree " *A primis* "

Because the Sacred Congregation of the Council's Decree " *A primis* " of July 20, 1898,[324] was a promised reply given to certain Bishops who were seeking a shorter method of acquiring new subjects for ordination by way of domicile, the explanation of its origin was more properly discussed in article I of this Chapter, under the heading " The Proper Bishop for Ordination

[321] *Collectanea S. C. P. F.*, n. 1918. Cf. *supra*, pp. 97, 192-3.

[322] Cf. *supra*, p. 193.

[323] Cf. *supra*, p. 193.

[324] *ASS*, XXXI (1898-9), 49 ss.; *Fontes*, n. 4307.

of Diocesan Clerics."[325] Since, however, its contents are of grave importance here, its full text is given for better and closer study.

S. C. C., decr. "*A primis*," 20 iulii 1898 (De Clericorum Excardinatione et ordinatione).

A primis Ecclesiae saeculis plura Concilia decreverunt, quod recentius confirmavit Tridentinum *cap. 8, sess. 23 de reform.*, neminem nisi a proprio Episcopo posse ordinari.

Proprius autem alicuius Episcopus, iuxta ea quae praefinivit in primis Bonifacius VIII in Sexto Decret. cap. *Cum nullus, De tempore Ordin.* "intelligitur in hoc casu Episcopus de cuius dioecesi est is, qui ad ordines promoveri desiderat, oriundus, seu in cuius dioecesi beneficium obtinet ecclesiasticum, seu habet (licet alibi natus fuerit) domicilium in eadem." Deinde cum consuetudo invaluerit, ut Episcopi familiares suos, etsi alienae dioecesis, sacris initiarent, et sancta Tridentina synodus *cap. 9, sess. 23 de reform.* id certis sub conditionibus probaverit, obtinuit, ut tribus prioribus titulis, originis, domicilii et beneficii, quibus ius fiebat Episcopis aliquem ad ordines promovendi, quartus quoque accenseretur, scilicet familiaritatis. Cum autem de huiusmodi titulis disceptaretur, Innocentius XII app. litt. incipientibus "*Speculatores*" datis die 4 nov. 1694, determinavit ac constituit quo sensu et extensione iidem essent accipiendi ad eum effectum, ut quis proprius fieret alicuius Episcopi subditus, quo legitime ordinari valeret. Quae constitutio ut suprema lex deinde habita est, eaque duce omnes quaestiones diremptae.

Verum nostris temporibus novae contentioni frequens se praebuit occasio. Pluribus enim in locis usu receptum est ut clerici, qui e sua dioecesi digredi et in alia sibi sedem constituere desiderarent, excardinationem, quam vocant, id est plenam et perpetuam dimissionem a suo Ordinario peterent; eaque innixi in alia dioecesi incardinationem seu adscriptionem implorarent: qua obtenta, eo ipso ut proprii novi Episcopi subditi ad ulteriores ordines suscipiendos admitterentur. Quae agendi ratio, ubi caute prudenterque adhibita fuit, absque querelis processit, sed nonnullis in locis, ubi necessaria cautio defuit, controversiis et abusibus viam saepenumero patefecit.

Quapropter Eñi S. C. Concilii Patres, rebus omnibus mature perpensis, praesenti generali decreto haec statuenda censuerunt:

[325] Cf. *supra*, pp. 113-115.

1°. Excardinationem fieri non licere nisi iustis de causis, nec effectum undequaque sortiri, nisi incardinatione in alia dioecesi executioni demandata.

2°. Incardinationem faciendam esse ab Episcopo non oretenus, sed in scriptis, absolute et in perpetuum, id est nullis sive expressis sive tacitis limitationibus obnoxiam; ita ut clericus novae dioecesi prorsus mancipetur, praestito ad hoc iuramento ad instar illius quod Constitutio "*Speculatores*" pro domicilio acquirendo praescribit.

3°. Ad hanc incardinationem deveniri non posse, nisi prius ex legitimo documento constiterit alienum clericum a sua dioecesi fuisse in perpetuum dimissum, et obtenta insuper fuerint ab Episcopo dimittente, sub secreto, si opus sit, de eius natalibus, vita, moribus ac studiis opportuna testimonia.

4°. Hac ratione adscriptos posse quidem ad ordines promoveri. Cum tamen nemini sint cito manus imponendae, officii sui noverint esse Episcopi, in singulis casibus perpendere, an, omnibus attentis, clericus adscriptus talis sit, qui tuto possit absque ulteriori experimento ordinari, an potius oporteat eum diutius probari. Et meminerint quod sicut "nullus debet ordinari qui iudicio sui Episcopi non sit utilis aut necessarius suis Ecclesiis" ut in *cap. 16, sess. 23 de reform.* Tridentinum statuit; ita pariter nullum esse adscribendum novum clericum, nisi pro necessitate aut commoditate dioecesis.

5°. Quo vero ad clericos diversae linguae et nationis, oportere ut Episcopi in iis admittendis cautius et severius procedant, ac numquam eos recipiant, nisi requisiverint prius a respectivo eorum Ordinario, et obtinuerint, secretam ac favorabilem de ipsorum vita et moribus informationem, onerata super hoc graviter Episcoporum conscientia.

6°. Denique quoad laicos, aut etiam quoad clericos, qui excardinationis beneficio uti nequeunt vel nolunt, standum esse dispositionibus const. *Speculatores*, quae, nihil obstante praesenti decreto, ratae ac firmae semper manere debent.

Facta autem de his omnibus relatione SSm̃o Domino Nostro per infrascriptum Cardinalem S. C. Concilii Praefectum, Sanctitas Sua resolutionem Em. Patrum benigne approbare et confirmare dignata est, contrariis quibuscumque minime obstantibus.

Datum Romae ex aedibus S. C. Concilii die 20 Iulii 1898.

A. Card. Di Pietro, *Praefectus.*

B. Archiepiscopus Nazianzenus, *Pro-Secret.*

In its preamble this document, after commemorating the famous *dicta* on proper Bishops for ordination, as enunciated by Pope Boniface VIII, by the Council of Trent, and by the Constitution "*Speculatores*" of Pope Innocent XII, indicates that something further must be said on the same subject, which, in the body of it, it then proceeds to do, and thereby takes its place of honor next to these same illustrious enactments as the last link in the long chain of legislation. For the next nineteen years, until the promulgation of the Code of Canon Law, it was referred to and quoted by all eminent authorities, including the various Sacred Roman Congregations, as the last word on the subject of excardination and incardination of diocesan clerics.

It is because of that finality with which it was regarded that it caused no little amount of discussion as to its effect on previously existing provincial and general laws or customs. Likewise, that is the reason for considering it as the beginning of a distinct historical period, brief though it be.

B. Opinions on Influence of Decree as to Abrogation of Previous Methods

1°. Affirmative opinion

Less than seven months after the decree was promulgated doubts arose as to its abrogation (in n. 6) of existing customs of transferring laymen from one diocese to another through the medium of letters ("quasi-excardination and quasi-incardination").[326] So ambiguous was the wording, and so uncertain the intent, of n. 6 of the "*A primis*" on this question that a new decree was issued less than nine years later to rescue the custom of laymen's written transfers from abrogation and to reorder that entire field of legislation.[327]

Sometime, also, after the promulgation of the "*A primis*" a similar doubt arose as to its abrogation of the method of "presumptive incardination" of priests, which had been adopted for the United States of America by the III Plenary Council of

[326] For a full discussion of this difficulty, cf. *supra*, pp. 91 ff.

[327] S. C. C., decr. 24 novem. 1906—*ASS*, XXXIX (1906), 600 ss.; *Fontes*, n. 4330.

Baltimore in 1884.[328] In a letter to the Sacred Congregation for the Propagation of the Faith the Apostolic Delegate to the United States noted that the "*A primis*," n. 2, had stated: "Incardinationem faciendam esse ab Episcopo non oretenus, sed in *scriptis*, absolute et in perpetuum," whereas the aforesaid Council of Baltimore had decreed: "Praesumptam incardinationem haberi declaramus, si Episcopus, elapso triennio vel respectivo quinquennio probationis, *actum adscriptionis formalem omiserit*," which latter was certainly not in agreement with the former. Hence his Excellency asked: 1st. whether presumptive incardination had been abrogated by the "*A primis*"; and, if so, 2nd. whether this abrogation was retroactive, so as to affect cases completed before the issuance of the decree.

The problem was forwarded by the Sacred Congregation for the Propagation of the Faith to the Sacred Congregation of the Council in order that the latter might interpret its own decree. Arguing that excardination and incardination was a real alienation of a cleric from one diocese to another, the juridic effects of which should be capable of proof beyond all doubt, and that that could not be done without a written instrument, the Consultor of the latter Sacred Congregation held that the requirement of written incardination in the "*A primis*" was essential, and, from its very purpose of ending difficulties, as well as from its final legal sanction, invalidated any contrary form, although it was not retroactive, since it did not expressly state this.

Accordingly, to the above questions proposed to it the Sacred Congregation of the Council replied: "Ad I affirmative, ad II negative." [329]

Then there arose the question whether or not the "*A primis*" abrogated the previous method of incardination by the reception of a residential benefice in an alien diocese with the consent of the cleric's own Ordinary. A classic decision on this question, to which all authorities have referred ever since, was issued by the Sacred Roman Rota in its case *Londonen.* Incardinationis, 9 ianuarii 1912.[330] A summary of it is this: Peter Mendosa

[328] Cf. *supra*, pp. 210-212.

[329] *Romana et aliarum*, 15 septembris 1906—ASS, XXXIX (1906), 498-499.

[330] *AAS*, IV (1912), 249 ss.

Roussel was born in Quebec, Canada, in the year 1874. As a layman, at the age of 25, he was quasi-incardinated into the archdiocese of Sante Fé. By the year 1902 he had received all sacred orders through the authorization contained in the *litterae dimissoriae* issued by the Archbishop of Santa Fé because of the fact that the cleric was making his studies nearer to home, and consequently had not yet set foot in Santa Fé. When this cleric was scarcely ordained as a priest, he received, upon request, a leave of absence from the archdiocese of Santa Fé, and for four years (1903-1907) labored in the sacred ministry, first as assistant or vicar, and then as pastor, in various places in the diocese of London, Canada. In 1903 he was ordered by his Archbishop to come to Santa Fé, or to ask for excardination. He did the latter, but there was no more than oral testimony to the granting of the same. Neither was there any more than oral testimony to his incardination into the diocese of London; and no trace of an oath taken to remain there could be found. On the strength of this orally established excardination, and his appointment to a pastorate in London, together with the oral testimony of incardination by the old and sickly Bishop who had appointed him, he claimed that he belonged to the diocese of London.

To the question, however, "An constet de legitima incardinatione sacerdotis Roussel dioecesi Londonensi, ita ut dicta incardinatio omnes canonicos effectus sortita sit." the Sacred Roman Rota replied: " Negative."

Since this disputed transfer occurred in 1903, i. e., after the promulgation of the "*A primis*," it was regarded as a test case on the validity of oral and equivalent incardination in the Pre-Code Period. The negative decision was based on: 1. the theory that the "*A primis*" was the universal law for all canonical transfers after 1898; 2. the necessity, after 1898, of written letters, for the validity of both excardination and incardination in any given case; and 3. the necessity, after 1898, of the oath to remain in the new diocese, for the validity of the incardination.[331] In this particular instance there were no written letters of any kind, and no reliable proof that the oath had been taken; but, on either one of these counts alone, apparently the same decision would have been rendered, namely, the decision against the validity of the incardination.

Those, however, who regard this decision as settling in the affirmative the question of abrogation of all previous methods of incardination, contrary to that specified by the "*A primis*," are mistaken. It was admitted by the Consultor in the case that oral and equivalent (or implicit) methods of incardination had been valid before the "*A primis*," as long as the consent of both Bishops was clearly established, but he expressly stated that in the London case there was no need of entering into any judgment on their abrogation.[332] This was simply a judgment of one single case on its own merits, and could not be regarded as an authoritative general conclusion. Its value lay in its revelation of the mind of the Sacred Roman Rota.

A far clearer case, after the "*A primis*," of equivalent incardination, i. e., by the reception of a residential benefice in an alien diocese with the permission of the cleric's own Bishop, was that of Adria, Italy, submitted to the Sacred Congregation of the Council for a decision, which was rendered on February 14 and July 11, 1925.[333] The facts were these: A certain priest *N.* was born, ordained, and assigned to a position with the care of souls, in the diocese of Adria, Italy. In 1907 he was transferred

[331] This third basis was disputed by the Consultor of the S. C. C. in *Bismarckien. et aliarum*, incardinationis, 31 ianuarii 1913: "Iam vero defectus solius iuramenti non videtur certo invalidam reddere incardinationem; nam argumenta quibus id probat Rota in citata causa Londonensi non sunt convincentia, iuramentum namque in const. Speculatores non requiritur ad valide acquirendum domicilium, quae est res in iure inaudita, sed ad acquirendum domicilium qualificatum quod requiritur ut episcopus legitime ordinet subditum ratione domicilii."—*AAS*, V (1913), 37.

[332] "Veteri iure, praeter scriptam incardinationem, etiam oralis, immo equipollens seu implicita incardinatio, scilicet mediante sacra Ordinatione vel beneficii collatione, in usu erat, dummodo certo constaret de voluntate utriusque episcopi clericum perpetuo et absolute dimittendi eumque item perpetuo et absolute recipiendi. Utrum huiusmodi incardinatio per decretum A primis, quod expresse scripturam requirit, abrogata fuerit necne, non est cur inquiramus."—S. R. R., *Londonensi*, 9 ian. 1912 (*AAS*, IV [1912], 249 ss.).

[333] *AAS*, XVIII (1926), 48-55.

by formal letters of excardination and incardination to the Italian diocese of Cervia, where he obtained an outstanding parochial benefice. He resigned this, however, in 1914 and, with the permission of the Ordinary of Cervia, went to another diocese in Italy, that of Montefiascone, where he obtained from its Bishop a parochial benefice. Because of ill health, he had to resign this also in 1918, and, after a period of other employment in Assisi and later in Sardinia, he was forced to return to his Ordinary. But to whom was he to return? Adria's Bishop had formally excardinated him to Cervia; the Ordinary of Cervia was unwilling to receive him because, with due permission, *N*. had been equivalently incardinated into Montefiascone, through the residential benefice which the Bishop of that city had conferred on him; and, finally, the Bishop of Montefiascone refused to accept him, because he denied that equivalent incardination could be sustained in law.

The question submitted to the Sacred Congregation of the Council, therefore, was: "Ad quamnam dioecesim sacerdos N. pertinere dicendus sit in casu." The answer was: "Ad dioecesim Cerviensem." [334]

Here was what would have been recognized in the Innocentian Period as a clear case of incardination into Montefiascone by the permitted acquisition of a residential benefice there, but the Sacred Congregation of the Council in 1925 called it invalid, not as a result of the Decree "*A primis*," but because its Consultors contended that equivalent incardination never had been valid for priests. They went further and said that, even if it had ever been valid, it would now be abrogated by the "*A primis*," because that was a general law which prescribed written letters of incardination as well as of excardination for the validity of a transfer to another diocese, when such was being accomplished independently of ordination, and because the "*A primis*" contained an invalidating clause against any other form of canonical transfer in the words "*contrariis quibuscumque minime obstantibus*."

[334] S. C. C., *Adrien.*, incardinationis, 11 iulii 1925—*AAS*, *ibid.*, p. 55. According to *Il Monitore Ecclesiastico* (XXXVIII [1926], 259-260) there were three Consultors used on this case, one of whom was believed to be the learned canonist of Hungary, D. Giustiniano Serèdi, O.S.B.

The Consultor of the Sacred Congregation of the Council in the case of the Bishop of Bismarck, North Dakota, in the United States of America,[335] held that the mode of incardination prescribed by the "*A primis*" was the form of the act, so that, when there was a substantial departure from this form, the incardination did not become effective, even apart from the absence of any express invalidating clause. This he concluded from the very purpose of the law—to put an end to controversies and abuses—and from the agreement of all authors that, whenever ecclesiastical law prescribes a certain form for an act or a contract, it implicitly invalidates an act which is placed without that form.

The Sacred Roman Rota made another decision on this matter, which, however, does not directly add to the weight of the affirmative argument, since the invalidity of the act was insisted on for a different reason.[336] Francis, a priest who originated in diocese *M* in Poland, received the *litterae dimissoriales* of his Bishop on Feb. 16, 1902. He labored for a year in diocese *A* as a pastor, though for what reason is not stated. Under date of April 2, 1903, he received a letter from the Bishop of *K* in America, promising to receive him in that diocese as rector of the Polish parish of St. Mary, provided that he obtained the permission and Testimonial Letters of his Bishop. No *dimissoriales* or *testimoniales* were issued from diocese *A*, but Francis did receive the promised parish and labored in it until 1910, when he was requested to resign and leave the diocese because of a life of moral turpitude. The Rota did not consider his incardination into *K* as valid, but it was rather because there was no trace of the necessary taking of the oath to remain in diocese *K*, and because there was no special permission obtained from the Sacred Congregation for the Propagation of the Faith[337] for his entry into the United States of America.

[335] *Bismarckien. et aliarum*, incardinationis, 31 ian. 1913—*AAS*, V (1913), 34 ss.

[336] *Decisio* XXII, 17 aprilis 1913—*S. Romanae Rotae Decisiones seu Sententiae*, V, 249 ss.

[337] Cf. *supra*, p. 216.

2°. Negative opinion

At the outset of this article comment was made on the intricate involvement of this subject with that of ordination, proper Bishops, ordination titles, etc., so that a series of schedules was provided to help clarify the entire field. A glance at the same will show that the general subject of this study affected laymen, clerics, and priests in different ways, and that in each category there was a general process of change with the times.[338] One need not wonder, then, at the elusiveness of the subject, or at the spectacle of even the masters being trapped into erroneous conclusions. It is considered rash to deny a scholastic's major proposition, but in the affirmative evidence just given,[339] that which is taken for granted, and about which the least, if anything at all, is offered by way of proof, is the general fundamental proposition that the Decree " *A primis* " applied to all canonical transfers, of *priests* as well as of *clerics;* yet it is that very foundation which is most open to attack.

A more tenable opinion is that the Decree " *A primis* " was issued to take care of only one subject—the establishment of the fifth title of proper Bishop for the ordination of *inferior clerics*—and, therefore, had nothing to do with the methods of canonically transferring *priests,* regardless of the relationship of these methods to the past, to the present, or to the future. Like an avalanche, the original misunderstanding of the scope of the decree has picked up in the course of years so many endorsements and repetitions of the original error as to make it now appear a formidable opinion.

To substantiate this claim that the " *A primis* " referred only to inferior clerics there are submitted the following arguments:

1) The origin of the " *A primis* " was the query made to Rome by certain Bishops whether inferior clerics incardinated by them could, by that very fact, be immediately promoted to sacred orders; that is, in other words, the query if they, the incardinating Bishops, could be considered as the proper Bishops for ordination at once, or, if that could not be done, how else they

[338] Cf. *infra,* pp. 263-284.

[339] *Supra,* pp. 221-223.

were to solve the perplexing modern difficulties which gave rise to such a custom of immediate ordination on the strength of incardination.[840] The answer "*Provideatur per Decretum*" (which eventually proved to be the Decree "*A primis*") was, therefore, a promise solely to provide the Bishops with a new legal title by which they could properly ordain, or authorize to be ordained, their newly incardinated subjects, without making it necessary for the latter to fulfill the provision of the "*Speculatores,*" namely, of previously establishing a domicile through at least three years of residence in the new diocese. It was in no sense a notification that the whole field of incardination and excardination was to be recast.

2) Internal evidence shows that it was intended only for inferior clerics: a) its sub-title was "De Clericorum excardinatione *et ordinatione*"; b) its first words, from which it derives the name "*A primis,*" state that from the first ages of the Church a proper Bishop for ordination was necessary; c) its second paragraph rehearses the history of the four various titles of proper Bishop for ordination that had come into vogue up to that time; d) its third paragraph explains how a custom of still a fifth title of proper Bishop, namely, incardination, had appeared, but was giving rise to contentions because it was not regulated by law; e) the rest of the decree is in the nature of a remedy for these contentions, so that the custom will have the protection of law; f) the oath prescribed in n. 2 is for the acquisition of a new domicile by an abbreviated method, so as to make the Bishop the proper one for ordination much sooner than had been done theretofore; this oath has to be fashioned after the example of the oath required by the "*Speculatores*" (*ad instar illius*), but does not have to be identical with it, because this latter required residence before the oath could be taken, but the "*A primis*" did not; g) n. 4 of the decree is its kernel, establishing the fifth title of proper Bishop with warnings of caution to be observed in the use of it; h) n. 6 left clerics the alternative of acquiring a proper Bishop for higher ordination by any of the other titles of proper Bishops; and that manifestly would apply only to inferior clerics, who alone would

840 Cf. *supra*, pp. 113-114.

be interested in further ordination; i) the decree did not mention the word " priest " even once.

3) The supplementary Decree of Nov. 24, 1906, confirmed the same opinion, because it referred to the " *A primis* " as having made certain regulations " circa excardinationem et incardinationem clericorum eorumque *subsequentem ordinationem.*"

4) The Decree " *A primis* " included no regulations whatever for transfers of secular clerics to religion or *vice versa,* which were naturally to be expected if the decree had been intended as a reordering of the entire subject.

5) It contained no provisions for the incardination of Orientals—an omission which would give rise to many new difficulties if this was to be considered a new, complete, general law.

If all this be so, certainly the " *A primis* " did not aim to abrogate the existing customs and laws of transferring *priests,* and particularly by the method of equivalent incardination, as is shown from the following considerations:

1st. Contrary to what the Consultor held in the Adria case,[341] the custom of incardinating priests by conferring residential benefices on them was as old as the institution of the benefice itself and the concomitant ordination title of patrimony, which made it to be of about seven hundred years' standing. All through the preceding pages of this study the history of that very thing has been traced. After 1179 those who had been ordained to the priesthood for the title of patrimony were free to continue as itinerant priests until they found a diocese from which they received a residential benefice, whereupon they became attached to it for life. The term *incardination* certainly was not used, since that is principally a nineteenth century word, but the idea was the same. In succeeding centuries, the liberty of a priest ordained for the title of patrimony, or of a simply beneficed priest, to find himself a residential benefice, no matter where, was variously restricted, but at no time entirely cancelled. In the Innocentian Period this very freedom of the priests to depart perpetually from their dioceses, even sometimes without the consent of their Bishops, as based on various de-

[341] S. C. C., *Adrien.*, 14 feb. et 11 iul. 1925—*AAS*, XVIII (1926), 48-55.

cisions of the Holy See, caused consternation in the minds of many Bishops, who feared their dioceses would be drained of priests because of the scarcity of residential benefices.[342] There was no question in any of these cases of the benefice being obtained merely to acquire a proper Bishop for ordination, as the Consultor in the *Adria* case would have it. Intentionally, priests were considered separately from clerics in this article to keep that point clear.

Now a custom of seven hundred years is immemorial and can be abrogated only by a specific invalidating clause such as " quavis contraria consuetudine etiam centenaria et immemorabili non obstante," which is not found in the " *A primis*."

2nd. The terms " incardination " and " excardination " were used in the " *A primis* " in the restricted sense of a canonical transfer of an inferior cleric by letters only, whereas in the present study they have been used generically to designate any method of transfer for any cleric. This restricted use is apparent from n. 6 of the decree, which leaves those clerics, who cannot or do not wish to use *excardination*, the alternative of becoming transferred to another diocese through the indirect and more lengthy method of acquiring a new proper Bishop for ordination by one of the other four titles, already recognized and regulated in the Constitution " *Speculatores*," i. e., origin, acquired domicile, adequate benefice, or service in a Bishop's household. All through the present study, that kind of transfer also has been termed an *excardination*. But in the decree a distinction is implied between the two, even though the " *A primis* " apparently recognizes the validity of both. Hence, one is forced to conclude that the decree set out to regulate solely the restricted field of transfers of inferior clerics by letters, which alone it termed *excardination*, and that it left untouched the wider field of indirect transfers. Furthermore, by its very mention of the latter in n. 6 as being a legal alternative for inferior clerics, it implicitly ratified for priests as well the notion of transfer by the acquisition of a residential benefice, because, as pointed out earlier in this article,[343] the mere obtain-

[342] Cf. *supra*, pp. 193-195.

[343] *Supra*, pp. 161-2, 170, 189-192.

ing of a new proper Bishop by any one of the four titles listed in the "*Speculatores,*" and even the reception of orders from the same, did not bring about a canonical transfer, except when that Bishop conferred on his new subject a residential benefice. On this point the Consultor of the Sacred Congregation of the Council in the *Adria* case was completely wrong when he regarded ordination, and not the conferring of a residential benefice, as the operative cause of incardination.[344] It was by no means an unusual thing for a cleric to be advanced in orders by the Bishop who had become his proper Bishop for ordination through the conferring of a simple benefice, and yet it is readily admitted by all that such a procedure did not establish any permanent bond between the ordained cleric and the diocese in which that benefice existed.

3rd. The decisions of the Sacred Roman Congregations, adduced in support of the affirmative opinion, were not official interpretations, but only responses to particular questions, with the one exception of that decision of the Sacred Congregation of the Council entitled *Romana et aliarum,*[345] which expressly declared that presumptive incardination was nullified by the "*A primis.*" Some of those cases wherein invalidity was predicated on non-conformance to the "*A primis*" were not clear-cut and could be held invalid for other reasons. In others, the Consultor's recommendations, on which the decisions were based, were the result of a misunderstanding either of the complex involvement of ordination with incardination, e. g., in the Adria case,[346] or of the legal terminology.[347] Even the various Sacred Congregations were not always of one mind on important things, e. g., on the necessity of the oath for the validity of incardination of priests.[348]

[344] S. C. C., *Adrien.*, 14 feb. et 11 iul. 1925—*AAS*, XVIII (1926), 50-52.

[345] Cf. *supra*, pp. 219-220.

[346] Cf. *supra*, footnote 344.

[347] E. g., the word *dimissoriis* occurring in S. C. Ep. et Reg., *Viterbien.*, 14 iul. 1905 (*ASS*, XXXIX [1906], 207) is interpreted as perhaps meaning *dimissorialibus* by the Consultor in S. C. C., *Adrien.*, 14 feb. et 11 iul. 1925 (*AAS*, XVIII [1926], 53). It is to avoid the misinterpretation of these terms in English that the Latin is resorted to so frequently in this study.

[348] Cf. *supra*, p. 222, footnote 331.

4th. Though the "*A primis*" insisted on an oath of permanent service and on an unconditional acceptance of the cleric as prerequisites for the incardination of inferior clerics, the Sacred Congregation of the Council declined to state that the absence of the oath in the incardinations of priests in the United States of America after 1898 invalidated the process; and its Consultor argued in favor of the continued validity, in the Pre-Code Period, of the American formal incardination of priests,[349] even though it was conditional in character.[350]

5th. Quite a number of Roman decisions recognized as valid the method whereby priests or clerics changed dioceses by the acquisition of alien residential benefices before 1898.[351]

6th. Equivalent incardination by the permitted reception of an alien residential benefice was accepted as a valid method in the Code of Canon Law (can. 114) only nineteen years after the "*A primis*" was supposed to have abrogated it.

349 Cf. *supra*, pp. 208-210.

350 S. C. C., *Bismarckien. et aliarum*, 31 ianuarii 1913—*AAS*, V (1913), 34, 37. This latter was a considerable admission, especially for cases where the distance was great between the *a qua* and the *ad quam* dioceses. Previous provincial councils and instructions from the Holy See had required the Bishop "*a quo*" to know that the Bishop "*ad quem*" was willing both to receive the priest and to confer on him an office before the written dismissal could be issued. By formal incardination an American Bishop would signify his willingness to receive the priest and to supply an office for him, but only in a provisory way over a three or five-year period, during which the immigrant priest would have to make good, under penalty of not being incardinated, and of having to depart elsewhere or of returning home. The "*A primis*" (n. 4) spoke of a trial *after* unconditional incardination before further ordination of an inferior cleric, but nothing of a trial after priestly ordination as a condition for incardination. On the contrary, it said (n. 2) that incardination had to be absolute and perpetual, i. e., subject to no express or tacit limitations. This, it would seem, would have abrogated the law concerning the *formal* incardination described in the III Plenary Council of Baltimore, i. e., if the "*A primis*" were meant to refer to priests. Yet the Consultor of the S. C. C. was of the opinion that this law continued in force.

351 E. g., S. C. Ep. et Reg., *Rottenburgen.*, 26 martii 1886—*ASS*, XIX (1886), 91; S. C. Ep. et Reg., *Viterbien.*, 14 iulii 1905—*ASS*, XXXIX (1906), 207 ss.; S. C. C., *Romana et aliarum*, 15 sept. 1906—*ASS*, XXXIX (1906), 486 ss.; S. R. R., *Londonen.*, 9 ianuarii 1912—*AAS*, IV (1912), 249 ss.; S. C. C., *Adrien.*, 14 feb. et 11 iul. 1925, at least admitted the existence of a legal incardination before 1898 when both Bishops' consent was clear, even though it was not a written consent, which is, after all, the very basis of incardination, when it is effected by means of the conferment of a residential benefice.—*AAS*, XVIII (1926), 48-55.

3°. Which opinion to be followed in practice

Though the negative opinion seems to be better substantiated by evidence, it is the affirmative alone which has received recognition from the Sacred Roman Congregations. There is a period of only nineteen years which would be affected by the practical adoption of the negative opinion, but very probably it would change the status of many a priest throughout the world. In practice, therefore, it is best not to disturb the present accepted doctrine, namely, that from 1898 to 1917 any cleric's transfer from one diocese to another except through the medium of formal letters of excardination and equally formal letters of incardination must be held as invalid.

C. Methods of Excardination and Incardination

1°. Formal letters

According to the practical conclusion just given there is no need for treating priests separately from clerics in this Pre-Code Period. No matter in what grade, the cleric could directly secure a change of diocese in no other way than by an exchange of formal letters. Indirectly, a cleric in lower orders could secure the same through the process of acquiring a new proper Bishop, as will be explained below.[352]

The translation of the Decree "*A primis*" was given in Chapter IV.[353] Its prescriptions are clear enough to need but little comment here.

1) In point of time, according to it, letters of excardination had to be issued first. Though it was not expressly so stated, these could not be general, but had to be addressed to a definite Bishop, who, through informal channels, was known to be willing to accept the candidate. No matter how absolute and perpetual these first letters were, they did not have their complete effect until the letters of incardination were executed. There is nothing said about the validity of the process being suspended

[352] Cf. *infra*, pp. 236 ff.

[353] Cf. *supra*, pp. 115-6.

until the Bishop "*a quo*" is notified of the incardination. Apparently it was assumed in the decree that the exact date of the canonical transfer would be that on which the letters of incardination were signed by the Bishop "*ad quem.*" A just cause was necessary for the lawfulness, but not for the validity, of the excardination; and the judge of the same was the dismissing Bishop. Hence, a transfer prompted by a cleric's avarice would be valid, but sinful.

A sample formula for letters of excardination, drawn up by the Plenary Council of Latin America in 1901, is as follows:

> N. Episcopus N.—Dilecto in Christo N.
>
> Petiisti a Nobis, ut tibi concederemus litteras excardinationis a Nostra Dioecesi, cui ratione originis (seu domicilii) adscriptus hucusque fuisti, et in qua ad Clericatus honorem promotus es, quo integrum tibi sit ad Ecclesiam et Dioecesim N. transire, eique adscribi. Quum igitur Nobis compertum sit Illustrissimum et Reverendissimum Dominum N. Episcopum Ecclesiae N. paratum esse ad te adscribendum Ecclesiae suae; et tu nullo alio canonico vinculo Dioecesi Nostrae ligatus sis, nec ullum in ea habeas beneficium (vel et beneficium, quod in ea habebas, canonica ex causa dimiseris et resignaveris) iustae praeterea habeantur causae huius excardinationis concedendae, nec tu ad eam petendam levitate aut ambitione movearis, gratiam, quam expostulasti, tibi duximus concedendam. Quare Nostris hisce litteris te N.N. dioecesis nostrae clericum et in minoribus (vel maioribus, et exprimantur Ordines quibus est insignitus) ordinibus constitutum e Dioecesi Nostra absolute et in perpetuum excardinamus et excardinatum edicimus et declaramus, in eum tantum finem ut Dioecesi N. adscribi valeas, et sub conditione, ut hae Litterae suum plenum sortiantur effectum tunc solummodo, quum Dioecesi N. rite fueris adscriptus.
>
> In quorum fidem etc.—Datum etc.—N. Episcopus N.—N. Cancellarius Episcopalis.[354]

2) Second in point of time were perpetual letters of incardination. The Bishop was the only competent authority to grant them. No conditions could be stipulated in them, as was for-

[354] *Concilium Plenarium Americae Latinae* (a. 1901), II (Appendix), 759-760—*AER*, XLVI (1912), 282.

merly done at times,[355] because such a procedure would only have served to multiply the possibilities of swelling the ranks of a vagrant clergy. Besides, the secret Testimonials furnished by the Bishop "*a quo*," if they were conscientiously drawn up, obviated the need of any conditional acceptance on the part of the Bishop "*ad quem*." However, Bishops were solemnly cautioned not to venture upon the incardination of any new cleric in their dioceses except for the reasons of necessity and utility in their churches.

A sample formula for letters of incardination, likewise adopted in 1901 by the Plenary Council for Latin America, is as follows:

> N. Episcopus N.—Dilecto in Christo N.
>
> Quum Nobis constiterit te N.N. in minoribus (vel maioribus, et exprimantur Ordines, quibus insignitus est) ordinibus constitutum, qui hucusque Dioecesi N. fueras adscriptus, ab illius Illustrissimo ac Reverendissimo Episcopo Domino N.N. iustis de causis excardinationis litteras obtinuisse, nec non ex praedicti Domini Episcopi testimonio certum Nobis sit te legitimis esse natalibus, integris moribus et sufficienti praeditum scientia; quum praeterea tu praestito iuramento declaraveris velle te in hac Nostra Dioecesi semper manere et huic Nostrae Ecclesiae iugiter deservire, Nos moti studio, quo exardescimus, bonum huius Ecclesiae Nostrae curae commissae procurandi, te, quem utilem (vel necessarium) Ecclesiae huic Nostrae pro praesentibus eius adiunctis existimamus, absolute et in perpetuum Ecclesiae et Dioecesi Nostrae adscribimus et adscriptum renuntiamus et declaramus, sperantes te alacri animo in futurum bono animarum in hac Nostra Dioecesi adlaboraturum, et omnibus fidelibus Nostrae curae commissis bonum Christi odorem futurum.
>
> In quorum fidem etc.—Datum etc.—N. Episcopus N.—N. Cancellarius Episcopalis.[356]

[355] E. g., in the Sacred Congregation of the Council's Rottenburg case, March 26, 1886, when the priest, after being asked for by the Bishop "*ad quem*," was told: "... receptionem petitam tunc tantum posse evenire, si ipse per longius tempus bonis moribus se commendasset."—*ASS*, XIX (1886), 90.

[356] *Concilium Plenarium Americae Latinae* (a. 1901), II (Appendix), 760—*AER*, XLVI (1912), 282-283.

The oath, which was held by various decisions of the Sacred Congregations to be necessary for the validity of the process,[357] was the sworn promise of the new cleric to remain subject throughout his whole life to the jurisdiction of the Bishop of the diocese "*ad quam*," and to work under his direction for the service of that diocese.[358] Even though he was thousands of miles away, such an oath taken by a cleric would bind him to the diocese adopting him. He could not swear, as was demanded of him in the "*Speculatores*," that he really and truly had the intention of "remaining" in the diocese, for as yet he was not present in the diocese; consequently this oath was only to be similar to that (*ad instar illius*) which the Constitution "*Speculatores*" prescribed for acquiring a domicile. By such an oath he did not assume any greater obligations towards the diocese than did its native clergy. Hence, it did not bar him from being loaned out, or from entering a Religious Congregation, with his new Bishop's permission, or even from entering a Religious Order without that permission, as long as he at least sought it.

3) The Bishop "*ad quem*" could not issue letters of incardination until he had first received the petitioner's letters of perpetual excardination; this incidentally showed that the Bishop "*a quo*" could proceed without fear of violating any law in issuing such letters. Neither could the receiving Bishop act until he had received reliable Testimonial Letters from the dismissing Bishop as to the cleric's birth, life, morals, and studies. Responsibility for the truth of these rested on the conscience of the Bishop issuing them.

4) The effects of this incardination were threefold: a) The cleric became attached to the new diocese in the same way as if he had been born there, with the enjoyment of all the rights and privileges of its native clergy; b) for the accepted cleric who was not yet in priestly orders, the receiving Bishop at once became exclusively the proper Bishop, by the title of incardination, for the conferring of any higher orders, so that he could issue the

[357] Cf. *supra*, pp. 221-2, 224.

[358] Many, *De Sacra Ordin.*, n. 70.

litterae dimissoriae to any other Bishop to ordain the new subject, even though the latter was a great distance away from his new diocese and had never even been seen by his new Bishop; and c) the newly incardinated cleric relinquished as proper Bishops for his ordination all those who previously had enjoyed that status, and the possibility of variation among them was definitely foreclosed.

This new title, which established the proper Bishop for ordination and the rights consequent thereto, and which by comparison with the past loomed up as an almost incredible reality, had to be used with great caution. There still obtained the ruling of the Council of Trent that no one be ordained hastily, and that the newly incardinated be advanced to orders solely in view of the necessity or utility of the diocese. However, the period of trial and probation to which clerics in non-priestly orders were subject before their eventual admission to priestly ordination, even if it proved unfortunate in its results, did not affect the validity of the incardination, for any misdirected quest of priestly orders could still be halted in good time.[359]

5) The incardination of clerics who, from a national standpoint, were foreigners was to be attended with even greater care. These were not even to be allowed to depart from their homeland for the appointed destination until the Bishop "*ad quem*" had first requested and received from their respective native Ordinary secret information of a favorable character about their life and morals, and this under pain of grave sin for both Bishops.

6) Whenever a layman wanted to secure a diocese different from that in which he was residing, or whenever a cleric in the lower orders wanted to do the same, without going through the process just explained, he had to follow the old law of the "*Speculatores*" by first acquiring the Bishop of the diocese of his choice as his proper Bishop for ordination through any one of the recognized titles, namely, origin, acquired domicile, adequate benefice or *familiaritas,* and in the course of time merit acceptance into the clergy of that diocese.

[359] *Ibid.*, n. 69.

2°. Indirect method—acquisition of a new proper Bishop

This method of canonical transfer, by acquiring a new proper Bishop for ordination, was available for only the clerics in the lower orders, as just stated, and as already explained relative to the preceding periods of history.[360] Right here, however, there results a peculiar dilemma. The very Decree "*A primis*," which was supposed to have abrogated all other types of clerical transfers except those executed by formal letters, in n. 6 makes available also an indirect method which functions independently of letters.[361] Stranger still, this indirect method never takes effect until a residential benefice has been conferred by the new proper Bishop [362]—the very thing which the affirmative opinion about the abrogatory force of the Decree "*A primis*" declared could no longer be done.[363]

It is easy to understand how a cleric, desiring to disengage himself from the diocese of his place of origin, could obtain a new proper Bishop. For instance, he could move to a new territory, taking with him most of his household possessions, and after three years' residence, fortified by an oath to remain perpetually, as was required by the Constitution "*Speculatores*" for the acquisition of a domicile, claim its Bishop as his proper Bishop *ratione domicilii.* Many angles for investigation would enter into it: where he had been studying; at whose expense; for what title, if any, he had been thus far ordained; whether or not he was dismissed from the seminary, etc.; all of which would have to be solved satisfactorily before higher orders could be received from the Bishop of his place of domicile, lest the cleric be convicted of acting "*in fraudem.*" The original Bishop's permission was needed for the cleric to change his

[360] Cf. *supra*, pp. 161-2, 170, 189-192.

[361] Wernz, *Ius Decretalium*, II, p. I, n. 28, Scholion II.

[362] Gasparri, *De Sacra Ordin.*, II, nn. 858-859. Many (*De Sacra Ordin.*, n. 42), explaining why a cleric may vary from one Bishop to another in receiving holy orders, says: "...ex se enim ordinatio non inducit vinculum rigorosum cum dioecesi episcopi ordinantis, nec ulla lex canonica inducit hoc vinculum *ex facto solius ordinationis.*"

[363] Cf. *supra*, pp. 219-224.

domicile, since all clerics were considered assigned in the diocese to minister to the necessity or utility of its churches by the very fact that they were ordained; still, that permission could not be withheld unless the cleric was obliged for one or the other of the above stated reasons to remain; and ordinarily this permission was included in the *litterae testimoniales* which the Constitution "*Speculatores*" required the ordaining Bishop to obtain.[364]

But could a cleric in minor orders, who suddenly moved into a new diocese and lived there with his parents for a period of even ten years, make a demand on the Bishop of the place for the reception of higher orders or for inclusion among the diocesan clergy? By no means. Through the title of the cleric's acquired domicile, that Bishop had indeed the right to ordain him, but did not have any obligation to do so. If he decided to ordain the cleric, the Bishop would first seek the *litterae testimoniales* of the cleric's original Bishop, which served to notify the latter of his cleric's intention and thus gave him an opportunity to protest the ordination or refuse the letters. If no objection was raised, the Bishop of the cleric's place of acquired domicile would confer a new order on him, and since, by the law of the Council of Trent, a Bishop could not do that except for the sake of consulting the necessity or utility of the churches in his diocese, by the very fact of ordination the cleric was regarded as linked with the diocese of his place of domicile. Still, even this full procedure did not rigidly bind the cleric to that diocese and, therefore, could not be called incardination. The cleric could leave the diocese without express permission just as he had come into it. The only absolute way in which the proper Bishop *ratione domicilii* could block such a cleric who was only in minor orders from leaving the diocese was by appointing him to a residential benefice. Then other proper Bishops would still be competent to ordain, but it would be of no avail for them to do so. They could not act without the permission of the Bishop *ratione domicilii,* and he, indeed, had a full right to refuse. Then, and only then, could the cleric be rightly regarded as canonically transferred to the diocese of his new proper Bishop.

364 Gasparri, *ibid.*, n. 857.

A similar ordeal had to be followed by a cleric in minor orders in acquiring a new proper Bishop by the obtaining of an adequate benefice, or by spending three years in the service of another Bishop's household. The conferring of a simple but adequate benefice on the cleric by the Bishop in either of these cases would satisfy the law of the Constitution "*Speculatores*" for making the new Bishop competent to ordain the incumbent of such benefice, but it did not permanently link the ordained cleric with the diocese within which he held this benefice. That could be accomplished only by the conferring of a permanent residential benefice.

D. Special Requisites for Certain Groups

1°. Those in sacred orders *titulo missionis*

Nothing in the Decree "*A primis*" indicated any change in the legislation regarding this group. Their oath was of a stricter nature than that required in n. 2 of this decree, which still permitted entrance into religion.[365] Permission for them to become excardinated still had to come from the Sacred Congregation for the Propagation of the Faith,[366] unless, as already explained,[367] the excardination was to a diocese in the same ecclesiastical province in England or in the United States of America.

From the practically accepted view that all forms of transfers other than those by formal letters of excardination and incardination were abrogated, it follows that after 1898 even the clerics and priests ordained *titulo missionis* could be transferred in only this way.

Ordinarily a transfer required a new oath, which was to be taken for a certain diocese, vicariate, or mission, and required also a new title of ordination. In those countries which in 1885 obtained the special grant that permitted the oath of service to be taken in relation to the entire ecclesiastical province, the transferred clerics needed only a new title, if their transfer

[365] Cf. *supra*, p. 234.

[366] Cf. *supra*, p. 144.

[367] Cf. *supra*, pp. 144-5, 192.

did not take them beyond that province; if it did, then both a new oath and a new title were required. Clerics ordained in these countries before 1885 had to take a new oath of service to the province in connection with their initial transfer to a diocese within that province. Thereafter any new transfer within the province could be effected for them without an oath.[368]

2°. Those dismissed from other seminaries

The special requisites for incardinating clerics who had been dismissed from other seminaries or Institutes of Religious were contained in the Decree "*Vetuit,*" issued by Pope Pius X, through the Sacred Congregation of the Council, on December 22, 1905.[369] Bishops were advised to make sure of the antecedents of clerics from other dioceses before even receiving such into their seminaries, and to refuse admittance to those who were judged unworthy by other Bishops (n. 1).

When such clerics who had been dismissed from other seminaries were admitted in good faith, and the Bishop was willing, after a period of trial, to incardinate and later ordain them, one special restriction was decreed—that they never return to establish their domicile in the same diocese from which they had been dismissed (n. 2).

If the dismissed cleric had belonged to a Religious Institute which was located in the Bishop's own diocese, the Bishop was to obtain secret written information from the moderators of the Institute about the morals, the character, and the ability of the cleric, and was not to receive him unless these attributes conformed to the moral integrity required in the priestly state. Obviously the above requirement against establishing a domicile did not apply in this particular instance (n. 4).

3°. Foreign-born minor clerics emigrating to the United States of America

Two years prior to the enactment of the Decree "*A primis*" an instruction to the Bishops of the United States of America

[368] Cf. *supra*, pp. 144-145.

[369] *ASS*, XXXVIII (1905-1906), 407 ss. Cf. *supra*, p. 96, where a translation of this decree is given.

was given on this subject by the Sacred Congregation for the Propagation of the Faith.[370] The " *A primis* " (n. 5) was general enough in language to embrace the first part of this instruction, which obliged immigrants from any country to present *litterae dimissoriales* and *litterae testimoniales* from the Bishop of their place of origin, but it was silent about the second part, which had added a special requisite for those from Poland, namely, that they bring Testimonial Letters from the Sacred Congregation for the Propagation of the Faith.[371]

Apparently that second part was still binding from 1898 until 1908, despite the omission of at least an implied mention of it in the Decree " *A primis*," for the instruction was withdrawn only in 1908 by Pius X's Constitution " *Sapienti consilio*." [372] In this Papal Constitution it was declared that thereafter the " *A primis* " (n. 5) would take the place of the above mentioned instruction of 1896, and that, if the immigrant clerics had been dismissed from seminaries abroad, their reception here was to be made by following the prescriptions of the Decree " *Vetuit*." [373]

The only new features added by the " *A primis* " to the ordinary requirements for this group, therefore, were greater caution and strictness, and mandatory instead of optional secret Testimonials from the original Bishop.

4°. Emigrating priests

The Pre-Code Period was one of emigration, largely from Europe to America, to provide spiritual services in the mother tongues of the vast numbers of people of every nation who had come to establish their homes here; and the development of the

[370] Cf. *supra*, pp. 192-3, 216.

[371] The United States of America was then under that Sacred Congregation's jurisdiction.

[372] *AAS*, I (1909), 7-19; *Fontes*, n. 682. Cf. also *AAS*, II (1910), 102. It was by this Constitution that the United States of America was exempted from the jurisdiction of the S. C. de Prop. Fide and placed under common law—Const. Apost., "*Sapienti consilio*," § 1, *Sacrae Congregationes*, 6° *Congreg. de Prop. Fide*, n. 2 (*AAS*, I [1909], 12).

[373] Cf. *supra*, footnote 369.

Philippine Islands under the American government intensified the movement.

In the preceding period it was, of course, required of all foreign-born priests emigrating here to be supplied with written permission from their Ordinary to depart, and with a Testimonial Letter from the same as to their freedom from censures and their enjoyment of good morals.[374] In addition, there were special requirements for priests emigrating from Italy and from Poland, most outstanding of which were that permission for the former had to come from the Sacred Congregation of the Council, and Testimonials for the latter had to be issued by the Sacred Congregation for the Propagation of the Faith.[375]

From the beginning of the Pre-Code Period, the "*A primis*," doubtfully at best referring to priests, established a general requirement that the receiving Bishop obtain secret Testimonial Letters from the respective Ordinary of each immigrant priest under pain of grave sin for both Bishops.

In 1903 the Sacred Congregation of the Council augmented its earlier encyclical letter of 1890 to the Bishops of Italy and America with a general decree to the world,[376] in which, under pain of nullity, it renewed, except for temporary sojourns, the prescriptions of the former encyclical letter, as far as Italian priests emigrating to America were concerned, but extended these prescriptions to include also other groups of priests as follows:

I. Renewal of the same law for Italian priests.[377]

II. For other European priests emigrating to America: (a) secret Testimonial Letters must first be sent to the Bishop "*ad quem*" by the dismissing Bishop; (b) consent of the Bishop "*ad quem*" to accept the priest must be received; and (c) the Bishop "*a quo*" himself must then issue to the priest the *litterae discessoriales* addressed to the Bishop "*ad quem*."

374 Cf. *supra*, p. 216.

375 Cf. *supra*, pp. 214-216. The latter condition was removed in 1908.

376 "*Clericos peregrinos*," 14 novem. 1903—*ASS*, XXXVI (1903-1904), 355 ss.; requoted in *AAS*, I (1909), 694 ss.

377 Cf. *supra*, pp. 214-215.

III. For any priests emigrating to the Philippine Islands: (a) the same procedure as for Italian priests emigrating to America must be followed; [878] (b) the Apostolic Delegate to the United States of America is authorized to grant the permission to American priests; for all others, the Sacred Congregation of the Council.

A little more than ten years later, i. e., in 1914, the entire field of legislation for priests emigrating from any country to America or to the Philippine Islands was renewed, recast, and amplified, in another general decree, issuing this time from the Sacred Consistorial Congregation.[879]

The following is an abbreviated condensation of its features as far as secular clerics are concerned:

Law for Secular Priests of the Latin Rite who emigrate permanently or for a long time.

1. No one to go to { America or Philippine Islands } unless:

   he has good testimony of a blameless life thus far in the sacred ministry;

   he offers solid hope that he will edify the faithful anywhere;

   he gives moral certainty that he will never stain his sacerdotal dignity.

2. Those with good testimony, not to emigrate until:

   Bishop "*ad quem*" agrees to accept them;

   grants an ecclesiastical office; and

   proper Ordinary grants letters *discessoriales* in specific form.

3. *Ordinarius loci* "*ad quem*" bound *sub gravi* not to give or promise acceptance until:

   after secret letters directly exchanged with proper Bishop "*a quo*,"

[878] *Loc. cit.*

[879] "*Ethnografica studia*," 25 martii 1914—*AAS*, VI (1914), 182-186.

he has certain testimony that candidate is worthy according to n. 1.

Ordinarius loci " a quo " forbidden *sub gravi* to give *discessoriales* unless:

priest pertains to his diocese by some canonical title;
Ordinarius " a quo " can justly give good Testimonials;
letters of *Ordinarius loci " ad quem "* are received,

agreeing to accept priest,
and
promising an ecclesiastical office.

4. Letters *discessoriales* by *proprius Ordinarius loci* for validity must:

be in specific form, i. e., addressed to a definite *Ordinarius loci;*
contain customary testimony;
contain individuating notes of priest, e. g., age, etc.

In Italy—Bishops must first fulfill the requirements; then refer these to the S. C. Consist.
S. C. Consist. gives the written permission.
It is then communicated to both Ordinaries.

5. Emigrations to the Philippine Islands

from Europe—S. C. Consist. issues the permission;
from America—Apostolic Delegate issues the permission.

6. New transfers { in perpetuity or for long time } of immigrated priests not allowed unless:

Proper Ordinary consents;
Ordinary of diocese of 1st immigration consents; and if from Italy—S. C. Consist. consents.

8. Priests who emigrate without observing these laws:

are suspended *a divinis ipso facto;*
if they violate it, they become irregular.

Absolution from these censures from S.C.Consist. alone.

9. Extension of these laws is made to priests, even in Europe, who leave homeland to labor among emigrated farmers or workers.

10. Bishops of America and other places to get rid, within time limit, of immigrant priests unless they have:

    an Indult to remain;

    a right to remain:

    by reason of incardination, or

    by reason of 10 years' legitimate residence.

    Bishops of Europe:

    to do same for priests in their dioceses who are engaged in sacred ministry among immigrated farmers, etc.

11. Bishops of those regions from which people emigrate:

    to make plans to provide priests for the emigrated people;

    to constitute one Bishop to represent all these Bishops;

    Ordinaries in need of priests to communicate with him.

For a clearer view of the practical way in which this decree should be observed there is appended here also a topical and chronological summary of its provisions, in which the part each individual concerned was to play is listed under separate headings, and the order of each step in point of time is indicated by consecutive numbers:

I. The emigrating priest:

1. must have led a blameless life in the sacred ministry, giving him the basis for good Testimonials;
2. must belong to the diocese of the Bishop "*a quo*";
3. writes to the Bishop "*ad quem*" seeking acceptance;
12. awaits letters of dismissal (*discessoriales*);
14. journeys with them to Bishop "*ad quem.*"

II. The Bishop "*a quo*":

6. receives letter from Bishop "*ad quem*" requesting Testimonials;

7. sends secret Testimonial Letters to Bishop "*ad quem*";
11. receives letter from Bishop "*ad quem*"
    { consenting to accept priest, and
    promising to confer an ecclesiastical office;
*13. gives letters of dismissal (*discessoriales*) to priest
    { addressed to Bishop "*ad quem*,"
    containing individuating and identifying notes of priest.

III. The Bishop "*ad quem*":
4. receives from priest petition for acceptance;
5. writes letter to Bishop "*a quo*" requesting Testimonials;
8. receives from Bishop "*a quo*" secret Testimonial Letters;
9. must become convinced of priest's worthiness;
10. sends letter to Bishop "*a quo*"
    { consenting to accept priest, and
    promising to confer an ecclesiastical office;
15. receives priest with his *discessoriales;*
16. confers on him an ecclesiastical office.

* S. C. Consist. issues these, after the data have been obtained by the Bishop "*a quo*," for:
{ Italians going to America or the Philippines;
Europeans going to the Philippines.
Apostolic Delegate in the United States of America issues them for:
Americans going to the Philippines.

Further provisions of this decree were as follows:

1) Priests who had already emigrated, and had not become incardinated, but who wanted to change in perpetuity to still another diocese needed: (a) the consent of their proper Ordinary ("*a quo*"); (b) the consent of the Ordinary of their present place; (c) the consent of the Sacred Consistorial Congregation, if they were Italians.

2) Exclaustrated Religious desiring to emigrate: (a) if incardinated in their present diocese, followed the same law as given above for seculars; (b) if not incardinated, needed an Indult from the Sacred Consistorial Congregation.

The fulfillment of the various rules herein given did not constitute excardination and incardination.[380] That had to be effected by a separate process, but these regulations supplied the incardinating Bishop with the knowledge he needed about the candidate before completing the written instrument of incardination, which was to be unconditional and perpetual.

ARTICLE V

CONSENT OF A CLERIC TO HIS OWN EXCARDINATION

There is no clear text extant that legally proves the necessity of a cleric's consent to his own excardination, but there is quite sufficient evidence to show that it was always an accepted rule. A cleric was considered a most precious possession which a Bishop could not easily be led to sacrifice; he yielded rather to the pleas of other Bishops in need, or to those of the cleric himself, whenever he did grant letters of release. Confirmation of this is found in c. 18 of the Synod of Rome (a. 826) as it is recorded in the Decree of Gratian: " Episcopus subiecto sibi sacerdoti, vel alii clerico, nisi ab ipso postulatus, dimissorias non faciat, ne quis quasi perdita aut errans inveniatur." [381] The words "*ab ipso postulatus,*" it is true, are variously interpreted. The Glossa considers them as referring to another Bishop, since it explains "*ab ipso*" as "*ab eo qui habere desiderat et postulat.*" Likewise the text itself of the Synod of Rome supplies a good foundation for this view by rendering the passage "*nisi ab alio pos-*

[380] S. C. Consist., decr. "*Ethnografica studia,*" 25 mart. 1914, n. 10: "Episcopi Americae aliorumve locorum, de sacerdotibus advenis, qui in suas migraverunt dioeceses, diligenter inquirant, habeantne ii legitimum permanendi indultum, aut certum quoddam permanendi ius consecuti sint vel *per incardinationem* vel per decennalem legitimam commorationem; quos, si eiusmodi indulto aut iure carere et ceteroqui fidelibus inutiles esse cognoverint, congruenti termino iis praefinito, ad Ordinarios proprios dimittant."—*AAS,* VI (1914), 184.

[381] C. 1, D. LXXII.

tulatus," [382] which, of course, would mean "*ab alio episcopo."* [383] To this interpretation, too, it must be admitted, the motive for the Roman synod's prohibition would more accurately correspond, i. e., "*ne quis quasi perdita aut errans inveniatur,"* because, if the cleric were dismissed without another Bishop having signified his willingness to accept him, he would be wandering around without a shepherd. Still, the same could be said of a cleric who, unwillingly excardinated, would leave indeed but would refuse to go to the new Bishop's diocese. Moreover, for a cleric to be forced to go to another Bishop willing to receive him would have the character of a punishment visited on a man who had done no wrong, which is quite foreign to the idea of ecclesiastical penalties.[384]

The other interpretation of "*ab ipso postulatus*" as referring to the petition for release by the cleric himself is favored by Hallier,[385] and is borne out by various examples of early dimissorial letters (*litterae dimissoriae seu formatae*), in which the dismissing Bishop expressly states that he is acting on the request of the cleric himself. Thus the *litterae dimissoriae* of Atticus, Archbishop of Constantinople, which were adopted as a formula by the Council of Nicaea (a. 325) and later incorporated in the Decree of Gratian, read in part: ". . . iste clericus, Hermannus nomine, nostra in parrochia instructus ac detonsus, *parvitatem nostram rogavit,* quatinus illi commendaticias litteras conscriberemus, . . . *cuius voluntati consentientes* . . . litteras ei dimissorias dedimus . . ." [386] Similar expressions are found in the *dimissoriae* of Wolfeon, Bishop of Constantia (a. 807), to Bernaltus, in favor of a cleric, Anno; [387] in the letter of Heidilon, Bishop of Noyon, to Rodulphus, Bishop of Laon, in behalf of Rotgerus, a deacon; [388] and in that of Durandus,

[382] Hardouin, V, 63.

[383] Hefele, Vol. IV, Pars II, p. 49.

[384] Cf. Bouix, "De l'exeat,"—*Revue des sciences ecclésiastiques,* V (1862), 35 ff.

[385] *De Sacris Elect. et Ordin.*, P. II, sec. V, cap. III, art. X, § 7—*MTC,* XXIV, 1043.

[386] Cf. *supra*, p. 156, footnote 170; c. 2, D. LXXIII.

[387] Hallier, *ibid.*, § 8—*MTC,* XXIV, 1046.

[388] *Ibid.*, § 7—*MTC,* XXIV, 1044.

Bishop of Auvergne (ab. 1088), to Rodulfus, Archbishop of Tours, concerning a certain subdeacon of the former diocese.[889] That expulsion from a diocese would rather be a punishment for wickedness can be gathered from the *dimissoriae* of Burchard, Bishop of Worms, to Walter, Bishop of Speyer, in favor of a priest, Herman: ". . . presens frater noster, harum litterarum portitor, nomine Hermannus, non pro sua nequicia expulsus est a nobis . . ." [890] Even, therefore, if another Bishop did ask for a cleric, the Bishop to whom he appealed would not send one who was unwilling to go, because the incardination of a cleric was likened to the adoption of a child, in which the will of the child could not be absolutely disregarded.[891] Through most of the Church's history, in fact, *litterae dimissoriae* were addressed to a particular Bishop, which meant that either the second Bishop of his own accord had requested a cleric from a Bishop who had a surplus number of clerics, or that the cleric himself, with a desire to work elsewhere, had gained a benevolent receiving Bishop.

A significant fact of the cleric's consent always being presumed is that, throughout all the legislation reviewed in the preceding pages of this study, there is a constant insistence on the permission of the dismissing Bishop being obtained for the release of a cleric, but that nothing at all is said about the cleric's consent. Certainly, in the course of eighteen centuries or more, some discussion or legislation would have been evoked, if there had been a practice of evicting clerics, for the solicitude of the Church was ever devoted to her clergy, that they have a place to work, a decent sustenance, a guaranteed security even in old age, and peace between themselves and the Bishop in each diocese.

The bond established between cleric and diocese immediately upon the acceptance or incardination of a cleric was a sacred contract, in which he pledged perpetual service in return for the Bishop's provision of a permanent home, of an ecclesiastical

[889] Cf. *supra*, p. 158, footnote 174.

[890] Cf. *supra*, p. 159, footnote 177; c. 1, D. LXXIII.

[891] Cf. *supra*, p. 158.

office, and of a just claim for sustenance. Clerics were considered absolved from their contract if the Bishop failed to provide these necessities for them. The Bishop, on the other hand, would be absolved from his contract only if the cleric became insubordinate.

This does not mean that a cleric could not be constrained to return to a diocese which he had deserted either without his Bishop's permission or through an illegal method of excardination.[392] Rome's standard for deciding to which diocese a cleric under disputed allegiance belonged was to determine in which diocese he was last validly incardinated, no matter in how many places after that he had labored.

The consent of the cleric did not necessarily have to be written. Just as in the case of equivalent incardination on the Bishop's part, so an act normally implying the cleric's consent would be a legal presumption of the same, for instance, if, with the permission of his Bishop, he accepted a permanent residential benefice from another Bishop, or if, after the legal execution of letters of excardination and incardination, he accepted an appointment from the new Bishop.[393]

Some contend that a cleric could give consent in advance, at the outset of his clerical life, to his own future excardination, if and when it seemed advisable to his own and to some outside Bishop. That opinion cannot be accepted without qualification. If such prior consent were to be restricted in scope to one or several known and designated dioceses, its practical possibility and legal sufficiency would seem plausible; hardly so, if the consent given in advance were to be regarded as altogether unrestricted. The reason is that no one but a unique character could blindly consent to spend his life anywhere regardless of location or climatic conditions, near his home or thousands of miles from it, within his fatherland or outside of it, in the frozen North or in the blazing sun of the equatorial regions; and laws do not deal with such fanciful possibilities. Previously

[392] E. g., S. R. R., *Londonen.*, 9 ian. 1912—*AAS*, IV (1912), 249 ss.; cf. *supra*, pp. 220-2.

[393] Cf. De Becker, "The admission of secular priests into a diocese of the United States,"—*AER*, XVIII (1898), 145.

in this Chapter it was seen that clerics had to be excardinated, because of unfavorable climate, to dioceses only fifty miles away!

Following up this contention, some say that the Holy See legalized anticipated consent in England and the United States of America, when it relaxed or widened the scope of the oath of service to include the entire ecclesiastical province for those ordained for the title of the mission in those countries.[394] Such was not the intention of Rome at all. Prior to the relaxation every excardination of a cleric in those countries had to be submitted to the Sacred Congregation for the Propagation of the Faith for a dispensation from the oath of service to a single diocese. Application for the same had to be made by the receiving Bishop six months in advance of the anticipated incardination.[395] The process was cumbersome and slow, and it had the effect of deterring clerics from accepting the mission title, inasmuch as such a rigid oath presented the aspect of a life confined within too narrow limits. All that the Bishops of those countries did was to request the Holy See to relieve them of all that strict formality as long as the excardinations were only to nearby dioceses, thereby also giving their clerics at least a prospect of a wider field of work. Hence, the granted relaxation was just a waiver on the part of Rome of its right to pass approval upon every such excardination, thus making them easier to obtain. The actions of the I Provincial Council of St. Louis (a. 1855) and of the II Plenary Council of Baltimore (a. 1866) give support to this interpretation, because, long before, they had besought Rome to do away with the oath altogether, on the plea that its confining character was too formidable for their

[394] Cf. *supra*, pp. 144-5. Thus, De Becker, *art. cit.*, p. 146: "The meaning of the Indult, if we may venture to express our opinion, is this: Generally speaking, and apart from special decisions in cases of canonical recourse to Rome, priests ordained for the mission, after 1885, may be transferred from one diocese to another within the same province, provided such transfer would be deemed lawful, if made within his own diocese, even against the wish of the priest. The reason of this is that in taking the oath of allegiance, the meaning and import of which should have been clear to the priest, he pledged himself in advance to consent to such removal, if deemed expedient to the Ordinaries."—*AER*, XVIII (1898), 145.

[395] Cf. *supra*, p. 213.

prospective clerics; but their ultra-liberal appeal was refused.[396] Hence it was not the Bishops who were trying to force their clerics to consent in advance to be excardinated if and when that proved opportune; it was rather the clerics themselves who were constraining the Bishops to procure from the Holy See more liberal provisions for their future excardination whenever they grew dissatisfied with their first mission field.

What a mission cleric did promise in advance by his oath was to go wherever he was sent by his Ordinary, even temporarily out of the diocese, but in such manner as to be lent, not to be excardinated, so that either his proper Bishop or he himself could ask for his recall at any time.[397]

In a class by itself was the matter which dealt with the allotment of the incardinated clerics of a diocese which was being divided or of which the territory was being reapportioned by the Holy See. Usually the pertinent papal document in each particular case expressly stated which priests and clerics were to be considered subject to the jurisdiction of the Bishop of the new diocese or of the Bishops of the two or more dioceses wherein the territories had been reapportioned. This, too, was desirable in order to forestall uncertainties and consequent disputes. The formula of the Sacred Consistorial Congregation varied, but usually was like this:

> Constituatur et adiudicetur eidem novo Episcopatui N. universum territorium, quo nunc constat praesignatus districtus N; proindeque praelaudata civitas N. caeteraeque cunctae vel civitates vel oppida vel paroeciae, quae intra territoriales eiusdem districtus N. terminos nunc comperiuntur, insimulque omnes eis in locis extantes ecclesiae sive parochiales succursales, sive simplices, oratoria, coenobia, monasteria, pia instituta et tam saecularia quam regularia, quae extant, Beneficia, itemque utriusque sexus personae sive saeculares sive regulares (non tamen exempti), tam Clerici quam Presbyteri, omnes demum incolae cuiuscumque status, gradus et conditionis simili modo subiiciantur ordinariae iurisdictioni, regimini, potestati ac superioritati Episcopi N. pro tempore exis-

[396] Cf. *supra*, p. 143.

[397] Cf. *supra*, p. 144, (n. 4).

> tentis eique respective pro civitate, dioecesi, clero et populo assignentur atque adtribuantur.

Apparently, then, the papal bull ordinarily attached to the new diocese anything and anyone within its boundaries at the time of the reapportionment—cities, towns, parishes, churches, monasteries, benefices, persons of both sexes whether secular or regular (except the exempt Religious), clerics, priests and all inhabitants.

In the absence of any express provision in the papal bull, some other sound basis for the division of the clergy had to be countenanced, e. g., the place of their origin. In 1867, for instance, a certain archdiocese *N* in America was divided into two, the archdiocese retaining its name *N* and the new diocese being called *G*, but in the papal bull nothing was said about the allotment of the clergy. The Bishop of *G*, hampered by a lack of priests, then proceeded to claim jurisdiction over all those clerics who had been born in the *G* section of the former archdiocese and who had not yet been released from its initial claim on them in view of the acquisition by them in the present *N* section of a residential benefice or of a ministry with the care of souls. In a test case before the Sacred Congregation of the Council, August 12, 1871, the Bishop of *G* won a favorable decision.[398]

[398] *ASS*, VI (1870), 571-588. The case was as follows: A priest, Alexius, had been born in the *G* section of the old archdiocese *N*, and his parents still had their home there. At the time of the division he was a professor in the Seminary of *N*, for which reason the Bishop of *G* considered him valuable to his new diocese, and had the consent of the Archbishop of *N* to have him. Alexius, however, was unwilling to go, and gave as his reasons that he had long since left *G* and received holy orders with the idea that he would remain a subject of the Archbishop of *N*, and that he had elected and acquired a domicile there where he was serving as a professor. Moreover, in his behalf it was argued that, since he was not assigned or residentially beneficed in the confines of *G*, he was free to be out of it perpetually even against its Bishop's will. However, the canonist of the case proved that Alexius could never have lost his original domicile unless and until he had acquired a new domicile or had received a residential benefice elsewhere with his Bishop's permission, neither of which he had done. A professor's position was not a residential benefice; and he could never acquire a domicile by the mere discharge of an office, no matter how many years it lasted and no matter what his intentions were. Furthermore, the liberty once recognized for unbeneficed and unassigned clerics to

After the Vatican Council, when the *service of the diocese* became popular as an ordination title, a priest was assigned to the diocese as a unit by the very fact of his ordination. Hence, in the division of a diocese, the place wherever the priest was holding an office of any kind at the time of the division determined the diocese to which he was to belong for the future. Usually in later times the Apostolic Constitution, by which a diocese was divided and a new one was erected from the portion that was cut off from it, contained some such formula as the following: "Quod vero ad clerum praecipue spectat, decernimus ut, simul ac dismembrationes praefatae et novae dioecesis erectio, ut supra statutae, exsecutioni mandatae fuerint, eo ipso clerici omnes Ecclesiae illae censeantur adscripti, in cuius territorio legitime exstant."[399] For those who have accepted perpetual residential benefices in the portion forming the new diocese this is quite understandable, because by that very fact they equivalently have given their consent to reside in that section for life. For other clerics engaged in a temporary capacity as vicars, chaplains, etc., in the dismembered portion, it would seem in some cases to be excardination without their consent. Yet even for them, it must be remembered that it is still the same territory as that to which they attached themselves at incardination; if not the actual spot of their origin or acquired domicile, it is at least close to it. It is the region where they voluntarily labored and dwelt under the direction of the Bishop prior to the time of the division. Hence it is not an excardination in the strict sense. How else, it might be asked, could the Holy See provide for the spiritual care of the new diocese? If all clerics laboring in the portion lately created into a new diocese wanted to return to the mother see, there would be no one left to provide spiritual care for the people. Furthermore, the

leave the diocese had long since been cancelled by the nineteenth century interpretations of the Roman Congregations (cf. *supra*, pp. 195 ff.).

Hence to the Dubia proposed by the Bishop of G: "I. An et ad quas personas Episcopi iurisdictio porrigatur in casu. II. An Episcopus ius habeat revocandi ad suam dioecesim Sacerdotem (Alexium) in casu." the S. C. C. responded: "Ad I. Providebitur in casibus particularibus. Ad II. Affirmative, dummodo Episcopus eidem provideat de congruo officio et Beneficio."—*ASS*, VI (1870), 587.

[399] Const. Apost. "*Ad maius Religionis*," 3 iulii 1928—*AAS*, XXI (1929), 466.

common motive which would impel many to seek a return would be the less worthy and worldly one of hope for material advancement, which could never be favored by the Church in preference to the spiritual needs of the people. Besides, any cleric having a just reason for wanting to regain affiliation with the mother see could later seek and obtain a return to it through the medium of formal letters. A general exodus through this method could easily be controlled until there were enough clerics in the new section to substitute for them.

ARTICLE VI

STATUS OF THE ORIENTAL CLERGY IN THE UNITED STATES OF AMERICA

The East was considerably in advance of the West in the Ancient Period of the Church in the matter of legislation on the bond between the clergy and the Bishop or diocese. In later years their discipline on the subject did not differ substantially from that of the Latin Church, and, consequently, no distinction was made between the two in this study. Even in the nineteenth century their councils are found to renew early Church legislation, which had been adopted by East and West alike.[400]

One important point to be noticed was that no Oriental cleric could be tonsured, or ordained in any of the grades of minor or major orders, by a Bishop of the Latin rite without special permission of the Apostolic See, under pain of perpetual suspension.[401] Similarly, no cleric could transfer to another rite, or, after a legitimate transfer, resume his native rite, without the permission of the Holy See.[402]

[400] E. g., in the Prov. Counc. of the Armenians in Mount Libanus (a. 1851), cap. III, nn. LXVI ss.—Mansi, XL, 815 ss.

[401] "Ut in ordinibus conferendis quaelibet rituum confusio et commixtio penitus tollatur, et unius ritus antistes alterius ritus clericos initiare in posterum minime valeat, sub perpetuae suspensionis a divinis poenis prohibemus, ne Latinus quicumque episcopus etiam subjectos suae jurisdictioni Graecos, neque Graecus quilibet antistes Latinos quovis praetextu, sine speciali sedis apostolicae licentia, ad primam tonsuram, vel ullum ordinem sive minorem sive majorem promovere praesumat";—Benedict XIV, *De dogmatibus et ritibus ab Italo-Graecis tenendis atque servandis*, 26 maii, 1742 (Mansi, XXXVIII, 373).

[402] Duskie, *The Canonical Status of the Orientals in the United States*, p. 66.

After 1880 Oriental Catholics representing several rites and especially the Greek-Ruthenians began to reside in the United States in considerable numbers. Some years elapsed, however, before the Sacred Congregation for the Propagation of the Faith for the Affairs of the Oriental Church provided canonical legislation for either their laity or their clergy in this country. At first, they were all made subject to the Latin Ordinary of the district; then the Greek-Ruthenians were given a Bishop of their own, but with powers merely delegated to him by the Latin Bishop; finally, the same group were given an Ordinary of their own.[403] It was the Greek-Ruthenian Bishops of Europe who promoted the first efforts to provide for the spiritual care of their fellow nationals in the United States, sending from time to time priests of their own rite to labor here. Though these first Oriental missioners were approved by their own Bishops, and even sanctioned by the Sacred Congregation for the Propagation of the Faith, it soon was seen to be necessary to enact certain restrictions, by means of regulations designed to overcome scandals and difficulties arising from their married state and from their insubordination to the Latin Ordinary. Accordingly, on Oct. 1, 1890, the Sacred Congregation for the Propagation of the Faith issued an Instruction to the Greek-Ruthenian Bishops of Europe,[404] prescribing: 1) that all priests of the Greek-Ruthenian rite desiring to go and remain in the United States of America be celibates; 2) that they notify the Sacred Congregation for the Propagation of the Faith in writing of their diocese of destination, so that the matter could be brought to the notice of that local Latin Ordinary; 3) that they report to that same Ordinary for their faculties; and 4) that they subject themselves to his jurisdiction.

It was on June 14, 1907, that Pius X issued the Apostolic letter "*Ea semper,*"[405] in which the Greek-Ruthenians in the

[403] *Ibid.*, pp. 30 ff.

[404] *Collectanea S. C. P. F.*, n. 1966, footnote 2. This was communicated to the American Bishops on May 10, 1892, in a letter addressed to the Archbishop of Baltimore, and therein also it was extended so as to include all other Oriental priests, irrespective of rite—*Decretum de Sacerdotibus Ruthenis* (*AER*, VII [1892], 66-67).

[405] *ASS*, XLI (1908), 3 ss.

United States of America were given a special status distinct from other Oriental Catholics here; in which, too, they were given their first Greek-Ruthenian titular Bishop. This arrangement was still unsatisfactory to their native clergy; and so, on May 28, 1913, the Holy See promoted the Titular Bishop to become the first Ordinary of the Greek-Ruthenians in the United States.[406]

In order to provide for this new canonical status, which removed them from the jurisdiction of the local Latin Ordinaries, the Sacred Congregation for the Propagation of the Faith for the Affairs of the Oriental Church issued the Decree "*Cum Episcopo*" on August 17, 1914, *ad decennium*,[407] which was subsequently renewed on June 21, 1924, for an indefinite period by the Sacred Congregation for the Oriental Church.[408] Chapter II of this decree dealt with the Greek-Ruthenian clergy who still had to be recruited from abroad through the Bishops of the same rite in Galicia and Hungary, due to an insufficient supply of their native clergy here in the United States of America. The formalities required for the admittance of such priests were as follows:

1) The Greek-Ruthenian priest must receive a call for mission service from the Greek-Ruthenian Ordinary in the United States.

2) The cleric must be approved by the Sacred Congregation for the Oriental Church.

3) *He is always to remain incardinated in the diocese of his origin*, but the Bishop of his place of origin retains no jurisdiction over him.

4) He is solely under the jurisdiction of the Greek-Ruthenian Ordinary in this country.

5) The priest in question may not return to Europe without the written permission of the Greek-Ruthenian Ordinary in the United States. The Ruthenian Bishop of Europe who might

[406] Letter of the Apostolic Delegate (Washington, D. C.) to the American Ordinaries, August 25, 1913,—*AER*, XLIX (1913), 473.

[407] *AAS*, VI (1914), 458 ss.

[408] Duskie, *The Canonical Status of the Orientals in the United States*, p. 43.

presume to readmit clerics without this required permission must notify the Sacred Congregation for the Oriental Church.

6) A Greek-Ruthenian priest who comes to the United States on his own accord, without necessary authorization, cannot be granted faculties to perform sacred functions or to exercise the ministry.[409]

Here, then, was the unique status of an Oriental priest of the Greek-Ruthenian rite in the United States of America: he could not be incardinated here, since his was a personal rather than a territorial diocese;[410] but still he remained solely under the jurisdiction of the Greek-Ruthenian Ordinary here, so that his own proper Bishop in Europe could not recall him without the written permission of the Ordinary in the United States of America.

Priests of other Oriental groups, who had no Ordinary of their own rite in the United States of America, continued, as formerly, under the jurisdiction of the local Latin Ordinary, which meant that they too could not be incardinated.[411]

409 S. C. de Prop. Fide pro negotiis Ritus Orientalis, decr. "*Cum episcopo*," 17 augusti, 1914, art. 11, 13—*AAS*, VI (1914), 458; Duskie, *op. cit.*, pp. 47-48.

410 Maroto, *Institutiones Iuris Canonici*, I, n. 183, footnote 2.

411 Cf. Duskie, *op. cit.*, p. 35, who also quotes, on p. 106, footnote 20, a letter from the Sacred Congregation for the Oriental Church to the Apostolic Delegate, Washington, D. C., under date of May 29, 1925, in which this fact is reaffirmed.

CHAPTER V

THE COMPETENT AUTHORITY FOR EXCARDINATING AND INCARDINATING DIOCESAN CLERICS

IN the Ancient Period of the Church, when the method of excardinating clerics who were only in minor orders consisted in the issuance of perpetual dimissorial letters (called *dimissoriae*), the Bishop of a cleric's place of origin was the only authority in a diocese competent to use it. To him alone it belonged to ordain a cleric; to him alone to dismiss him, whether before or after the priesthood; and, since it was the Bishop of the diocese who assigned his clergy to the churches and holy places, he it was who had the authority to incorporate new clerics from other dioceses when they were needed. Hence, all the councils and legal sources of the time, as frequently cited in this study, spoke of the permission or letters of the *Bishop* as necessary in order that one of his clerics might be transferred to another diocese; and they warned Bishops not to usurp or solicit for incorporation another Bishop's cleric. The examples already shown [1] of such dimissorial letters (*dimissoriae*) likewise gave proof of their authorship by the solemnity with which they were prepared, i. e., in the Bishop's own hand-writing or, at least, with his own signature, with the names of himself and the addressee together with the see cities of each formally expressed, and with the impression of the seal of his office.

In those days, moreover, a Bishop did not ordain a cleric without the counsel of his clergy. *A fortiori* he did not or could not excardinate a cleric without the same, because that was a form of alienation of ecclesiastical persons. Rightly, therefore, must it be concluded that no one else but the Bishops with residential sees possessed the competent authority to excardinate or incardinate clerics, and even they could do so only with the advice of their clergy.[2]

[1] *Supra*, pp. 156, 158, 159.

[2] Hallier, *De Sacris Elect. et Ordin.*, P. V, sec. V, cap. III, art. X, n. 21—*MTC*, XXIV, 1048-1049.

Then in the thirteenth century came the distinction of proper Bishops for ordination, with the possible multiplication of them for even a single cleric. The more generic term " Superior " was used to indicate from whom the cleric needed permission for a release from the diocese. Pope Boniface VIII (a. 1294-1303) was the first to describe who was meant by " Superior," and he made some fine distinctions which are still used in the modern legislation.[3] Though he was speaking of an alien Bishop's power to authorize an ordination, his words apply equally to excardination and incardination, which process in early times was so intimately bound up with the dismissal of a cleric for ordination elsewhere. He described the " Superior " of a cleric as the Bishop of his place of origin, benefice or acquired domicile, all of whom were competent. Next he evaluated the powers of other inferior Prelates, religious and secular, as follows: a) all such inferior Prelates were unable to grant permission for a diocesan cleric to be ordained by an alien Bishop unless that power were granted to them by an Apostolic Indult; b) the *Officialis* of the Bishop was likewise incompetent, since his office did not extend that far; c) the Vicar General in spiritual matters could do so if the Bishop was far from his see; d) the Cathedral Chapter could do so when the see was vacant; or e) he who was legally authorized to administer the spiritualities of the diocese when the see was vacant could likewise do so.[4]

The next important change in the matter came in the Council of Trent, which limited the competence of Cathedral Chapters, in the issuance of *dimissoriae* during the first year of the vacancy of the see, to those only who had to become ordained to some holy order within the space of a year by reason of a benefice which they had or were about to receive.[5]

[3] C. 3, *de temp. ordin.*, I, 9, in VI°. See full text above, p. 49.

[4] A thorough discussion of these distinctions may be found in Hallier, *ibid.*, art. XI, nn. 7-14—*MTC*, XXIV, 1053-1058.

[5] " Non liceat capitulis ecclesiarum, sede vacante, infra annum a die vacationis, ordinandi licentiam, aut litteras dimissorias, seu reverendas, ut aliqui vocant, tam ex juris communis dispositione, quam etiam cujusvis privilegii, aut consuetudinis vigore, alicui, qui beneficii ecclesiastici recepti, sive recipiendi occasione arctatus non

In another decree, the same Council inferentially made this limitation apply to any person or group whatsoever (e. g., Vicar Capitular) succeeding to the jurisdiction of the Bishop during the vacancy of the see,[6] and it also abrogated any privileges or customs which inferior or exempt Prelates, whether religious or secular, had enjoyed of dismissing diocesan clerics for ordination elsewhere.[7]

The spirit of this legislation of the Council of Trent sought to prevent any inferior or substitute from burdening or harming a diocese over which he had only a short term rule. The unity of government was thought best secured by leaving all important questions to be solved by the permanent Superior, namely, the residential Bishop, who would thus not have to suffer for any other mistakes than his own if courageous restraint and forbearance were necessitated by any earlier misdirected energies in the government of the diocese.

In reference to extra-diocesan transfers of clerics in normal times, the Council of Trent insisted on the consent of their

fuerit, concedere: si secus fiat, capitulum contraveniens ecclesiastico subjaceat interdicto: et sic ordinati, si in minoribus constituti fuerint, nullo privilegio clericali, praesertim in criminalibus, gaudeant: in majoribus vero, ab executione Ordinum, ad beneplacitum futuri praelati, sint ipso jure suspensi."—Sess. VII, *de ref.* (a. 1545), c. 10. It was quite common for major clerics to acquire curatial benefices under the condition that they receive the priesthood within a year, so that the administration of such benefices by vicars would not be prolonged too far.

6 "...Poenam quoque impositam iis, qui contra hujus sanctae Synodi sub Paulo III decretum [i. e., sess. VII, *de ref.*, c. 10], a capitulo, episcopali sede vacante, litteras dimissorias impetrant; ad illos, qui easdem litteras non a capitulo, sed ab aliis quibusvis, in jurisdictione episcopi loco capituli, sede vacante, succedentibus, obtinerent, mandat extendi. Concedentes autem dimissorias contra formam decreti, ab officio et beneficio per annum sint ipso jure suspensi."—Sess. XXIII, *de ref.* (a. 1563), c. 10.

7 "Abbatibus, ac aliis quibuscumque, quantumvis exemptis, non liceat in posterum, intra fines alicujus dioecesis consistentibus, etiamsi nullius dioecesis, vel exempti esse dicantur, cuiquam, qui regularis subditus sibi non sit, tonsuram, vel minores Ordines conferre: nec ipsi abbates, et alii exempti, aut collegia, vel capitula quaecumque, etiam ecclesiarum cathedralium, litteras dimissorias aliquibus clericis saecularibus, ut ab aliis ordinentur, concedant: sed horum omnium ordinatio, servatis omnibus, quae in hujus sanctae Synodi decretis continentur, ad episcopos, intra quorum dioecesis fines existant, pertineat: non obstantibus quibusvis privilegiis, praescriptionibus, aut consuetudinibus, etiam immemorabilibus... "—*Loc. cit.*

Bishop,[8] i. e., the one among the various proper Bishops who could claim them as his own because he had assigned them to his churches in the diocese after ordaining them in his own right. In extraordinary times, such as during the Bishop's absence or grave illness, or during an *interregnum,* the laws of Boniface VIII and their extensions and limitations by the Council of Trent, as just given, concerning the competency to issue *dimissoriae,* applied to excardinations and incardinations also, since they were closely allied acts and there was no other specific law to decide otherwise.[9]

[8] Sess. XXIII, *de ref.,* c. 16: "Cum nullus debeat ordinari, qui judicio sui *episcopi* non sit utilis... Quod si locum inconsulto *Episcopo* deseruerit, ei sacrorum exercitium interdicatur..."

[9] An example of this is found in a decision of the S. C. C. on June 22, 1871, as follows: Dubium—"An et quas literas et qua forma suis subditis concedere liceat Decano S. Michaelis . . . in casu." Resolutio—"Non licere Decano concedere literas dimissoriales ac testimoniales ad ordines recipiendos, neque remissoriales seu excardinationis, quibus alieno Episcopo potestas fiat dimissos Clericos suae ecclesiae incardinandi: posse tamen dare literas dimissoriales ad tramites iuris, addita clausula ut illae approbentur ab Archiepiscopo."—*ASS,* VI (1870), 495.

HISTORICAL SUMMARY

OF

RELATIONS BETWEEN BISHOPS AND CLERICS

LAYMEN

(Candidates for Clerical State)

ANCIENT PERIOD (1–1100)

Proper Bishop for Ordination	Origin (i. e., original domicile)
Ordination Title	A particular church
Obligation of Residence	At particular church
Canonical Transfer	By *litterae perpetuae* { *dimissoriae*, *commendatitiae*, *formatae*, *canonicae*, *reverendae* } of Bishop of { origin, incardination }

LAYMEN

(Candidates for Clerical State)

MEDIEVAL PERIOD (1100 to Council of Trent, 1563)

Proper Bishop for Ordination	Origin Acquired domicile { 10 years' residence; indefinite residence with proofs of probable intention
Ordination Title	Required—none
Obligation of Residence	None
Canonical Transfer	Potential method—by acquisition of new domicile

LAYMEN

(Candidates for Clerical State)

TRIDENTINE PERIOD (Council of Trent, 1563, to 1694)

Proper Bishop for Ordination	Origin Acquired domicile { 10 years' residence; indefinite residence with proofs of probable intention *Familiaritas*
Ordination Title	Required—none
Obligation of Residence	Assignment to some church or religious place Attendance at diocesan or provincial seminary Exception—University students
Canonical Transfer	Potential methods { by acquisition of new domicile; by *familiaritas* extending over a period of 3 years

LAYMEN

(Candidates for Clerical State)

INNOCENTIAN PERIOD (1694–1898)

Proper Bishop for Ordination	Origin Acquired domicile { 10 years' residence together with oath; 3 years' residence together with sworn intention } *Familiaritas*
Ordination Title	Required—none
Obligation of Residence	Assignment to some church or religious place Attendance at diocesan or provincial seminary Exception—University students
Canonical Transfer	Potential methods { by acquisition of new domicile; by *familiaritas* extending over a period of 3 years }

LAYMEN

(Candidates for Clerical State)

PRE-CODE PERIOD (1898 to Code)

Proper Bishop for Ordination	Origin Acquired domicile { 10 years' residence together with oath; 3 years' residence together with sworn intention } *Familiaritas* Quasi-incardination (after 1906)
Ordination Title	Required—none
Obligation of Residence	(Assignment to some church or religious place)—Obsolete Within diocese—if unassigned Attendance at diocesan or provincial seminary Exception—University students
Canonical Transfer	By letters of perpetual quasi-excardination and quasi-incardination (after 1906) Potential methods { by acquisition of new domicile; by *familiaritas* extending over a period of 3 years }

MINOR CLERICS

Ancient Period (1–1100)

Proper Bishop for Ordination	Origin (i.e., original domicile)
Ordination Title	A particular church
Obligation of Residence	At particular church
Canonical Transfer	By *litterae perpetuae* { *dimissoriae*, *commendatitiae*, *formatae*, *canonicae*, *reverendae* } of Bishop of { origin, incardination }

MINOR CLERICS

Medieval Period (1100 to Council of Trent, 1563)

Proper Bishop for Ordination	Origin Acquired domicile { 10 years' residence; indefinite residence with proofs of probable intention } Benefice (either one or several)
Ordination Title	Required—none Potential title—benefice { simple; residential }
Obligation of Residence	None At residential benefice, if one was held Exception—University students
Canonical Transfer	With no residential benefice { by acquisition of residential benefice; potential methods { by acquisition of new domicile; by acquisition of any simple benefice } } With residential benefice { by acquisition of residential benefice along with permission of Bishop; potential methods { by acquisition of new domicile along with permission of Bishop; by acquisition of a simple benefice } }

MINOR CLERICS

TRIDENTINE PERIOD (Council of Trent, 1563, to 1694)

Proper Bishop for Ordination	Origin Acquired domicile { 10 years' residence; indefinite residence with proofs of probable intention } Benefice (either one or several) *Familiaritas*
Ordination Title	Required—none Potential title—benefice
Obligation of Residence	Assignment to some church or religious place At residential benefice, if one was held Attendance at diocesan or provincial seminary Exception—University students
Canonical Transfer	Formally assigned or Residentially beneficed } by acquisition of residential benefice along with *litterae* { *testimoniales* of resignation; *commendatitiae* of Bishop } which had to be granted { if cleric's service was not necessary or useful to diocese; if cleric was not receiving suitable sustenance; if cause of departure was just and reasonable } Simply beneficed—by acquisition of residential benefice along with *litterae commendatitiae* of native Bishop Unassigned—by acquisition of residential benefice along with compellable *litterae commendatitiae* of Bishop All clerics—potential methods { by acquisition of new domicile together with permission of Bishop; by acquisition of a simple benefice; by *familiaritas* together with permission of Bishop }

MINOR CLERICS

Innocentian Period (1694–1898)

Proper Bishop for Ordination	Origin Acquired domicile { 10 years' residence together with oath; 3 years' residence together with sworn intention } Adequate benefice *Familiaritas*
Ordination Title	Required—none Potential title—benefice
Obligation of Residence	Assignment to some church or religious place At residential benefice, if one was held Within diocese, if unassigned Attendance at diocesan or provincial seminary Exception—University students
Canonical Transfer	Assigned or Residentially beneficed } by acquisition of residential benefice along with *litterae* { *testimoniales* of resignation; *commendatitiae* of Bishop } which had to be granted { if cleric's service was not necessary or useful to diocese; if cleric was not receiving suitable sustenance; if cause of departure was just and reasonable } Unassigned—same, with compellable *litterae commendatitiae* By letters of excardination along with oath to remain permanently Potential methods { by acquisition of new domicile along with permission of Bishop; by acquisition of an adequate simple benefice; by *familiaritas* along with permission of Bishop }

MINOR CLERICS

Pre-Code Period (1898 to Code)

Proper Bishop for Ordination	Origin Acquired domicile { 10 years' residence together with oath; 3 years' residence together with sworn intention } Adequate benefice *Familiaritas* Incardination
Ordination Title	Required—none Potential title—benefice
Obligation of Residence	(Assignment to some church or religious place)—Obsolete At residential benefice, if one was held Within diocese—if unassigned Attendance at diocesan or provincial seminary Exception—University students
Canonical Transfer	By letters of perpetual excardination and incardination By acquisition of residential benefice along with *litterae dimissoriales* of Bishop Potential methods { by acquisition of new domicile along with permission of Bishop; by acquisition of an adequate simple benefice; by *familiaritas* along with permission of Bishop }

MAJOR CLERICS

Ancient Period (1-1100)

Proper Bishop for Ordination	Origin (i.e., original domicile)
Ordination Title	A particular church
Obligation of Residence	At particular church
Canonical Transfer	By *litterae perpetuae* { *dimissoriae*, *commendatitiae*, *formatae*, *canonicae*, *reverendae* } of Bishop of { origin, incardination }

MAJOR CLERICS

Medieval Period (1100 to Council of Trent, 1563)

Proper Bishop for Ordination	Origin Acquired domicile { 10 years' residence; indefinite residence with proofs of probable intention } Benefice (either one or several)
Ordination Title	Required { benefice { simple; residential }; patrimony }
Obligation of Residence	None At residential benefice, if one was held Exception—University students
Canonical Transfer	With no residential benefice { by acquisition of residential benefice; potential methods { by acquisition of new domicile; by acquisition of a simple benefice } } With residential benefice { by acquisition of residential benefice along with permission of Bishop; potential methods { by acquisition of new domicile with permission of Bishop; by acquisition of a simple benefice } }

MAJOR CLERICS

TRIDENTINE PERIOD (Council of Trent, 1563, to 1694)

Proper Bishop for Ordination	Origin Acquired domicile — 10 years' residence; indefinite residence with proofs of probable intention Benefice (either one or several) *Familiaritas*
Ordination Title	Ordinary—benefice, adequate — simple; residential Extraordinary — patrimony, adequate; pension, adequate; mission, together with oath of stability (after 1631)
Obligation of Residence	Assignment to some church or religious place At residential benefice, if one was held Attendance at diocesan or provincial seminary Exception—University students
Canonical Transfer	Formally assigned or Residentially beneficed — by acquisition of residential benefice along with *litterae* — *testimoniales* of resignation; *commendatitiae* of Bishop which had to be granted — if cleric's service was not necessary or useful to diocese; if cleric was not receiving suitable sustenance; if cause of departure was just and reasonable Simply beneficed—by acquisition of residential benefice along with *litterae commendatitiae* of native Bishop Unassigned—by acquisition of residential benefice along with compellable *litterae commendatitiae* of Bishop All clerics—potential methods — by acquisition of new domicile with permission of Bishop; by acquisition of a simple benefice; by *familiaritas* together with permission Mission intituled—special permission from S.C.P.F. together with letters of receiving Bishop

MAJOR CLERICS

Innocentian Period (1694–1898)

Proper Bishop for Ordination	Origin Acquired domicile { 10 years' residence together with oath; 3 years' residence together with sworn intention } Adequate benefice (either one or several) *Familiaritas*
Ordination Title	Required { Ordinary—benefice, both adequate and permanent { simple; residential }; Extraordinary { patrimony, adequate; pension, adequate; mission, together with oath of stability; service of diocese (in XIX cent.) } }
Obligation of Residence	Assignment to some church or religious place At residential benefice, if one was held Within diocese, if unassigned Attendance at diocesan or provincial seminary Exception—University students
Canonical Transfer	Assigned or Residentially beneficed } by acquisition of residential benefice along with *litterae* { *testimoniales* of resignation; *commendatitiae* of Bishop } which had to be granted { if cleric's service was not necessary or useful to diocese; if cleric was not receiving suitable sustenance; if cause of departure was just and reasonable } Unassigned—same, with compellable *litterae commendatitiae* By letters of excardination along with oath to remain permanently Potential methods { by acquisition of new domicile along with permission of Bishop; by acquisition of an adequate simple benefice; by *familiaritas* along with permission of Bishop } Mission intituled { special permission from S. C. P. F. together with letters of proper mission Bishop; after 1885—note change below for U.S.A. and England. (Cf. Pre-Code Period) }

MAJOR CLERICS

Pre-Code Period (1898 to Code)

Proper Bishop for Ordination	Origin Acquired domicile: { 10 years' residence together with oath; 3 years' residence together with sworn intention } Adequate benefice *Familiaritas* Incardination
Ordination Title	Ordinary—benefice, both adequate and permanent: { simple; residential } Extraordinary: { patrimony, adequate; pension, adequate; mission, together with oath of stability; service of diocese }
Obligation of Residence	(Assignment to some church or religious place)—Obsolete At residential benefice, if one was held Within diocese, if unassigned Attendance at diocesan or provincial seminary Exception—University students
Canonical Transfer	By letters of perpetual excardination and incardination By acquisition of residential benefice along with *litterae dimissoriales* of Bishop Potential methods: { by acquisition of new domicile along with permission of Bishop; by acquisition of an adequate simple benefice; by *familiaritas* along with permission of Bishop } Mission intituled: { special permission of S.C.P.F. together with letters of proper mission Bishop; in U. S. A. and England: { same—for transfers out of province; both Bishops' permission alone—for transfers within province } }

PRIESTS

ANCIENT PERIOD (1–1100)

Proper Bishop for Ordination	
Ordination Title	
Obligation of Residence	At particular church
Canonical Transfer	By *litterae* { *dimissoriae*, *commendatitiae*, *formatae*, *canonicae*, *reverendae* } of Bishop of { origin, incardination }

PRIESTS

MEDIEVAL PERIOD (1100 to Council of Trent, 1563)

Proper Bishop for Ordination	
Ordination Title	
Obligation of Residence	None At residential benefice, if one was held
Canonical Transfer	With no residential benefice—by acquisition of a residential benefice With residential benefice—by acquisition of residential benefice along with permission of Bishop

PRIESTS

TRIDENTINE PERIOD (Council of Trent, 1563, to 1694)

Proper Bishop for Ordination	
Ordination Title	
Obligation of Residence	At church or place of assignment At residential benefice, if one was held At mission, if priest was ordained for the title of mission
Canonical Transfer	Formally assigned or Residentially beneficed — by acquisition of residential benefice along with *litterae* { *testimoniales* of resignation; *commendatitiae* of Bishop } which had to be granted { if priest's service was not necessary or useful to diocese; if priest did not receive suitable sustenance; if cause of departure was just and reasonable } Simply beneficed—by acquisition of residential benefice along with *litterae commendatitiae* of native Bishop Unassigned—by acquisition of residential benefice along with compellable *litterae commendatitiae* of Bishop Mission intituled—special permission from S.C.P.F. together with letters of receiving Bishop

PRIESTS

Innocentian Period (1694–1898)

Proper Bishop for Ordination	
Ordination Title	
Obligation of Residence	At church or place of assignment At residential benefice, if one was held Within diocese, if unassigned At mission, if priest was ordained for the title of mission
Canonical Transfer	By acquisition of residential benefice along with *litterae commendatitiae* of Bishop which had to be granted { if priest's service was not necessary or useful to diocese; if priest did not receive suitable sustenance; if cause of departure was just and reasonable } By general *litterae* { *dimissoriales* and *testimoniales* } of proper Bishop accepted *in perpetuum* In U. S. A. { formal exchange of letters after a trial (after 1884); presumptive acceptance of priest after a trial (after 1884) } Mission intituled { special permission from S. C. P. F. together with letters of proper mission Bishop; after 1885—note change below for U.S.A. and England. (Cf. Pre-Code Period) }

PRIESTS

PRE-CODE PERIOD (1898 to Code)

<table>
<tr><td>Proper Bishop for Ordination</td><td></td></tr>
<tr><td>Ordination Title</td><td></td></tr>
<tr><td>Obligation of Residence</td><td>(At church or place of assignment)—Obsolete
At residential benefice, if one was held
Within diocese, if unassigned
At mission, if priest was ordained for the title of mission
Within diocese, if he was ordained for the title of service of diocese</td></tr>
<tr><td>Canonical Transfer</td><td>By letters of perpetual excardination and incardination
By acquisition of residential benefice along with litterae dimissoriales of Bishop
Mission intituled { special permission of S.C.P.F. together with letters of proper mission Bishop
in U. S. A. and England { same—for transfers out of province
both Bishops' permission alone —for transfers within province</td></tr>
</table>

SECTION II

CANONICAL COMMENTARY

CHAPTER VI

Canonical Assignment

Can. 111 - § 1. **Quemlibet clericum oportet esse vel alicui dioecesi vel alicui religioni adscriptum, ita ut clerici vagi nullatenus admittantur.**

There are four chief considerations in this initial enactment of the group of canons comprising this study: 1) the meaning of canonical assignment; 2) its necessity; 3) the definition of a diocese; and 4) affiliation with a Religious Institute.

ARTICLE I

THE MEANING OF CANONICAL ASSIGNMENT

In every diocese or Religious Institute there are two distinct classes of subjects, laity and clergy. The former are bound to the jurisdictional authority by reason of habitation, i. e., they have a domicile or quasi-domicile in the place.[1] This can be effectively relinquished, when it is a voluntary habitation, by the simple fact of departure with the intention of not returning to it.[2] The bond which encompasses the clergy, on the other hand, is a much firmer one, because they are more than just inhabitants (*incolae*), or temporary residents (*advenae*), but form a class of ecclesiastical public servants.[3] To be in that class, they must, by the very nature of their position, be subject permanently to a definite ecclesiastical Superior from the time of their first reception into the clerical state. From his sphere of jurisdiction they are unable ever to withdraw at will, but may do so only according to definite legal norms. That bond of subjection is what is meant by canonical assignment. In the present law it may, therefore, be defined as " a certain special aggregation and consociation which, when consisting of clerics, links them with

[1] Can. 94, § 1.

[2] Can. 95.

[3] " Qui divinis ministeriis per primam saltem tonsuram mancipati sunt, clerici dicuntur."—Can. 108, § 1.

some particular diocese, and which, when composed of Religious, affiliates them with some particular approved Institute of religion." [4]

In past centuries the connotations of the terms *adscriptus* and *adscriptio* were less comprehensive, but more formal, in character. These terms were intimately associated with the title of ordination, of which the historical development was traced in Chapters III and IV. There it was explained how, in the early ages of the Church, as soon as a layman was inducted into the clerical state, he became attached for life, not to a whole diocese, but to a particular church, and to the Bishop who ordained him for the service of the same; and many texts were adduced to show how illegal it was for the cleric to forsake his assignment. That was his title of ordination and also his place of registered service. Bishops were forbidden, under grave penalties, to ordain any layman without at the same time linking his service with some particular and specified church.

It was not until the twelfth century that that rigorous discipline weakened. Due to the circumstances already explained, "absolute" ordinations, i. e., such as were unaccompanied with any title or assignment, became common, and the Church was afflicted with the plague of a numerous band of "*acephali*" and "*vagi*"—unassigned and unattached clerics—who were without either a place where they labored or a Superior whom they recognized as their own.

Then followed the Council of Trent's efforts to restore the original discipline by decreeing that no one be ordained without being assigned to that church or religious place for the service of which he was being assumed into the clerical state [5]—a decree which met with little success. In succeeding centuries, interpreters of the Council's decrees and other canonists read into that law a formality which, if followed, secured the cleric to his Bishop and diocese, but which, if not followed, left him his freedom. It was an act, separate and distinct from the conferring of first tonsure, in which the Bishop made some such

[4] Cf., e. g., Maroto, *Institutiones Iuris Canonici* (2 vols., Romae, 1919-1921), I, n. 492.

[5] Sess. XXIII, *de ref.*, c. 16.

declaration as: "I assign you, N————, to the church of N————."[6] In all documents affecting the cleric afterwards the name of the church of his assignment was included. Still, many Bishops overlooked, neglected, or disdained this formality; and so the Church was still burdened with many clerics who could withdraw from their dioceses at will.

In the nineteenth century, two big factors had a strong influence in shaping the present legislation, namely, the vast reduction in the number of ecclesiastical benefices, and the consequent introduction of new titles of ordination for those major clerics who were absolutely needed for religious ministrations to the faithful. The most prominent of the new titles was that of the "service of the diocese." Clerics ordained *in sacris* for this title had to be judged by the Bishop to be necessary or useful to the service of the many churches of his diocese, instead of to some one of them in particular; and hence, once ordained, they were considered as bound or assigned to the service of the diocese as a whole. The widespread use of this and other extraordinary titles forced the Sacred Roman Congregations to modify their interpretations and applications of the old principles, and to recognize as bound to the diocese even clerics who were not formally assigned to some particular church or place.[7] Though the title of service was neither needed nor applied until sacred orders were about to be received, still, the layman, immediately after being accepted as a candidate for the clerical state, was usually educated gratis at a diocesan seminary with a view to the title of service, and such free education was recognized by Rome as binding him to the diocese also during the time he was a cleric in minor orders. Consequently, it was *practically* a bond which was coexistent with the clerical state itself.[8]

In the present legislation of canon 111, § 1, assignment to a particular church has been abandoned in favor of the nineteenth

[6] Hence it was that Pope Innocent XIII could command the Bishops of Spain to supply the neglected assignments many years after the first tonsure had been received —Cf. *supra*, p. 83.

[7] Cf. *supra*, p. 174.

[8] Cf. *supra*, Chapters III and IV, especially pp. 64-84, 88-89, 148-154, 172-186, wherein this matter is treated more extensively. Cf. also Wernz-Vidal, *Ius Canonicum*, II, n. 60; Chelodi, *Ius de Personis* (2 ed., Tridenti: Libr. Edit. Tridentum, 1927), n. 106.

century title of diocesan service, but now, legally, as well as practically, this takes effect at the reception of first tonsure.[9] The words *quemlibet clericum* show that it applies to every cleric without exception from first tonsure onwards.

This bond which attaches every cleric to his diocese, even when it is the original bond established through tonsure, is now termed *incardinatio.*[10] That is the canonization of a modern term which became popular only in the last century.[11] Still, it is a new acceptation of the term. Formerly the word was used to signify absorption into a new diocese after a transfer from another. In the Decree " *A primis* " it was used in a still narrower sense of incorporation into a diocese by the formal process of letters after a transfer from elsewhere.[12] It is in its present sense of the attachment of a cleric to a diocese, no matter by what method, that it is to be used throughout the second section of this study.

ARTICLE II

ITS NECESSITY

A number of reasons were previously cited [13] for the existence of a strict bond between the clergy and the Bishop of a diocese, but most fundamental of all is the age-old principle that no one can be raised to the clerical state except for the necessity or utility of the service of the Church.[14] Mere private devotion, honor, or convenience is not a sufficient reason. The Bishop who ordains, or who issues a request for one to be ordained, cannot do so except to supply the needs in his own definite territory. If he is to have the responsibility of providing spiritual ministrations for his diocese, he must have the right and power to select, train, and maintain his own proper clergy.

[9] Can. 111, § 2.

[10] Can. 111, § 2.

[11] Cf. *supra*, Chapter I.

[12] Cf. *supra*, p. 228.

[13] *Supra*, pp. 36-39.

[14] Can. 969, § 1.

The law must protect him in that right. Hence, it is necessary when a layman is first inducted into the clerical state that he become answerable at once to that Bishop, and subject to the service of that diocese or territory, to whom, and for which, he willingly presented himself, so that thereafter he cannot forsake the same except by concession of the Bishop, and that only when another Bishop is willing to receive him.[15] If there were no such law of canonical affiliation of clerics with their diocese, the world would be filled with clerics who would have no immediate Superior to obey, and no particular field for their ministry. Such clerics have always been realistically termed *vagi, vagantes,*[16] or *acephali,*[17] and have been universally held in disesteem wherever they existed.

It is true that the term *vagus,* when referring to a lay person, has a respectable place in Canon Law. But under this supposition the meaning of the term is different. A lay *vagus* is one who has not anywhere a domicile or quasi-domicile, either parochial or diocesan.[18] In other words, he is a traveller who has given up his home permanently and has not yet established another. Still he has a proper pastor and Ordinary assigned to him by law, i. e., those of the place where he is actually staying.[19]

The clerical *vagus,* on the other hand, were it assumed that he had a domicile or quasi-domicile as a private individual, would, nevertheless, as a cleric, be without both a juridical seat and an immediate Superior whose commands he would have to obey wherever he might be staying. The Church not only does not recognize this type of *vagi,* but it also has attempted to suppress them wherever found. The many prohibitions against absolute ordinations and against clerics who had abandoned by their own free will their place of assignment through ordination,

15 Wernz-Vidal, *Ius Canonicum,* II, nn. 57-59.

16 From *vagor, ari, atus sum,* to wander—Freund-Leverett, *Lexicon,* "*vagor.*"

17 From α + κεφαλή = wanting the head—*Ibid.,* "*acephalus.*" An erudite discussion of this term is given by Piontek, "De acephalis in iure canonico,"—*Jus Pontif.,* XIV (1934), 194-215, 284-294; XV (1935), 55-63, 202-208; XVII (1937), 64-82.

18 Can. 91.

19 Can. 94, § 2.

the warnings to Bishops not to give letters of dismissal to their clerics unless another Bishop asked for them, and the efforts to have every cleric assigned to some church or place at ordination, as recorded in the historical section above, all bear witness to the unrelenting attitude of the Church towards this illegal group. In the early ages clerical *vagi* were forbidden to exercise their ministry; Bishops were prohibited from receiving them; and the obstinate were punished with perpetual degradation; [20] most drastic of all, the Council of Chalcedon (a. 451) called their absolute ordination itself "*irritam . . . et in actu invalidam,*" which, however, meant suspension rather than actual invalidity.[21]

Consistently, the present legislation aims to make it impossible for a clerical *vagus* to exist at all. The attachment of a cleric to a diocese (i. e., incardination) is now an automatic process instead of a separate formality. It takes place through the very act of tonsure itself, and the diocese to which the new cleric becomes attached is that for the service of which he was promoted by his proper Bishop.[22] Once attached, he has it as his juridical seat and its Bishop as his Superior, no matter where he may be. Even should he arbitrarily leave his diocese, he cannot now expect admission anywhere else except through the formalities of canons 112 to 117, and hence he cannot be classified as a *vagus*, because, regardless of his personal wishes, he has an immediate Superior to whom he must eventually return under penalty of being reduced to the lay state. Neither can the Bishop arbitrarily set him loose and make him a *vagus*. Canon 116 prevents that; unless the dismissal follows its requisites, one of which is legitimate incardination elsewhere, it is invalid, and the cleric still belongs to his first diocese. Though there might be a long interval between the excardination or dismissal and the subsequent incardination, there is not a single moment at which the cleric is without a diocese, because of the provident way in which the Code has interlocked the two external acts into a single juridical one.

[20] Cf. *supra*, p. 67.

[21] *Supra*, pp. 67-68.

[22] Can. 111, § 2.

The words "*ita ut clerici vagi nullatenus admittantur*" constitute a result clause, as is gathered from the introductory adverb *ita,* giving to understand that, under the present law of automatic incardination, the Church has left absolutely no legal way in which clerics can become *vagi,* such as it did once when Pope Alexander III (a. 1179) unwittingly authorized ordinations without a title on the strength of patrimony alone.[23] Today, regardless of what the title of ordination is or will be, the *tonsuratus* becomes inevitably bound to a diocese just the same.

There are, however, illegal ways by which clerical *vagi* can be created, but they deserve only a mention because of being so highly improbable in actuality. They are deducible from the clause "*pro cuius servitio promotus fuit*" in § 2 of this canon; for if the ordaining Bishop has no diocese of his own, i. e., if he be a titular Bishop only, and yet, without any authorization, tonsures a man; or if he be a residential Bishop, and tonsures a man who is not his proper subject without the intention of *incardinating* him in his diocese, the terms of the clause are not fulfilled, and incardination does not result. The ordination is valid, by canon 951, but unlawful, because contrary to canon 955, § 1, in the first case, and also to canon 969, § 1, in the second.[24] The penalty of canon 2373, § 1, namely, *ipso facto* suspension from the conferring of orders for a year, with the absolution from the same reserved to the Holy See, descends upon the ordaining Prelate. The candidate, in the first case, if in bad faith, becomes *ipso facto* suspended by virtue of canon 2374; in the second case, he is not censured, but acts sinfully. To correct his illegal status, it is necessary that his proper Bishop ordain him to a higher order for his own diocese, either perpetually, or temporarily with a view to later excardination by virtue of canon 969, § 2, and thereby supply the intention missing at the outset; or that some other willing Bishop have the cleric go and establish a domicile in his diocese, thus rendering

[23] Cf. *supra,* pp. 75 ff.

[24] Vermeersch-Creusen, *Epitome,* I, n. 203. Cf. also Cappello, "Collatio primae tonsurae,"—*Periodica,* XIX (1930), 38*-40*.

himself a proper Bishop to raise him to higher orders for the title of service to that new diocese. In the event that neither remedy is applied, a reduction to the lay state according to canon 211, § 2, or a recourse to the Holy See for a solution, are the last alternatives.[25] Cappello, it may be remarked, also takes into consideration the intention that the recipient had when he received tonsure in an unlawful way.[26]

ARTICLE III

THE DEFINITION OF A *Diocese*

Since it is a diocese to which a secular cleric becomes attached in a permanent way by incardination, it is necessary to define the meaning of that term as it is to be understood in this canon. The entire world itself is the territory committed to the universal Church, but efficacious ministry and rule requires organization, both territorial and personal. The universal Church is divided into many particular churches, each of which has a determined territory, called a diocese. Then each territorial division, in addition to having its own particular church, must have assigned to it a definite segment of the people, and a definite Superior, who will rule it as its proper pastor for the necessary care of souls. Consequently, a *diocese* may be defined as " that determined part of territory, in regions where the ecclesiastical hierarchy has been established, which is committed to some Bishop to rule in his own name as its legitimate pastor." [27]

Even in places where the hierarchy has been established, there are some territories which are kept separate from the rest and not placed under any Bishop, but are committed to inferior Prelates to rule in their own name. These territories are called abbacies *nullius* or prelatures *nullius*, and their rulers, Abbots *Nullius* and Prelates *Nullius*, respectively. Since the Abbot and the Prelate *Nullius*, for the same reason as a diocesan Bishop,

[25] Vermeersch-Creusen, *Epitome*, I, n. 203.

[26] *Art. cit.—Loc. cit.* Cf. *infra*, p. 306, for a fuller explanation of Cappello's view.

[27] Badii, *Institutiones Iuris Canonici*, I, nn. 154, 155; Vermeersch-Creusen, *Epitome*, I, n. 291.

must have their own clergy, the law expressly places the territories over which they rule on the same basis as dioceses, so that, wherever in the common law the word *diocese* occurs, it applies to abbacies and prelatures *nullius* also, unless the contrary is apparent from the nature of the matter or from the context of the canon.[28] In a corresponding way, the word *Bishop* applies also to this group of inferior Prelates.[29] In the absence of any evidence to the contrary in canon 111, § 1, therefore, incardination is possible also in an abbacy or prelature *nullius*.

In regions where the hierarchy has not been established or restored, the Church is territorially organized into apostolic vicariates and apostolic prefectures, and they are governed, respectively, by Vicars Apostolic and Prefects Apostolic. The former group usually are titular Bishops, but both groups rule, not in their own name, but in that of the Sovereign Pontiff himself.[30] Since they are bound to institute their own native clergy as soon as possible,[31] and are very much restricted in their power to grant their missionaries permission to leave the vicariate or prefecture perpetually;[32] since, also, the " title of the mission," accepted by the new legislation, still requires an oath of perpetual service to the mission under the authority of its Ordinary;[33] and since, finally, the Code unconditionally outlaws clerical *vagi;* it is evident that these missionary territories, too, are implicitly included in the word *diocese* in canon 111, § 1, so that secular clerics may be incardinated in them also.[34]

In each of these cases, the Superior to whom the cleric becomes subject in a permanent way, independently of where he may live thereafter, is the one appointed by the Church to rule over that particular territorial division in which he lives, i. e., the residential Bishop (in the case of a diocese), the Abbot *Nullius*, the Prelate *Nullius*, the Vicar Apostolic, or the Prefect Apostolic.

28 Can. 215, § 2.

29 Can. 215, § 2.

30 Badii, *ibid.*, n. 155.

31 Can. 305.

32 Can. 307, § 1.

33 Can. 981, § 1.

34 Vermeersch-Creusen, *Epitome*, I, n. 202.

These five categories cover all the fundamental units of the Church's territorial organization as listed in canon 215, § 1; but there is still another category which is not mentioned by any author thus far consulted. What is to be said of the possibility of incardination in a *vicariatus castrensis?* In the United States of America there is at the present time (1941) a Military Ordinariate with both an Ordinary and an auxiliary Bishop acting in the respective capacities of Military Vicar and Military Delegate, a force of 361 chaplains, and an estimated population of 238,000 people. One might argue that, regardless of what the practice is, a priest should be able to obtain an excardination from his own diocese in order that he might devote his life exclusively to this field of spiritual endeavor. The practice, of course, is for all chaplains to be lent by their dioceses for the work. In the Official Catholic Directory for 1941,[35] for example, the proper diocese of each priest in the organization is listed beside his name. Underlying the practice, however, is the fact that this, like all others of its kind, is just a personal, and not a territorial, diocese. Its subjects are determined, not by reason of domicile, but by reason of the character they bear, namely, because they are active members of Military or Naval Units of the country. While the Church sometimes does allow incardination in a personal diocese, it does so only when the ones thus incardinated are so different in rite, customs, language, and nationality as to cause no conflict with the territorial diocese in which they *de facto* live, e. g., it allows the Greek-Ruthenian clergy in the United States of America and Canada to be incardinated in the personal Ordinariates of the Greek-Ruthenians in these countries,[36] but does not allow them to be incardinated in the territorial diocese in which they live and serve.

Since a personal diocese embraces under its jurisdiction many who, as far as domicile is concerned, are in a territorial diocese distinct from the former, one can well imagine what complications would arise if incardination in a personal diocese were allowed where there was no easily marked distinction between

[35] (New York: Kenedy & Sons), pp. 664-668.

[36] Cf. *infra*, pp. 545-7.

its clerics and those of the territorial diocese. The *Ordinarius Castrensis,* for example, would have the problem of finding and educating his own clergy. A youth born of two civilian employees in a United States Army Reservation, and having his domicile there, could be claimed for orders by both the residential and the Military Bishop with equal right—the very confusion which the new law seeks to prevent. Or, it might be argued that the *Ordinarius Castrensis* would have no right to claim any candidate, since the only foundation for subjection *quoad ordinationem* is domicile,[37] and so he would have an obligation without an enabling faculty—a contradiction in law. It must be concluded, therefore, that canon 111, § 1, does not include the possibility of incardination in a *vicariatus castrensis.*

ARTICLE IV

AFFILIATION WITH A RELIGIOUS INSTITUTE

The canons which are entitled "*De clericorum adscriptione alicui dioecesi*" in the Code deal solely with secular clerics, barring one exception, namely, canon 115. Other aspects of the subject affecting Religious are placed more appropriately elsewhere. Here, however, in the declaration of a general principle in canon 111, § 1, mention must be made also of Religious: "*vel alicui religioni adscriptum.*" Briefly, then, an explanation of its connotation is in order.

The word *religioni* here, as elsewhere in the Code, means a society, approved by legitimate ecclesiastical authority, in which, according to the laws proper to the society itself, the members take public vows, either perpetual or temporary, but renewable each time their term expires, and thus strive for evangelical perfection.[38]

Candidates become canonically affiliated with such a society or Religious Institute when they make their profession of vows. From that time on they become attached to the society in a permanent way, so that they are no longer free to withdraw at will, and they receive a religious Superior, whose commands

37 Can. 956.

38 Can. 488, 1°.

they are bound to obey wherever they themselves may be.[39] Manifestly, in religion, laymen as well as clerics are thus bound. The general term "*adscriptio*" is used by the Code to denote this affiliation for all. Therefore, Religious are not properly said to become "incardinated" in their Religious Institute.[40]

Canon 111, § 1, as a matter of principle is concerned with the necessity of a candidate in the religious life becoming affiliated with a Religious Institute before being made a cleric by first tonsure. Religious profession must come before the induction into the clerical state, as canon 567, § 2, states: "Ad ordines (i. e., including first tonsure),[41] durante novitiatu, ne promoveantur." The reason is simple enough—to prevent the creation of clerical *vagi.* When a Religious receives first tonsure, he does not become incardinated into his own or any other diocese, because it is not for their service that he is being promoted,[42] but rather for the use and ministrations proper to the Religious Institute to which he belongs.[43] Hence, if he were not already validly affiliated with his Religious Institute at tonsure, he would become a clerical *acephalus* or *vagus,* since he would have no immediate Superior whom he would be bound to obey. By decreeing that every cleric be attached to some diocese or to some Religious Institute, the Church prohibits the ordaining Bishop from tonsuring, unless he has the service of a definite diocese in mind for the candidate, or unless he knows that the candidate has already made his religious profession. In either case, the newly made cleric immediately has both a juridical seat and a proper immediate Superior, and can not be a *vagus.*[44]

[39] Maroto, *Instituts.*, I, n. 492; Wernz-Vidal, *Ius Canonicum,* II, n. 59: "...cui (religioni) illum (religiosum) ipsa natura vinculi professionis religiosae permanenti modo adscribit."

[40] Maroto, *op. et loc. cit.;* Blat, *Commentarium textus Codicis Iuris Canonici* (6 vols., Romae: F. Ferrari, 1921-1927), II, n. 45: "Verbum 'incardinatio' non adhibetur ad significandum adscriptionem alicui religioni."

[41] Cf. can. 950.

[42] Can. 111, § 2.

[43] Wernz-Vidal, *Ius Canonicum,* II, n. 59; Maroto, *ibid.*, n. 493.

[44] Chelodi, *Ius de Personis,* n. 108, presents this difficulty, that a temporarily professed member of an exempt Religious Institute, receiving tonsure after temporary profession, but later legitimately leaving the Institute, becomes an *acephalus.* Discussion of that point would not be *ad rem* in this study of secular clerics only.

CHAPTER VII

Initial Diocesan Incardination

Can. 111. - § 2. **Per receptionem primae tonsurae clericus adscribitur seu, ut aiunt, incardinatur dioecesi pro cuius servitio promotus fuit.**

ARTICLE I

FIRST TONSURE THE VALID INSTRUMENT OF INITIAL INCARDINATION

1. *Singleness of the Process*

In the words of canon 111, §2, there is clearly restated, with some modifications, the ancient principle of Canon Law that it is the reception of the very first order at the hands of the Bishop which binds the cleric perpetually to the place of his spiritual ministry. Clerical tonsure now takes the place of the first minor order, and the diocese at large supplants the particular church, but the general significance of the process is the same. The cleric becomes wedded to his diocese the minute that the ordaining Prelate performs the tonsure ceremony. As long as ordination was conferred for ecclesiastical service alone, the single character of this process remained the same; the two effects followed from the one act. It was only when ordination for honor or personal convenience was recognized that a separate act became necessary for incardination, as distinct from elevation to the clerical state. So, in the Code, canon 969, § 1, reaffirms the old principle that ordination can only be for service, and that, specifically, in a diocese; and the canon under consideration makes permanent attachment or incardination to the diocese in question an *ipso facto* effect of the subject's promotion to first tonsure.

2. *Validity an Absolute Requisite*

The validity of initial incardination depends solely on the valid reception of first tonsure.[1] Since first tonsure is also included in the words *ordain, orders, ordination,* or *sacred ordination,* wherever they occur, unless the contrary be apparent,[2] its validity is likewise determined according to the same standards as those that are employed with reference to any holy order. Briefly, this would mean valid matter, form, minister, and subject, with the necessary intention in minister and subject alike.

Valid analogous matter and form for tonsure is the clipping of the subject's own hair, not that of a wig, and the recital by him at the same time of the formula "*Dominus pars*" etc.[3] The ordinary minister is any consecrated Bishop;[4] the extraordinary is one who, though lacking the episcopal character, has received from the law, or from the Holy See through a special Indult, the power to confer it.[5] Thus, Vicars and Prefects Apostolic, if they lack the episcopal character, receive from the law the power to confer tonsure during their time in office.[6] Likewise, a regular Abbot *de regimine,* even though without a territory *nullius,* is empowered by the law to confer it on those who are his subjects through simple profession at least, provided that he himself is a priest and has legitimately received the abbatial blessing.[7] The subject is to be a baptized male.[8] The minister must seriously perform the external cere-

[1] Maroto, *Instituts.*, I, n. 497, B.

[2] Can. 950.

[3] Gasparri, *De Sacra Ordin.*, II, n. 1014; Many, *De Sacra Ordin.*, n. 292. Canon 1002 enjoins strict observance of this ritual as it is contained in the Roman Pontifical.

[4] A titular Bishop, therefore, validly tonsures, but, unless he is authorized by the *dimissoriae* of some residential Bishop or religious Superior, no incardination results—Cf. *supra*, p. 293. Hence, every valid incardination requires valid tonsure, but not every valid reception of tonsure produces valid incardination.

[5] Can. 951.

[6] Can. 957, § 2.

[7] Can. 964, 1°.

[8] Can. 986, § 1.

mony, and at the same time have at least a virtual or an implicit intention of doing what the Church does, not just a habitual or an interpretative one; [9] and the subject is required to have at least a habitual intention of receiving tonsure, i. e., an intention which once he had and has never retracted.[10]

ARTICLE II

LICITNESS OF INITIAL INCARDINATION

The licit as well as the valid character of initial incardination is absolutely dependent on that of first tonsure. If, for any reason, the latter is unlawful, the incardination will stand as valid, but illicit, and sometimes rescissible. Requisites for the licitness are the same as for the reception of any holy order, because of the assimilation of tonsure with orders in the scope of the law. They proceed from three sources: the subject, the minister, and the ceremony itself. Concerning the last nothing more need be said, except that tonsure be received first, before any order.

1. *Requisites on the Part of the Subject*

In a general way canon 968, § 1, states that that subject licitly receives sacred ordination who, in the judgment of his proper Ordinary, is endowed with the necessary qualifications according to the standards of the sacred canons, and who is not restrained by any irregularity or other impediment.[11] The qualifications for the candidate are: 1. that his service be necessary or useful for the churches of the diocese, in the judgment of his proper Bishop; [12] 2. that he have the intention not only of being a cleric but of ascending to the priesthood itself, and that he give his Superior good grounds for conjecturing that he

[9] Cf. Gasparri, *ibid.*, nn. 966-967, where this is amply explained.

[10] *Ibid.*, I, nn. 626, 627.

[11] The irregularities and impediments are those enumerated in canons 984, 985, and 987. Anyone who maliciously presents himself for any order while still bound by a censure, irregularity, or other impediment, is to be punished severely according to the circumstances of the case—Can. 2374.

[12] Can. 969, § 1.

will make a worthy priest; [13] 3. that he have received the sacrament of Confirmation; 4. that he be adorned with a character befitting the clerical state; and 5. that he have the proper knowledge and age, i. e., that he at least have begun the theological course.[14]

It is not necessary that he have a canonical title, for by canon 974, § 1, 7°, that pertains to the licit reception of major orders only.

2. *The Proper Bishop* (*Canon 956*)

On the part of the minister, the only requisite is that he be the proper Bishop of the subject, or that he be authorized by the legitimate dimissorial letters (*litterae dimissoriae*) of the proper Bishop.[15] Concerning this a great deal must be said, because in the new law considerable confusion and division of opinion has developed in its regard. The pertinent canon 956 reads as follows:

> Can. 956. - **Episcopus proprius, quod attinet ad ordinationem saecularium, est tantum Episcopus dioecesis in qua promovendus habeat domicilium una cum origine aut simplex domicilium sine origine; sed in hoc altero casu promovendus debet animum in dioecesi perpetuo manendi iureiurando firmare, nisi agatur de promovendo ad ordines clerico qui dioecesi per primam tonsuram iam incardinatus est, vel de promovendo alumno, qui servitio alius dioecesis destinatur ad normam can. 969, § 2, vel de promovendo religioso professo, de quo in can. 964, n. 4.**

In this law the word *Episcopus* means not only a diocesan Bishop, i. e., one who rules a diocese in his own name as its legiti-

[13] Can. 973, § 1.

[14] Cans. 974, § 1; 976, § 1.

[15] Any Bishop who ordains an alien subject (lay or clerical) without *litterae dimissoriae* incurs *ipso facto* suspension from the conferring of orders for a year, which suspension can be lifted only by the Holy See.—Can. 2373, 1°. Likewise, any subject who maliciously presents himself for any order before a Bishop who is not his proper Bishop, without having any dimissorial letters (*litterae dimissoriae*), or with false ones, is *ipso facto* suspended from the exercise of the order received. —Can. 2374.

mate pastor, but also a Vicar Apostolic, a Prefect Apostolic, an Abbot *Nullius*, or a Prelate *Nullius*, provided they be endowed with the episcopal character.[16] But even when these latter have no episcopal consecration, they are made equal to a Bishop as far as the conferring of first tonsure and the effecting of incardination are concerned within their own territory during their time of office, but only for their own secular subjects, and for those who present legitimate dimissorial letters from other Bishops or Superiors.[17]

When a diocese or a quasi-diocese is vacant or is otherwise substantially impeded in its normal functions, then those who by law succeed to the administration of the territory act as the Bishop in those things which pertain to ordination, except insofar as their faculty is limited by lack of the power of orders or by prescript of law.

Thus, for a diocese: an Apostolic Administrator, if appointed by the Holy See, enjoys all the rights of a residential Bishop or of a Vicar Capitular, according to whether he is appointed perpetually or only temporarily.[18] If such a one is not appointed, the regime descends upon the Cathedral Chapter or the Board of Diocesan Consultors, who in turn choose a Vicar Capitular or Administrator, respectively, within eight days.[19] He, in turn, is restricted by law from exercising any faculty concerning ordination within the first year of the vacancy, except in behalf of those who must be promoted in orders either in view of a benefice already conferred upon them, or soon to be conferred, or also in view of their being needed to fill a diocesan office, appointment to which brooks no delay. After the year is over, he can issue dimissorial letters (*litterae dimissoriae*); [20] if he is a Bishop, he can also confer tonsure itself,[21] but in all cases he

[16] Cans. 957, § 1; 215, § 2. Cf. *supra*, pp. 294-5.

[17] Can. 957, § 2.

[18] Can. 315.

[19] Cans. 431; 432.

[20] Can. 958, § 1, 3°. Cf. can. 34, § 3, 3°, for the method of reckoning this year.

[21] Can. 959.

needs the consent of the Cathedral Chapter or of the Diocesan Consultors to act validly.[22]

For a quasi-diocese: canons 309 and 310 provide for the government of apostolic vicariates and prefectures during a vacancy by having the Vicar or Prefect Apostolic, as soon as he arrives in his territory, depute from his own clergy a suitable Pro-vicar or Pro-prefect. When the latter succeeds to the government of the territory, he, too, must choose at once an ecclesiastic who is potentially to succeed him as administrator. If no administrator has been thus chosen, the senior missionary in the territory is authorized by law to assume the government as a delegate of the Holy See. In all these instances the administrator succeeds to the ordinary and delegated faculties of the Vicar or Prefect, except to those that had been committed to these latter Superiors on personal grounds. This would mean, then, that the Pro-vicar and Pro-prefect, the administrator selected by either, and the senior missionary in the defect of any designated administrator, would succeed during the vacancy of the see to the ordinary faculty contained in canon 294, § 2, and in canon 957, § 2, of tonsuring and incardinating, with, however, the limitations just stated above [23] relative to territory, time, and subjects.

On the succession to even a more important ordinary faculty, namely, that of granting *litterae dimissoriae* for major orders, as contained in canon 958, § 1, 4°, the Pontifical Commission for the Interpretation of the Code decided affirmatively in favor of the Pro-vicar,[24] and, as Schaaf points out,[25] this should apply also to the Pro-prefect, the administrator, and the senior missionary acting as regent. Hence, there is no doubt that it would also apply to all of these in the case of the lesser faculty of tonsuring and incardinating. It is to be noted that the law itself places no express restrictions as to faculties pertaining to ordination on those who succeed to the *regimen* of quasi-dioceses,

[22] Cf. can. 105, 1°, for the import of the phrase "*cum consensu.*"

[23] P. 303.

[24] July 20, 1929, ad I—*AAS*, XXI (1929), 573.

[25] "Episcopus Proprius Ordinationis,"—*AER*, XC (1934), 353, note 4. Cf. also Davis, *Moral and Pastoral Theology* (3. ed., 4 vols., London: Sheed and Ward, 1938), IV, 23.

such as it does on the Vicar Capitular or Administrator in a diocese. According to the decision just referred to, the Provicar (and anyone upon whom the *regimen* of a quasi-diocese falls during a vacancy) does not have to wait for a year before acting, as does the Vicar Capitular.

An abbacy *nullius* or prelature *nullius* follows during its vacancy the same procedure as a diocese—the Chapter of Religious or the Chapter of Canons is constituted the immediate successor in power, but chooses a Vicar Capitular within eight days, and he in turn is limited in the same way as any such Vicar.[26]

When a diocesan see or an abbacy or prelature *nullius* is impeded in its normal functions, the Vicar General succeeds to the administration,[27] and, if he enjoys, by special mandate of the Bishop, the right to issue *litterae dimissoriae*,[28] he is able at once to grant them for tonsure and concomitant incardination, but not in favor of candidates already refused by the Bishop; if he be a Bishop, he can confer the tonsure himself.

The note of *proprius*, in the sense to be expounded later in this article,[29] designates that Bishop who can *lawfully* tonsure and incardinate. It is a most ancient principle of the Church legislation. Its history was amply traced through the centuries in the first section of this study. When, then, a Bishop who is not the proper Bishop of the candidate tonsures him with the intention of incardinating him into his own diocese, the conferring of tonsure is valid, but it violates canon 956 and is therefore illicit, which rule also applies to the concomitant incardination—the incardination to the alien diocese is valid, but unlawful.[30] Nevertheless, it is recognized that this unlawful act is detrimental in character to the diocese of the rightful Bishop,

[26] Can. 327, § 1.

[27] Cans. 429, § 1; 327, § 2.

[28] Cans. 368, § 1; 958, § 1, 2°.

[29] Cf. *infra*, pp. 310 ff.

[30] Chelodi, *Ius de Personis;* n. 106, note 2; Vermeersch-Creusen, *Epitome*, II, n. 239; S. C. C., *Dioecesium N. et X.*, 10 martii 1923, *Votum Consultoris—AAS*, XVI (1924), 54.

who, consequently, has a right to restitution, that is, he can reclaim the cleric for his own diocese if he so desires.[31]

Cappello, in discussing this question, holds the same view, but he adds a new requisite on the part of the subject for initial incardination, namely, the intention of being incardinated into the diocese of the ordaining Prelate. Hence, he concludes: 1. If the subject had that intention, and through error was unaware that the ordaining Prelate was not his proper Bishop, incardination into the diocese of the ordaining Bishop follows, but the new cleric must at once take an oath to remain there perpetually, i. e., as soon as the mistake becomes known; 2. if the subject did not have the intention of being incardinated into the diocese of the ordaining Prelate, and it was through deception or trickery that he was being ordained by a non-proper Bishop, incardination does not follow; and 3. in any case the proper Bishop can reclaim his cleric, but is not bound to do so, even to prevent him from becoming a *vagus*. With regard to the second conclusion, the cleric would be a *vagus* and would have a choice of five alternatives: to elect his proper diocese if his Bishop would accept him, to elect the diocese of his ordaining Prelate, to find some other benevolent Bishop to accept him, to return to the lay state, or to apply to Rome for a solution of his case.[32]

When a Prelate of a quasi-diocese who lacks episcopal consecration, but enjoys the faculty accorded by law of tonsuring subjects, goes beyond his scope and tonsures a layman who is not his subject, his act is invalid, and hence no incardination results.[33]

The process of reclamation of a cleric who has been validly but unlawfully incardinated in an alien diocese is clear. The cleric's proper Bishop, who is acknowledged to have the right to

[31] Vidal, "Il Nuovo Codice di Diritto Canonico," (Lib. III, Parte 2ª): "Se un vescovo, senza essere vescovo proprio, conferisce ad un secolare la tonsura, lo incardina nella sua diocesi; ma siccome questo atto è illegittimo e contro il diritto del vescovo proprio, questi ha il diritto di richiamarsene, esigendo che gli sia reso il soggetto, che egli solo aveva diritto di ordinare."—*La Civiltà Cattolica*, LXIX (1918), 219. Wernz-Vidal, *Ius Canonicum*, II, n. 67; Vermeersch-Creusen, *op. et loc. cit.*; Vermeersch, "Quaesita Canonica," I—*Periodica*, XV (1926), (115).

[32] Cappello, "Collatio Primae Tonsurae,"—*Periodica*, XIX (1930), 38*-40*.

[33] Can. 957, § 2.

reclaim him, uses the formal method of canon 112. The Bishop who had performed the illegal ceremony is required to issue letters of excardination, releasing the cleric whom he had usurped.

Authors, however, are silent about the process of initial incardination for a clerical *vagus*, that is to say, about the method which a Bishop would use to incardinate in his diocese a cleric who, through a deliberate intention to thwart the law, had received tonsure validly, but in such a way that its conferment had not simultaneously effected his incardination to any diocese. Canon 112 would not be applicable in this case, because, since no Bishop recognizes the cleric as pertaining to his diocesan clergy, there is no Bishop who can issue letters of excardination to him. The more probable solution is the following: The clerical *vagus* first finds a Bishop who is willing to receive him, then establishes a domicile in the receiving Bishop's diocese, fortifying with an oath his intention of perpetually remaining there, according to the provisions of canon 956, whereupon the receiving Bishop initially incardinates the cleric when he confers on him the first or next minor order. This would correspond to the practice of the Ancient Period of the Church in which a cleric became linked with the service of a particular church, not at the reception of first tonsure as such, but rather at the reception of the first minor order, regardless of the sequence of the minor orders that was followed in the ordination. One of the mistakes of the Tridentine Period was to accentuate too much the *formality* of linking a cleric with his diocese at the reception of tonsure, so that the opinion came to be accepted by many that whenever this formality was neglected at tonsure it could not be supplied later.[34] When canon 111, § 2, states that incardination is effected *ipso facto* by the reception of first tonsure, this must not be understood *taxative*, but rather in the sense that *a fortiori* it would be effected by the reception of a minor order, or especially of a major order wherein a title of ordination is necessary.[35]

[34] Cf. *supra*, p. 164, footnote 190.

[35] Cf. *infra*, pp. 526 ff.

The next words of canon 956 *quod attinet ad ordinationem* distinguish the *Episcopus proprius* treated of in this section from the *Ordinarius* or *Episcopus proprius* of canon 94. Confusion results from a disregard of this distinction.[36] A youth secures a proper Bishop, to whom he becomes subject, by acquiring a quasi-domicile, i. e., by spending six months in a diocese, albeit with the intention of not remaining; in fact, he secures one in the place where he stays even if he is a *vagus,* not having a domicile or quasi-domicile anywhere; but in neither case is the Bishop the proper Bishop for ordination. To be that, he must fulfill the qualifications hereinafter explained.

Saecularium is a word used in the Code to designate non-religious. It is equally applicable, therefore, to laymen [37] and to clerics.[38] It was claimed by some authors that in the old law laymen did not have a proper Bishop for ordination [39]—a contention with which this thesis took issue [40]—and interpreters of the Code at first thought that that was to be the sense of the new law on proper Bishops. They based their reasoning on the fact that, whereas the advance *Schemata* of the Code contained, in canon 234, lib. III, "*De rebus,*" express mention of "conferment of first tonsure" being performed by a Bishop who was not the proper Bishop by reason of domicile, the final edition of the Code kept silent on that point.[41] Against such a negative argument was the clear wording of canon 955, § 1, "Unusquisque a proprio Episcopo ordinetur aut cum legitimis

[36] "Episcopus sive Ordinarius *proprius* de quo in can. 94, § 1 non est idem ac Episcopus sive Ordinarius *proprius* de quo in can. 956. Iste canon loquitur de Episcopo proprio quoad ordinationem; ille e contra loquitur de Episcopo sive Ordinario (atque etiam de parocho) quoad subiectionem. Can. 94, § 1 respicit omnes fideles universim, sive mares sive feminas; can. 956 respicit dumtaxat alumnos saeculares ad ordines promovendos."—Cappello, "Quaestiones Canonicae de Ordinatione, domicilio et incardinatione," (*Periodica,* XX [1931], 131*-132*).

[37] E. g., in can. 957, § 2.

[38] E. g., in cans. 640, § 1, 1°; 964, 4°.

[39] Thus, Hofmann, "Die Excardination einst und jetzt,"——*ZkT,* XXIV (1900), 115-123; Gasparri, *De Sacra Ordin.,* II, n. 802.

[40] Cf *supra,* pp. 40 ff.

[41] D'Angelo, "De Collatione primae Tonsurae—Animadversiones,"—*Apollinaris,* III (1930), 243.

eiusdem litteris dimissoriis," in which the pronominal adjective *unusquisque* was all-embracing, and the verb *ordinetur* was manifestly applicable to first tonsure by the definition of the law itself in canon 950. To settle all doubts, the Pontifical Commission for the Interpretation of the Code on Feb. 17, 1930, answered in the negative to the question: " An vi canonis 111, § 2, conlati cum canone 955, § 1, Episcopus alienum subditum sine legitimis proprii Episcopi litteris dimissoriis ad primam tonsuram promovere licite possit." [42] By a unique twist of fate it is now seen to be true, and will be developed below,[43] that not only are laymen included in canon 956, but they are the only ones to whom it applies.

The restricted specification of the proper Bishop for orders is shown in the words *est tantum.* There is, and can be, only one foundation upon which a Bishop can become the proper Bishop for the ordination of a lay subject, namely, domicile in that Bishop's diocese. There may be many proper Bishops *quoad subiectionem,* because of the possibility of a plurality of domiciles, but no more than one *quoad ordinationem,* because the candidate himself must add the formality which will designate one Bishop alone as his choice for his life's service.[44] This is a welcome change from the much involved previous legislation, in which it was possible to have as many as five proper Bishops for the same lay candidate. Moreover, even after one of the five had been selected for the conferring of the first tonsure, the rest still remained competent to advance this cleric to higher orders on various scores.

Since domicile is made the only foundation for competency, it follows that the proper Bishop must be one exercising jurisdiction over the territory in which the candidate resides. Hence the canon says *Episcopus dioecesis,* a diocesan Bishop, not just a titular one. The phrase, however, includes also any Bishop or Prelate of a quasi-diocese,[45] but not any honorary Prelate.

[42] *AAS,* XXII (1930), 195.

[43] Pp. 359 ff.

[44] Vidal, " Il Nuovo Codice di Diritto Canonico,"—*La Civiltà Cattolica,* LXIX (1918), 219.

[45] Vermeersch-Creusen, *Epitome,* II, n. 239. Cf. *supra,* pp. 302-303.

A. For Promotion of Laymen to the Clerical State

There now follows in canon 956 the definition of the grounds upon which a Bishop becomes the proper one for ordination, particularly and primarily for the initial elevation to the clerical state, because lay candidates for tonsure (*promovendi*) are the first to need a proper Bishop. Two bases for competency are given: 1) domicile together with origin in a diocese, i. e., original diocesan domicile; and 2) simple domicile in a diocese without origin, i. e., acquired diocesan domicile. In other words, the Code has reverted to the old grounds for competency enumerated by Popes Clement IV (a. 1265-1268) and Boniface VIII (a. 1294-1303),[46] because with them the idea of origin was that of original domicile, and the idea of domicile was that of acquired domicile.[47] With the passage of time, however, origin or original domicile came to be considered as a basis of competency even after a new domicile had been acquired, whereas in the thirteenth century they were meant to be mutually exclusive. When modern authors say that the Code has abrogated origin alone as a title,[48] they merely mean that it has reverted to that mutually exclusive idea, and that it no longer recognizes the original domicile as a title of competency after it has been abandoned by the candidate.

1°. Through original diocesan domicile still retained (*Domicile together with origin*)

. . . dioecesis in qua promovendus habeat domicilium una cum origine . . . —Can. 956.

a) Domicile

§ 1. *Meaning.*—The first and oldest definition of domicile given by Alfenus Varus in the Digest is as follows: " Sed de ea re constitutum esse, eam domum unicuique nostrum debere existimari, ubi quisque sedes et tabulas haberet suarumque rerum

46 Cf. *supra*, pp. 45 ff.

47 Cf. *supra*, pp. 49-50.

48 E. g., Bondini, " De incardinatione et excardinatione clericorum," p. 7—*Jus Pontificium*, IX (1929), 205-213.

constitutionem fecerit."[49] Therefore, it is the place where one has settled and has set up his possessions.[50] There is no definition of domicile given in the Code, but the conditions required for securing one are very concisely stated in canon 92.

§ 2. *How secured.*—" A domicile is secured by residence in a parish or quasi-parish, or at least in a diocese, apostolic vicariate, or apostolic prefecture; which residence must be either joined with the intention of remaining there always, if nothing unforeseen occurs, or be continued for ten complete years."[51] Hence, there are two methods recognized in the Code for the acquisition of a diocesan domicile: 1. residence in a diocese or quasi-diocese, coupled with the intention of remaining perpetually, if nothing calls one away; and 2. residence in a diocese or quasi-diocese, independent of the intention, but protracted over a period of ten years. One can discern therein two elements, the material, of the body, and the formal, of the mind. In the first method, the two elements concur and are verified, and the domicile is established at that same moment. In the second, the formal element is missing, and the domicile is not established until the material element has been in existence continuously for ten years in the diocese or quasi-diocese.

The type of residence (*commoratio*) required has aroused considerable discussion. Many authors, in explaining it, declare that it must fulfill special requisites.[52] Upon analysis of their

[49] D. (50.16) 203.

[50] Costello, *Domicile and Quasi-Domicile*, The Catholic University of America, Canon Law Studies, n. 60 (Washington, D. C.: The Catholic University of America, 1930), p. 12.

[51] Can. 92.

[52] E. g., Cappello, *Summa Iuris Canonici* (2 vols., Romae: apud Aedes Universitatis Gregorianae, 1928-1930), I, p. 216: " Censetur commorari qui domum, sive propriam sive conductam, more aliorum civium per tempus requisitum colit. Non sufficit mera residentia etiam diuturnior."; Vermeersch-Creusen, *Epitome*, I, n. 183: " De priore modo [namely, where material and formal elements are united] haec observanda veniunt. Commoratio non sufficit ad modum visitantis, itinerantis, sed requiritur ad modum inhabitantis: sive domum habeas propriam, sive conductam, sive excipiaris diversorio, hospitio . . . De altero acquirendi modo, per decem annos completos, haec notamus. Commorationem instar inhabitantis esse debere, per se perspicitur . . . "; Farrugia: " Locus commorationis est ille ubi iuxta communem hominum aestimationem etc."—" *De ecclesiastico domicilio*," (*Il Monitore Eccles-*

statements and a comparison of their requisites with canon 1097 on the *commoratio* for marriage, they mean nothing more than this: the residence must be more than mere physical presence; it signifies staying or tarrying in a place, making it one's abode or place of rest for a time; it implies that one sleeps there, makes the place one's *sedes,* which also involves keeping some of one's belongings there. It does not require the purchase of a house or the bringing of one's furniture; it is quite compatible with living in a hotel or inn, an automobile trailer, or a tent, and it is distinguished from the place of one's work or business during the day by the journey made back to the *sedes* at the end of the day's work.[58]

To exemplify the point, let it be supposed that a certain layman, Matthew, is engaged in an official capacity by the government. He has the eastern part of the State of Pennsylvania as his territory. He travels from city to city and lives in hotels. Each hotel at which he temporarily resides is used as a base from which he travels by automobile to the nearby towns. Let it also be supposed that the various hotels where he has been staying are all located within the archdiocese of Philadelphia, but that the greater portion of his working days throughout the year are spent in cities and towns in the dioceses of Harrisburg and Scranton. In which diocese does Matthew have *commoratio?* In the archdiocese of Philadelphia. Certainly he is physically present in Harrisburg and Scranton more than in Philadelphia, but that mere physical presence is not enough to be termed residence. His various temporary dwelling places or *sedes commorationis* are all located in the archdiocese of Philadelphia, and they may form the material element for his eventual acquisition of a domicile in the archdiocese of Philadelphia.

The territory within which this residence is verified, let it be remembered, can now be as extensive as the diocese or quasi-

iastico [*ME*], 5 series, VII [1935], 313-314). A basis for these opinions is found in S. C. S. Off., *litt. encycl.*, 7 iun. 1867: "Praeterea manifestum quoque est, actualem habitationem ineptam esse ad quasi domicilium pariendum, si quis in ea regione more vagi ac itinerantis commoretur, non autem vere proprieque habitantis, quemadmodum scilicet ceteri solent qui in eodem loco verum proprieque dictum domicilium habent."—*Fontes*, n. 1001.

[58] Browne, "The Meaning of 'Commoratio'," —*IER*, XLVII (1936), 81-83.

diocese, since diocesan domicile is all that is required in canon 956. One need not reside, therefore, in the same house or hotel all the time, but can vary from place to place within the diocesan limits, as long as in each place the true notion of residence, as just explained, is fulfilled.

A peculiar observation to be made here is that regional or interdiocesan seminaries, if established as such by authority of the Holy See in accordance with canon 1354, § 3, are considered to be the very territory of the dioceses which they serve, just as an embassy is regarded as the soil and territory of the nation it represents, so that a youth studying there is considered to have residence in the diocese for which he is studying. This is taught by various canonists,[54] and is supported by the Consultor's argument and the consequent decision in the Sacred Congregation of the Council's case *Dioecesium N. et X.*, Mar. 10, 1923.[55] It has no practical value in the United States of America because there are no such seminaries here.[56]

In the first method of securing a domicile, the formal element of the mind, i. e., the intention, must be joined with that of residence. This intention is to remain in the place permanently, if nothing unforeseen occurs to call one away. It is not, therefore, absolute and irrevocable; it admits journeys away from the place of domicile, even though protracted over long periods, provided always there be the mind to return.[57] The clause " *si nihil inde avocet* " shows how far it can be limited. The prevision of some future possibility of changing residence does not suspend the present will to remain; it puts no term on it. On the other hand, the will is suspended if made conditional on some future event.[58] A conditional will is very important

[54] E. g., Meysztowicz, "Domicilium et Quasi-Domicilium,"—*Jus Pontif.*, VI (1926), 46, n. 37; Browne, "Incardination and Ordination: a Recent Reply,"—*IER*, XLVIII (1936), 532.

[55] *AAS*, XVI (1924), 51-55.

[56] Schaaf, "Episcopus proprius ordinationis,"—*AER*, XC (1934), 356, note 7.

[57] "... unde cum profectus est, peregrinari videtur, quo si rediit, peregrinari iam destitit."—C. (7.40) 40 (39).

[58] Meysztowicz, "Domicilium et Quasi-Domicilium,"—*Jus Pontif.*, VI (1926), 35, n. 3.

in this study because the will to reside in a place permanently *if* one succeeds in becoming ordained there destroys at once the possibility of acquiring a domicile by the first method.

The second method of securing a domicile dispenses with the formal element altogether. The residence, in the sense just expounded, must continue for ten complete years, after which the domicile is established. This is a new feature of the Code. Formerly, the mere continuity of the residence only created a presumption of law that the formal element was present, but the presumption ceased in the face of the truth, e. g., if the subject openly stated that he had no intention of remaining. In the present law of canon 92, the continuity of residence over a ten-year period gives a true domicile, and does not merely establish a presumption, so that the domicile is effectively established despite protestations of an opposite intention.[59]

The ten-year period is to be computed in the ordinary way, i. e., according to canon 34, § 3, 1°, 3°. The months and years are to be taken as they are in the calendar. Since, as a general rule, the starting point does not coincide with the beginning of the day, the first day, being incomplete, is not counted, and the time ends with the completion of the last day of the same number.[60] Canon 92, § 1, expressly states that the ten years' residence must be complete, and it is quite clear that it must be morally, though not physically, continuous.[61]

There is a difference of opinion among canonists as to the way in which this moral continuity of residence is definitely broken. Costello defends the opinion that a brief departure with the intention of not returning does not destroy the continuity of residence.[62] This is quite acceptable, because the acquisition of a domicile through the sole material element of residence is a distinct departure from the legislation of the past, and purposely leaves mental attitudes out of consideration.

[59] *Ibid.*, 46, n. 38; Farrugia, "De ecclesiastico domicilio,"—*ME*, 5 series, VII (1935), 312-313.

[60] Costello, *Domicile and Quasi-Domicile*, p. 127.

[61] *Loc. cit.*

[62] *Ibid.*, pp. 130-135.

A more difficult question to solve is, what length of absence alone would break this moral continuity of residence. The same author, basing his argument on a similar law—the month's residence of canon 1097, § 1, 2°—and on the common interpretation of canonists, concludes that a continuous absence of one year would certainly break it, and that more probably a continuous absence of *over* six months would have the same effect.[63] There is a strange lack of parity in this conclusion. It admits that a *total* absence of four days would break the moral continuity of a thirty-day period, and yet tolerates a total absence of 1800 days (6 months every year for ten years) in a 3652-day period! A person might be led to wonder why the legislator should have been so meticulous about the method of reckoning the precise day on which the ten-year period of residence would be completed, if at the same time he intended to regard as complete a ten-year period out of which a total of almost five years had been deleted.

Vermeersch, by whom Costello has been considerably influenced, is even more liberal. He, in speaking expressly of the method of acquiring a domicile by the material element of residence alone, says:

> Quocirca, si quis per decem annos locum quempiam stabiliter per quattuor menses, singulis annis, inhabitaverit, nec umquam animo linquendi locum discesserit, sed contra, ex conducta domo, etiam absens corpore, censeatur inhabitans, completo decimo anno, habebit domicilium in illo loco, donec discesserit sine animo revertendi.[64]

Hence, he would allow a total of six and two-third years to be deleted from a ten-year period of residence and still call the latter complete.

The fault with these ultra-liberal views is that, doubtless unwittingly, they introduce the formal element of intention into the new method of acquiring a domicile by residence alone. They confuse the new type of domicile with the old, forgetting

[63] *Ibid.*, p. 129.

[64] Vermeersch-Creusen, *Epitome*, I, n. 183.

that at the present day a man with a valise or two who registers in a hotel is commencing residence (*commoratio*), and that, when he leaves to go elsewhere, he checks out of the hotel and takes his belongings with him. They base their argument too much on the legislation of the past, in which this new method of acquiring a domicile was unknown. They forget that domicile may now be diocesan in scope, and, most of all, they make the mistake of taking for granted the premise that one can acquire three or four domiciles simultaneously by the method of material residence alone, whereas a plurality of benefices can be gained simultaneously only when the method of residence *with intention* is used.

In the words of Vermeersch just quoted it can be readily seen how he injects the formal element—a man is " considered " to be present, even though absent corporally, if he has never departed from the place with the " intention " of leaving it. Vermeersch's sole requirement of four months of residence each year for a materially acquired domicile apparently is made to avoid a conflict with what he writes a little later about the acquisition of a plurality of domiciles:

> Verum nihil repugnat quin aliquis duo vel tria domicilia voluntaria habeat . . . Tria autem domicilia tribuemus ei qui soleat per aliquot menses, singulis annis, in tribus locis habitare.[65]

Yet, a plurality of domiciles is possible only because the residence, whenever interrupted, is reputed or considered to be continuous because of the *intention* the dweller has of returning. This is impossible whenever a domicile is being acquired absolutely independently of intentions. Hence, it is justifiable to conclude that the completed ten years' residence necessary for the acquisition of a diocesan domicile by the informal method does admit of brief interruptions for journeys such as are common to all humans, but, whenever interrupted for a considerable period of time, must be reckoned as having commenced anew from the day that the diocesan residence was reëstablished. The same should be held as true whenever the residence is broken by

[65] *Loc. cit.*

brief absences so frequently repeated as to exceed the normal custom of the average individual.

Blat has a unique opinion in this regard. Striving to interpret the completed ten-year period of canon 92, in which there is no express prescript of law about interruptions, he invokes canon 20 to justify his adoption of the norm of canon 556 on the interruptions in the continuous and complete year of novitiate, which he considers an analogous bit of legislation. There, it is expressly prescribed that for a period of 365 days to be entire and continuous, absences aggregating less than 15 days (= .0447 of the total) need not be supplied at all; absences aggregating from 15 to 30 days (= .0447 to .082 of the total) must be supplied; and absences aggregating over 30 days (i. e., over .082 of the total) break the continuity and force the year to be commenced anew. Apparently by adopting the same proportionate scale, Blat states that for a ten-year period (i. e., 3652 days) to be complete, absences aggregating less than five months (163 days would equal .0447 of the total period) need not be supplied later; absences aggregating from five months to ten months (163 days to 299 days = .0447 to .082 of the total) must be supplied; and absences aggregating over 10 months (i. e., over .082 of the total period) break the continuity and force the ten-year period to be commenced anew.[66]

The important objection to Blat's interpretation is that the year of novitiate is expressly required to be continuous, but not so the ten-year period. Hence a greater rigidity is expected in the former than in the latter, but to apply the rigid prescriptions concerning the year of novitiate to the ten-year period of residence for a domicile would be, contrary to canonical principles, amplifying rather than restricting the scope of onerous requirements.[67] Nevertheless, canonists, interpreting the month's residence of canon 1097, § 1, 2°, which does not expressly prescribe a continuous month, admit that, if a total absence of four days intervened, the month would be seriously interrupted

[66] Blat, *Commentarium Textus Codicis Iuris Canonici*, II, n. 11.

[67] Cf. Meysztowicz, "Domicilium et Quasi-Domicilium,"—*Jus Pontif.*, VI (1926), 47, n. 38.

and would have to be begun again. An absence of four days in a total of even thirty-one days is only .129 of the total, which is certainly not a much higher percentage of allowance than the .082 of Blat. It must be admitted, then, that, though Blat's insistence on the ten-year period being extended, to compensate for interruptions aggregating more than five months but less than ten months, is an unwarranted provision, nevertheless, his verdict that total interruptions of over ten months would necessitate an entirely new reckoning point for the completion of the ten years' residence is a fair norm. But to extend liberality to the limit, by adopting the proportion used by the canonists in interpreting the month's residence of canon 1097, § 1, 2°, it should be concluded that a ten-year period of residence is not completed if there have been intervening interruptions aggregating 1.3 years (which would be .129 of the total period of ten years), and that in such a case the ten-year period would have to be begun again. Likewise, it should be concluded that a continuous absence of more than four months definitely breaks the *commoratio,* and requires the ten-year period to be reckoned anew from the day that diocesan residence is reëstablished, since four months is a liberal limit to an average individual's vacation or sojourn.

§ 3. *Legal or necessary domicile.*—From ancient Roman Law the Code in can. 93, § 1, has adopted the principle that sometimes the law itself can supply both elements for acquiring a domicile. This means that there are some on whom the law imposes the obligation of retaining their domicile in a certain place, and they are considered to be residing in that place, and not where they *de facto* are found to be; and, further, they are considered to have that intention which is prescribed for them by the law, not that which proceeds from their own will. Thus in Roman Law, the following had their domicile prescribed for them: prisoners, in the place of the detention or imprisonment; public officials, in the place of the office; soldiers, where they are officially serving; legitimate wives, in the place of their husband; freedmen, in the place of their patron; and, to a certain extent, children (*filii familias*), in the place of their father, that is, unless these were permitted to establish a separate domicile.[68] In the Code, only three groups have a domicile expressly prescribed for them as a necessary or legal one, namely: a wife who is not legitimately separated has the domicile of her husband; an insane person, that of his legal guardian; and a minor, that of the person to whom he is subject.[69]

The case of the minor, i. e., a person who has not yet completed his twenty-first year of age,[70] is the only one with which this study is concerned. No matter where he is or goes, his domicile is still where his father, or at least his guardian, has his domicile. Though not mentioned in the Code, canonists generally think that, as in Roman Law, a minor can acquire a separate domicile if he obtains the special permission of his father or guardian.[71] When a youth at the age of 21 still remains in his father's or guardian's house, his domicile there becomes voluntary in place of necessary. At that age he is free to contract a new one wherever he wishes, but mere excursions from home for the sake of temporary employment and the like do not constitute a renunciation of the paternal hearth.[72]

The Code's enumeration in canon 93, § 1, of those who have necessary domiciles is to be considered as applying only to those which are borrowed (*mutuata*) from others, according to some authors, for, they say, there are other groups who are required by other canons of the Code to dwell in a certain place independently of their own will, but it is their own and not somebody else's domicile which they thus acquire. Hence it should be called *necessarium sed proprium et personale*. In this category they enumerate the following: the beneficed cleric, in the place of the benefice; the Religious, in the convent to which they are affiliated; Cardinals, in the city of Rome (except those

[68] *Ibid.*, n. 5.

[69] Can. 93, § 1.

[70] Can. 88, § 1.

[71] Browne, "Questions about domicile,"—*IER*, XLVII (1936), 633. The guardian functions if the parent no longer retains the child as the result of a court order, a separation, disease, etc.—*Ibid.*, p. 632.

[72] *Ibid.*, pp. 633-634.

who are Bishops of non-suburbicarian dioceses); life prisoners, in the prison itself; and soldiers, in their stationary garrisons.[73] One author [74] places in this list also secular clerics, in the diocese in which they are incardinated, on the strength of canon 111, where clerical *vagi* are outlawed, and of canons 143 and 144, where the secular cleric is shown to have no free will in selecting any residence outside the diocese. In addition to all these types of domiciles being proper instead of borrowed, another point of differentiation between them and those mentioned in canon 93, § 1, is that only one element, the formal, is supplied by law. There is no evidence to show that any one of these categories would have a legal residence in a place where they never yet had been. It is their will alone which has been constrained by law to consent actually to go to a certain place and remain there, and, since they are not free to leave on their own authority, they are considered as still belonging there even if they later leave without permission. Hence, it is not justifiable to put them in the same category with wives, the insane, and minors, for whom even the basic element of residence itself is supplied by law, nor may the same juridical effects be invoked.[75]

§ 4. *How lost.*—A domicile is lost by departure from the place with the intention of not returning.[76] For those with legal domiciles, this departure and intention must be on the part of the one from whom the necessary domicile is borrowed. No matter by which method the domicile was acquired, both of these elements must concur for its loss. The intention of not returning, by analogy with the intention of remaining when acquiring the domicile, must not be considered absolute and irrevocable, as terminating every remote possibility of ever returning as an inhabitant. Rather it is a present positive act of the will excluding any future foreseen return as an ordinary

[73] E. g., Farrugia, "De ecclesiastico domicilio,"—*ME*, 5 series, VII (1935), 316; Meysztowicz, "Domicilium et Quasi-Domicilium,"—*Jus Pontif.*, VI (1926), 47-48, n. 42.

[74] Meysztowicz, *loc. cit.*

[75] Cf. Costello, *Domicile and Quasi-Domicile*, pp. 169-174.

[76] Can. 95.

resident. It readily admits of the intention of returning as a visitor, e. g., in the case of a priest leaving his home for a distant diocese in which he has been incardinated. The loss of a domicile, however, is a fact which the law will not concede lightly. Once constituted, it is regarded as an acquired right—a *res favorabilis*. It enjoys the favor of the law. Its loss, being a *res odiosa*, must be strictly interpreted. The loss must be clearly proved, and, in cases of doubt, the presumption is in favor of its retention. Hence, even if a person has been absent for many years, or has left with the intention of being absent for many years, the domicile is considered to exist until it is clearly proved that the person has actually left with the certain intention of abandoning his domicile, never to return.[77] Apparently, then, a conditional intention when leaving the domicile would not become effective until the condition had been fulfilled, and the domicile would not be lost in the meantime. Thus a youth, who leaves his parental home to study for the priesthood in a distant diocese with the view of devoting his life to the service of that or of still another more distant diocese, has the intention, indeed, of not returning, but it is conditioned on his being finally ordained a priest. If it later happens that he is rejected, or incurs some major physical disability, such as the loss of an arm in an accident, or the contraction of some incurable disease, he will return whence he came, not as a visitor, but as a resident coming back home; and such contingencies can be foreseen easily in every cleric's life. Hence, the conditional or suspensive intention which he had upon leaving home prevents his loss of the domicile.

§ 5. *Plurality of diocesan domiciles.*—Although the Code does not expressly treat this question, it is quite certain that the old Roman Law principle of a plurality of domiciles still obtains its full force, because canon 20 states that "if there is no express prescription of law, whether general or particular, covering a certain matter, a norm is to be taken . . . from the practice of the Roman Curia and from the common and constant teaching

[77] Costello, *op. cit.*, pp. 143-146.

of the doctors," and they, in turn, have been unanimous in admitting the present possibility of plural domiciles. Besides, canon 1216, § 2, allowing a plurality of proper parishes, implies it also as one of the possibilities. To acquire a domicile in more than one place, it is commonly taught that it is necessary to establish oneself in a *morally* equal way in each place, e. g., spring, summer, and part of autumn in one place, the balance of autumn and winter in another. For a continuance of these domiciles, it is not necessary that at each moment a person shall be prepared to dwell in or even retain his homes for equal terms of succeeding years. All that is required to retain any one of them is the perseverance of at least one of the two elements, actual residence or intention. It is only when both elements cease to exist for one of the domiciles that it ceases to be a domicile. In other words, to lose one of them, the person once having it must not only not live there at all, but must have the mind not to return to it as a resident. Canonists have struggled with the question of how many domiciles a person can have simultaneously, and the general conclusion is that not more than four are admissible.[78]

No more than a bare mention need be made here of the fact that a plurality of domiciles can be acquired simultaneously only by the method wherein the material element of residence is combined with the formal element of intention.[79]

b) Origin

The place of origin of a youth, or also of a convert, is that place in which his father had a domicile or, in defect of it, a quasi-domicile at the time of his son's birth. If the son be illegitimate or posthumous, it is the domicile (or quasi-domicile) of his mother which determines the place of his origin.[80] For lay *vagi*, the very place of the birth is the place of origin; and for foundlings, it is the place where they were discovered.[81]

[78] Costello, *op. cit.*, pp. 151-154; De Meester, *Compend.*, I, n. 316.

[79] Cf. *supra*, pp. 315-316.

[80] Can. 90, § 1.

[81] Can. 90, § 2.

In all cases it is actual birth, and not just conception or adoption, which is spoken of; and by place is meant diocese or quasi-diocese.

Since quasi-domicile enters into the possible determination of place of origin, a few words concerning it are also in order.

Similarly to domicile, a diocesan quasi-domicile may be acquired in two ways: 1) by residence in a diocese or quasi-diocese, with the intention of remaining there for at least the greater part of a year, if nothing unforeseen occurs; and 2) by residence in such a place, actually protracted beyond a period of six months, regardless of the intention.

There are no legal or necessary quasi-domiciles, because the Code is silent on that point, significantly giving to minors and to wives who are not legitimately separated from their husbands the power of acquiring a quasi-domicile of their own. Most canonists after the Code are agreed that a necessary quasi-domicile does not exist any longer.[82]

A quasi-domicile is lost in exactly the same way as a domicile, that is, by departure from the place with the intention of not returning.[83] This clears up the legal obscurity which previously existed. It used to be considered that an intention not to return for over six months was enough to forfeit the quasi-domicile, but not so now. As long as the intention is to return, no term need be placed on it; the quasi-domicile is preserved.[84]

For the same reason a plurality of quasi-domiciles, acquired by the first method of residence and intention, is possible, though not expressly mentioned in the Code. When a person absents himself from one quasi-domicile to acquire another, he has the intention of remaining in the second for over six months but of afterwards returning to the first. Such a mind is sufficient to acquire the second and still retain the first.[85]

[82] Costello, *op. cit.*, pp. 174-177.

[83] Can. 95.

[84] Costello, *op. cit.*, pp. 147-150.

[85] *Ibid.*, pp. 158-159.

c) How original diocesan domicile makes a Bishop the proper Bishop

In view of the manifold phases of domicile (or quasi-domicile) and of origin when considered separately, it is inevitable that one should expect complications when the two notions are combined. To consider all possible combinations of the two with reference to a cleric's ordination without sacrificing clarity, the appended chart is utilized in order to show in brief the key to each solution prior to explaining these possibilities more in detail. In this chart, the capital letters will represent dioceses: *A* and *C* will represent the dioceses of the place of domicile; *D* and *E*, the dioceses of the place of quasi-domicile (except in columns four and five, wherein they represent the dioceses of former places of quasi-domicile which have now been changed to places of domicile); and *B*, the diocese of the incidental place of birth. The various contingencies as affecting the father will be represented in the first vertical column; the various possibilities accompanying the son's actual birth, in the second; and the indications of the son's legal place of origin, by application of canon 90, in the third. Since a youth's quasi-domicile means nothing as far as ordination is concerned, column four merely furnishes the indications of the domicile it is possible for him to hold at the time he comes up for ordination. Whenever the letter in column three corresponds to that in column four, it designates the Bishop of that same diocese as the proper Bishop *ratione domicilii una cum origine* for the ordination of the youth, and the same letter will appear in column five in identification of this Bishop. But, whenever the letters in columns three and four are not identical, a dash (—) is employed in column five to indicate that the youth has for his proper Bishop of ordination the Bishop of his current domicile (*ratione simplicis domicilii sine origine*), but has no proper Bishop in view of any *domicilium una cum origine*. This latter consideration of simple domicile without concomitant origin will be further discussed later in this present article. Each of the cases here adduced in the list of possible combinations carries its own distinctive number in order to facilitate reference to it.

PROPER BISHOP FOR ORDINATION *ratione DOMICILII una cum ORIGINE*

Case No.	I Place of Father's Domicile or Quasi-domicile	II Place of Son's Birth	III Place of Son's Legal Origin	IV Place of Youth's Domicile at time of Ordination	V Proper Bishop for Ordination
1	A	A	A	A	A
2	A	A	A	A and C	A
3	A	A	A	C	—
4	A	B	A	A	A
5	A	B	A	B	—
6	A	B	A	C	—
7	A and C	A or C	A and C	A	A
8	A and C	A or C	A and C	C	C
9	A and C	A or C	A and C	A and C	A and C
10	D	D	D	D	D
11	D	D	D	A	—
12	D	B	D	D	D
13	D	B	D	B	—
14	D and E	D or E	D and E	D	D
15	D and E	D or E	D and E	E	E
16	D and E	D or E	D and E	D and E	D and E
17	A and D	A	A	A	A
18	A and D	A	A	D	—
19	A and D	B	A	A	A
20	A and D	B	A	B	—
21	A and D	B	A	D	—
22	A and D	D	A	A	A
23	A and D	D	A	C	—
24	A and D	D	A	D	—
25	A and D	D	A	A and D	A

Key: A and C = the dioceses of the place of domicile
D and E = the dioceses of the place of quasi-domicile
B = the diocese of the incidental place of birth

Case 1. The candidate still has at ordination the same diocesan domicile, e. g., at Chicago, which his father had at the time of the candidate's birth and where also the latter was actually born. Hence, the Archbishop of Chicago is the proper Bishop for ordination.

Case 2. The candidate still has at ordination the same diocesan domicile at Chicago which his father had at the time of the candidate's birth and where also the latter was actually born, but he also has a second domicile at St. Paul in addition to his original one. The Archbishop of Chicago, the place of his original domicile, is the proper Bishop *ratione domicilii una cum origine*, but the candidate also has the Archbishop of St. Paul as a proper Bishop *ratione simplicis domicilii sine origine.* The latter possibility, however, is not under consideration here and now.

Case 3. At the time of ordination the candidate has changed from his original domicile at Chicago, which is both his actual and legal place of origin, to a new domicile at St. Louis. Neither Archbishop is the proper Bishop for his ordination on the score of domicile together with origin.

Case 4. The candidate was born at Los Angeles, while his mother was on a journey away from the father's domicile at San Francisco. The son's legal place of origin is, nevertheless, at San Francisco. If he still has San Francisco as a domicile at the time for tonsure, its Archbishop is the proper Bishop for the ordination.

Case 5. The candidate was born at Los Angeles, while his mother was on a journey away from the father's domicile at San Francisco. His legal place of origin is still San Francisco, but at the time for tonsure he has changed his domicile to Los Angeles, where he had actually been born (i. e., while his mother was on a journey). The Archbishop of Los Angeles, the place of birth, is not the proper Bishop *ratione domicilii una cum origine,* because in the case the actual birthplace is not identical with the legal place of origin.

Case 6. The candidate was born at Los Angeles, while his mother was on a journey away from the father's domicile at San Francisco. The son's legal place of origin is San Francisco. Yet, at the time for tonsure he has established his domicile in a new diocese, San Diego, which is different both from the diocese of his legal place of origin and from the diocese where he had actually been born. Manifestly the Bishop of San Diego is not constituted the proper Bishop for ordination *ratione domicilii una cum origine,* but merely *ratione simplicis domicilii sine origine.*

Cases 7, 8, and 9. The candidate can claim two dioceses as his legal place of birth, e. g., Philadelphia and Camden, because his parents had a winter home in the former and a summer seashore home in the latter diocese at the time of his birth. Even if he was born in their summer domicile he would still have Philadelphia as a legal place of origin as well as Camden. If, at the time for tonsure, his sole domicile was Camden, its Bishop would be the proper Bishop; or if his sole domicile at the time for tonsure was Philadelphia, its Archbishop would be the proper Bishop; and if at the time of tonsure he still retained both domiciles, he could select either the Bishop of Camden or the Archbishop of Philadelphia to tonsure him, and the one he selected would thus be acknowledged as the proper Bishop by reason of domicile together with origin.

Case 10. At the time of the candidate's birth the father had only a quasi-domicile at Baltimore, and there the candidate was born. Baltimore thus became the candidate's legal place of origin. Later on, the candidate acquires a domicile at Baltimore, and still retains it when he is admitted for tonsure. The Archbishop of Baltimore is the proper Bishop.

Case 11. At the time of the candidate's birth the father had only a quasi-domicile at Baltimore, and there the candidate was born. Baltimore thus became the candidate's legal place of origin. Before tonsure, however, the candidate acquires a domicile in the diocese of Richmond. Neither the Bishop of Richmond nor the Archbishop of Baltimore is competent as a proper Bishop *ratione domicilii una cum origine.*

Case 12. With nothing but a quasi-domicile at Baltimore, the parents make a journey to New York, and there a son is born to them. The legal place of the son's origin is still Baltimore, and if, at the time for tonsure, the candidate has acquired a domicile at Baltimore, its Archbishop is competent to ordain.

Case 13. With only a quasi-domicile at Baltimore, the parents make a journey to New York, and there a son is born to them. The legal place of the son's origin is still Baltimore. If, prior to ordination, the candidate has acquired a domicile at New York, he could not look upon either Archbishop, whether of Baltimore or of New York, as being competent for the ordination by reason of domicile together with origin.

Cases 14, 15, and 16. The parents have two quasi-domiciles, one in Harrisburg and one in Pittsburgh, and a son is born to them either in one or in the other diocese. Both dioceses are considered the son's legal place of origin. If, when the son becomes a candidate for tonsure, he has acquired a domicile at Harrisburg, its Bishop will be the proper Bishop; if at Pittsburgh, the Bishop of that diocese will be the proper Bishop; if he happens to have acquired both places simultaneously as domiciles, both Bishops will have equal competence for the ordination, and the candidate himself will have to make a choice.

Case 17. When the candidate was born at Wilmington, his parents had a domicile in that city, and a quasi-domicile at Raleigh. Wilmington is the legal place of origin, and, if the domicile at Wilmington is still retained at the time for tonsure, the Bishop of Wilmington is the proper Bishop.

Case 18. When the candidate was born at Wilmington, his parents had a domicile in that city, and a quasi-domicile at Raleigh. Wilmington is the legal place of his origin. In the event that the domicile at Wilmington was given up, and one at Raleigh was acquired prior to the conferment of tonsure, neither Bishop will be the proper Bishop by reason of domicile together with origin.

Case 19. While having a domicile at Wilmington and a quasi-domicile at Raleigh, the parents make a business trip to Savannah, and while there a son is born to them. The son's legal place of birth is still considered to be Wilmington, and the Bishop of that city will be the proper Bishop to tonsure the youth, if his parents still have their domicile at Wilmington when he becomes a clerical candidate.

Case 20. While having a domicile at Wilmington and a quasi-domicile at Raleigh, the parents make a business trip to Savannah, and while there a son is born to them. The son's legal place of birth is still considered to be at Wilmington. If the parents have changed their domicile to Savannah at the time their son becomes a candidate for tonsure, he will not be able to consider any of the three Bishops, namely, of Wilmington, of Raleigh, or of Savannah, as the proper Bishop for conferring his tonsure by reason of domicile together with origin.

Case 21. While having a domicile at Wilmington and a quasi-domicile at Raleigh, the parents make a business trip to Savannah, and while there a son is born to them. The son's legal place of birth is still considered to be at Wilmington. Should the parents change their domicile to Raleigh prior to their son's entrance into the clerical state, he will not be able to consider any of the three Bishops, namely, of Wilmington, of Raleigh, or of Savannah, as the proper Bishop for conferring his tonsure by reason of domicile together with origin.

Case 22. Let it be supposed that the parents had a domicile at Boston and a quasi-domicile at Portland, and a son was born to them at Portland. The legal place of origin is Boston. The Archbishop of Boston would be the proper Bishop for the son's later tonsure, if at that time he still had his domicile at Boston.

Case 23. The parents had a domicile at Boston and a quasi-domicile at Portland, and a son was born to them at Portland. The legal place of origin is Boston. If, at the time for tonsure, the candidate's parents had abandoned the domicile at Boston, and had acquired a new domicile at Providence, no Bishop would be the proper Bishop for their son's ordination under the heading of domicile together with origin.

Case 24. The parents had a domicile at Boston and a quasi-domicile at Portland, and a son was born to them at Portland. The legal place of origin is Boston. If, at the time for tonsure, the parents had established a full domicile at Portland, and had lost their former domicile at Boston, neither the Archbishop of Boston nor the Bishop of Portland would be the proper Bishop for their son's ordination under the heading of domicile together with origin.

Case 25. The parents had a domicile at Boston and a quasi-domicile at Portland, and a son was born to them at Portland. His legal place of origin is Boston. At the time when he is preparing for tonsure it so happens that his parents still have their domicile at Boston, but in addition have established a full domicile also at Portland. The Archbishop of Boston is the only proper Bishop for the son's ordination on the score of domicile together with origin. The Bishop of Portland is not his proper Bishop on this score, because Portland, while being the actual place of his birth, is not his legal place of origin.

2°. Through simple acquired diocesan domicile fortified by an oath

. . . **aut simplex domicilium sine origine; sed in hoc altero casu promovendus debet animum in dioecesi perpetuo manendi iureiurando firmare** . . . —Can. 956.

In the chart given above,[86] whenever the candidate for ordination has a newly acquired domicile different from the legal place of his origin, the proper Bishop in column five is not designated. This is to signify that the candidate has no proper Bishop on the first basis of " domicile together with origin," but has one on the second basis of domicile alone, provided that his intention of remaining there permanently be fortified by an oath. In all these cases the proper Bishop will, of course, be the one of the diocese designated in the fourth column of the chart, i. e., where the candidate has a domicile at the time of his ordination.

a) The oath

§ 1. *Reason for oath.*—Pope Innocent XII, in his Constitution "*Speculatores,*" [87] was the first to demand an oath as a requisite

[86] P. 325.

[87] Nov. 4, 1694, § 5—*Fontes*, n. 258.

for acquiring a domicile for ordination whenever this domicile differed from the candidate's original one. It was the purpose of this oath to strengthen the formal element of the mind to remain permanently, since that could be no more than conjectured from other facts such as the transference of one's goods or an actual stay of ten years. Since ordination required a life's service in the diocese or locality for which one offered himself, it was plain that at the time of ordination the formal element of intention to remain permanently in one's domicile was most important, and could not be left to conjecture. Especially did the oath become necessary when, in 1898, the material element of residence for acquiring a domicile was reduced to a minimum.[88] It was insisted upon in the Sacred Congregation of the Council's Decree of Nov. 24, 1906,[89] for laymen who were candidates for tonsure in a new diocese; and, not long afterwards, it was adopted into the Code in the canon under discussion. Here, as in its original form in the "*Speculatores,*" it applies to all laymen who have an acquired, instead of an original, domicile at the time they seek to be elevated to the clerical state, no matter whether the same was acquired by ten years of residence, or by mere entrance into the place *per modum inhabitantis* as prescribed in canon 92, § 1. This latter canon does not mention the oath because it gives the requisites for acquiring a domicile in general, not one *quoad ordinationem.*

At first sight one might be inclined to argue that another reason for the oath is the limiting of the competency for ordination to one Bishop. A man might have two acquired domiciles simultaneously for all purposes except ordination, for then he must make a choice and take the oath to remain in one of them permanently, making its Bishop competent to ordain him on the score of "simple acquired domicile fortified by an oath," whereas the diocesan Bishop of the other place of domicile, by the same oath, is automatically ruled out as a proper Bishop for ordination.

[88] S. C. C., decr. "*A primis,*" 20 iulii 1898, 2°—*ASS*, XXXI (1898-1899), 49 ss.; *Fontes*, n. 4307.

[89] N. 3—*ASS*, XXXIX (1906), 600 ss.

This argument, however, would not be strictly correct. In the same manner as a man can have the intention required to obtain two, or even as many as four, domiciles simultaneously,[90] so too he can emit an oath to guarantee each one of these intentions without contradiction or perjury. The question is hardly more than theoretical, because he could be making his studies in only one seminary, and that is where he would be summoned to take the oath. But, even granted that he had taken an oath to guarantee the stability of two or more domiciles, all Bishops, except the one for whose diocese he becomes tonsured, lose their competency to ordain him as soon as he is thereby incardinated into the one.

From the above interpretation of the oath as a part of the requisites for the very acquisition of a domicile for ordination purposes, there arises the question whether or not a minor can elicit it. Logically the answer must be in the negative. A minor necessarily has the domicile of his father; his own mind does not enter into it. Hence an oath to fortify his own intention would be useless. If it were assumed that the minor could take the oath to remain where his father's domicile now is, and suddenly, after tonsure, the father had to answer the call of his employer to take up a position and residence several thousand miles away, it equivalently would exile the son from his father's house, and the oath's fulfillment would weigh very heavily on young shoulders. For that reason the Sacred Congregation of the Council, in its Decree of Nov. 24, 1906,[91] warned Bishops not to admit to tonsure, and consequently to the eliciting of its preliminary oath of permanent residence, any youth, who had left his original domicile, until after he had reached his majority and was able to choose a domicile of his own. Is this warning still to be heeded? The Code does not mention age in canon 956, but it does say that the oath is to fortify the intention of establishing a simple domicile in the diocese. Whose domicile, one might ask,—the youth's? If he be a minor, by canon 93, § 1, he does not have a domicile of his

[90] Cf. *supra*, pp. 321-322.

[91] *ASS*, XXXIX (1906), 600 ss.

own. Hence, for a minor, the domicile spoken of in canon 956 is that of the candidate's father or guardian. Consequently, the oath should not be taken by the candidate until he is 21 years of age and able to make his necessary domicile a voluntary one.[92] The only exception to this would be the case in which a father or guardian expressly allowed his son or ward in his minority to establish his own domicile.[93]

§ 2. *Nature of oath.*—There are four different oaths which might enter into the ordination process. The first is the present one of canon 956, by which a layman, desirous of being included among the clergy of a diocese other than the one that connotes his legal place of origin, guarantees his intention of establishing a domicile in the new diocese. This is required of him in order that he may obtain a proper Bishop for his promotion to the clerical state. Hence it must be emitted before tonsure can be received. The second, treated of in canon 117, 3°, is prescribed for the cleric who is formally excardinated, and by it he pledges perpetual service to the new diocese. The third, made mandatory by canon 981, is exacted of the cleric who is a candidate for major orders for the " title of service of the diocese," and consists in his sworn promise to devote himself perpetually to the service of the diocese in which he is already incardinated. This oath is new and differs from the mission oath inasmuch as it does not include a promise not to enter the religious state. The fourth, likewise prescribed by canon 981, is taken by the cleric who is a candidate for major orders for the " title of the mission," in places subject to the jurisdiction of the Sacred Congregation for the Propagation of the Faith. By it he promises to devote himself perpetually to the service of the particular mission to which he is to be sent.

Note that the first of these oaths, which alone is being considered here, does not refer to the service of the diocese, but rather simply qualifies or fortifies the election of a domicile. It adds the weight of religion to the formal element required

92 D'Angelo, " De prima tonsura—Consultatio,"—*Apollinaris* (*Apoll.*), I (1928), 181-182; Cappello, " Collatio primae tonsurae,"—*Per.*, XIX (1930), 39*.

93 Cf. *supra*, pp. 318-319.

for the acquisition of a domicile for any purpose as contained in canon 92, § 1. Since, then, the intention in that canon admits the contingency expressed in the clause "*si nihil inde avocet,*" so too does the oath of canon 956. There is no prescription that the oath be taken immediately before tonsure. It may be taken several years in advance of that occasion, e. g., at the inception of the philosophical or theological course, provided, however, that the youth has reached his majority. The mere foreseeing of contingencies which might cause him to withdraw from that domicile in the intervening period prior to tonsure would not nullify his oath any more than it would his initial intention. Once tonsure is received, he becomes subject to the Bishop by a new tie, and loses his right to change his domicile at will. Thereafter he needs excardination to effect a legitimate change.

On the other hand, it has been stated above [94] that the will or intention is suspended if made conditional on some future event, for then the intention to establish a domicile does not become effective until the expected event has taken place. Such an intention is insufficient to establish a domicile, and, similarly, such a conditioned oath would be inadmissible in canon 956. Would a youth's intention to remain in a diocese provided that he succeed in being ordained a priest be absolute or suspensive? Vermeersch,[95] Woywod,[96] and Moeder [97] consider it as no more suspensive than any other intention. With this opinion it is difficult to agree. That would make the rejection of candidates for the priesthood such a rarity as to be classifiable with such unforeseen contingencies as earthquakes and the loss of fortune, which is certainly not the experience of the average seminarian, even after he is admitted to theological studies. A case of this

[94] P. 313.

[95] *Epitome* (4. ed., 1930), I, n. 183.

[96] *A Practical Commentary on the Code of Canon Law* (2 vols., New York: J. Wagner, 1925), I, 40.

[97] *The Proper Bishop for Ordination and Dimissorial Letters*, The Catholic University of America, Canon Law Studies, n. 95 (Washington, D. C.: The Catholic University of America, 1935), p. 51.

nature came up for consideration before the Sacred Congregation of the Council from the diocese of Manizales, Colombia, South America, in 1905.[98] True it is that it referred to the law of the "*Speculatores*," but at least it is illustrative of the mind of the Consultors of that Sacred Congregation with regard to conditional intention for domicile. The Bishop of Manizales had a number of youths in his seminary who, for just reasons, had left their families and homes in the diocese of their birth, and had come to his diocese with the intention of remaining, provided that they were admitted to holy orders. Because of their conditional intention, and his inability to get the Bishop of their place of origin to issue *litterae dimissoriae* for them, he doubted that he could be considered their proper Bishop for ordination on the score of acquired domicile, and submitted his doubts to Rome. In the "*animadversiones*" it is written: "In casu deesse videtur animus perpetuo manendi; praefati enim adolescentes ita animo dispositi exhibentur, ut in dioecesi Manizalensi perpetuo manerent, si tamen ad ordines promoverentur. Eorum igitur animus esset consequens non autem antecedens ordinationis actum contra sacros Canones domicilium constitutum et non constituendum pro ordinibus praescribentes." The decision was not based on this particular point; it merely gave to the Bishop of Manizales for a three-year period the privilege of ordaining such youths without fulfilling the conditions of the common law. But this case is quoted by Kinane[99] to substantiate his view that a youth's intention to remain "if I get ordained" is not sufficient to acquire a new domicile.

More recently, Maroto, likening the intention of a clerical candidate who abandons his old domicile to take up a new one in the place where he expects ordination to that of a woman who departs from her old home to take up her residence in the place where her intended husband lives, held that both intentions were conditional and, therefore, insufficient to effect either the loss of the old or the acquisition of the new domicile, at least unless the contrary, unusual, and unnatural intention in a

[98] *ASS*, XXXVII (1904-1905), 775 ss.

[99] *IER*, 5th series, XIV (1919), 320-322.

specific case were established by indubitable proof.[100] This view indeed seems to be the correct one.

A young layman, let it be supposed, leaves his home in Ireland and comes to the United States of America to study for the priesthood with a view to laboring in Los Angeles, but he makes his studies in Baltimore. If it so happens later that he is rejected for ill health or unsatisfactory studies, what does he do? He either returns to his home in Ireland, or he travels around the United States until he finds a position to his liking. His mind upon coming here, therefore, is certainly not to settle down in Los Angeles for life, come what may. It takes some event such as the finding of a position to settle his mind for him. The fact that he proceeded at once to Los Angeles to make his studies would not alter this conditional state of mind.

A sample formula of the oath required to establish an ordinational domicile [101] might be the following:

> Ego ———— habens simplex domicilium, at non originem, in dioecesi X coram Domino voveo ac juro in eadem dioecesi me perpetuo manere velle. Sic me Deus adjuvet et haec Sancta Evangelia quae manibus tango. In quorum fide subsigno ———, die ———.[102]

The clause "*si nihil inde avocet,*" or similar ones, such as "*nisi sanitati officiat*" or "*dum alia commodior vel sanior non se offerat habitatio,*" might be inserted into the oath after the word "*velle,*" if so desired, but of course they would lose all force as soon as first tonsure had been received.[103]

As in the case of a newly incardinated cleric, the oath should be taken before the Ordinary or his delegate, in which latter event a written declaration of the fact should be made and subscribed by the delegate.[104]

100 "De episcopo proprio quoad ordinationem,"—*Apoll.*, V (1932), 238-245.

101 By this term, wherever hereinafter used, understand an acquired domicile fortified by an oath.

102 Mahoney, "The Tonsure and Incardination,"—*AER*, LXXXII (1930), 398.

103 Gasparri, *De Sacra Ordin.*, II, n. 834.

104 Mahoney, *art. et loc. cit.*

b) Exceptions from the oath

... **nisi agatur de promovendo ... —Can. 956.**

One of the problems of the codification of Canon Law was to make the laws agree with one another, so that there would be no contradictions. This is admirably achieved through the use of technical wording, as well as through careful, explicit exceptions. Frequently in the statement of one canon there must be inserted such an expression as "*salvo praescripto canone*—," e. g., in canon 95, to save another canon from being nullified. It is an old adage that the exception attests the rule. In the matter of acquiring an ordinational domicile, the general rule of canon 956 must suffer exceptions because of the implicit contradictions that would otherwise exist in canons 111, § 2; 969, § 2; and 964, 4°.

From the punctuation in canon 956 it must be admitted that the "*nisi agatur*" clause introducing the exceptions really does modify the immediately preceding clause concerning the oath, inasmuch as that is separated from *nisi agatur* by only a comma, and not the second preceding clause concerning the proper Bishop, which is closed off from the rest of the sentence by a semicolon.[105] The sense of the *nisi agatur* clause, therefore, is this: "Although all candidates for ordination who have lost their original domicile must acquire a new domicile, and take an oath to their present intention of establishing it as such, this oath need not be taken by the cleric who is already incardinated into a diocese through first tonsure according to the norm of canon 111, § 2; nor by the layman who is to be incardinated only temporarily into the diocese of his domicile, with a view to future excardination to a more needy diocese, as is expressly allowed in canon 969, § 2; nor, finally, by the professed Religious whose ordination is governed by the law for seculars, as described in canon 964, 4°." The reason for each of the exceptions will be given at greater length below.

105 Vermeersch-Creusen, *Epitome*, II, n. 239; Woywod, *The New Canon Law* (New York, 1918), p. 799; Meehan—*AER*, LVII (1917), 499; Macerlean—*Cath. Ency.*, *Canon Law Supplement*, p. 54.

§ 1. *Clerics already incardinated by first tonsure* (. . . **nisi agatur de promovendo ad ordines clerico qui dioecesi per primam tonsuram iam incardinatus est . . .**)—Can. 956.

This clause has caused much trouble to the interpreters of the Code. It is out of place in its present setting. The Pontifical Commission for the Interpretation of the Code has shown beyond doubt in recent responses that canon 956 deals only with the proper Bishop for seculars' first elevation to the clerical state.[106] After a youth has been tonsured, his domicile, whether original or acquired with or without an oath, makes little difference as far as future orders are concerned. His proper Bishop is the one into whose diocese he has been incardinated. Knowing that, one finds it difficult to explain why a cleric's status should be put down as an exception to a layman's requirement. The lapse of twenty-three years before an authoritative opinion was given on the scope of canon 956, during which time many eminent authors taught the contradictory opinion, leads one to believe that the framers of the canon must have intended it to apply to clerics as well as to laymen, and that only after the years had brought to light the unwieldy consequences of such a wide interpretation, has a limitation been officially declared by the Committee wisely appointed for that purpose. But more of this below under C.

In order to clarify the meaning of this particular clause, one may assume three hypotheses:

1st Hypothesis.—Charles, a layman of twenty-one years of age, had the legal place of his birth in the diocese of Altoona, but moved with his parents some years later to the archdiocese of Baltimore, where they fixed their domicile. Charles begins to study for the priesthood for the service of the archdiocese of Baltimore. Before he can be tonsured, he must take the oath of canon 956 that it is his intention to establish his own voluntary domicile at Baltimore. He is then tonsured for the same archdiocese, and thereby becomes incardinated into it by force of canon 111, § 2. A year later, when, as a cleric, Charles becomes a candidate for minor orders, he does not need to take again the

[106] Cf. *infra*, pp. 369-370.

oath for the establishment of a domicile. In the first place, the oath which he did take fixed his own domicile in perpetuity, and hence need not be renewed; and secondly, since he is already incardinated in Baltimore, his obligation to remain springs from the fact of incardination rather than from any oath.[107]

2nd Hypothesis.—Charles, after leaving his birthplace at Altoona, comes with his parents to Baltimore, where they establish their domicile. Some time later, hearing of the paucity of priests in the diocese of Baker City, thousands of miles away, he obtains permission from both Bishops, viz., of Baltimore and of Baker City, to study for the service of the latter diocese. He makes his studies at Baltimore or at nearby Emmitsburg, and when the time comes for him to be tonsured, although ordinarily he would first have to take the oath of canon 956, in this case he cannot take it, because he does not intend to make Baltimore his voluntary domicile. He is tonsured by the Archbishop of Baltimore, his sole proper Bishop, for the service of the diocese of Baker City, by which he becomes *ipso facto* incardinated into the latter diocese. Still he remains at the same seminary. When he is ready for minor orders, it is the Bishop of Baker City who is the proper Bishop to ordain him or to issue the necessary dimissorial letters for his ordination by some other Bishop, even though Charles never yet has set foot in the diocese of Baker City. Before receiving minor orders, manifestly he will not have to take an oath to establish his domicile at Baltimore, first, because he has no intention to stay, and secondly, because it is not the Bishop of his place of domicile, but the Bishop of his diocese of incardination, who is now the proper Bishop to ordain him. Nor will he have to take any preliminary oath to establish a domicile in Baker City, first, because one cannot swear to remain where one has not yet been, and secondly, because, even if he proceeds to his destination, it is not on the score of domicile anyhow that the Bishop of Baker City is the proper Bishop for his ordination.

3rd Hypothesis.—Abandoning Altoona for Baltimore, Charles remains in the domicile of his parents there, but later seeks and

107 Vidal, "Il Nuovo Codice di Diritto Canonico,"—*La Civiltà Cattolica,* LXIX (1918), 218.

obtains permission to study at Little Rock Seminary for the service of the diocese of Little Rock. His stay in that diocese does not constitute a new domicile, because of his conditional intention to remain there only if he succeeds in becoming ordained. At tonsure, it is the Archbishop of Baltimore, who is still the proper Bishop over him, who will issue dimissorial letters (*litterae dimissoriae*) to the Bishop of Little Rock to tonsure him for the service of Little Rock. This will immediately incardinate him in that latter diocese, and make its Bishop the proper Bishop for all future orders. No oath is taken by Charles before tonsure to establish his domicile at Baltimore, because he does not intend to remain in Baltimore, even though the material element of residence in that archdiocese still perdures during a part of every year. Nor is any oath to acquire a domicile at Little Rock taken before tonsure, because the Bishop of that city is not as yet his proper Bishop. When, as a cleric he is to be admitted to the reception of minor orders, he does not need to take an oath to establish his intention of residing in the diocese of Little Rock, because the obligation of residing there already springs from the fact of incardination.

In these hypothetical cases the immediate concern is with the exemption from the oath for Charles, not as a *lay* candidate for tonsure, but only as a *cleric* ascending to higher orders. Whatever might be said for or against the propriety of the clause under consideration in this particular canon, one thing is certain, that the oath need not be taken by any *cleric* in Charles' position.

Some difficulty in the interpretation is occasioned by the words "*per primam tonsuram.*" First tonsure is not the only way by which incardination is brought about. It is also and more properly effected by formal letters,[108] and by the legally permitted acquisition of an alien residential benefice.[109] When canon 956 exempts from the domiciliary oath clerics who have been incardinated through first tonsure, does it mean to make the taking of the oath obligatory on clerics incardinated by the

[108] Can. 112.

[109] Can. 114.

other two methods? If the opinion that canon 956 establishes domicile as the only basis for a proper Bishop for clerics as well as for laymen were to be followed, the reply would have to be given affirmatively, especially since the words "*per primam tonsuram*" apparently were inserted designedly. Even then, it would seem to be a superfluous obligation, because those who are incardinated formally are already implicitly bound to residence by the oath of perpetual service prescribed in canon 117, and those incardinated by a residential benefice are already bound to residence by the very nature of the benefice. However, it is now known that canon 956 applies only to lay candidates for tonsure, and hence the oath for an ordinational domicile is a requisite for them only, and not for clerics already canonically attached to a diocese, no matter by what method they became attached. In either sense of the canon, the phrase *per primam tonsuram* as well as the entire clause *nisi agatur de promovendo ad ordines clerico* etc. is unwarranted. Even by disregarding the punctuation, and by considering the exceptions as pertaining to the proper Bishop rather than to the oath, there would still remain the difficulty of establishing who is the proper Bishop for minor clerics incardinated in a diocese by formal letters or by the conferring of a residential benefice. Indeed, the identity of the proper Bishop for any of the exempted classes would then be a matter for speculation.

The word *dioecesi* gives a little help in the elucidation of the exception, because it is without a modifier, and, therefore, signifies any diocese whatsoever. At least it shows that the legislator, in exempting an incardinated cleric from taking the domiciliary oath, did not have in mind merely the ordination of a cleric to higher orders for the diocese wherein he has already acquired a domicile and wherein he had previously emitted the same oath before tonsure. Otherwise it would have been modified to read "*suo dioecesi.*"

§ 2. *Lay candidates for tonsure destined for deferred alien incardination* (. . . **vel nisi agatur de promovendo alumno, qui servitio alius dioecesis destinatur ad normam can. 969, § 2 . . .**) —Can. 956.

A full discussion of canon 969, § 2, is reserved for its more appropriate place in article III of this Chapter. Suffice it to say here that, despite the age-old law that no one be ordained unless he be necessary or useful to the churches of his diocese, a special exception is made by which a Bishop may ordain his own laymen, even though they be unnecessary in their proper diocese, as long as he foresees a future demand for them in other dioceses. Since the exact diocese of destination is presumed to be unknown, the Bishop must incardinate such candidates into his own diocese temporarily, until the time when they will be excardinated from his own and incardinated into that alien diocese which seeks them.

In the event that these lay candidates have only an acquired domicile in the diocese of the ordaining Prelate, the question arises, must they obey the general law of canon 956 to emit an oath guaranteeing domicile in their present diocese? The answer is "no." They are explicitly exempted from doing so by the above-quoted clause of canon 956. The reason is plain. They know the conditions under which they are to be tonsured, and hence have no intention of perpetually remaining in their present well-supplied diocese.

This excepting clause does not refer to the further promotion of the same subjects after they have become clerics, because such a category was already exempted in the preceding clause.

§ 3. *Professed Religious of non-exempt Congregations and those belonging to non-exempt societies without vows* (. . . **vel nisi agatur de promovendo religioso professo, de quo in can. 964, n. 4 . . .**)—Can. 956.

Canon 964 deals with the proper Bishop for the ordination of Religious. For ordination purposes it is necessary to divide all Religious into two categories, exempt and non-exempt from the jurisdiction, namely, of the local Ordinary. The exempt include all members of Religious Orders, properly so-called, and all those who, by reason of their constitutions, make solemn profession.[110] These are said to be exempt by common law.

[110] Canons 488, 2°, 7°; 615.

The non-exempt by common law include all members of Congregations with simple vows, whether temporary or perpetual. However, some of these Congregations enjoy a special papal privilege exempting them; and some others have received an Indult to grant dimissorial letters to their members. For the purpose of ordination these two latter groups are included among the exempt class. Then, there are societies of men living in common without vows, to which many of the canons concerning Religious apply. Some of these societies also have received an Indult to issue dimissorial letters to their members, and they, too, for ordination purposes are enumerated amongst the exempt Religious.

To summarize, exempt Religious, as far as ordination is concerned, include those who belong: a) to a Religious Order or to an Institute wherein the constitutions require solemn profession; b) to a Congregation with simple vows, but exempted from the jurisdiction of the local Ordinary by special papal privilege; c) to a non-exempt Congregation, which has an Indult to grant *litterae dimissoriae;* or d) to a society of men living in common without vows, which has an Indult to grant *litterae dimissoriae.*

Non-exempt Religious, as far as the ordination laws are concerned, include those who belong: a) to non-exempt Congregations which make perpetual profession, no matter whether the individual's vows at the time are perpetual or temporary, provided, however, that the Congregation have neither a privilege of exemption nor an Indult to issue *litterae dimissoriae;* b) to non-exempt Congregations which make only temporary profession, and which do not possess a special privilege or Indult; or c) to societies of men without vows, which have no special Indult to issue *litterae dimissoriae.*

N. 4 of canon 964 in the words "*ordinatio ceterorum omnium alumnorum cuiusvis religionis*" refers to all in the non-exempt group,[111] and it rules that their ordination is to follow the same laws as govern secular clerics' ordination.

[111] Moeder, *The Proper Bishop for Ordination and Dimissorial Letters*, p. 107.

One of these laws is that of canon 956, that the proper Bishop is the Bishop of the place of original domicile or of the place of acquired ordinational domicile (i. e., of domicile without origin, but guaranteed with an oath). This means that anyone in the non-exempt group has for his proper Bishop for tonsure and minor orders the same Bishop whom he had as a proper Bishop before he entered religion. That Bishop alone can licitly ordain him or issue *litterae dimissoriae* for him to be ordained, although the religious Superior is empowered to present him as a candidate to the Bishop. When perpetual profession has been made, the cleric, by virtue of canon 585, loses the diocese, domicile, and Bishop he had in the world, and from then on is considered to have a domicile in the place where he is stationed as a member of the religious family of a certain house,[112] and the Bishop of that place becomes the proper Bishop for his elevation to higher, especially major, orders. It follows that non-exempt Religious, who belong to Congregations whose members never take perpetual vows, or to societies of men without vows, even though they take a final oath or promise to remain perpetually in the society, never lose the proper Bishop of the domicile they had in the world.

What canon 956 means, in excepting all those in the non-exempt religious category from the obligation of taking the oath of domicile, is that when these are to receive tonsure, even though they had left their original domicile and, before entering religion, had acquired only a simple domicile for general purposes according to canon 92, § 1, nevertheless, that simple domicile alone makes the Bishop of that diocese the proper one to tonsure them after presentation by their religious Superior. This exception is granted for good reasons. A person becomes affiliated with a religion by any religious profession. Assignment or affiliation, as spoken of in canon 111, § 1, is not the same as incardination in § 2 of the same canon. Rather it is to incardination as a *genus* is to a *species*. Prior to perpetual profession, however, religious affiliation is not absolute, as any incardination would be, since the law itself states in canon 585

[112] *CpR*, II (1921), 304.

that only by perpetual profession is the diocese which the Religious had in the world lost.[113]

When anyone in the non-exempt religious category spoken of in canon 964 [114] receives tonsure, by that very fact he becomes a cleric, but does not thereby become incardinated into the diocese of his place of domicile, since he is already by temporary profession, or by something similar, such as an oath or promise in societies without vows, affiliated with his respective Religious Congregation or society. All that canon 111, § 1, demands is that every cleric be attached to some diocese or Religious Institute. In the case of the Religious, this is guaranteed by having him affiliated with the religion before he can be made a cleric. For non-exempt Religious, by canon 964, 4°, coupled with canon 956, it is the Bishop of the place of original or acquired domicile who is the proper Bishop. If it should be the Bishop of the place of acquired domicile in a given case, of what use would it be to require the *religiosus tonsurandus* to emit an oath guaranteeing his intention to make that his permanent domicile? He belongs to a Religious Congregation or society which, as long as his vows or promises are in force, is to have the authority to station him wherever the religious Superiors see fit; and in addition to that, no matter where they send him, the common law itself still safeguards him in retaining his claim of the diocese where he has domicile, as long as his vows or promises are only temporary. Even if he be hundreds of miles away, it is his Bishop back home who must issue the dimissorial letters for his reception of tonsure or of higher orders, and that by force of the common law. When the Religious makes his perpetual profession, he loses the diocese and domicile he had in the world, because his intention then is definitely never to return to it. From that time on it is the Bishop of the place where the religious house in which he lives is situated who is the proper Bishop for ordination. Perchance that might be the Bishop of the very same diocese as before, but no longer on the score of the candi-

[113] Piontek, *De Indulto Exclaustrationis Necnon Saecularizationis*, The Catholic University of America, Canon Law Studies, n. 29 (Washington, D. C.: The Catholic University of America, 1925), p. 178.

[114] Cf. *supra*, p. 343.

date's former acquired domicile, but rather on the score of his present religious domicile.[115] Manifestly, there would be no sense in his taking an oath to establish his religious domicile, since he has perpetually submitted his will to that of his religious Superiors in this matter.

It is not within the province of this study to discuss the status of non-exempt Religious who, after receiving orders during temporary profession, later return to their diocese.[116]

§ 4. *Lay candidates for tonsure destined for immediate alien incardination.*—Only the three categories just enumerated are explicitly excepted from the oath of domicile in canon 956, and yet, for a far greater reason, a fourth category must be considered as implicitly excepted, namely, those lay candidates for the clerical state who have a simple acquired domicile, but who are to be tonsured by the Bishop of the place of that domicile for the service of an alien diocese. The fundamental truth that this type of immediate alien incardination is possible is contained in canon 111, § 2, and has been clarified by the Pontifical Commission for the Interpretation of the Code; but this will be better discussed in article III of this Chapter. What matters here is merely the question whether or not such a candidate needs an ordinational domicile (i. e., an acquired domicile, with a confirming oath) or just a simple acquired domicile [117] to have a proper Bishop to tonsure him.

Not only does he not need to take the oath, but he would be committing perjury if he did so. He cannot have the intention of permanently continuing in his present simple acquired domicile, because he is entering the service of another diocese altogether, and the imminent ceremony of tonsure will immediately incardinate him in that other diocese, whereupon his continuance or non-continuance in his present domicile will depend, not on his own will, but on that of the Bishop of incardination. If the candidate who is destined ultimately for the service of a diocese other than that of his simple acquired

[115] Cf. *supra*, p. 344, note 112.

[116] For discussion of this point cf. Piontek, *op. cit.*, esp. pp. 202-204, 222-224; Moeder, *op. cit.*, esp. pp. 106-114.

[117] Can. 92, § 1.

domicile is excused from the oath (exception § 2 above), *a fortiori* is the candidate in this case excused, and that is the opinion of eminent authors.[118]

A further question arises whether or not such a candidate would be obliged to take this oath as a guarantee of his intention of permanently residing in the future in the diocese of destination. At least a few authors hold that he is,[119] but their opinion seems to be incorrect. For one reason, the old method of acquiring a domicile by an oath alone has been abolished by canon 92, § 1, and in the present law there are two constituent elements to a domicile, material and formal, but the more fundamental of the two is the material.[120] Through it by itself a domicile can be acquired, but not through the formal element alone. The wording of canon 92, § 1, indicates that the material element of residence is in existence first, and the formal element of mind qualifies it. In the case under consideration, however, the material element of residence in the diocese of destination is not yet existent, and may not be for many years. The formal element of intention, posited prior to residence, would have no canonical effect as far as domicile is concerned. Again, to consider the oath of canon 956 as a means of insuring the cleric's going to his diocese of destination is to distort the meaning of the oath, and to add a superfluous bond where that of incardination will amply supply the need, for the cleric's obligation of going to the diocese of destination when its Bishop calls will flow canonically from the fact of incardination, not from any superadded oath. Finally, in view of recent decisions it is now certain that the Bishop of destination will be the proper Bishop for the candidate's elevation to higher orders on the score of incardination, and not on that of domicile, so that the oath guaranteeing domicile is unnecessary.[121]

118 Vermeersch-Creusen, *Epitome*, II, n. 239; Vermeersch, *Theologiae Moralis, Principia-Responsa-Consilia* (2. ed., 4 vols., Romae: Università Gregoriana, 1926-1927), (*Theol. Mor.*), III, n. 685; Maroto, "De episcopo proprio quoad ordinationem,"—*Apoll.*, V (1932), 243, n. 10.

119 E. g., Moeder, *The Proper Bishop for Ordination and Dimissorial Letters*, p. 61; Mahoney, "The Tonsure and Incardination,"—*AER*, LXXXII (1930), 404.

120 Cf. *supra*, p. 311.

121 Cf. *infra*, pp. 369-370.

B. For Promotion of Laymen Who Have No Domicile

For the first tonsure of a layman the only Bishop given as the proper Bishop in canon 956 is that of his place of domicile. It was just shown above that the exceptions mentioned in that canon did not relate to the Bishop of the place of domicile but to the oath qualifying that domicile. Not every layman, however, has a domicile. Though clerical *vagi* are not permitted by canon 111, § 1, lay *vagi* are by canon 91; and, furthermore, lay *vagi* are granted a proper Ordinary in canon 94, § 2, namely, the Ordinary of the place where the *vagus* actually resides, no matter how briefly. The question now arises, is the proper Ordinary of the lay *vagus* also the proper one *quoad ordinationem;* and if not, who is? Then, too, there are laymen who are *advenae,* i. e., who have a quasi-domicile only,[122] and these also have a proper Ordinary.[123] Does his designation as their proper Ordinary extend to the act of ordination as well?

1°. Who come under this heading

By " laymen who have no domicile " are meant both lay *vagi* and lay *advenae.* The expression does not refer to laymen who are *incolae* (living in the place where they have a domicile) or *peregrini* (on a journey away from their established domicile or quasi-domicile), except *peregrini* who were only *advenae* before they set out.

While a *clerical vagus* is a cleric who is not attached to any diocese or Religious Institute, even though he may have a domicile, a *lay vagus* is a lay person who does not have a domicile or quasi-domicile anywhere.[124] This last word is to be noted. While ever a lay person retains a domicile or quasi-domicile in any part of the world he is not a lay *vagus.* He can become such only if he has never had either one or the other, or, if he had them, has lost them. A domicile or quasi-domicile is lost only by actual departure from the place with the absolute in-

122 Can. 91.

123 Can. 94, § 1.

124 Can. 91.

tention of not returning as an inhabitant.[125] A good illustration of how well the possession of a domicile is protected by law as a *res favorabilis* is shown in the case of Religious who take only temporary vows. Though they remain in religion many years, the temporary character of their vows shows that they have not yet made the decision to abandon their home permanently, and so their domicile in the world still continues. Similarly, a layman's domicile is preserved for him, even when he leaves it, until it is clearly proved that he has formed the intention of abandoning it permanently. Of particular importance in this connection is the conditional intention when leaving. With such an intention a domicile is not lost. Thus, when a lay person who has reached his majority leaves his home diocese in quest of an alien Bishop who will accept him as a candidate for the priesthood in the service of the alien Bishop's diocese, his intention in abandoning his domicile is usually presumed to be conditioned on his success in securing a benevolent Bishop and on his subsequent actual reception of the order of priesthood. The contrary would have to be plainly and certainly established by sound arguments.[126] Even if he resided in the alien diocese for a considerable period of time, the same would hold true. A lay person who is still in his minority when he leaves his home does not lose his necessary domicile there, regardless of his intention, as is apparent from the words "*salvo praescripto can. 93*" in canon 95.

A lay *advena* is numbered amongst those who have no domicile because, while he resides in a definite place, his intention is such as to make his residence no more than a quasi-domicile. Thus, in the example cited above, if it were established with certainty that the lay person who is in his majority had really lost his former domicile, his residence in the alien diocese would still be a mere quasi-domicile because of the conditional intention; and it would become a domicile only when it were proved that he intended to stay there permanently, whether or not he would ultimately be accepted for the priesthood.

[125] Cf. *supra*, pp. 320-1, 323.

[126] Maroto, "De episcopo proprio quoad ordinationem,"—*Apoll.*, V (1932), 239-241.

When a lay *advena* starts to travel and thereby becomes a *peregrinus,* he is still a man with no domicile, even though he continues to retain his quasi-domicile.

It seems that much of the confusion which has surrounded this whole problem could have been avoided if writers had adhered to the technical terminology of the Code.[127]

2°. Reply of the Pontifical Code Commission in 1919

The canonical world was rife with discussion on this problem chiefly between the years 1919 and 1924, following a private reply by the Pontifical Commission for the Interpretation of the Code. The reply, made by letter to Cardinal Logue, Archbishop of Armagh, on Aug. 3, 1919, was in answer to four *dubia* which he had proposed, the first of which the Commission solved as follows:

> I. Quisnam sit Episcopus proprius pro ordinatione illorum qui nullum domicilium habent (c. 956).
>
> Resp. Ad I. Prout dubium exponitur: est Episcopus loci in quo fit ordinatio, modo tamen ordinandus praevie acquirat domicilium cum iuramento ad normam canonis 956.[128]

Immediately, consternation was displayed by the *Irish Theological Quarterly* [129] and the *Irish Ecclesiastical Record,*[130] both of which claimed that there had been a misunderstanding at Rome, and that the Pontifical Commission for the Interpretation of the Code had not grasped Ireland's difficulty at all. The Cardinal's query was about those who had no domicile, and the answer referred only to those who at the moment of ordination had a domicile. *Il Monitore Ecclesiastico* [131] defended the reply

[127] As an instance of this confusion cf. *The Irish Theological Quarterly,* XV (1920), 194, which cites as an example of those "who have no domicile" the student "with a domicile" in Cashel who intends to be ordained for Dublin and who spends three years at Maynooth in the archdiocese of Dublin with that in mind.

[128] *ITQ,* XIV (1919), 391-392; *ME,* XXXII (1920), 57. It was never published in the *Acta Apostolicae Sedis.*

[129] *Loc. cit.*

[130] Article by Kinane—5th series, XIV (1919), 320-322.

[131] *Loc. cit.,* and pp. 156 ff. of the same volume.

on the grounds that it was the questioner who was at fault for poorly wording his *dubium,* and that that was why the Commission intentionally said "*Prout dubium exponitur.*" If the query had been differently worded, no doubt a more satisfactory answer to the real problem would have been drawn.[132]

In analyzing the considerations *pro* and *contra,* one cannot fail to come to these conclusions with regard to the misunderstanding: 1) The Irish Cardinal had in mind, not those who "had no domicile," but those who at the time for tonsure "could not have one" as yet, either: (a) because of the defect of the material element of residence, although the formal element of intention was present; or (b) because of the defect of the proper formal element, even though the material element was present; or (c) because of a defect of both elements. 2) The Pontifical Commission for the Interpretation of the Code had interpreted the words of the query in their primary sense of lay *vagi, advenae,* and *advenae peregrini,*[133] and in that sense had correctly answered the question.

Ireland, it seems, at that time had a peculiar difficulty. There were no diocesan seminaries. There was but one National College for the Irish Church and several missionary colleges. When a young man over 21 years of age left his parental home to study in one of these missionary colleges for the foreign missions, it seems that according to the writers in the various Irish Ecclesiastical publications he made a complete break with his home, definitely and absolutely determined never to return again as a resident, and, consequently, that he lost his domicile, from which plight arose the difficulty as to which Bishop could later tonsure him.

In the United States of America, at least, it is difficult to understand this situation. Prior to the age of twenty-one, of course, a youth retains the domicile of his parents, no matter where he goes and no matter what his intention may be,[134]

132 For further discussion, cf. *ITQ*, XV (1920), 192-195; *Jus Pontif.*, III (1923), 7-9; *Per.*, XII (1924), 74-76.

133 Cf. *supra,* pp. 348-350.

134 Can. 95.

unless by special permission of his parents he be allowed to acquire a new domicile of his own. Unmistakably, it seems, this latter permission does not grant him the faculty of becoming a lay *vagus*. He still retains his parental domicile until he has actually established his residence with the proper intention in the new one.

After the age of twenty-one, a lay youth who leaves his home to study in a distant seminary, either for the diocese in which that seminary exists, or for some more distant one, is still considered to retain a voluntary domicile at his parents' home, because he returns " home " there during his vacation periods, and will ordinarily return there also if rejected for the priesthood.[135] Even if he should leave the country in search of a diocese for his clerical service, and go, for instance, to the West Indies, the same would still be true because of his conditional intention. His domicile is not lost until, after departure, his intention also of remaining away is shown to be final.

These methods of retaining a domicile are strictly in accordance with Canon Law, and would apply to any youth in Ireland or elsewhere if the circumstances were the same. Granted, however, that a lay youth over twenty-one years of age has actually lost his domicile, or has never had one, he becomes an *advena* or a *vagus* according to whether he has, or has not, at least a quasi-domicile. As soon as a question is raised about the ordination of such a one, at once it becomes automatically clear that the *advena* or *vagus* has in mind to settle down somewhere for life and to cease his temporary or wandering status, or, in other words, to establish a diocesan domicile, because to be ordained at all means to become incardinated into a definite diocese perpetually. The first and logical answer to the question regarding the one who is to tonsure him is to say that it is the Bishop of the place where he has decided to settle down and render his life's service. Anomalous as it may seem, therefore, the very notion of ordination for a *vagus* or an *advena*, who hitherto has had no domicile, means the intentional establishment of one, with the

[135] Schaaf, " Episcopus Proprius Ordinationis,"—*AER*, XC (1934), 354.

additional emission of an oath guaranteeing the intention according to canon 956. That was precisely what the Pontifical Commission said.

A distinct additional question is raised when it is premised that the *advena* or the *vagus* has, indeed, the mind to settle down and to become attached to a definite diocese, but that such an intention is impossible of execution at the present: (a) because the location of the diocese is too far distant here and now to establish residence immediately; or (b) because his mind is still conditioned on the reception of the priesthood; or (c) because his mind is thus conditioned and in addition the prospective diocese is too far away.

3°. The solution

Before Cardinal Logue submitted his queries, little, if anything, was known of the present interpretation of canon 111, § 2, as admitting of immediate alien incardination.[186] Hence, while one can excuse the general perplexity in the face of the original problem readily enough, it is easier still to understand the surprise and puzzled attitude of canonists towards the official interpretation of canon 111, § 2, when it was first issued simultaneously with the Pontifical Commission's response to Cardinal Logue's first query.

To give a complete solution to the question, "Who is the proper Bishop for the ordination of those who have no domicile?" one should, therefore, proceed as follows:

a) If the layman be a mere *advena* (whether *peregrinus* or not) or a *vagus*, the response *ad I^{um}* of the Pontifical Commission for the Interpretation of the Code on Aug. 3, 1919, is still valid. The Bishop of that diocese for whose service the candidate wishes to be tonsured becomes the proper Bishop for the initial ordination, after the candidate has arrived there with the absolute intention of remaining, and has, furthermore, in the presence of that Bishop or his delegate, taken an oath to guarantee this intention.

[186] Cf. *infra*, pp. 373 ff.

b) If the layman be an *advena* (whether *peregrinus* or not) or a *vagus* who has formed his mind to labor for life as a priest in some definite or indefinite diocese other than the one where he now is, and cannot yet posit both conditions, material and formal, together with the confirmatory oath for the acquisition of an ordinational domicile in that diocese,[187] then he has no proper Bishop for ordination at all. In that case, the Bishop of the diocese where the layman is making his studies needs to obtain for himself an Apostolic Indult, dispensing him from the requirement of obtaining dimissorial letters, so that he can tonsure the candidate for the service of the diocese of destination, if it be definite, or for his own diocese, with a view to later excardination by canon 969, § 2, if the diocese of destination be still indefinite.[188]

c) If the layman knows in advance that he is going to study for the priesthood, he can anticipate and prevent the problem from arising at all. If a lay youth over twenty-one years of age has a diocesan domicile, and yet desires to study for the service of an alien diocese, he should take care not to lose his domicile,[189] and, while still retaining it, either through correspondence or by a temporary journey, seek a Bishop willing to receive him. If he succeeds, his Bishop of domicile by canon 111, § 2, will still be the proper Bishop to tonsure him or to issue *litterae dimissoriae* relative thereto for the definite diocese of destination. If he does not succeed in finding a benevolent receiver, his Bishop of domicile by canon 969, § 2, will still be the proper Bishop to ordain him for his own diocese with a view to future excardination to the diocese of destination.

[187] Manifestly he is not one of those excused from the oath by the "*nisi agatur*" clause of can. 956, because all of them are *incolae*.

[188] *ME*, XXXII (1920), 156 ff.; Vermeersch, *Theol. Mor.*, III, n. 240; Davis, *Moral and Pastoral Theology*, IV, 22; Aertnys-Damen, *Theologia Moralis* (13. ed., 2 vols., Taurini: Domus Editorialis Marietti, 1939), II, n. 570, *Notanda*, 1; Mahoney, "The Tonsure and Incardination,"—*AER*, LXXXII (1930), 399-400, Case VI.

[189] It must not be overlooked that residence in a regional seminary, established as such by the authority of the Holy See (can. 1354, § 3) and supplying one's diocese of destination, is the same as residence in the destined diocese—S. C. C., *Dioecesium N. et X.*, 10 mar. 1923 (*AAS*, XVI [1924], 51-55); Schaaf, "Episcopus Proprius Ordinationis," (*AER*, XC [1934], 356, note 7). Cf. *supra*, p. 313.

It is to be observed that the Pontifical Commission for the Interpretation of the Code understood the original query as applying only to lay candidates for tonsure, as is evident from the adjoined phrase "*cum iuramento,*" for clerics were excused from the oath of canon 956 by its clause "nisi agatur de promovendo ad ordines clerico qui dioecesi per primam tonsuram iam incardinatus est." In this the Commission was correct, because canon 956, on which the first query was based, applied only to laymen, as will now be discussed more fully.

C. For the Elevation of Tonsured Clerics to Higher Orders

As consequent upon the detailed explanation of the grounds on which a Bishop becomes the proper Bishop for those who first need such a Bishop for ordination, namely, lay candidates for tonsure, logical sequence requires that the next consideration deal with the question, Who is the proper Bishop for these same men after they have become tonsured clerics? In the historical section it was seen that, prior to the Code, there were five titles of competency to promote this group to higher orders, and that none of the five titles except the last, namely, the title based on incardination, was exclusive of the rest. That was certainly not an ideal condition. As for laymen, so also for clerics, unity of competence was desirable. The result was that in the Code competence to ordain by reason of mere origin, of benefice, and of *familiaritas,* was eliminated. Canon 956 speaks of the Bishop of the place of domicile, that is, either of the original domicile or of the acquired ordinational domicile, as being the only proper Bishop for the ordination of seculars. Nowhere, either, is there a word of the proper Bishop by reason of incardination. Is it, then, true that the Code has also abolished this last title of competence, so that domicile is the only title by which a Bishop can be a proper Bishop for the ordination of clerics as well as of laymen? If so, it means that very often the Bishop of the diocese in which a cleric is incardinated is powerless, not only to advance in orders his own cleric, but even to issue dimissorial letters (*litterae dimissoriae*) for his advancement. Opinion on this question has been divided.

1°. Contending opinions

a) The Bishop of the place of domicile alone is the proper Bishop

Many good canonists adhered to the view that the Bishop of the place of domicile is the sole proper Bishop for the advancement in orders even of incardinated clerics.[140] Their arguments might be summarized thus: 1st) Canon 956 makes no distinction between laymen and clerics, and consequently must be applied to all indiscriminately, especially since the exceptions to the oath manifestly apply to clerics also. 2nd) The framers of the Code must have had before them the two famous pre-Code decrees of the Sacred Congregation of the Council through which the title of proper Bishop *ratione incardinationis* had been introduced, namely, the Decree " *A primis* " of July 20, 1898,[141] and that of Nov. 24, 1906,[142] and yet did not incorporate that particular feature from them—an omission which must have been deliberate, since they did incorporate other features of the same. 3rd) The precise reason why the titles of proper Bishops other than that of domicile were abolished was to insure the Bishop's having a sufficient knowledge of his *ordinandi.* Particularly the Bishop of incardination might never have seen the ordinand and be thousands of miles distant from him. 4th) This view does not interfere with the rights of the Bishop of incardination. He still remains the judge on the necessity or

[140] Bouuaert-Simenon, *Manuale Iuris Canonici* (2. ed., 3 vols., Wetteren, Belgium: De Meester et fils, 1930), n. 734; O'Donnell—*IER*, XI (1918), 363; Wernz-Vidal, *Ius Canonicum*, II, n. 61; Biederlack, "Inkardination und Ordination der Saekularkleriker nach dem jetzigen Kirchenrecht,"—*ZkT*, *XLVII* (1923), 50-58; d'Angelo, "De prima tonsura,"—*Apoll.*, I (1928), 181-182; Kinane—*IER*, XXXIV (1929), 410; Mahoney, "The Tonsure and Incardination,"—*AER*, LXXXII (1930), 405-406; Maroto, "De Episcopo proprio quoad ordinationem,"—*Apoll.*, V (1932), 245; Schaaf, "Episcopus Proprius Ordinationis,"—*AER*, XC (1934), 352-365; Cappello, *Tractatus Canonico-Moralis de Sacramentis*, Vol. II, Pars III, *De Sacra Ordinatione* (Romae: Marietti, 1935), 277-279; Woywod, "Proper Bishop for ordination of men transferred to another diocese by first tonsure,"—*HPR*, XXXVII (1937), 522-527; Browne, "Incardination and Ordination: a Recent Reply,"—*IER*, XLVIII (1936), 531-537.

[141] *ASS*, XXXI (1898-1899), 49 ss.; *Fontes*, n. 4307.

[142] *ASS*, XXXIX (1906), 600 ss.

utility of his diocese, and makes the decision whether or not, and when, the candidate is to be ordained. He also still retains authority over his clerical subject by virtue of canons 127 and 143, so that even the cleric's continued residence in the diocese of the place of domicile depends on his will. 5th) The reply of the Pontifical Commission for the Interpretation of the Code *ad IIum*, Aug. 3, 1919,[143] does not militate against this opinion, because it was only a private reply, and would need promulgation to change the import of canon 956 of the Code. 6th) The reply of the Pontifical Commission for the Interpretation of the Code to the Bishop of Santa Fé, Argentina, on Dec. 7, 1931,[144] does not overthrow canon 956, because it, too, was a private reply, needing promulgation if it is to be considered as extending, restricting, or clarifying the law; and because its terminology "*superiores ordines recipere debeat . . . ab Episcopo dioecesis cui rite iam incardinatus est,*" does not define who is the proper Bishop for a cleric, but merely declares it to be the incardinated cleric's duty to go to the diocese of destination and receive his higher orders from its Bishop, and not from some other Bishop through dimissorial letters. If followed out, the Bishop by title of incardination becomes also the Bishop by title of domicile.[145] 7th) Canon 956 would need a general change in its wording if the Bishop of incardination were to be recognized, and that can be done only by the Supreme Pontiff.

Some of the authors who championed the doctrine that the sole proper Bishop for ordination relative to all candidates alike is the Bishop of their place of domicile were apparently under the impression that, when a cleric became incardinated into an alien diocese, he likewise became domiciled there, either by going to it directly, or by acquiring it as a necessary domicile in virtue of canon 143.[146] Vidal [147] seemed to presume that every cleric

143 *ME*, XXXII (1920), 57.

144 For text cf. *infra*, p. 361.

145 For full treatment of this point cf. Browne, "Incardination and Ordination: a Recent Reply,"—*IER*, XLVIII (1936), 531-537.

146 Thus Cappello wrote: "Eo ipso quod clericus excardinatur a sua dioecesi et incardinatur alienae, *per se* necessario amittit domicilium, quod habebat in dioecesi excardinationis illudque obtinet in dioecesi incardinationis. Sane, cum clericus in-

was tonsured for his own home diocese, and so the Bishop of his place of domicile alone was competent to confer higher orders, because he was identical with the Bishop of incardination.

cardinatur *formaliter*, debet iureiurando coram Ordinario eiusve delegato declarare 'se *in perpetuum* novae dioecesis servitio velle adiici ad normam sacrorum canonum' (117, 3°). Haec autem voluntas de servitio novae dioecesi *in perpetuum* praestando, quomodo conciliari potest cum intentione *perpetuo* manendi in alia quoque dioecesi?

"Ubi agitur vero de excardinatione et incardinatione tacita aut aequivalenti, necesse est ut clericus ab Ordinario alienae dioecesis beneficium *residentiale* obtineat cum consensu sui Ordinarii in scriptis dato, vel cum licentia ab eodem in scriptis concessa e *dioecesi discedendi in perpetuum* (c. 114).

"Voluntatis actus, quo clericus in casu beneficium *residentiale* acceptat, vix videtur simul exsistere posse cum voluntate *perpetuo* manendi etiam in alia dioecesi.

"Quae huc usque diximus, confirmantur praescripto can. 143 et 144. Nam clericus ita manet adscriptus suae dioecesi, cui incardinatus est, atque in ea residere tenetur, ut, licet beneficium aut officium residentiale non habeat, nequeat tamen per notabile tempus ab illa discedere sine licentia saltem praesumpta proprii Ordinarii (can. 143); quod si in aliam dioecesim cum licentia sui Ordinarii transierit, semper potest revocari, iusta de causa et naturali aequitate servata (144). Quibus positis, voluntas perpetuo manendi in una dioecesi videtur manifeste opponi voluntati *perpetuo* item manendi in alia dioecesi, sicuti *perpetua residentia* in una dioecesi necessario excludit *perpetuam residentiam* in alia."—"Quaestiones Canonicae de Ordinatione, domicilio et incardinatione," II, 3 (*Per.*, XX [1931], 130*-131*). Earlier in this same article Cappello seemed to defend the competency of the Bishop of incardination thus: "Per incardinationem clericus *propriam* dioecesim ac *proprium* Episcopum sortitur, ut liquet ex dictis. Idcirco laicus qui recipit primam tonsuram servitio alius dioecesis, huic plane incorporatur, ita ut ipsa *propria* fiat eiusque Episcopus *proprius* sit.

"Iuxta disciplinam Codicis, clericus *uni* tantum dioecesi potest esse incardinatus et *unum* dumtaxat habere potest Episcopum *proprium* quoad ordines suscipiendos. Quare ea dioecesis, in qua laicus recipit primam tonsuram pro servitio alius dioecesis, ipsi *aliena* iuridice est, et Episcopus ordinans nec est nec manet proprius. Posito facto incardinationis determinatae dioecesi, necessario consequitur eum illius Episcopum fieri proprium, ac propterea ius habere promovendi clericum incardinatum seu subditum suum. Episcopus autem, qui primam tonsuram contulit laico promoto servitio alius dioecesis, eatenus potest altiores ordines eidem conferre, quatenus licentiam seu litteras dimissorias habeat Episcopi proprii ordinandi, seu Episcopi illius dioecesis cui, receptione tonsurae, clericus incardinatus fuit."—I, 6 (*Ibid.*, p. 129*). However, in a later article he denied this and held out for the Bishop of domicile alone ("De Episcopo proprio quoad ordinationem," —*Per.*, XXIII [1934], 134), which seeming reversal is quite understandable in view of what he has already been quoted as writing in respect of the *necessary* domicile of a cleric in the diocese of incardination. In his treatise "*De Sacra Ordinatione*," (*Tractatus Canonico-Moralis de Sacramentis*, Vol. II, Pars III, 277-279) he still kept his opinion on the sole competency of the Bishop of the place of domicile, but seems also to have deserted the idea of clerics having a necessary domicile. That at least indicated a preference for the competency of the Bishop of incardination and an effort to reconcile the preference with canon 956.

[147] *Ius Canon.*, II, n. 61.

A general feeling was discernible among the canonists who professed the opinion outlined above that the framers of the Code were guilty of a "*lapsus memoriae*," which would have to be corrected some day by the Holy See itself, but that until that time the sole competency of the Bishop of the place of a candidate's domicile had to be accepted.

Possibly that, too, was the reason why a number of eminent authors maintained silence on the question whether or not the Bishop of incardination is the proper Bishop for clerics' ordinations.[148]

b) The Bishop of incardination is exclusively the proper Bishop

Behind the opinion that the Bishop of the diocese of incardination is the sole proper Bishop for the conferring of higher orders on incardinated clerics there also has stood a number of canonists and moralists of undeniable authority.[149] The first important fact to be noted in the defense of this opinion is that

[148] E. g., Vermeersch-Creusen, *Epitome*, II, n. 239; Pruemmer, *Manuale Theologiae Moralis* (2. ed., 3 vols., Friburgi Brisgoviae: Herder, 1923), III, n. 597; Blat, *Commentarium*, III, pars I, 366-368; Genicot-Salsmans, *Institutiones Theologiae Moralis* (*Instit. Theol. Mor.*), (10. ed., 2 vols., Bruxellis: Alb. Dewit, 1922), II, n. 431; Aertnys-Damen, *Theol. Mor.*, II, n. 570.

[149] As early as 1919 an unknown author wrote in *Il Monitore Ecclesiastico*, XXXI (1919), 179: "... quindi Ordinario proprio per gli ordini successivi alla tonsura è solo il Vescovo alla cui diocesi si è incardinati." In succeeding years others wrote in the same vein, e. g., Ferreres, *Compendium Theologiae Moralis* (ed. 1921), II, n. 869, note 1: "Per susceptionem tonsurae, incardinatur clericus dioecesi, pro cuius servitio promotus fuit (n. 870); unde Ordinarius huius dioecesis erit Episcopus proprius pro subsequentibus ordinibus, nisi ordinandus legitime excardinetur, et alteri dioecesi incardinetur (n. 870). Tunc Episcopus proprius erit Ordinarius novae dioecesis." ; Noldin, *Summa Theologiae Moralis* (18 ed., revised by A. Schmitt, 3 vols., Oeniponte: Felician Rauch, 1927), III, *De Sacramentis*, n. 464: "Quoad ordinationem saecularium ex triplici titulo episcopus potest esse proprius ordinandi episcopus: ... c) Si in dioecesi incardinatus est aut a. per primam tonsuram aut b. per beneficium residentiale, quod in dioecesi obtinuit."; Eichmann, *Lehrbuch des Kirchenrechts* (2. ed., 1926), p. 312: "Inkardination eines Klerikers nach erfolgter Exkardination (c. 112); der inkardinierende Bischof wird zur Weihe des inkardinierenden Klerikers zustaendig weil er jetzt dessen Herr geworden ist."; Davis, *Moral and Pastoral Theology* (3. ed., 1938), IV, 22: "If he receives tonsure from his own bishop for service elsewhere, his bishop of ordination is the bishop of the latter diocese."

the Code in canon 111, § 2, made attachment to a single definite diocese an *ipso facto* effect of first tonsure, whereas formerly it had to be a separate and distinct act. For the lower clerics, their attachment to or assignment in a church or diocese was the forerunner of the title of ordination, and all through history was the equivalent of the same. In ancient times, as soon as a cleric was assigned or had received a title, no other Bishop but the one who assigned him or gave him a title in his diocese could ordain him. The various bases of competence for the proper Bishops of ordination were introduced much later to settle definitely the question which Bishop could assign a layman.

In the course of time proper Bishops ordained laymen without assigning or titling them (absolute ordinations), and that was the general reason for the multiplication and extension of the bases of competence of the proper Bishops relative to the ordination of clerics also. The Church tried valiantly to enforce the law which called for such assignment, but never fully succeeded until 1917, when clerical diocesan attachment was made an automatic process in the Code. The culmination of this historic effort should, therefore, mean that, under the present law, the basis of the proper Bishop for ordination[150] should merely decide which Bishop is entitled to tonsure the layman. As soon as tonsure is conferred, attachment to a definite diocese automatically follows, and, when a cleric is attached to a Bishop's diocese, no other Bishop may dare to assume the authority to ordain him. That makes the Bishop of incardination not only a proper Bishop, but the exclusively proper Bishop for ordination. True it is that such an express statement is not found in canon 956, but neither is there any necessity for it to be there if the basis of competence of a proper Bishop really refers to the ordination of laymen only. Implicitly it is included in canon 111, § 2. Another reason for its not being found in canon 956 might be derived from what was said above,[151] namely, that the framers of the section of the Code which dealt with orders originally meant canon 956 to apply

[150] Can. 956.

[151] P. 338.

to clerics as well as to laymen, and that only afterwards was it noticed that in the simple wording of canon 111 was couched a new substitute for the former letters of quasi-excardination, in the form of tonsure for a distant diocese, which of itself effected incardination there immediately. Consequently it was not until after the Code was promulgated that the difficulty in reconciling canon 956 with canon 111 was discovered.

The second important line of defense for the opinion under consideration is the private reply of the Pontifical Commission for the Interpretation of the Code to the Bishop of Santa Fé, Argentina, on Dec. 7, 1931. The *dubium,* concerning the Bishop from whom higher orders should be received by a cleric already incardinated into a distant diocese, was proposed and answered as follows:

> Dubium.—An ille qui promotus fuit ad primam tonsuram a proprio Episcopo, sed pro servitio alius dioecesis cui eo ipso est incardinatus ad normam can. 111, § 2, et responsi Pontificiae Commissionis diei 17 aug., 1919, ad II, superiores ordines recipere debeat a priori Episcopo, an potius ab Episcopo dioecesis cui rite jam incardinatus est, etsi studia theologica absolvere teneatur in alia dioecesi.
>
> Responsum fuit: Negative ad primam partem, affirmative ad secundam.[152]

The natural and obvious meaning of this reply is that, as soon as incardination has taken place through first tonsure, the proper Bishop for the conferring of higher orders on the cleric is the Bishop of the diocese in which the cleric is incardinated.

Browne, writing in the *Irish Ecclesiastical Record,*[153] takes exception to this meaning, but his arguments are far from convincing. In fact they do violence to the text. He claims: 1) The query does not state clearly that the candidate still has a domicile in the diocese of the Bishop who gave him tonsure and that he has *not* a domicile in the diocese in which he is incardinated. 2) The meaning of the last clause, introduced by

[152] Cappello, *Tractatus de Sacramentis,* II, Pars III, n. 333.

[153] XLVIII (1936), 531-537.

etsi, is not clear. *In alia dioecesi* may mean in the diocese of adoption or in some third diocese. If the former, the candidate has a domicile in the diocese of adoption; if the latter, he still may have such a domicile by reason of residence in the adopted diocese's regional seminary. 3) The expression "*ordines recipere ab*" signifies the actual reception of orders, and not the grant of dimissorial letters. Hence, the query was not, which Bishop has the right to ordain or to issue *litterae dimissoriae* for the ordination of the cleric, but, from which Bishop should he actually receive the higher orders. 4) In the reply of Aug. 3, 1919,[154] the Pontifical Commission for the Interpretation of the Code likewise omitted all mention of a grant of *litterae dimissoriae,* and insisted on actual ordination by the Bishop of the candidate's place of domicile. In a parallel way, the same was meant here. 5) Since the reply was not promulgated, it is a strong indication that its meaning was not contrary to the words of canon 956, else it would have to be promulgated. But, if it meant to make the Bishop of incardination the proper Bishop, it certainly would have been contrary to canon 956, as many eminent canonists show who wrote against the doctrine of the competency of the Bishop of incardination in the new Code.

To these arguments, respectively, it can be answered: 1) If it were meant that the candidate no longer had a domicile in the diocese of tonsure, but did have one in the diocese of incardination, there would be no *dubium* at all. The only reason for the doubt is an apparent clash between the rights of the first and second Bishops. 2) If the *etsi* clause implied the continuance of studies in the diocese of tonsure, there would be no sense in making it an opposition clause. If it connected the place of these studies with the diocese of destination, there would be no clash of Bishops, and hence no *dubium.* Therefore, it must have pointed to a third diocese, and was inserted to show that the candidate had not yet established residence in the diocese of incardination. 3) To see such a specific meaning as "actual reception of orders" attached to the simple expression "*ordines recipere ab*" in its present setting taxes one's credulity. To

[154] *ME,* XXXII (1920), 57.

ascribe such a meaning to the text is plainly to distort it. Moreover, the assumption of this meaning for the text "*ordines recipere ab*" would argue a most peculiar, if not abnormal, conception of duty in the Most Reverend Bishop who submitted the question. It must not be forgotten that one of the alternatives in the question was, whether the higher orders were to be received from the "first Bishop." Would the Bishop in South America ordinarily be asking whether a youth, whom he tonsured for a diocese in Cuba and who is pursuing his studies at Louvain, should come back to Argentina and receive orders personally from himself? And why would it concern the Bishop of Argentina to ask whether the same young man should come back and receive his higher orders personally from the Bishop in Cuba? The real doubt rather is, which Bishop should issue the *litterae dimissoriae* to the Bishop at Louvain: the Bishop in Argentina or the Bishop in Cuba. The question, "From which Bishop ought he to receive higher orders?" is merely the popular way of saying, "From which Bishop will the authority come for the conferring of higher orders?" 4) The Pontifical Commission's reply of 1919 is no parallel. There was question there of a layman who had no domicile at all. Consequently, there could be no question of *litterae dimissoriae*, but rather of finding a willing Bishop and of establishing the necessary domicile in his diocese. 5) The Santa Fé reply is not contrary to canon 956 if this canon deals with the proper Bishop for lay candidates only, as it is here contended that it does. It is merely declaring what is contained already in canon 111, § 2. Hence it needed no promulgation. If, for the sake of argument, it would be admitted that it did clarify a doubt, its non-promulgation might only mean that the Pontifical Commission for the Interpretation of the Code was treading cautiously before promulgating to the world an authentic interpretation.[155]

With a view to the consideration of the negative arguments, an effort must be made to refute what was cited above in favor of the sole competence of the Bishop of the place of domicile for

[155] An authentic interpretation was promulgated by the C. I. C., July 24, 1939 —*AAS*, XXXI (1939), 321. For text and discussion cf. *infra*, pp. 369 ff.

the ordination of clerics.[156] In this the respective order of the negative arguments will be followed.

1st. Canon 956 does not apply to clerics as well as laymen. It has, however, a clause referring to clerics which is out of place, no matter what the interpretation of the scope of the canon may be.[157] It has another clause "*nisi agatur . . . de promovendo religioso professo, de quo in can. 964, n. 4,*" to which canonists point as manifestly including clerics, but upon close scrutiny it does not necessarily do so. Assuming for the moment that canon 956 deals exclusively with the proper Bishop for laymen, the clause exempting the professed Religious from taking the oath of domicile is still required and can even remain in its present form. Hence its presence is not a conclusive argument that canon 956 does extend to clerics. But, says the opposition, if canon 956 deals only with laymen, who is the Bishop who is to authorize advancement in orders for the professed Religious cleric who is ruled *iure saecularium?* Until the Holy See gives an authentic interpretation, it is still the Bishop of the candidate's place of domicile in the world, because by canon 585 he still retains that diocese until he has made his perpetual profession, just as though he were incardinated in it, even though he is not actually, but instead is affiliated with a Religious Institute. It is to be remembered that the affiliation of a Religious with his religion does not happen *ipso facto* through first tonsure as incardination to a diocese does for a secular cleric. The lay Religious is already affiliated through temporary profession before he is tonsured at all. Hence there is no possible change in proper Bishops for him after tonsure as there is for the secular layman.

The rest of canon 956 contains no word or expression which would prove conclusively that it refers to clerics. *Saecularium* is in opposition to *religiosorum. Tantum* indicates the exclusiveness of the proper Bishop of the place of domicile for those to whom this canon extends. *Promovendus* and *alumno* are non-committal. Take out the superfluous and misplaced

[156] Cf. *supra*, pp. 356-7.

[157] Cf. *supra*, pp. 338-341.

clause exempting tonsured clerics from the oath of domicile, therefore, and there is nothing in canon 956 to show with any degree of certainty that it is applicable to any others than laymen.

This interpretation of it, too, coincides with the history of the foundation of proper Bishops for ordination.[158]

An unnamed writer in the *Periodica*[159] adopted this opinion of canon 956 because of the incongruity which would follow from the opposite. The case proposed to him ran thus: Titius received first tonsure from the Bishop of diocese *A*. Then he left diocese *A* and went to another diocese, no longer concerned in the first one. He continues his studies for the priesthood, however, and still has minor and major orders to receive. Who is his proper Bishop for the conferring of these orders? The canonist's answer was, the Bishop who tonsured Titius, who still remains his proper Bishop until he becomes excardinated. If one were to hold that canon 956 applies to clerics also, the Bishop of the new diocese, where, in violation of canon 143, Titius *de facto* established his domicile, would have to be considered the proper Bishop. As a matter of fact, the Bishop of the second diocese cannot receive, much less ordain, the candidate until he has received the authority, through the medium of letters of excardination, from the Bishop of diocese *A*.[160] Nor can it be argued that in this case the candidate does not really have a domicile in the second diocese because he still retains a necessary domicile in *A*. It was pointed out above that necessary domiciles are not assigned to clerics in the Code.[161]

Incongruities like this could be multiplied indefinitely if it were held that canon 956 applies to clerics.

2nd. It was precisely the effort to incorporate and simplify the titles of proper Bishops by both incardination and quasi-incardination that has probably caused the confusion in canon 956. In the historical section of this study it was pointed out

158 Cf. *supra*, p. 360.

159 XXIV (1935), 39*-40*.

160 Can. 117, 2°.

161 P. 320.

that both these titles were in reality the equivalent of the title of domicile acquired by short methods in order to overcome the cumbersomeness of three-year or ten-year periods of residence. The framers of the section of the Code on holy orders very likely noted that practically every title, by means of which a Bishop could become the proper Bishop for ordination, was rooted in domicile. Origin meant original domicile; *familiaritas* implied at least a three-year residence; of the conferred benefices many, though not all of them, were residential benefices; and incardination and quasi-incardination simply betokened abbreviated methods for the acquisition of domicile. Might they not have reasoned that, if domicile as a title were reduced to a requisite of simpler form, it would include all the rest? And, thus, the requisite of domicile was made so simple that its achievement could be verified by only a moment's stay in a diocese, if this abbreviated sojourn was coupled with the proper intention of permanent residence. But there was one big difference. No residence at all was necessary to acquire a domicile in the Pre-Code Period, if the method of incardination or quasi-incardination was employed, for by this method the domicile was obtained through a mere exchange of letters. Hence, through the medium of letters of incardination or quasi-incardination a cleric or a layman could, *ratione domicilii,* claim as his proper Bishop for ordination a Bishop who, thousands of miles away, ruled over a diocese in which the candidate for ordination had never set foot.[162]

By the Code, however, that same domicile can be secured only by travelling the intervening thousands of miles to initiate the necessary material element of residence in the diocese of destination. Was it the purpose of the Code, then, legally to forestall the distant Bishop from becoming competent for the ordination? If so, why does it allow him at all to incardinate a cleric in minor orders, as it does in canon 111, § 2, when formal excardination and incardination after the reception of priesthood, by

[162] An example of this is the case of Rev. Peter Roussel of Quebec who had been quasi-incardinated into the diocese of Santa Fé and received all sacred orders through the dimissorial letters of its Bishop without ever having been there.—S. R. R., *Londonen.*, 9 ian. 1912 (*AAS*, IV [1912], 249 ss.)

virtue of canon 969, § 2, would accomplish the same result with far less trouble? One is rather inclined to think that the framers of the Code set out to incorporate the titles of incardination and quasi-incardination, but then failed to accomplish this with clear precision because of the changed requirements in the present law relative to the acquisition of a clerical domicile.

Furthermore, if the interpretation is accepted that canon 956 is applicable to laymen only, then the Code did incorporate the titles of incardination and quasi-incardination, because, as soon as a layman is tonsured, he becomes automatically attached to that diocese alone for which he was promoted, and, if he later is excardinated by formal letters, he at once becomes exclusively attached to the new diocese which incardinates him, no matter how far away. Attachment to a diocese, as was said, in its original significance made the Bishop of that diocese the solely competent one to ordain the subject.

3rd. It is true that the Bishop who ordains or authorizes an ordination must examine carefully the character of the candidates beforehand and be satisfied as to their fitness. This was emphasized since the promulgation of the Code by the Sacred Congregation of the Sacraments on Dec. 27, 1930, especially in § 2, n. 6.[168] However, that proves nothing more than that it is the Bishop of the candidate's place of domicile who is naturally expected to be the best qualified to give responsible authorization for the conferring of first tonsure. After the reception of tonsure, the candidate is under the constant surveillance of Superiors in some seminary, and information as to his worthiness for higher orders is communicated to the proper Bishop by Testimonial Letters. Hence, it matters not whether the proper Bishop of a cleric be one hundred miles or one thousand miles away: in either case he can obtain reliable information regarding the candidate before authorizing his promotion in orders.

4th. For the Bishop of the place of domicile to be the sole authority who can ordain, or cause to be ordained, another Bishop's incardinated cleric and, yet, not to be able to do so without the permission of the Bishop of incardination seems a

[168] *AAS*, XXIII (1931), 123.

contradiction. Under that assumption, all that the Bishop of incardination could say is, " My diocese is in need of one of my clerics." If he went further and said to the Bishop of the place of domicile, " Proceed to ordain one for me," he would really be authorizing the ordination, and that, according to the theory under attack, he cannot do. Such an interpretation of canon 956 would give any cleric who did not yet have a domicile in the diocese of incardination two proper Bishops, one *quoad omnia* and one *quoad ordinationem.* Many places in the Code speak of the *episcopus proprius* without distinguishing. This would lead to confusion of rights. Particularly is this so in canon 969, where it would be necessary to consider *proprii episcopi* in § 1 as referring to the Bishop of incardination, and *Episcopus proprium promovere subditum* in § 2 as referring to the Bishop of the place of domicile. Again, in canon 970 who would be the *episcopus proprius* who could block a candidate's ascent to higher orders, the Bishop of the place of domicile, the Bishop of incardination, or both? Divided responsibility is no one's responsibility.

5th. The reply of the Pontifical Commission for the Interpretation of the Code *ad II*^{um} on Aug. 3, 1919, merely explained the relative scopes of canons 111, § 2, and 969, § 2, the latter of which, at least, should have been clear already, particularly when read in conjunction with § 1 of the same canon. It does not establish the assumption that only the Bishop of the place of domicile is the proper Bishop over a cleric, because it speaks only of first tonsure, not of later orders. In pointing out that a *tonsuratus* becomes incardinated at once in the diocese of destination, it merely reiterates canon 111, § 2.

6th. The meaning of the reply of the Pontifical Commission for the Interpretation of the Code on Dec. 7, 1931, to the Bishop of Santa Fé, Argentina, was discussed above.[164] It certainly did proclaim the competency of the Bishop of incardination for the higher ordination of clerics, and yet it did not militate against canon 956, since that canon deals with the proper Bishop of the place of domicile solely for the ordination of laymen. It is only when one insists on extending the law of canon 956 to

164 Pp. 361-3.

clerics also that he has to assail the Pontifical Commission's reply as changing the law and therefore needing promulgation.

7th. As explained above,[165] canon 956 needs no general change of wording to confine its scope to laymen. The only clause which does not agree well with that restricted interpretation is the one exempting clerics from the oath, but the inclusion of this same clause in canon 956 strikes upon a note of similar discord for the wider interpretation as well.

2°. The authoritative interpretation

All doubt on the question as to who is the proper Bishop for the higher ordination of tonsured clerics was removed by two promulgated decisions of the Pontifical Commission for the Interpretation of the Code on July 24, 1939. They read as follows:

> D. I. Whether a layman, who is promoted to first tonsure by his proper Bishop for the service of another determined diocese with the consent of its Bishop, is incardinated to this latter diocese according to the rule of canon 111, § 2.
>
> R. Yes.
>
> D. II. Whether the Bishop of the diocese, for the service of which a layman was promoted to first tonsure by his proper Bishop, has the proper and exclusive right to confer orders on him or to give dimissorial letters for his ordination according to the rule of canon 955, § 1, even though he has not yet acquired a domicile in the same diocese.
>
> R. Yes.[166]

The first of these is an official promulgation of the old private reply *ad II^um^* to the Archbishop of Armagh in 1919.[167]

165 Pp. 364-5.

166 D. I. An laicus, qui a proprio Episcopo ad primam tonsuram promotus sit in servitium alius determinatae dioecesis de consensu huius Episcopi, huic dioecesi incardinatus sit ad normam canonis 111, § 2. R. Affirmative.

D. II. An Episcopus dioecesis, in cuius servitium laicus ad primam tonsuram a proprio Episcopo promotus fuerit, illi iure proprio et exclusivo ordines conferre aut litteras dimissorias dare valeat ad normam canonis 955, § 1, licet ipse in eadem dioecesi domicilium nondum acquisiverit. R. Affirmative.—Pont. Comm. Int. Cod., 24 iul. 1939 (*AAS*, XXXI [1939], 321).

167 *ME*, XXXII (1920), 57. For text cf. *infra*, p. 375.

The second is an official promulgation of the old private reply to the Bishop of Santa Fé, Argentina, in 1931,[168] but by reason of a better worded *dubium* it solves the problem in a clearer and more accurate fashion. The *dubium* specifically states that the tonsured cleric has not yet acquired a domicile in the diocese of destination, and yet the reply attributes to the Bishop of incardination the proper and exclusive right to confer orders himself or to authorize any other Bishop through dimissorial letters to confer orders on his incardinated cleric. This puts an end to the possible confusion of two proper Bishops for the one cleric.

Though the *dubium* only asked about those who were immediately incardinated into alien dioceses through first tonsure, it is quite certain that the same solution must avail those clerics who are formally incardinated into an alien diocese before the priesthood. Some day another specific reply may be given in their regard.

The obvious result of this decision is that canon 956 must be understood to refer to the initial tonsure of laymen only, and canon 111, § 2, must be considered as settling the identity of the proper Bishop for clerics even as regards their ordination to higher orders.

The first canonist who is found to comment on the reply is Coussa.[169] He interprets it in the manner just stated, and finds it based on the norms handed down from the most ancient times, and calculated to remove the incongruity of a diocesan Ordinary giving his cleric permission to remain in another diocese and yet, because of that very fact, being deprived of the power to ordain him. Strange to say, he considers the troublesome clause "*nisi agatur de promovendo ad ordines clerico*" in canon 956 as a sufficient indication that the canon treats only of the promotion of laymen to tonsure!

[168] Cappello, *Tractatus de Sacramentis*, II, Pars III, *De Sacra Ordinatione*, n. 333. For text cf. *supra*, p. 361.

[169] *Apoll.*, XII (1939), 321-325.

ARTICLE III

THE *Terminus* OF INITIAL INCARDINATION

Can. 111. - § 2. . . . **Clericus adscribitur seu, ut aiunt,** ***incardinatur*** **diocesi pro cuius servitio promotus fuit.**

The meaning of the term *diocese* in this canon was sufficiently elaborated above.[170] The service of which it speaks is the rule of the faithful and the ministry of divine worship,[171] to furnish which in the various churches of a diocese men are ordained to be clerics and set apart from the laity. The only justification for the ordination of a cleric, therefore, is his ability to supply that rule and ministry where it is needed or useful.[172]

1. *Incardination in One's Proper Diocese*

A Bishop can lawfully tonsure for his own diocese only his proper lay subjects, and they must be proper to him, not merely in a general way,[173] but in the particular way required by canon 956 for *ordinandi,* as described in the last article. Furthermore, he alone has the right to say, through the medium of dimissorial letters, when these same subjects may be tonsured by an outside Bishop for their own diocese of domicile, for the ordaining Prelate's, or for some other alien diocese.[174] When, then, a Bishop confers tonsure upon subjects who are proper to him *quoad ordinationem* or issues dimissorial letters for the conferring of tonsure upon them, he ordinarily does this for the service of his own diocese, and the conferring of tonsure incardinates them in his diocese. A contrary intention on the Bishop's part must be clearly established in one of the ways to be shown below.[175] The contrary intention of the lay subject himself has no force unless it coincides with that of his proper Bishop. The

[170] Pp. 294-7.

[171] Can. 948.

[172] Can. 969, § 1. Cf. also *supra,* pp. 38-39, 290-1.

[173] Can. 94.

[174] C. I. C., 17 feb. 1930—*AAS,* XXII (1930), 195.

[175] Pp. 373-382.

subject's intention is revealed by a sufficiently manifested *propositum* of dedicating himself to the service of, and obedience to, the Ordinary of the diocese for which he is being promoted.[176] It matters not if afterwards he does not actually render that service, for that does not prove that he was not ready to render it at the time he was tonsured.[177] A sufficient manifestation of willingness to become incardinated is the candidate's very presence and submission to the tonsure ceremony at the hands of his proper Bishop. What happens when he is tonsured by an unauthorized, non-proper Bishop was discussed above.[178]

2. *Lawful Methods by Which Proper Lay Subjects Become Incardinated in Alien Dioceses*

From the twelfth century onward, i. e., after the idea of proper Bishops for ordination developed, lay subjects who wished to devote their life's service to a diocese alien to their own first had to secure its Bishop as a proper Bishop on one or other of the various bases of competency.

A briefer and more satisfactory method, introduced by the Sacred Congregation of the Council in its Decree of November 24, 1906,[179] was the issuance and exchange of letters of quasi-excardination from and quasi-incardination into other dioceses.[180]

The Code, however, abolished this latter practice. In its place it introduced two new lawful methods by which laymen may become incardinated in dioceses different from their own. These might be termed " direct methods " in order to distinguish them from the still existing indirect method, whereby a layman can become incardinated in an alien diocese by first making it his proper diocese through the acquisition of a domicile therein, and by then becoming tonsured for its service.

[176] *Synopsis disceptationis*, S. C. C., *Dioecesium N. et X. Incardinationis*, 10 mar. 1923—*AAS*, XVI (1924), 51 ss.

[177] *Loc. cit.*

[178] Pp. 305-307.

[179] *ASS*, XXXIX (1906), 600 ss.

[180] Cf. *supra*, pp. 89-96.

A. Direct Methods

1°. Initial incardination in a definite alien diocese (Can. 111, § 2)

Of the two direct methods this is the more unique, inasmuch as it is without precedent. Canon 111, § 2, states that through the reception of first tonsure a cleric becomes incardinated in the diocese for the service of which he was promoted. If a proper lay subject now wishes to become incardinated in an alien diocese, instead of receiving letters of quasi-excardination to the same he simply obtains the permission of both his proper Bishop and the alien Bishop who is willing to receive him, then receives tonsure from his proper Bishop, but for the service of the alien diocese, and thereby directly and immediately becomes incardinated in it, no matter how distant it may be. The *terminus* of the initial incardination must be definite and known if this method is to be used. Certain formalities also are to be observed.

a) The preliminary agreement

A cleric cannot be forced upon a Bishop without the latter's knowledge and consent. Hence, the first step in this process calls for an agreement to be entered into between the proper Bishop and the receiving Bishop at the behest of the lay subject.[181] In the first private reply of the Pontifical Commission for the Interpretation of the Code, on August 3, 1919,[182] wherein was indicated the lawfulness of this new method of transferring proper lay subjects, nothing was said about the preliminary agreement between the Bishops. In the most recently promulgated reply, however, it is expressly mentioned. The Pontifical Commission for the Interpretation of the Code was asked whether a lay person, who is promoted by his proper Bishop to first tonsure *with the consent of the Bishop of another determined diocese* for the service of that diocese, is incardinated into the same in accordance with canon 111, § 2. The reply was in

[181] Schaaf, "Episcopus Proprius Ordinationis,"—*AER*, XC (1934), 357.

[182] *ME*, XXXII (1920), 57. For text cf. *supra*, p. 350.

the affirmative.[183] Such consent would necessarily be in writing, both because of the possible distance separating the receiving from the proper Bishop, and because of the proper Bishop's need of incontrovertible proof that the incardination had not been to his own diocese, as would be presumed ordinarily.

No legal form is prescribed for this agreement. The lay subject (usually a seminarian) might take the initiative by making a journey or by writing some letters to offer his service in the priesthood to various alien Bishops of other dioceses. The alien Bishop who is found to be in need of clerics and well disposed toward the candidate then writes to the candidate's proper Bishop expressing his consent to receive the candidate if the same is not needed in his diocese of domicile. If the proper Bishop has enough clerics for his own diocese and is willing to relinquish the candidate, he in turn communicates with the alien receiving Bishop, telling him of his willingness to relinquish the subject, whereupon the receiving Bishop writes back that he wishes to have the lay candidate tonsured for his alien diocese as soon as the proper Bishop finds him qualified. These letters are kept in the files of both Chanceries. The proper Bishop is still the judge of the worthiness of the candidate, being the Bishop of his place of domicile, either original or acquired, and cannot proceed to the conferring of tonsure until all requisites are fulfilled.[184] Naturally the candidate will have knowledge of the above process and agreement, and when finally he is tonsured by his proper Bishop he will know that it is for the service of the alien diocese.

b) The reception of tonsure for its service

The proof that it is by reception of first tonsure that a lay subject becomes automatically incardinated to a definite alien diocese was supplied in a semi-official way for the first time by the private reply of the Pontifical Commission for the Interpretation of the Code to the queries of the Archbishop of Armagh. The second and third queries were as follows:

[183] July 24, 1939, ad I—*AAS*, XXXI (1939), 321. For full text see above, p. 369.

[184] Cf. *supra*, pp. 301 ff.

2. Utrum ille qui ordinetur a proprio Episcopo servitio alius dioecesis, incardinetur huic alii dioecesi iuxta canonem 111, § 2, an potius dioecesi proprii Episcopi iuxta canonem 969, § 2.

Et quatenus negative ad primam partem,

3. Quonam tempore incardinari debeat dioecesi cuius servitio ordinetur.

On Aug. 3, 1919, the Commission responded:

Ad II. Affirmative ad primam partem; negative ad secundam.
Ad III. Provisum in responsione ad II.[185]

Elucidation was needed at the time to reconcile canon 111, § 2, with canon 969, § 2, for they seemed to present contradictory solutions to the status of a man destined for the service of an alien diocese but tonsured at home. To which diocese did he belong after tonsure? Canon 111, § 2, pointed to the alien diocese, and yet canon 969, § 2, said he was to be formally excardinated to the alien diocese at a later time, and therefore was to belong to his proper diocese in the *interim.* Supporting the latter solution as more correct was the wording of canon 956 which, in dispensing from the oath of domicile those who were destined for the service of another diocese, mentioned only the method of canon 969, § 2. Apparently the Archbishop of Armagh expected the decision to be in favor of canon 969, § 2; that was the reason for his third query. When the decision was made in favor of immediate alien incardination according to canon 111, § 2, the canonists began to realize that these two canons were not contradictory, but referred to two different types of cases. When the diocese of destination was already known and agreed upon in advance, tonsure for its service had the effect of immediately incardinating the new cleric into it; when the diocese of destination was still unknown, tonsure could not be conferred for an indefinite territory, and so the proper Bishop tonsured for his own diocese temporarily, until a receiving Bishop could be secured, who would then formally incardinate the cleric.

[185] *ME*, XXXII (1920), 57 ss. For discussion of the same cf. *ITQ*, XIV (1919), 391; Kinane—*IER*, 5th series, XIV (1919), 320-322; *ME*, XXXII (1920), 156 ss.; *ITQ*, XV (1920), 192-195; *Jus Pontif.*, III (1923), 7-9; *Per.*, XII (1924), 74-76.

Although the above reply of the Pontifical Commission for the Interpretation of the Code was private, it at least afforded an insight into the mind of the Commission, and it was even arguable that it was binding, on the ground that it did nothing more than restate that which was already contained in the law. All doubts as to its authenticity, however, were settled on July 24, 1939, when the same Pontifical Commission promulgated the following *dubium* and response:

> D. I. An laicus, qui a proprio Episcopo ad primam tonsuram promotus sit in servitium alius determinatae dioecesis de consensu huius Episcopi, huic dioecesi incardinatus sit ad normam canonis 111, § 2.
>
> R. Affirmative.[186]

c) Exception from the oath of domicile

When a layman is thus destined for immediate alien incardination by first tonsure, the proper Bishop for his ordination is determined either by the layman's legal place of origin which is still retained as his domicile, or by the layman's present place of simple domicile acquired through one or the other of the two methods indicated in canon 92, § 1. In the latter case, the layman is exempted from taking the domiciliary oath which canon 956 requires whenever a lay candidate is to become incardinated in the diocese wherein he has only a simple domicile.[187] Of course, here as elsewhere, it must be kept in mind that to designate a Bishop as the proper Bishop for ordination means that he is the one who possesses the authority in the matter. If no just cause impedes him, he himself must actually confer the tonsure;[188] otherwise he issues dimissorial letters for some other Bishop to do so.[189] In this particular instance, his issuance of dimissorial letters would carry with it the instruction that the lay candidate is to be tonsured for the alien diocese of destination. It might even happen that the proper Bishop will issue the dimissorial

[186] *AAS*, XXXI (1939), 321. Cf. *supra*, p. 369.

[187] Cf. discussion above, pp. 346-7.

[188] Can. 955, § 2.

[189] Can. 955, § 1.

letters to the very receiving Bishop himself, who will then tonsure the candidate on the proper Bishop's authority, but by that act will incardinate the new cleric *ipso facto* in his own diocese. Even in that event no oath of domicile is taken, because the alien Bishop does not confer tonsure on the basis of a domicile already possessed by the candidate in the latter Bishop's diocese, but rather on the strength of the dimissorial letters issued by the Bishop of the candidate's place of present domicile.

2°. Deferred incardination in an indefinite alien diocese

Can. 969. - § 1. **Nemo ex saecularibus ordinetur, qui iudicio proprii Episcopi non sit necessarius vel utilis ecclesiis dioecesis.**

§ 2. **Non prohibetur tamen Episcopus proprium promovere subditum, qui in futurum, praevia legitima excardinatione et incardinatione, servitio alius dioecesis destinetur.**

The second direct method of disposing of superfluous lay candidates for the priesthood has been introduced into the Code in the form of an exception to an ancient canonical principle still in force. The principle, restated in the first paragraph of canon 969, is that no secular is to be ordained who in the judgment of his proper Bishop is not necessary or useful to the churches of the diocese. The history of this principle need not be repeated here. It was aimed to keep a balance between supply and demand for the clergy. Especially since the Council of Trent, it has deterred Bishops from tonsuring worthy candidates within their own confines. As stated above, the words *qui . . . non sit* indicate that the necessity or utility must be a present, not even a prudently foreseen future one.

Some of the superfluous candidates in a well-supplied diocese succeed on their own efforts in finding alien Bishops willing to receive them, and these can be disposed of by initial incardination to such dioceses. Others, not so fortunate but equally qualified and zealous, might be kept waiting so long in the lay state that their vocations would be lost. Some, but certainly not all, might avert that catastrophe by journeying afar to needy dioceses and acquiring therein new domiciles. But what of the rest? In paragraph 2 of canon 969 the Code has wisely allowed their admittance to the clerical state, and even their advancement to the priesthood, by way of an exception to the general principle.

a) Legal procedure of canon 969, § 2

At the outset it is to be noticed that this is a permission, not a command. *Non prohibetur* shows that it is still up to the proper Bishop's judgment whether he should use this faculty or not. It is supposed, therefore, that he will use it when it is indicated in a worthy case.

Proprium promovere subditum puts no limit to the degree of orders that may be conferred on the subject. The one obstacle will be a title of ordination for major orders. Since the cleric will not be needed in his proper diocese and has not yet a destination, the title of benefice is impossible, and neither can he be ordained for the title *servitii dioecesis.* The title of the mission cannot be used in a country not subject to the jurisdiction of the Sacred Congregation for the Propagation of the Faith.[190] An ecclesiastical pension is destined only for diocesan service. The only possibilities left are the title of patrimony or an apostolic Indult to ordain without a canonical title. If the proper Bishop ordains such a subject to major orders without either title or Indult, he is bound to support him out of his own funds, if the cleric be in need, and as long as no other provision is made for his proper sustenance.[191]

Qui in futurum indicates that the service of the diocese of destination is something to be realized only in the future. For the present, the newly tonsured cleric remains in his home diocese, and, since no cleric can be without a diocese,[192] he is incardinated in it, even though not tonsured for its service. It also indicates what mind the proper Bishop has in tonsuring him. The Bishop knows that there are always some dioceses which lack a sufficient number of priests for their needs. He is morally certain that at a future date the clerics whom he tonsures in excess of his own diocesan needs will be absorbed by those needy

[190] Can. 981, § 1.

[191] Can. 980, § 2.

[192] Can. 111, § 1.

dioceses. Their diocese of service will be determined, therefore, from some one of the petitions he receives from those definite alien Bishops.[193]

Praevia legitima excardinatione et incardinatione describes and decrees the methods by which the transfer will be made as soon as a definite call is received and accepted. They are twofold: by formal letters of excardination and incardination,[194] or by the permitted reception of a residential benefice in the diocese of destination.[195]

Servitio alius dioecesis destinetur shows clearly the indefiniteness of the diocese of destination at the time tonsure is conferred, but it also unmistakably classifies the subject as one who has nothing else to expect but future excardination. Still, there would be nothing to prevent the proper Bishop from using the cleric in his own diocese, if a vacancy occurred, before he became absorbed by an alien diocese.

In the interval between tonsure and excardination the cleric is able to exercise his orders. If elevated to the priesthood, he is able to celebrate Mass daily, and might even become a welcome temporary substitute on some odd occasion when an extraordinary number of temporary vacancies occur, such as at the time of a diocesan pilgrimage, or during an epidemic.

b) Exception from the oath of domicile

It has already been seen [196] that the superfluous lay subject who is tonsured for an indefinite destination is expressly exempted in canon 956 from guaranteeing by oath his acquired domicile in case he has left his original domicile before becoming a candidate for tonsure.

If the proper Bishop, justly impeded, issues *litterae dimissoriae* for the conferring of tonsure, the ordaining Prelate's act invariably results in incardination in the diocese of the proper Bishop. To suppose that the ordaining Prelate might want the

[193] *Per.*, XII (1924), 76.

[194] Can. 112.

[196] Cf. *supra*, pp. 341-2.

new cleric for his own diocese would be a contradiction of the case in hand, wherein it is presumed that no needy Bishop is yet known. It would be nothing more than a recurrence of the first method described above.[197]

c) Assurance of execution of deferred incardination

None of the authors consulted mention the problem of how a proper Bishop is to be assured that the superfluous lay candidate whom he tonsures will eventually become incardinated elsewhere after a willing Bishop has been found. One can well imagine how reluctant a Bishop would be to use canon 969, § 2, if he had no assurance that the temporary incardination to his own diocese of a supernumerary would not actually become permanent.

Before an answer be given this difficulty it must be remembered that the Bishop who tonsures a lay subject who is neither necessary nor useful to the churches of his own diocese must act very cautiously and circumspectly. He is presumed to be normally unwilling, but in specific cases is persuaded to make use of the privilege mainly for two reasons: 1st. To save the vocation of one who is found well qualified for the priesthood; and 2nd. because of a moral certainty that some other diocese will be in need of a cleric, and he will have someone already prepared to supply it. At the very outset, then, he is supposed to have pretty certain guarantees that the cleric will be willing to go when called for and that there will be a Bishop to call for him.

Even granted, however, that the process failed of execution, the result need not cause much fear. To assume that the diocese would suffer from the cleric being in it even permanently is unwarranted. A supernumerary tonsured or minor cleric is no burden on any diocese unless he becomes a source of scandal, whereupon he can be reduced to the lay state.[198] A supernumerary major cleric is a burden on a diocese if his title of ordination is a drain on its resources, or if he too becomes a source of scandal. But, in the problem under consideration, the cleric is not raised to major orders for any title that will be a drain on the diocese; rather, the title of patrimony is used. In

197 Pp. 374-6.

198 Can. 211, § 2.

the event that the Bishop should ordain him *in sacris* without a title, the burden is not on the diocese, but on the Bishop personally,[199] and he has only himself to blame for it. If the major cleric should become a source of scandal, the Bishop has merely the extra inconvenience of dealing with him in the same fashion as he would with any of his diocesan clergy who acted in like manner.

If, however, the proper Bishop wants something stronger than moral guarantees that the cleric will be excardinated when a diocese is found for him, he should adopt the following procedural steps: I. He should require of the candidate before tonsure an oath similar to that taken by those ordained *titulo missionis,* namely, that he will consent to his future incardination in any diocese, within a certain agreed area, that will be in need of a cleric; and II. When a receiving Bishop has been found, he should formally excardinate the cleric on the strength of his original free consent, expressed or understood.[200]

Step I.—It is to be understood that such an oath is not prescribed by law, but the proper Bishop could justly refuse to confer tonsure unless it were emitted. The candidate should be over twenty-one years of age, because the oath includes the willingness to acquire a domicile in the diocese of destination, and that cannot be done ordinarily by anyone until after his majority.[201] The formula of the oath might be as follows:

> Ego N. ————, filius N. ————, dioecesis (vel vicariatus) N. ————, sciens laborem meum ac operam propriae meae dioecesi neque necessariam esse neque utilem propter eius sufficientem numerum sacerdotum, spondeo, et iuro, quod postquam ad primam tonsuram promotus fuero, in quacumque dioecesi vel vicariatu cuius Ordinarius servitio meo egebit desiderabitque intra limites patriae meae (*vel substituantur limites*) incardinationem accipiam et posteaquam eiusdem pro tempore Ordinarii mandatis stabo.

[199] Can. 980, § 2.

[200] Cf. *supra*, p. 249.

[201] Cf. *supra*, pp. 332-3.

Item voveo, et iuro, me praedictum iuramentum et eius obligationem intelligere, et observaturum. Sic me Deus adiuvet et haec sancta Dei evangelia.

Step II.—The sole obstacle to formal excardination and incardination would be lack of consent on the part of the cleric, for, as has been seen,[202] it is the rule, though not the express law, to require it because of the similarity of incardination to the legal adoption of children. Consent would not be wanting in a cleric tonsured according to canon 969, § 2, because antecedently he would know that his tonsure is only by way of exception, and that he is in the category of those who are destined for service outside their proper diocese. For every such *tonsurandus* the consent to work in an alien diocese and to be incardinated in it would at least be tacit at the time of the initial ceremony. From some it might be obtained as an express declaration before witnesses. Still others would gladly put it in writing in order to receive the desired advancement to the clerical state.

After the exchange of formal letters of excardination and incardination the cleric would belong legally to the receiving Bishop's diocese. If he refused to go and take up his residence in it when told to do so by that Bishop, he would be violating canon 143, and could be punished in the same way as any recalcitrant cleric.

B. Indirect Method—Acquisition of a New Proper Bishop

All through the centuries the one ever valid method by which a layman could become ordained for a diocese different from his own was the acquisition of a new proper Bishop. In the Code that is still a valid, but not the ordinary, method. The only basis for a Bishop to be a proper Bishop over laymen is domicile. Hence they must acquire a new domicile to obtain a new proper Bishop. That is not so easy for candidates for the clerical state because of the conditional intention that most of them have upon entering a new diocese. In order that the

[202] Cf. *supra*, pp. 246-254.

acquisition of a domicile be effective, they must have the intention of remaining perpetually, whether they become ordained or not. This cannot be had by minors, because they have a necessary domicile in the home of their parents or guardians, but it can be had by those who have reached their majority. Such, too, is the significance of this reply of the Pontifical Commission for the Interpretation of the Code on Feb. 17, 1930:

> D. An vi canonis 111, § 2, conlati cum canone 955, § 1, Episcopus alienum subditum sine legitimis proprii Episcopi litteris ad primam tonsuram promovere licite possit.
>
> R. Negative.[203]

In other words, as long as the candidate remains a subject of the previous Bishop by domicile, an alien Bishop cannot tonsure him without dimissorial letters; if he leaves his domicile and acquires another after his twenty-first year of age, and simultaneously guarantees his intention by an oath, he does not need the *litterae dimissoriae* of his former Bishop. In this way he succeeds in becoming tonsured and incardinated to the new diocese without even having to approach his former proper Bishop. It was once required that laymen, even though over twenty-one years of age, have their proper Bishop's permission before changing their domicile. Today no such permission is necessary.

All this is *per se* applicable even to those laymen who are students in seminaries. The law does not make any special distinction concerning them, so neither should we.

Per accidens, however, lay seminarians might be bound to remain in their diocese for another reason, e. g., because of an oath or pact they have made in return for a free education. In this exceptional case the Bishop would certainly have the right to prohibit their departure, but only because of that special agreement.[204]

[203] *AAS*, XXII (1930), 195.

[204] D'Angelo, "De prima tonsura,"—*Apoll.*, I (1928), 181-182; Cappello—*Per.*, XIX (1930), 39*. Cf. also *supra*, p. 289.

CHAPTER VIII

FORMAL EXCARDINATION AND INCARDINATION OF SECULAR CLERICS

Can. 112. - **Praeter casus de quibus in can. 114, 641, § 2, ut clericus alienae dioecesi valide incardinetur, a suo Ordinario obtinere debet litteras ab eodem subscriptas excardinationis perpetuae et absolutae; et ab Ordinario alienae dioecesis litteras ab eodem subscriptas incardinationis pariter perpetuae et absolutae.**

ARTICLE I

GENERAL NOTIONS

AFTER a candidate for the priesthood has been tonsured and thereby incardinated in a definite diocese, one of the effects is his inability to transfer his incardination to another diocese except through a canonical process.[1] Two things must be achieved by the process: a legal separation of the cleric from the diocese to which he is already attached, called excardination, and a legal attachment of the cleric to a new diocese. This latter was the original significance of the term *incardination.* Both effects must be so coördinated that canon 111, § 1, will not be violated by the lapse of any interval between the one and the other.

For secular clerics to be transferred from one diocese to another there are only two alternative processes recognized by Canon Law. The first is formal excardination and incardination, namely, through the instrumentality of written letters; [2] the second is a type of virtual excardination and incardination,[3] through the permitted reception of an alien residential benefice.[4]

For religious clerics to be transferred to a diocese, there are likewise two processes: one is an express reception of the re-

[1] Cf. *supra,* p. 292.

[2] Can. 112.

[3] Cf. Maroto, *Institutt.,* I, n. 495.

[4] Can. 114.

ligious cleric by the benevolent episcopal receiver (either with or without a period of trial), and the other is a tacit reception after a period of trial has ended.[5] Excardination of a secular cleric transferring to a Religious Institute takes place *ipso facto* by the cleric's perpetual religious profession.

In canon 112 the Code deals solely with the first process for seculars. Hence it mentions, but eliminates from consideration for the time being, the other processes of both seculars and Religious by the words "*Praeter casus de quibus in can. 114, 641,* § 2." In this study consideration of the processes for Religious is entirely eliminated as alien to its scope.

Clericus, in the sense of canon 108, § 1, shows that canon 112 has nothing to do with the transfer of laymen from one diocese to another. That question was already treated in canon 111, § 2. Throughout this study a clear-cut division has been made between the law for laymen and that for clerics. The Code does the same. All canons of the title *De clericorum adscriptione alicui dioecesi* from 112 to 117 inclusive deal with clerics, not with laymen. Authors only confuse, instead of clarify, when, for the sake of unity of classification, they put reception of first tonsure in the same category with reception of a residential benefice, and call them both *virtual* incardination.[6]

Alienae is the word used in contradistinction to *propriae* to indicate a diocese to which one does not here and now belong. For clerics, then, it means a diocese to which they are not now incardinated, because even if a layman has several proper dioceses by domicile prior to his reception of tonsure, all except the one for which he is tonsured at once become juridically *alienae.*[7] This is so true that it holds even for all his dioceses of domicile, in the event that he becomes initially incardinated in a diocese where he has never been. Consequently, there arises the paradox that a layman, who still retains his original domicile in the diocese, for example, of Trent, in Italy, and then, after

[5] Can. 641, § 2.

[6] E. g., Maroto, *op. et loc. cit.*

[7] Cappello, "Quaestiones canonicae de Ordinatione, domicilio et incardinatione," —*Per.,* XX (1931), 129*, n. 6.

receiving tonsure from his proper Bishop for the service of the archdiocese of New York, still pursues his studies in Trent, must juridically consider New York as his proper diocese and Trent as *aliena;* and if, after a period of years in Trent, he should change his mind and wish to serve that diocese perpetually, he would be numbered amongst those who are to be incardinated in an alien diocese, even though it was the one in which he had been born and which he had never actually left. Likewise, the term *aliena* must be given to that diocese in which a cleric was incardinated at one time, and from which he later became excardinated. If ever there was question of his being reincardinated in the first diocese, he would in that case have to adopt one of the two processes required for the transfer of clerics to any other alien diocese.

Dioecesi retains here the broad significance which was already seen attached to it.[8]

Valide indicates that what is contained in canon 112 concerning the formal process of incardinating secular clerics is for the validity, not merely for the licitness, of the same. It is not to be taken, therefore, as extending to any other canon or to any of the other processes enumerated above. If even a single item of what is to follow is lacking, the entire formal process eventuates in an invalid procedure.[9] When the omission of a requisite for validity is not noticed at the time, the later fulfillment by the cleric of all obligations proceeding from a valid incardination does not rectify or remedy the original mistake. No matter how many canonical transfers to different dioceses the cleric has after that, a Sacred Congregation or Tribunal investigating the matter would have to render a decision in favor of the diocese which had the last unquestionably valid claim on him.

Incardinetur is here used in its original significance of the attachment of a cleric to a diocese to which he did not theretofore belong. Some speak of it as second incardination.

[8] Cf. *supra*, pp. 294-7.

[9] Toso, *Ad Codicem Juris Canonici . . . Commentaria Minora* (*Comment. Minora*), (5 vols., Taurini-Romae: P. Marietti, 1920-1934), in can. 112.

ARTICLE II

THE ORDINARIES

The canon goes on to say that the cleric must obtain letters *a suo Ordinario* and also *ab Ordinario alienae dioecesis.* The meaning of *Ordinarius* is given in canon 198, § 1, and that of *Ordinarius loci* in § 2 of the same canon. The only difference is that the latter does not include religious Superiors. In canon 112, which deals only with seculars whose present and prospective Superiors have territories, obviously it is *Ordinarius loci* that is meant by both of the above phrases. This term embraces all those previously mentioned as included in the word *episcopus* of canon 956,[10] as it must, to be coextensive with the term *dioecesis* just interpreted.

In canon 198, § 1, however, provision is made, through the words "*nisi quis expresse excipiatur,*" for exceptions to the general scope of the term *Ordinarius* in some fields of legislation where it occurs. In canon 113 some exceptions are made to the scope of the term *Ordinarius* in the field of excardination and incardination. Hence in the reading of canon 112 it must be kept in mind that the local Ordinaries from whom the letters are to be obtained may be any one of those included in canon 198, § 2, subject, however, to the exceptions of canon 113.

Suo designates the Ordinary of that diocese to which the cleric is now incardinated, because that diocese alone is *propria* to him.

Alienae dioecesis, on the other hand, serves to describe the Ordinary of a diocese in which he is not now incardinated (because all such are juridically called *alienae*),[11] but in which he desires to become incardinated.

[10] Cf. *supra*, pp. 302-303.

[11] Cf. *supra*, pp. 385-6.

ARTICLE III

THE LETTERS

1. *Their Character*

The cleric who seeks the transfer must obtain a letter of excardination (*obtinere debet litteras . . . excardinationis*) from his present Ordinary; he must also obtain a letter of incardination (*et . . . litteras . . . incardinationis*) from the Ordinary of the alien diocese for which he is destined.

The history of these letters was traced quite fully in the historical section. The terms "excardination" and "incardination" were used sporadically during the Innocentian Period to designate that type of letter by which a Bishop gave up all rights over his cleric, including the right to ordain, to another Bishop, who in turn accepted the same. It was the Decree "*A primis*" of the Sacred Congregation of the Council [12] that officially adopted the idea of a canonical transfer by letters and brought the pertinent terms into common usage.

Both types of letters must be permanent (*perpetuae*) in their scope and absolute (*absolutae*) in their specification.

The first of these characteristics means that there must be no term placed on them. A Bishop who would issue a letter of excardination containing a time limit would not really be excardinating, but only lending his cleric with the expectation of recovering him when the term expired. It is vitally necessary that the letters be permanent in scope. In 1898 they were considered to provide a short form in the acquisition of a domicile for ordination, and domicile always included the intention of remaining permanently. If they were anything else but permanent, it would be unfair to the Bishops as well as to the clerics. The Bishops have to supply their dioceses adequately with clergy, and they take appropriate measures to do so. If, after bringing in an alien cleric and spending time and efforts, not to say money, on making him a valuable adjunct to the diocese, a Bishop suddenly discovered that the cleric's release from his home diocese was only temporary, and that now he must return, the diocese *ad quam* would suffer through losing an efficient cleric

[12] July 20, 1898—*ASS*, XXXI (1898-1899), 49 ss.

on whom it had depended; the Bishop *ad quem* would suffer through having to search for another available cleric, whereupon he would need to initiate the work of preparation all over again; and the cleric himself would no doubt suffer because of the difficulty in disengaging himself from various works of zeal in which he had become vitally interested in the diocese wherein he had been incardinated. Similar unfair results would follow for the excardinating Bishop if incardination proved to be only temporary. The excardinating Bishop, after having endured considerable trouble and expense in having one of his supernumerary clerics incardinated in another diocese, would be plagued with a repetition of the process if the exchange eventuated as only a temporary one. In the Decree " *A primis* " it was expressly stated that the incardination had to be *in perpetuum* (n. 2), and that it had to be evident, first of all, from a legitimate document that the cleric had been *in perpetuum dimissus* (n. 3). The Code in incorporating the idea has also insisted on perpetuity.

The second of the characteristics, absoluteness, means that the letters must be free from all conditions, whether express or tacit, which would suspend their effect. For instance, a letter of incardination would not be absolute if it contained the clause " provided that the candidate proves worthy." Any factor which would make the excardination and incardination process rescissible would be equally damaging in its effects on the Bishops and clerics concerned therein, regardless of whether that factor happened to be an uncertainty about the duration or an uncertainty about the execution of the incardination process. When these letters were recognized as short forms for acquiring a new domicile, a condition in them was also regarded as forestalling their effect altogether, just as a conditional intention even today would be inadequate for acquiring a domicile. Hence the " *A primis* " had to insist on the incardination being made " absolute " (*id est nullis sive expressis sive tacitis limitationibus obnoxiam*).

Some years before the issuance of the " *A primis*," letters of excardination and incardination were made a legitimate method of transfer for priests in the United States of America by the

Third Plenary Council of Baltimore (a. 1884).[13] In the case of priests, the formation of a domicile was not so important, and so for them there was instituted formal, *conditional* incardination, in which the subject had to prove worthy through a three or five-year period of trial before he was definitely incardinated. Meanwhile, the effect of the excardination had to remain suspended. This was certainly a hardship for the priests being transferred. Their lifetime could be absorbed in successive five-year experiments without incardination to a new diocese ever resulting.

By decreeing that letters of excardination and incardination must be *absolute* the Code has lifted all that uncertainty, and now there should be no considerable interval of time between the issuance of the one and the other. The incardinating Bishop must rely on the character testimony he receives from the dismissing Bishop rather than on knowledge attained from experiments of his own.

In canon 112 both the formal process of the Third Plenary Council of Baltimore, stripped of its conditional features, and that of the Decree "*A primis*" have been brought together. The Code, be it noticed, places no restrictions regarding the status of the subjects for whom the formal process may become of avail. It is equally applicable to priests and to lower clerics still pursuing their studies, even though the "*A primis*" had embraced the latter group only.

The essential features to be included in a letter of incardination should be:

a) the name of the incardinating Bishop,
b) the name of his diocese,
c) the name of the subject,
d) the designation of whether he is a priest or cleric,
e) his consent to be excardinated from his proper diocese,
f) the name of the excardinating Bishop,
g) the name of his diocese,
h) an account of his issuance of excardinatory letters in favor of the incardinating Bishop,
i) a declaration of incardination,

[13] Cf. *supra*, pp. 208-210.

j) express mention that it is perpetual and absolute,
k) a reference to the canon on formal incardination,
l) the name of the place,
m) the date of the month and year,
n) the signature of the incardinating Ordinary, and
o) the seal of the same.

A letter of excardination, similarly, should contain:

a) the name of the excardinating Bishop,
b) the name of his diocese,
c) the name of the subject,
d) the designation of whether he is a priest or cleric,
e) the subject's consent to his own excardination,
f) the name of the incardinating Bishop,
g) the name of his diocese,
h) an account of his preparatory consent,
i) a declaration of excardination,
j) express mention that it is perpetual and absolute,
k) some explanation of what it entails,
l) express mention of the justice of the causes,
m) a definite designation of the Bishop and diocese in whose favor it is given,
n) a reference to the canon on formal excardination,
o) the name of the place,
p) the date of the month and year,
q) the signature of the excardinating Ordinary, and
r) the seal of the same.

It is neither necessary nor desirable that all of the requisites contained in canons 116 and 117 for the validity and lawfulness of the entire juridical process be included. All that is needed for the validity of the letters as such is to be found expressed or implied in canon 112. Formerly, Testimonial Letters were sometimes made one with the "*exeat.*" The Code makes the execution of them a distinct act.

Strictly to be avoided in a letter of excardination is any authorization or direction as to the conferring of higher orders on a transferred lower cleric. That is a relic of ancient times, when *litterae perpetuae dimissoriae* were used as a means of effecting a transfer. Today the incardinating Bishop at once becomes the proper Bishop for the conferring of all future orders and needs no authorization or direction from the cleric's past Superior. Of course, the incardinating Bishop will need Testimonials when the time comes for conferring higher orders on his cleric.

2. *The Signatures*

Letters of both excardination and incardination must be signed personally by the respective Ordinaries issuing them. *Ab eodem subscriptas* leaves no room for any other interpretation. Normally this will be the Bishop's signature; but in the various contingencies wherein others besides the Bishop must assume the rule of the diocese, the signature will be that of the Ordinary who by common law is competent also to excardinate or incardinate clerics.[14] Usually the Chancellor or the Bishop's Secretary also signs the letters, but these signatures are not required *ad validitatem.* The Chancellor, being *eo ipso* an ecclesiastical notary,[15] by his signature gives to the letters a public documentary value.[16]

Nothing is said in canon 112 about the seal of the Bishop needing to be impressed upon the letters. Hence its absence would not invalidate them.[17] Nevertheless, a wise Ordinary will use both seal and Chancellor's signature in addition to his own to make assurance doubly sure.

3. *Sample Formulae*

Before a Bishop can make out a letter of excardination he must know the destination of the cleric, and, consequently, the prospective incardinating Bishop must inform him, preferably by letter, that he is prepared to incardinate. The form which this as well as the actual letters of excardination and incardination might take is varied. The following sample formulae, embodying the essential features mentioned above, are given by way of suggestion, not of direction:

[14] Cf. *supra*, p. 387.

[15] Can. 372, § 3.

[16] Can. 1812, § 1, 2°.

[17] Blat, *Commentarium*, II, n. 46.

I. Preparatory Consent of Incardinating Bishop

Petrus | scutum | Andreas

Miseratione Divina et Apostolicae Sedis Gratia

Episcopus N.——————

Omnibus quorum interest

Salutem in Domino.

Per has praesentes litteras declaramus Nos paratos esse Dominum (vel Reverendum Dominum) —————— Dioecesis —————— clericum / presbyterum, (et in ordine ————— constitutum), accipere et in subditos clerumque Dioecesis ————— incardinare, quando Illmus. et Revmus. D.D. ——————, Episcopus ——————, jurisdictionem et auctoritatem quam super Dominum (vel Reverendum Dominum) ——————— hucusque habuit in manus Nostras successorumque Nostrorum transtulerit.

Datum ———————

die ——— mensis ——— A.D. ———

———————————

Episcopus

II. Letter of Excardination

Joanes [scutum] Joseph

Dei et Apostolicae Sedis Gratia

Episcopus N.————

Dilecto Nobis in Christo

Dno. (vel Rev. Dno.)————

Dioecesis Nostrae Alumno (vel Presbytero)

Salutem in Domino.

Precibus tuis propter iustas causas a Nobis cognitas et admissas libenter annuentes, cum Nobis compertum sit Illm̃um. et Revm̃um. D.D.————, Dioecesis ———— Episcopum, paratum esse ad te incardinandum, per has praesentes litteras te ab hac Dioecesi Nostra perpetuo et absolute excardinamus et excardinatum edicimus et declaramus ad normam canonis 112 Codicis Iuris Canonici, omnem jurisdictionem et auctoritatem quam in te habemus ad eundem Antistitem vel Successores ejus in sede ———— in perpetuum transferentes.

In quorum fidem, praesentes Excardinationis litteras manu Nostra subscriptas sigilloque Nostro munitas fieri jussimus.

Datum ———— ex aedibus Nostris,

die ———— mensis ———— A.D. ————

————————————

Episcopus N. ————

————————————

Cancellarius

III. Letter of Incardination

Petrus scutum Andreas

Miseratione Dei et Apostolicae Sedis Gratia
Episcopus N.———

Dilecto Nobis in Christo
Dno. (vel Rev. Dno.)———
Salutem in Domino.

Quum per litteras excardinationis perpetuae et absolutae, die ——— mensis ——— anni ———, subscriptas, certo Nobis compertum sit Illm̃um. ac Revm̃um. D.D. ———, Episcopum ———, hactenus Ordinarium tuum, votis tuis annuentem, jurisdictionem et auctoritatem quam super te hucusque habuit in manus Nostras successorumque Nostrorum transtulisse, per has praesentes litteras te in clerum Dioecesis ——— perpetuo et absolute incardinamus ad normam canonis 112 Codicis Iuris Canonici incardinatumque declaramus.

In quorum fidem, has litteras manu Nostra subscriptas sigilloque Nostro munitas fieri jussimus.

Datum ——— ex aedibus Nostris,

die ——— mensis ——— A.D. ———

———

Episcopus N. ———

———

Cancellarius

ARTICLE IV

COMPETENCY FOR ORDINATION TO HIGHER ORDERS

The proper Bishop *quoad ordinationem* for incardinated clerics was discussed at length in a previous Chapter.[18] There it was stated that the authentic interpretation given by the Pontifical Commission for the Interpretation of the Code on July 24, 1939,[19] which settled this question for those who are directly incardinated in an alien diocese by first tonsure, certainly must extend also to all clerics *formally* incardinated in an alien diocese. In other words, the Commission settled a question of principle, not merely one of method. The underlying doubt was: "Is incardination still a basis on which a Bishop has a right to ordain?" This the Commission answered affirmatively, contrary to the opinion of many eminent canonists. It was only accidental to the main issue that the incardination spoken of in the *dubium* had been effected through first tonsure. Whether by first tonsure, by formal letters, or by residential benefice, the jurisdiction over a cleric arising from incardination is the same. If it extends to the conferring of orders in one instance, so does it also in the others. This is held as certain, though, of course, the Holy See may still further clarify it.

As soon, then, as a Bishop concludes the transfer process by executing letters of incardination and informing the excardinating Bishop of the same,[20] he is immediately competent to ordain the incardinated cleric to higher orders, or to issue dimissorial letters to some other Bishop to ordain the cleric to higher orders, even though the cleric has not yet established residence for a domicile in the incardinating Bishop's diocese. The incardinating Bishop, however, must first obtain the necessary Testimonials as to character, etc., and fulfill all other canonical requisites.[21]

Letters such as these can be exchanged by mail, by messenger, or at a personal meeting of the two interested Bishops.

[18] Cf. *supra*, pp. 355 ff.

[19] *Supra*, p. 369.

[20] Can. 116.

[21] Cf. *infra*, pp. 524 ff.

CHAPTER IX

Exceptions to the Power of Granting Excardination and Incardination

Can. 113. - **Excardinationem et incardinationem concedere nequit Vicarius Generalis sine mandato speciali, nec Vicarius Capitularis, nisi post annum a vacatione sedis episcopalis et cum consensu Capituli.**

THE authority competent to grant formal excardination and formal incardination to secular clerics was expressly stated in canon 112 to be the Ordinary of a diocese. The wide meaning of the term "Ordinary" was defined in connection with that canon.[1] There also it was stated that the term in canon 112 suffers some exceptions, which are logically listed in the very next canon, and which now merit some explanation. In view of the general wording of canon 113, however, it must be concluded that its restrictions apply to any form of excardination and incardination of clerics, but not to laymen. The use of the two terms as correlatives, joined by the conjunction *et,* insinuates that. A layman can be incardinated by first tonsure, but, since he cannot be excardinated, it is not possible to consider him a subject for the double canonical transfer process of "excardination *and* incardination" expressly referred to here.[2] The power of the Ordinary, *sede vacante vel impedita,* initially to incardinate clerics, by issuing dimissorial letters for first tonsure, is likewise restricted, but by another canon, namely, canon 958, § 1, 3°. However, the issuance of a written permission to a

[1] *Supra,* p. 387.

[2] Many authors without offering any semblance of argument cling more or less definitely to the opinion that can. 113 modifies the formal process alone, e. g., Maroto, *Institutt.,* I, n. 498; Chelodi, *Ius de Personis,* n. 107, a; Augustine, *A Commentary on the New Code of Canon Law* (8 vols., St. Louis: B. Herder, 1918-1922), II, 54; Badii, *Institutt.,* I, n. 98; De Meester, *Compendium,* I, n. 349; Wernz-Vidal, *Ius Canonicum,* II, n. 62. This can hardly be sustained. For canonists holding the opposite opinion, cf. *infra,* p. 407.

diocesan cleric to accept an alien residential benefice, or to depart from the diocese perpetually, is a form of excardination, as will be seen in connection with canon 114, and hence it, too, must be considered, by virtue of this same canon, as restricted in its use by Vicars Capitular and Administrators. The power to incardinate by the conferring of a residential benefice is regulated and restricted by the canons on benefices, but suffers further curtailment from this canon as well.[3]

It is readily admissible that the act of excardinating is a form of perpetual alienation, and that the act of incardinating has the effect of increasing a diocese's liabilities. Since both acts primarily affect the diocese and its ruler, it is no more than just that the permanent diocesan authority, the residential Bishop, have the controlling voice in their execution. Hence certain exceptions are made to safeguard his rights.

In mission territories there is not the same reason for a check; in fact, the opposite is true. It is all important that a quasi-diocese incardinate as many clerics as it can secure to fill its vast needs. Hence no express limitations are found placed on the incardinatory power of those who rule a quasi-diocese *sede vacante vel impeditæ.* Since they do not have to wait a year after the vacancy to issue dimissorial letters,[4] *a pari* it can be argued that neither are they restricted in the issuance of letters of incardination, because of the close alliance between the two. In the last analysis, dimissorial letters issued for a layman's ordination for his proper vicariate or prefecture is initial incardination.

With regard to the excardinatory power of these temporary rulers of quasi-dioceses, another consideration enters in. Many of the priests laboring in quasi-dioceses are sent there by the Holy See through the Sacred Congregation for the Propagation of the Faith. They take the strict oath of the mission title not to desert their mission, even to enter religion, and *a fortiori* not to desert it for another territory, without express permission from the Holy See. Hence, the excardinatory power, not only

[3] Cf. *infra,* pp. 416-7.

[4] Cf. *supra,* pp. 304 ff.

of those who rule the quasi-diocese *sede vacante vel impedita,* but also of the Vicars and Prefects Apostolic themselves, is limited by canon 307, § 1. They must first consult the Holy See and obtain its approval before any action is taken that leads to excardination.

ARTICLE I

THE VICAR GENERAL

The first exception to the term "Ordinary," as it is used in canon 112, is the Vicar General, who is the Bishop's other self. Normally he is termed an Ordinary because he exercises ordinary jurisdiction in the diocese, that is to say, the power he possesses is attached to his office by the common law itself. The same law, however, also places specific restrictions on his jurisdiction, in which matters it requires him to have a "special mandate" from the Bishop.[5] There are twenty-nine cases in which the Vicar General can not act without a mandate.[6] The very first of these is in the matter of excardinating and incardinating secular clerics.[7] This is not strange, in view of what was just said, and, besides, this is a graver matter than merely issuing dimissorial letters (*litterae dimissoriae*) for ordination, and that power is withheld from the Vicar General in canon 958, § 1, 2°.[8]

In the letter of appointment of a Vicar General the Bishop is able to incorporate a special mandate for all or for some of the entire twenty-nine cases which are listed in the Code as needing such, or he can content himself with issuing singly, and separately from the original appointment, a special mandate for each type of jurisdictional matter as the occasion arises. Creusen [9] holds that the Vicar General's power in the specified matters in the first instance is ordinary, because annexed to and made ac-

[5] Can. 368, § 1.

[6] Campagna, *Il Vicario Generale del Vescovo,* The Catholic University of America, Canon Law Studies, n. 66 (Washington, D. C.: The Catholic University of America, 1931), pp. 130-131.

[7] Can. 113.

[8] Maroto, *Instituts.,* I, n. 498.

[9] Vermeersch-Creusen, *Epitome,* I, n. 436.

cessory to the office itself, but that in the second instance his power in each specified matter is delegated. Campagna[10] disagrees with this opinion of Creusen, and strongly inclines to the view that whatever a Vicar General does per *mandatum speciale*, whether the power be conceded *in globo* or *in individuo*, he does as a delegate of the Bishop.

The only effect that this difference of opinion might have on the subject at hand is the length to which the Vicar General can go in using his power to excardinate and incardinate diocesan clerics. If it be admitted that the Vicar's power is ordinary in the jurisdictional matter of excardinating and incardinating, because it had been given to him at the time of his appointment, he can use that power without further consulting the Bishop, until the Bishop dies, or removes him from office, or until the Vicar himself resigns his office, whereupon all of his jurisdiction ceases at once.[11] If the Vicar's power in this matter be conceded to be no more than delegated, it can be used only according to the will of the Bishop. This is always true whenever the special mandate is given separately from the Vicar General's original appointment, because then the power is definitely a mere delegation. If the Bishop grants to his Vicar General a special mandate to excardinate and incardinate, but only during a certain emergency, e. g., while the Bishop is absent from his diocese to recover health, the Vicar is able to use the power if needed until the mandate is ended. In all cases, however, wherein a Vicar General, enjoying a special mandate, signs the letter of excardination or incardination, he must include in the formula mention of his special mandate.[12] Furthermore, the Vicar General with a special mandate cannot validly excardinate or incardinate a cleric whose petition the Bishop himself has already refused, but the Bishop can validly grant the favor, even though it was already refused by the Vicar General, provided that in his petition the cleric makes known the latter's refusal.[13]

[10] *Op. cit.*, pp. 133-135.

[11] Can. 371.

[12] Toso, *Comment. Minora*, in can. 113.

[13] Can. 44, § 2.

ARTICLE II

THE VICAR CAPITULAR OR THE ADMINISTRATOR

The second " Ordinary " who is excepted from the power of granting excardination and incardination as delineated in canons 112 and 114 is the Vicar Capitular, or, in dioceses where the Cathedral Chapter has not yet been instituted or restored, and where a Board of Diocesan Consultors functions in its place, the Administrator.[14] The law expressly states in canon 427 that all those powers which are attributed by Canon Law to the Cathedral Chapter for the government of a diocese, either when the see is filled or when it is impeded or vacant, are likewise to be considered as granted to the Board of Diocesan Consultors. Hence, too, whatever exceptions are made to the power of the Chapter or of the Vicar Capitular must apply also to the Consultors and to the Administrator.

There was given above a brief outline of the way in which the rule of a diocese is provided for *sede vacante vel impedita.*[15] According to canon 435, § 1, the Vicar Capitular (or Administrator) who is elected succeeds to the ordinary jurisdiction of the Bishop in all spiritual and temporal things, except those which are expressly forbidden to him in the law. In canon 113 there is explicitly denied him the power of granting excardination and incardination, except after a year from the time the see becomes vacant, and then only with the consent of the Chapter (or Consultors). Historically this restriction can be traced to that placed by the Council of Trent on the power of a Cathedral Chapter, or of any person or group succeeding to the *regimen* during the vacancy of a see, to issue dimissorial letters,[16] because the exercise of such a power was so closely allied to the power of granting excardination and incardination that the reason for a limitation was the same in both, even as it is today.[17]

[14] Can. 423.

[15] Pp. 303-4.

[16] Cf. *supra*, pp. 259-261.

[17] Cf. can. 958, § 1, 3°, where exactly the same restriction is still placed on the Vicar Capitular's (or Administrator's) power of issuing *litterae dimissoriae.*

The Code says that the power is not granted until after a year (*nisi post annum*) from the vacancy of the episcopal see. The computation of the year follows the rule of canon 34, § 3, 3°, which supposes that the *terminus a quo* does not coincide with the beginning of the day. Hence the actual day of the Bishop's death is not counted, no matter at what time it occurs, and the year is not completed until the end of the same calendar day of the following year. If the Bishop died on January 2, 1941, at 1:10 A. M., for example, the year would not be completed until January 2, 1942, at 12 midnight, and the Vicar Capitular or Administrator would have the power formally to excardinate or incardinate on January 3, 1942, even though he himself had not been elected until January 9, 1941.[18]

The " consent " (*cum consensu*), and not merely the advice or the hearing, of the Cathedral Chapter or Board of Diocesan Consultors is required. This means that the Vicar Capitular or Administrator would act invalidly if he attempted to overrule their vote.[19]

An Apostolic Administrator appointed only temporarily has no more rights or duties than a Vicar Capitular, and hence he, too, would be restricted in the same way,[20] but not so if he was appointed permanently.[21]

Whenever the jurisdiction of a Vicar Capitular or Administrator lasts over a year from the vacancy of the see, if he uses his power formally to excardinate or incardinate, in order to act lawfully he must make explicit mention in the letters that the two conditions have been fulfilled: to wit, that a full year has elapsed, and that he has the consent of the Cathedral Chapter or of the Board of Diocesan Consultors. Otherwise the letters of excardination or incardination are faulty because of an understatement of the truth (*subreptio*),[22] though this does not interfere with the validity of the process.[23]

[18] Blat, *Commentarium*, II, n. 47, who also notes that this would not apply to an Apostolic Administrator who had been given while the see was still occupied.

[19] Can. 105, 1°.

[20] Can. 315, § 2, 1°.

[21] Can. 315, § 1.

[22] Toso, *Comment. Minora*, in can. 113.

[23] Cf. can. 42.

CHAPTER X

Virtual Excardination and Incardination of Secular Clerics Through a Residential Benefice

Can. 114. - **Habetur excardinatio et incardinatio, si ab Ordinario alienae dioecesis clericus beneficium residentiale obtinuerit cum consensu sui Ordinarii in scriptis dato, vel cum licentia ab eodem in scriptis concessa e dioecesi discedendi in perpetuum.**

THIS is the second of the two alternative processes which are recognized by Canon Law for the transfer of secular clerics from one diocese to another.[1] It consists in a cleric's procuring the written permission of his Ordinary, either to accept a residential benefice elsewhere, or simply to depart from the diocese in perpetuity, and his later acquisition from the Ordinary of an alien diocese of a definite residential benefice. Excardination and incardination take place, not by any formal document, but by the very fact whereby there is conferred upon the cleric an alien residential benefice, which by its nature has the power and effect of disengaging the cleric perpetually from his former proper diocese and attaching him to the spiritual service of the new diocese, in which the benefice is located. The act of conferring the benefice has several effects, of which excardination is one, but not the direct and immediate one.[2] For these reasons the process is called *virtual* excardination and incardination, although it is also variously named by different authors as implicit, tacit, equivalent, and *ipso iure* excardination and incardination.[3]

[1] Cf. *supra*, pp. 384-5.

[2] Maroto, *Institutts.*, II, n. 494.

[3] Cf. Suarez, "De incardinatione ratione beneficii,"—*Angelicum*, XIII (1936), 193, note 1.

ARTICLE I

EXISTENCE OF THIS METHOD PRIOR TO THE CODE

Considerable difference of opinion exists over the question whether or not this virtual process is born of the Code. Some present day writers have no hesitation in saying that it is.[4] Nevertheless, it has been shown above [5] not only that it existed prior to the promulgation of the Code, but that for a long time it was the usual method.[6]

1. *Before 1898*

The point which confused many was the common practice of lower clerics obtaining a benefice in an alien diocese to acquire thereby a proper Bishop for ordination on the title or basis of that benefice. That did not bring about incardination at all, as was profusely explained in the historical section of this study. Even ordination on the strength of such a benefice did not necessarily effect incardination, as many claim. Side by side with the title of proper Bishop *ratione beneficii* was the ordination title of benefice (*titulus beneficii*), which could be acquired in an alien diocese also by a priest, especially if he did not have a sufficient *titulus ordinationis* in his proper diocese. When this *titulus beneficii* was a residential one, and was acquired with due observance of the law of the period relative to the proper Bishop's consent, it undoubtedly resulted in an *ipso facto* excardination from the former diocese and incardination into the alien diocese.

One important difference between equivalent (*aequipollens*) incardination, as it was mostly called then, and virtual incardination, as it is popularly known today, is that equivalent incardination was based on an informal expression of the will of the two Bishops to excardinate and incardinate, whereas virtual incardination in canon 114 is effected *ipso facto* by the fulfillment of

[4] E. g., Creusen, "De excardinatione et incardinatione implicita,"—*Jus Pontif.*, XV (1935), 37-40; Francia, "Animadversiones circa incardinationem,"—*Apoll.*, IX (1936), 216-218.

[5] Pp. 227-230.

[6] Cf. Suarez, *art. cit.*, pp. 192-201, for a very fine defense of its previous existence.

the requirements, regardless of the intention.[7] When a diocesan Bishop conferred a residential benefice on an alien cleric, prior to 1898, it had to be evident from his words and actions that he meant to incardinate; otherwise it was not effected. After 1918, however, if a Bishop confers a residential benefice on an alien cleric, it is useless for the Bishop to protest later that he did not intend to bring about incardination; it is effected *ipso facto,* provided, of course, that the cleric has written permission from his proper Ordinary, and that he has not acted fraudulently in securing the benefice. It is because of this new feature that the canon is called dangerous for those Bishops who are prompted more by charity than by caution in admitting alien clerics to serve in their dioceses.[8]

2. *Between 1898 and 1918*

When the Decree "*A primis*" was issued,[9] it was immediately assumed by canonists that it abrogated all other previously existing methods of excardination and incardination for both lower clerics and priests, and that it made the formal process the only canonical one for all. In fact the Consultors of the Sacred Congregation of the Council itself apparently agreed that it did so, by their decision that the presumptive incardination of priests, as established by the III Plenary Council of Baltimore (a. 1884), was abrogated by it.[10] Therein, too, was a misunderstanding. The Decree "*A primis*" had not been issued for the regulation of priests, but only for lower clerics, and even the Consultors of the Sacred Congregation of the Council could not justify its application and abrogatory power to both classes.[11]

[7] "At veteri iure, praeter scriptam incardinationem, etiam oralis, imo et aequipollens seu implicita incardinatio in usu erat, dummodo certe constaret de voluntate utriusque Episcopi clericum perpetuo et absolute dimittendi eumque item perpetuo et absolute recipiendi."—Conclusio 2 post responsum S. C. Ep. et Reg., *Viterbien.,* 14 iul. 1905 (*ASS,* XXXIX [1906], 211). Compare this with "*Habetur* excardinatio et incardinatio si . . ." in can. 114.

[8] "*Incautis episcopis periculosi*"—Chelodi, *Ius de Personis,* n. 107, note 4.

[9] Cf. text above, pp. 217-218.

[10] S. C. C., *Romana et Aliarum,* 15 sept. 1906—*ASS,* XXXIX (1906), 486 ss.

[11] Cf. Suarez, "De incardinatione ratione beneficii,"—*Angelicum,* XIII (1906), 196-201. Cf. also *supra,* pp. 220 ff., 227 ff.

In reality, then, equivalent incardination still existed after the Decree "*A primis*" and continued up to the promulgation of the Code. It was merely to avoid the possibility of wholesale court suits that this study adopted the practical conclusion that in the interval between 1898 and 1918 there was no equivalent incardination existent.[12]

The virtual incardination of the Code is really a continuation of the old equivalent process, inasmuch as both are achieved in the same way and without formalities, except that the Code has placed it on a firmer, surer basis.

ARTICLE II

VIRTUAL EXCARDINATION

The opening words of canon 114 "*Habetur excardinatio . . . si . . .*" indicate that this is now a canonical method of real excardination. It is not just based on informal indications or presumptions; rather it is had *ipso iure* as soon as certain posited conditions are fulfilled. If any one of them is unfulfilled, the act is null and void as far as virtual excardination is concerned.[13] Canon 114 proceeds to outline these conditions. Since, then, the act by which the cleric is permitted to leave his diocese is a real excardination, it must follow the general requisites for all excardinations wherever that term is used in a generic way. Principally it must be coördinated with canons 113, 116, and 117. Not every Ordinary can give it, as will be presently explained; and, when it is given, it must be only for a just cause. The permission to depart, likewise, is so correlated to the reception of the benefice that it does not have the canonical effect of excardination until the benefice is actually obtained.[14] If, for some reason, the cleric bearing his proper Bishop's consent or permission is never installed in the benefice for which he was elected, he still remains incardinated in his first diocese. The Curia of the dismissing Ordinary must also issue Testimonials about the cleric, and the Ordinary himself is charged in conscience, under

[12] Cf. *supra*, p. 231.

[13] Toso, *Comment. Minora*, in can. 114.

[14] Maroto, *Instituts.*, I, n. 497, A, a.

pain of grave sin, for the truth of them. Finally, a very old condition is that the securing of the benefice be not done *in fraudem*. This would be the case, for instance, if the cleric concealed his perpetual departure permission from an alien Bishop who, while appointing him to a parish, did not intend to incardinate him.

1. *The Cleric*

No layman is eligible for a benefice of any kind.[15] A cleric (*clericus*) alone can profit by the virtual method of incardination. Though not likely in days when benefices are scarce, a mere *tonsuratus*, being included in the term cleric,[16] can acquire a residential benefice which does not have attached to it the care of souls,[17] can provide for it by a vicar, and thereby can be virtually excardinated to the diocese of the place in which the benefice exists.

2. *The Dismissing Ordinary*

The one whose consent is needed for a cleric to depart from a diocese is his own proper Ordinary (*sui Ordinarii*). This means not only the Bishop of the diocese to which he was hitherto attached, either by first tonsure or by some other canonical method, but also anyone who comes under the name of the " Ordinary of the place " according to canon 198, § 2, subject, however, to the limitations placed on such a one in canon 113. A Vicar General, Vicar Capitular, or Administrator, therefore, cannot give to a cleric consent to accept an alien residential benefice, or grant to him permission to depart from the diocese in perpetuity, except under the conditions therein described and explained above.[18]

Those who succeed to the rule of apostolic vicariates and prefectures, *sede vacante vel impedita*, are not included in the

[15] Can. 118.

[16] Can. 108, § 1.

[17] Cf. can. 154.

[18] Pp. 397 ff. Cf. Blat, *Commentarium*, II, n. 48; Toso, *Comment. Minora*, in can. 114; Vermeersch-Creusen, *Epitome*, I, n. 204; Suarez, " De incardinatione ratione beneficii,"—*Angelicum*, XIII (1936), 205-206.

list of exceptions to the power of excardinating, but, because of the oath of the mission title which many of their priests have taken, the excardinatory power of all rulers of quasi-dioceses is limited by the Holy See, as was previously explained.[19]

The permission to depart from the diocese in perpetuity is likewise conceded by the same Ordinary (*ab eodem*), i. e., the one whose proper subject the cleric is, since "*eodem*" manifestly refers back to the proximate phrase "*sui Ordinarii.*"

3. *The Permission*

For excardination and incardination to follow from the obtaining of an alien residential benefice, the cleric must have his proper Bishop's permission (*cum consensu . . . vel cum licentia*). This is an age-old requirement, insisted upon with more or less severity in the various periods of history.[20] It is a natural consequence of the perpetual, special attachment of a cleric to his Bishop. It might be given in either one of two forms: Consent of the Ordinary for his cleric to receive a residential benefice in an alien diocese, or permission of the Ordinary for his cleric to depart perpetually from the diocese. Both of these will now be examined in detail.

A. Consent to Accept an Alien Residential Benefice

The consent of a Bishop for his cleric to obtain a certain residential benefice in another diocese, when given, is the same as formal excardination without the solemnity. From his standpoint, the Bishop in giving this absolutely disengages the cleric from his own diocese, because thenceforth the cleric will be bound to reside perpetually in the other diocese, and will be subject to the jurisdiction of the other Bishop, at least as far as the benefice, and therefore his life's service, is concerned.

This consent must be written, for the Code says "*cum consensu sui Ordinarii* in scriptis *dato,*" but there are no special formalities to it. It is addressed to the cleric, not to a Bishop, and it suffices for its validity if it contains the mere declaration:

[19] *Supra*, pp. 398-9.

[20] Cf. *supra*, pp. 165, 167-9, 174, 193-5.

"I hereby grant my consent for you to accept ———————, a residential benefice in the diocese of ———————." From the wording of the Code "*si . . . beneficium residentiale obtinuerit cum consensu . . ., vel cum licentia . . .*" it can be inferred that consent is given only when the particular residential benefice to be received is known in advance, e. g., when the cleric already has some title to it by nomination or election.[21] When the particular benefice is not known in advance, it is the permission of perpetual departure which is given to the cleric.

To illustrate, let it be supposed that public notice has been given of a *concursus* for a residential benefice in diocese *A*, and that there is no restriction that the applicants be clerics of diocese *A*. The successful competitor might be a cleric of diocese *B*. He must then approach his own Ordinary for consent to accept in actuality that to which he has already secured a title. On the other hand, a cleric of diocese *B* might be anxious to find a new diocese where the climate will be more agreeable for his health. Not knowing of any diocese where a *concursus* is to be held, he might obtain from his proper Bishop a mere permission to depart permanently from diocese *B*. Fortified with this, he goes in search of a possible haven, and eventually finds that there is a residential benefice, as yet unconferred, in diocese *A*. He applies for it, and wins it, either by open competition or otherwise, but needs no further permission from his proper Bishop of *B* to accept it.

Must the consent be in writing to be *valid?* Authors are not unanimous in their answer to this question, but the preponderance of the arguments is in favor of the affirmative. "All authors agree," says the Consultor of the Sacred Congregation of the Council in the case *Bismarckien. et Aliarum*,[22] "that when ecclesiastical law prescribes the form of an act, the act lacking its form is invalid." Canon 11 gives the general principle for discerning invalidating laws. It says: "Irritantes aut inhabilitantes eae tantum leges habendae sunt, quibus aut actum

[21] Ayrinhac, *General Legislation in the New Code of Canon Law (General Legislation)*, (New York: Benziger Brothers, 1923), n. 246.

[22] 31 ian. 1913—*AAS*, V (1913), 36.

esse nullum aut inhabilem esse personam expresse vel aequivalenter statuitur." According to Maroto,[23] "it is equivalently laid down that the act is null or the person incapacitated when the form or solemnities with which the act is to be executed, or the conditions which are required to make or keep capacity, are determined." Now, canon 114 prescribes the form of excardination with a view to incardination by reason of an acquired residential benefice. Consequently, when the form is not strictly fulfilled, excardination does not result.[24] Followers of this opinion, besides Suarez,[25] are Creusen,[26] Chelodi,[27] Toso,[28] and De Iturre,[29] not to speak of others who hold it in a more obscure way.[30] The only opponent to it seems to be Coronata.[31]

The written consent must also be *signed* by the Ordinary "*a quo.*" This is a consequence of the preceding conclusion. Though canon 114 does not say "*subscriptas,*" like canon 112 does for the formal letters, nevertheless, as long as written letters are necessary for *validity*, it logically follows that they have to be signed by the one authorized to issue them. Otherwise one could not speak of consent or permission given in writing by the releasing Ordinary. Rather it would be consent, perhaps oral, attested as the Ordinary's by the letter of a notary.

A final and very important question is: Must the written consent of the Ordinary for the cleric to receive the residential benefice be *perpetual* and *absolute* (or unconditional) for the validity of virtual excardination? Canon 114 does not expressly state that this consent must be either perpetual or abso-

[23] *Institutt.*, II, n. 225, A.

[24] Suarez, "De incardinatione ratione beneficii,"—*Angelicum*, XIII (1936), 202-203.

[25] *Loc. cit.*

[26] Vermeersch-Creusen, *Epitome*, I, n. 204.

[27] *Ius de Personis*, n. 107, b.

[28] *Comment. Minora*, in can. 114.

[29] "Quid requiritur ad beneficium in aliena dioecesi possidendum,"—*Illustracion del Clero*, fas. 514 (1928), 202-203.

[30] Cf. those listed by Suarez, *art. cit.*—*Angelicum*, XIII (1936), 202, note 1.

[31] *Institutiones Iuris Canonici* (*Institutt.*), (5 vols., Taurini: Marietti, 1928-1936), I, n. 175, 2, b.

lute. Yet, with regard to the permission of the Ordinary for his cleric to depart perpetually from the diocese, the same canon manifestly states that it must be given in perpetuity (*in perpetuum*), but does not state that it should be absolute. Does the omission of both qualifications in the first instance, and the insertion of only one of them in the second, have any juridical significance? At least it affords the foundation for a dispute whether or not these omitted qualifications are necessary for the validity of the consent.[32] Hence it will be of assistance to discuss both qualifications more in detail.

The most likely reason why canon 114 does not include *perpetuity* as a qualification for the validity of the Ordinary's written consent for his cleric to receive an alien residential benefice is that it is of the very nature of a residential benefice to be conferred *in perpetuum,* not *ad tempus;* [33] and hence the consent for a cleric to receive one can not be anything else but *perpetual* before the law. Even if a Bishop gave his written consent for his cleric to receive an alien residential benefice " for a period of five years," that restriction would be juridically inoperative, because contrary to the common law. Nevertheless, it would be a valid consent, enabling the cleric to accept the benefice, and the cleric would become virtually incardinated in the new diocese. He would not be bound to return to his former proper Bishop after the five years had elapsed. Only the supreme ecclesiastical power, through an Apostolic Indult, could authorize a Bishop to add such a condition contrary to the common law and have it juridically recognized.[34]

This does not mean, of course, that a Bishop, who gives his cleric permission to work in an alien diocese for any limited period of time, *ipso facto* loses him. By canon 144 an Ordinary can certainly grant that permission, and the cleric still remains incardinated in his own diocese, and can be recalled for a just

[32] Cf. Maroto, *Instituts.*, II, n. 497, A, note 1; Ayrinhac, *General Legislation,* n. 246.

[33] Can. 1438.

[34] Cappello, " Quaestiones Canonicae de Ordinatione, domicilio et incardinatione," III—*Per.*, XX (1931), 133*-136*; Creusen, " De excardinatione et incardinatione implicita,"—*Jus Pontif.*, XV (1935), 38; Toso, *Comment. Minora,* in can. 114.

cause at any time, even before the time limit, provided the recall does not harm the diocese where he is serving. But, in such a temporary permission to work in an alien diocese, the Ordinary "*a quo*" must be careful not to say that he is granting permission for the cleric to accept this or that particular parish, canonry, etc., in the other diocese, because thereby, regardless of the time limit to the permission, he would be juridically excardinating the cleric. A safer course would be definitely to state that he is granting his cleric permission to labor in the other diocese, but *not* to accept therein any residential benefice.

Canon 114 does not make it a requisite for validity that the written consent of the Ordinary for a cleric to receive an alien residential benefice be *absolute* or unconditional, because virtual excardination, unlike formal excardination, can and does admit of conditions which are capable of fulfillment before the excardination process is completed. Conditions attached to the letter of consent might be divided thus: 1. those that are impossible of fulfillment at any time; 2. those that are capable of fulfillment only after the excardination process is completed; and 3. those that can be fulfilled before the excardination process is completed. Conditions of the first type would not even suspend the consent; from the very outset they would negate it. Hence, a conditional consent of this type would really be no consent at all. The second type of appended conditions would outwardly reduce the consent to a temporal one, but it was pointed out above [35] that a Bishop's consent for his cleric to receive an alien residential benefice is always considered perpetual before the law. Therefore, a condition of this type, attached to the Bishop's consent, would be juridically inoperative, and would not mar the validity of the virtual excardination process. The third type of condition is entirely compatible with the virtual excardination process, in which there can be a considerable lapse of time between the issuance of the Bishop's consent and the execution of the excardination, which latter takes place only when the alien residential benefice is actually conferred. Such a condition would suspend the Bishop's consent

[35] P. 411.

temporarily, but, as soon as the condition had been fulfilled, the consent would automatically become both absolute and perpetual.

The following examples will illustrate the three types of conditional consent: 1st type—" I consent to your acceptance of the parish of St. John in the diocese of ————, provided that no other priest can be found who is capable and worthy of receiving it "; 2nd type—" I hereby consent to your acceptance of the parish of St. Philip in the diocese of ————, on condition that, if for some reason you resign it, you will be bound to return to this diocese "; 3rd type—" I hereby grant my consent for you to accept the parish of St. James in the diocese of ————, if you succeed in obtaining a title to it." [86]

It is also to be noted that a permission for a cleric to enter a *concursus,* even though it be accompanied by Testimonial Letters about the cleric's life, character, and service thus far rendered, does not include consent for the cleric to accept the residential benefice if he should be successful in the *concursus.* Priests very often enter a *concursus* in another diocese without the idea of gaining a particular benefice. Sometimes it is just to obtain a good record for the future from their meritorious success in the examinations; sometimes, too, it is with the idea of accepting the benefice best suited to them out of several that may be offered to them. In any case, another permission is needed by the cleric before he can actually accept this or that particular residential benefice in another diocese. This does not prevent the Ordinary " *a quo* " from combining both permissions in one document.[87]

B. Permission to Depart Perpetually from the Diocese

This is the second form which the permission from the Ordinary " *a quo* " might take (*vel cum licentia ab eodem in scriptis concessa e dioecesi discedendi in perpetuum*). It is expressly stated that it is to be written, which is a requisite for its validity, just as that consent which the Ordinary gives his cleric

[86] Cf. Suarez, " De incardinatione ratione beneficii,"—*Angelicum,* XIII (1936), 204; Blat, *Commentarium,* II, n. 48; Badii, *Instituts.,* I, n. 98, note 1.

[87] Suarez, *art. cit.*—*Ibid.,* p. 205.

to accept an alien residential benefice must be in writing in order to be valid; [38] and, in a parallel way, the permission must also be signed by the dismissing Ordinary.[39] It consists in a blanket permission issued to the cleric to leave the diocese perpetually. Its purpose is to give a cleric, who has a just cause for desiring to transfer his life's service to another diocese, an opportunity of going in search of a diocese more satisfactory to his personal needs and of a Bishop able and willing to use him, so that when he does become satisfied, and is offered a residential benefice, he may become excardinated without delay. An example of how it operates will be shown in the discussion below on canon 117.[40] Foreign-born clerics from regions outside Europe receive from their proper Bishops letters of perpetual dismissal, armed with which they come to the United States of America and give their labor to some diocese here, still remaining incardinated in their home diocese. However, there may come a time when they will become incardinated in the diocese here, either by accepting a parish on the strength of their dismissal letters, or by having formal letters of excardination and incardination prepared and exchanged. The virtual method is obviously the easier where the home diocese is so far away.

It may be argued that, for these foreign-born clerics, a definite diocese and Bishop must be known in advance; hence, a letter of perpetual dismissal should give the cleric his liberty only to serve in a certain alien diocese. The fallacy in that is that the prescription for the Bishop of destination to be known in advance applies only to Europeans coming to America or to the Philippine Islands, and to Americans going to the Philippines; it does not apply to other long-distance loans of clerics.

It may seem somewhat like the creation of clerical *vagi* again, but it really is not, because these clerics still belong to their diocese "*a qua*" until they are incardinated elsewhere; and, in accordance with canon 116, notice of their incardination elsewhere is to be transmitted to their proper Ordinary "*a quo*" as soon as possible.

[38] Cf. *supra*, pp. 409-410.

[39] Cf. *supra*, p. 410.

[40] Cf. pp. 538-545.

One distinct precaution against their becoming *vagi* in fact if not in law is the insertion of a condition into their perpetual dismissal, e. g., "I grant you permission to depart from this diocese perpetually, provided that you obtain a residential benefice within a year from this date." [41] It is definitely expressed in canon 114 that the permission must be *perpetual,* but it does not say that it must be *absolute,* i. e., unconditional. What was said above concerning the consent of an Ordinary for his cleric to accept an alien residential benefice [42] applies here also to the permission for a cleric's perpetual departure from the diocese—any condition which is capable of fulfillment prior to the execution of the virtual excardination is admissible. The example just given does not interfere with the perpetuity of the permission, nor with the perpetual and absolute character of the virtual excardination itself; as soon as the condition is satisfied the permission is in force for life.

Care must be taken to distinguish a permission for perpetual departure from temporary or indefinite leaves of absence. A temporary leave of absence designates the term at which the leave will expire, e. g., after two, five, or ten years. An indefinite leave of absence is one which contemplates a termination at the pleasure of the dismissing Ordinary. Thus he might say: "I grant you permission to be absent from this diocese until you are recalled," or simply, "You have my permission to depart from the diocese." Even this latter is not a perpetual permission, but only an indefinite one. To be perpetual, it must leave no doubt about the dismissing Ordinary's mind, just as there is no doubt about the receiving Ordinary's mind when he confers a residential benefice, which *per se* is perpetual. The word *perpetual* (*in perpetuum*) must therefore be expressed, not implied. When a doubt exists, since excardination is an alienation and, therefore, a *res odiosa,* a permission to depart from a diocese must be strictly interpreted, and hence is presumed not to be perpetual.

[41] Suarez, "De incardinatione ratione beneficii,"—*Angelicum,* XIII (1936), 204.

[42] Pp. 412-413.

In the United States of America, at least, it must be concluded that this permission is almost unknown. Of twenty-five leading Chanceries questioned on the matter, not one admitted ever having granted it. The general answer from all was, "The Bishop always insists on a formal excardination and incardination process."

ARTICLE III

VIRTUAL INCARDINATION

Since the conferring of a residential benefice on an alien cleric after all other requirements have been met is now a real incardination (*Habetur . . . incardinatio*), it follows that it must be considered in the canons which speak of "incardination" as a genus, and must satisfy their requirements too. Thus, the conferring of the benefice will have to satisfy: canon 113, as to the authority of the one who bestows it; canon 116, as to its correlativity with the dismissing Bishop's permission, and as to the obligation of the Ordinary who confers the benefice to notify as soon as possible the Ordinary who gave the cleric his dismissal; and canon 117, as to all the general requisites to be discussed in Chapter XII.[43]

1. *The Receiving Ordinary*

"*Ab Ordinario alienae dioecesis*" are the words with which canon 114 identifies the authority by which the benefice must be conferred. "*Dioecesis*" has no different significance from that which it has elsewhere in this study.[44] "*Alienae*" is in opposition to *propriae;* it means "not proper," alien, one that is foreign to a person's present diocese. "*Ordinarius*" is to be understood here as the "Ordinary capable of incardinating," because the limitations of canon 113 affect the power of conceding excardination and incardination, no matter by which method it proceeds.[45] Hence, a Vicar General, a Vicar Capitular, and

[43] Cf. *infra,* pp. 524 ff.; Suarez, "De incardinatione ratione beneficii,"—*Angelicum,* XIII (1936), 209.

[44] Pp. 294 ff.

[45] Pp. 397 ff.

an Administrator, cannot confer a residential benefice which will incardinate the alien cleric, except under the limitations placed on them in canon 113. A Vicar Capitular has, by law, certain restricted faculties, even within a year from the vacancy of the see to fill vacant parishes which are not of free conferment.[46] Thus, within the year he can confirm an election, or accept a presentation, for such a vacant parish, and can concede institution in the parish to the one who is elected or presented.[47]

Let it be supposed that the one elected or presented is from another diocese, and bears with him the consent of his proper Ordinary, may the Vicar Capitular then institute him in the vacant parish? No, he cannot, because that would be going beyond the faculty of canon 455, § 2, 2°, inasmuch as it would be also incardinating an alien priest, and that he cannot do within a year from the vacancy, and, even after the lapse of a year, he can do it only with the consent of the Cathedral Chapter, by reason of canon 113.[48]

No such restrictions, however, are placed on those who by law succeed to the regime of apostolic vicariates and prefectures, when the see is impeded in its normal functions or is vacant. They can confer a benefice, even if it results in incardination, provided that the alien cleric, on whom a residential benefice is to be conferred, is not bound by the oath of the mission title, or, if he be thus bound, that a dispensation from the same has been secured from the Holy See.

2. *Conferring of the Benefice*

A. Actual Conferment

The cleric must have obtained the residential benefice in order to be incardinated virtually (*si . . . obtinuerit*). This means that the Ordinary controlling it actually conferred it upon him, not just promised it to him or committed it to him for a time.[49]

[46] Can. 1432, § 2.

[47] Can. 455, § 2, 2°.

[48] Cf. Suarez, "De incardinatione ratione beneficii,"—*Angelicum,* XIII (1936), 206-207.

[49] Blat, *Commentarium,* II, n. 48; Ojetti, *Commentarium in Codicem Iuris Canonici* (*Comment.*), (4 vols., Romae: apud Aedes Universitatis Gregorianae, 1927-1931), II, 36, note 1; Suarez, *art. et loc. cit.*

To be appointed a Vicar *Oeconomus* (Administrator) in a parish is not the same as being appointed a pastor; it does not entail the acquiring of a benefice.[50] Neither does the appointment to a parish for a summer season, in place of an absent, journeying pastor, bring about the acquisition of a benefice. It is nothing more than the position of Vicar Substitute.[51]

B. Its Formality

The provision of any ecclesiastical office is to be made in writing.[52] This extends to beneficial offices also.[53] Hence, when a cleric has obtained a title to a residential benefice, or is offered it, and accepts with the written permission of his Ordinary, the actual conferring of the benefice is accomplished by means of a letter of appointment to him, signed by the receiving Ordinary. A double written record of this should be made, one copy of which is to be kept in the Chancery archives, and the other is to be sent to the Ordinary who released the cleric.[54] Even without the letter, the conferring is an external fact, which is as easily and evidently proved as letters of incardination. With the written appointment, the proof is doubly secure, so that at no time can virtual incardination be upset or overthrown if the remainder of the prescribed form in canon 114 is fulfilled.[55] Nevertheless, the failure to consign the appointment to writing does not invalidate the act.[56]

C. Perpetuity

The need for perpetuity in the very conferment of the benefice, or, in other words, the need for *subjective* perpetuity in the benefice, is a disputed question. A benefice is always

[50] Cans. 472; 473.

[51] Can. 474.

[52] Can. 159.

[53] Cans. 146; 1413, § 2.

[54] O'Dwyer, *Incardination and Excardination,* MS. (Washington, D. C.: The Catholic University of America, 1923), p. 114.

[55] Wernz-Vidal, *Ius Canon.*, II, n. 64.

[56] O'Dwyer, *op. cit.*, pp. 115-117.

objectively perpetual; [57] but one of the divisions of benefices in the Code is " manual, temporary or *beneficia amovibilia,* and perpetual or *beneficia inamovibilia,* according as they are conferred revocably or perpetually." [58] This has to do only with subjective perpetuity.

In the old Innocentian law there was no difficulty about this. Equivalent incardination was based on the presumed will of both Ordinaries, and, unless the benefice was also conferred in perpetuity (i. e., unless it was a *beneficium inamovibile*), the receiving Bishop could not be presumed to have the will to attach the cleric to his diocese in perpetuity, and no incardination resulted.

In the present law the qualifying adjective *inamovibile* is not to be found, even though canon 1411, 4°, wherein the distinction between *amovibile* and *inamovibile* is contained, is just as much the expressed will of the legislator as is the law here discussed. The virtual process is no longer based on a presumed will, but is an *ipso facto* result of the observance of the proper form of the act as prescribed in canon 114. Hence, regardless of the subjective perpetuity of the benefice, if the requisites of canon 114 are fulfilled, incardination results. Despite this, some authors still cling to the old opinion that the benefice must be an irrevocably conferred one.[59] The more probable opinion that a revocably conferred benefice will suffice is still held by Coronata,[60] Ojetti,[61] Chelodi,[62] Creusen,[63] and Suarez.[64] The difference between these two types of benefices today lies

[57] Cf. *infra,* pp. 453 ff.

[58] Can. 1411, 4°.

[59] Thus Wernz-Vidal, *Ius Canon.,* II, n. 64; Cappello, *Summa Iur. Can.,* I, n. 223, 4, 1; Saegmueller, *Lehrbuch des katholischen Kirchenrechts* (4. ed., Freiburg im Breisgau: Herder, 1925-1934), I, § 64.

[60] *Instituts.,* I, n. 175.

[61] *Comment.,* II, 36.

[62] *Ius de Personis,* n. 107, note 4.

[63] " De excardinatione et incardinatione implicita,"—*Jus Pontif.,* XV (1935), 38.

[64] " De incardinatione ratione beneficii,"—*Angelicum,* XIII (1936), 208-209.

solely in the mode of procedure in removing the incumbent from them. For a grave cause, the possessor of any ecclesiastical office or benefice may be removed.[65] The process, however, is much more difficult in the case of an irrevocably conferred parochial benefice[66] than it is in the case of a revocably conferred one.[67] In both instances the Ordinary must provide the removed cleric with another benefice, office, or pension.[68] Therefore, there is no point to the argument that, unless the residential benefice were irrevocably conferred, the cleric incardinated through it would not enjoy the stability required for his canonical attachment, and, if removed, would have to return to his former diocese. The cleric so incardinated would not be in any different position than the native cleric who, deprived of either type of benefice, still remains incardinated.[69]

D. Acceptance

A cleric cannot be validly instituted in a benefice against his own will.[70] Canon 128 does speak of the obligation of a cleric to undertake and to fulfill faithfully any position (*munus*) committed to him by his Bishop, if in the judgment of his Ordinary the necessity of the Church requires it, unless he be excused for some legitimate reason. This would mean that he could be constrained to accept a benefice in his own diocese;[71] it would not mean that he could be forced by his proper Bishop to accept a benefice in an alien diocese. That would amount to excardination, and, as was seen,[72] no one is to be excardinated against his own will.

65 Can. 192.

66 Cans. 2147-2156.

67 Cans. 2157-2161.

68 Cans. 2154-2156; 2161, § 2.

69 Suarez, *art. et loc. cit.*; Creusen, *art. et loc. cit.*

70 Can. 1436.

71 Vermeersch-Creusen, *Epitome*, II, n. 768. If he later deserted such a position he would be suspended *a divinis* for a period set by the Ordinary (can. 2399).

72 *Supra*, pp. 246-254.

E. Installation

There are two distinct acts in the process of conferring a benefice on a cleric. The first is the act of appointing, which gives to the new beneficiary a title or right by law to possess the benefice. The second is the act of installation, which gives real possession to the cleric who has already been appointed. A cleric who would take possession of a benefice without having any title to it would be an intruder and a thief. But, by canon 1443, § 1, even after a cleric has received an appointment to a benefice, he cannot take real possession of it on his own authority. He must be installed in it by the proper ecclesiastical authority. The ceremony by which the proper ecclesiastical authority really installs a cleric in his benefice is called " corporal institution." Only that authority who is competent to confer the particular benefice is able to install the beneficiary in it. When the benefice is non-consistorial, e. g., a parish, it is the duty of the local Ordinary thus to install the cleric, although he may delegate another ecclesiastic to represent him.[73] The installation is performed according to the manner prescribed in the particular law of the diocese or province, or in the manner canonized by legitimate custom.[74] Corporal institution is a very ancient prescription of the Church. A cleric could never be said to have really obtained a benefice without it. Hence, even though the Code does permit the Ordinary to dispense from it,[75] such dispensation can be given only for a just cause, of which the Ordinary is the judge, and it must be given in writing. This written dispensation can be combined with the letter of appointment, or given separately, but in either case it must expressly, not just equivalently, state that the Ordinary is dispensing from the solemnity of corporal installation in the benefice.[76] In that case the written dispensation itself becomes a substitute for the act of taking possession of the benefice.

[73] Can. 1443, § 2.

[74] Can. 1444, § 1.

[75] Can. 1444, § 1.

[76] Pistocchi, *De Re Beneficiali iuxta Canones Codicis Iuris Canonici* (*De Re Benef.*), (Taurini: Marietti, 1928), p. 230.

For that reason the dispensation must fulfill all the requirements just stated, or else the very conferment of the benefice will be invalid.[77]

It is true that canon 1443, § 1, does not contain any express invalidating clause. Yet, canon 2394, obviously referring back to canons 1443 and 1444, states that anyone who would take possession of a benefice on his own authority, or who would corporally install himself in a benefice, for which he had already been elected, presented, or nominated, before having received and properly exhibited his letter of appointment to those who by law should see it, becomes *ipso iure inhabilis,* and is to be punished by the Ordinary in other ways as well. That sufficiently shows that the prescriptions of canons 1443 and 1444, at least as far as corporal installation are concerned, are for the validity of the very conferment of a benefice.[78] Hence, before a cleric can be considered virtually incardinated in a diocese, he must either have been canonically installed in the residential benefice, personally or through a procurator,[79] or at least be able to produce a letter from the Ordinary "*ad quem*" expressly dispensing him from the solemnity of corporal installation.

By virtue of canon 1406, § 1, Canons, dignitaries, pastors, and all those who receive a curatial benefice of any kind, must make a profession of faith before the Ordinary or his delegate. This, too, is an ancient prescript of law. Canon 1443, § 1, also forbids those so bound to take possession of a benefice without having made their profession of faith. This portion of canon 1443, however, is not a requisite for the validity of the conferment itself of the benefice. Canon 2403 deals with the penalties against delinquents on this score, but it contains no inhabilitating clause. It merely states that those who are bound to make the profession of faith and who, while not hindered by any just impediment, neglect to do so, are to be admonished to conform to the law within a reasonable, specified time. If their negli-

[77] *Loc. cit.*

[78] Coronata, *Instituts.*, II, n. 996.

[79] Can. 1445.

gence becomes contumacious, they are to be penalized even to the extent of privation of their benefice, office, dignity, or position, and of the accrued revenue from the same. The fact that the canon speaks of privation of the benefice indicates that at least the conferment of the benefice is valid. Therefore, if a cleric had been virtually incardinated in a diocese, and had fulfilled all requisites except the making of the profession of faith, his incardination would remain valid, even though he were penalized by the privation of the very residential benefice which wrought his incardination.

3. *The Residential Benefice*

Virtual incardination of secular clerics is concluded only when the cleric has actually obtained a residential benefice in the alien diocese (*si . . . beneficium residentiale obtinuerit*). What, then, is a residential benefice? Which positions in a diocese fulfill such a notion? These are important questions, on the answers to which will depend the solution of *post-factum* litigations about incardination. In the United States of America, particularly, this is now of paramount concern. Prior to 1918, benefices were almost unknown here,[80] and laws concerning them were of little interest; but the changes introduced by the Code, especially in the notions of a parish and of a benefice, had the effect of changing the character of the missions in this country into that of real canonical parishes and ecclesiastical benefices;[81] and it still remains a matter of doubt whether or not other forms of benefices have been or will be introduced here in a similar manner as a result of the new legislation. Thus, within recent years it was a debated question whether or not since the Code the Assistant to a Pastor was to be considered as the possessor of a residential benefice, and both views were defended with equal sincerity and vigor.[82]

[80] Creagh, "Benefice,"—*Cath. Ency.*, II, 474.

[81] Cf. Golden, *Parochial Benefices in the New Code,* The Catholic University of America, Canon Law Studies, n. 10 (Washington, D. C.: The Catholic University of America, 1925), pp. 97-103; Resp., Commission for the Interpretation of the Code, Sept. 26, 1921, as contained in the letter of the Apostolic Delegate in the United States to the American Hierarchy, Nov. 10, 1922.

[82] Cf. *AER*, LXXVI (1927), 317-319; LXXVII (1927), 74-79, 306-312.

In order to solve the difficulty as to which diocesan positions may be considered residential benefices, a fundamental study is required of the elements of an ecclesiastical benefice, and particularly of an ecclesiastical office on which it is founded.

A. Notion of an Ecclesiastical Office

1°. In the pre-Code legislation

Fundamentally a sacred or ecclesiastical office has a particular relation to the hierarchy of jurisdiction in the Church. Christ gave to His Apostles and their successors a twofold power, that of orders, for providing men with the supernatural means of salvation which He instituted, and that of jurisdiction, for ruling and governing men towards the attainment of their eternal destiny. By divine institution these two powers exist in the Church in hierarchies, i. e., in various degrees they are participated in by a special body of men known as the clergy. The hierarchy of orders is made up of Bishops, priests and ministers; that of jurisdiction is made up of the Supreme Pontiff and the subordinate Bishops, but these two grades of jurisdiction, established by divine authority, have by ecclesiastical law been augmented with others, which partake of their power in various degrees.[83]

There are a number of differences between the powers of orders and jurisdiction, but the one of chief interest here is the mode of acquisition. The power of orders is acquired by sacred ordination alone; that of jurisdiction, either by a properly performed deputation, in the case of the Supreme Pontiff, or, for all other grades, by a canonical mission, namely, a legitimate mandate of a Superior, the validity of which mission is regulated by the power and the laws of the Church.[84]

Hence, it can be seen that among the clergy there are a number of grades of jurisdiction, some established by divine, others by ecclesiastical authority, each limited, except in the case of the Pope, to a certain territory, class of persons, or something

[83] Maroto, *Institutt.*, I, n. 486; Wernz, *Ius Decretalium*, II, n. 4; De Meester, *Compen.*, I, n. 439.

[84] Maroto, *Institutt.*, I, n. 487, c.

similar, each subject to the grades superior to it, and, finally, acquired not by ordination but by one of the modes just mentioned. Such a grade of jurisdiction, when perpetually established, was the primary, strict, and objective meaning of a sacred office in the law prior to the Code. Hence an office in this sense was defined by Wernz as follows:

> . . . gradus quidam iurisdictionis ecclesiasticae quoad personas, causas, locum legibus Christi vel Ecclesiae in perpetuum ita institutus, ut iura et onera spiritualia ipsi adnexa nomine proprio et ratione quadam stabili sint exercenda.[85]

In addition to such jurisdictional offices, however, there existed in the Church for centuries various other positions which were given the name of offices, although they had no power connected with them beyond that of orders or of a mere administration of ecclesiastical things. Thus, in Cathedral and Collegiate Chapters, in addition to dignities (*dignitates*), i. e., canonries to which the right of precedence and the power of jurisdiction in the external forum were annexed, e. g., archdeacons, there were also personable rankings (*personatus*) or simple canonries, to which the right of precedence without any power of jurisdiction in the external forum had been attached, e. g., the ranking functionaries (*primicerii*), and also offices (*officia*) or simple canonries, which included neither right of precedence nor power of jurisdiction in the external forum but merely the right to administer certain ecclesiastical goods, e. g., sacristans or treasurers (*sacristae*). All of these classes of positions were equally considered as sacred offices, and fully capable of being made benefices in the present-day sense by the attachment of *praebendae*.[86]

For clarity's sake, then, distinctions had to be made, between a sacred and a profane office on the one hand, the former of

[85] *Ius Decretalium*, II, n. 240, § II.

[86] Cf. c. un., X, *de officio primicerii*, I, 25; c. un., X, *de officio sacristae*, I, 26; cc. 1-2, X, *de officio custodis*, I, 27; Reiffenstuel, *Jus Canon. Univ.*, l. I, t. XXV-XXVII; Schmalzgrueber, *Jus Eccles. Univ.*, P. IV, t. XXIII, Introd.; t. XXV-XXVII; Wernz, *Ius Decretalium*, II, n. 767, III; Devoti, *Instit. Can.*, lib. I, tit. III, §§ 10-11.

which alone could underlie a benefice,[87] and between the various acceptations of a sacred office on the other.[88]

2°. In the Code

The essential notion of an ecclesiastical office has not been substantially changed by the Code, but its classifications have been altered. There are now two acceptations in which it can be understood: a) the broad sense; and b) the strict sense.

a) An office in the *broad* sense is any employment whatsoever which is legitimately practiced for the attainment of a spiritual end.[89] It does not necessarily contain any ecclesiastical power of orders, of jurisdiction, or of administration, and, hence, can be obtained by lay persons, male or female, as well as by clerics; and it cannot form the basis of a benefice. A few examples of such offices explicitly contained in the Code are those of notaries,[90] judicial messengers (*cursores*), court beadles (*apparitores*),[91] and Superioresses.[92]

b) An office in the *strict* sense, on the other hand, now embraces not only a grade of, or participation in, jurisdiction, but also any type of position which has attached to it nothing more than a participation in the power of orders. It is defined by the Code in the following important terms:

> Officium ecclesiasticum . . . stricto autem sensu est munus ordinatione sive divina sive ecclesiastica stabiliter constitutum, ad normam sacrorum canonum conferendum, aliquam saltem secumferens participationem ecclesiasticae potestatis sive ordinis sive iurisdictionis.[93]

This definition merits analysis.

87 Aichner, *Compendium Iuris Ecclesiastici* (6. ed., Brixinae, 1887), n. 76, 1.

88 Wernz, *Ius Decretalium*, II, n. 240, II.

89 "Officium ecclesiasticum lato sensu est quodlibet munus quod in spiritualem finem legitime exercetur; . . ."—Can. 145, § 1.

90 Can. 374, § 1.

91 Can. 1591, § 2.

92 Cans. 2412; 2413, § 1; 2414.

93 Can. 145, § 1.

1) A type of employment (*est munus*). An office in the strict sense is no longer defined as a grade of jurisdiction, but is rather called a *munus*, which means a post, an employment, or a charge;[94] and herein lies a distinction in the new definition which seems to have been overlooked by many authors; and much confusion in other matters bearing a relation to ecclesiastical offices has resulted. The distinction is that this is the definition of an office *in genere*, not *in specie*. It embraces under its extension kinds or *genera* of ecclesiastical positions or posts, not specific ones, which, namely, have been actually erected in a definite locality. Thus, it would be applicable to the position or post of a Bishop as distinct from that of a pastor, Vicar General, etc.; it would not be applicable, for example, to the specific position of the Bishop of Pittsburgh as distinct from that of the Bishop of Harrisburg, although each of these would be an office *in specie*. Hence, the term *munus* in the definition must be taken in the sense of an ecclesiastical post, position, or charge in general. This will become clearer by a comparison with the old law.

In the law preceding the Code an office in the strict sense was a grade in the hierarchy of jurisdiction.[95] With the exception of the singular office of the Supreme Pontiff such a grade was certainly a generic entity. There were only two such grades established by Christ, that of the Supreme Pontiff, and that of the Bishops. The original Bishops, the Apostles, were twelve in actual number, but, with the exception of St. Peter, who was more than a Bishop, they constituted only the one grade of jurisdiction, only the one office, because the same degree of power was given to them all. Subsequent grades established by the Church in the hierarchy of jurisdiction were of the same form as the office of Bishops, i. e., in each case a distinct grade of power was determined upon to be exercised within a particular sphere, and that same degree of power was to belong to every individual who acquired that grade in the hierarchy, with this sole difference, that, in the case of each individual, the particular

94 Freund-Leverett, *Lexicon*, "munus."

95 *Supra*, p. 425.

sphere for the exercise of his power also had to be individuated by circumstances of place. Hence, in each case there was but one grade of power, and, therefore, only one generic office, although specifically there were many individuals participating in that office. Thus, the Church instituted the office of Metropolitans, of Archdeacons, of ordinary ecclesiastical Judges, and the like. Each of these was only one office in the strict sense, because each represented only one distinct grade of jurisdiction, yet each was actually possessed by many men in various parts of the world. In the former sense, the office is generic; in the latter, specific.

From this comparison with the idea of an office in the old legislation it is evident that, granting the similarity of the new law with the old in the matter, the term *munus* in the definition under consideration should certainly be taken in the generic sense, so as to mean a generic form of ecclesiastical position or post. It remains to be seen whether or not the new law is similar to the old, and, in particular, why *munus* is used, and not a " grade of jurisdiction."

The simplest answer to this is that *munus* here is a wider term, embracing not only the jurisdictional office, but also any kind of an ecclesiastical position with power other than jurisdiction; and, as will be seen below, an office in the strict sense now includes that latter type. An established grade in the hierarchy of jurisdiction, e. g., that of Bishop, obviously comes under the notion of *munus* in the generic sense, because, in whatever specific case it is acquired, it is a position of public government, bearing with it rights and duties towards a particular section of Christ's Church. Besides jurisdictional positions, however, there have existed in the Church for centuries various other kinds of public positions, constituted by the Church in the same manner as the grades of the hierarchy, and involving the exercise of some power of orders or administration, which positions, while not directly concerned with the government of the Church, nevertheless contribute towards it. These, too, can be classed as *munera,* and it is to include them that the present concept of an office has been extended. Nevertheless, it can readily be seen that the jurisdictional position is the more important of the two, and is the one which is primarily included in the notion of a *munus*. That is why the authors almost unanimously agree that the power belonging to an ecclesiastical office in the strict sense is primarily and principally that of jurisdiction.[96]

That the present law is similar to the old in its concept of an ecclesiastical office, is likewise shown from the fact that the generic interpretation of the definition under discussion is the only one which explains other relevant expressions and laws in the Code. More of this will be seen in subsequent paragraphs.

2) How constituted (*ordinatione sive divina sive ecclesiastica . . . constitutum*). In these words the old concept of an office in the strict sense is further preserved. There were two grades of the hierarchy of jurisdiction which were constituted by divine law, those of the Sovereign Pontiff and of the Bishops; and all the rest which arose in the course of time were of ecclesiastical origin. At the present day the two of divine origin naturally still exist and fulfill the definition of an office in the strict sense, as do also, with a few exceptions, those of ecclesiastical origin. Likewise, the various public positions for the exercise of power other than jurisdiction have been established by ordinance of the Church. In order to embrace all these the definition uses the terms just stated.[97] Naturally, constitution by civil authority is excluded, because civil authority is totally incompetent whenever there is question of the powers of orders and ecclesiastical jurisdiction.

Here, too, there is question, not of the constitution or erection of an ecclesiastical position or post *in specie* (in a definite place), but rather of the constitution or initiation of the position in its generic form. The position of a Bishop, for instance, is of divine constitution, even though every specific bishopric is constituted by ecclesiastical authority. In like manner, the position of a pastor (*parochus*) fulfills the requirements of this clause of the definition, not because a specific parish is constituted by the diocesan ecclesiastical authority, but because the generic

[96] De Meester, *Compen.*, I, n. 394, 2°, d; Chelodi, *Ius de Personis*, n. 131; Wernz-Vidal, *Ius Canon.*, II, n. 140, III; Pruemmer, *Manuale Iuris Can.*, Q. 72, 3; Badii, *Instituts.*, I, n. 126, c; Toso, *Comment. Minora*, in can. 145.

[97] Cf. Maroto, *Instituts*, I, n. 579; De Meester, *Compen.*, I, n. 394.

position of pastor was constituted by the Church back in the early centuries. A distinction must always be made, therefore, between the constitution or erection of a position or post *in genere* and the multiplication of that position *in specie*. Usually the position is constituted by the Holy See in common law and for the universal Church, and then it is multiplied by an inferior, that is, diocesan authority. It would be possible, however, also for an inferior ecclesiastical authority, e. g., a Bishop, to constitute *in genere* a new position not already constituted by any authority superior to him, but merely for his own territory; from then on such a position could be multiplied *in specie* either by himself or by inferiors to whom the proper authority would be given.[98]

The constitution of a position or office *in genere* is usually accomplished by the law itself, when it determines the kind of position which is to be started, the limits of its powers, the circumstances and conditions under which it is to be multiplied *in specie*, and the like.[99] A position is constituted or erected *in specie*, on the other hand, by an initial canonical provision [100] or appointment in a definite place, by the competent Superior, and according to the norms of Canon Law for the erection of such a position, which latter may involve the definition of boundaries and the like, as in the case of a parish.[101]

3) Its stability (*stabiliter constitutum*). The stability of constitution here required obviously refers to the position itself, that is to say, to objective stability, as distinct from subjective, which would mean irremovability of the incumbent. This is evident not only from the grammatical construction, but also from the fact that the Code nowhere requires subjective stability for the incumbent of an office as such. Authors, too, are unanimous in this declaration.[102]

[98] Cf. Maroto, *Institutš.*, I, n. 582, B; Chelodi, *Ius de Personis*, n. 132.

[99] Maroto, *op. et loc. cit.*; Chelodi, *op. et loc. cit.*

[100] Cf. cans. 147-182.

[101] Can. 216, §§ 1, 3.

[102] Maroto, *Instituts.*, I, n. 579; De Meester, *Compen.*, I, n. 394; Chelodi, *Ius de Personis*, n. 131; Wernz-Vidal, *Ius Canon.*, II, n. 140; Badii, *Instituts.*, I, n. 126; Toso, *Comment. Minora*, in can. 145.

The distinction, however, which almost all the authors have again overlooked is that the *objective* stability here required has reference only to the constitution of a position or office *in genere*. Creusen alone in a large field has sensed the point and has thus expressed it:

> Officium stricte dictum his notis distinguitur: . . . stabile est, stabilitate sc. obiectiva, ita ut ex institutione Christi aut iure ecclesiastico constituatur in Ecclesia modo perpetuo certus potestatis spiritualis gradus, certus iurium spiritualium complexus clerico conferendus aut semper aut quotiens adiuncta iure definita recurrunt, puta munus episcopi, Vicarii Capitularis, administratoris dioecesis, etc. . . .[103]

In other words, it is the generic type of ecclesiastical position or post, the grade of power constituted once for all in the universal Church by Christ or by ecclesiastical law, which must have an abiding existence about it, i. e., it must have some degree of permanence in the Church as a whole, capable of being multiplied *in specie* wherever the law calls for it. It is not necessary that each specific multiplication of it be of permanent constitution. In fact, the law itself may prescribe that it be specifically erected only under certain temporary circumstances. Hence, it is quite possible to have a public ecclesiastical position or post, which, in its generic constitution, is stable and thoroughly fulfills the notion of an ecclesiastical office in the strict sense, but which, in its specific constitution, is only temporary, e. g., the position of parochial administrator (*vicarius oeconomus*).[104] Ecclesiastical law brought this public position into existence in the Church, and determined that it should always be specifically erected in a certain set of circumstances, namely, whenever a parish became vacant, and until such time that a new pastor would be appointed. In its generic sense this position is, therefore, permanently established in the Church, but in every single specific instance it is only temporary, and quite ordinarily expected not to continue longer in exis-

103 Vermeersch-Creusen, *Epitome*, I, n. 227.

104 Cans. 472-473.

tence than for a period of six months.[105] Of a like nature are the positions of diocesan Administrator,[106] Vicar Capitular,[107] parochial vicar substitute (*vicarius substitutus*),[108] parochial vicar adjutant (*vicarius adiutor*),[109] and others.

Furthermore, a difference must be acknowledged between stability and perpetuity. Even generically, an ecclesiastical position need not be constituted in perpetuity before it can become an office in the strict sense, although this was required in the old definition. It is sufficient that it have some degree of stability or permanency. Of course, any generic position described in the Code is *per se* perpetual, with the exception of the office of diocesan consultors, which is a temporary expedient; but it is not impossible to conceive of a post-Code law which would constitute a new position to last even in its generic form only for an extended period of time, e. g., during the persistence of some heresy, and yet such a position might verify the definition of an office in the strict sense. An office of this kind when erected *in specie* would naturally also be of a temporary nature.

All this has a practical bearing upon the relation between ecclesiastical offices and benefices. A public ecclesiastical position, which is only temporary in its specific constitution, regardless of whether its generic form is perpetual or not, may well fulfill the notion of an office in the strict sense, but it can never be made a benefice. The reason for this is clear. A benefice cannot exist except in specific form, because any moral person, including a benefice, must be based on a material foundation.[110] The perpetuity of constitution, therefore, which is required in a benefice is a *specific* perpetuity, and, consequently, an office such as just described, which in its specific nature would not be perpetual, could never form the proper basis for a benefice.

[105] Cf. cans. 155; 458.

[106] Can. 431, § 2.

[107] Can. 432, § 1.

[108] Can. 474.

[109] Can. 475.

[110] Cf. *infra*, p. 451.

One further observation remains to be made, and that in the face of the opposite teaching of many authors. An ecclesiastical office in the strict sense, as such, is *not a moral person.* It is not so in its generic constitution, because a moral person cannot exist except in specific form. In its specific form it is not so: a) By prescript of law, because the law cannot recognize any entity as a moral person unless perpetuity belongs to its specific nature, as required by the very nature of a moral person, and that is lacking in an office in the specific form. Besides, the Code does not refer to an office as a moral person, nor does it speak of it as having the capacity to acquire property, as it does for various other entities which acquire moral personality by prescript of law.[111] b) By erection to the status of a moral person through a formal decree, because, on the one hand, those offices which are only temporary, e. g., that of some parochial vicar adjutant (*vicarius adiutor*), could not possibly be made moral persons, since they lack the necessary specific perpetuity; and, on the other hand, for those offices which are perpetual, there is no mention made in the Code of the possibility of erecting them as moral persons by a formal decree. Even these latter, therefore, are not and cannot be made moral persons unless and until they are made benefices, for canon 1409 shows that the office and the right to receive revenues attached to the office from a definite endowment, when joined in perpetuity by the proper authority, go together to make up the one *ens iuridicum* or moral person.

4) How conferred (*ad normam sacrorum canonum conferendum*). Reference has been made above to the fact that, when a public ecclesiastical position is constituted *in genere*, provision is made by the law itself concerning the circumstances and way in which it is to be multiplied or constituted *in specie*, and this is done separately for each position according to its character. It is for this reason that the Code contains no general Chapter on the constitution or erection of offices, but deals with each singly. A few examples will illustrate the point: Canon 216, § 1, contains norms for the erection of specific parishes;

[111] E. g., cans. 531; 1410.

canon 350 legislates on the constitution of specific Coadjutor Bishops; canon 366, § 1, deals with the specific constitution of the position of Vicar General; canon 398 treats of the constitution of a Canon Theologian and a Canon Penitentiary in a Cathedral or Collegiate Chapter; canon 432, § 1, of a Vicar Capitular; canon 471, § 1, of an actual parochial vicar (*vicarius actualis*), etc.

Since, however, as a rule an office is founded *in genere* by the supreme ecclesiastical authority for the entire Church, it likewise is reserved to that universal authority to legislate concerning that which it has founded; and so it is reserved to common law to prescribe the norms according to which such an office, when erected *in specie*, will be *conferred* upon an individual, not only in the initial, but also, if such there be, in succeeding instances. Hence it is that the definition of an office in the strict sense contains the condition that it must be conferred, in specific instances, according to the norm of the sacred canons. An inferior authority, then, such as a Bishop, when specifically constituting one of the common law offices, is not always free to confer it on anyone according to his judgment, but must obey the laws of the Code concerning the concession of that particular office. Maroto apparently claims that, even if an inferior authority generically constituted an office not previously existing in common law, he would, nevertheless, be bound by common law when conferring it.[112]

The norms which the Code prescribes for the *conferring* of all specific offices are contained in a general section embracing canons 147 to 182; those which affect the conferring of any particular specific office are to be found in that part of the Code which contains the legislation on the particular office in question. Thus canons 366, § 2, and 367 give the particular norms for the provision of the office of a Vicar General; canons 403-404 do the same for the office of a Canon in a Cathedral or Collegiate Chapter; canons 432, 434, and 438, for that of a Vicar Capitular; and canons 452-461 for that of a pastor.

[112] *Instituts.*, I, n. 579, note 3.

5) Its participation in power (*aliquam saltem secumferens participationem ecclesiasticae potestatis sive ordinis sive iurisdictionis*). In these words is contained the most outstanding difference between an ecclesiastical office in the broad and in the strict sense. The former does not necessarily include any ecclesiastical power whatsoever; the latter invariably must include at least some participation in the power of orders or of jurisdiction.

§ 1. Power of orders.—It has already been noted that a position, to which is annexed only a participation in the power of orders, is now included in the idea of an office in the strict sense, and is, consequently, capable of entering into the foundation of a benefice, provided that all the other requisites are fulfilled. This possibility gives rise to a difficulty. A power or right attached to an office is something which is obtained *ipso facto* by the acquisition of the office itself. If, then, as is true, the power of orders is acquired once for all through ordination, how can it be said to be acquired also through an ecclesiastical office? Vidal answers this difficulty by stating that the power of orders, mentioned in canon 145, § 1, as being possibly the sole power attached to an office in the strict sense, must be understood as a special power, distinct from that which is acquired by the simple fact of ordination.[113] A number of other authors either explicitly or implicitly state that any participation in the power already received in ordination suffices, and as examples they cite the celebration of Mass, the recitation of the Breviary, and the like.[114]

Neither of these opinions seems completely correct. It is true that the power of orders attached to an office can be special and distinct from that acquired in priestly ordination, when, namely, it is annexed to an office by a privilege of law, which is effectively equivalent to the law itself.[115] This is confirmed by canon 210,

[113] Wernz-Vidal, *Ius Canon.*, II, n. 140, II.

[114] Maroto, *Instituts.*, I, n. 579, e; De Meester, *Compen.*, I, n. 394, 2°, d; Chelodi, *Ius de Personis*, n. 131; Cocchi, *Commentarium in Codicem Iuris Canonici* (8 vols., Taurinorum Augustae: Marietti, 1920-1930), l. II, p. I, sec. I, n. 59, 2°; Raus, *Institutiones Canonicae* (Parisiis, Lugduni: Vitte, 1924), n. 70, I.

[115] Maroto, *Instituts.*, I, n. 699, 4; *ibid.*, n. 291, B.

and an example of it is found in canon 294, § 2, where, in addition to jurisdiction, certain powers of episcopal orders, such as consecrations, the power of confirming, and the like, are given in the law to Vicars and Prefects Apostolic who lack the episcopal character. That, however, is not the only sense in which an office can exist on the power of orders alone. It is also possible for it to include merely a participation in the power already received in ordination, but that must be understood in the correct manner. To this end a distinction must be made between the power of orders itself, and the strict right to exercise that power in a determined sphere. The former is acquired through ordination, but it is the latter which is usually obtained through an ecclesiastical office. If the office be of such a nature as to require the exercise of some power of orders in a given sphere, and with a view to that end bears with it a right to such exercise, then it must be said to include in itself some participation in the power of orders. An example is the office of a Coadjutor Bishop attached to a see. Obviously this was constituted by the Church primarily for the purpose of relieving thickly populated dioceses in the discharge of the more frequent pontifical functions; and so the Code itself attaches to this office the right to exercise pontifical orders, with the exception of ordinations, in the territory of the see,[116] as well as the obligation of doing so when required.[117] In like manner, a pastor has, through his office, the right and obligation to administer the sacraments in his own parish, and no priest from outside the parish can lawfully do so without his permission.[118] If, however, he should become completely unable to perform the functions of a pastor, a parochial coadjutor (*vicarius adiutor*) would be appointed, and would acquire that right and obligation by the very fact of his appointment to the office, without any permission or delegation being necessary.[119] This distinction between the power and the right to exercise it is strikingly similar

[116] Can. 352.

[117] Can. 351, § 4.

[118] Cf. cans. 462; 738, § 1; 846, § 2; 848; 938, § 2; 467, § 1.

[119] Can. 475, § 2.

to the difference between the power of orders and jurisdiction in the sacrament of penance; and in fact some authors held that the right to exercise any power of orders was a part of jurisdiction;[120] but this can hardly be sustained except in relation to the sacrament of penance, where the right to administer is a right to rule consciences, and in relation to the magisterial power.[121]

It is possible, then, for an office in the strict sense to include merely a participation, according to the above explanation, in a power of orders already possessed; but it must be a real power of orders acquired through sacred ordination (*ecclesiasticae potestatis . . . ordinis*). It certainly would not extend, for instance, to the right of reciting the Divine Office in choir, as the authors would have it, for that is in no sense whatsoever a power of orders. Furthermore, not every post or charge which includes a participation in the power of orders already possessed can be said to be an office in the strict sense, but only those which fulfill the other requirements in canon 145, § 1. A pious foundation may require the celebration of Mass in a particular church or chapel daily, but it is certainly not a specific office, because it is not a public position which has been generically and durably constituted by ecclesiastical law. It is rather merely a sum of temporal goods which are given in perpetuity to some already existing ecclesiastical moral person, with the obligation that from the revenues accruing from those goods a certain number of Masses will be said or some other ecclesiastical functions will be performed every year.[122] The obligation is merely assumed in addition to all the others which the moral person already has. Similarly, a priest who is engaged simply to take the place of a temporarily absent parochial assistant (*vicarius cooperator*) assumes the obligation and acquires the right to exercise his orders in that particular parish, but for the same reason as above that does not make his charge an office.

120 E. g., Pirhing, *Jus Canon.*, l. I, tit. XXXI, n. II; Aichner, *Compen.*, n. 24, 2b; Sägmüller, "Jurisdiction"—*Cath. Ency.*, VIII, 569.

121 Cf. *infra*, p. 439.

122 Cf. cans. 1544, § 1; 1546, § 1; Augustine, *Commentary*, VI, 611.

He is rather just one of the priests assigned to a parish, as mentioned in canon 478, § 2. Any public ecclesiastical position, however, which fulfills the other requirements of canon 145, § 1, as to stability of constitution and the rest, but of which the sole right and obligation is lawfully limited to the celebration of Mass in a particular place, must, nevertheless, be acknowledged as an office in the strict sense.

§ 2. Power of jurisdiction.—As of old, the definition of an ecclesiastical office in the strict sense also naturally embraces those positions which include some participation in the power of jurisdiction. Formerly this was the only type of position which was considered an office in the primary and strict sense, for the very idea of such an office was a grade in the hierarchy of jurisdiction,[123] although those in the less strict sense could also become benefices. Even today, authors are wont to consider positions with jurisdiction attached as representing the primary type of office; [124] and so they treat ecclesiastical offices in a section concerning the hierarchy of jurisdiction, a practice which is apparently founded on the method of treatment in the Code itself.

The question now arises as to what is included in the general expression "ecclesiastical power of jurisdiction." In Roman Law jurisdiction meant *judicial* power alone.[125] In Canon Law it has a much wider significance. It is described in the Code as a power of rule,[126] and so it may be defined as "The public power of ruling the faithful towards the attainment of eternal salvation." [127] This is one of those powers which were given by Christ to His Church, and the commonly accepted teaching among Catholic authors is that there were only two such powers, orders and jurisdiction,[128] so that all public ecclesiastical power

[123] Wernz, *Ius Decretalium*, II, n. 240, II.

[124] Cf. *supra*, pp. 428-9.

[125] Maroto, *Instituts.*, I, n. 573.

[126] "Potestas iurisdictionis seu regiminis . . ."—Can. 196.

[127] "Potestas publica regendi fideles in ordine ad salutem aeternam."—Chelodi, *Ius de Personis*, n. 125. For variations of this cf. Wernz, *Ius Decretalium*, II, n. 3, § 1; Maroto, *Instituts.*, I, n. 573; De Meester, *Compen.*, I, n. 437; Badii, *Instituts.*, I, n. 142; Cocchi, *Comment.*, l. II, p. I, n. 113.

[128] Cf. Wernz, *op. et loc. cit.*; De Meester, *ibid.*, n. 436.

can be classed under one or the other of these. Some add a third division, the teaching power (*magisterium*), but, since it is authoritative, and can command the assent or will of the faithful in matters to be believed, it is only a form of rule coming under the general power of jurisdiction.[129]

Since jurisdiction is a general power, it embraces various species, each one of which, taken separately, is real jurisdiction. Just how to classify these species in such a way as will make the categories complete and yet mutually exclusive has long been a problem for authors; but the classification commonly accepted is the threefold one of legislative, judiciary, and coactive powers; [130] and this, too, has been incorporated in the Code.[131] Some authors make a separate category of executive power,[132] but whether this be correct or not is disputed.[133] In any event, under these main species there can be grouped as subdivisions various particular powers, such as those of authoritatively teaching, of dispensing, of granting privileges, and the like.

There are various other divisions of jurisdiction made in the Code according to different viewpoints, but they are only different ways of classifying those powers which are already conceded to be included in jurisdiction. For example, there is a division into judicial and non-judicial power,[134] the latter of

[129] Wernz, *ibid.*, § III; De Meester, *op. et loc. cit.;* Maroto, *ibid.*, n. 486, b, note 2.

[130] Wernz, *Ius Decretalium*, II, n. 3; n. 4, § III, d; Badii, *Instituts.*, I, n. 142; Cocchi, *Comment.*, l. II, p. I, n. 113; Toso, *Comment. Minora*, in can. 196, n. 1.

[131] E. g., cans. 335, § 1; 2220, § 1; 2221. Roberti, *De Processibus* (2 vols., Romae, apud Aedes Facultatis Iuridicae ad S. Apollinaris, 1926), I, n. 38 sq., restricts the term jurisdiction, when strictly taken, to judicial power, and claims that the Code does the same in canon 201, § 2. This does not appear true; in canon 201, § 1, a general principle for the power of jurisdiction is stated, and then in the two succeeding paragraphs this power is divided into judicial and non-judicial, for each of which a particular principle is enunciated. The Code certainly applies the term jurisdiction to judicial power, e. g., in canon 1637, but it also and equally applies it to the other above-named species, e. g., in canon 368, § 1.

[132] Maroto, *Instituts.*, I, n. 573, e; Chelodi, *Ius de Personis*, n. 125.

[133] Cf. Wernz, *Ius Decretalium*, II, n. 4, § III, d.

[134] Can. 201, §§ 2, 3.

which embraces any power of jurisdiction which is exercised by a Superior according to his prudent judgment without the form of a trial; [135] consequently, it can embrace the power of making laws, of attaching punishments to them, of granting dispensations, privileges, etc., of paternal correction, of governing, and of other similar functions.[136] This non-judicial or voluntary type is what is meant by administrative, as distinct from judicial power,[137] although many authors seem to give it a much more particular, though vague, meaning.[138]

Whatever may be said for or against the above classifications, one thing is certain, that all the types of public power above mentioned, not only the main categories, but also their subdivisions, are universally acknowledged as parts of jurisdiction, for the dispute among authors is not whether they do or do not pertain to jurisdiction, but how they may be best classified.

§ 3. Participation in these powers.—An essential requisite of an ecclesiastical office in the strict sense is that it include at least some participation (*aliquam saltem . . . participationem*) in the power of orders or of jurisdiction. This requirement is obviously very broad. In regard to orders, it has already been shown that participation can signify either a real, distinct power of orders attached to the position, or merely a right to exercise the power already possessed. In regard to jurisdiction, it can readily be seen that the Supreme Pontiff alone possesses it entirely and without limit, and that all those under him merely participate in one or all forms of it, but always to a limited extent. This is the very notion of the hierarchy of jurisdiction. Hence, not only can that general power of ruling the faithful be divided into forms, thus giving rise to the classifications listed above, but also any single form of it can be limited as to territory, persons, matters, causes, and the like; and yet, any form,

[135] De Meester, *Compen.*, I, n. 443.

[136] Wernz, *Ius Decretalium*, II, n. 4, § III, d; Maroto, *Instituts.*, I, n. 724, 2°; De Meester, *op. et loc. cit.*; Badii, *Instituts.*, I, n. 144; Cocchi, *Comment.*, l. II, p. I, n. 116, § 3; Chelodi, *Ius de Personis*, n. 125, not. 2.

[137] Roberti, *De Processibus*, I, n. 52.

[138] E. g., Maroto, *Instituts.*, I, nn. 573, 724; De Meester, *Compen.*, I, nn. 439, 443; Chelodi, *Ius de Personis*, nn. 125, 190.

however limited, is a participation in the power of jurisdiction, and, if attached to an ecclesiastical position, can make of it an office in the strict sense.

§ 4. Inclusion of the power within the office itself.—A final and exceedingly important requisite of such an office is that the participation in the power be included in the position itself (*munus . . . secumferens*). The value of the word *secumferens* as meaning " including in itself " is derived from the following passage in canon 66, § 3:

> Concessa facultas *secumfert* alias quoque potestates quae ad illius usum sunt necessariae; quare in facultate dispensandi *includitur* etiam potestas absolvendi a poenis ecclesiasticis, si quae forte obstent, . . .

This significance of the term is further supported by similar usage elsewhere in the Code.[139]

An observation of far-reaching importance in connection with this part of the definition is that, since the word *secumferens* agrees with and modifies *munus,* and since the latter has already been shown to signify a generic position,[140] the participation in power must be included in the position as it generically exists. This would, consequently, embrace not only that power which was included in it when it was first generically constituted, but also any power which was later attached to the entire *genus.* Later additions can be made to the original powers of a generic office by the law which is competent to govern it. Practically, this means the common law, for that is the supreme law of the Church which can at any time attach further powers to generic offices that already exist.[141]

In the light of the explanation just concluded of the Code's definition of an ecclesiastical office in the strict sense it would seem to be a natural conclusion that all offices in the strict sense enjoy *ordinary* power. A discussion of that point is now in order.

[139] E. g., cans. 154; 497, § 2; 1053; 1138, § 1; 2243, § 1; 2259, § 2; 2275, n. 1; 2277; 2300; 2303, § 1.

[140] Cf. *supra,* pp. 427 ff.

[141] Cf. Maroto, *Instituts.,* I, n. 697, 7ª.

1st. The difference between ordinary and delegated power.—In practically all cases the power included in an office will be ordinary power, which, although properly a division of jurisdiction, namely, from the standpoint of the title by which it is acquired, is, nevertheless, used by analogy also of orders. Ordinary power is defined to be that which is annexed by the law itself to an office,[142] and is so distinguished from delegated power, which is defined as that which is committed to a person.[143]

There are three main differences between these two divisions of power:

(α). The *terminus*. Power is ordinary only when it is annexed to an office, whereas it is delegated when given to a particular person or persons, either physical or moral. In the Code an office is always to be understood in the strict sense unless the broad sense is apparent from the context,[144] but in the definition of ordinary power there is nothing to indicate that the broad sense is to be taken. On the contrary, the strict sense is imperative, because, if common law should annex power to a generic position which was an office only in the broad sense, e. g., to that of notary, it would by that very fact be changing it to an office in the strict sense, for it would be establishing it as a permanent position with a participation in the power of orders or jurisdiction, and hence capable of being conferred only according to the canonical rules for the provision of offices. But, when taken in the strict sense, an office is something generic; consequently, power is ordinary only when attached to an office *in genere,* so that it must pertain to every specific office of that genus which is ever erected. Hence, no authority whatsoever which has not the power over an office as a genus can ever attach ordinary power, either to the entire office, or to any specific multiplication of it. A provincial Council, for instance, might bestow new powers on all the pastors of the province, but these powers would not be ordinary, because they would not

142 "Potestas iurisdictionis ordinaria ea est quae ipso iure adnexa est officio; . . ."—Can. 197, § 1.

143 ". . . delegata, quae commissa est personae."—Can. 197, § 1.

144 Can. 145, § 2.

pertain to the office of pastor as it exists throughout the Church. Similarly, even though the diocesan statutes, in accordance with canon 476, § 6, would extend full parochial powers to the assistants (*vicarii cooperatores*) in the diocese, these would, for the same reason, not be ordinary powers. They would be given to a number of physical persons, each one of whom occupies the specific position or office of an assistant,[145] but they would not be attached to the office as it exists in the universal Church. Contrarily, if common law should ever attach certain powers to the office of parochial assistant, these powers would be ordinary.

Delegated power can be given only to persons, and, since the Code does not distinguish, the persons spoken of may be either physical or moral. It cannot be extended to a generic office as such, because that is not a moral person, since it lacks the necessary material foundation; it cannot be extended to a specific office as such, because, for the reasons stated above,[146] that is not a moral person either. In the first case, it is possible outside of law for power to be delegated to all those who possess a certain office in the strict sense, for example, the Sovereign Pontiff during a Holy Year may grant extraordinary faculties to pastors, but then the power is rather given to persons in whom the possession of the office is an essential qualification. In the law itself, powers conveyed in that fashion could not be considered as delegated, because any power attached by law to an office in the strict or generic sense is ordinary. If there were no question of an office in the strict sense, then, naturally, these powers would be delegated, e. g., the powers conveyed by the Code to simple confessors.[147] In the second case, though power cannot be delegated to a specific office as such, it can always be delegated to the incumbent of the office. If a specific office be a benefice, it is then a moral person, and power can be delegated to it independently of any incumbent.

145 Cf. *infra*, pp. 486 ff.

146 Cf. *supra*, p. 433.

147 Cf. Maroto, *Institutt.*, I, n. 705, B.

(β). The conveying source. Ordinary power is granted solely by the law itself, whereas no such limitation is made on the source of delegated power. The words of the Code show that the law which is here meant is primarily the Code itself. Nevertheless, it can also be taken in a wide sense, and then it embraces not only the written law, including privileges in the broad sense, which are the same as law, but also unwritten or customary law.[148]

At all events, the law must be competent to govern the office as a *genus*. Thus, to an office existing in the universal Church, ordinary power cannot be attached except by common law, by a privilege extending to all who possess that certain office, or by a custom of the universal Church. For an office constituted *in genere* by an inferior power, e. g., by a Bishop for his own territory, ordinary power can be attached also by particular law, by a privilege extended to all who possess the office, or by a diocesan custom; but particular law, such as diocesan statutes, cannot possibly add ordinary power to an office which exists in common law, for therein it is incompetent.

For delegated power there is no such requisite or limitation as to the source. In most cases it is simply conceded by a person who has authority (*ab homine*), but it can also be given by law (*a iure*), or by a privilege,[149] either in the strict sense of a favor granted to an individual person, or in the broad sense of a favor granted to an entire class of persons. When delegation is conceded by law, or by a privilege of law, it is always discernible from ordinary power, because it is not given to an office, but to a person or class of persons who do not possess an office in the strict sense.[150] Thus, in the Code, certain powers are given to pastors, and these are ordinary, because the position of a pastor is an office in the strict sense; other powers are given to simple confessors, and these are delegated, because a simple confessor has not an office in the strict sense.

148 *Ibid.*, n. 699, 4ª.

149 Maroto, *Instituts.*, I, nn. 704, 291.

150 *Ibid.*, nn. 704; 699, 4ª.

(γ). The stability. The annexation of ordinary power to a generic office is made once for all, and so is something permanent, whereas the mere commission of delegated power to an ecclesiastical person is only something temporary. The ordinary power annexed to an office is never lost, unless the office itself is lost,[151] whereas power committed to a person can be lost in many ways, but especially by the mere revocation of it at any time.[152]

2nd. Must an office in the strict sense include ordinary power? —From the foregoing the warranty of the statement that the power attached to an office in the strict sense will practically always be ordinary is established. It is the generic office which must have the power attached to it; but competent law alone can attach power to generic offices; and, hence, the definition of ordinary power is fulfilled. In fact, it would seem from this that an office in the strict sense could not exist at all without at least some ordinary power, either of jurisdiction, or, analogically, of orders. Canonists too have come to this conclusion.[153] This view, however, cannot be sustained in the face of contrary facts. It is certainly true that ordinary power cannot exist without an office in the strict sense, by reason of the definition in canon 197, § 1; but the converse of this is not true, that an office in the strict sense cannot exist without

[151] Can. 208.

[152] Can. 207, § 1. From these three differences between ordinary and delegated power it can be seen that Ojetti errs when he identifies certain notable powers which the Code attributes to Ordinaries as powers which are delegated to them *a iure* or by the law ("De natura potestatis Ordinariorum secundum Codicem," —*Gregorianum*, VI (1925), 436-441). The word Ordinary (*Ordinarius*) is merely an arbitrary expression used in designation of any of the offices in the strict sense enumerated in canon 198, § 1, and, hence, any power given in the Code to Ordinaries is power attached by law to each one of those generic offices, and is consequently ordinary power. Furthermore, contrary to what that illustrious author claims (*ibid.*, 439), the identification of such power with delegation by law would be opposed to the very nature of delegated power, which can be given solely to persons, whereas an office in the generic sense such as the one implied by the word *Ordinarius* is certainly not a moral person (cf. *supra*, p. 433).

[153] Wernz, *Ius Decretalium*, II, n. 240, § II; Wernz-Vidal, *Ius Canon.*, II, n. 140, § III; Maroto, *Instituts.*, I, nn. 579, c; 699, 10ª; Chelodi, *Ius de Personis*, n. 131; Pruemmer, *Manuale Iuris Canonici*, Q. 72, 3; Badii, *Instituts.*, I, n. 126; Toso, *Comment. Minora*, in can. 145.

ordinary power. There is one possibility, founded on actual facts in the Code, which practically all authors have overlooked. It is that the common law can bring into permanent existence a type or genus of ecclesiastical position, which of its very nature requires only some variable participation in the power of orders or jurisdiction. The common law does not attach to such a type of position any definite powers, but merely the efficacious right that some definite power be *delegated* to the incumbent of each specific position by the proper authorizing Superior. A position of this character would fulfill the definition of an office in the strict sense. Each specific position would necessarily bear with it some delegated power, and so the generic position itself would have to be said to bear with it some participation in power. It is to be noted that in the definition in canon 145, § 1, it is not required that the participation in power be given by the law itself, and, furthermore, that the words *aliquam saltem participationem* are broad enough to embrace even delegated power.

The actual examples in the Code of offices of this character are few, but clear. They are the offices of episcopal and parochial partial coadjutors, which have been established permanently in the Church for the purpose of assisting the titular incumbent of the benefice to a limited extent in the exercise of orders or jurisdiction. A participation in these powers is, therefore, of the very nature of the offices, so that, in any specific case, it would be a contradiction for a coadjutor to be instituted without simultaneously being accorded some powers of assistance; but, since the extent of the powers required in any partial coadjutor is dependent upon the circumstances of the particular case, and since ordinary power in such a one would inevitably create conflicts with the titular possessor of the benefice, the Code does not attach any powers to these offices, but merely provides that determined powers be delegated to them in each specific case. Thus, a Coadjutor given to the person of a Bishop, who is not completely incapable of fulfilling his duties, has only those powers which the letters of appointment in a particular case, or, if they are silent, which the Bishop himself commits or delegates to him.[154] Again, a parochial adjutant vicar (*vicarius adiutor*) who is given to a pastor hampered by a personal disability in order to supply his place only in part, has only those powers which the letters of appointment in a given case delegate to him.[155] Finally, a parochial assistant (*vicarius cooperator*), who, for the purpose of helping in the care of souls, is given to a pastor, who by himself is unequal to the task, has only those powers which are delegated to him by the diocesan statutes, by the letters of appointment, and by the pastor himself.[156] To all three offices the Code obviously connects the efficacious right to hold and exercise power, because it speaks of rights and obligations as pertaining to them, and determines from what source these rights or powers are to be conveyed, so much so that, if those sources would not delegate any powers whatsoever, neither would there be any specific office whatsoever, for an adjutant without the power of helping is no adjutant at all. The last mentioned of these offices especially forces the conclusion that there can be an office in the strict sense with only delegated power. In canon 477, § 2, it is clearly shown that it is possible for the position of a parochial assistant to be a benefice—how and when will be determined later.[157] To be a benefice, it must be an office in the strict sense, and yet no powers are connected with it by the Code; on the contrary, it is rather presupposed in the Code that its powers are only delegated,[158] but, as just pointed out, the delegation is imposed as a requisite. It is only when the three potential sources of the assistant pastor's delegated power—the diocesan statutes, the letter of appointment by the Ordinary, and the pastor himself—fail to grant any power at all to the assistant pastor that the common law itself intervenes in his behalf and grants to him the power to assist the pastor in the entire parochial ministry. This is nothing more than universal delega-

[154] Can. 351, §§ 1, 2.

[155] Can. 475, § 2.

[156] Can. 476, § 6.

[157] Cf. *infra*, pp. 498 ff.

[158] Cf. cans. 874, § 1; 1096, § 1.

tion *a iure.* It is not ordinary power, because it is not attached to the generic office of *vicarius cooperator.* Rather it is attached only to the specific offices of those assistant pastors who are bereft of power. The expression *ratione officii* in canon 476, § 6, shows the reason for the universal delegation *a iure,* namely, that it is of the very nature of the generic office to have some power of assisting. Furthermore, even after a specific assistant pastor has received the universal delegation here spoken of, it is still possible for his power to be limited later by any one of the three agencies named in canon 476, § 6. Such a limitation could not be countenanced if the universal power of assisting conferred on him by the law were ordinary power, because loss of ordinary power is contingent on the loss of the office itself to which the power is attached.[159]

B. Notion of a Benefice

The idea of an ecclesiastical office, as just elaborated, constitutes the foundation for a benefice. Let a proper authority exercise his power to erect *in specie* one of the sacred offices generically established by common law, and let him attach to this specific foundation the right to receive revenues from a perpetual source, and then a benefice is established. In fact, one might term a benefice " a beneficial office." [160]

To arrive at a more accurate understanding of it, it will be necessary to analyze the definition given in the Code. An ecclesiastical benefice is there defined to be: " A juridical entity constituted or erected in perpetuity by competent ecclesiastical authority, and consisting of a sacred office together with the attached right to receive the revenues accruing to that office from an endowment."

> Beneficium ecclesiasticum est ens iuridicum a competente ecclesiastica auctoritate in perpetuum constitutum seu erectum, constans officio sacro et iure percipiendi reditus ex dote officio adnexos.[161]

[159] Can. 208. For further discussion of this question see below, pp. 486-8.

[160] Can. 1411, 3°.

[161] Can. 1409.

1°. A juridical entity

It is said to be a juridical entity (*ens iuridicum*), but that is only another way of saying that it is a moral person. The terminology of the Code is not constant in the matter of moral personality. In many canons the expression *persona moralis* is used,[162] whereas in others the more accurate expression *persona iuridica* is used to designate the same generic idea, and, furthermore, it is used indiscriminately of the collegiate and the non-collegiate type of moral person, e. g., of associations of the faithful, as well as of hospitals, orphan asylums, and similar institutes.[163] In canons 1409 and 1410 the term *ens iuridicum* is used, and there is nothing to indicate that it is anything more than a synonym for the other two expressions,[164] for the capacity of owning property is attributed to it. This is confirmed by canon 99, which cites the benefice as an example of a non-collegiate moral person.

Being a moral person, then, a benefice is distinct from a physical and a collective person.

The prime difference among these three types of persons in the Church is the manner of their constitution. A physical person is constituted in the Church by baptism.[165] A collective person is constituted by a mere agreement or union of physical or moral persons simply with the approbation of ecclesiastical authority.[166] It lacks a corporate existence that is independent of its members, e. g., an association of the faithful or a pious union which has been approved but not canonically erected.[167]

[162] E. g., cans. 99-103; 106; 471, § 1; 536, §§ 1, 2; 1208, § 3; 1278; 1491, § 1; 1495, § 2; 1498; 1499, § 2; 2255, § 2.

[163] Cans. 687; 1489, § 1; 1495, § 2. In can. 1495, § 2, both terms are used in the same paragraph, and in a way which, on first sight, would seem to indicate that it was possible to have a moral person which was not a juridical person, but which, on further examination, shows that the opposition is not between those two terms, but between clauses in that paragraph and in the preceding one concerning the manner in which the Church itself, on the one hand, and inferior ecclesiastical institutes, on the other, have juridical personality.

[164] Chelodi, *Ius de Personis*, n. 97, note 4.

[165] Can. 87.

[166] Cans. 686, § 1; 708. Maroto, *Instituts.*, I, n. 475.

[167] Can. 687.

In other words, it is not a moral person,[168] and hence does not enjoy the capacity of acquiring and exercising rights,[169] except by special concession in a determined matter.[170] A moral person, finally, is constituted within the Church solely by public ecclesiastical authority,[171] either by a prescript of law, or by the special concession of a competent ecclesiastical Superior through the medium of a formal decree.[172]

In law a person is a subject capable of acquiring and exercising rights and of being bound by duties or obligations.[173] Etymologically it originally meant a masked character, but by a process of development it successively came to mean a theatrical character, a rôle as distinct from the individual enacting it, and also the part which an individual played in society.[174] Hence there was a foundation for the distinction between the person and the individual underlying it, and so the Romans defined a person, that is to say a natural or physical person, as a man endowed with a civil status.[175] Even in Roman Law, however, there was felt the need of having a legal subject, different from the ordinary natural person, with a capacity for certain rights and duties aiming at the accomplishment of ends which transcended the good of individuals; and so the collegiate moral person was brought into existence, consisting of a legally recognized union of individuals with two fundamental characteristics, perpetuity of existence independently of the identity of the individuals underlying it, and a separate status over and above them, with a capacity for rights and duties.[176] From Roman

168 Can. 708.

169 Can. 691, § 1.

170 E. g., can. 708.

171 Can. 99.

172 Can. 100, § 1.

173 Cf. Maroto, *ibid.*, n. 390.

174 Brown, *The Canonical Juristic Personality with Special Reference to its Status in the United States of America*, The Catholic University of America, Studies in Canon and Civil Law, n. 39 (Washington, D. C.: The Catholic University of America, 1927), p. 62.

175 Maroto, *ibid.*, note 2.

176 Cf. Brown, *op. cit.*, p. 63.

Law this institution was adopted by Canon Law, and, under the influence of Christianity, the other (non-collegiate) form of moral person, such as a charitable institution, also made its appearance.[177] A moral person in Canon Law may now, therefore, be defined as follows: " A juridical entity, formally constituted by public authority, existing in a permanent manner, through a concession of law, regardless of the identity of any individual physical persons who might form its material basis, and endowed with the capacity of acquiring and exercising rights." [178]

2°. Constitution by competent ecclesiastical authority

A benefice is constituted or erected by competent ecclesiastical authority (*a competente ecclesiastica auctoritate . . . constitutum seu erectum*). This clause refers to the assembling by the proper ecclesiastical authority of the material elements requisite for the formation of a benefice. Every moral person, it must be observed, is based on a material foundation, to which, however, a juridical existence is added. Thus, a collegiate moral person is primarily made up of a number of physical persons, while a non-collegiate moral person fundamentally consists in determined material things destined for a certain religious or charitable end, and those things take the form of an institute, such as a church, seminary, hospital, and the like.[179]

The juridical existence is given to the material foundation in one of two ways, either by prescript of law, or by the special concession of a competent ecclesiastical Superior through the medium of a formal decree.[180]

In the first way the law itself extends juridical existence to certain types of material foundations, on condition that they contain all the elements required by law, and have been brought into being by the proper ecclesiastical authority. Thus, the

177 Cf. Chelodi, *Ius de Personis*, n. 97.

178 " Definiri potest: ens iuridicum, publica auctoritate formaliter constitutum, independenter à personis singularibus ex iuris concessione subsistens, atque capacitate iuris acquirendi exercendique donatum."—Maroto, *Instituts.*, I, n. 458.

179 Cf. Maroto, *ibid.*, n. 459, b; Wernz-Vidal, *Ius Canon.*, II, n. 28.

180 Can. 100, § 1.

Code itself in canon 531 implicitly extends juridical existence or personality to religious houses, but that presupposes that the religious house verifies the canonical notion of such a house, for instance, that it is not merely a summer villa, and also that it has been erected by the proper authorization according to canons 495-497. It can thus be seen that for those moral persons which derive their juridical existence or personality from the law a twofold authority enters in: a competent ecclesiastical authority for the material foundation, and the law itself for the superadded juridical existence. Now all this is verified of a benefice. It is one of those types of entities which derive juridical existence or personality from the law itself, as is evident from various parts of the Code, in which the characteristics of a moral person are attributed to all benefices without exception. Thus, in canon 99 benefices are cited as examples of moral persons; in canon 1356, § 1, there is placed on them the obligation of paying the seminary tax; and in canon 1410 their capacity for owning property is acknowledged.

This extension of juridical existence or personality to a benefice, however, is dependent in any particular instance on the condition that the material foundation be all that it should be, that it contain all the elements and conditions necessary to make up a benefice, namely, a specific sacred office with such concrete limitations as those of place and territory, a sufficient and determined endowment from which the revenue of the beneficiary is to be derived, and an established perpetuity, both of the sacred office and endowment individually, and of the union of the two; and, furthermore, that this material foundation be assembled by a competent ecclesiastical authority. It is for this latter reason that the Code contains the clause under discussion, that the benefice be constituted or erected by competent ecclesiastical authority.

The second way in which some types of material foundations receive their juridical personality is by formal decree, e. g., associations of the faithful,[181] hospitals, orphan asylums, and the like.[182] In the constitution of benefices there is no need for

[181] Can. 687.

[182] Can. 1489, § 1.

any such decree, since they receive their juridical personality from the Code itself as soon as their material establishment is properly effected. The document attesting the erection of a benefice, as prescribed in canon 1418, has no reference to this formal decree, but is merely a documentary proof of the material establishment of the benefice, and even as that it is not an essential requisite, since the law neither expressly nor equivalently states so.[183]

From all this it can be readily understood why the Pontifical Commission for the Interpretation of the Code [184] expressly declared that for the erection of a canonical parish it was not necessary that there be issued a formal decree explicitly declaring that a certain district is thereby erected into a parish, but that it was sufficient that the Bishop fulfill the material requirements of canon 216, § 1, namely, that he define the territorial limits, and assign a rector and a church within the limits. Likewise, it is understood from the above why the Cardinal President of the aforesaid Commission added in the same reply that a parish is always an ecclesiastical benefice, as long as it fulfills the above requirements together with those concerning the endowment, as prescribed in canons 1410 and 1415, § 3.

The determination in a general way of the ecclesiastical Superior competent to erect the material foundation of a benefice is made in canon 1414. According to it, the Holy See alone is competent to erect consistorial benefices, whereas the Pope, the Ordinaries, and, in some circumstances, also Vicars General and Cardinals are competent in erecting non-consistorial benefices.

3°. Perpetuity of constitution

A benefice must be constituted or erected in perpetuity (*in perpetuum constitutum seu erectum*). By this it is shown that perpetuity of the material foundation of the benefice is one of the conditions which the law presupposes in extending juridical existence or personality to such a foundation. A moral person

183 Cf. can. 11.

184 Sept. 26, 1921, as contained in the letter of the Apostolic Delegate to the American Hierarchy, dated Nov. 10, 1922.

by its very nature is perpetual,[185] i. e., it continues to exist independently of the identity of the individual physical persons who may be its material basis. This was one of the essential characteristics of the moral person as it was created in Roman Law, and its purpose was to protect the common good for which the moral person was brought into existence from being dependent on the vicissitudes of individuals. Hence, that characteristic became natural to all moral persons, non-collegiate as well as collegiate. This perpetuity, however, is not absolute, but only as far as humanly can be foreseen; and so the law itself provides for the suppression of a moral person under certain circumstances.[186] Since this is so, it is necessary that, before a material thing can be given perpetual juridical existence, the perpetuity of its material existence also, as far as can be foreseen, must be secure, at least in the sense that a material foundation will always be provided, even though it be not always identically the same. It would be impossible to extend juridical or moral personality to a thing which of its very nature could not be indefinitely renewed, for then the perpetuity essential to moral personality could not be verified. The independence of existence of a moral or juridical person does not mean that it continues to exist even though its material foundation has totally and permanently ceased. It rather means an independence from the vicissitudes of the underlying foundation; but when the underlying material foundation ceases to exist in such a way that it is not renewed, then the moral person likewise ceases to be (*esse desierit*), although it is still capable of revivification, if a new material foundation be provided within a century.[187]

To give an example, a Cathedral Chapter remains identically the same collegiate moral person for centuries, even though the individual members are different in every generation; but if a time comes when all the members are dead, and no new members are appointed, the Chapter itself as a moral person ceases to exist, since there is no longer any subject capable of rights;

185 Can. 102, § 1.

186 Cans. 102, § 1; 1419-1422.

187 Can. 102, § 1.

nevertheless, if before a century elapses new members are again appointed in the same Cathedral, then the same moral person as before revivifies; if, however, new members are not appointed, then that moral person is no longer capable of revivifying, and a new Cathedral Chapter cannot exist in the same church without a new decree of erection from the Holy See.

By transferring all this into the realm of benefices, it can now be seen why the Code requires that the material foundation be constituted in perpetuity. Since a benefice by prescript of law is a moral person, and therefore juridically perpetual, it is necessary that those material things which go to make up a benefice have likewise an assured perpetuity. Concretely, this means that the specific sacred office must be of its very nature perpetual, that the endowment furnish a moral certainty of permanent existence, and that the right to receive the revenues from the endowment be perpetually linked with the office by the authority of the competent authorizing Superior.

It need scarcely be added that the perpetuity here spoken of deals exclusively with the objective existence of the benefice, and has no relation to the stability of the beneficiary's position, which is known as subjective perpetuity.[188] In the law of the Code subjective perpetuity is not a part of the nature of a benefice. It is true that the law prescribes that all secular benefices should be conferred in perpetuity,[189] but at the same time it admits of many exceptions, and in canon 1411, 4°, the manual or subjectively temporary benefice is given official recognition.[190]

4°. Constitutive elements: office and revenues

A benefice is said to consist of a sacred office together with the attached right to receive the revenues accruing to that office from an endowment (*constans officio sacro et iure percipiendi reditus ex dote officio adnexos*). In these words the Code sums up the materially constitutive elements of a benefice,

[188] For that cf. *supra*, pp. 418 ff.

[189] Can. 1438.

[190] Cf. Wernz, *Ius Decretalium*, II, n. 240, note 7; Wernz-Vidal, *Ius Canon.*, II, n. 141, note 3; Vermeersch-Creusen, *Epitome*, II, n. 742.

and at the same time shows thereby that a benefice is of the non-collegiate type of moral person, since its material foundation consists, not in physical persons, but in determined material things. Likewise it is apparent from this clause that a benefice is at least partly a sacred office. From other canons [191] it is conclusively shown that a benefice is principally a sacred office, and that permanent revenue is attached only as an accessory element, for in them a benefice is called a beneficial office, that is to say, an office to which permanent revenue is attached. *Office* there is obviously the genus, since it is shown that not every office need be a benefice, whereas it is evident from canon 1409 that every benefice must be an office. Hence, benefices are governed not only by the laws proper to themselves, but also by those concerning specific sacred offices.[192] This two-fold aspect of a benefice caused considerable confusion in the law prior to the Code, although enunciations of the correct present-day view were not lacking among the authors.[193] All doubts are now dispelled by the decisive wording of the Code.

The first constitutive element, the sacred office, was amply considered above.[194]

The accessory element—the right to receive the attached revenue—has in the present Code law undergone considerable change in its qualifications. Formerly a real endowment was exacted in the durable and fixed form of a principal, to the annual revenues of which the beneficiary had an exclusive right. Now, the idea of an endowment is very much broadened, so as to include even the voluntary offerings of the faithful, as long as they have some certainty about them.[195]

It is not the endowment itself which forms a part of the benefice, but rather the right to receive the revenues accruing from the endowment. Nevertheless, the one involves the other,

[191] E. g., Cans. 146; 1413, § 2.

[192] Cf. Wernz-Vidal, *Ius Canon.*, II, n. 138.

[193] E. g., Wernz, *Ius Decretalium*, II, n. 240; Aichner, *Compen.*, n. 76.

[194] Pp. 424-448.

[195] Can. 1410; cf. Vermeersch-Creusen, *Epitome*, II, n. 743; Wernz-Vidal, *Ius Canon.*, II, n. 141.

and so a benefice cannot be erected until some form of endowment in the sense of canon 1410 is designated, and then the right to receive the revenues from that source is perpetually and exclusively united to the office, and through it to the holder of the office, by the authority of the authorizing Superior.

In conclusion, a few remarks must be made concerning the division of moral persons into collegiate and non-collegiate, to the latter of which types the benefice belongs. An attempt was made to show that the term *ens iuridicum* in canon 1409 conveyed no further notion than the generic moral person. It was left for the constitutive elements of the benefice to differentiate this as non-collegiate. The Code wisely abstains from defining these two types of moral persons, but it describes them in such a way as to make clear what is meant. A collegiate moral person is one whose material foundation consists of physical persons, and in Canon Law the number of these must be at least three.[196] A non-collegiate moral person, on the other hand, is one whose material foundation consists in determined things destined for some religious or charitable end.[197] A benefice is not made up of physical persons but of determined things, namely, an actual specific sacred office and the attached right to receive certain definite revenues, and hence it is non-collegiate.

C. The Annexed Obligation of Residence

Upon the previous successive study of the notions of ecclesiastical office and ecclesiastical benefice, it now remains to say what is meant by the residential benefice of canon 114.

A residential benefice is simply described in the Code as "An ecclesiastical benefice which, in addition to the beneficial office, has annexed to it the obligation of residence." [198] Residence here means an almost continuous stay in the place where an office

196 Can. 100, § 2.

197 Cf. Maroto, *Instituts.*, I, n. 459; De Meester, *Compen.*, I, n. 324; Cocchi, *Comment.*, l. II, p. I, n. 6.

198 "Beneficia ecclesiastica dicuntur: . . . 3°. Duplicia seu residentialia, vel simplicia seu non residentialia, prout, praeter officium beneficiale, adnexam habent, vel minus, obligationem residendi: . . . "—Can. 1411, 3°.

or benefice exists for the purpose of personally fulfilling the duties inherent in that office.[199]

In the early ages of the Church, before the advent of benefices, all clerics were bound by the law of residence in the church of their ordination. Later, when separate benefices came into existence, all beneficiaries without distinction were bound to reside in the place of their benefice, because then the conferring of a benefice was merely the way by which a cleric was assigned at ordination to the service of a particular church as the law demanded, and also because it was invariably the will of the founder of a benefice that certain duties pertaining to divine worship be permanently fulfilled by a cleric in the particular church where the benefice was erected, which duties involved the necessity of personal residence.[200] All benefices, therefore, whether or not they involved the care of souls; whether, too, they were double or simple in the former sense of these terms—i. e., whether they involved jurisdiction, preëminence, administration, or the care of souls, on the one hand, or just simply a participation in orders, on the other—all were residential benefices, and that by the common law.[201] By a general custom of the entire Church, however, the latter class, i. e., simple benefices, with some exceptions, became exempt from the law of residence, so that the beneficiary could obtain a permanent substitute for himself. The exceptions were the simple benefices of Canons in Cathedral or Collegiate Chapters, and also all those benefices to which the obligation of residence had been attached by the approved will of the founder, by a statute of the church, or by particular custom.[202] Hence arose the distinction between residential and non-residential benefices, but there was no official cognizance taken of it until about the year 1230 in a letter of Pope Gregory IX to the Patriarch of Antioch and

[199] Cf. Schmalzgrueber, *Jus Eccles. Univ.*, l. III, t. IV, 1 sq.; Reiffenstuel, *Jus Canon. Univ.*, lib. III, tit. IV, 1, n. 2; Henry, *De Residentia Beneficiatorum* (Lovanii, 1863), pp. 4-5.

[200] Henry, *op. cit.*, pp. 8-12; Wernz, *Ius Decretalium*, II, nn. 469, 470.

[201] III General Council of the Lateran (1179), can. 13 (c. 3, X, *de cler. non resid. in eccl.*, III, 4); Henry, *op. et loc. cit.*; Wernz, *op. et loc. cit.*

[202] Henry, *op. cit.*, pp. 12, 222 ff.; Wernz, *op. et loc. cit.*

Legate of the Holy See, whereafter the distinction became a part of the common law.[203] The Council of Trent furthered this distinction by vigorously renewing the obligation of residence with the invocation of canonical sanctions in favor of those benefices which included either the care of souls or the power of ruling, yet omitting all mention of simple benefices, with the sole exception of cathedral and collegiate Canonries.[204] In fact, in one of the reform sessions the Council recognized the distinction explicitly, by speaking of " those benefices which by law or by custom require personal residence." [205] Finally, the Sacred Roman Congregations, after the Council of Trent, repeatedly and explicitly admitted that simple benefices did not bind to personal residence, unless they were Canonries, or unless the obligation of residence had been established through some source of authority other than the common law.[206] Thus, simple benefices, in the sense of *non-curata,* gradually passed from a condition in which lawful subjection to the demand of residence gave way to lawful exemption from that obligation.[207]

The condition prior to the Code, therefore, was as follows: All benefices which had annexed to their office the care of souls, as in the case of Bishops or pastors, subjected their incumbents to the obligation of personal residence by the common law, and, according to the more probable opinion, also by divine law.[208] Of those whose office did not include the care of souls, the benefices of cathedral or collegiate Canons subjected their incumbents to the same obligation. All other simple benefices, from the viewpoint of the common law, did not demand residence.

[203] C. 17, X, *de cleric. non resid. in eccl.*, III, 4; Henry, *op. cit.*, p. 13.

[204] Sess. VI, *de ref.*, cc. 1, 2; sess. XXIII, *de ref.*, c. 1; sess. XXIV, *de ref.*, c. 12; Henry, *De Resid. Benef.*, p. 14.

[205] Sess. VI, *de ref.*, c. 2.

[206] Henry, *op. cit.*, pp. 16, 17.

[207] Though mention has constantly been made in this brief sketch of benefices as subjecting their incumbents to the obligation of residence, this has been done merely for the sake of clarity, for it must be remembered that it is always from the ecclesiastical office, which underlies a benefice, that such obligations derive (cf. Henry, *De Resid. Benef.*, p. 3).

[208] Henry, *op. cit.*, pp. 17-23.

If, nevertheless, some simple benefice had the obligation of residence connected with it, then such a duty was derived from some particular legal source in any one of the three following ways: From the specific will of the founder as expressed in the foundation, from the statutes of a particular church, or from some localized custom.[209]

In the Code certain changes have been introduced in the terminology that specifies the various classes of benefices. Unlike the former usage, a double is now made synonymous with a residential, and a simple with a non-residential benefice, without any direct reference to the kind of power that is involved.[210] Thus, a Canonry is now a double instead of a simple benefice. The important distinction between the *curata* and the *non-curata,* according to whether or not there is annexed the care of souls, is still retained.[211]

Apart from these and other rather minor changes the former legislation on the obligation of residence is incorporated into the Code. The obligation is attached by the law itself to all offices in the strict sense which have the care of souls, such as those of residential Bishops,[212] pastors,[213] Vicars and Prefects Apostolic,[214] Vicars Capitular,[215] actual parochial vicars,[216] parochial vicar administrators,[217] certain parochial vicar substitutes,[218] and full parochial adjutant vicars.[219] As for those offices which have not the care of souls, the common law still attaches the obligation of residence to the office of cathedral or collegiate Canons, but

209 Henry, *De Resid. Benef.*, pp. 3-4, 222-227; Wernz, *Ius Decretalium*, II, n. 470.

210 Can. 1411, 3°.

211 Can. 1411, 5°.

212 Can. 338.

213 Can. 465.

214 Can. 301, § 1.

215 Can. 440.

216 Can. 471, § 4.

217 Can. 473, § 1.

218 Can. 474.

219 Can. 475, § 2.

in a modified way. Some are bound to daily choir duty; others are not. For the former the obligation of residence is absolute; for the latter it admits of a greater latitude.[220] In addition to this the Code also attaches the obligation of residence to certain other *non-curata* offices, which however contain some participation in jurisdiction.[221] For the remainder, the Code simply provides for the possibility of the obligation of residence being attached by particular law, whether by the canonically approved will of the founder, in the case of a benefice,[222] or by particular statute or custom, in the case of either a benefice or a specific office.[223] It is now possible, consequently, for a benefice to be residential, either because the Code has attached the obligation to the generic office underlying it, or because particular statute or custom has attached the obligation to all the specific offices underlying benefices in a certain territory, or, finally, because in the erection of an individual benefice the founder, in conjunction with the proper ecclesiastical authority, has attached the obligation to that one specific beneficial office.

4. *Which Diocesan Offices Can Be Residential Benefices*

In consequence upon the determination of the principles of a residential benefice, it is logical to examine existing diocesan positions or offices in the light of them, so as to discover which positions are apt to effect excardination and incardination according to the method of canon 114. The order of the Code in this affords a good standard of sequence.

A. The Diocesan Curia

The Curia of a diocese consists of those persons who help the Bishop, or him who is in the Bishop's place, in the rule of the entire diocese.[224] It is divided into two departments, the non-

220 Cans. 418, § 1; 419, § 1; 420; 421.

221 E. g., that of Cardinals in the Curia (can. 238).

222 Can. 1417.

223 E. g., can. 476, § 5.

224 Can. 363, § 1.

judiciary and the judiciary. The former comprises the Vicar General, the Chancellor, the Notaries, the Synodal Examiners, and the Parish Priest Consultors; the latter includes the *Officialis,* the Promoter of Justice, the Defender of the Bond, the Synodal Judges, the Auditors, and the Court Beadles.[225]

1°. The Vicar General

The position of a Vicar General is undoubtedly an ecclesiastical office in the strict sense. It has been constituted generically in a permanent manner by the common law; [226] a specifically defined participation in the power of jurisdiction has been annexed to it by the Code,[227] which power is consequently ordinary; and in each specific instance it must be either constituted or conferred according to the general and particular norms of the Code.[228] Despite all this, the specific office of a Vicar General can never become an ecclesiastical benefice, for the simple reason that, although generically permanent, it has not the necessary objective *specific* perpetuity, because the objective existence of the office of a Vicar General in any particular diocese is entirely dependent on the needs of the diocese,[229] so that when the need ceases, the objective specific office can be abolished at will. It might also be added that the objective specific office also ceases indirectly whenever the episcopal see becomes vacant, for then the incumbent loses his office, [230] and, as it was shown above,[231] an office has no objective existence independent of any incumbent, since it is not a moral person. It follows from this that, although a priest be brought in from another diocese, as the Code itself permits,[232] to assume the office of Vicar General,

[225] Can. 365.

[226] Cans. 366-371.

[227] Cans. 366, § 1; 368, §§ 1, 2.

[228] Cans. 147 ff.; 366; 367.

[229] Can. 366, § 1.

[230] Cans. 371; 308; 183, § 2.

[231] P. 433.

[232] Can. 367, § 3.

excardination and incardination can never result from that mere fact. That explains why the Code does not mention any possibility of such an effect arising when a Vicar General is selected from an outside diocese.

2°. The Chancellor

However much opposed it may seem to the common estimation of men, the position of a diocesan Chancellor is not even an ecclesiastical office in the strict sense, for, although it is a position which is generically and permanently constituted by the common law,[233] it does not have included in itself any participation whatsoever in the power of orders or of jurisdiction, either by the law itself, or by order of the law. Rather, its chief function is to care for the contents of the diocesan archives, to keep them in chronological order, to make indices of them, and the like.[234] Any powers which a particular Chancellor may have superior to this are merely delegated to him by the Bishop, and do not belong to his position. At most, then, he has an office only in the broad sense, but that is certainly not sufficient to form the foundation of a benefice. The same is obviously true of the position of a Vice-Chancellor.[235]

3°. The Notaries

Somewhat akin to that of Chancellor is the position of a diocesan Notary. This position likewise has no power of orders or of jurisdiction attached to it, and its main duty, as outlined in canon 374, is to draw up various forms of documents, decrees, sentences, and the like. Hence it is not an office in the strict sense, and cannot become a benefice. The Code itself permits it to be held by lay persons.[236]

4°. The Synodal Examiners and Parish Priest Consultors

These positions have no power attached to them beyond that of conducting certain clerical examinations and of acting as an

[233] Can. 372.

[234] Can. 372, § 1.

[235] Can. 372, § 2.

[236] Can. 373, § 3.

advisory board to the Bishop in various processes.[237] Hence they are not offices in the strict sense and cannot be benefices.

5°. The *Officialis* and *Vice-Officialis*

The position of *Officialis* in a diocese fulfills all the requirements of an ecclesiastical office in the strict sense. It has been constituted in a generic and fixed manner by the common law; [238] it has definite judicial power of jurisdiction attached to it by the same law, which, therefore, is ordinary power; [239] and it must be conferred according to the general and particular norms of the Code.[240] Furthermore, unlike the office of Vicar General, each specific creation of this office entails objective perpetuity, for in every diocese it is made mandatory on the Bishop, and its duration in existence is unconditional.[241] Hence in a particular diocese it can be made into a benefice, namely, if a determined endowment in one of the forms enumerated in canon 1410 be constituted, and the right to receive the income from that endowment be perpetually attached by the Bishop to the office of the *Officialis,* either through the instrumentality of a formal document, or in some other way, if such there be, whereby the attachment of the two could be perpetually proved in the external forum. It is true that in any specific case this office is not subjectively perpetual, for the incumbent is removable at the mere will of the Bishop,[242] but that is not contrary to the nature of a benefice in the law of the Code.[243] Consequently, in the erection of an office of this type into the status of a benefice, the founder, with the consent of the Bishop, could make the condition that the beneficiary be removable at the will of the Bishop, and that would be nothing more than one of those conditions which are permitted by canon 1417, § 1; or again,

[237] Cf. cans. 389; 2144, § 1; 2153, § 1; 2154, § 1; 2165.

[238] Can. 1573.

[239] Can. 1573, § 1.

[240] Cans. 147 ff.; 1573, §§ 1, 4, 5.

[241] Can. 1573, § 1.

[242] Can. 1573, § 5.

[243] Can. 1411, 4°.

the Bishop could obtain an Indult to permit him to make the office of his diocesan *Officialis* a benefice which would be revocable at his own will.

The obligation of residence is not attached by the Code to the generic office of the *Officialis,* and so, even though in a specific case it were enhanced into the status of a benefice, it would not be a residential one, unless the obligation of residence were attached to it in one of the three ways spoken of above,[244] namely, by the canonically approved will of the founder as expressed in the law of the foundation, by provincial statute, or by custom, affecting all the *Officiales* in a province. An examination into the individual case would have to be made, therefore, before it could be determined whether the office was a benefice, and, if so, whether or not it was a residential benefice.

The position of a *Vice-Officialis* is also an office in the strict sense. Like that of the *Officialis,* it is permanently constituted in its generic form by common law; [245] the conferring of it must follow the norms established by the Code; [246] and from the Code, too, it has attached to it ordinary judicial power of jurisdiction.[247] It differs from the office of the *Officialis,* however, in one major respect, which destroys the possibility of its ever becoming a benefice, and that is that it lacks objective specific perpetuity. In any particular case its nature is nothing more than a coadjutorship in the office of the *Officialis,*[248] and so its objective existence is always dependent on a temporary need.

6°. The Promoter of Justice and the Defender of the Bond

These two positions have been constituted in a generic and perpetual way by the Code, and at the same time they have objective specific perpetuity, because their constitution in a diocese is mandatory and absolute.[249] Likewise they are con-

244 P. 461.

245 Can. 1573, § 3.

246 Can. 1573, §§ 4, 5.

247 Cans. 1577, § 2; 1578. Cf. Roberti, *De Processibus,* I, n. 97.

248 Can. 1573, § 3.

249 Can. 1586.

ferrable only according to the norms of the law.[250] Nevertheless, neither of these positions includes in itself any participation in the power of orders or of jurisdiction.[251] Rather, they are nothing more than the positions of officially recognized contending parties in certain kinds of judicial trials, for the purpose of promoting and defending justice.[252] As their names suggest, the former is established to prosecute justice in criminal trials, and in contentious trials wherein the public good is concerned; the latter is constituted for the purpose of defending the bond of ordination or of matrimony in trials wherein that bond is attacked.[253] Since, then, there is no power of orders or of jurisdiction connected with either of these positions, they are not offices in the strict sense and cannot be made benefices.

7°. The Synodal and Pro-Synodal Judges

Although the Judge of the first instance in every diocese is the Ordinary of the place for all causes which are not expressly withdrawn by law from his competence,[254] and although the *Officialis* and *Vice-Officialis* enjoy that same distinction except in those causes wherein the Bishop of the place reserves judgment for himself,[255] still the Code restricts the judgment over certain causes to a collegiate tribunal of three, and in other causes to a tribunal of five, Judges.[256] In order to make this possible the Code demands that besides the Bishop and the *Officialis* there are to be selected in every diocese not less than four and not more than twelve priests proven in character and skilled in the science of Canon Law, and they are to be constituted as Judges. They are to be designated Synodal Judges or Pro-

[250] Cans. 1588; 1589; 1590.

[251] Cf. Roberti, *De Processibus*, I, nn. 40, 120.

[252] E. g., cans. 1616; 1688, § 2; 1696, § 2; 1729, § 4; 1745, § 1; 1759, § 2; 1773, § 2; 1786; 1793, § 2; 1824, § 1; 1830, § 3; 1837; 1839; 1841 etc. Cf. Roberti, *loc. cit.*

[253] Can. 1586; cf. Roberti, *op. cit.*, I, nn. 122, 123.

[254] Can. 1572, § 1.

[255] Can. 1573, § 2.

[256] Can. 1576, § 1, 1°, 2°.

Synodal Judges according to whether their election takes place at a diocesan synod or at a time apart from a diocesan synod.[257]

The Code ordains that they are to have a part in judging disputes by virtue of power delegated by the Bishop.[258] That, however, is to be taken in the sense that they exercise a communicated rather than a native power.[259] In truth they have ordinary judiciary power, because it is the common law itself which attaches to the generic position of Synodal and Pro-Synodal Judge the right to give a definitive sentence when acting in a collegiate tribunal. The fact that the Ordinary is empowered to select the membership of the tribunal in specific cases by turn, unless he in his prudence deems some other method more advantageous,[260] does not imply that the Ordinary delegates jurisdiction to the selected Judges each time they are chosen, but merely that he determines the order in which the the individual Judges are to function.[261] The collegiate tribunal in which the Synodal and Pro-Synodal Judges function is placed in the Code under the sub-heading "*De tribunali ordinario primae instantiae*," and in canon 1578 it is likewise termed the *ordinary* tribunal. This is in contradistinction to another sub-heading of the Code "*De tribunali delegato*," which refers to Judges who are not elected to such a position but are merely delegated for a certain case. It is admitted by all canonists that the president of the ordinary tribunal of the first instance, the Bishop, the *Officialis*, or the *Vice-Officialis*, acts with ordinary power. Yet, when the collegiate tribunal delivers a sentence, it does so as a unit; the persons comprising the tribunal are "the Judge," not Judges. It would be incompatible with this idea for one of the judicial persons to have ordinary power and the others only delegated power.[262] Therefore, the judiciary power

[257] Can. 1574, § 1; cf. Roberti, *De Processibus*, I, n. 103.

[258] Can. 1574, § 1.

[259] Roberti, *loc. cit.*

[260] Can. 1576, § 3.

[261] Roberti, *loc. cit.*

[262] *Ibid.*

which Synodal and Pro-Synodal Judges have is ordinary power, attached to their generic position by the common law itself. Hence the position of a Synodal or Pro-Synodal Judge is an ecclesiastical office in the strict sense. Furthermore, in accordance with what was said above,[263] it must be admitted that that would still be true even if the power which they exercise were only delegated, because the Code apparently demands that there be attached to the office *in specie* at least some delegated power.

The conferring of these offices must follow the express norms of the common law.[264] Then, too, the offices of Synodal and Pro-Synodal Judge in any particular diocese have objective perpetuity. The Code requires that they be constituted in every diocese without exception, and places no limit to their duration.

It follows that the office of a Synodal or Pro-Synodal Judge in any specific diocese can be elevated to the status of a benefice if the Bishop of the diocese attaches to the office in a perpetual manner the right to receive the income from a determined endowment in the sense of canon 1410. Since subjective perpetuity is not a part of the nature of a benefice,[265] the fact that the office of a Synodal or Pro-Synodal Judge is conferred merely for a term of ten years[266] does not militate against its potential erection to the status of a benefice.

The obligation of residence, however, is not expressly attached by the Code to the office of Synodal or Pro-Synodal Judge. Consequently, it would not be a residential benefice unless the obligation of residence were attached to the specific office in one of the ways already enumerated.[267]

8°. The Auditors

An Auditor is one to whom is committed the execution of all the procedural acts which are required for the proper preparation of a case.[268] His commission can originate from the Ordinary

263 P. 446.

264 Cans. 1574, § 2; 385-388.

265 Cf. *supra*, p. 455.

266 Cans. 1574, § 2; 387, § 1.

267 Cf. *supra*, p. 461.

268 Roberti, *De Processibus*, I, n. 110.

of the place or from the Judge,[269] and, since the identity of the latter is unspecified, it can be the *Officialis* or *Vice-Officialis*, the collegiate tribunal itself, or even a delegated Judge. When the Ordinary of the place appoints an Auditor, the appointment may be merely for one certain case, or it may be permanent for all cases. The question naturally arises, "Is the position of Auditor a generic one established in a perpetual manner by the Code?" This can be answered in the affirmative only with regard to the permanently appointed Auditor. The provisions of the Code for an Auditor to be appointed for only a certain case are merely a substantiation in a particular matter of the general principles of delegation and subdelegation contained in canon 199. Especially is this evident when the Auditor for a particular case is appointed by a delegated Judge. The Auditor at best is just an auxiliary Judge,[270] an executor of the Judge's will, and so his power depends almost entirely on the will of the Judge who appoints him.[271]

The permanently appointed Auditor derives at least some limited and limitable participation in the power of jurisdiction from the common law itself, inasmuch as there is attached to his position the power and authority to cite witnesses, to hear testimony, and, in general, to conduct the trial up to, but exclusive of, the definitive sentence.[272] It can be safely held, therefore, that the jurisdictional power of the permanently appointed Auditor is ordinary, and that his position is an office in the strict sense.[273] Furthermore, the conferment of this office is regulated by canons 1580, § 1, and 1581. However, the specific office lacks objective perpetuity because its constitution in any diocese is voluntary, not mandatory. Even after a Bishop has elected an Auditor for all cases he can not only remove the incumbent at any time for a just cause,[274] but he can also use his

[269] Can. 1580.

[270] Cf. can. 1614, § 1.

[271] Roberti, *loc. cit.*

[272] Can. 1582; cf. Roberti, *De Processibus*, I, n. 110; Vermeersch-Creusen, *Epitome*, III, n. 40.

[273] Roberti, *loc. cit.*

[274] Can. 1583.

discretionary power to abolish the office altogether. Therefore, even the office of a permanently appointed Auditor could never be raised to the status of a benefice.[275]

9°. The Court Beadles

Though these are attached to the diocesan Curia, they are nothing more than a chosen group of persons who may be commissioned by the Judge to put his sentences or decrees into execution,[276] i. e., into material execution, so that they merely partake of the nature of police and messengers.[277] There is no power of orders or of jurisdiction connected with the position, for only lay persons are to be appointed to it, unless in a particular case prudence dictates otherwise,[278] and, consequently, it is not an office in the strict sense, and cannot be a benefice.

B. Canons Capitular

A Chapter of Canons is a college of clerics, instituted in a cathedral or other church, for the purpose of performing therein the more solemn divine worship and, in the case of a Cathedral Chapter, for the purpose of acting as the senate of the Bishop, and of supplying his place in the rule of the diocese when the see becomes vacant.[279] It is called a Cathedral or a Collegiate Chapter, according to whether it is instituted in a cathedral, or in an ordinary church. It is made up of two classes of members, known as "Dignities" and "Canons," among the latter of whom are distributed various offices. In addition to these two classes there are minor officers, who assist the members of the Chapter, but these are not included in the Chapter itself.[280]

[275] Cf. *supra*, p. 455.

[276] Can. 1591, § 1.

[277] Cf. S. C. Ep. et Reg., instr., 11 iun. 1880, n. 14; *Regulae servandae in iudiciis apud S. R. Rotae Tribunal*, 4 aug. 1910, § 24, nn. 1-2; *Regulae servandae in iudiciis apud Suprem. Signaturae Ap. Tribunal*, 6 mar. 1912, art. 16; Roberti, *De Processibus*, I, n. 125.

[278] Can. 1592.

[279] Can. 391, § 1.

[280] Can. 393, §§ 1, 3.

In attempting to discover which of these positions are sacred offices in the strict sense, and possible benefices, a process of elimination may be followed. The position of the " Dignities " need not be considered, because it can only be conferred by the Holy See,[281] and hence will never verify the supposition of canon 114. The minor beneficiaries need not be discussed here, because they comprise either simple substitutes, who are beneficed and obliged to choir duty in order to increase the number present by substituting for the absentees,[282] or else mere chaplains, whose appointment includes the obligation of serving those who are engaged in the choir service, or of helping the parochial vicar of the Chapter in the care of souls.[283] The first do not differ as to their beneficiary status from simple Canons; the latter will receive consideration under the section concerning Chaplains. Even the major offices, those of the Canon Theologian, the Canon Penitentiary, and the Canon who functions as actual vicar in a parish united to the Chapter, may be passed over, because they are only conferred on those who are already Canons. Hence the position of Canon alone needs to be considered at length.

In the position of a Canon Capitular all the requirements of an ecclesiastical office in the strict sense are found. It has been constituted in a generic and fixed way by the common law; [284] it must be conferred according to the laws of the Code; [285] and finally, in the case of both Cathedral and Collegiate Chapters, it includes some participation in the power of orders and of jurisdiction, for it gives a Canon a right according to his rank to assist the Bishop in the functions of divine worship, to administer the sacraments to him in his sickness, to perform the funeral

281 Can. 396, § 1.

282 Cf. Bouix, *Tractatus De Capitulis* (Parisiis, 1882), p. I, sec. II, capp. XIII-XIV.

283 De Meester, *Compen.*, II, n. 750, 1°, e; S. C. C., *Aretina*, 20 dec. 1851 (Lingen-Reuss, *Causae Selectae*, n. 494); Ferraris, *Bibliotheca*, " Cappellania," n. 48; " Cappellanus," n. 21.

284 Cans. 391 ff.

285 Cans. 403-405.

rites over him upon his death, and to convoke and preside over the Chapter; [286] it gives him a voice in the Chapter,[287] and, consequently, a part in the power of making capitular statutes; [288] and, lastly, it obliges him and gives him the right to function according to his order in the conventual mass and in the service of the altar.[289] In Cathedral Chapters, in addition, the Canons participate in the ordinary jurisdiction over the diocese whenever the see becomes vacant and no other provision is made for its rule.[290]

Not only is this position an office; it is also in its specific constitution almost always a benefice. Honorary Canons, of course, are Canons practically only in name and participate in only a few of the honors and privileges connected with the position.[291] Supernumerary Canons, or those who are constituted without the right to receive revenues, are the exception, and can be created only with the special permission of the Holy See.[292] Normally, therefore, canonries already existing and those which the Bishop constitutes have attached to them the perpetual right to receive revenues, either from separate endowments (*praebendae*) or from some other source,[293] in accordance with the definition of canon 1410. Finally, the obligation of personal residence in the place where the Chapter exists is imposed by the Code on all Canons who have benefices, although this admits of some latitude for those who are not bound to daily choir duty.[294] Consequently, the office of a Canon Capitular is, in most instances, a residential benefice.

[286] Can. 397.

[287] Cans. 405, § 1; 411, § 3.

[288] Can. 410, § 2.

[289] Cans. 413; 416; 417.

[290] Cans. 431, § 1; 435, § 1.

[291] Can. 407, § 2.

[292] Can. 393, § 3.

[293] Can. 394, § 1.

[294] Cans. 418; 419.

C. Diocesan Consultors

The position of Diocesan Consultors is created by the Code as a substitute for the office of Canons of the Cathedral Chapter until such time as these latter may be constituted or restored in a diocese.[295] For that reason the generic position of Diocesan Consultors cannot be said to be perpetually established by the Code. Since, however, it will doubtless be many years before all dioceses in the world will be able to conform to the will of the legislator by canonically erecting the Cathedral Chapter, it must be admitted that the generic position of Diocesan Consultors has a considerable degree of stability about it, enough at least to satisfy the requirement for an office in the strict sense.[296] Moreover, the generic position of Diocesan Consultors fulfills the other requirements for an office in the strict sense, because the conferring of it is regulated by the Code[297] and it has attached to it at least some participation in the power of jurisdiction, namely, in the rule of the diocese during the potential period of eight days subsequent to its vacancy, if the Holy See has made no contrary specific provision.[298]

No similar degree of stability, much less objective perpetuity, can be attributed to the *specific* office of Diocesan Consultors in whatever particular diocese they are constituted, because a particular diocese might be able to constitute or restore the Cathedral Chapter in a relatively brief space of time. As long as there is no Cathedral Chapter existing the Bishop of the diocese not only can, but must, appoint Diocesan Consultors, but that does not excuse him from a prudent effort to have the Cathedral Chapter canonically erected in his diocese as soon as that is possible.[299] Now, objective perpetuity, and not merely objective stability, is required of a specific ecclesiastical office before

295 Can. 423.

296 Cf. *supra*, p. 432.

297 Cans. 424-426.

298 Cans. 427; 431, § 1; 435, § 1. Cf. also Chelodi, *Ius de Personis*, n. 215; Wernz-Vidal, *Ius Canon.*, II, n. 699.

299 Wernz-Vidal, *ibid.*, n. 698.

it can be elevated to the status of a benefice.[300] For that reason the specific office of Diocesan Consultors in any particular diocese cannot be made a benefice. In fact, it might be said that any Bishop who would attempt to make it so would equivalently be refusing to conform to the will of the legislator as it is expressed in canon 423.

D. Vicar Capitular

Whenever a residential Bishop comes to such misfortune that he cannot physically communicate with his flock even by letter, or when the episcopal see becomes vacant, if the rule of the diocese is not otherwise legally provided for, the Cathedral Chapter or the Board of Diocesan Consultors elects a Vicar Capitular or an Administrator who temporarily rules the diocese.[301] There is no doubt that the position of the Vicar Capitular is an office in the strict sense, since it is permanently constituted in the common law,[302] is conferred according to law,[303] and includes the power of jurisdiction over a diocese.[304] Upon every specific election, however, the office is only temporary, since it ceases with the accession of a new Bishop,[305] and so it can never become a benefice.

E. Vicars Forane

This is a position concerning which the determination of its nature causes some difficulty. Undoubtedly it is a position which has been generically and perpetually constituted by the common law,[306] and which can only be conferred according to the prescriptions of that law,[307] but whether or not it includes in itself some participation in the power of orders or of jurisdic-

300 Cf. *supra,* p. 432.

301 Cans. 429, §§ 1, 3; 432, § 1.

302 Cans. 429 ff.

303 Cans. 429, § 3; 432, §§ 1, 2; 434, § 1.

304 Cans. 429, § 3; 432, § 1; 435, § 1; 438.

305 Can. 443, § 2.

306 Cans. 217; 445 ff.

307 Can. 446.

tion is a much disputed point. Some authors claim that these vicars have ordinary power of jurisdiction;[308] others equally contend that they have only delegated jurisdiction; [309] and still others hold that they have also ordinary power, which, however, they are loathe to call real jurisdiction.[310] The dispute centers about the nature of the rights or powers which are given to Vicars Forane in canons 447-449. It cannot be denied that in these canons the Code attaches to that generic position some very definite rights, subject to modification by the provincial or diocesan synod or by the Bishop. If these rights are to be considered as parts of jurisdiction, then certainly Vicars Forane have ordinary jurisdiction, but such is not the case. Jurisdiction in any of its forms is a power of ruling the faithful, but the rights enumerated in these canons simply imply an authorization to watch over certain events and practices, and to report the acquired observations to the Bishop,[311] for not a single one of these canons authorizes the Vicar Forane to act on his own authority in any way which would imply the rule of others. Hence he cannot be said to have ordinary jurisdiction, nor can it be properly asserted that he has ordinary power, for that expression is used exclusively by the Code as a division of jurisdiction, though implicitly it is also extended to assistance at marriages.

Furthermore, if in accordance with canon 447 particular law, such as that of a provincial council or of a diocesan synod, should attach real jurisdictional powers to all Vicars Forane within a certain territory, these powers would not be ordinary, as some authors erroneously believe, but merely delegated, for the reason

[308] E. g., Maroto, *Instituts.*, I, nn. 700; 702, B; Wernz-Vidal, *Ius Canon.*, II, n. 716, § III; Toso, *Comment. Minora*, in can. 447; Zaplotnik, *De Vicariis Foraneis*, The Catholic University of America, Canon Law Studies, n. 47 (Washington, D. C.: The Catholic University of America, 1927), pp. 69, 70, 73, 76.

[309] E. g., De Meester, *Compen.*, II, n. 803; Vermeersch-Creusen, *Epitome*, I, n. 487; Badii, *Instituts.*, I, n. 267; Bargilliat, *Praelectiones Iuris Canonici* (37. ed., 2 vols., Parisiis: apud Baston, Berche et Pagis, 1923), II, n. 855; Fanfani, *De Iure Parochorum ad Normam Codicis Iuris Canonici* (Taurini-Romae: Ex officina Libraria Marietti, 1924), p. 369.

[310] E. g., Chelodi, *Ius de Personis*, n. 221.

[311] Chelodi, *loc. cit.*

adduced above,[312] namely, that jurisdiction is not ordinary unless it is attached to the entire generic office by that law which is competent to regulate it in its entirety. Since the position of Vicar Forane has been constituted in the universal Church, it follows that only the common law can attach ordinary power to it.

It is true that Vicars Forane have no real jurisdiction except that which is delegated to them, but it does not follow that their position is not an office in the strict sense. It has already been discussed above,[313] how an office in the strict sense can exist with only delegated power, when namely the Code itself provides that in each specific erection of the office power be delegated to the incumbent. That is the case here. In canon 447 the Code presupposes that faculties are delegated to all Vicars Forane by their respective provincial or diocesan synods, but in canon 899, § 2, it explicitly commands that the faculty to absolve from sins reserved to the Ordinary be habitually delegated to all these Vicars, so that it becomes true that every single Vicar Forane, and consequently their position as a whole, includes in itself at least some participation in the delegated power of jurisdiction.

Not only has the office of a Vicar Forane objective generic perpetuity, but it has also perpetuity in each specific constitution of it.[314] In a particular instance, therefore, it could be made a benefice. The only obstacle to this is that the office is subjectively revocable at the will of the Bishop,[315] but this could be remedied in the foundation by a condition, such as the one permitted in canon 1417, § 1, that the office would become revocable only by process of law, or by a clause permitting it to remain revocable at will, in accordance with canon 1438.

Finally, the office of Vicar Forane has the obligation of residence attached to it by common law,[316] and that would make

312 Pp. 442 ff.

313 Pp. 445-6 ff.

314 Can. 217.

315 Can. 446, § 2.

316 Can. 448, § 2. Cf. Zaplotnik, *De Vicariis Foraneis*, pp. 123-125.

the benefice residential. The point which would have to be determined and proved in each case, therefore, would be that the Bishop had made the office a benefice.

F. Pastors

There is no difficulty in identifying the position of a pastor as an office in the strict sense. It has been perpetually constituted in its generic form by common law; [317] the laws of the Code govern the conferring of it; [318] and it has attached to it by the Code itself a participation in the power both of orders and of jurisdiction.[319] In addition to this each specific erection of a pastorate or parish *per se* has objective perpetuity.[320] Before the Code this meant that a canonical parish could be erected into the status of a benefice, if by the authority of the Bishop it acquired the ownership of some capital which would produce a sufficient annual revenue for the support of the pastor. Consequently, not every canonical parish was a benefice. The Code, however, so widened the notion of the endowment required for a benefice, and in particular for a parochial one,[321] as to make it impossible for a canonical parish to exist without at the same time being a benefice. This caused some agitation, especially in the United States, where, for various reasons, it had been doubtful whether or not the so-called parishes or missions were canonical parishes. If not, they would not be benefices, and their rectors would not be real pastors. On August 1, 1919, the Sacred Consistorial Congregation solved the doubt by declaring that, in view of canon 216, definite parts of dioceses to which particular rectors had been assigned for the care of souls were to be considered as real parishes.[322] That Sacred Congregation created a new difficulty, however, by stat-

[317] Cans. 451 ff.

[318] Cans. 453; 455; 459.

[319] Cans. 451, § 1; 461; 462; 464, § 1; 467, § 1; 873, § 1; 1044; 1045, § 3; 1245, § 1.

[320] Can. 216, §§ 1, 3.

[321] Cans. 1410; 1415, §§ 1, 3.

[322] *AAS*, XI (1919), 346.

ing that all that was required for constituting a parish was a decree of the Ordinary determining the boundaries, the parochial see, and the endowment both for the conduct of divine worship and for the support of the pastor. Existing parishes had not been erected by a special decree, and, in view of the above declaration, that omission seemed to militate against their canonical nature. The new difficulty was solved by a decision of the Pontifical Commission for the Interpretation of the Code,[323] in which it was declared that, for the erection of a parish, no special decree of the Ordinary was necessary, but that it was sufficient for him to define the territorial limits, and to assign a rector and a church, as prescribed in canon 216, § 1. Furthermore, it declared that all parishes, so established before the Code, became canonical parishes *ipso facto* on the promulgation of the Code. In the same decision it was noted by the President of the Commission that a parish is always an ecclesiastical benefice with the care of souls attached, no matter whether it have the proper endowment, as defined in canon 1410, or whether it be simply erected with the prudent foresight that the necessary revenues will not be lacking from some other source, as is permitted in canon 1415, § 3. It may be concluded, therefore, that, since the promulgation of the Code, every parish, the erection of which fulfills the requirements of canon 216, § 1, and the financial support of which is provided for after the manner of canons 1410 or 1415, § 3, is a benefice, and that, too, regardless of whether the pastorate be subjectively revocable or irrevocable, inasmuch as these terms merely refer to different degrees of stability.[324] Furthermore, since the obligation of personal residence is attached by the Code to the office of a pastor,[325] the benefice is residential.

Thus far reference has been made only to the ordinary territorial parish. What is to be said about the so-called national parish or the personal, e. g., colored, parish? Are they also residential benefices? The answer depends on whether or not

[323] Sept. 26, 1921, contained in a letter of the Apostolic Delegate in the United States to the American hierarchy under date of Nov. 10, 1922.

[324] Can. 454, §§ 1, 2.

[325] Can. 465.

the national or the personal parish is a real canonical parish and its rector a real pastor. If they are, undoubtedly the office of the pastor is no different from that considered above, and the pastorate is a residential benefice.

Although canon 216, § 1, describes a parish as a distinct territorial part of a diocese, nevertheless, if it is to be reconciled with § 4 of the same canon, it must be admitted that a definite and distinct territory is not essential to a parish in the canonical sense,[326] and, consequently, that § 1, in mentioning it, is dealing particularly with the ordinary type of parish. By combining these two paragraphs of canon 216, then, it can be deduced that there are three different types of parishes: territorial, personal, and mixed, according to whether their subjects are designated by mere residence in a territory, by personal characteristics alone, or by a combination of both.[327] Since all of these types are expressly designated in the Code as parishes, it follows that they must be such in the canonical sense, provided, of course, that they fulfill the other requirements of canon 216, § 1. Therefore, also, the particular rectors assigned to them are real pastors.

Have these parishes the objective perpetuity required for benefices? Canon 216, § 4, likewise supplies the answer to this question, for it makes it impossible to erect them without a papal Indult, and, when once erected, to suppress or change them without the authority of the Holy See. As for national and racial parishes, the usual kind in this country, though they be founded on accidental differences among men, it can hardly be claimed that these parishes are by nature only temporary, for as long as there are different nations and races on the face of the earth and they are still permitted to emigrate from one country to another, and as long as they continue to follow the propensities of human nature of bonding themselves together in colonies, a parish of this type will continue to be a necessity, and will be just as abiding as any ordinary territorial parish. Hence, whenever the pastor, church, and people are designated

326 Cf. De Meester, *Compen.*, II, n. 491; Maroto, *Instituts.*, II, n. 767, § II; n. 771, §§ I-II; Vermeersch-Creusen, *Epitome*, I, n. 292; Wernz, *Ius Decretalium*, II, n. 821; Toso, *Comment. Minora*, in can. 216.

327 Vermeersch-Creusen, *loc. cit.*

as in canon 216, § 1, and at the same time one of the approved sources of revenue is provided for, a national or a personal parish will also be a residential benefice.[328]

G. Parochial Vicars of Moral Persons

When a parish is united in full right (*pleno iure*) to a religious house, to a Cathedral or Collegiate Chapter, or to some other moral person, then this moral person itself is thereby constituted in a permanent manner as the pastor invested with the title (*parochus habitualis*), but a parochial vicar must be constituted to exercise the actual care of souls in its place.[329] Various names are given to such a vicar by different authors, e. g., *vicarius actualis, vicarius perpetuus, vicarius curatus,* but all these titles are either ambiguous or incorrect; the title employed in the heading above, and used by De Meester,[330] seems the best of all, because it completely distinguishes this type of parochial vicar from the other four types as mentioned by canons 472-476.

The details of the constitution of such a vicar are respectively different, according to whether it is a religious house to which the parish is united, or some other moral person.

In the first instance, it is the religious Superior of the house who ordinarily presents the vicar to the local Ordinary for approval and appointment; [331] the candidate whom he presents must be a priest of his own religious Order or Congregation; [332]

[328] Cf. Golden, *Parochial Benefices in the New Code*, pp. 106-107. It is to be noted that in the United States the term "Rector" is often used to designate a pastor (*parochus*). In such instances the above conclusions apply to a priest so named. On the other hand, the term "Rector *pro tem*" is nothing more than a way of designating some forms of temporary parochial vicars, of whom more will be said shortly, and, consequently, the above conclusions are not applicable to priests who are appointed in that capacity.

[329] Cans. 452, § 2; 471, § 1.

[330] *Compen.*, II, nn. 867, 868.

[331] Cans. 471, § 2; 1425, § 2.

[332] Can. 1425, § 2, uses the word *potest*, which would seem to give the Superior the liberty to present even a secular priest, and this opinion is, in fact, held by Pistocchi, *De Re Beneficiali*, pp. 103-104. From a comparison of reasons for and against this interpretation it appears that it can hardly be sustained. It was an old law in the Church that churches or benefices which were accustomed to be governed by Regulars were to be conferred only on Religious of the same Order

the religious priest who is appointed is removable at the will, not only of the local Ordinary, but also of the Superior, in accordance with canon 454, § 5; [333] and, of course, the revenues assigned will cede, not to himself, but to his Institute or to the Holy See.[334]

In the second instance, the presentation of the vicar is made by the moral person itself. The candidate must be a secular priest. Once appointed, he is not removable at all by the moral person, and only through process of law by the Ordinary; and, finally, a fair portion of the revenues, to be determined by the Bishop, must be assigned to him.[335] In both instances the vicar obtains from the Code itself the full care of souls, with all the rights and obligations of a pastor, subject, however, to some modification by the diocesan statutes and customs.[336]

From this single canon, i. e., canon 471, it is apparent that the position of parochial vicar of a moral person has been generically established in a stable way by the Code, that the conferring of it must follow the laws of the same, and that it includes from the Code itself participation in the power both of orders and of jurisdiction in the internal forum, just as is provided for pastors, which power is, consequently, ordinary.[337] In other

(cf. c. 10, X, *de rebus ecclesiae alienandis vel non*, III, 13; c. 32, *de praebendis et dignitatibus*, III, 4, in VI°; c. 1, *de electione et electi potestate*, I, 3, in Clem.; Conc. Trid., sess. XIV, *de ref.*, c. 10). This law has been extended to all Religious in no uncertain terms in canon 1442. Canon 1425, § 2, itself expressly states that in a union in full right the parish becomes a religious one, and in canon 1411, 2°, a religious benefice is described as pertaining to religious clerics only. Canon 456, to which Cardinal Gasparri refers in the notes to this canon, in treating of parishes entrusted (*concreditae*) to Religious, i. e., not united to a particular religious house, makes no provision for the presentation of any priest as pastor except one of the same Religious Society. In conclusion, therefore, it seems that the word *potest* in canon 1425, § 2, is used as a part of an antithesis of clauses, the contradistinction being between *Superior potest . . . nominare* and *sed Ordinarii loci est . . . probare et instituere*. In this sense the nomination of a priest of the same Religious Society would be the only choice. For exactly the same use of the word cf. Wernz, *Ius Decretalium*, II, n. 840, § III b, in conjunction with n. 306.

333 Can. 471, § 3.

334 Cans. 580, § 2; 582.

335 Can. 471, §§ 1-3.

336 Can. 471, § 4.

337 De Meester, *Compen.*, II, n. 868, § IV; Badii, *Instituts.*, I, n. 276, b; Toso, *Comment. Minora*, in can. 471; cf. also cans. 452, § 3, 2°; 873, § 2.

words, it is an office in the strict sense, and, indeed, it hardly differs from the office of pastor except in name. It also has objective specific perpetuity, because the union of a parish in full right to a moral person is *per se* perpetual, and the moral person, which is made the canonically vested pastor of the parish, cannot possibly ever exercise the actual care of souls except through its constituted vicar.[338] Moreover, the Code directs that in every particular case a suitable portion of the revenues of the parish (*congrua fructuum portio*) be permanently attached by the authority of the Bishop to the office of the vicar.[339] Certainly the parochial vicar of the moral person does not have the title to the parish itself. The moral person has that, and because of it receives the full beneficial revenue. Yet, the moral person has the obligation by command of the Code to set aside a determined portion of the beneficial revenue, to be fixed by the Bishop, for the support of the parochial vicar. Even this portion can be considered an endowment for a benefice in accordance with canon 1410, which states: "*Dotem beneficii constituunt . . . certae et debitae praestationes alicuius familiae vel personae moralis. . . .*" It is not unlike an ecclesiastical pension, which, when constituted in perpetuity by an episcopal decree as deriving from the revenues of a church and as due to be conferred on a cleric by canonical institution, does not differ from a benefice, and is regulated accordingly.[340] As soon, then, as a Bishop determines the amount of the pension, and decrees that it be permanently attached as revenue to the ecclesiastical office of the parochial vicar of the moral person, a new benefice within, and in addition to, the parochial benefice is created. It is precisely because he possesses a benefice that the parochial vicar of a moral person in the case of seculars cannot be removed from office except by process of law.[341]

[338] Can. 452, § 2.

[339] Can. 471, § 1.

[340] Cf. *supra*, p. 138.

[341] Can. 471, § 3. Cf. also Pirhing, *Ius Canon.*, lib. I, tit. XXVIII, nn. III, V, VIII, IX, XIII; Aichner, *Compen.*, § 129, n. 1; Wernz, *Ius Decretalium*, II, n. 840, § III e; Badii, *Instituts.*, I, n. 276 b; Toso, *Comment. Minora*, in can. 471.

Finally, it is stated by the Code that this vicar has all the rights and obligations of pastors.[342] One of those obligations is that of personal residence. Hence the office of a parochial vicar of a moral person in the case of seculars is always a residential benefice.

Allied to the question of the status of a parochial vicar of any moral person is that of the status of the secular priest who is appointed to a parish which has been united by the Holy See to a religious house *ad temporalia tantum.*[343] A brief elucidation of this question would seem to be in order here.

As canon 1425, § 1, expressly states, when a union of this type is made, two effects follow: the religious house itself becomes a participant in the income which accrues from the endowment of the parochial benefice, and the religious Superior obtains the right of presenting to the local Ordinary the secular priest who is to be appointed to the parish. The spiritual rights of the parish are not touched by the union. The parochial church receives no change in its status; it continues to be a secular parochial benefice,[344] and the secular priest who is appointed to it becomes a pastor, not a vicar. Moreover, by virtue of canon 454, § 3, this parochial benefice is irrevocably conferred (*paroecia inamovibilis*) unless particular statutes or the Bishop, with the advice of the Cathedral Chapter or of the Diocesan Consultors, has decreed otherwise.[345] Instead of receiving the full income of the benefice, however, the pastor receives only that suitable portion of it which must be assigned to him by the religious Superior with the knowledge of the local Ordinary.[346] Having all the rights and duties of a pastor, this secular priest appointed to a parish thus united *ad temporalia tantum* to a religious house has also the obligation of personally residing at the place where the benefice exists, and, therefore, he is the incumbent of a residential benefice.

[342] Can. 471, § 4.

[343] Can. 1425, § 1.

[344] Vermeersch-Creusen, *Epitome*, II, n. 753.

[345] Pistocchi, *De Re Beneficiali*, p. 102.

[346] Pistocchi, *ibid.*, p. 103.

H. Parochial Administrators (*vicarii oeconomi*)

When a parish becomes vacant in any one of the usual ways,[347] the local Ordinary has a duty to constitute therein as soon as possible a parochial vicar administrator to rule it until a new pastor is appointed. In the United States this vicar is often called a " rector *pro tem.*" Although the specific position is, obviously, only temporary, and for that reason incapable of being made a benefice, yet, in conformity with the principles already laid down concerning the nature of an ecclesiastical office,[348] the position of such a vicar fulfills the notion of an office in the strict sense.[349] It is founded permanently in its generic form by the common law; appointment to it is based upon the enactments of the same law; and there are attached to it all the powers that belong to a pastor in the fulfillment of his official duties regarding the care of souls.[350] Its powers for that reason are ordinary.[351]

I. Substitute Pastors (*vicarii substituti*)

When a pastor leaves his parish for an absence which will extend beyond a week, and also when, after a sentence of privation of his parish, he appeals to the Holy See, a parochial vicar substitute must be constituted therein to exercise the care of souls during the meantime. This type of vicar also is often designated in the United States as " rector *pro tem,*" e. g., the priest who is appointed to a parish during the illness of the pastor. Just as is the case for a parochial vicar administrator, so too here, the position in a particular instance is only temporary and can never be a benefice; nevertheless, as a genus it fulfills the notion of an office in the strict sense. As a generic position it is permanently established by the Code for the whole

[347] Cf. cans. 183, § 1; 430, § 1; 2150 ff.

[348] Cf. *supra*, pp. 424 ff.

[349] Can. 2189, § 1.

[350] Cans. 472, 1°; 473, § 1.

[351] Cf. cans. 451, § 2; 873, § 1; S.C.C., 9 maii et 12 sept. 1874 (*ASS*, VIII [1875], 129); C.I.C., 20 maii 1923, ad V, n. 1 (*AAS*, XVI [1924], 114); De Meester, *Compen.*, II, n. 869, § III; Chelodi, *Ius de Personis*, n. 229 b; Vermeersch-Creusen, *Epitome*, I, n. 516; Toso, *Comment. Minora*, in can. 473.

Church;[352] it is only conferred in accordance, particularly, with the provisions of canons 465, §§ 4-5, and 1923, § 2; and it has annexed to it by the Code all the powers of a pastor with regard to the care of souls, subject, however, to some modification by the local Ordinary and the pastor.[353] Its powers are, therefore, also ordinary.[354]

J. Parochial Adjutants (*vicarii adiutores*)

When a pastor, by reason of old age, weakness of mind, deficient capability, blindness, or some other permanent cause, becomes unable properly to perform his duties, the local Ordinary must give him a vicar adjutant to supply his place either in whole or in part.[355] Here provision is made by the Code for two distinct types of positions. In canon 475 both are permanently established, and the norms according to which they are conferred are indicated, but in each the participation in power is different. To the position of the full parochial adjutant the Code itself annexes all the powers of a pastor,[356] thereby making it an office in the strict sense and its powers ordinary.[357] To the position of partial parochial adjutant, on the other hand, the Code does not annex any power, but simply rules that whatever powers are necessary in the particular instance be determined and delegated to the vicar through his letters of appointment. Consequently, none of his powers are more than delegated.[358] This is one of those cases in which an office in the strict sense can exist on only delegated power. Every particular parochial adjutant must have at least some participation in the power of orders or of jurisdiction, both because of the very nature of his

352 Cans. 474; 465, §§ 4, 5; 1923, § 2.

353 Cans. 474; 452, § 2.

354 Cf. cans. 451, § 2; 873, § 2; C.I.C., 20 maii 1923, ad V, n. 2 (*AAS*, XVI [1924], 114); De Meester, *Compen.*, II, n. 870, § III; Toso, *Comment. Minora*, in can. 474.

355 Can. 475, §§ 1, 2.

356 Can. 475, § 2.

357 Cans. 451, § 2; 873, § 2; C.I.C., *loc. cit.*, n. 5; De Meester, *ibid.*, n. 875 a; Chelodi, *Ius de Personis*, n. 230 a; Vermeersch-Creusen, *Epitome*, I, n. 519; Toso, *op. cit.*, in can. 475.

358 Can. 475, § 2; Chelodi, *Ius de Personis*, n. 230 b; Toso, *op. et loc. cit.*

position, which would not be what it is if he did not have some power to help, and that not merely in economic but in spiritual matters, and also because of the evident will of the legislator as expressed in canon 475, § 2. With delegation of some power thus assured to each particular vicar, the position as a genus must also be admitted to include some participation in power, and hence all the requirements for an office in the strict sense are verified.

Though both types of parochial adjutants are offices, neither of them has the objective specific perpetuity to be made a benefice. In any given case the adjutancy as such does not last, at most, beyond the death of the disabled pastor. Even when the right of succession is connected with it, the office of adjutant definitely ends when the office of pastor begins. Hence in no case is the office a benefice.[359]

K. Assistant Pastors (*vicarii cooperatores*)

1°. The position of an assistant pastor is an office in the strict sense

One of the most perplexing problems in connection with this whole matter is the determination of the character of an assistant pastor's position, and the possibility of its ever being made a benefice in a particular case. In view of the general principles established above, it can be said with considerable certainty that this position is an office in the strict sense. As a generic form of ecclesiastical position it has been perpetually established for the entire Church by the common law; [360] it can be conferred only according to the special norms of the Code; [361] and it involves a participation in the power of orders or of jurisdiction.

To understand this last clause it is to be remembered that an office in the strict sense can exist on mere delegated power, provided that each specific erection of the office is guaranteed at least some delegated power through a provision of the law.[362]

[359] Cf. can. 1412, 3°; Pistocchi, *De Re Beneficiali*, p. 35.

[360] Can. 476, § 1.

[361] Can. 476, §§ 1, 3, 4.

[362] Cf. *supra*, pp. 445 ff.

The assistant pastor's is just such an office. The very reason for its generic constitution by the common law, and, consequently, for each specific actualization of it in any particular place, is to assume a share in the care of souls, and thereby partially to relieve the pastor's burden.[363] Presupposing, then, that in every instance the assistant pastor is to have some powers of orders or of jurisdiction, the Code proceeds to legislate on how the powers which each individual is to have are to be determined. Briefly, they are to be determined and delegated by the diocesan statutes, by the letters of the Ordinary, and by the pastor. If, however, in any particular instance none of these three agencies expressly define and delegate his powers, the assistant, by reason of the very character of the office to which he is appointed, is obliged and, therefore, is delegated by the common law itself to assist the pastor in the entire parochial ministry, except in the application of the *Missa pro populo*.[364]

There is absolutely no question here of ordinary power.[365] Since the office is generically established in common law, ordinary power could be obtained only if the Code attached powers to the office as it exists everywhere throughout the Church. Yet, this is not the case. In the clause wherein the Code mentions diocesan statutes, letters of the Ordinary, and commission of the pastor, ordinary power is obviously not meant because none of these agencies is competent to attach power to all assistant pastors who exist as well as to those who ever will exist throughout the Church, but only to the limited few who may come under their restricted domain. In the other clause, introduced by the words "*sed, nisi aliud expresse caveatur,*" there is no concession of ordinary power by the Code, such as some authors erroneously claim for assistant pastors,[366] because there, too, the clause does not refer to *all* assistant pastors, but only to those individuals whose powers are not expressly determined and delegated by one of the three above-mentioned sources. This

[363] Can. 476, §§ 1, 7.

[364] Can. 476, § 6.

[365] Cf. *supra*, pp. 447-8.

[366] E.g., Fanfani, *De Iure Paroch.*, n. 251, B, 6; Augustine, *Commentary*, II, 575 (at least virtually); Maroto, *Instituts.*, I, nn. 700, d, g; 702, A, C.

conclusion is further substantiated by canons 874, § 1, and 1096, § 1, which show that the assistants' power in the sacraments of penance and matrimony is only universal delegation at most. It is confirmed also by the fact that an assistant pastor cannot have full parochial power and be in the place of a pastor in the sense of canons 451, § 2, and 873, § 1, since the very nature of his position is not completely to supplant a pastor, as is the case with most of the other parochial vicars mentioned in canons 471-475. Rather it is the nature of an assistant's position only to assist a pastor who is present and actually performing his share of the parochial duties.

From the above it may be concluded that, through the dispositions of the Code, each individual assistant pastor is sure of participating in some delegated power. In fact, if he were not given any power, he would no longer be an assistant pastor, as is evident from canon 476, § 1. Consequently, the position as a genus verifies the requisites for an office in the strict sense.

2°. Can an assistant pastorate be a benefice?

The important question now arises whether the office of a particular assistant pastor can be erected into a benefice. Canon 477, § 2, apparently signifies that it can, and, relying on it, some authors have been led to declare, at least implicitly, that any assistant pastorate could be made a benefice if erected as such by the Bishop,[367] and one writer actually claimed that all assistant pastorates, at least in the United States of America, in reality are benefices, and the assistants themselves irremovable except by process of law.[368] That both of these opinions are incorrect interpretations of canon 477, § 2, and therefore false, will appear from what is to follow.

The office of assistant pastor has objective perpetuity in its generic form, inasmuch as it has been constituted in the Church once for all in order to fill a certain need wherever and whenever that need arises. Nevertheless, in its specific form, and in

[367] E.g., Wernz-Vidal, *Ius Canon.*, II, n. 744, § IV; Chelodi, *Ius de Personis*, n. 231, b; Toso, *Comment. Minora*, in can. 477; Badii, *Institutś.*, I, n. 280, b.

[368] Art. "Benefice of Assistant Pastorate,"—*AER*, LXXVII (1927), 74-79, 309-312.

the sense in which it is used in canon 476, i. e., of an assistant attached to the parish church or to one of the temporary chapels in a particular part of the parish, no particular assistant pastorate ever has, or can have, objective perpetuity, for the simple reason that a limit is set to its existence by the law itself. It is by its very nature, as determined by the Code, an office which is to be erected temporarily in any parish where the pastor is in real need of assistance in the care of souls.[369] As soon as that need ceases, the sole reason for the existence of an assistant ceases, and it is the Bishop's duty definitely to remove him. Even though the need may be foreseen to be of indefinite duration, e. g., because of the great number of people in a big city parish, the essential nature of the office is not thereby changed, just as the temporary nature of the office of a parochial adjutant is not changed even though the pastor live to be a hundred years old. Likewise, the fact that the assistant's office does not cease automatically when there is no further need for it does not alter its temporary nature.[370] The office of an assistant is, therefore, quite different from that of a pastor. The division of a diocese into parishes or pastorates is mandatory. Their objective existence is not made dependent by law on any external circumstances. But in the matter of assistant pastorates, not only their creation, but also their duration, is made dependent by law on the changing needs of parishes.

Since, then, an assistant pastorate in the sense of canon 476 has no objective specific perpetuity, it cannot be erected into a benefice. Even if it could, the form of erection claimed by the writer in the American Ecclesiastical Review [371] would certainly not suffice. In his opinion all the assistant pastorates of a diocese become permanently erected and canonically endowed through the provisions of the diocesan synod,[372] when, namely, the diocesan statutes merely state the norms according to which

369 Can. 476, § 1.

370 Can. 477, § 1. Cf. De Meester, *Compen.*, II, n. 894.

371 Art. "Benefice of Assistant Pastorate,"—*AER*, LXXVII (1927), 74-79, 309-312.

372 *Ibid.*, 79.

assistants are to be appointed, and at the same time define their powers and stipulate their salary. Thus, Articles 103 and 481 of the *Statuta Synodalia* of the twenty-seventh diocesan Synod of Buffalo, held in 1924, and adduced among others by the aforesaid writer to prove his contention, read as follows:

ART. 103

§ 1. Si parochus propter populi multitudinem aliasve causas nequeat, iudicio Ordinarii, solus convenientem curam gerere paroeciae, eidem detur unus vel plures vicarii cooperatores quibus congrua remuneratio assignetur (can. 476, § 1).

§ 2. Vicarii cooperatores iuxta consuetudinem vigentem, omnes constituuntur ad universitatem causarum, nisi expresse aliud caveatur.

§ 3. Non ad parochum, sed ad loci Ordinarium, audito parocho, pertinet ius nominandi vicarios cooperatores (*ibid.* § 3).

§ 4. Vicarii cooperatoris iura et obligationes ex statutis dioecesanis, ex litteris Ordinarii et ex ipsius parochi commissione desumantur, et nisi aliud expresse caveatur, ipse debet ratione officii parochi vicem supplere eumque adiuvare in universo paroeciali ministerio, excepta applicatione Missae pro populo (*ibid.* § 6).

CAPUT III

DE REDITIBUS NON-BENEFICIARIIS NOSTRIS DEBITIS

ART. 481

§ 1. Reditus vicariorum cooperatorum (de quibus in can. 476) vicariorumque adiutorum (de quibus in can. 475) determinatum est ad summam mille centum scutatorum ($1100.00) per annum; de qua quingenta scutata ($500.00) parocho pro sustentatione sunt solvenda.

§ 2. Reditus vicariis substitutis, locum parochorum absentium tenentibus, debitus, potest esse vel idem ac emolumentum parochi cum omnibus obligationibus parochi in spiritualibus et temporalibus (si forte parochus nullum salarium pro tempore absentiae sumeret) vel idem ac salarium vicariorum cooperatorum, prout a parocho vel, si parochus id negligat, a Nobis determinatur.

§ 3. Reditus vicariorum oeconomorum, administratorum paroeciarum vacantium, (de quibus in cann. 472, 473) idem est ac emolumentum parochorum, cum omnibus parochorum in spiritualibus temporalibusque obligationibus.

It is very apparent that here the statutes are merely repeating the general laws of the Code concerning assistants, and at the same time supplying that which is left by the Code to be supplied—the definition of powers and of remuneration. Obviously they are not erecting any particular assistant pastorates; much less are they erecting any benefices. If any further proof be needed that the Bishop of Buffalo had no intention whatsoever of so erecting them, it may be found unmistakably in the title "*De Reditibus* **Non-Beneficiariis** *Nostris Debitis* under which article 481 of the statutes appears as well as from the following, apparently overlooked, words of article 468:

ART. 468

§ 1. Vi declarationis S. Cong. Consistorialis, die 1 Augusti 1919, nostrae missiones, uti vocatae sunt, verae sunt paroeciae, i. e., beneficia; ac illarum missionum rectores veri sunt parochi, cum omnibus parochorum iuribus et obligationibus ad normam iuris canonici.

§ 2. *Alia beneficia non-consistorialia in Nostra dioecesi non existunt.*[373]

A benefice, being a moral person, is always an individuated entity, made up of a specific sacred office, erected in perpetuity in a particular place, and of the perpetual right to receive revenues from a definite source. Hence benefices are not ordinarily erected *in globo,* but only individually, and if the erection is to have any legal value, it must be done in a way which later offers the possibility of establishing legal proof, e. g., by a document defining the exact place, the endowment, and the beneficiary's rights and duties.[374]

3°. Perpetual and temporary parochial vicars in the pre-Code legislation

The fact that an assistant pastorate in the sense of canon 476 cannot be made a benefice is quite in conformity with the past history of that office. The Code, it may be noticed, has made

[373] Italics inserted.

[374] Can. 1418.

the primary division of parochial vicars according to an aspect different from that used in previous legislation. In the old law and among all the pre-Code authors, all vicars were primarily divided, not, by reason of the purpose which they served, into parochial administrators, substitutes, adjutants, etc., but, by reason of their stability, into perpetual and temporary vicars. Both of these classes are mentioned in the Decretals and their classification is taken from the rescripts of the Popes of the twelfth and thirteenth centuries.[375] Perpetual vicars were defined in the Glossa to c. 6, X, *de officio vicarii,* I, 28, as follows:

> Vicarii perpetui dicuntur, qui authoritate Episcopi canonice sunt instituti ad deserviendum cuipiam Ecclesiae loco principalis Rectoris, cum assignatione congruae portionis fructuum, quos inde percipere debet.[376]

A temporary vicar, on the other hand, was defined in the following terms:

> Temporalis Vicarius dicitur ille, qui auctoritate alicujus in locum alterius ad tempus, vel ad voluntatem constituentis sufficitur; nimirum in officio beneficiali.[377]

These two classes of vicars differed from each other in subjective stability. Perpetual vicars were irremovable, except by privation for a cause recognized by law; [378] temporary vicars were removable at the will of the one appointing, or at least at the expiration of a certain time. The difference between them,

[375] E.g., c. 27, X, *de rescriptis,* I, 3; cc. 1, 3, 6, X, *de officio vicarii,* I, 28; c. 30, X, *de praebendis et dignitatibus,* III, 5; c. 3, X, *de ecclesiis aedificandis vel reparandis,* III, 48; c. 7, X, *de officio archidiaconi,* I, 23; c. 33, X, *de praebendis et dignitatibus,* III, 5; c. 1, X, *de celebratione missarum,* III, 41; c. 34, *de electione et electi potestate,* I, 6, in VI°.

[376] Cf. Reiffenstuel, *Jus Canon. Univ.,* lib. I, tit. XXVIII, n. 23; Schmalzgrueber, *Jus Eccles. Univ.,* lib. I, p. II, tit. XXVIII, n. 1; Pirhing, *Jus Canon.,* lib. I, tit. XXVIII, n. 2; Leurenius, *Forum Beneficiale* (ed. noviss., 2 vols., Coloniae, 1742), t. I, q. 109; Ferraris, *Biblioth.,* "Vicarius Parochialis," n. 2.

[377] Leurenius, *op. et loc. cit.;* Ferraris, *op. et loc. cit.*

[378] Cf. c. 3, X, *de officio vicarii,* I, 28; c. 30, X, *de praebendis et dignitatibus,* III, 5; Pirhing, *op. et loc. cit.;* Schmalzgrueber, *op. et loc. cit.*

however, was not merely a subjective one. A perpetual vicarage (*vicaria perpetua*) was constituted in perpetuity independently of the man placed in charge of it. It signified the office of caring for souls in a church which was perpetually united to some other church, Chapter of Canons, monastery, or the like, so that as a result the church so united would always have to be ruled and attended by a resident vicar of the principal rector.[379] On the other hand, a temporary vicarage was instituted to last only for a time,[380] and signified chiefly the position of caring for souls in a parish during its vacancy or during the absence, sickness, or permanent disability of its pastor.[381]

4°. A perpetual vicarage was a benefice

In consequence of this essential objective difference between them, a perpetual vicarage, having attached to it the right to receive revenues, was a real benefice wherever it was erected,[382] whereas a temporary vicarage, lacking the required perpetuity, neither was, nor could be made, a benefice, but was considered

379 C. 30, X, *de praebendis et dignitatibus*, III, 5; Conc. Trid., sess. VII, *de ref.*, c. 7; Reiffenstuel, *Jus Canon. Univ.*, lib. I, tit. XXVIII, nn. 27-29; Schmalzgrueber, *Jus Eccles. Univ.*, lib. I, tit. XXVIII, n. 3; Pirhing, *Jus Canon.*, lib. I, tit. XXVIII, n. 5; Leurenius, *Forum Benef.*, t. I, q. 115.

380 "Et Vicaria temporalis, [dicitur illa] quae ad tempus, non in perpetuum duratura est; scilicet usque dum cesset causa, vel elapsum sit tempus, ob quam, vel usque ad quod talis Vicaria concessa est."—Barbosa, *Iuris Ecclesiastici Universi Libri Tres* (Lugduni, 1660), l. III, cap. 6, n. 50; Leurenius, *Forum Benef.*, t. I, q. 109. "Cum vicaria temporalis sit illa, quae ad tempus, non in perpetuum duratura est, puta cessante causa vel lapso tempore, ob quam, vel usque ad quod talis vicaria concessa est; . . ."—Barbosa, *ibid.*, n. 58; Garcia, *De Benef. Eccles.*, p. I, cap. II, n. 93; Pellegrini, *Praxis Vicariorum* (Venetiis, 1706), p. I, sect. 8, n. 22; Ferraris, *Biblioth.*, "Vicarius Parochialis," n. 41.

381 Leurenius, *ibid.*, qq. 111-112; Pirhing, *ibid.*, n. XX; Reiffenstuel, *ibid.*, nn. 47. 50; Schmalzgrueber, *ibid.*, n. 7.

382 ". . . Non enim beneficio carere debet dici, cui competenter de perpetuae vicariae proventibus est provisum. . . ."—C. 27, X, *de rescriptis*, I, 3. "Respondeo primo: Vicarias perpetuas in parochialibus esse vera beneficia Ecclesiastica. . . ."—Leurenius, *Forum Benef.*, t. I, q. 111, n. 1. Garcia, *De Benef. Eccles.*, p. I, cap. II, n. 93; Pirhing, *Jus Canon.*, lib. I, tit. XXVIII, nn. 8-9; Reiffenstuel, *Jus Canon. Univ.*, lib. I, tit. XXVIII, nn. 30-31; Schmalzgrueber, *Jus Eccles. Univ.*, lib. I, tit. XXVIII, n. 4.

merely the position of a clerical employee, to whom a stipend or salary was paid for services rendered.[383]

5°. To which class the position of an assistant pastor belonged

To which of these classes belonged the position of an assistant pastor, working either along with the pastor in the parochial church, or alone in one of the temporary, outlying missions within the parish? From the above it is beyond the shadow of a doubt that in neither case did his position fulfill the notion of a perpetual vicarage, and hence he was not considered to be a perpetual vicar. Nay more, in the strict sense of the term some authors apparently did not even consider him a temporary vicar, since, according to the definition above, they understood that term in the sense of one who was temporarily but completely substituted in the place of, and who obtained the same power as, the beneficiary.[384] Though this may have been the correct usage of the word *vicar*, nevertheless, in Canon Law it came to be used in several senses, embracing also that of parochial "*coöperator.*"[385] Hence it was that Pope Innocent XIII expressly called assistant pastors "*Vicarios temporarios*";[386] and among the reasons for constituting temporary vicars authors adduced the following: when a pastor was given charge of more than one parochial church, when he was placed in charge of a nationality different from his own, and when, because of numerous other duties, infirmity, or other reason, he was unable alone to perform his parochial duties adequately, and so needed the

[383] "At Vicaria temporalis seu ad nutum amovibilis non est beneficium, nec titulus beneficialis; quia non confertur in titulum, sed est simplex salarium seu stipendium." —Garcia, *De Benef. Eccles.*, p. I, cap. II, n. 93. "Hujusmodi enim Vicariae ad nutum removibiles, non sunt tituli beneficiales, nec impetrabiles."—S.R.R., 15 mar. 1596, dec. 2 (Garcia, *ibid.*, n. 94). Leurenius, *Forum Benef.*, t. I, q. 111, n. 2; Reiffenstuel, *Jus Canon. Univ.*, lib. I, tit. XXVIII, nn. 45, 46; Schmalzgrueber, *Jus Eccles. Univ.*, lib. I, tit. XXVIII, n. 10; Ferraris, *Bibliotb.*, "Vicarius parochialis," n. 41.

[384] E.g., Pirhing, *Jus Canon.*, lib. I, tit. XXVIII, nn. 22, 24.

[385] Leurenius, *Forum Benef.*, t. I, q. 108.

[386] "Quoties itaque in aliis Parochialibus Ecclesiis, quae, ut praefertur, unitae non sint, oportuerit ex aliqua iusta causa provideri per Coadiutores Parochorum, aut per Vicarios temporarios, curae erit Episcopis etc."—Const. "*Apostolici ministerii,*" 23 maii 1723, § 13 (*Fontes*, n. 280).

help of a vicar.[387] Among these there may be recognized the reasons for constituting assistant pastors even today. In other words, both then and now the assistant pastor (*vicarius cooperator*) was, at most, a temporary vicar, whereas perpetual vicars alone had benefices.

6°. Perpetual chaplaincies

Those who contend that an assistant pastorate can be a benefice adduce in support of their opinion various instances wherein benefices actually existed in parish churches in the form of perpetual chaplaincies with the attached obligation of helping the pastor in the care of souls.[388] That situation truly existed. There are numerous examples of such perpetual chaplaincies,[389] but in law a chaplaincy is entirely different from a parochial vicarage, even though outwardly it may appear the same, just as a parochial administrator is not a pastor, though really he has the same rights and duties. A chaplaincy is a pious institute, to be conferred on some cleric, consisting of the obligation of celebrating Mass on stated days at some altar or in some church, and of performing such other sacred duties as may be stipulated, together with the right of receiving the revenues from an endowment given by the founder.[390] It may be ecclesiastical (collative) or lay (non-collative), according to whether or not the endowment passes into the possession of the church and the erection is made by the authority of the Bishop; in the first case it is always a benefice; in the latter, it is nothing more than a pious legacy.[391] Again, an ecclesiastical chaplaincy may

387 Leurenius, *ibid.*, q. 112; Reiffenstuel, *ibid.*, n. 50; Schmalzgrueber, *ibid.*, n. 7; Ferraris, *Biblioth.*, " Vicarius parochialis," n. 42.

388 E. g., Wernz, *Ius Decretalium*, II, n. 838, note 115; Wernz-Vidal, *Ius Canon.*, II, n. 744, note 9.

389 E. g., S.C.C., 24 iul. 1875 (*ASS*, IX [1876], 116-123); *Reatina*, 16 dec. 1854 et 22 dec. 1855 (Lingen-Reuss, *Causae Selectae*, n. 498); *Aretina*, 20 dec. 1851 (Lingen-Reuss, *op. cit.*, n. 494); *Praenestina*, 9 iun. 1855 (Lingen-Reuss, *op. cit.*, n. 497).

390 Pistocchi, *De Re Beneficiali*, p. 33. Cf. also Leurenius, *Forum Benef.*, t. I, q. 85.

391 Leurenius, *ibid.*, q. 86; Garcia, *De Benef. Eccles.*, p. I, cap. II, nn. 81, 82, 95, 102-104; Laymann, *Theologia Moralis* (9. ed., Moguntiae, 1723), l. IV, tract. II,

be either perpetual or manual (revocable at will), according to the stability of the incumbent; but in both cases it is a benefice, since subjective perpetuity in office does not pertain to the essential nature of a benefice.[392] Finally, according to the conditions made at the time of its foundation, a chaplaincy may have attached to it the obligation of helping in the care of souls, and then the chaplains are called *cappellani curati* or *cappellani coadjutores*,[393] or it may be a simple chaplaincy without such an obligation.[394] A chaplaincy, then, is erected merely through the pious wish of some individual founder. Its objective existence is absolutely independent of any real necessity in the church where it is erected. It involves no obligation whatsoever of helping a pastor in the care of souls, unless that condition be expressly placed in its foundation; whereas, on the other hand, that obligation may be present even though it be but a lay chaplaincy.[395] A simple chaplaincy can be obtained by a mere cleric, who may then fulfill the obligations through another;[396] and, consequently, more than one can be obtained by a single person.[397] From all this it is more than apparent that chaplaincies, even though coadjutorial, are entirely different from assistant pastorates.[398]

cap. IV, n. 6; S.C.C., *Firmana*, 29 aug. 1772, § *Sed* (Pallottini, *Conc. Trid.*, V, 536, n. 73); S.C.C., 3 iul. 1819, § *Primum* (Pallottini, *op. cit.*, V, 527, n. 18).

[392] Laymann, *op. et loc. cit.*; Garcia, *ibid.*, nn. 79, 82, 85, 95; Leurenius, *op. et loc. cit.*

[393] E. g., S.C.C., 24 iul. 1875 (*ASS*, IX [1876], 116-123); *Reatina*, 16 dec. 1854 et 22 dec. 1855 (Lingen-Reuss, *Causae Selectae*, n. 498); *Aretina*, 20 dec. 1851 (Lingen-Reuss, *op. cit.*, n. 494); 16 feb. 1867 (*ASS*, III [1867], 92-96); Ferraris, *Biblioth.*, "Cappellanus," nn. 41-43.

[394] Leurenius, *Forum Benef.*, t. I, q. 100; S.C.C., 18 dec. 1847 et 29 iul. 1848 (Lingen-Reuss, *op. cit.*, n. 499); *Aretina*, 20 dec. 1851 (Lingen-Reuss, *op. cit.*, n. 494).

[395] E.g., S.C.C., 16 feb. 1867—*ASS*, III (1867), 92-96.

[396] Ferraris, *Biblioth.*, "Cappellania," nn. 19-21.

[397] S.C.C., *Spoletana*, 28 mar. 1744—Pallottini, *Conc. Trid.*, V, 528, n. 27.

[398] For further differences cf. Leurenius, *Forum Benef.*, t. I, qq. 85-141; Ferraris, *Biblioth.*, "Cappellania," "cappellanus," "vicarius parochialis"; Caponi, *Institutiones Canonicae* (2 vols., Coloniae Allobrogum, 1734), lib. I, tit. XXVI.

That perpetual chaplaincies actually existed in many parochial churches prior to the Code need cause no surprise. The office of "assistant pastor" (*vicarius cooperator*) as it is known today is really a development from that of chaplain. As early as the thirteenth century, in England, France, and Germany, whenever a pastor was in need of assistance, the necessity was supplied by chaplains, whom the pastor himself, as a rule, appointed.[399] In the Council of Trent this practice became universal law, so that busy pastors incurred the obligation of securing and appointing as many *priests* as were needed to administer the sacraments and to conduct the divine worship.[400] Manifestly, the appointment of chaplains was sufficient to satisfy that law, since the wide term *sacerdotes,* and not *vicarios,* was used. In 1723 Pope Innocent XIII, legislating for Spain, interpreted that canon in the sense of parochial coadjutors or temporary vicars, and commanded that, wherever the people were too numerous, the pastors should appoint such vicars, and, if they neglected to do so, the Bishop himself should do it.[401] Nevertheless, for the Church at large the law of the Council of Trent remained.[402] The priests so appointed were frequently called "parochial coöperators" by the authors; but, as far as the common law was concerned, and prescinding from local customs, one of the normal ways of supplying the needs of large parishes prior to the Code was through chaplaincies, which by their very nature were of perpetual foundation. The Code changed this by the clear constitution of the office of "vicar coöperator," and by the mandate that it be created in any parish where there was need of assistance. In the Code, chaplaincies, both ecclesiastical and lay, are still recognized, but they are clearly distinct from the coöperatorial vicarages or assistant pastorates.[403] From canon 1412, 2°, it is evident that

399 De Meester, *Compen.*, II, n. 878.

400 Sess. XXI, *de ref.*, c. 4.

401 Const., "*Apostolici ministerii,*" 23 maii 1723, § 13—*Fontes*, n. 280.

402 Cf. Benedict XIV, Const. "*Ad militantis,*" 30 mar. 1742, § 1—*Fontes*, n. 326.

403 Can. 1412, 1°, 2°.

any particular ecclesiastical chaplaincy is always a benefice. There is no distinction made about its erection, because by its very nature it is always erected in perpetuity; while subjective perpetuity, of course, does not pertain to the nature of a benefice.[404] An assistant pastorate, on the other hand, is included in the category of parochial vicarages in canon 1412, 1°, and is a benefice only when objectively erected in a particular place in perpetuity.

7°. How an assistant pastorate can now become a benefice when constituted as a perpetual assistant vicarage

A return must now be made to the primary purpose of this discussion. From canon 477, § 2, it is clear that an assistant pastorate can, in some way or other, be a benefice; canon 1412, 1°, shows that that can happen only when it is erected in perpetuity in a particular place; yet, from what has gone before, it may be concluded that for an assistancy, in the sense of canon 476, i. e., in a parochial church or in a temporary mission within the parish, such perpetual erection is impossible. In what sense, then, is it possible? The answer is found in canon 1427.

When the faithful live such a distance from the parochial church that they have great difficulty in reaching it, or when their number is so great that their spiritual welfare cannot be properly served, even through the aid of assistant pastors in the parish, then there is canonical reason for the Ordinary either to divide the parish or to reapportion its territory.[405] If he reapportions it, a part of its territory together with the faithful living therein is simply subtracted and assigned to another already existing parish.[406] If, however, he divides the parish, and consequently the parochial benefice, two benefices result,[407] the newer of which, according to particular circumstances and to his own judgment, may take one of two forms. If the

[404] Can. 1411, 4°.

[405] Cans. 476, § 8; 1427, §§ 1, 2.

[406] Can. 1421.

[407] Can. 1421.

proper conditions are present he may erect a new parish, presided over by a real pastor, and then, except for the honorary deference which it may have to show to the mother parish, it is an independent entity. If, however, conditions do not warrant the erection of a new parish, for instance, if the number of parishes agreed upon by a Concordat with a Civil Government which pays the pastors' salaries be already filled, then the Ordinary may simply erect a perpetual vicarage, i. e., he may designate a second church and perpetually establish there and endow the office of a vicar, with the care of souls, and the consequent obligation of residence, and at the same time unite this new *beneficium curatum* in a less principal way, by subjection, to the mother parish,[408] so that the pastor of the parish becomes also the pastor of the filial church,[409] and the resident vicar who is to be perpetually constituted there becomes subject to him.[410]

Such a perpetual vicarage, the objective existence of which is obviously independent of any passing necessity,[411] is nothing more than an assistant pastorate (*vicaria paroecialis cooperatorialis*) for the reason that the office of the vicar is really linked with the parish, and the incumbent has no proper power from the Code, but is the vicar of, and subject to, the pastor. Consequently he does not differ from a simple assistant except in the fact that his office is objectively perpetual, and a benefice.[412]

408 Can. 1419, § 3.

409 Can. 1420, § 3.

410 Cf. Pistocchi, *De Re Beneficiali*, pp. 114-116; De Meester, *Compen.*, III, n. 1407; Vermeersch, *Periodica*, XIV (1925-1926), (12)-(17), in which he changes the opinion which he formerly held (*Epitome*, II, n. 757).

411 Can. 1423, § 3.

412 It cannot be denied that such a priest is a parochial vicar of some kind or other. The Code's new division of parochial vicars is set forth in cans. 471-476. It would be rash to hold that the framers of the Code after their ten years of labor on it completely overlooked in that section an entire and important species of vicar. Yet, it is apparent that the one here spoken of is not included in any of the categories of cans. 471-475. Consequently it must be concluded that he is a *vicarius cooperator*, with the added qualifications of can. 1427. To designate him merely as a "perpetual vicar," as most authors do, is either to confound him with the vicar of a *moral person* (can. 471), or else to reject the new primary division of vicars in the Code, and to revert to that of the old law. To classify him as a *vicarius*

This, then, is the one way in which an assistant pastorate can admit of objective perpetuity and be a benefice, and it is likewise that which is referred to in canons 477, § 2, and 1412, 1°.

That the perpetual parochial vicarage is really a benefice follows, as has been indicated, from canons 1412, 1°, 1421, and 1427, § 3; and, indeed, it has long been such, as will be seen below.

The rights, powers, and duties of the perpetual assistant vicar are stable, because determined and attached by the Ordinary to each vicarage in its foundation. The Code itself does not annex any powers to the office, and, consequently, the only powers which the vicar can have are delegated, but they may comprise a delegation either of all or only of some parochial powers in the vicarage. Ordinary power remains with the principal pastor, who, as a physical and not a moral person, has the actual as well as the vested care of souls in the vicarage.[413]

Finally, the perpetual assistant vicar, having a benefice, is subjectively irremovable except by process of law; but to the causes for which other parochial beneficiaries, such as pastors, can be removed must be added that of insubordination to the pastor in the exercise of his functions, for, being an assistant vicar, he is subject to the pastor.[414]

The interpretation given above of the nature of a perpetual vicarage is confirmed by past history. During the reign of Pope Alexander III (a. 1159-1181), the first instance of what is considered a perpetual vicarage is found. In a letter to the Archbishop of York he ordered that, since a certain village was so far

cooperator or parochial assistant, on the other hand, best agrees both with past history and with cans. 477, § 2, and 1412, 1°; nor is can. 476, § 8 opposed to this, because that merely refers to assistant pastors in the parish church, and to those sent out temporarily to missions of the parish. Cf. also Fanning, "Filial Church,"—*Cath. Ency.*, VI, 72; Ferreres, *Compen. Theol. Mor.*, II, n. 1075.

413 Can. 1420, § 3.

414 Can. 477, § 2. A perpetual vicarage such as here described must not be confounded with a temporary one, such as that provided for in can. 476, § 2, in virtue of which a Bishop can place an assistant vicar in a chapel in some outlying section or village within a parish, when there is some passing need for such assistance, e.g., to minister to a large number of men who are to be engaged for several years on construction work in a particular locality. Such a temporary vicarage is not a benefice (can. 1412, 1°).

away from the parochial church that the parishioners experienced great difficulty in getting there, and since the parish was sufficiently rich to get along without the revenues from that village, the Bishop was to erect a filial church there, and to install, upon presentation by the pastor, a priest who was to receive the revenues from the village as his support.[415] Certainly there was question there of a division of the old benefice, and many authors held that it meant the erection of a perpetual vicarage rather than that of a new parish.[416]

The Council of Trent seemed to interpret the letter cited above of Pope Alexander III as a norm for the erection of new parishes only. Without mentioning perpetual vicarages, the Council stated that whenever the people could not attend their parish church without grave inconvenience, because of its distance or because of some other difficulty, the Bishop could erect a new parish according to the form of the Constitution "*Ad audientiam*"[417] of Pope Alexander III.[418] Yet, Pope Innocent XIII, in interpreting the Tridentine law for Spain,[419] as well as the Sacred Congregation of the Council, the official interpreter of the decrees of the Council of Trent, both provided for the erection of these perpetual vicarages. In fact, in the early part of the eighteenth century the Sacred Congregation of the Council only with difficulty gave permission for the division of a parish and the erection of a new one,[420] and rather insisted on the erection of a perpetual vicarage wherever the need could thereby be satisfied.[421]

415 C. 3, X, *de ecclesiis aedificandis vel reparandis*, III, 48.

416 E.g., Pirhing, *Jus Canon.*, lib. I, tit. XXVIII, n. 5; Reiffenstuel, *Jus Canon. Univ.*, lib. I, tit. XXVIII, n. 29; Schmalzgrueber, *Jus Eccles. Univ.*, lib. I, tit. XXVIII, n. 3. Cf. Vermeersch, "De Canone 1427 et de vicariis perpetuis,"—*Per.*, XIV (1925-1926), (13)-(14).

417 C. 3, X, *de ecclesiis aedificandis vel reparandis*, III, 48.

418 Sess. XXI, *de ref.*, c. 4.

419 Const., "*Apostolici ministerii*," 23 maii 1723, § 14—*Fontes*, n. 280.

420 Cf. Richter, *Conc. Trid.*, sess. XXI, *de ref.*, c. 4, n. 7; Pistocchi, *De Re Beneficiali*, p. 115.

421 E.g., S.C.C., *Brixinen.*, 28 ian., 16 mar., 22 iun. 1743 (Richter, *ibid.*, n. 5); *Lunen. Sarzanen.*, 27 sept. 1732, 24 ian. 1733 (Richter, *ibid.*, n. 6; *Thesaurus Resolutionum*, V [1730-1732], 284, 376).

That this vicarage was nothing more than an assistancy for the parish is evident from the way in which it was conceived as still being *within* the parish, even though the parochial benefice had to be divided in order to erect it, and also from the designation of the vicar as "*Parochi Coadjutor*" and "*vicarius perpetuus*," subject in all cases to the pastor.[422]

In agreement with the above authorities the canonists of the early eighteenth century likewise interpreted the Constitution "*Ad audientiam*," of Pope Alexander III,[423] as authorizing the erection of perpetual vicarages. Consequently, among the reasons for constituting a "perpetual vicar," which type alone possessed a benefice,[424] they included not only the case wherein a parish was fully united to some monastery, Chapter of Canons, or other moral person, and had to be cared for by a vicar of the moral person, such as is provided for now in canon 471, but also the situation wherein a parish was too large or too populous and when, in order to provide for the spiritual needs of a section of it, a subsidiary or filial church had to be erected, and endowed, in a distant part of the parish, and presided over by a vicar of the pastor.[425]

[422] Innocent XIII, Const., "*Apostolici ministerii*," 23 maii 1723, § 14—*Fontes*, n. 280; Richter, *op. et loc. cit.*

[423] C. 3, X, *de ecclesiis aedificandis vel reparandis*, III, 48.

[424] Cf. *supra*, pp. 493-4.

[425] "In quibus Ecclesiis, et quibus ex causis Vicarius perpetuus constitui possit? Respondetur: Vicarius perpetuus, authoritate Episcopi, inprimis constitui potest, ac solet in Ecclesiis parochialibus, . . . Deinde etiam interdum, ob populi multitudinem, seu Parochiae amplitudinem, praeter Ecclesiam parochialem, Capella, seu Ecclesia filialis erigitur, et aedificatur, quae accessorie, et in perpetuum unita, ac subjecta est Ecclesiae principali, seu Matrici, in eaque etiam Vicarius perpetuus, cum consensu, et approbatione Episcopi, a principali Rectore constituitur, juxta c. Ad audientiam 3, de Eccles. aedific. detracta etiam ex reditibus Ecclesiae principalis justa, ac debita portione ad commodam sustentationem Vicarii."—Pirhing, *Jus Canon.*, lib. I, tit. XXVIII, n. 5.

"A quo, quibusque de causis, instituendus sit Vicarius perpetuus? Resp. III. Quando Parochia nimis ampla existit, ac populus multus, potest praeter Ecclesiam Parochialem alia Ecclesia filialis aedificari, quae sit unita et subjecta Ecclesiae Parochiali, et in ea ad praesentationem Rectoris Ecclesiae majoris, atque institutionem Episcopi, una cum congrua proventuum assignatione, poni perpetuus Vicarius. Patet hoc ex c. Ad audientiam 3, de Eccles. aedifican."—Reiffenstuel, *Jus Canon. Univ.*, lib. I, tit. XXVIII, n. 29.

These filial churches exist in many places in Europe, e. g., in Germany and Spain, but in the United States of America they are unknown. Hence, a priest cannot become virtually incardinated in this country by being appointed as an assistant pastor.

L. Rectors of Churches (*rectores ecclesiarum*)

The term " rector " as it is often used in the United States to designate a pastor (*parochus*) is canonically incorrect. A " rector of a church " in Canon Law signifies only one thing—a priest who has charge of a church which is *not parochial*, or capitular, or annexed to the house of a religious community for use in celebrating the divine offices.[426] There is question here, not of an oratory, but of a real church, i. e., a place of worship destined primarily for the use of all the faithful,[427] and one which is not subject to the pastor of the parish, but to the Bishop directly.[428]

It refers, for instance, to those churches which are erected to cultivate some special devotion, e. g., the National Shrine of the Immaculate Conception, Washington, D. C., or to the church of a confraternity or pious union.[429] The rector of such a church is not a mere chaplain. His position is permanently established by the Code, and the rights, duties, and powers attached to it are there determined.[430] It is conferred according to the regulations of the law.[431] It does not involve any partici-

"In quibus beneficiis, et quibus ex causis vicarius perpetuus constitui possit? Resp. Fere tantum constitui solet in beneficiis, et ecclesiis parochialibus: idque ex duplici praecipue causa. . . . Altera, eaque non infrequens, quando parochia reditibus abundans valde numerosum, et distantem populum habet; tunc enim ecclesia, seu capella filialis erigitur, eique vicarius perpetuus, assignata congrua portione, praeficitur, qui ab ecclesia matrice sejunctos, et longe remotos curet juxta c. ad audientiam 3, de eccl. aedif."—Schmalzgrueber, *Jus Eccles. Univ.*, lib. I, tit. XXVIII, n. 3.

426 Can. 479, § 1.

427 Can. 1161.

428 Cf. can. 483; De Meester, *Compen.*, II, n. 898.

429 Can. 716, § 1.

430 Cans. 481-485.

431 Can. 480.

pation in the power of jurisdiction, but *per se* it does carry with it the right to celebrate in the church the divine offices. It is, therefore, an ecclesiastical office in the strict sense, and, since there is no limit whatsoever placed to its objective existence in any particular place, it can be made a benefice through the regular formalities of attaching an endowment and the like.[432] In such an event the law of the foundation would have to determine whether or not the rector was to be removable at the will of the local Ordinary.[433] There is no obligation of residence attached by the Code to this office, and, consequently, even if in a particular case it were made a benefice, it would not be a residential one, unless the diocesan statutes, particular custom, or the law of the foundation made personal residence a requisite.[434]

M. Chaplains (*cappellani*)

Originally, as the etymology of the Latin term suggests,[435] a chaplain was a priest who, through a provision of the law, and in virtue of an income from a stable endowment left by some pious founder, was obliged to celebrate Mass a certain number of times every year in some particular church or chapel (*cappella*).[436] This position was, or was not, a benefice according as the foundation was made by the authority of the Bishop, or merely by some other person; and this is the meaning of a chaplaincy in canon 1412, 2°. The term *chaplain*, however, has come to have a much wider signification, and today, even in the legal sense, it designates a priest who, in virtue of the position which he obtains, and prescinding from the presence or absence of remuneration in any form, has the right and duty to perform certain spiritual functions for the benefit of particular individuals or groups of persons.[437] Under this genus

432 Chelodi, *Ius de Personis*, n. 233, e; Wernz-Vidal, *Ius Canon.*, II, nn. 747, 750; Toso, *Comment. Minora*, in can. 480.

433 Can. 486.

434 *Supra*, p. 461.

435 Cf. Leurenius, *Forum Benef.*, t. I, q. 85.

436 Cf. *supra*, p. 495.

437 Cf. can. 479, § 2; De Meester, *Compen.*, II, n. 903.

come: 1) Chaplains of non-exempt lay Religious Institutes, whether of men or of women; 2) chaplains of pious associations of the faithful, particularly of confraternities and pious unions; 3) chaplains of non-collegiate ecclesiastical institutes, such as hospitals, schools or colleges, orphan asylums, etc., of prisons, or of units of a nation's armed forces; and 4) simple Mass chaplains, such as may exist in Cathedral and Collegiate Chapters.

As far as the houses of non-exempt lay Religious or any pious houses are concerned, as long as they remain under the care of the pastor in whose parish they are situated, they are ministered to by him or by his assistant vicar, and there is no question of a chaplain. However, it is in the Bishop's power to remove these houses from the care of the pastor for a just and grave cause.[438] When that is done, the Ordinary must appoint a chaplain, subject directly to himself, to provide for the care of souls in these houses.[439] Official notification of such a decision would most probably have to be given to the pastor by the Bishop, for, in a matter so important as the care of souls, no pastor already having the obligation would be justified in acting on a mere presumption of release from such care. The chaplain who is thus appointed by the Bishop certainly must have some share in the power of orders or of jurisdiction in the internal forum. For chaplains in the houses of non-exempt lay Religious, whether the Institute be of men or of women, some powers are obtained from the Code itself, e. g., the right to administer Holy Viaticum and Extreme Unction to the sick and dying; [440] the rest must be determined and delegated through the diocesan statutes or the letters of appointment.[441]

As for the chaplains of pious associations of the faithful in general, as well as of confraternities and pious unions in particular, there is no question of the care of souls or of exemption from parochial care. Nevertheless, the nomination of the

[438] Can. 464, § 2.

[439] Cans. 514, § 3; 529.

[440] Can. 514, § 3.

[441] Cf. De Meester, *Compen.*, II, n. 904. Cf. also cans. 529; 1338, § 3.

chaplain pertains to the local Ordinary, and his rights and duties as mentioned in the Code participate to some slight extent in the exercise of the power of orders through his faculties to bless insignia, scapulars, etc., and to perform certain non-parochial functions.[442]

Chaplains of the third group are appointed by the Ordinary, and may have the care of souls in place of the pastor, within the confines of whose parish the institutes exist, in the same way as is provided for chaplains of non-exempt lay Religious Institutes. Military chaplains, in particular, are regulated as to their rights and duties by special prescripts of the Holy See.[443]

Finally, the simple Mass chaplains have at least the right to celebrate Mass in the church or chapel where they are located. This right is common also to practically all the other types.

These four main groups of chaplains are permanently established by the Code, and laws concerning their appointment are given. As was pointed out, they participate at least to some slight extent in the power of orders. They can, therefore, be considered as the occupants of ecclesiastical offices in the strict sense. Furthermore, since the objective existence of these offices is not dependent on anything, they can be made benefices. This can only be done in a particular case in the ordinary way, i. e., by the special act of the Bishop erecting that particular chaplaincy in perpetuity, attaching to it the perpetual right to receive a definitely assured income, and clearly defining the rights and duties of the beneficiary.

In the absence of any specific regulation in the Code concerning an obligation of residence being imposed upon the various types of chaplains, the norm must be taken from laws enacted for similar groups. Since pastors have the obligation of residence because of the care of souls,[444] it should be concluded that those chaplains who have the care of souls in place of the pastor also have the obligation of residence. If their chaplaincy is

[442] Cans. 698, § 2; 716, § 1.

[443] Can. 451, § 3.

[444] Can. 465, § 1.

made a beneficial one, it, consequently, is a residential benefice. Any chaplaincy which does not involve the care of souls, even if it be made beneficial, is not a residential benefice, unless the obligation of residence is attached in one of the three usual ways, namely, by the law of the very foundation of the benefice, by immemorial custom, or, finally, by particular Indult. Virtual incardination into a diocese through the reception of some such chaplaincy is not effected except in the face of both facts, namely, its erection as a benefice and the concomitant obligation of residence. To assure the claim of incardination both facts have to be capable of proof.

N. Ordinary and Extraordinary Confessors

A simple confessor is merely a priest, who, in addition to his power of orders, has also, even though only temporarily, the power of jurisdiction. Therefore, it is not an ecclesiastical position or office which he enjoys, but simply a power. An ordinary or extraordinary confessor, on the other hand, has an office in the strict sense. Both are positions generically established in the Code,[445] which must be constituted for houses of lay Religious whether of men or of women,[446] for religious novitiates,[447] and for seminaries.[448] Appointment to these positions is made in accordance with special laws; [449] and, of its nature, such an appointment implies a participation in the power of jurisdiction for the one appointed. The offices of one ordinary and of one extraordinary confessor in every house are established by the common law as objectively perpetual, for the appointment of additional confessors would be required only as long as a large membership at the religious house necessitated it.[450] Consequently, the offices of only two confessors—the one ordinary,

445 Cans. 518 ff.; 566; 1361.

446 Cans. 520, § 1; 521, § 1; 528.

447 Can. 566.

448 Can. 1361.

449 Cans. 524-527; 566, § 1; 1361, § 1.

450 Cans. 520, § 1; 521, § 1; 528; 566, §§ 1, 2, 1°, 4°.

the other extraordinary—at each house could be enhanced to the status of a benefice; and even these would never imply any subjective perpetuity. As is obvious, the office of confessor does not involve any obligation of residence, except the residence in the novitiate which is demanded of the ordinary confessor appointed for the novices of a clerical Religious Institute, which confessor in all normal cases would be a member of the same Institute.[451] Thus, the office of ordinary or extraordinary confessor could hardly ever imply the existence of a residential benefice.

O. Rectors of Seminaries

The generic position of the rector of a seminary is permanently established in the Code,[452] and the general and particular norms there given regulate the conferring of it.[453] A seminary is exempt from the care of the pastor in whose territory it exists, and, by virtue of the Code, the rector of the seminary is empowered to fulfill the office of pastor for all those within it, except in certain matters expressly mentioned.[454] His position has, therefore, annexed to it a certain participation in the power of jurisdiction, e. g., in the dispensing power of canon 1245, § 1, as well as in that of orders, namely, in the various functions of divine worship. That makes it an office in the strict sense. The office of rector, too, has objective perpetuity because the law which commands its erection does so absolutely; when once erected it is to continue without any temporal restriction. Finally, by the authority of the Bishop, the office of rector includes a right to receive revenue from a permanent source, namely, from the voluntary offerings given by the faithful of the diocese in support of the seminary, or from the tax which the Code authorizes the Bishop to levy in his diocese for that end.[455] As a result, the office of rector of a seminary *ipso facto*

451 Can. 566, § 2, 2°.

452 Cans. 1358 ff.

453 Can. 1360, § 1.

454 Can. 1368.

455 Cans. 1355-1356.

becomes a benefice as soon as it is constituted in a diocese by the Bishop who is empowered to do so, in the same way as a parish becomes a benefice by the very fact of its erection by the competent authorizing Superior. Furthermore, since the rector fulfills the office of a pastor for all those within the seminary, it follows that he has also a pastor's obligation of residence, which same must be satisfied either personally or through a substitute; and so, wherever the office of the rector of the seminary has been established, it is by that very fact a residential benefice.

P. Other Seminary Positions

All the other positions which pertain to a canonical seminary manifestly have no participation whatsoever by law in the powers of orders or of jurisdiction, but are merely instituted for the spiritual, moral, mental, and physical development of the seminarians. Consequently, they are not offices in the strict sense, and cannot be benefices. Of such a character are the positions of the spiritual director,[456] the members of the board of discipline,[457] the professors,[458] and the procurator.[459]

Q. Secretaryships

There is no mention in the Code of private secretaries. They hold positions which the Ordinaries establish for the purpose of assistance, either for themselves or for others, in the material work of their offices. Such positions neither by their nature nor by the provision of law require any participation in the power either of orders or of jurisdiction. If, in individual cases, they may be given some delegated faculties, that does not make of the position one which everywhere postulates some such powers. Hence, it is neither an office in the strict sense, nor a possible basis for the creation of a benefice.

[456] Cans. 1358; 1360, § 1.

[457] Cans. 1359, §§ 1, 3; 1366, § 1.

[458] Cans. 1358; 1360, § 1; 1366, § 1.

[459] Can. 1358.

ARTICLE IV

RETROACTIVITY OF THE VIRTUAL METHOD

A final question with regard to canon 114 is this: "Does the ruling of this canon have retroactive force, so as to validate a virtual or equivalent incardination which when undertaken before 1918 remained void of its desired juridical effect?"

There are a few examples of what might seem to imply an automatic retroactivity in the law of the Code. Thus, Religious who were secularized before the Code became binding as law are affected by canon 642, which prevents them from obtaining certain offices and positions, according to a decision of the Pontifical Commission for the Interpretation of the Code, ad V, on Nov. 24, 1920.[460] Terms of religious Superiors, though they had already been started before the advent of Code law, thereafter were regulated by the current law.[461] On the other hand, no *ipso facto* convalidation was given by the Code to marriages which were null and void because of a diriment impediment now no longer retained in the law.[462]

Retroactivity is thus treated in canon 10: "Laws affect future, not past acts, unless it is explicitly declared that they are retroactive." Explicit declarations that the law does affect the past are found, for instance, in canons 1138, §§ 1-2; 2226, § 2; and 2232, § 2. The principle expressed in canon 10 is found in Roman Law, in the Law of the Decretals, in the Civil Code of Italy, and in the Constitution of the United States.[463] Mere declaratory interpretations may affect the past, but that is not retroactivity, because they merely explain more clearly the laws then already existing, and decree nothing new.

By the exception to its rule, canon 10 vindicates the right of the legislator to enact laws concerning past acts when the public welfare demands that the force of old laws be extended

[460] *AAS*, XII (1920), 575.

[461] *CpR*, II (1921), 65-70.

[462] C.I.C., 2-3 iun. 1918, IV—*AAS*, X (1918), 346; *Per.*, IX (1921), 150, 154.

[463] Cicognani, *Canon Law* (2. ed., Philadelphia: The Dolphin Press, 1935), pp. 553-554.

or restricted, changed or corrected. But, if he does so, he is obliged to state explicitly that they are retroactive. When he does so, he does not touch an act already posited, but exercises his authority over its effects that still endure.[464]

These, then, are the principles in the scales of which the proper legal effect of the law of canon 114 must be weighed. Now, in this canon there is not found any express mention of a retroactive force attaching to the law in question. The conclusion, then, follows necessarily that the law begets no retrospective operation. Thus, the effect of the law on the past remains entirely inoperative, and, therefore, does not rectify the status of an incardination which under the previous legislation remained null and void in its juridical effect for any reason whatsoever.[465]

It remains to summarize what this entails in a practical way.

1. Equivalent excardination and incardination completed between 1898 and 1918—Let it be supposed that a cleric, with the full permission of his Ordinary to accept an irrevocably conferred residential benefice in another diocese during the Pre-Code Period (1898-1918), actually departed and obtained the benefice which he still holds after the promulgation of the Code. Is that cleric incardinated in the new diocese now? The answer theoretically is "yes," but, if the incardination were contested by either Bishop, the case would need to be submitted to Rome for a decision.

The reason is that the Decree "*A primis*" was mistakenly understood by so many canonists to have abrogated all methods of excardination and incardination of priests, other than the formal one, that it would take a Roman Congregation or Court to decide that particular point for the period between the "*A primis*" and the Code. Evidence was adduced in Chapter IV [466] to show that the equivalent method for priests was not affected by the "*A primis,*" but it was simultaneously recommended there that in practice one should not take that for granted.

[464] *Ibid.*, p. 555.

[465] Francia, "Animadversiones circa incardinationem,"—*Apoll.*, IX (1936), 218.

[466] *Supra*, pp. 225 ff.

Hence, the answer is only theoretically " yes " to the above case. Canon 114 does not affect the case in any way, because, according to the way of thinking outlined above, the excardination and incardination by the equivalent process was both complete and valid before the Code became effective.

2. Incardination that was invalid any time before 1918—Let it be supposed that an equivalent incardination undertaken before 1918 remained invalid, but that the cleric at present still remains in the benefice. Does the Code now render that incardination valid? The answer must be given in the negative.

In this case it is presumed that the permission to depart from the diocese " *a qua* " was all that it should be, but that the will of the incardinating Bishop was not clear, and, therefore, no incardination resulted. The Bishop " *ad quem* " may have conferred a residential benefice revocably. In pre-Code law that was not sufficient evidence of his will to incardinate. Or again, the diocese " *ad quam* " may have been in the United States of America and the Bishop may have conferred a *paroecia inamovibilis,* indeed, but with the mind that it was not a residential benefice at all. In that case, too, his will to incardinate was not evident.

Although the cleric remained in the benefice or parish, he was there only as an alien, and not as a properly incardinated cleric. His status continues the same after the Code. Canon 114, with its automatic incardination regardless of the subjective perpetuity of the benefice, did not make the cleric, who was still a member of the first diocese, instantly become a member of the second. Nor did the declaration, that by the law of the Code parishes in the United States of America *ipso facto* became residential benefices,[467] alter the mind that the receiving Bishop had of them when he first acted. In both variations of the case, the receiving Bishop's act was not posited with a view to effecting incardination. A new act is now needed for that, and canon 114 will not supply it. The new act may be either formal incardination, or virtual incardina-

[467] Cf. *supra,* pp. 477-8.

tion by a faithful observance of canon 114, with the receiving Bishop issuing a letter of appointment to the parish as a benefice.

3. Excardination that was invalid any time before 1918—Finally, let it be supposed that an equivalent excardination undertaken before 1918 remained invalid, but that the residential benefice was actually conferred, and is still retained after 1918. Does a permission which was given only after 1918 for the acceptance of a benefice actually obtained before 1918 have the effect of convalidating the excardination, so that on the strength of this the entire process stands rectified? The answer again is in the negative. The proper adjustment of the case calls for the conferring of the benefice anew.

There was no valid equivalent excardination, either because no permission at all was issued, or because it was only a temporary permission and contemplated a return of the cleric. No receiving Bishop could validly confer a residential benefice on an alien cleric without the written consent of the cleric's proper Ordinary. That was shown by abundant evidence in the historical section of this study. If the benefice was *inamovibile*, this consent had to be perpetual. Since the original act by which the benefice was conferred remained void of all juridical effect, the presence of an assured permission and valid consent supplied only after the Code became binding would still entail the necessity of a new collative act to make the transfer to the new diocese juridically effective.

CHAPTER XI

Excardination of Secular Clerics—General Requisites

Can. 116. - **Excardinatio fieri nequit sine iustis causis, et effectum non sortitur, nisi incardinatione secuta in alia dioecesi, cuius Ordinarius de eadem priorem Ordinarium quantocius certiorem reddat.**

After describing the two methods by which excardination and incardination may be effected for diocesan clerics, together with the requisites peculiar to each method, the Code next treats separately of the general requisites for excardination and incardination themselves. It deals with the requisites for excardination first, because it is the first step in either method.

Canon 116 has two proximate sources: the Sacred Congregation of the Council's Decree "*A primis*" of July 20, 1898, n. 1,[1] and the III Plenary Council of Baltimore (a. 1884), n. 67.[2] Both of these sources, dealing as they did with the formal process alone, give good ground for the opinion, based on canon 6, 2°, that also the canon derived from them respects formal excardination solely.[3] However, it can be argued equally well that canon 116 makes no distinction and neither should we (*ubi lex non distinguit nec nos distinguere debemus*). The qualifying adjectives "formal" and "virtual" are inventions of the

[1] "Excardinationem fieri non licere nisi iustis de causis, nec effectum undequaque sortiri, nisi incardinatione in alia dioecesi executioni demandata."—*ASS*, XXXI (1898-1899), 49 ss.; *Fontes*, n. 4307; cf. text above, pp. 217-218.

[2] "Declaramus porro sacerdotem, sive ad nostras provincias pertineat, sive ex Europa aliundeve advenerit, etsi a proprio suo Episcopo literas excorporationis (*Exeat*) jamjam obtinuerit, a vinculo communionis et subjectionis erga ipsum solutum haberi non posse, donec alteri dioecesi vel formaliter vel praesumptive adscriptus sit; simulque, si de formali adscriptione agatur, Episcopus proprius de ea peracta authenticum monitum acceperit. Ejus enim jurisdictio in sacerdotem tantum cessat post hanc monitionem."—*Acta et Decreta Conc. Plen. Balt. III.*, 1884, p. 34.

[3] Cf. Chelodi, *Ius de Personis*, n. 107; Wernz-Vidal, *Ius Canon.*, II, n. 63.

canonists, not of the legislator. Incardination is practically defined in canon 111, § 2, to be the attachment of a cleric to a diocese, and, correlatively, excardination must be the severance of a cleric's attachment to a diocese, no matter by which method these effects are secured. Again, in canon 112 it is apparent that incardination (and, correlatively, excardination) is the generic term for a certain effect, which is obtainable differently in various "cases." There seems to be no cogent reason why the term should have a narrower meaning in canon 116. Besides, to argue that any clause taken from the "*A primis*" must refer only to formal incardination or excardination is misleading, because in the "*A primis*" the formal process was the only one to which the term "incardination" itself was applied, whereas in the Code a far wider application is given to it. Most authors, too, hold that canon 116 is applicable to the virtual excardination of canon 114, even if it be granted that its primary application is to the formal excardination of canon 112.[4]

The next issue relative to canon 116 is whether its prescriptions are necessary for the sake of the validity of the act, for the sake of licitness only, or for the sake of satisfying the claims of both considerations. With many canonists it must be admitted that the correct interpretation rests with the adoption of the third of the proposed demands,[5] and accordingly the subsequent discussion will espouse that view.

ARTICLE I

FOR LICITNESS OF EXCARDINATION

The requisite for licitness alone is that there must be just causes for granting an excardination (*Excardinatio fieri nequit sine iustis causis*).

This is a very ancient principle. Even from the beginning clerics were not allowed to depart from their diocese unless

[4] Cf. De Meester, *Compen.*, I, n. 350; Maroto, *Instituts.*, I, n. 497; Cocchi, *Comment.*, l. II, p. I, n. 26; Vermeersch-Creusen, *Epitome*, I, n. 204.

[5] E.g., Maroto, *op. et loc. cit.*; Cocchi, *op. et loc. cit.*; Wernz-Vidal, *Ius Canon.*, II, nn. 62-63; Bondini, *De Incardinatione et Excardinatione Clericorum*, Monographia Juridica ex Ephemeride "Jus Pontificium" excerpta, Series II, fasc. X (Romae: Jus Pontificium, 1929), pp. 14-15.

another Bishop was in need and sought them, or unless some catastrophe forced their exit, such as the capture of their territory by infidels. In the *litterae dimissoriae* (excardinatory letters) of Bishop Luitadus (a. 768) it is to be noted that the text contained the following clause: ". . . Nunc autem quia scitis eum propter causas necessarias in partibus vestris morari, sicut mihi commendatus erat, vobis eum committo. . . ."[6] Similarly, in other periods, particularly after the Council of Trent, just causes were required for any canonical transfer, because, since no cleric was supposed to exist except for the necessity or utility of his diocese,[7] to allow a cleric to leave perpetually was equivalent to bringing damage and harm to the spiritual welfare of the diocese to which he was previously attached.[8] From the outline of the Tridentine and Innocentian Periods in the accompanying historical schema it will be noticed that not only was the Bishop allowed, but, when all other requirements were met, even bound, to grant his cleric permission to depart from the diocese to receive a residential benefice elsewhere, as long as this cleric's cause for departure was just and reasonable. Hence, just causes were a necessity for virtual excardination as well as for formal. In the Pre-Code Period the Decree "*A primis*" stated the law thus: "*Excardinationem fieri non licere nisi iustis de causis. . . .*" From the verb *non licere* it is clear beyond doubt that the just cause was a requisite for licitness only, and it was this very paragraph of the "*A primis*" which was the pattern for canon 116.[9] In the proposal of this doctrine the authors are unanimous.[10] Such unanimity of thought must be well founded. A possible reason to doubt

[6] Cf. *supra*, p. 158.

[7] Sess. XXI, *de ref.*, c. 2.

[8] Cf. *supra*, pp. 162 ff.

[9] Blat, *Commentarium*, II, n. 50.

[10] Cf. Chelodi, *Ius de Personis*, n. 107; Maroto, *Instituts.*, I, n. 497; Cocchi, *Comment.*, l. II, p. I, n. 26; Blat, *op. et loc. cit.;* Vermeersch-Creusen, *Epitome*, I, n. 204; Wernz-Vidal, *Ius Canon.*, II, n. 63; De Meester, *Compen.*, I, n. 350; Bondini, *De Incardinatione et Excardinatione Clericorum*, p. 15; Toso, *Comment. Minora*, in can. 116.

its correctness would be the change of terminology from "*non licere*," as it is in the "*A primis*," to "*fieri nequit*," as it is rendered in the Code. It is a fundamental canonical norm that only those laws are invalidating in their force wherein the nullity of an act is either expressly or equivalently established.[11] Can it be maintained that the clause "*Excardinatio fieri nequit sine iustis causis*" in canon 116 expressly or equivalently lays down a condition which is necessary for the *validity* of excardination? It cannot. Expressions similar to *fieri nequit* are of frequent occurrence in the Code. Often they stand alone without adverbial modifiers, just as in the case at hand.[12] Frequently, however, they are modified by the adverb *valide*,[13] which establishes their meaning beyond question. Where the adverb *valide* is not present the expression can refer to a condition for the licitness of an act equally as well as to a condition for the validity of an act. In canon 759, § 2, for example, there is no doubt that the clause "... *baptismum privatum loci Ordinarius permittere nequit, nisi*" etc. establishes a condition solely for the licitness of the local Ordinary's act. Hence, in the absence of clear proof to the contrary, the expression *fieri nequit* in canon 116 must be assumed to define a condition for the licitness only of the excardination. This conclusion is further confirmed by canon 6, 4°, which states that, whenever the Code retains in part at least the discipline which was current in 1917 in a certain matter, and there arises a doubt whether or not some prescription of the canons is a change from the former legislation, the former law is to be considered retained. It was pointed out above that much of the present legislation on excardination and incardination was taken from the Decree "*A primis*"—current law in 1917—and in particular is that true of canon 116. There is no doubt that a just cause was a condition for the licitness only of the excardination in the Decree "*A primis*." There-

[11] Can. 11.

[12] E.g., cans. 81; 120, § 2; 123; 167, § 1; 195; 201, § 2; 374, § 2; 452, § 1; 454, § 3; 481; 759, § 2; 1056; 1063, § 1; 1423, § 2.

[13] E.g., cans. 44, § 2; 147, § 1; 154; 157; 1075; 1436.

fore, if there be any doubt about it now, the former law must be considered as retained or renewed.

What is a just and reasonable cause? The canonists, to whom reference was made above as holding that a just cause was a requisite for licitness only, give the following examples: provision for or recuperation of one's health because of great difficulties experienced in the diocese, e. g., on account of its damp climate; difficulty on the part of the diocese to support the cleric; impediments by which his ministry is rendered useless or harmful; the greater need for or usefulness of the cleric in another diocese. Sometimes the just cause for excardination might proceed from the cleric himself who is to be excardinated, e. g., some little displeasure or even some great aversion which has arisen within him towards or against his Bishop "*a quo*." [14] Some of the causes which the Sacred Congregation of the Council considered sufficient for granting excardination were: a strong desire amounting to a demand for a certain priest by the people of a parish in an alien diocese; ill health coupled with the acquisition of an inheritance in another diocese; the moral need of retaining a position of which the revenue was necessary for the support of the cleric's parents; long years of service spent in the diocese "*ad quam*," especially when coupled with old age and infirmity.[15]

Common examples of unjust and unreasonable causes are cupidity and ambition.

Since it is the dismissing Bishop whose conscience becomes burdened with sin if he grants an excardination without a just reason, it is he alone who must decide on the justice of the cause.[16] If his judgment seems unreasonable to the cleric, recourse should be made to the Holy See, which will pass on the merits of the case and instruct the Bishop "*a quo*" accordingly, as was done in the cases previously mentioned from the records of the Sacred Congregation of the Council.[17]

[14] Ojetti, *Comment.*, II, in can. 116.

[15] Cf. *supra*, pp. 199-201.

[16] Chelodi, *op. et loc. cit.*; Blat, *op. et loc. cit.*

[17] *Supra*, pp. 199-201.

Though not contained in canon 116, another requisite for the licitness of excardination should here be noted, namely, that the excardinating Ordinary is bound under pain of grave sin to transmit nothing but truthful testimony concerning the cleric he is dismissing.[18]

ARTICLE II

FOR VALIDITY OF EXCARDINATION

To insure the observance of canon 111, § 1, namely, the attachment of every cleric to some diocese or to some Religious Institute, so that the legally possible existence of clerical *vagi* is entirely excluded, it is absolutely necessary that no act of excardination be recognized as valid unless and until the correlative act of incardination of the same cleric in another diocese has been executed. The words of canon 116 are: ". . . *et* [*excardinatio*] *effectum non sortitur, nisi incardinatione secuta in alia dioecesi. . . .*" This clause is likewise borrowed from n. 1 of the Decree "*A primis,*" which read: ". . . *nec* [*excardinationem*] *effectum undequaque sortiri, nisi incardinatione in alia dioecesi executioni demandata.*" The word *invalida* does not occur, but it is clear that when excardination does not obtain its effect this is the same as when it remains unaccomplished. By no stretch of the imagination could one consider an excardination as being unaccomplished simply because it connoted an unlawful procedure. Canonists quite generally agree that this particular clause of canon 116 points to a requisite for validity; [19] Maroto and Creusen, moreover, regard this requisite as entering into the virtual as well as the formal method of excardination.

The history of the correlativity or interdependence of excardination and incardination is as old as the clerical state itself. Even in the Ancient Period, the formulae used [20] showed that the letters of dismissal were issued by a cleric's ordaining Prelate to some other definite Bishop, and only with the idea of the

[18] Can. 117, 2°.

[19] E.g., Maroto, *op. et loc. cit.*; Cocchi, *op. et loc. cit.*; Wernz-Vidal, *op. cit.*, II, n. 62; Bondini, *op. et loc. cit.*

[20] Cf. *supra*, pp. 156, 158-9.

cleric's becoming attached to the latter Bishop's diocese. If they failed to accomplish that, the cleric still belonged to his former church or territory.[21] Confirmation of this is found in the 18th canon of the Synod held at Rome in the year 826, which also was incorporated into the Decree of Gratian as follows: "Episcopus subiecto sibi sacerdoti, vel alii clerico, nisi ab ipso postulatus, dimissorias non faciat, ne quis quasi perdita aut errans inveniatur." [22] Many other proofs from history were given above, especially in the Tridentine and later Periods.[23] It was the wish and the law of the Church that at no time should a cleric be released from his allegiance, such as would be the case if excardination could be valid without a corresponding incardination.

In the Tridentine and Innocentian Periods practically all the canonical transfers were effected by the reception of residential benefices in alien dioceses, as can be seen at a glance from the accompanying schema, but, until a cleric had actually obtained a residential benefice he could still be recalled to his home diocese, even when in his travels he could produce letters of his Bishop which authorized him to accept such a benefice wherever it was offered to him.

In the latter part of the nineteenth century transfers by letters became the more usual method. The variously named letters of release had to be accepted *in perpetuum* by a receiving Bishop before the process of transfer was completed and the release really effected. Formal excardination according to the III Plenary Council of Baltimore [24] allowed a period of trial as long as five years, and, if after that time the trial Bishop refused to incardinate the priest, he simply remained incardinated in his proper diocese, because his excardination had not yet become

[21] Claeys-Bouuaert, *De Canonica Cleri Saecularis Obedientia* (Lovanii, 1904), pp. 194-195.

[22] C. 1, D. LXXII. The point is more clearly made from the genuine text of the canon which reads: ". . . nisi ab *alio* postulatus, dimissorias non faciat, ne ovis quasi perdita . . . , sed per consensum unius in alterius inveniatur ovili."—Hardouin, V, 67.

[23] Pp. 162 ff.

[24] *Acta et Decreta Conc. Plen. Balt. III.*, 1884, n. 63.

effective.[25] Then the Sacred Congregation of the Council in paragraphs 1 and 2 of its Decree "*A primis*" of July 20, 1898, adopted the formal process for the universal Church, eliminated the trial period, and coördinated the two types of letters, namely, the letters of excardination and the letters of incardination.[26]

According to the present law of the Code on excardination, two points affecting validity must be attended to: The letters for formal, or the permission for virtual, excardination must fulfill the requirements of canons 112 and 114 respectively in order to be in valid form; but then, even when issued in valid form, the process itself is not valid until incardination has followed. That is the import of canon 116. It is already implied in both canons 112 and 114, but it is made a distinct requisite here to guard against any mistake. After a cleric has obtained an express promise of incardination from an alien Bishop, and his reason for desiring it is considered just, his proper Bishop need have no hesitation about issuing to him a formal letter of excardination, because it will not take effect under any circumstances until a valid act of incardination has been executed. Meanwhile, therefore, the Bishop can still exercise control over the cleric, no matter where the latter may be, because he is still a subject. Similarly, if there be a just reason for excardination, and no receiving Bishop is yet known, the proper Bishop does no wrong in issuing to his cleric a letter permitting him to depart from the diocese perpetually, because neither will that have the effect of actually disengaging the cleric from his diocese of incardination until he has obtained a residential benefice in another diocese. No matter how long he may be absent prior to that happening, he is not without a permanent Superior, and must obey if his Bishop of incardination orders him back home.

Corollary.—Excardinating Bishop to be notified of the subsequent incardination

In the III Plenary Council of Baltimore it was provided that an excardinated priest, whether from the United States of

[25] Cf. *supra*, p. 514, note 2.

[26] ASS, XXXI (1898-1899), 49 ss.; *Fontes*, n. 4307. For text cf. *supra*, pp. 217-218.

America, Europe, or elsewhere, could not be considered absolved from the bond of communion with and subjection towards his proper Bishop, until this same proper Bishop had received an official notification that the receiving Bishop had signed the formal document of incardination. It was only after that notification that the dismissing Bishop's jurisdiction ceased.[27] This was understood as a condition for the validity of the excardination whenever the correlative process of incardination was only conditional, that is, when a definite decision to incardinate the candidate did not have to be rendered for three or five years. But, when this provision for the proper notification of the dismissing Bishop about the completed incardination was incorporated in the Code, according to the law of which incardination must be absolute and no lapse of time can intervene between excardination and incardination, there was not the same necessity that the notification be made a condition for valid excardination. Hence a marked difference may be discerned in the wording of this provision as included in canon 116: ". . . *cuius Ordinarius de eadem* [*incardinatione secuta in alia dioecesi*] *priorem Ordinarium quantocius certiorem reddat.*" Evidently, the notification is now nothing more than a mandate placed on the incardinating Bishop, which he is to fulfill as soon as possible.[28] The adverb *quantocius* insinuates that as long as the notification is not made the validity of the excardination is, nevertheless, not held in suspense, for even a belated act of notification would of course no longer fulfill the mandate as it now stands.[29]

[27] *Acta et Decreta Conc. Plen. Balt. III.*, 1884, n. 67: ". . . a vinculo communionis et subjectionis erga ipsum solutum haberi non posse, donec alteri dioecesi . . . adscriptus sit; simulque, si de formali adscriptione agatur, Episcopus proprius de ea peracta authenticum monitum acceperit. Ejus enim jurisdictio in sacerdotem tantum cessat post hanc monitionem."

[28] For that reason some authors include this among the general requisites for the licitness of incardination, e.g., Maroto, *Institutt.*, I, n. 497; Cocchi, *Comment.*, l. II, p. I, n. 26.

[29] Bondini (*De Incardinatione et Excardinatione Clericorum*, p. 14), among the authors consulted by the writer, stands alone in his contention that when the notification has been neglected the cleric is still to be considered as juridically attached to his proper native diocese. Indeed, this opinion is not only unwarranted by canon 116, but also gainsaid by canons 112 and 114, for in these latter two canons no mention at all is made of this notification.

The inclusion of the mandate in canon 116 follows quite naturally as a corollary of the preceding clause on the correlation of excardination with incardination. Excardination is not valid until incardination has been executed. As soon as that takes place, the process is complete and valid on both sides. However, the dismissing Bishop is not free of all concern for the cleric as soon as the latter has departed. His solicitude continues until the cleric has reached his new home and has been incardinated there. Since the dismissing Bishop will not ordinarily know about the fact of incardination until he has received the official notification of the same, he is justified in still claiming jurisdiction over the excardinated cleric until it is proved to his satisfaction that his jurisdiction over this cleric no longer exists, but has been transferred to the receiving Bishop by virtue of the completion of the canonical transfer process.

Courtesy on the part of the receiving Bishop and solicitude for a sense of security on the part of the dismissing Bishop require that the notification be made as soon as that be possible. Since the canon does not indicate what medium of information should be used, the method and manner of notification will be determined by the incardinating Bishop according to his own good pleasure and discretion, but they should be such as to furnish certitude to the dismissing Bishop.[30] A formal document is surely not contemplated as the one and only means by the mandate contained in canon 116.

This notification must be made also by the Bishop who, by conferring a residential benefice, virtually incardinates another's cleric after he has received the proper Bishop's consent. It is of far greater urgency in this instance than it is in the case of formal incardination, because there might be a very considerable lapse of time between the issuance to the cleric of the permission to depart from the proper diocese and the conferring on him of the residential benefice in the new diocese.

30 Blat, *Commentarium*, II, n. 50.

CHAPTER XII

Incardination of Secular Clerics—General Requisites for Licitness

Can. 117. - **Ad incardinationem alieni clerici Ordinarius ne deveniat, nisi:**

1°. Necessitas aut utilitas dioecesis id exigat, et salvis iuris praescriptis circa canonicum ordinationis titulum;

2°. Ex legitimo documento sibi constiterit de obtenta legitima excardinatione, et habuerit praeterea a Curia dimittente, sub secreto, si opus sit, de clerici natalibus, vita, moribus ac studiis opportuna testimonia, maxime si agatur de incardinandis clericis diversae linguae et nationis; Ordinarius autem dimittens, graviter onerata eius conscientia, advigilare debet ut testimonia sint veritati conformia;

3°. Clericus iureiurando coram eodem Ordinario eiusve delegato declaraverit se in perpetuum novae dioecesis servitio velle addici ad normam sacrorum canonum.

What is contained in canon 117 applies to the incardination of *clerics* from dioceses other than the Bishop's own (*Ad incardinationem alieni* clerici), and not to the initial incardination, through first tonsure, of proper or alien subjects. The question of initial incardination is governed by other canons, and the requirements for the licit and valid effecting of it were amply discussed above.[1]

Only *secular* clerics are here contemplated, for the entire group of canons 111-117 is arranged under the title "*De clericorum adscriptione alicui dioecesi.*"

Both methods of incardination, the formal of canon 112 and the virtual of canon 114, are included in the scope of canon 117,

[1] Pp. 299 ff.

because the same arguments apply here with regard to the term "incardination" as for the interpretation of the corresponding term "excardination" in canon 116.[2] In this the opinion of De Meester,[3] Maroto,[4] and Toso[5] is followed. These authors, however, qualify their assertions with such expressions as *iuxta modum* or *mutatis mutandis.* Most authors are silent on the scope of the canon.

The one primarily affected by these requisites is the same local Ordinary (*Ordinarius*) who was designated in canon 112 as competent to sign letters of incardination, and in canon 114 as competent to confer a residential benefice. Even as in those canons, therefore, the Ordinary must be understood in the sense of canon 198, § 2, subject to the limitations of canon 113.[6]

The words "*ne deveniat*" constitute a prohibition for the local Ordinary. To violate this prohibition would be a sinful act of disobedience. The conjunction *nisi* introduces the requirements under which the proper authority may act without sin. Hence what follows is stated entirely with reference to the licitness, and not the validity, of the act of incardination.[7] To these requirements must be added also the obligation specified in canon 116, namely, that the incardinating Ordinary notify the Ordinary "*a quo*" as soon as possible of the incardination he has executed. This, of course, applies to both formal and virtual incardinations. The opening clause of canon 117 is taken almost *verbatim* from paragraph 3 of the Decree "*A primis,*" which reads: "*Ad hanc incardinationem deveniri non posse, nisi . . .,*" after which there follows mention of the requisites for a lawful procedure. These latter, too, are closely paralleled by the Code, as will be seen.

[2] *Supra,* pp. 514-515.

[3] *Compen.,* I, n. 350.

[4] *Instituts.,* I, n. 497.

[5] *Comment. Minora,* in can. 117.

[6] *Supra,* pp. 397 ff.

[7] Toso, *op. et loc. cit.*

ARTICLE I

THE CANONICAL TITLE

The very first thing about which a Bishop who contemplates the incardination of an alien cleric must make certain is that he has a pious place in which to use the cleric's services, and a source of sustenance for him. These two provisions were closely allied throughout history, as was seen in Chapter III, article III, and in Chapter IV, article III, and, consistently, they are placed together in n. 1 of canon 117.

In the beginning the attachment of a cleric to a definite church in the diocese created the source of sustenance or title of ordination for him. Then there was a divorce of the two ideas, and titles became concrete entities, conferrable upon those clerics who were needed in the diocese. A third step was the invention of titles of ordination, e. g., patrimony and pension, which were obtainable by those also who were not needed. The final step in the process of the evolution, taken by the Council of Trent,[8] was to bring the two ideas together again, so that even those who possessed the titles of patrimony or pension could not be ordained unless they were also necessary for or useful to the diocese. A canonical title today, therefore, signifies both a place of service and a source of sustenance.

1. *The Place of Service*

A general principle is enunciated in canon 969, § 1: "Let no secular be ordained who, in the judgment of his proper Bishop, is not necessary or useful to the churches of the diocese." This is a good safeguard against the otherwise inevitable emergence of an idle clergy, whose presence in the Church has ever brought the clerical state into disrepute. However, the incardination of an alien cleric is, like ordination, the addition of another individual to the ranks of the diocesan clergy. If the above rule is needed as a check upon admissions to the clergy of a diocese by ordination, a similar one is needed for second incardinations. And, in fact, this was insisted upon by the Holy See in the Sacred Congregation of the Council's Decree "*A primis*" of

[8] Sess. XXIII, *de ref.*, c. 16.

July 20, 1898, 4°, in the following terms: ". . . Et meminerint quod sicut 'nullus debet ordinari qui iudicio sui Episcopi non sit utilis aut necessarius suis Ecclesiis' ut in cap. 16, sess. 23 de reform. Tridentinum statuit; ita pariter nullum esse adscribendum novum clericum, nisi pro necessitate aut commoditate dioecesis." So, in the Code, a similar provision is incorporated into the canon under discussion: "*Ad incardinationem alieni clerici Ordinarius ne deveniat nisi 1°. Necessitas aut utilitas dioecesis id exigat. . . .*" Practically, this means that the incardinating Bishop must have some office or position to which he can assign the incoming cleric and wherein the cleric's time and faculties will be utilized in the service of religion. For the lower clerics still preparing for the priesthood this means the same as it did after the Council of Trent, which decreed the institution of seminaries to take the place of the private training and of the exercise of clerics' orders in the individual churches, which up to that time had been the practice. It means, then, that the Bishop should have a place for the incardinated cleric in his own or some other seminary, and should be morally certain that he can assign the cleric to an office or position when the time for priestly ordination arrives.

2. *The Source of Sustenance*

A. Canonical Titles of Ordination in the Code

No change has been made by the Code in the previously existing titles. Canon 979 shows that the ordinary canonical title is that of benefice—secure, adequate, and perpetual, according to the norms established by the Ordinaries for different countries and times. The first two extraordinary titles mentioned in the same canon are those of patrimony or pension, which likewise must be secure, adequate, and perpetual. In case none of these are possible to obtain, canon 981, § 1, allows the substitution of the extraordinary title of "service of the diocese." In missionary territories, subject to the jurisdiction of the Sacred Congregation for the Propagation of the Faith, it allows the extraordinary "title of the mission." In both these latter cases, however, the major cleric ordained for them is required by canon 981 to take an oath that he will devote himself to the perpetual service of his destined diocese or mission under the authority of its local Ordinary. The oath for the title of " the mission " excludes even entrance into religion except with the permission of the Holy See; the oath for the title of " service of the diocese " does not.[9]

For Religious who are ordained *iure saecularium,* if they be of an Institute which takes perpetual vows, the title of ordination to major orders is the title *mensae communis, Congregationis,* or something similar, as prescribed by their constitutions;[10] if they be of an Institute which takes only temporary vows, or of a society whose members live in common without vows, they use the same titles as secular major clerics.[11]

In order to make the titles of " service of the diocese " or of " the mission " effective, the Ordinary who ordains a priest for his diocese or mission using one of these as the ordination title must confer on him a benefice, an office, or a subsidy, from the income of which the priest will be able to sustain himself in a manner becoming his state.[12]

B. For Whom is a Canonical Title Necessary?

Among the requisites for the licitness of any ordination there is included in canon 974, § 1, 7°: "*Titulus canonicus, si agatur de ordinibus maioribus.*" Hence every minor cleric who is about to receive major orders must have a canonical title. Any Bishop who elevates such a one to sacred orders without a title acts unlawfully, and the Bishop himself is required to support the cleric so ordained, in the event that the cleric later becomes reduced to a state of want, until some other proper provision has been made for his sustenance.[13] The Bishop who is guilty of ordaining the cleric without a title also incurs an *ipso facto* suspension from

[9] Vermeersch-Creusen, *Epitome,* II, n. 250.

[10] Can. 982, § 2.

[11] Can. 982, § 3.

[12] Can. 981, § 2.

[13] Can. 980, § 2.

the conferring of orders for a year, the lifting of which suspension during the year is reserved to the Holy See.[14]

A mere tonsured cleric, or one ascending to any of the minor orders, stands in no need of a title at that time, but the Bishop who incardinates such a one must prudently foresee that there will be a title available for him when the time for his reception of major orders arrives.

C. Substitution or Provision of a Canonical Title for an Incardinated Major Cleric

When canon 117, 1°, says "... *et salvis iuris praescriptis circa canonicum ordinationis titulum*," it means that the incardinating Bishop must be careful to provide in his own diocese a canonical title of ordination for the cleric he is receiving, if the cleric be in major orders. Failure to do so renders his act of incardination illicit, and most probably burdens him with the responsibility of supporting this cleric out of his own personal funds, if the cleric should be reduced to a state of distress, just as he would be obliged to do if he had ordained the same to sacred orders without a title.[15]

The reason for this prescription is that ordinarily a canonical title in one diocese is lost by the transfer of a cleric to another, and canon 980, § 1, states that whenever a cleric in sacred orders loses his title he should be provided with another, unless, in the judgment of his Bishop, his sustenance in a manner befitting his state is secured in some other way. That is especially true when the title of ordination which is being given up is a benefice. His own proper Ordinary may not allow him to give it up, unless it is clear that he has the necessaries for an honest livelihood from some other source; [16] and, in fact, the resignation of such a benefice is invalid unless another legitimate title of ordination is substituted for it.[17] Yet, a residential benefice in the diocese

[14] Can. 2373, 3°.

[15] Can. 980, § 2; cf. Wernz-Vidal, *Ius Canon.*, II, n. 63, note 21; Toso, *Comment. Minora*, in can. 117.

[16] Can. 1484.

[17] Can. 1485.

"*a qua*" must be given up, if excardination is to take place, unless there be an agreement between the two Bishops to allow the cleric to retain it for awhile; but ultimately it will most certainly have to be substituted by a new title in the diocese "*ad quam.*" A non-residential benefice in the diocese of excardination could still remain the excardinated cleric's title of ordination after his transfer, and that perpetually (though he would have to be also necessary or useful to the churches of the new diocese), but such a situation is very unlikely, because Bishops quite generally reserve the benefices in their own territory for their own clerics. That holds true for ecclesiastical pensions as well.[18]

The only title which is not lost by transfer to another diocese is patrimony. No substitute is needed for it, but the incardinating Bishop must ascertain if it be adequate for a decent livelihood in the new locality, and if it be secure and perpetual. Even when he is satisfied of that, he must still assign the new cleric to a position. If the patrimony is inadequate, he must substitute a new title for it.

The extraordinary titles of "service of the diocese" and of "the mission" are manifestly lost by incardination to a new diocese or mission, and a new title must be conferred.[19] This is comparatively easy to do, since it merely means an act whereby the Bishop gives to the incardinated cleric a right to receive his sustenance from the voluntary oblations of the people in the new diocese or mission territory.[20]

For the virtual incardination of a cleric by the conferring of a residential benefice there is no difficulty in fulfilling the demand of this first paragraph of canon 117, because, if the newcomer were not necessary, there would not be a benefice to give him; and, no matter what his former title of ordination, the residential benefice conferred on him, if it be secure, adequate, and perpetual, can well be made his title in the new diocese.

[18] Wernz-Vidal, *Ius Canon.*, II, n. 63, note 21.

[19] Cf. *supra*, pp. 147, 154.

[20] Wernz-Vidal, *op. et loc. cit.*

ARTICLE II

THE DOCUMENTS

The history of the subject of incardination was shown to be replete with examples of particular and general laws which made the exhibition of a letter of release and of recommendation an important requisite for the reception of an alien cleric into any diocese. Especially after the Council of Trent was this the rule.[21] Even for a temporary sojourn a letter of permission had to be shown, in order to protect the receiving Bishop against the charge of usurpation, as well as to prevent the Church in his diocese from being duped by impostors and scandalous men. At the present time ordination and incardination are still, as they always have been, closely allied. Sometimes the newly incardinated clerics are in the lower grades of orders and need to be ordained to higher orders. Church law has always been strict about the knowledge a Bishop should have of the men whom he ordains or authorizes to be ordained. It must be equally strict about his knowledge of the men he intends to incardinate for diocesan priestly service. Since he presumably has no personal knowledge of them, it must be gathered from official documents, which he can rely upon inasmuch as they are issued by his fellow members of the hierarchy. Hence, this second paragraph of canon 117 deals with the informative documents he needs and the character of their reliability.

1. *Legal Document of Legitimate Excardination*

The first and most important document is that which certifies to the cleric's freedom to come to the new diocese. As the Code puts it, " Let not the Ordinary proceed to the incardination of an alien cleric unless . . . 2° it has become evident to him from a legal document that a legitimate excardination was obtained " (*nisi . . . 2° Ex legitimo documento sibi constiterit de obtenta legitima excardinatione*). This is apparently fashioned from the Decree " *A primis*," n. 3, which read: ". . . nisi prius

[21] Cf. schema included in this work, *supra*, pp. 265-284.

ex legitimo documento constiterit alienum clericum a sua dioecesi fuisse in perpetuum dimissum. . . ." [22]

The common sense of equity is itself the basis for such a requisite. The process of excardination precedes that of incardination both in principle and in fact, somewhat like the establishment through investigation of a person's status of freedom to marry precedes his actual contraction of the marriage bond. For a Bishop to execute an act of incardination before knowing whether the alien cleric has received his excardination is to invert the proper order, and to set at naught the requirement of a just cause for the cleric's release from his present diocese.[23]

Two distinct points are, therefore, included in this requisite of the production of a document of excardination prior to the effecting of incardination: a) The document itself must be lawfully executed; and b) it must be clear from it that an excardination has been granted, not merely promised, and that the excardination has been granted in a lawful manner.[24]

The document may take the form of formal letters of excardination,[25] of a written permission to obtain an alien residential benefice,[26] or of a written permission to depart perpetually from the diocese.[27] The document itself is lawfully executed if it follows the norms enacted in canons 112 and 114. Whether or not the document really grants excardination will be ascertained from its wording; and the lawfulness of the grant will depend on whether or not the causes for the excardination were known and admitted to be just by the excardinating Ordinary, who alone is the judge of that. Hence, every letter of perpetual release should contain, among other things, a declaration that it is being given for just reasons.[28] A receiving

[22] Cf. text, *supra*, pp. 217-218.

[23] Can. 116.

[24] Toso, *Comment. Minora*, in can. 117.

[25] Can. 112.

[26] Can. 114.

[27] Can. 114.

[28] Cf. *supra*, pp. 391, 394.

Bishop who would act upon the strength of a document of excardination without making certain of its justice would equivalently coöperate in the unlawful performance.

All of this, be it remembered, is only for the licitness of the incardination; it would still be valid, even if the incardinating Bishop had not seen the document of excardination, provided that it had actually been issued.[29]

From this it can be seen that tacit excardination is not made possible at all by the Code, even though there is recognized in the Code one species of incardination that is effected tacitly, namely, the incardination of ex-Religious when they are received into a diocese and thereupon, without the interposition of their dismissal from the diocese, have served it for the time beyond which the period of their probation can not be prorogued by the Bishop.[30]

2. *Testimonial Letters*

A. For Native-born Clerics

The second document required is the one that contains the character testimonials. Canon 117, 2°, goes on to state: "Let not the Ordinary proceed to the incardination of an alien cleric unless . . . 2° . . . he also has had in addition from the dismissing Curia, secretly if need be, appropriate testimony concerning the cleric's ancestry and origin, life, character, and studies . . ." (*et habuerit praeterea a Curia dimittente, sub secreto, si opus sit, de clerici natalibus, vita, moribus ac studiis opportuna testimonia*). The parallel section of the Decree "*A primis,*" its proximate source, reads: " 3° . . . et obtenta insuper fuerint ab Episcopo dimittente, sub secreto, si opus sit, de eius natalibus, vita, moribus ac studiis opportuna testimonia." [31]

Once again the nexus between ordination and incardination is seen. Of old the points on which candidates for orders had to pass an examination for fitness were listed in the Decree of

[29] Maroto, *Instituts.*, I, n. 497.

[30] Can. 641, § 2.

[31] Cf. full text above, pp. 217-218.

Gratian as: "genus, vita, patria, aetas, institutio, locus, ubi educati sunt, si sint bene litterati, si in lege Domini instructi." [32] In the year 1206 Pope Innocent III instructed the Patriarch of Constantinople not to recognize, and not to advance to higher orders, clerics coming to him without letters of their ordaining Bishop in proof of the grade of orders which they claimed to possess.[33] Then the Council of Trent [34] commanded that whenever a cleric sought *litterae dimissoriae* to be ordained by a Bishop other than his proper Bishop such permission should not be granted him "*nisi ejus probitas ac mores Ordinarii sui testimonio commendentur.*" Two famous Papal Constitutions, namely, "*Speculatores*" of Innocent XII [35] and "*Apostolicae Sedis*" of Pius IX,[36] likewise ordered that Testimonial Letters be obtained in certain cases. The former of these two declared that a cleric who had already received tonsure or some minor orders from his proper Bishop could not be promoted to higher orders by another Bishop on the basis of a conferred benefice, "nisi ante eorumdem susceptionem Testimoniales Literas proprii Episcopi tam originis, quam domicilii super suis natalibus, aetate, moribus, et vita sibi concedi obtinuerit, easque Episcopo Ordinanti in actis illius Curiae conservandas exhibuerit."

In the Code it is required for the licit reception of any order that the candidate, in the judgment of his proper Ordinary, be endowed with the proper qualities, and that he labor not under any irregularity or other impediment.[37] Hence, before he is ordained to any grade, his proper Bishop must be in possession of testimony on the following counts: 1°) Reception of baptism and confirmation, if he be a candidate for tonsure, or, if he be already a cleric, the last order received; 2°) Completion of the

[32] C. 5, D. XXIV. By historians it is thought that this text of Gratian's Decree was derived from a canon of a council which was held at Nantes during the seventh century.

[33] C. 2, X, *de clericis peregrinis*, I, 22.

[34] Sess. XXIII, *de ref.*, c. 8.

[35] Nov. 4, 1694, § 3—*Fontes*, n. 258.

[36] Oct. 12, 1869, § V, n. 3—*Fontes*, n. 552.

[37] Can. 968, § 1.

studies required for the particular order he is about to receive; 3°) Seminary rector's report on his good character, or, if he be not in a seminary, his priestly guardian's report on the same; and 4°) Testimonial Letters from the Ordinary of any place where he stayed long enough to become liable to the contraction of a canonical impediment.[38]

When the candidate is to be ordained by some Bishop other than his proper one, he is not to be given dimissorial letters for the ordination until his proper Bishop has all the testimonies required, not only in the canon just cited, but in canons 994-1000 as well.[39]

After incardination the receiving Bishop becomes solely the proper Bishop in perpetuity over the new cleric. He acquires exclusive responsibility for him in whatever grade of orders he then is established, just as though he himself had ordained the man. It is entirely reasonable, therefore, that he, too, should have confidential and reliable testimony about the cleric before he accepts such a responsibility. When higher orders are necessary it will be he who must judge of the cleric's fitness, and, upon the strength of it, either ordain, or issue dimissorial letters for the ordination. The latter procedure appears the more likely one whenever the cleric is not domiciled in the new diocese of incardination.

It follows from this that the testimony the Bishop needs to incardinate lawfully is substantially the same as to ordain lawfully, namely: 1) The parentage and origin of the candidate (*de clerici natalibus*), which would include not merely the bare facts of his date of birth and legitimacy but also his moral, cultural, and social background. Though it is presumed that the first ordaining Prelate verifies the necessary facts of the candidate's legitimacy as well as of his reception of the sacraments of baptism and confirmation, nevertheless, it still remains

[38] Can. 993. Failure to observe this results in the proper Bishop becoming *ipso facto* suspended from the right to confer orders for a year. The Holy See has reserved to itself the lifting of this suspension (Can. 2373, 2°).

[39] Can. 960, § 1. Anyone who maliciously advances a candidate to any order without these Testimonial Letters is to be gravely punished according to the circumstances of the case (Can. 2374).

the prerogative of any Bishop who is interested in incardinating a cleric to judge of the cleric's desirability from the standpoint of his family history. 2) His life (*de clerici . . . vita*), which means his record for righteousness, goodness, or moral integrity, for it must be known whether or not he is enmeshed in any irregularity or canonical impediment, whether or not he spent all his time in the diocese " *a qua,*" and, if not, how long elsewhere, and what was his record for good conduct while away. 3) His character (*de clerici . . . moribus*), by which is signified the traits, habits, etc., which reveal it, such as zeal or indifference, a spirit of sacrifice or one of selfishness, and the like. 4) His studies (*de clerici . . . studiis*), i. e., his creditable completion of the prescribed course of studies for the order which he presently has and his mental ability to pursue the requisite higher studies with at least some promise of success.

The source from which all this testimony is to emanate is the Curia of the diocese from which the cleric is excardinated (*a Curia dimittente*). The Curia is defined in canon 363, § 1, as consisting of those persons who assist the Bishop, or the one who heads the diocese in place of the Bishop, in the rule of the diocese as a whole. Among others it includes the Vicar General, the Chancellor, and the Notaries.[40] In the Decree " *A primis* " it was from the excardinating Bishop himself that the testimony had to be obtained. That feature has been relaxed in the Code in favor of the above-mentioned officials, but, as will be seen below, the Ordinary must oversee what they write.

Occasions may arise when the testimony concerning the cleric is more or less unfavorable. In these instances it should be transmitted secretly to the receiving Bishop (*sub secreto, si opus sit*), so that he may make his decision without fear or pressure. The norms that he would use in order to decide whether or not ordination should be conferred may also be employed in order to determine whether or not incardination should be granted. They are threefold:

1st. If the facts revealed are such as would show the candidate to be unworthy of sacred orders, he must be refused. A case in

[40] Can. 363, § 2.

hand would be one in which the candidate is addicted to inebriety, impurity, or dishonesty. Moral deficiencies are not corrected by a mere change of territory, and, if a cleric gave scandal in one diocese, it is to be feared that he will possibly give worse scandal in another, where he is less well known, and where in consequence his misconduct is likely occasion for still greater moral bewilderment on the part of observers. No dire need of priests should justify the perpetual acceptance of an unworthy cleric.

2nd. If the testimony reveals that the cleric had evil traits in the past, but that these have been definitely corrected, so that he is now considered worthy of sacred orders, he may be admitted, if the receiving Bishop is satisfied that the amendment is of sufficiently long standing to give solid hope that it will be permanent.

3rd. If the cleric is revealed to have evil traits which can be corrected, but it is not yet certain that he has amended to the extent required of one who is to be, or already is, in sacred orders, he should not be received until his amendment of life is certain and long established.[41]

Ex-seminarians, whether such by dismissal or by voluntary departure, if they be clerics, are still incardinated in the diocese for the service of which they were promoted. To be accepted elsewhere they need to be excardinated. Naturally, the Testimonials must include the fact and cause of their departure or dismissal. Mere departure carries with it no stigma, and hence the law is unconcerned about it. Nevertheless, the receiving Bishop must look for that steadfastness of purpose in reaching the priesthood which should be found in every candidate for the clerical state.[42]

Dismissal from a seminary, on the other hand, does attach some stigma to the cleric. In the Pre-Code Period certain regulations for the incardination of such a cleric were made by Pope Pius X in the Decree "*Vetuit*" of the Sacred Congregation of

[41] Many, *De Sacra Ordin.*, n. 128.

[42] Can. 973, § 1.

the Council.[43] In place of these the Code has substituted the easier provisions of canon 1363, § 3, by which a Bishop is forbidden to admit to a seminary anyone dismissed from another seminary, unless he has first received from its Superior, secretly if necessary, knowledge of the cause for dismissal, and of the student's character, nature, and talent, and has discovered with certainty that there is nothing in him which is unbecoming to the priestly state. These regulations apply to any non-tonsured, dismissed, ecclesiastical candidate. Whenever the student is already a cleric, the information required by canon 1363, § 3, will be gathered and sent to the receiving Bishop by the Curia of the diocese to which the cleric still belongs. The point to the discussion is that the Bishop "*ad quem*" can incardinate even a dismissed cleric, if in his judgment the testimony presented shows nothing incompatible with the sacerdotal state. However, the Superior of the seminary from which the cleric was dismissed is bound under pain of grave sin to report the truth to the proper Bishop of the cleric, and he, in turn, is equally bound in conscience to transmit truthful testimony to the incardinating Bishop.[44]

B. For Foreign-born Clerics

1°. In general

It has always been a problem to regulate transfers of clerics from far-distant, and especially foreign, dioceses in such a way as to eliminate all deception and danger. Because of the distance separating the dioceses "*a qua*" and "*ad quam*," the slowness of inter-communication, and the language difficulty, frauds were easily perpetrated, and it was most difficult and laborious to detect and avert them. Nevertheless, the Church in the course of ages sincerely tried by repeated legislation to lessen the dangers.[45] In the Decree "*A primis*" the pertinent paragraph n. 5, which forms the basis of the present law, reads as follows:

[43] Cf. *supra*, p. 239.

[44] Cans. 1363, § 3; 117, 2°.

[45] E.g., letter of Pope Alexander III (a. 1159-1181) to the Bishop of Le Mans in France—C. 1, X, *de clericis peregrinis*, I, 22. Cf. also *supra*, pp. 192, 214-216, 239-246.

> Quo vero ad clericos diversae linguae et nationis, oportere ut Episcopi in iis admittendis cautius et severius procedant, ac numquam eos recipiant, nisi requisiverint prius a respectivo eorum Ordinario, et obtinuerint, secretam ac favorabilem de ipsorum vita et moribus informationem, onerata super hoc graviter Episcoporum conscientia.[46]

This was merely paraphrasing what the decree had already stipulated in paragraph n. 3 for the reception of any alien cleric, except that it admonished the Bishops in these cases to act with greater caution and strictness.

The Code, in canon 117, parallels the "*A primis*" in its requirement of documentary proof of perpetual dismissal from the diocese "*a qua,*" and of appropriate character Testimonials from its Bishop, antecedent to any act of incardination. Since this, however, is equally valid for the acceptance of any cleric, the Code goes on to say "*maxime si agatur de incardinandis clericis diversae linguae et nationis.*" The lower clerics are not usually lent out for the practical ministry as are priests. When one of these seeks a foreign diocese, it is to become incardinated, to continue his studies, and to serve perpetually as a priest the diocese of his choice. The Code amply covers that exchange. A Bishop sins grievously if he attempts to incardinate a foreign-born cleric without first procuring the two types of documents, and satisfying himself that they are genuine and that the testimony contained in them is favorable. The Bishop "*a quo*" likewise commits grave sin if he does not give testimony that is truthful. The receiving Bishop must be extra-cautious and strict with regard to the legality of the documents themselves, e. g., the genuinity of signature and seal and the absence of erasures, and with regard to the identity of the one who bears them, and the favorable character of the contents. It was stated above that a Bishop can accept for his diocese a cleric whose Testimonial Letters reveal former bad traits, if they are now corrected. That would not hold true if the cleric were from a foreign country, because of the Code's warning in canon 117,

[46] For full text cf. *supra*, pp. 217-218.

2°, "*maxime si agatur etc.*" The spirit of the law can be detected from the regulations, presently to be seen, concerning the incardination of foreign-born priests. They must have led exemplary lives all through their career, and must offer a solid basis for hope that they will never stain their priesthood.

2°. Priests emigrating from Europe and the Mediterranean countries to America and the Philippine Islands

Unlike the lower clerics, priests are often lent out from one diocese to another, while they still remain juridically linked with their native see. They actively exercise their ministry for definite or indefinite periods of time, and sometimes, on the strength of their service, are eventually incardinated in the diocese where they are laboring. The countries which made the emigration of priests most necessary in the nineteenth century were America and the Philippine Islands. The Decree "*Ethnografica studia,*"[47] prior to the Code, was made necessary in order to regulate the release and reception of these diocesan missionary priests, including, however, also those who would later become permanently incardinated in their new fields of labor. After the Code was promulgated, the Holy See wished to coördinate the above decree with the canons on diocesan incardination; it also concluded from experience that the provisions of the decree should be added to and tempered a little, so as to make its ultimate purpose more fully and easily realized. The result was that the Sacred Consistorial Congregation issued a new decree, "*Magni semper,*" on December 30, 1918,[48] in which it readopted most of the features of its former Decree, "*Ethnografica studia,*" but abrogated the remainder.

The principal additions made to the old decree are: 1) The priest must serve his own diocese some years before emigrating; 2) he must have a just cause for going; 3) the ecclesiastical office or ministry promised to the incoming priest must imply more than the mere celebration of Mass, whenever the priest

[47] S. C. Consist., 25 mar. 1914—*AAS*, VI (1914), 182 ss.; *Fontes*, n. 2088; cf. *supra*, pp. 242 ff.

[48] *AAS*, XI (1919), 39 ss.

is young and active; 4) the Bishop "*ad quem*" cannot accept an immigrant unless for the necessity or utility of his diocese, or some other just and reasonable cause; 5) the letters of permission to depart (*litterae discessoriales*) must include, for validity, the express mention of the consent of the Bishop "*a quo*," and of the acceptance of the Bishop "*ad quem*"; 6) in Spain and Portugal, it is the Apostolic Nuncio who is to issue the *litterae discessoriales;* 7) priests traveling to their destination with the proper letters are to be admitted to exercise their ministry also in places *en route* where they stop because of sickness or any other just reason; 8) the proper Ordinary "*a quo*" is to be notified, if they change from one diocese to another in the country where they are laboring; for priests from Italy, Spain, or Portugal, the Holy See is to be notified of the same by the latest receiving Bishop; and 9) the immigrant priests may not live privately in houses or hotels, but are to live in ecclesiastical institutions fitted for that purpose, or with some pastor, or with a community of male Religious.

The principal changes made from the old decree are: 1) The Bishop, and not the Ordinary of the place (including the Vicar General, Vicar Capitular, or Administrator), is the one empowered to issue the *litterae discessoriales* (similar to the provision of canon 113); 2) the Bishops of America can now grant the letters of departure to priests of America going to the Philippine Islands; 3) for all of Europe, except Italy, Spain, and Portugal, the Bishops can do likewise; 4) the extension of the law to include European priests, who journey to other parts of Europe to labor among emigrated peoples of their own nationality, no longer applies; 5) actual residence even of ten years' duration does not give a cleric a right to remain in a diocese;[49] and 6) the constitution of a single Bishop, to act as a representative of all the Bishops of a single nation and to receive requests for the emigration of priests, is discontinued.

The following is an abbreviated summary of the contents of the Decree "*Magni semper*," which still remains in force:[50]

[49] Can. 143.

[50] Wernz-Vidal, *Ius Canon.*, II, n. 67, Scholion III; De Meester, *Compen.*, I, n. 350, note 3; Cocchi, *Comment.*, l. II, p. I, n. 26.

"*MAGNI SEMPER*"

Things to be observed in the emigration of priests of the Latin Rite.

1. For priests going { from Europe or the Mediterranean coast } to { America or The Philippine Islands }

for { a long time / an indefinite time / perpetual service.

It is right for Bishops (not for { Vicar General or Vicar Capitular }) to issue

litterae discessoriales to these, under the conditions that:

a) They be secular priests, proper to them by reason of some canonical title;

b) They have served the original diocese for at least some years after their ordination;

c) They gave certain signs of a blameless life throughout,
are possessed of sufficient knowledge, and
offer a solid hope that they will edify the people anywhere, and
will never stain the sacerdotal dignity;

d) They have a just cause for emigrating;

e) Both Ordinaries observe this law, under pain of grave sin, that:
Bishop "*a quo*" first directly deal with Bishop "*ad quem*,"
tell him of priest's age, life, character, studies, and cause of departure, and
find out from him if he is disposed:
to accept the priest,
to give him an ecclesiastical ministry
(not just saying Mass, if he is young);

Bishop "*a quo*" will issue *litterae discessoriales* only after receiving an affirmative answer to both questions;

f) Bishop "*ad quem*" not to accept the priest unless

necessity or utility of diocese
or
other just cause } requires it.

2. *Discessoriales litterae* for *validity* must be furnished in *specific* form, i. e., they must express:

consent of Bishop "*a quo*" { temporary,
perpetual, or
until revocation;

acceptance of Bishop "*ad quem*";

individuating notes of priest, e. g., age, origin, etc.

3. For Ordinaries of Italy—

Requirements of No. 1 to be fulfilled by Bishops.

S. C. Consist. to issue the written permission to both Ordinaries.

4. For Spain and Portugal—

Requirements of No. 1 to be fulfilled by Bishops.

Apostolic Nuncio to issue the written permission to both Ordinaries.

5. Those without these letters—not to be admitted to exercise ministry.

Those with these letters—to be admitted to exercise ministry even at necessary stops *en route*.

6. Priests from Europe may be incardinated into the dioceses of

{ America
or
The Philippine Islands } provided that

these norms are observed,
Code is observed, and
both Ordinaries consent.

7. Priests from Europe may *change* dioceses in { America or The Philippine Islands } if

Bishop "*a quo*" and Bishop "*ad quem*" consent,

substance of Nos. 1 and 2 are observed,

proper Ordinary is notified of the change *quamprimum,* and

Holy See is notified of change by Bishop "*ad quem,*"

if the priests are from { Italy, Spain, or Portugal.

8. Ordinaries of America and the Philippine Islands:

must not let the priests stay in private homes or hotels;

if they will not obey—Ordinaries are to interdict them the celebration of Mass.

9-15. (Not *ad rem*).

16. Priests who emigrate without observing these laws are *ipso facto* suspended *a divinis;*

if they violate the suspension they become irregular;

they can receive absolution from the censure from S. C. Consist. alone.[51]

Emigration, as was said before, does not mean excardination. Priests who come from abroad to labor merely for a term of years among their fellow nationals in the United States, or in the Philippine Islands, must follow the decree just synopsized. If they come to be incardinated in the new country, *a fortiori* the decree must be obeyed, because then it is supplementary to canon 117, 2°, and is part of the extra caution alluded to in that canon's clause "*maxime si agatur de incardinandis clericis diversae linguae et nationis.*" Incardination of these foreign-born priests may occur through the formal process, either before they leave their native country, or after a term of years of

[51] S. C. Consist., 30 dec. 1918—*AAS,* XI (1919), 39 ss.

service in the new country; it may also occur through the virtual process of conferring on them a residential benefice (a parish) instead of a mere ecclesiastical office or ministry, whenever their permission to emigrate is given in perpetuity. In both these types of incardination the regulations of the Decree "*Magni Semper*," as just outlined, have to be observed, regardless of the country in Europe or on the Mediterranean coast from which the priest originated, provided his destination was America or the Philippine Islands. The reason should be clear. The "*Magni Semper*" was issued precisely in order to coördinate the former Decree "*Ethnografica studia*" with the canons of the Code on the diocesan incardination of priests, including, therefore, the canons on both formal and virtual incardination. There is nothing in the Decree to indicate that its provisions are restricted to either formal or virtual incardination alone; also there is nothing to indicate that any particular class of foreign-born priests is exempted from its regulations. From an examination of the foregoing it is apparent that it is still quite possible for a priest to be assigned in a probationary capacity for a long time in a diocese before he becomes perpetually and canonically attached thereto.

C. For Orientals in the United States of America

In Chapter IV an account was given of the status of this group before the Code.[52] It was shown that at that time they were not to be incardinated in this country.

A second Ordinary for the Greek-Ruthenians in the United States of America was appointed, and, by a decree of the Sacred Congregation for the Affairs of the Oriental Church on May 8, 1924,[53] the two Ordinariates were founded, one for the people of this rite originating in Galicia, with its see in Philadelphia, Pa., and the other for those of the same rite originating in Russian Podocarpathia, Hungary, and Jugoslavia, with its see in Homestead, Pa. After this had been done, the same Sacred Congregation for the Affairs of the Oriental Church issued a decree on the spiritual administration of the two Ordinariates.[54]

52 *Supra*, pp. 254-7.

53 Cf. *AAS*, XXI (1929), 152.

54 Mar. 1, 1929—*AAS*, XXI (1929), 152-159.

In that decree it departed from the former traditional practice, and stated that "any priest coming from Europe to North America for the spiritual care of the faithful of the Greek-Ruthenian rite will remain incardinated in the diocese of his origin, unless, after having observed all that by law is to be observed, he be incardinated by one or the other Greek-Ruthenian Ordinary of the United States."[55] Meanwhile, if not incardinated, during his stay here he is to depend solely on the jurisdiction of the Greek-Ruthenian Bishop in this country, and he is not allowed to return to his native land without the express written permission of the same. The Bishop of his place of origin is not to exercise jurisdiction over him in any way, and, if this Bishop should ever receive him back into his native diocese without the above-mentioned permission of the Greek-Ruthenian Ordinary in the United States of America, this same Bishop of the place of origin will have to answer for it to the Sacred Congregation for the Affairs of the Oriental Church.

The incardination spoken of is to be concluded "*servatis de iure servandis.*" This means that it must be executed according to the regulations of canons 111-117.[56]

An identical arrangement was made by the Sacred Congregation for the Affairs of the Oriental Church on May 24, 1930,[57] for Greek-Ruthenian priests emigrating to Canada to assume the care of souls. There, too, an Ordinariate for Greek-Ruthenians had been established in 1912.

For all other emigrant groups, of whatever Oriental rite, the original precaution still stands, that they are not to be incardinated into the diocese where they are serving, but are to remain bound to the Patriarch or Bishop of their place of origin, subject, however, while in an alien country, to the jurisdiction of the local Ordinary alone.[58]

[55] *Ibid.*, art. 14, p. 155.

[56] Cf. can. 1.

[57] Art. 16—*AAS*, XXII (1930), 346-354.

[58] S. C. pro Eccl. Orient., decr., "*Qua sollerti,*" 23 dec. 1929, nn. 11, 18—*AAS*, XXII (1930), 104-105; S. C. pro Eccl. Orient., instr., 26 sept. 1932, n. 2—*AAS*, XXIV (1932), 344.

When Orientals emigrate to the United States of America, naturally they also need character Testimonials, but in both the Decree "*Ethnografica studia*" and the Decree "*Magni semper*" it was expressly stated that the enactments contained therein were meant only for Latins, and that the emigration of Orientals would still be ruled by the laws issued for them by the Sacred Congregation for the Propagation of the Faith and by the Sacred Congregation for the Affairs of the Oriental Church.

In Articles 11 and 12 of the decree of March 1, 1929, issued by the Sacred Congregation for the Affairs of the Oriental Church,[59] the laws covering this for the Greek-Ruthenians are: a) A major and minor seminary, at least for the two Ordinariates combined, is to be erected, as soon as opportunity permits, for the education in this country of clerics of the Greek-Ruthenian rite; b) meanwhile, the Greek-Ruthenian Ordinaries here are to ask for priests from the Bishops of the Greek-Ruthenian rite in Galicia, Hungary, and Jugoslavia, through the mediation of the Sacred Congregation for the Affairs of the Oriental Church. Any Greek priests who come here, without having been asked for by one or the other of the two Greek Bishops in the United States of America, and without having been sent here by the Sacred Congregation for the Affairs of the Oriental Church, may not receive any faculties from the Greek-Ruthenian Bishops here to celebrate Mass, to administer the sacraments, or to perform any other ecclesiastical duties. Besides, those who are sent here must be celibates.[60]

3. *Responsibility for Truth of the Testimonial Letters*

The key to the success of the incardinational processes lies in the reliability of the testimony concerning the candidates. It is that which assures the distant receiving Bishop that he knows as much about the cleric's character as the proper Bishop himself. Take away that, and incardination, instead of being a boon to dioceses in which there is a scarcity of priests, would become a positive danger to the welfare of the Church. Excardination would be nothing more than an elimination by large and well-

[59] *Supra*, p. 545.

[60] *AAS*, XXI (1929), 154-155.

manned dioceses of their undesirable and unworthy clerics and priests, and the dioceses least able to utilize them would be the very ones overburdened with them. Testimonial Letters for ordination are a most serious requirement; by relying on them a Bishop justifies his conscience for entrusting to a man the most sacred power of holy orders. The Testimonials for incardination are equally serious, and their truth just as essential. For that reason their conformity to truth is an obligation of justice, binding, under pain of serious sin, the Ordinary who is releasing the cleric ("*Ordinarius autem dimittens, graviter onerata eius conscientia, advigilare debet ut testimonia sint veritati conformia*").

The actual gathering and the ultimate forwarding of the testimony is attended to by the Curia of the excardinating Ordinary. However, it is his responsibility to know what his Curia does, and to see to it that everything contained in its testimony about a cleric who is to be excardinated is absolutely truthful and reliable, regardless of whether it be good or bad.

ARTICLE III

THE OATH OF PERPETUAL SERVICE

Can. 117, 3°. - **Clericus iureiurando coram eodem Ordinario eiusve delegato declaraverit se in perpetuum novae dioecesis servitio velle addici ad normam sacrorum canonum.**

1. *Nature of the Oath*

Whenever a cleric is to be canonically transferred to a new diocese through excardination and incardination, by either the formal or the virtual process, the Ordinary "*ad quem*" may not lawfully proceed to the act of incardination, unless the cleric has declared by oath before him, or his delegate, that he wishes to be attached in perpetuity to the service of the new diocese, in accordance with the standards of the sacred canons of the Code. This is the second of the oaths, enumerated above,[61] which enter into the legislation on ordination and its allied subject, incardination. It must not be confused, therefore, with

[61] P. 333.

the oath for acquiring an ordinational domicile,[62] nor with those for receiving sacred orders *titulo missionis* or *titulo servitii dioecesis*.[63] These as a usual rule are necessary only *before* ordination, whereas the oath of canon 117, 3°, must be taken in every instance also by priests.

This oath is a sworn *assertion* of the cleric's actual intention of perpetually linking himself with the service of the new diocese. But it is not a promissory oath. Hence, it does not effect that the newly incardinated clerics are bound to the diocese with any stronger ties than are those who were ordained for its service while having their original domicile in it. In other words, clerics who have taken this oath may still be excardinated from the diocese or, also, enter religion at some later time.[64] Like all oaths which are required for effecting a valid or lawful process, the particular oath here in question should exist in written form and be preserved in the diocesan Curia.[65] One author, Blat, holds that an oral oath suffices, but that even then a documentary record of it should be kept in the Curia.[66]

The simple formula of the oath may be as follows:

> Ego N. ————————, hactenus dioecesis ———————— clericus, nunc spondeo et juro me in perpetuum dioecesis ———————— servitio velle addici ad normam canonis 117, n. 3, Codicis Juris Canonici.
>
> Sic me Deus adjuvet et haec Sancta evangelia quae manibus tango.
>
> ————————————————
>
> Die ———— mensis ———— A.D. ————
>
> Juramentum rite coram nobis
> emissum testamus
>
> Ordinarius ————————
>
> ———————————— Ordinarii ———————— Delegatus

[62] Can. 956.

[63] Can. 981, § 1.

[64] Chelodi, *Ius de Personis*, n. 107.

[65] Cocchi, *Comment.*, l. II, p. I, n. 26.

[66] *Commentarium*, II, n. 51.

2. *Reason for the Oath*

A cleric who enters the service of a diocese in which he was born and in which he still continues to retain his domicile is attracted by a natural reason to remain there perpetually. For him a departure would normally be neither welcome nor easy, for it would imply a farewell to all he holds near and dear. When, however, a cleric leaves the diocese in which he was born in order to offer his life's service elsewhere, his permanent continuance of residence in the new diocese is very much more, if not exclusively, dependent on the resolution of his will and the strength of the intention manifested by him. It can readily be visualized that in general circumstances this will and intention must derive support and confirmation through an oath.[67] This is the natural explanation for the oath which is demanded of everyone before his reception of tonsure to guarantee his intention of the acquisition or retention of a domicile which is different from the domicile of his place of birth, as also, partly at least, for the oath which is taken by those who receive ordination for the title of "the mission." In a similar manner the same reason obtains relative to the oath of perpetual service.

The genesis of this oath may be traced thus: Pope Innocent XII in the Constitution "*Speculatores*"[68] required an oath, in addition to a number of other proofs, as full guaranty of intention when someone established a domicile in a place different from the place of his birth. This oath was not required for the acquisition of a domicile in general, but for the acquisition of an ordinational domicile in particular (*ad effectum suscipiendi Ordines*). The oath provided an additional support and strength for the will, needed by a youth who was to receive an ordination whereby he would offer his life's service to a strange or alien diocese. The case contemplated the future reception of orders, and, hence, there was required an actual residence in the new place before the taking of the oath. Then came the Decree "*A primis,*" which with relation to ordination purposes provided a quicker method for the acquisition of a

[67] Toso, *Comment. Minora,* in can. 117.

[68] Nov. 4, 1694, § 5—*Fontes,* n. 258.

domicile distinct from the natal one. It made possible for the cleric the acquisition of a new diocesan domicile, not merely by actual residence together with the transfer of the greater part of his belongings, but also through the medium of formal letters of excardination and incardination. Here, too, the cleric's expression of will needed bolstering by an additional assertory oath. The case presupposed the future reception of orders from a Bishop who had thus become the proper Bishop for ordination by reason of his domiciliary title, even though as yet the cleric had not occupied the newly acquired domicile. Hence a mere assertory oath of the cleric's intention to remain in the diocese, as demanded in the Constitution "*Speculatores,*" did not always suffice. Instances could occur in which there was need of a promissory oath to take up residence in the new diocese, and to work under the direction of its Bishop.[69]

In the Code, however, these concepts were readapted. Domicile was made the basis for a Bishop to become the proper Bishop for the ordination of a layman. However, if the latter's domicile at the time of ordination was different from his natal domicile, there was still necessary the taking of an assertory oath to remain in his acquired domicile. This is the oath as required by canon 956. Yet, domicile was not made the necessary basis by which a Bishop could become the proper Bishop for a cleric's promotion to higher orders. Complete authority, not only to ordain personally, but also to issue dimissorial letters for the cleric's ordination by some other Bishop, as well as to grant letters of excardination, was acquired by the Bishop of that diocese for the service of which the cleric had been tonsured, even though the latter had not ever set foot in that diocese.[70]

Tonsure itself automatically attached the cleric in perpetuity to the diocese for which his service was thus preëmpted. If the Bishop of this diocese excardinated the cleric, and another Bishop incardinated him, then the new Bishop gained complete authority over him, both to ordain, and likewise to excardinate

[69] Cf. *supra,* p. 234.

[70] Cf. *supra,* pp. 355 ff., and especially p. 369.

him if need be. Incardination, as the Code conceives it, is no longer just a means of acquiring a domicile. Hence, in the second incardination of an already tonsured cleric there is no reason for the *assertory* oath of his present intention to remain perpetually in the new diocese, because he need not yet be there; nor is there any reason for the *promissory* oath to reside in the new diocese and to subject himself perpetually to the jurisdiction of its Bishop, because domicile is not needed to enable that new Bishop to advance him to higher orders; and, anyway, his obligation relative both to residence and subjection will flow automatically from the fact of his incardination, and not from any oath.

Still, a second incardination, whether formal or virtual, does imply a cleric's change of service in favor of a strange diocese for life. His decision to make that change must be definite, not wavering. His intention needs to be strengthened. Hence, there is a reason for the new oath required by canon 117, 3°, which is merely *assertory* of his present will to be attached to the service of the new diocese in perpetuity.

It is to be noted that this assertory oath may not be regarded as something practically identical with, or even as a necessary accompaniment of, the ordination title of " service of the diocese." The latter can stand altogether unaccompanied with any oath, because in itself it does not involve a cleric's change from his native to new territorial surroundings. The " service of the diocese " is the ordination title employed in the United States of America for all secular clerics, just as invariably when they are ordained in and for their own native dioceses by their own episcopal Ordinary as when they receive ordination at the hands of any properly authorized Bishop in or for an alien diocese, or when they become incardinated in a new diocese distinct from the one in which or for which they were initially ordained.[71]

[71] For an explanation of how this assertory oath differs from the oath of the title of " the mission " the reader may consult the historical conspectus of this study, pp. 142 ff.

3. *The Proper Ordinary for Receiving the Oath*

It is the incardinating Ordinary, or his delegate, who is to receive the oath of perpetual service (*coram eodem Ordinario eiusve delegato*). "*Eodem*" cannot refer to the "*Ordinarius dimittens*" of the last clause in canon 117, 2°, because there is a complete break in the continuity of thought between canon 117, 2°, and canon 117, 3°. The latter portion of the canon deals with an altogether different phase of the subject of incardination. But the opening clause of the canon is followed by a colon, which manner of punctuation draws all the subsequent subsidiary clauses into its own proper orbit. Hence it is that the phrase "*eodem Ordinario*" in canon 117, 3°, must look for its proper identification to the opening clause of canon 117, in which that Ordinary is mentioned as the "*Ordinarius ad incardinationem deveniens.*"[72]

The incardinating Ordinary here contemplated is identical with the "*Ordinarius alienae dioecesis*" mentioned in canon 112. Thus the limitations indicated by canon 113 must here as there be properly kept in mind.

If the cleric is actually present in the new diocese, whither he has come to present in person his document of excardination, the incardinating Ordinary may and can himself receive the oath of perpetual service. A delegate of the Ordinary, e. g., the rector of the seminary, or a priest member of the diocesan Curia, could be employed for this act if the Bishop is preoccupied at the time with other important cares in his diocese. But a delegate would actually become necessary in almost all cases in which a formal process of incardination would be utilized in favor of a cleric still pursuing his studies in some distant diocese. In that eventuality the Ordinary "*ad quem*" could readily authorize the Ordinary of the diocese in which the cleric is making his studies, or also some definite priest in the vicinity of the seminary, to act as his delegate in receiving the cleric's oath. This Ordinary or priest delegate would then forward the written and properly signed copy of the oath to the desired destination.

[72] Blat, *Commentarium*, II, n. 51.

CONCLUSIONS

In addition to its juridical exposition of the present-day law on the canonical transfer of laymen and clerics, it is felt that the above study has contributed its mite to canonical jurisprudence, inasmuch as it has brought to light or clarified a number of points on which knowledge has hitherto been meager or non-existent.

This contribution may be summed up in the following brief conclusions:

1. While the terms *to incardinate* and *cardinal* were derived from the same Latin root *cardo,* a hinge, they were not interchangeable in meaning to the extent that *to incardinate* always meant *to make a cardinal* and *vice versa,* as many authors have hitherto held; but, at least from the sixth century until the promulgation of the Code, the term *to incardinate,* when used ecclesiastically, meant to attach a person, particularly a cleric, to a new diocese after transferring him from another.

2. The changing of clerics, as well as of candidates for the clerical state, from one diocese to another is a practice as old as the Church.

3. Throughout Church history laymen as well as clerics always had at least one proper Bishop for ordination.

4. Not until near the end of the nineteenth century did the incardination of a non-diocesan cleric officially confer on the receiving Bishop the right to ordain the new subject in a higher grade.

5. To receive different orders from various simultaneously proper Bishops was permissible from the thirteenth century to the Code, with this exception, that, from 1898 until 1917, any cleric who became formally incardinated in a diocese also became exclusively subject to the Bishop of that diocese for the reception of all higher orders.

6. The permitted acquisition of a residential benefice in an alien diocese was not merely a method by which an inferior cleric gained a new proper Bishop for higher ordination, but was one of the ways in which excardination and incardination was effected for priests as well as for inferior clerics throughout the last seven hundred years, and, in fact, was the more normal and favored method of the same.

7. Formal excardination and incardination became popular only in the nineteenth century, and the missionary countries, especially the United States of America, contributed much to making it so.

8. Tacit or presumptive incardination of secular priests in the United States of America did not exist except during the years 1884 to 1898.

9. The Decree "*A primis*" in 1898 was not a reordination of the whole subject of diocesan transfers for clerics of any grade, as all authors have hitherto believed, but was rather merely the establishment of a new and fifth title of proper Bishop for the ordination of inferior clerics. It did not, therefore, abrogate previously existing methods of canonical transfers, and did not apply at all to priests.

10. The term *to incardinate* in the Code has a new and wider significance than it ever had before. It now means the attachment, initial or otherwise, of a cleric to a diocese through any legitimate method whatsoever.

11. Canon 956 establishes the sole title of proper Bishop for ordination for laymen only.

12. Any layman, aspiring to the clerical state, who injudiciously loses his domicile and becomes a *vagus* cannot be raised to the clerical state until he has acquired a new domicile and proper Bishop. In defect of that he needs an Apostolic Indult.

13. In the present law the Bishop of incardination becomes exclusively the proper Bishop for the ordination of his subject clerics.

14. Though the quasi-excardination and quasi-incardination of laymen no longer exists, the Code provides in canons 111 and

969 two methods by which the same result can be directly obtained.

15. Formal letters of excardination and incardination are mutually complementary, and hence neither one, taken separately, has any juridical effect at all until its complement has been executed. The logical sequence requires the document of excardination to be executed first.

16. The idea of an ecclesiastical office according to the Code has been so thoroughly clarified as to make a benefice, which it underlies, readily discernible.

17. The various sacred offices or positions in a diocese which are, or possibly may become, residential benefices, and can thereby form the basis for virtual excardination and incardination, have been carefully investigated and determined.

18. It is now evident that canon 113, which limits the competent authority for excardinating and incardinating, applies to clerics only, not to laymen, and to all methods, not just to one.

19. An unmistakable distinction has been made among the various types of oaths which enter into the different phases of the ordinational and incardinational process.

20. A clearly defined way has been opened through the former haze of confusing terminology and the complex labyrinth of canonical legislation regarding this multi-phased subject.

BIBLIOGRAPHY

Sources

Acta Apostolicae Sedis, Commentarium Officiale, Romae, 1909—

Acta et Decreta Concilii Plenarii Americae Latinae in Urbe Celebrati, A. D. MDCCCXCIX, 2 vols., Romae: Typis Polyglottis Vaticanis, 1902-1910.

Acta et Decreta Concilii Plenarii Baltimorensis Tertii, A. D. MDCCCLXXXIV, Baltimorae: John Murphy, 1886.

Acta et Decreta Sacrorum Conciliorum Recentiorum, Collectio Lacensis, 7 vols., Friburgi Brisgoviae, 1870-1890.

Acta Sanctae Sedis, 41 vols., Romae, 1865-1908.

Bullarium Diplomatum et Privilegiorum Sanctorum Pontificum Taurinensis Editio, 24 vols., Augustae Taurinorum, 1857-1872.

Bullarium Pontificium Sacrae Congregationis de Propaganda Fide, Romae, 1839.

Bullarium Romanum Luxemburgense (Bullarium Magnum), 8 vols., Luxemburg, 1727.

Canones Apostolorum et Conciliorum saec. IV-VII, ed. Bruns, Berolini, 1839.

Canones et Decreta Sacrosancti Oecumenici Concilii Tridentini, Editio novissima ad Fidem Optimorum Exemplarium Castigate Impressa (XIX reimpressio stereotypa), Taurini, 1913.

Codex Iuris Canonici Pii X Pontificis Maximi iussu digestus Benedicti Papae XV auctoritate promulgatus, Romae: Typis Polyglottis Vaticanis, 1919.

Codicis Iuris Canonici Fontes cura Emi Petri Card. Gasparri editi, 9 vols., Romae, later Civitate Vaticana: Typis Polyglottis Vaticanis, 1923-1939. (Vols. VII-IX, ed. *cura et studio Emi Iustiniani Serédi*).

Collectanea in Usum Secretariae Sacrae Congregationis Episcoporum et Regularium, A. Bizzarri, Romae, 1885.

Collectanea S. Congregationis de Propaganda Fide, Romae: Typographia Polyglotta S. C. de Propaganda Fide, 1893.

Collectanea S. Congregationis de Propaganda Fide, 2 vols., Romae: Typographia Polyglotta S. C. de Propaganda Fide, 1907.

Concilii Plenarii Baltimorensis II., in Ecclesia Metropolitana Baltimorensi, a die VII. ad diem XXI. Octobris, A. D. MDCCCLXVI., Habiti, et a Sede Apostolica Recogniti, Acta et Decreta, Baltimorae: John Murphy, 1868.

Corpus Iuris Canonici, Editio Lipsiensis II (Richter-Friedberg), 2 vols., Lipsiae, 1879.

Corpus Iuris Civilis, Krueger-Mommsen-Schoell-Kroll, 5. ed., 3 vols., Berolini: Weidman, 1928-1929.

Corpus Scriptorum Ecclesiasticorum Latinorum, Editum Consilio et Impensis Academiae Litterarum Caesariae Vindobonensis (*Corpus Vindobonense*), Vindobonae, 1866—

Hardouin, Jean, *Conciliorum Collectio Regia Maxima*, 12 vols., Parisiis, 1715.

Hartzheim, Joseph, *Concilia Germaniae*, Coloniae Augustae Agrippensium, 1759-1790.

Ius Pontificium de Propaganda Fide, Auspice Emo ac Rmo Dño S.R.E. Card. Ioanne Simeoni, Cura ac studio Raphaelis de Martinis, Pars I, 7 vols., Romae, 1888-1898.

Labbeus, Philippus, et Cossartius, Gabriel, *Sacrorum Conciliorum Nova et Amplissima Collectio*, 17 vols., Florentiae, 1760.

Lingen, C., et Reuss, P. A., *Causae Selectae in S. Congregatione Cardinalium Concilii Tridentini Interpretum propositae per summaria precum ab anno 1823 usque ad annum 1869*, Ratisbonae, 1871.

Mansi, Joannes Dominicus, *Sacrorum Conciliorum Nova et Amplissima Collectio*, 53 vols., Paris-Arnhem-Leipzig, 1901-1927.

Migne, J. P., *Patrologiae Cursus Completus, Series Graeca*, 161 vols., Parisiis, 1856-1866.

——— *Patrologiae Cursus Completus, Series Latina*, 221 vols., Parisiis, 1844-1864.

Pallottini, Salvator, *Collectio Omnium Conclusionum et Resolutionum Quae in causis propositis apud Sacram Congregationem Cardinalium S. Concilii Tridentini Interpretum Prodierunt ab eius institutione anno MDLXIV ad annum MDCCCLX, distinctis titulis alphabetico ordine per materias digesta*, 17 vols., Romae, 1868-1893.

Pii IX Acta, 9 vols., Romae, 1854-1880.

Pii X Pontificis Maximi Acta, 5 vols., Romae, 1905-1913.

Regulae Servandae in iudiciis apud S. Romanae Rotae Tribunal, Romae, 1910.

Regulae Servandae in iudiciis apud Supremum Signaturae Apostolicae Tribunal, Romae, 1912.

Richter, A. L., *Canones et Decreta Sacrosancti Oecumenici Concilii Tridentini*, ex Editione Romana a. MDCCCXXXIV. Repetiti. Accedunt S. Congr. Card. Conc. Trid. Interpretum *Declarationes ac Resolutiones* etc., Lipsiae, 1853.

S. *Romanae Rotae Decisiones seu Sententiae quae . . . prodierunt anno 1909-1932*, 24 vols., Romae: Typis Vaticanis, 1912-1940.

Synodus Dioecesana Buffalensis Vigesima Septima, Die 14 maii 1924.

Theiner, Augustin, *Acta Genuina SS. Oecumenici Concilii Tridentini*, Opus Posthumum, 2 vols., Zagrabiae (Croatiae), 1874.

Thesaurus Resolutionum Sacrae Congregationis Concilii, 167 vols., Romae, 1718-1908.

Authors

Aertnys, J. – Damen, C. A., *Theologia Moralis*, 13. ed., 2 vols., Taurini: Domus Editorialis Marietti, 1939.

Aichner, Simon, *Compendium Juris Ecclesiastici*, 6. ed., Brixinae, 1887.

Alexander, Natalis, *Historia Ecclesiastica Veteris Novique Testamenti*, ed. novissima, 18 vols., Parisiis, 1740-1744.

Alphonsus Maria De Ligorio, St., *Theologia Moralis*, ed. absolutissima, 2 vols., Augustae Taurinorum, 1827.

Alzog, John, *Manual of Universal Church History*, Transl. from 9th German ed. by F. J. Pabisch and T. S. Byrne, new ed., 4 vols., Dublin, 1889.

Antiquus, Abbas, *Lectura aurea super quinque libros Decretalium*, Argentinae, 1510.

Ayrinhac, H. A., *General Legislation in the New Code of Canon Law*, New York: Benziger Brothers, 1923.

Baart, Peter A., *Legal Formulary*, 2. ed., New York, 1898.

[Bachofen], Charles Augustine, *A Commentary on the New Code of Canon Law*, 8 vols., St. Louis: B. Herder, 1918-1922.

Badii, Caesar, *Institutiones Iuris Canonici*, 3. ed., 2 vols., Florentiae: Libreria Editrice Fiorentina, 1921-1922.

Barbosa, Agostino, *De Officio et Potestate Episcopi*, 2 vols., Lugduni, 1656.

——— *Iuris Ecclesiastici Universi Libri Tres*, Lugduni, 1660.

——— *Summa apostolicarum decisionum*, Lugduni, 1645.

Bargilliat, M., *Praelectiones Iuris Canonici*, 37. ed., 2 vols., Parisiis: apud Baston, Berche et Pagis, 1923.

Bastnagel, Clement Vincent, *The Appointment of Parochial Adjutants and Assistants*, The Catholic University of America, Canon Law Studies, n. 58, Washington, D. C.: The Catholic University of America, 1930.

Bellarmine, R., *Omnia Opera*, 8 vols., Naples, 1858.

Benedictus XIV, *De Synodo Dioecesana*, 2 vols., Romae, 1806.

——— *Institutiones Ecclesiasticae*, Prati, 1844.

Bingham, Joseph, *The Antiquities of the Christian Church*, 9 vols., London, 1843-1845.

Blat, Albertus, *Commentarium Textus Codicis Iuris Canonici*, 6 vols., Romae: F. Ferrari, 1921-1927.

Bondini, A., *De Incardinatione et Excardinatione Clericorum*, Monographia Juridica ex Ephemeride "Jus Pontificium" excerpta, Series II, Fasc. X, Romae: Jus Pontificium, 1929.

Bouix, D., *Tractatus De Capitulis*, Parisiis, 1882.

——— *Tractatus De Episcopo*, 2. ed., 2 vols., Parisiis, 1873.

——— *Tractatus De Jure Regularium*, 2. ed., Bruxellis, 1867.

Bouuaert-Simenon, *Manuale Iuris Canonici*, 2. ed., 3 vols., Wetteren, Belgium: De Meester et fils, 1930.

Brown, Brendan Francis, *The Canonical Juristic Personality with Special Reference to its Status in the United States of America*, The Catholic University of America, Studies in Canon and Civil Law, n. 39, Washington, D. C.: The Catholic University of America, 1927.

Calepinus, Ambrosius, *Dictionarium*, ed. noviss., Lugduni, 1681.

Campagna, Angelo, *Il Vicario Generale del Vescovo*, The Catholic University of America, Canon Law Studies, n. 66, Washington, D. C.: The Catholic University of America, 1931.

Caponi, Julius, *Institutiones Canonicae*, 2 vols., Coloniae Allobrogum, 1734.

Cappello, Felix, *Summa Iuris Canonici*, 2 vols., Romae: apud Aedes Universitatis Gregorianae, 1928-1930.

——— *Tractatus Canonico-Moralis de Sacramentis*, 2. ed., 3 vols., 1928-1935. Vol. II, Pars III, *De Sacra Ordinatione*, Romae: Marietti, 1935.

Catholic Encyclopedia, The, 15 vols. & Index, New York: The Encyclopedia Press, Inc., 1907-1914.

Chelodi, Joannes, *Ius de Personis*, 2. ed., Tridenti: Libr. Edit. Tridentum, 1927.

Cicognani, Amleto Giovanni, *Canon Law*, 2. ed., Philadelphia: The Dolphin Press, 1935.

Claeys-Bouuaert, Ferdinandus, *De Canonica Cleri Saecularis Obedientia*, Lovanii, 1904.

Coady, John Joseph, *The Appointment of Pastors*, The Catholic University of America, Canon Law Studies, n. 52, Washington, D. C.: The Catholic University of America, 1929.

Cocchi, Guidus, *Commentarium in Codicem Iuris Canonici*, 8 vols., Taurinorum Augustae: Marietti, 1920-1930. Lib. II, *De Personis*, 2. ed., 1925-1926.

Coronata, Matthaeus Conte a, *Institutiones Iuris Canonici*, 5 vols., Taurini: Marietti, 1928-1936.

Costello, John M., *Domicile and Quasi-Domicile*, The Catholic University of America, Canon Law Studies, n. 60, Washington, D. C.: The Catholic University of America, 1930.

D'Annibale, Josephus, *In Const. Apostolicae Sedis qua censurae l.s. limitantur commentarii editi iussu Illmi et Revmi Fr. Aegidii Mauri, O.P.*, episcopi Reatini (Comm. Reat.), Interamnae, 1873.

Daris, J., *Praelectiones Canonicae in seminario Leodiensi habitae.* Tom. I. *Tractatus de Hierarchia Jurisdictionis*, Leodii, 1863; tom. IV. *Quaestiones Canonico-Civiles de Statu Religioso*, Leodii, 1866.

Davis, Henry, *Moral and Pastoral Theology*, 3. ed., 4 vols., London: Sheed and Ward, 1938.

De Meester, A., *Juris Canonici et Juris Canonico-Civilis Compendium*, 3 vols. in 4, ed. nova, Brugis: Sumptibus et Typis Societatis Sancti Augustini, 1921-1928.

De Rossi, Giovanni Battista, *Roma Sotteranea Cristiana*, 3 vols. in 5, Romae, 1864.

Devoti, Joannes, *Institutionum Canonicarum Libri IV*, 2 vols., Leodii, 1883.

Digby, Kenelm H., *Mores Catholici* or *Ages of Faith*, 3 vols., New York, 1889.

Du Cange, C., *Glossarium ad Scriptores Mediae et Infimae Latinitatis*, 6 vols., Parisiis, 1733-1736.

Duchesne, Louis, *Christian Worship, Its Origin and Evolution*, Translated from third French edition by M. L. McClure, London, 1903.

——— *Liber Pontificalis*, Parisiis, 1886.

Duskie, John A., *The Canonical Status of the Orientals in the United States*, The Catholic University of America, Canon Law Studies, n. 48, Washington, D. C.: The Catholic University of America, 1928.

Eichmann, E., *Lehrbuch des Kirchenrechts auf Grund des Codex Iuris Canonici*, 2. ed., Paderborn: Schoeningh, 1926.

Eusebius, Pamphilius, *Historiae Ecclesiasticae Libri Decem*, ed. Hugo Laemmer, Scaphusiae, 1862.

Fagnanus, Prosperus, *Commentaria in Libros Decretalium*, 5 vols., Romae, 1661.

Fanfani, Ludovicus I., *De Iure Parochorum ad Normam Codicis Iuris Canonici*, Taurini-Romae: Ex officina Libraria Marietti, 1924.

——— *De Iure Religiosorum ad Normam Codicis Iuris Canonici*, 2. ed., Taurini-Romae: Ex officina Libraria Marietti, 1925.

Farren, Neil, *Domicile and Quasi-Domicile*, Dublin: M. H. Gill & Son, Ltd., 1920.

Ferraris, F. Lucius, *Bibliotheca Canonica, Iuridica, Moralis, Theologica, necnon Ascetica, Polemica, Rubricistica, Historica*, ed. noviss., 9 vols., Romae, 1885-1899.

Ferreres, Ioannes B., *Compendium Theologiae Moralis*, 14. ed., 2 vols., Barcinone: Eugenius Subirana, 1928-1929.

Forcellini, Aegidius, *Totius Latinitatis Lexicon*, Schneelbergae, 1831.

Freund-Leverett, *Lexicon of the Latin Language*, new ed., Philadelphia: J. B. Lippincott Co., [1850].

Funk, F. X., *Didascalia et Constitutiones Apostolorum*, 2 vols., Paderbornae, 1905.

——— *A Manual of Church History*, 3rd. impression of authorized translation from 5th German edition by Luigi Cappadelta, 2 vols., London, 1910.

Garcia, Nicolas, *De Beneficiis Ecclesiasticis Amplissimus et Doctissimus Tractatus*, 2 vols., Venetiis, 1618.

Gasparri, Petrus, *Tractatus Canonicus de Sacra Ordinatione*, 2 vols., Parisiis-Lugduni, 1893.

Genicot, E. – Salsmans, I., *Institutiones Theologiae Moralis*, 10. ed., 2 vols., Bruxellis: Alb. Dewit, 1922.

Giraldi, Ubaldus, *Expositio Juris Pontificii*, nova Romana editio, 2 vols., Romae, 1829-1830.

Golden, Henry F., *Parochial Benefices in the New Code*, The Catholic University of America, Canon Law Studies, n. 10, Washington, D. C.: The Catholic University of America, 1925.

Hallier, Francis, *De Sacris Electionibus et Ordinationibus ex Antiquo et Novo Ecclesiae Usu* (in Migne, J. P., *Theologiae Cursus Completus*, vol. XXIV), Parisiis, 1860.

Harper's Latin Dictionary, revised and enlarged by Lewis & Short, New York, 1888.

Hatch, Edwin, *The Organization of the Early Christian Churches*, 8th. impression, London, 1918.

Hefele, C. – Hergenröther, J., *Conciliengeschichte*, 2. ed., 9 vols., Freiburg im Breisgau, 1873-1890.

Henry, Ludovicus, *De Residentia Beneficiatorum*, Lovanii, 1863.

Hinschius, Paul, *Decretales Pseudo-Isidorianae et Capitula Angilrami*, Lipsiae, 1863.

——— *System des katholischen Kirchenrechts*, 4 vols., Berlin, 1869-1888.

Honorante, Romualdus, *Praxis Secretariae Tribunalis Cardinalis Urbis Vicarii*, 2. ed., Romae, 1762.

[Icard, H.], *Praelectiones Iuris Canonici*, 3 vols., Lutetiae Parisiorum, 1859.

Laymann, Paulus, *Theologia Moralis*, 9. ed., Moguntiae, 1723.

Lesêtre, Henri, *La Paroisse*, 3. ed., Paris, 1908.

Leurenius, Petrus, *Forum Beneficiale*, ed. noviss., 2 vols., Coloniae, 1742.

Lucidi, Angelus, *De Visitatione Sacrorum Liminum*, 3. ed. (aucta per Iosephum Schneider), 3 vols., Romae, 1883.

Many, S., *Praelectiones de Sacra Ordinatione*, Parisiis, 1905.

Maroto, Philippus, *Institutiones Iuris Canonici*, 2 vols., Romae, 1919-1921. Vol. I, 3. ed., Romae: Apud Commentarium pro Religiosis, 1921.

Meysztowicz, V., *Domicilium et Quasi-Domicilium*, Monographia Juridica ex Ephemeride " Jus Pontificium " excerpta, Series I, Fasc. XIV, Romae: Jus Pontificium, 1926.

Migne, J. P., *Theologiae Cursus Completus*, 28 vols., Parisiis, 1863-1866. Vol. XXIV, *De Sacris Electionibus et Ordinationibus*, auctore Francisco Hallier, Parisiis, 1860.

Moeder, John M., *The Proper Bishop for Ordination and Dimissorial Letters*, The Catholic University of America, Canon Law Studies, n. 95, Washington, D. C.: The Catholic University of America, 1935.

Monacelli, Fr., *Formularium legale practicum fori ecclesiastici*, 4 vols., Romae, 1713.

Moreno, Fr. Joseph, *Tractatus Moralis, Titulos Pro Promovendis ad Ecclesiasticos Ordines*, Romae, 1699.

Nilles, Nic., *De libertate clericorum religionem ingrediendi*, Ex selectis disputationibus academicis juris ecclesiastici, fasc. 1, Oeniponte, 1886.

Noldin, Henricus, *Summa Theologiae Moralis*, 18. ed., revised by A. Schmitt, 3 vols., Oeniponte: Felician Rauch, 1927.

O'Dwyer, Thomas J., *Incardination & Excardination*, The Catholic University of America, Canon Law Studies, Licentiate Dissertation, n. 639, Washington, D. C.: The Catholic University of America, 1923.

Official Catholic Directory, The, New York: Kenedy & Sons, 1941.

Ojetti, B., *Commentarium in Codicem Iuris Canonici*, 4 vols., Romae: apud Aedes Universitatis Gregorianae, 1927-1931.

——— *Synopsis Rerum Moralium et Iuris Pontificii*, 3 vols. & Index, Romae, 1909-1914.

Pallavicini, S., *Vera Concilii Tridentini Historia*, Antwerpiae, 1673.

Panormitanus, Abbas, (Nicolaus de Tudeschis), *Commentaria super quinque libros Decretalium*, 5 vols., Lugduni, 1547.

Panvinius, Onuphrius, *Romani Pontifices et Cardinales S.R.E. ab eisdem a Leone IX ad Paulam Papam IIII per quingentos posteriores a Christi Natali annos creati*, (Appendix—*De Episcopatibus, Titulis, et Diaconiis Cardinalium Liber*), Venetiis, 1557.

Pellegrini, Carolus, *Praxis Vicariorum*, Venetiis, 1706.

Petra, Vincentius, *Commentaria ad Constitutiones Apostolicas*, 5 vols., Venetiis, 1729.

Pighi, Jo. Baptista, *Institutiones Historiae Ecclesiasticae*, 2. ed., 3 vols., Veronae, 1906.

Pignatelli, Jacobus, *Consultationes Canonicae*, 11 tom. in 4 vols., Coloniae Allobrogum, 1700.

Piontek, Cyrillus, *De Indulto Exclaustrationis Necnon Saecularizationis*, The Catholic University of America, Canon Law Studies, n. 29, Washington, D. C.: The Catholic University of America, 1925.

Pirhing, Enricus, *Jus Canonicum in V Libros Decretalium distributum*, ed. noviss., 5 vols., Dilingae, 1722.

Pistocchi, Marius, *De Re Beneficiali iuxta Canones Codicis Iuris Canonici*, Taurini: Marietti, 1928.

Pruemmer, Dominicus, *Manuale Iuris Canonici*, 3. ed., Friburgi Brisgoviae: Herder, 1922.

——— *Manuale Theologiae Moralis*, 2. ed., 3 vols., Friburgi Brisgoviae: Herder, 1923.

Raus, J. B., *Institutiones Canonicae*, Parisiis, Lugduni: Vitte, 1924.

Reiffenstuel, Anacletus, *Jus Canonicum Universum*, 4 vols., Venetiis, 1735.

Riganti, Joannes Baptista, *Commentaria in Regulas, Constitutiones et Ordinationes Cancellariae Apostolicae*, Opus Posthumum, 4 vols. in 2, Coloniae Allobrogum, 1751.

Roberti, Franciscus, *De Processibus*, 2 vols., Romae: apud Aedes Facultatis Iuridicae ad S. Apollinaris, 1926.

Saegmueller, Johannes Baptist., *Lehrbuch des katholischen Kirchenrechts*, 4. ed., Freiburg im Breisgau: Herder, 1925-1934.

Schäfer, Timotheus, *De Religiosis ad Normam Codicis Iuris Canonici*, Münster i. W.: Ex Officina Libraria Aschendorff, 1927.

Schmalzgrueber, Franciscus, *Jus Ecclesiasticum Universum*, 12 vols., Romae, 1843-1845.

Schmidt, Antonius, *Thesaurus Iuris Ecclesiastici potissimum Germanici sive Dissertationes Selectae in Ius Ecclesiasticum*, 7 vols., Heidelbergae, Bambergae et Wircelburgi, 1772-1779.

Soramus, Basilius Fabrius, *Thesaurus Eruditionis Scholasticae*, Hagae-Comitum, 1735.

Tamagna, Giuseppe, *Origini e Prerogative de' Cardinali della S.R.C.*, 2 vols., Romae, 1790.

Tanquerey, Adrianus, *Synopsis Theologiae Dogmaticae ad Mentem S. Thomae Aquinatis Hodiernis Moribus Accomodata*, 19. ed., 3 vols., Romae-Tornaci (Belg.)-Parisiis: Desclée et Socii, 1922.

Thomassinus, Ludovicus, *Vetus et Nova Ecclesiae Disciplina circa Beneficia et Beneficiarios*, Magontiaci, 1787.

Toso, Albertus, *Ad Codicem Juris Canonici . . . Commentaria Minora*, 5 vols., Taurini-Romae: P. Marietti, 1920-1934.

Van Espen, Zegerus Bernardus, *Jus Ecclesiasticum Universum*, ed. noviss., 10 vols., Venetiis, 1769.

Vermeersch, Arthurus, *Theologiae Moralis, Principia - Responsa - Consilia*, 2. ed., 4 vols., Romae: Università Gregoriana, 1926-1927.

Vermeersch, Arthurus, et Creusen, Josephus, *Epitome Iuris Canonici*, 2. ed., 3 vols., Mechliniae-Romae: H. Dessain, 1924-1925.

Vitruvius, M., *De Architectura Libri Decem ad Caesarem Augustum*, Lugduni, 1552.

Vocabularium Latinum et Italicum, Romae, 1792.

Vosius, Gerardus Joannes, *Etymologicon Linguae Latinae*, Amstelodami, 1662.

Wernz, F. X., *Ius Decretalium*, 3. ed., 6 vols., Prati, 1915.

Wernz, F. X., et Vidal, P., *Ius Canonicum ad Codicis normam exactum*, vol. II: *De Personis*, 2. ed., Romae: Universitas Gregoriana, 1928.

Woywod, Stanislaus, *A Practical Commentary on the Code of Canon Law*, 2 vols., New York: J. Wagner, 1925.

——— *The New Canon Law*, new ed., New York: J. Wagner, 1918.

Zaplotnik, Johannes Leo, *De Vicariis Foraneis*, The Catholic University of America, Canon Law Studies, n. 47, Washington, D. C.: The Catholic University of America, 1927.

Zitelli, Zephyrinus, *Apparatus seu Compendium Juris Ecclesiastici*, Romae, 1886.

ARTICLES

Biederlack, J., "Inkardination und Ordination der Saekularkleriker nach dem jetzigen Kirchenrecht"—*ZkT*, XLVII (1923), 50-58.

Bondini, A., "De incardinatione et excardinatione clericorum"—*Jus Pontif.*, IX (1929), 205-213.

Bouix, D., "De l'exeat"—*Revue des sciences ecclésiastiques*, V (1862), 35 ff.

Browne, M. J., "Incardination and Ordination: a Recent Reply"—*IER*, XLVIII (1936), 531-537.

Browne, M. J., "The Meaning of 'Commoratio'"—*IER*, XLVII (1936), 81-83.

Browne, M. J., "Questions about domicile"—*IER*, XLVII (1936), 633.

Cappello, F., "Collatio primae tonsurae"—*Per.*, XIX (1930), 38*-40*.

Cappello, F., "De Episcopo proprio quoad ordinationem"—*Per.*, XXIII (1934), 133*-135*.

Cappello, F., "Quaestiones Canonicae de Ordinatione, domicilio et incardinatione"—*Per.*, XX (1931), 125*-136*.

Coussa, A., "Annotationes ad resp. C.I.C., 24 iul. 1939"—*Apoll.*, XII (1939), 321-325.

Creusen, I., "De excardinatione et incardinatione implicita"—*Jus Pontif.*, XV (1935), 37-40.

D'Angelo, S., "De Collatione primae Tonsurae—Animadversiones"—*Apoll.*, III (1930), 243-244.

D'Angelo, S., "De prima tonsura—Consultatio"—*Apoll.*, I (1928), 181-182.

De Becker, "The admission of secular priests into a diocese of the United States"—*AER*, XVIII (1898), 145.

De Iturre, "Quid requiritur ad beneficium in aliena dioecesi possidendum"—*Illustracion del Clero*, fas. 514 (1928), 202-203.

Farrugia, N., "De ecclesiastico domicilio"—*ME*, 5 series, VII (1935), 312-316.

Francia, E., "Animadversiones circa incardinationem"—*Apoll.*, IX (1936), 216-218.

Hofmann, M., "Die Excardination einst und jetzt"—*ZkT*, XXIV (1900), 92-124; 393-424.

Mahoney, E. J., "The Tonsure and Incardination"—*AER*, LXXXII (1930), 398-406.

Maroto, P., "De episcopo proprio quoad ordinationem"—*Apoll.*, V (1932), 238-245.

Meysztowicz, V., "Domicilium et Quasi-Domicilium"—*Jus Pontif.*, VI (1926), 34-55.

Ojetti, B., "De natura potestatis Ordinariorum secundum Codicem"—*Gregorianum*, VI (1925), 436-441.

Peries, "Titulus Ordinationis"—*AER*, XIII (1895), 353.

Piontek, C., "De Acephalis in iure canonico"—*Jus Pontif.*, XIV (1934), 194-215, 284-294; XV (1935), 55-63, 202-208; XVII (1937), 64-82.

Schaaf, V., "Episcopus Proprius Ordinationis"—*AER*, XC (1934), 352-365.

Suarez, E., "De Incardinatione Ratione Beneficii"—*Angelicum*, XIII (1936), 192-209.

[Vermeersch, A.], "De Canone 1427 et de vicariis perpetuis"—*Per.*, XIV (1925-1926), (12)-(17).

Vermeersch, A., "Quaesita Canonica—Iuridica condicio eius qui ab Episcopo non proprio primam tonsuram recepit"—*Per.*, XV (1926-1927), (115)-(117).

Vidal, P., "Il Nuovo Codice di Diritto Canonico"—*La Civiltà Cattolica*, LXIX (1918), 218-219.

Voltas, P., "De Domicilio Quoad Ordinatonem Religiosorum"—*CpR*, II (1921), 299-307.

Woywod, S., "Proper Bishop for ordination of men transferred to another diocese by first tonsure"—*HPR*, XXXVII (1937), 522-527.

Anonymous, "Conditions of Excardination and Diocesan Adoption"—*AER*, LXXVI (1927), 317-319.

Anonymous, "Benefice of Assistant Pastorate"—*AER*, LXXVII (1927), 74-79, 306-312.

Periodicals

Analecta Iuris Pontificii, Romae, 1855-1868; Parisiis, 1869-1890.

Angelicum, Romae, 1924—

Apollinaris, Romae, 1928—

Archiv für katholisches Kirchenrecht, Innsbruck 1857-1861; Mainz, 1862—

Civiltà Cattolica, La, Romae, 1850—

Commentarium pro Religiosis et Missionariis, Romae, 1920—

Ecclesiastical Review, The [originally *The American Ecclesiastical Review*], Philadelphia, 1889—

Gregorianum, Romae, 1920—

Homiletic and Pastoral Review, The, New York, 1900—

Illustracion del Clero, Madrid, 1909—

Irish Ecclesiastical Record, The, Dublin, 1864—

Irish Theological Quarterly, The, Dublin, 1906—

Jus Pontificium, Romae, 1921—

Monitore Ecclesiastico, Il, Romae, 1876—

Nouvelle Revue Théologique, Tournai, 1869—

Periodica de Re Canonica et Morali utili praesertim Religiosis et Missionariis, Bruges, 1905—

Razon y Fe, Madrid, 1901—

Revue des Sciences Ecclésiastiques, 70 vols., Lille, 1860-1897.

Zeitschrift für katholische Theologie, Innsbruck, 1877—

LIST OF ABBREVIATIONS

AAS—Acta Apostolicae Sedis.
AER—The American Ecclesiastical Review.
AkKR—Archiv für katholisches Kirchenrecht.
Anal. Jur. Pont.—Analecta Juris Pontificii.
Apoll.—Apollinaris.
ASS—Acta Sanctae Sedis.
Bruns—*Canones Apostolorum et Conciliorum saec. IV–VII*, ed. Bruns.
Bullarium Magnum—Bullarium Romanum Luxemburgense.
C.—*Codex* (Justinianus) vel *Causa.*
c.—canon seu caput (iuris antiqui).
cc.—canones seu capita (iuris antiqui).
can.—canon (novi Codicis).
cans.—canones (novi Codicis).
Cath. Ency.—The Catholic Encyclopedia.
C.I.C.—Pontificia Commissio ad Codicis Canones Authentice Interpretandos.
Collectanea S.C.*Ep. et Reg.* — Collectanea in Usum Secretariae Sacrae Congregationis Episcoporum et Regularium, A. Bizzarri.
Collectanea S.C.P.F.—Collectanea Sacrae Congregationis de Propaganda Fide, ed. 1907.
Collectanea S.C.P.F. (1893)—Collectanea Sacrae Congregationis de Propaganda Fide, ed. 1893.
Coll. Lac.—(Collectio Lacensis) Acta et Decreta Sacrorum Conciliorum Recentiorum.
Conc. Trid.—Concilium Tridentinum.
CpR—Commentarium pro Religiosis et Missionariis.
CV—(Corpus Vindobonense) Corpus Scriptorum Ecclesiasticorum Latinorum.
D.—*Digestum (Iustinianum)* vel *Distinctio.*
Fontes—Codicis Iuris Canonici Fontes.
Greg. Mag.—Sanctus Gregorius Magnus.
Hardouin—Hardouin, J., *Conciliorum Collectio Regia Maxima.*
Hartzheim—Hartzheim, Jos., *Concilia Germaniae.*
Hefele—Hefele, C., – Hergenröther, J., *Conciliengeschichte.*
HPR—The Homiletic and Pastoral Review.
Ibid.—*(Ibidem)* The preceding reference.
IER—The Irish Ecclesiastical Record.
ITQ—The Irish Theological Quarterly.
Jus Pontif.—Jus Pontificium.
kath.—katholisches.
KR—Kirchenrecht.
Labbe-Cossart—Labbe, P., – Cossart, G., *Sacrorum Conciliorum Nova et Amplissima Collectio.*
Lingen-Reuss—Lingen, C., – Reuss, P. A., *Causae Selectae in Sacra Congregatione Cardinalium Concilii Tridentini Interpretum propositae.*
Loc. cit.—Loco citato.
Mansi—Mansi, J. D., *Sacrorum Conciliorum Nova et Amplissima Collectio.*
ME—Il Monitore Ecclesiastico.

MPG—(Migne, Patrologia Graeca) Migne, Jacques Paul, *Patrologiae Cursus Completus—Series Graeca.*

MPL—(Migne, Patrologia Latina) Migne, Jacques Paul, *Patrologiae Cursus Completus—Series Latina.*

MTC—(Migne, Theologiae Cursus) Migne, Jacques Paul, *Theologiae Cursus Completus.*

Novell.—Novellae Constitutiones.

Op. cit.—Opere citato.

Pallottini—Pallottini, S., *Collectio Omnium Conclusionum et Resolutionum Quae in causis propositis apud Sacram Congregationem Cardinalium S. Concilii Tridentini Interpretum Prodierunt, MDLXIV–MDCCCLX.*

Per.—Periodica de Re Canonica et Morali Utili praesertim Religiosis et Missionariis.

Richter — Richter, A. L., *Canones et Decreta Sacrosancti Oecumenici Concilii Tridentini.*

S.C.C.—Sacra Congregatio Concilii.

S.C.Consist.—Sacra Congregatio Consistorialis.

S.C. de Prop. Fide—Sacra Congregatio de Propaganda Fide.

S.C.Ep. et Reg.—Sacra Congregatio Episcoporum et Regularium.

S.C.P.F.—Sacra Congregatio de Propaganda Fide.

S.C. pro Eccl. Orient.—Sacra Congregatio pro Ecclesia Orientali.

S.C. pro Negot. Eccl. Extraord.—Sacra Congregatio pro Negotiis Ecclesiasticis Extraordinariis.

S.C.S. Off.—Sacra Congregatio Sancti Officii.

S.R.R.—Sacra Romana Rota.

Thesaurus Resolutionum—*Thesaurus Resolutionum Sacrae Congregationis Concilii.*

ZkT—Zeitschrift für katholische Theologie.

BIOGRAPHICAL NOTE

James T. McBride was born on October 21, 1902, in Rush Township, Schuylkill County, Pennsylvania. He received his elementary education in the parochial school of St. Vincent de Paul, Germantown, Pa. His high school and College training were obtained during the years 1915-1923 at St. Joseph's College Preparatory School and at St. Joseph's College in Philadelphia, from which latter institution he received the degree of Bachelor of Arts in 1923. He entered the Seminary of St. Charles Borromeo, Overbrook, Pa., in September of the same year, and in the fall of 1927 was sent to the Catholic University of America in Washington, D. C., to pursue a graduate course of studies in the School of Canon Law. He was ordained to the priesthood at Philadelphia on June 2, 1928. His Baccalaureate in Canon Law was received from the Catholic University of America in November, 1927, and his Licentiate in Canon Law in June, 1928.

ALPHABETICAL INDEX

J

U

V

CANON LAW STUDIES

1. Freriks, Rev. Celestine A., C.PP.S., J.C.D., Religious Congregations in Their External Relations, 121 pp., 1916.
2. Galliher, Rev. Daniel M., O.P., J.C.D., Canonical Elections, 117 pp., 1917.
3. Borkowski, Rev. Aurelius L., O.F.M., J.C.D., De Confraternitatibus Ecclesiasticis, 136 pp., 1918.
4. Castillo, Rev. Cayo, J.C.D., Disertación Historico-Canonica sobre la Potestad del Cabildo en Sede Vacante o Impedida del Vicario Capitular, 99 pp., 1919 (1918).
5. Kubelbeck, Rev. William J., S.T.B., J.C.D., The Sacred Penitentiaria and Its Relations to Faculties of Ordinaries and Priests, 129 pp., 1918.
6. Petrovits, Rev. Joseph J. C., S.T.D., J.C.D., The New Church Law on Matrimony, X-461 pp., 1919.
7. Hickey, Rev. John J., S.T.B., J.C.D., Irregularities and Simple Impediments in the New Code of Canon Law, 100 pp., 1920.
8. Klekotka, Rev. Peter J., S.T.B., J.C.D., Diocesan Consultors, 179 pp., 1920.
9. Wanenmacher, Rev. Francis, J.C.D., The Evidence in Ecclesiastical Procedure Affecting the Marriage Bond, 1920. (Printed 1935).
10. Golden, Rev. Henry Francis, J.C.D., Parochial Benefices in the New Code, IV-119 pp., 1921. (Printed 1925).
11. Koudelka, Rev. Charles J., J.C.D., Pastors, Their Rights and Duties According to the New Code of Canon Law, 211 pp., 1921.
12. Melo, Rev. Antonius, O.F.M., J.C.D., De Exemptione Regularium, X-188 pp., 1921.
13. Schaaf, Rev. Valentine Theodore, O.F.M., S.T.B., J.C.D., The Cloister, X-180 pp., 1921.
14. Burke, Rev. Thomas Joseph, S.T.D., J.C.D., Competence in Ecclesiastical Tribunals, IV-117 pp., 1922.
15. Leech, Rev. George Leo, J.C.D., A Comparative Study of the Constitution "Apostolicae Sedis" and the "Codex Juris Canonici", 179 pp., 1922.
16. Motry, Rev. Hubert Louis, S.T.D., J.C.D., Diocesan Faculties According to the Code of Canon Law, II-167 pp., 1922.
17. Murphy, Rev. George Lawrence, J.C.D., Delinquencies and Penalties in the Administration and the Reception of the Sacraments, IV-121 pp., 1923.
18. O'Reilly, Rev. John Anthony, S.T.B., J.C.D., Ecclesiastical Sepulture in the New Code of Canon Law, II-129 pp., 1923.

19. MICHALICKA, REV. WENCESLAS CYRIL, O.S.B., J.C.D., Judicial Procedure in Dismissal of Clerical Exempt Religious, 107 pp., 1923.
20. DARGIN, REV. EDWARD VINCENT, S.T.B., J.C.D., Reserved Cases According to the Code of Canon Law, IV-103 pp., 1924.
21. GODFREY, REV. JOHN A., S.T.B., J.C.D., The Right of Patronage According to the Code of Canon Law, 153 pp., 1924.
22. HAGEDORN, REV. FRANCIS EDWARD, J.C.D., General Legislation on Indulgences, II-154 pp., 1924.
23. KING, REV. JAMES IGNATIUS, J.C.D., The Administration of the Sacraments to Dying Non-Catholics, V-141 pp., 1924.
24. WINSLOW, REV. FRANCIS JOSEPH, M.M., J.C.D., Vicars and Prefects Apostolic, IV-149 pp., 1924.
25. CORREA, REV. JOSE SERVELION, S.T.L., J.C.D., La Potestad Legislativa de la Iglesia Catolica, IV-127 pp., 1925.
26. DUGAN, REV. HENRY FRANCIS, A.M., J.C.D., The Judiciary Department of the Diocesan Curia, 87 pp., 1925.
27. KELLER, REV. CHARLES FREDERICK, S.T.B., J.C.D., Mass Stipends, 167 pp., 1925.
28. PASCHANG, REV. JOHN LINUS, J.C.D., The Sacramentals According to the Code of Canon Law, 129 pp., 1925.
29. PIONTEK, REV. CYRILLUS, O.F.M., S.T.B., J.C.D., De Indulto Exclaustrationis necnon Saecularizationis, XIII-289 pp., 1925.
30. KEARNEY, REV. RICHARD JOSEPH, S.T.B., J.C.D., Sponsors at Baptism According to the Code of Canon Law, IV-127 pp., 1925.
31. BARTLETT, REV. CHESTER JOSEPH, A.M., LL.B., J.C.D., The Tenure of Parochial Property in the United States of America, V-108 pp., 1926.
32. KILKER, REV. ADRIAN JEROME, J.C.D., Extreme Unction, V-425 pp., 1926.
33. MCCORMICK, REV. ROBERT EMMETT, J.C.D., Confessors of Religious, VIII-266 pp., 1926.
34. MILLER, REV. NEWTON THOMAS, J.C.D., Founded Masses According to the Code of Canon Law, VII-93 pp., 1926.
35. ROELKER, REV. EDWARD G., S.T.D., J.C.D., Principles of Privilege According to the Code of Canon Law, XI-166 pp., 1926.
36. BAKALARCZYK, REV. RICHARDUS, M.I.C., J.U.D., De Novitiatu, VIII-208 pp., 1927.
37. PIZZUTI, REV. LAWRENCE, O.F.M., J.U.L., De Parochis Religiosis, 1927. (Not Printed).
38. BLILEY, REV. NICHOLAS MARTIN, O.S.B., J.C.D., Altars According to the Code of Canon Law, XIX-132 pp., 1927.
39. BROWN, MR. BRENDAN FRANCIS, A.B., LL.M., J.U.D., The Canonical Juristic Personality with Special Reference to its Status in the United States of America, V-212 pp., 1927.
40. CAVANAUGH, REV. WILLIAM THOMAS, C.P., J.U.D., The Reservation of the Blessed Sacrament, VIII-101 pp., 1927.

41. DOHENY, REV. WILLIAM J., C.S.C., A.B., J.U.D., Church Property: Modes of Acquisition, X-118 pp., 1927.
42. FELDHAUS, REV. ALOYSIUS H., C.PP.S., J.C.D., Oratories, IX-141 pp., 1927.
43. KELLY, REV. JAMES PATRICK, A.B., J.C.D., The Jurisdiction of the Simple Confessor, X-208 pp., 1927.
44. NEUBERGER, REV. NICHOLAS J., J.C.D., Canon 6 or the Relation of the Codex Juris Canonici to the Preceding Legislation, V-95 pp., 1927.
45. O'KEEFE, REV. GERALD MICHAEL, J.C.D., Matrimonial Dispensations, Powers of Bishops, Priests and Confessors, VIII-232 pp., 1927.
46. QUIGLEY, REV. JOSEPH A. M., M.A., J.C.D., Condemned Societies, 139 pp., 1927.
47. ZAPLOTNIK, REV. JOHANNES LEO, J.C.D., De Vicariis Foraneis, X-142 pp., 1927.
48. DUSKIE, REV. JOHN ALOYSIUS, A.B., J.C.D., The Canonical Status of the Orientals in the United States, VIII-196 pp., 1928.
49. HYLAND, REV. FRANCIS EDWARD, J.C.D., Excommunication, Its Nature, Historical Development and Effects, VIII-181 pp., 1928.
50. REINMANN, REV. GERALD JOSEPH, O.M.C., J.C.D., The Third Order Secular of Saint Francis, 201 pp., 1928.
51. SCHENK, REV. FRANCIS J., J.C.D., The Matrimonial Impediments of Mixed Religion and Disparity of Cult, XVI-318 pp., 1929.
52. COADY, REV. JOHN JOSEPH, S.T.D., J.U.D., A.M., The Appointment of Pastors, VIII-150 pp., 1929.
53. KAY, REV. THOMAS HENRY, J.C.D., Competence in Matrimonial Procedure, VIII-164 pp., 1929.
54. TURNER, REV. SIDNEY JOSEPH, C.P., J.U.D., The Vow of Poverty, XLIX-217 pp., 1929.
55. KEARNEY, REV. RAYMOND A., A.B., S.T.D., J.C.D., The Principles of Delegation, VII-149 pp., 1929.
56. CONRAN, REV. EDWARD JAMES, A.B., J.C.D., The Interdict, V-163 pp., 1930.
57. O'NEIL, REV. WILLIAM H., J.C.D., Papal Rescripts of Favor, VII-218 pp., 1930.
58. BASTNAGEL, REV. CLEMENT VINCENT, J.U.D., The Appointment of Parochial Adjutants and Assistants, XV-257 pp., 1930.
59. FERRY, REV. WILLIAM A., A.B., J.C.D., Stole Fees, V-135 pp., 1930.
60. COSTELLO, REV. JOHN MICHAEL, A.B., J.C.D., Domicile and Quasi-Domicile, VII-201 pp., 1930.
61. KREMER, REV. MICHAEL NICHOLAS, A.B., S.T.B., J.C.D., Church Support in the United States, VI-136 pp., 1930.
62. ANGULO, REV. LUIS, C.M., J.C.D., Legislación de la Iglesia sobre la intención en la aplicación de la Santa Misa, VII-104 pp., 1931.

63. Frey, Rev. Wolfgang Norbert, O.S.B., A.B., J.C.D., The Act of Religious Profession, VIII-174 pp., 1931.
64. Roberts, Rev. James Brendan, A.B., J.C.D., The Banns of Marriage, XIV-140 pp., 1931.
65. Ryder, Rev. Raymond Aloysius, A.B., J.C.D., Simony, IX-151 pp., 1931.
66. Campagna, Rev. Angelo, Ph.D., J.U.D., Il Vicario Generale del Vescovo, VII-205 pp., 1931.
67. Cox, Rev. Joseph Godfrey, A.B., J.C.D., The Administration of Seminaries, VI-124 pp., 1931.
68. Gregory, Rev. Donald J., J.U.D., The Pauline Privilege, XV-165 pp., 1931.
69. Donohue, Rev. John F., J.C.D., The Impediment of Crime, VII-110 pp., 1931.
70. Dooley, Rev. Eugene A., O.M.I., J.C.D., Church Law on Sacred Relics, IX-143 pp., 1931.
71. Orth, Rev. Clement Raymond, O.M.C., J.C.D., The Approbation of Religious Institutes, 171 pp., 1931.
72. Pernicone, Rev. Joseph M., A.B., J.C.D., The Ecclesiastical Prohibition of Books, XII-267 pp., 1932.
73. Clinton, Rev. Connell, A.B., J.C.D., The Paschal Precept, IX-108 pp., 1932.
74. Donnelly, Rev. Francis B., A.M., S.T.L., J.C.D., The Diocesan Synod, VIII-125 pp., 1932.
75. Torrente, Rev. Camilo, C.M.F., J.C.D., Las Processiones Sagradas, V-145 pp., 1932.
76. Murphy, Rev. Edwin J., C.PP.S., J.C.D., Suspension Ex Informata Conscientia, XI-122 pp., 1932.
77. MacKenzie, Rev. Eric F., A.M., S.T.L., J.C.D., The Delict of Heresy in its Commission, Penalization, Absolution, VII-124 pp., 1932.
78. Lyons, Rev. Avitus E., S.T.B., J.C.D., The Collegiate Tribunal of First Instance, XI-147 pp., 1932.
79. Connolly, Rev. Thomas A., J.C.D., Appeals, XI-195 pp., 1932.
80. Sangmeister, Rev. Joseph V., A.B., J.C.D., Force and Fear as Precluding Matrimonial Consent, V-211 pp., 1932.
81. Jaeger, Rev. Leo A., A.B., J.C.D., The Administration of Vacant and Quasi-Vacant Episcopal Sees in the United States, IX-229 pp., 1932.
82. Rimlinger, Rev. Herbert T., J.C.D., Error Invalidating Matrimonial Consent, VII-79 pp., 1932.
83. Barrett, Rev. John D. M., S.S., J.C.D., A Comparative Study of the Third Plenary Council of Baltimore and the Code, IX-221 pp., 1932.
84. Carberry, Rev. John J., Ph.D., S.T.D., J.C.D., The Juridical Form of Marriage, X-177 pp., 1934.

85. Dolan, Rev. John L., A.B., J.C.D., The Defensor Vinculi. XII-157 pp., 1934.
86. Hannan, Rev. Jerome D., A.M., S.T.D., LL.B., J.C.D., The Canon Law of Wills, IX-517 pp., 1934.
87. Lemieux, Rev. Delisle A., A.M., J.C.D., The Sentence in Ecclesiastical Procedure, IX-131 pp., 1934.
88. O'Rourke, Rev. James J., A.B., J.C.D., Parish Registers, VII-109 pp., 1934.
89. Timlin, Rev. Bartholomew, O.F.M., A.M., J.C.D., Conditional Matrimonial Consent, X-381 pp., 1934.
90. Wahl, Rev. Francis X., A.B., J.C.D., The Matrimonial Impediments of Consanguinity and Affinity, VI-125 pp., 1934.
91. White, Rev. Robert J., A.B., LL.B., S.T.B., J.C.D., Canonical Ante-Nuptial Promises and the Civil Law, VI-152 pp., 1934.
92. Herrera, Rev. Antonio Parra, O.C.D., J.C.D., Legislación Ecclesiástica sobre el Ayuno y la Abstinencia, XI-191 pp., 1935.
93. Kennedy, Rev. Edwin J., J.C.D., The Special Matrimonial Process in Cases of Evident Nullity, X-165 pp., 1935.
94. Manning, Rev. John J., A.B., J.C.D., Presumption of Law in Matrimonial Procedure, XI-111 pp., 1935.
95. Moeder, Rev. John M., J.C.D., The Proper Bishop for Ordination and Dimissorial Letters, VII-135 pp., 1935.
96. O'Mara, Rev. William A., A.B., J.C.D., Canonical Causes for Matrimonial Dispensations, IX-155 pp., 1935.
97. Reilly, Rev. Peter, J.C.D., Residence of Pastors, IX-81 pp., 1935.
98. Smith, Rev. Mariner T., O.P., S.T.Lr., J.C.D., The Penal Law for Religious, VII-169 pp., 1935.
99. Whalen, Rev. Donald W., A.M., J.C.D., The Value of Testimonial Evidence in Matrimonial Procedure, XIII-297 pp., 1935.
100. Cleary, Rev. Joseph F., J.C.D., Canonical Limitations on the Alienation of Church Property, VIII-141 pp., 1936.
101. Glynn, Rev. John C., J.C.D., The Promoter of Justice, XX-337 pp., 1936.
102. Brennan, Rev. James H., S.S., A.M., S.T.B., J.C.D., The Simple Convalidation of Marriage, VI-135 pp., 1937.
103. Brunini, Rev. Joseph Bernard, J.C.D., The Clerical Obligations of Canons 139 and 142, X-121 pp., 1937.
104. Connor, Rev. Maurice, A.B., J.C.D., The Administrative Removal of Pastors, VIII-159 pp., 1937.
105. Guilfoyle, Rev. Merlin Joseph, J.C.D., Custom, XI-144 pp., 1937.
106. Hughes, Rev. James Austin, A.B., A.M., J.C.D., Witnesses in Criminal Trials of Clerics, IX-140 pp., 1937.
107. Jansen, Rev. Raymond J., A.B., S.T.L., J.C.D., Canonical Provisions for Catechetical Instruction. VII-153 pp., 1937.

108. Kealy, Rev. John James, A.B., J.C.D., The Introductory Libellus in Church Court Procedure, XI-121 pp., 1937.
109. McManus, Rev. James Edward, C.SS.R., J.C.D., The Administration of Temporal Goods in Religious Institutes, XVI-196 pp., 1937.
110. Moriarity, Rev. Eugene James, J.C.D., Oaths in Ecclesiastical Courts, X-115 pp., 1937.
111. Rainer, Rev. Eligius George, C.SS.R., J.C.D., Suspension of Clerics, XVII-249 pp., 1937.
112. Reilly, Rev. Thomas F., C.SS.R., J.C.D., Visitation of Religious, IV-195 pp., 1938.
113. Moriarity, Rev. Francis E., C.SS.R., J.C.D., The Extraordinary Absolution from Censures, XV-334 pp., 1938.
114. Connolly, Rev. Nicholas P., J.C.D., The Canonical Erection of Parishes, X-132 pp., 1938.
115. Donovan, Rev. James Joseph, J.C.D., The Pastor's Obligation in Prenuptial Investigation, XII-322 pp., 1938.
116. Harrigan, Rev. Robert J., A.M., S.T.B., J.C.D., The Radical Sanation of Invalid Marriages, VIII-208 pp., 1938.
117. Boffa, Rev. Conrad Humbert, J.C.D., Canonical Provisions for Catholic Schools, X-211 pp., 1939.
118. Parsons, Rev. Anscar John, O.M.Cap., J.C.D., Canonical Elections, XII-236 pp., 1939.
119. Reilly, Rev. Edward Michael, A.B., J.C.D., The General Norms of Dispensation, X-156 pp., 1939.
120. Ryan, Rev. Gerald Aloysius, A.B., J.C.D., Principles of Episcopal Jurisdiction, XII-172 pp., 1939.
121. Burton, Rev. Francis James, C.S.C., A.B., J.C.D., A Commentary on Canon 1125, X-222 pp., 1940.
122. Miaskiewicz, Rev. Francis Sigismund, J.C.D., Supplied Jurisdiction According to Canon 209, XII-340 pp., 1940.
123. Rice, Rev. Patrick William, A.B., J.C.D., Proof of Death in Prenuptial Investigation, VIII-156 pp., 1940.
124. Anglin, Rev. Thomas Francis, M.S., J.C.L., The Eucharistic Fast.
125. Coleman, Rev. John Jerome, J.C.L., The Minister of Confirmation.
126. Downs, Rev. John Emmanuel, A.B., J.C.L., The Concept of Clerical Immunity.
127. Esswein, Rev. Anthony Albert, J.C.L., The Extrajudicial Coercive Powers of Ecclesiastical Superiors.
128. Farrell, Rev. Benjamin Francis, A.M., S.T.L., J.C.L., The Rights and Duties of the Local Ordinary Regarding Congregations of Women Religious of Pontifical Approval.
129. Feeney, Rev. Thomas John, A.B., S.T.L., J.C.L., Restitutio in Integrum.
130. Findlay, Rev. Stephen William, O.S.B., A.B., J.C.L., Canonical Norms Governing the Deposition and Degradation of Clerics.

131. GOODWINE, REV. JOHN, A.B., S.T.L., J.C.L., The Right of the Church to Acquire Property.
132. HESTON, REV. EDWARD LOUIS, C.S.C., Ph.D., S.T.D., J.C.L., The Alienation of Church Property in the United States.
133 HOGAN, REV. JAMES JOHN, S.T.L., J.C.L., Judicial Advocates and Procurators.
134. KEALY, REV. THOMAS M., A.B., Litt.B., J.C.L., Dowry of Women Religious.
135. KEENE, REV. MICHAEL JAMES, O.S.B., J.C.L., Religious Ordinaries and Canon 198.
136. KERIN, REV. CHARLES A., S.S., A.M., S.T.B., J.C.L., The Privation of Christian Burial.
137. LOUIS, REV. WILLIAM FRANCIS, A.M., J.C.L., Diocesan Archives.
138. McDEVITT, REV. GILBERT JOSEPH, A.B., J.C.L., Legitimacy and Legitimation.
139. McDONOUGH, REV. THOMAS JOSEPH, A.B., J.C.L., Apostolic Administrators.
140. MEIER, REV. CARL ANTHONY, A.B., J.C.L., Penal Administrative Procedure Against Negligent Pastors.
141. SCHMIDT, REV. JOHN ROGG, A.B., J.C.L., The Principles of Authentic Interpretation in Canon 17 of the Code of Canon Law.
142. SLAFKOSKY, REV. ANDREW LEONARD, A.B., J.C.L., The Canonical Episcopal Visitation of the Diocese.
143. SWOBODA, REV. INNOCENT ROBERT, O.F.M., J.C.L., Ignorance in Relation to the Imputability of Delicts.
144. DUBÉ, REV. ARTHUR JOSEPH, A.B., J.C.L., The General Principles for the Reckoning of Time in Canon Law.
145. McBRIDE, REV. JAMES T., A.B., J.C.L., Incardination and Excardination of Seculars.

www.ingramcontent.com/pod-product-compliance
Lightning Source LLC
LaVergne TN
LVHW041117090826
844660LV00060B/669

9780813223346